LIVING IN THE TENTH CENTURY

LIVING

Mentalities

IN THE

and

TENTH

Social Orders

CENTURY

HEINRICH FICHTENAU

Translated by
PATRICK J. GEARY

THE UNIVERSITY OF CHICAGO PRESS

Chicago and London

Heinrich Fichtenau was president of the Institute for Austrian Historical Research from 1962 until his retirement in 1984. Patrick J. Geary is professor of history at the University of Florida.

THE UNIVERSITY OF CHICAGO PRESS, CHICAGO 60637
THE UNIVERSITY OF CHICAGO PRESS, LTD., LONDON
© 1991 by The University of Chicago
All rights reserved. Published 1991
Printed in the United States of America
00 99 98 97 96 95 94 93 92 91   5 4 3 2 1

Originally published as *Lebensordnung des 10. Jahrhunderts: Studien über Denkart und Existenz im einstigen Karolingerreich,* © 1984 Anton Hiersemann, Stuttgart.

Library of Congress Cataloging-in-Publication Data
Fichtenau, Heinrich.
    [Lebensordnungen des 10. Jahrhunderts. English]
    Living in the tenth century : mentalities and social orders / Heinrich Fichtenau ; translated by Patrick J. Geary.
        p. cm.
    Translation of: Lebensordnungen des 10. Jahrhunderts.
    Includes bibliographical references and index.
    ISBN 0-226-24620-5 (cloth)
        1. Holy Roman Empire—Church history. 2. Christian life—Middle Ages, 600–1500. 3. Holy Roman Empire—Social conditions.
    I. Title. II. Title: Living in the tenth century.
    BR735.F5313 1991   90-11134
    943'.022—dc20   CIP

CONTENTS

TRANSLATOR'S FOREWORD

An earlier work of Heinrich Fichtenau's is well known to the British and American public through an abridged translation of his 1949 *Das karolingische Imperium*. Long out of print in German, *The Carolingian Empire* has remained the first introduction to Carolingian history for the great majority of Americans since it first appeared in 1957. Professor Fichtenau wrote that brilliant synthesis in the ruins of postwar, occupied Vienna as a corrective both to the German glorification of Charlemagne as a great ruler and master of Europe and to the French cult of Charlemagne as father of a united Europe. His emphasis on the tensions, stresses, and failures of Charlemagne and his advisers displeased an older generation of German historians even while establishing Professor Fichtenau's reputation as a highly original, creative scholar whose independent, personal view of the past holds more in common with French *Annales* scholarship than with the mainstream of German constitutional history.

Professor Fichtenau's subsequent work as director of the Institute for Austrian Historical Research, his fundamental studies of medieval diplomatics, and even his broad contributions to the history of medieval culture, are largely unknown in Britain and America outside of a small circle of specialists. Nevertheless, they, even more than his study of Charlemagne, are the basis of his international reputation as one of the world's premier interpreters of medieval history. In the tradition of his institute, much of his time has been devoted to diplomatics. Before World War II he assisted his academic teacher Hans Hirsch in preparing the edition of the diplomas of Conrad III. After the war, with Erich Zöllner, he edited the three-volume collection of Babenberg charters (*Urkundenbuch zur Geschichte der Babenberger*, 1950, 1958, 1968.)

At the same time, he has been one of the rare diplomatists who relate diplomatics and paleography to cultural history and the history of mentalities. His *Mench und Schrift im Mittelalter* (1946), written during the war under the most difficult circumstances, examines the relations between literate communities and their productions. This extraordinary work anticipates by more than three decades current critical interest in textual communities and the interrelations between literacy and society. His study of diplomatic harangue formulas, *Arenga: Spätantike und Mittelalter im Spiegel von Urkundenformeln* (1957), remains an exemplary investigation of how archival sources can be exploited for the history of ideology. This path-breaking study again anticipates more recent criticism of the putative distinction between "literary" (self-reflective) and "documentary" (theoretically transparent) texts. Even his regional studies of diplomatics and paleography, *Das Urkundenwesen in Österreich vom 8. bis zum frühen 13. Jahrhundert* (1971) and *Die Lehrbücher Maximilians I und die Anfänge der Frakturschrift* (1961), reach far beyond their geographical limits in terms of European written culture and practice.

In the present study, published the year he retired from the Institute, he returns to some of the topics he treated in his *Carolingian Empire*. In exploring the tenth century, he faced a very different problem from that which he had encountered in studying the Carolingian Empire itself. Post-Carolingian Europe has often been seen as another "dark age," a time of confusion, decline, fragmentation, and ignorance. His goal was to examine the quest for order in the ensemble of regions that had once made up the Carolingian world. He does this through a wide-ranging study of the various ways in which tenth-century Europeans attempted to structure their political, social, and mental experience. However, just as in his earlier *Carolingian Empire*, he is constantly aware of the inadequacies, failures, and contradictions within this struggle. Thus, if the first parts of the book focus on "orders," familial, religious, and popular, the last examines confusion as an integral part of living in the tenth century. In writing this synthesis Professor Fichtenau draws on decades of specialized works on Italian, French, and German history. To these he adds his lifetime of reading and reflecting on primary sources. The book was clearly intended for both a scholarly and a more general audience. It is a meditation on human nature, human achievement, and human limitations.

The translator was privileged to serve as Visiting Professor at the University of Vienna in 1983, just as the final draft of *Lebensordnungen des 10. Jahrhunderts* was being completed. Professor Fichtenau kindly allowed me to read the manuscript, and I offered to translate

TRANSLATOR'S FOREWORD

it so that it could reach the wider audience that it, like his earlier Carolingian book, deserved. Translating another historian's work is always a tricky business: there are portions of the book I would have written differently, and I do not always share the methodological reflections of the author. Yet the process was immensely rewarding because it gave me the opportunity to observe in an intimate manner how one of the great historians of postwar Europe goes about plying the historian's craft.

The author's involvement in the translation has amounted to a true collaboration. Our original intention was to provide a complete translation of text and notes, but the financial realities of American publishing made this impossible. Were the full scholarly apparatus to be included, the English translation would have been impossibly expensive for any but a handful of research libraries. So Professor Fichtenau has provided a careful chapter-by-chapter bibliography of primary and secondary sources, which may prove even more useful to the general reader than the original notes. He has also closely reviewed the entire translation several times, made numerous corrections and revisions, incorporated necessary material from the notes into the text, and corrected a few minor errors in the German original. Thus the present book is more a second, revised edition than a simple translation.

It is a pleasure to acknowledge the vital assistance of those individuals who have made this translation possible. First and foremost, of course, has been Professor Fichtenau himself, who has labored more than an author should to see this project through. I wish to thank also Mrs. Fichtenau, whose warmth and hospitality made the long hours spent in their home reviewing and refining the translation a pleasure rather than a burden. Professor Herwig Wolfram, Professor Fichtenau's student and successor at the Institute for Austrian Historical Research, first introduced me to Professor Fichtenau and encouraged me to undertake the translation. In the United States, Professors John Freed, Barbara Rosenwein, and Daniel Callahan were extremely helpful in reviewing and commenting on large portions of the translation. Finally, I wish to thank my wife and daughters for their patience as I spent many hours away from them living in the tenth century.

PATRICK J. GEARY

Gainesville, Florida

INTRODUCTION

Approaching the end of the second millennium, historians should look back to the end of the first, asking themselves how people lived at that time and what they thought about their society. It should be interesting to see how much human life and human motivations have changed, and what has remained constant until our own epoch: Heraclitus was wrong: all is *not* flux, and even in antiquity many erred in placing their hopes on the changeability of human beings.

Some may welcome an attempt to present a synthesis of many elements of medieval life which for the most part have been studied separately. Some may also think it worthwhile to reconsider an epoch often misunderstood as a "dark age." This book can be called a synthesis with the reservation that no synthesis can be complete. For example, no great territorial differentiation will be found here. Can we treat the vanishing (or vanished) Carolingian Empire as a whole, at a time when parts had found their way to become Germany, France, and Italy? On the other hand, can we be content with studying the development of those continental countries alone, when England was becoming increasingly an integral part of post-Carolingian Europe?

What was intended here was not a monograph but a series of studies. Incomplete as they are, may they be a first step toward summarizing the rich sources of the tenth century as well as the research of historians living in different countries and using different methods. It will be up to younger scholars to go beyond this point.

Our chronological period is the tenth and early eleventh centuries. The Year of the Millennium quoted by some chroniclers and many modern scholars in reality changed nothing. Writing on two or more centuries is quite common, but it has some disadvantages. The picture thus presented is less precise; though rich in detail, it is somewhat faded. When focusing on the lifetime of a few generations, we hope not to disregard what was specific for that period. On the other hand, much of what will be treated here can be found in earlier or later centuries: it is the common ground of the Middle Ages.

One can write history from many different perspectives, most of which complement each other. The present study aims to show how people attempted to understand and set in order the fluctuating variety of human experience. Living in a society presupposes an *ordo,* which has formed the society. The German title of this book begins with the word *Lebensordnungen,* orders of living, with all its differentiation of rank and status. It is a vast topic, and we can approach it here only with the help of some examples.

We have a double task: first, we must speak of human groups and institutions that actually exist (or that are presumed by modern scholarship to have existed). Second, we must deal with the mental representations that contemporaries had of their social grouping and its *ordo.* Modern historians often used to pass over these representations, as they did not fit into what they considered reality. But reality, in a larger sense, can also be popular opinion, which produces concrete and, hence, real effects in history.

With incomplete knowledge and inadequate means of comprehension, people tried to comprehend and systematize their world—to create an *ordo.* Such a system seeks continuity within the flux of time; it needs a canon of fixed behavior. People feel less uneasy as members of an organized group with its standard feelings and ceremonial, in a fixed relationship with other groups and bound by "everlasting" custom. But the system was insufficient. Threatened by incomprehensible phenomena, the "legitimate order" often succumbed to ruse and passion. It was far from a homogeneous and rationally developed system, and some of its principles contradicted one another. This contradiction is often neglected by medievalists, although it was a painful experience of past generations. Seen from afar, medieval society may appear monolithic, closed, but it had grave problems, many of them unconnected with external exigencies.

The "dark age" of the tenth century also had its positive qualities and was occasionally praised as a golden age by subsequent generations. In modern times, many historians have seen it as an age of decadence and decay, the ruins of the Carolingian Empire. It is true that the period was closely bound to the Frankish heritage, which may justify our limiting this book to the old Frankish territories: we shall speak of France, the Frankish parts of Germany and Italy, and Catalonia, for which modern study exists by Pierre Bonnassie (see

Bibliography). Sources for the tenth century are not as meager as historians used to believe before they learned to use charters, saints' *vitae,* contracts, and so forth. Unfortunately, the documents of that period have uneven geographic representation and concern the upper classes more than the mass of the population. We know all too little about the lower strata, their daily life and their conceptions. This is also true, in part, for the upper levels of lay society. With meager sources, a "history of mentalities," such as is called for by our French colleagues, must be written piecemeal. It is a very important task, however, and one which has its background not only in Marc Bloch's work. This approach to history can be found here and there in the works of Max Weber and Oswald Spengler. Unlike Bloch's successors in the French *Annales* school, their suggestions found little echo among German historians.

Ultimately, all history is a history of mentalities. The word should not be overused. It will be employed in this book as rarely as other words that cannot be defined unambiguously and are in danger of becoming catchphrases. It would also be a pity if research into mentalities should be carried on in too abstract a manner and thereby fall into the errors of what was once called intellectual history: the products of thinking and meaning cannot be separated from the existence of people in this world.

Since the present book can be neither a monograph on the tenth century nor a synthetic presentation of its social order, the reader will think that much is missing or insufficiently treated. The author intentionally avoided referring the reader to the complete literature on each question treated, preferring to cite significant primary sources. Ideally, both should be provided: the orderly instruction of a textbook and a more discursive series of studies in which the specific evidence of the sources remains in view. This book is of the second type.

We begin with examples of medieval thinking about order. The examples show that those thoughts were rooted in reality and, in a sense, formed a part of this reality of life. People sought to give to all persons their due and to assign to each an appropriate place in the community. Restraining the individual impulse and making people fit into the collective order constituted an important part of "civilizing" mankind.

Given the small dimensions of the world as it existed before the age of modern mass society, this quest for order could be so intensive that everyone within one's own group might be assigned a rank, either permanent or changeable. This ranking, of course, had a practical basis, like the pecking order of the henhouse. Such a gradation could also foster a sense of security—the world was "in order."

In an age when abstract thinking was little developed, it was useful to have concrete indicators of what orders meant. Institutions were recognized by the people when they became "visible" in form of their functionaries; there was law, but rarely was it written law; it resided mostly in pronouncements and ceremonies. Above all there was custom, a practical knowledge of what was right, the appropriate conduct in all circumstances of daily life. Those who did not know or did not wish to follow these rules of the game lost their rank and excluded themselves from the group. Many of these rules, although they have largely lost their meaning and have been abandoned by some, exist even today.

After several examples from the broad area of tenth-century ceremony, ritual, and custom, the order of the family will be discussed, but family in the wider sense of the period as *familia*. Here our narrative sources are particularly poor. Attempts to arrive at a statistical evaluation of such an early period must remain incomplete. This topic has often been treated from the perspective that the family of the "feudal age" must have been essentially different from that of the bourgeois epoch. We must reject such a preconceived opinion and ask only what the sources can tell us about the central problems: the form of the household community; the position and authority of women; and the *Sippe* (or clan) as a wider kin group. Familial sense was strong enough to have served as the model for other forms of ordering.

So much has been said about political orders that repetition seems useless. We know that political institutions were filled by kings and nobility, and we can see the mutual influence of each of the groups— though some historians regard kingship and others nobility as the decisive factor. Our concern is with only one part of the subject: how far both institutions were perceived as a higher unity in the thought of the period. This question concerns the term *nobilitas,* which is usually equated with nobility. We must distinguish, however, between the nobles as a well-defined social group and "noble" in the sense of well-born, high-minded, and so on. In German, the "nobles" collectively are called *der Adel* (the nobility); the adjective "noble" is *edel.* Our sources were not yet acquainted with the rationally defined technical meaning of *Adel,* which is a product of a later period. Nobility, as a body of leading men, was not yet a "closed" group; it included the king as well as many ecclesiastics. We focus on these persons and groups as part of a developing nobility.

All medieval orders had both a certain independence and a larger or smaller overlap. When we speak of nobility, we must also think of royalty, clergy, and family. Between them there could be collisions of obligations, although those radical thinkers who wanted to separate them clearly from each other were not yet born. The "world" did not stop at the monastery door; indeed, from the monastery an attempt was made to educate the worldly. Clerics (or Church) and laity were seen not as a duality but simply as "Christendom."

Monasticism had separated itself from the world as an independent order, forming a spiritual family which renounced all that possessed value for the nobility. Discussing monasticism in this context cannot provide much that is new because so much has been done in this area during recent decades. Thus it may be best to sum up what is important from the perspective of the sources, that is, through the eyes of past generations.

It is obvious that monastic attitudes differed from those of nobility, but both lived together in peace. We no longer regard these differences from the moralistic point of view of the leaders of Cluniac and Gregorian reform ideologies. What they wanted was, in its own way, magnificent. But their program required a transformation of current customs. The attachment of their contemporaries to these customs often prevailed, and not only in the secular realm.

The clergy received a generally modest literary education, either alongside of or within their moral and religious formation. Lay education was, with few exceptions, nonliterate. It consisted mainly in knowledge of practical life, a rudimentary view of the world, and a similarly limited religious background. This knowledge was transmitted primarily within the family, although the local clergy was theoretically available for religious instruction. Thanks to the effort to assimilate this folk religion and morals to the teaching of the Church, we have references to the deviations in the former from the latter. Since we know little about the mass of the population of this period, these are precious indications of the thought and actions of the lower ranks of society beyond the sphere of material activity. We no longer speak of these customs as superstition or abuses, nor do we glorify them as a sacred inheritance. There are significant parallels with the evidence of ethnological studies on non-European societies.

These currents were long ignored by German scholars. Parallels of this kind show that continuity—whether with antiquity or with Germanic tradition—is not as important as some historians have believed.

Many scholars would happily trade our knowledge of popular beliefs for richer sources on the economic conditions under which this population lived. By the tenth century the age of the great polyptyches was past, and from only some regions do charters offer a partial compensation. One always learns more about great landlords, especially ecclesiastics, than about smaller land holders and their servants. Still, one can attempt to use the extant sources to extract what they have to say about the peasantry. Such an approach is less questionable methodologically than to make retrospective inferences about the tenth century from later periods richer in sources.

The first part of this book treats of order and orders; the last will be devoted to disorder. The two belong together like light and shadow, the striving for clarity and perfection and its very imperfect realization. Even a very conservative society with strict rules and customs has inherent tensions, since it lacks the unity, one might say the inhumanity, of an all-pervading system. Although the tensions do not seriously threaten the coherence of society, they are manifest in certain fissures. Symptomatic of this tendency to disorder are heretical groups, the excessive use of ecclesiastical power, the formalization of moral behavior, etc. So-called Chiliasm will not be considered, because there is no clear evidence that the people of that epoch feared the imminent end of the world.

In the late nineteenth century in Germany, a form of historical discourse, *Kultur- und Sittengeschichte* (history of culture and customs), was much in vogue. It purported to show how far behind the dark ages trailed in the enlightenment of general progress. Much of what had been unintelligible to bourgeois comprehension was explained as the stupidity, immorality, and raw barbarism of a gullible age. Such anachronistic mischief has ended, but cultural history remains a suspect discipline. It is time for it to reemerge renewed and strengthened, as our pride in our own age and its progress is greatly diminished. Knowing that we have little reason to look back with disdain upon the different world of the Middle Ages, we can study its motivations without emotional involvement. And as we do so, we will often find that men acted as they believed they ought to, whether the effects proved to be good or evil.

I wish to express my warmest thanks to Professor Patrick J.

Geary, of the University of Florida, who initiated this translation and completed it successfully despite various difficulties (including those of mentalities and behavior). I also thank my publishers, both German and American. Their common efforts will, I hope, serve to enlarge the understanding between scholars on two continents.

HEINRICH FICHTENAU

Vienna, Austria

I·ORDO

1 ❧ ORDER AS RANK ORDER

EVERY TENTH-CENTURY SCHOOLBOY learned from the Book of Genesis and from examples in the traditional curriculum of the *artes liberales* that the world was a well-ordered cosmos. The enemies of the divinely willed order were the devil and any person who allied himself with him. In them was to be found the cause whenever disaster struck, be it in human affairs or in natural catastrophes, epidemics, and famines. Only slowly did people come to accept the Christian teaching that the most significant conflicts between the powers of good and evil take place within the human soul. Even in the domain of law the sense of guilt was little developed. Some scholars have argued that until the middle of the twelfth century people had no notion of punishment but, rather, conceived of a sort of "restorative magic" which served as an antidote for "objective disorder." This may be an exaggeration; nevertheless *ordo* was primarily an external, strongly formalized order because people simply could not see and grasp internal qualities. A contrast between inner being and outward behavior, and hence hypocrisy, seldom existed or at least was seldom acknowledged as people generally trusted the behavior of their fellows. We should not underestimate the pedagogical effect of the constant practice of conduct prescribed by habit. What we dismiss as mere etiquette had a certain formative power.

Order (*ordo*) included the "orders" (*ordines*), as was already indicated in the social divisions of antiquity. Senators, equestrians, urban corporations and so forth were recognizable by means of clothing and badges; they formed groups with their own institutions and were clearly separated from each other. During the early Middle Ages, such distinctions diminished. In monasticism, order first meant a way of life; only later did the *Ordo Cluniacensis* become a legally founded association of monasteries. Contemporaries were generally satisfied to divide Christendom into three large groups according to the most significant function of each in society. Scholars such as Georges Duby have devoted much attention in recent years to the tenth- and eleventh-century sources that deal with this subject. A similar threefold division already existed in ancient India and Iran, among the Ionian Greeks, the Romans, the Celts, the Scandinavians, and others. The three groups normally consisted of priests, warriors, and agricultural workers. The haziness of this distribution is apparent in the fact that trade and crafts have no place in it. At the beginning of the High Middle Ages, however, it more closely approximated reality than at other periods, for at that time a peasantry made up of free and unfree began to consolidate into a unified group. Various attempts have been made to subdivide the three groups and thus to shape them more realistically.

ORDO AND ORDINES

The tripartite division, whose sequence—the priest first, the peasant last—indicates a specific value judgment, had to be harmonized with the fact that according to Christian teaching all men were equal. Adalbero of Laon got around it by ascribing equality to the divine order and inequality to the human. Similarly, Rather of Verona derived the latter from the "dissimilarity of customs," that is, of customary law. In that context he ventured the opinion that many are placed under other men in such a way that the better must serve the worse. Such social criticism remained isolated, and Rather did not deny that these circumstances were derived from the will of God and the sin of Adam, as Hincmar of Reims had explained by citing Gregory the Great. Elsewhere, Rather was more clearly under the influence of Isidore of Seville when he said that servitude was a fruit of sin and that lordship was necessary for the maintenance of order.

The absolute necessity of a hierarchical order beyond that of positive law resulted from the medieval reception of Neoplatonic thought. Saint Paul spoke of the *ordines* of the resurrected; that is, he seems to have assumed an ordering of men in the next world by groups, parallel to the earthly order. Later the orders of the heavenly hierarchy were seen as primary and were held out as models for earthly groupings. There were angels and archangels, explained Gregory the Great, different *in potestate et ordine* although both archangels and angels had the same nature. This shows us, Gregory continues, that created beings cannot live and be governed in equality. Hincmar, who in the monastery of Saint-Denis had studied the translations of Pseudo-Dionysius "the Areopagite," cited this sentence and further expanded the parallels between the earthly and heavenly worlds. The words of the Greek author also had some effect in the tenth and eleventh centuries: Abbot Maiolus of Cluny read his work, Adalbero of Laon referred to him. Later, references to the parallel between heavenly and earthly orders are numerous: in paradise the (nine) choirs of angels shine forth; radiant is the grandeur of the patriarchs, the order of the prophets, the choir of the apostles, and so forth.

Such a perception was of course more appropriate to clerics than to the laity. Nevertheless, the laity too imagined the heavenly world as a graduated order in which bishops and monks stood at the highest level—the holy bishop, monk, or hermit was, so to speak, the normal type of saint. Then followed the worldly, with a few great laymen venerated as holy. The "common people" were content to reach the position of servants in paradise. From the year 940 we have the story of a young girl named Flothilde who was a servant of the monastery Avenay sur Marne (dedicated to Saint Peter). Flothilde had a vision, in which she heard the Virgin Mary request Peter to give her this girl—apparently for personal service in heaven.

When the three groups were compared with each other, it was clear to the ecclesiastics that they ranked above the laity. Within the clergy, monks developed a tendency to place themselves next to and even above the secular clergy; this evaluation was related to practical matters, mainly to the exemption of monasteries from the power of the bishop in whose diocese the monasteries lay. In this spirit Abbo of Fleury developed his tripartite ranking of monks, bishops, and laymen. Rather of Verona, whom we must continue to cite for questions of rank, sided with the monastic party, to which he himself had belonged before he had become a bishop: monks justly reign in heaven with God and sit in judgment on the world, for they would rather command (in heaven) the owners of riches than seek (earlier, on earth) riches for themselves. Not only the laity but also the secular clergy have property and are therefore, according to Rather, under the (heavenly) lordship of monasticism. This is an unusual opinion, which becomes easier to explain when one realizes that a quite different view was generally held: namely that God, with the (holy) bishops, rules over and judges the world (monks included).

From a comparative evaluation of the *ordines,* no real lordship of one group over the others could be established, in spite of Rather. It was a kind of reputation, a kind of "social existence," that wielded a certain authority over the subordinated groups. And such authority was all the more important, the less the reputation of a major group was supported by institutions. Since the Constantinian period the bishops had held a specific rank among the holders of imperial office; now many of them had sunk to the position of mere agents or Frankish counts—the social prestige of the secular clergy was not fixed once and for all. For good reason, Bishop Adalbero of Laon felt called upon to defend polemically the position of the secular clergy in his poem to King Robert II: this monarch was attached to the monasticism of Fleury and the Cluniacs.

Not only the prestige of the entire group but that of each of its individual members was of great importance. Even in an association of formally equal partners, each can have an individual rank and prestige. That Christ was asked by his disciples who would be the greatest in heaven—and thus, by implication, who was greatest now in his earthly existence—shows how much rank is an issue of human concern. One could be content with the establishment of a *primus inter pares,* or one could order all the members according to rank, and hence give the group an internal structure. The tendency to do the latter was always present; how far it actually took place depended upon the number of persons, the criteria used, and so on. Within the secular clergy these criteria were established very early; the offices were firmly organized, and leaving these traditions was not easy. In the lay world, whose familial groupings constantly changed and in which high value was placed on personal prestige, no permanent internal order comparable to that of the clergy could be devised. Even feudalism did little to change this situation.

Christ had selected the apostles on the basis of equality; yet he had given one of them a leading position: on this precedent Pope Leo the Great and, after him, Hincmar of Reims based the argument that within the *ordo generalis* of priests there were various degrees or "dignities." No justification was required that the holders of such dignities should endeavor always and everywhere to "represent" these dignities. In a period when elevated forms of abstract thought were engaged in with difficulty, rank had to show itself in outward things. Atto, Bishop of Vercelli, critically described how many of the prelates of his age were intent on both representing and being recognized in their position (*honor*): they wanted to appear learned, they wanted to be greeted first, they wanted to take the first place at meals, they demanded the first seat (*primas cathedras*) in (ecclesiastical) assemblies. Later, in the eleventh century, Peter Damian wrote similarly of the clergy: "They love the best places at meals, the first seat in the synagogue (that is, at synods) and the greetings of the crowd, and they wish to be called Rabbi by the people." The biblical allusions in both cases stamp the clergy as modern Pharisees and show what had hardly changed in a millennium: esteem demands marks of esteem, and there can be no social rank without orders of greeting and seating. Conflicts over rank occur mainly in situations where rank is not unambiguously fixed in each case "from above" or when there is no power to make existing canons prevail. In Rome and in Byzantium, at least for a time, a strict government ruled, whose authority assigned to each his own (*suum cuique*). By contrast, the situation of the religious party of Pharisees presented in the New Testament, like that of the clergy in the Italian cities of the tenth century, was unstable.

In Ancient Rome there was a list (*album*) for members of boards, in which they appeared in a specific order (*certus ordo*). This list was intended to indicate in which order the members were to take their seats and to cast their votes. The etiquette in the imperial palace likewise required—at least in Byzantium—a written formulation. *Taktika* have survived from the ninth and tenth centuries, according to which the master of ceremonies of the palace assigned seats at the emperor's table and at the neighboring tables. The imperial order, even in seating at table, was an image of the divine world order, and it was actually God who assigned rank and office through the emperor. For the independent position of the Ottonians it was important that Liutprand of Cremona should formally protest that in Constantinople at the emperor's table he had been seated "behind" a Bulgar envoy.

Thus the high clergy took their place at the imperial table according to the dignity of their offices; a saint, Archbishop Epiphanios of Cyprus, is said to have drawn up the written order, which was then revised by Constantine Prophyrogennetos (913–59), the imperial author of the famous Book of Ceremonies. The order also held beyond the imperial table, for example, in the prelates' military service. The emperor and the patriarch had a good reason to concern themselves with this theme. At the beginning of the tenth century a conflict between the eastern ecclesiastical dignitaries and the prelates of the former Illyrian prefecture had degenerated into a brawl: "It appeared to us beneath all dignity that the servants (of God) should fight for the place of honor in front of the altar."

RANKING OF CITIES AND CHURCHES

When such unworthy squabbles even occurred in Byzantium, things could be no better in the West. Here there were lists, originating in Late Antiquity, of cities arranged according to provinces. They continued to be copied in the early Middle Ages because people consulted them for the rank of their churches as well as the age and the prestige of their city or region. These lists were more a mine of material than a firm guide for the *honor* of a community. For example, concerning the prestige of Châlons-sur-Marne, Fulbert of Chartres wrote to the bishop-elect of Soissons: "So that you do not slight the prestige of the church of Châlons, you should know that this city holds third place in the ancient description of the province of *Belgica secunda*, behind that of Reims." We shall frequently return to the notion that such historically based explanations were not simply the predilections of learned clerics but had real consequences. Apparently the bishop of Soissons had, as the senior pastor of the second church of *Belgica secunda* according to the *Notitia Galliarum,* the right to consecrate the archbishop of Reims.

That the *Notitia* distinguished between a *Belgica prima* and a *Bel-*

gica secunda also had significance in terms of rank: "primates (sunt) qui primas sedes tenent" (Primates are those who hold the first sees), reads the text of Pseudo-Isidore, which means that Trier, the metropolitan see of *Belgica prima,* had primacy over Reims! It is no wonder that Hincmar of Reims had a different opinion and secured papal confirmation of it.

In the foreground of classical thought stood neither regions nor provinces but *civitates,* cities with their adjacent territories. In survivals of this thought, as in poetic comparisons with Rome in the Carolingian and post-Carolingian periods, one likewise finds expressions of ranking. From the middle of the tenth century onward, the well-known historical forgeries of Trier call that city not "another" but "a second" Rome, and coins were struck at Trier with the inscription "Sanctus Petrus—secunda Roma." This was ammunition for the competition with Reims over precedence, as was the foundation legend of Trier developed around the year 1000: Trebeta, the son of Ninus and a contemporary of Abraham, had founded the city, while Reims could only look back to a comparatively recent foundation by Remus, the brother of Romulus. Next to this precedence based on pagan antiquity stood the "apostolic" primacy secured through two disciples of Saint Peter, to which we shall return.

To what extent bishops derived prestige from their cities is seen in Hincmar of Reims: bishops, he explained, must not have their see in castles or unseemly settlements because this would lead to the decay of episcopal dignity. They should be titled after an "honorable" city (*honorabilem urbem*). This view reflects that of the Roman church; such scruples still had to be developed in the secular, Germanic sphere.

Secular thought envisioned a rank order of tribes in which one's own tribe was placed first whenever possible. In the reign of Otto III, however, a connection with the different cultural position of the imperial lands becomes perceptible: books were decorated with miniatures in which four figures of serving women walk one behind the other. They are the personifications of Rome (or occasionally *Italia*), *Gallia, Germania,* and *Sclavinia.*

Both ecclesiastics and laity placed great emphasis on ancient descent. We have already seen this in the case of Trier and Reims. Just as Romulus was the founder of Rome, the expelled Remus and his followers established Reims, which was hence a sort of brother city to Rome. As we pointed out, the ecclesiastical rank of a city followed its secular rank; so the prestige of the metropolitan of Reims should, because of that historical link, approach that of the Roman see. The connections between the two cities and their ecclesiastical heads were ancient according to the declarations of Flodoard in his history of the church of Reims: "It is clear that the people of Reims (*populus Remorum*) was already in the earliest times bound in firm friendship with that of Rome," since Caesar wrote that the tribe of the "Remi" had sworn loyalty and friendship to the Romans. Also, the Apostle Peter himself had ordained an archbishop for Reims, Saint Sixtus (see Flodoard of Reims, Bib. sec. 1, 413 f.). There was another, simpler way to acquire the patina of age for an archbishopric, namely through papal privilege, as Magdeburg succeeded in acquiring from Pope John XIII in 967. The privilege said that Magdeburg should be "first with the first and ancient with the ancient (metropolitan towns)."

ECCLESIASTICAL DISPUTES OVER RANKING

From the rank of a city and its bishop within a specific province, the next step up was superintendence over a *Land*—a large territory or a realm. An expanded position of this kind was expressed in the ecclesiastical rank of metropolitan and led to a specific title reflecting this position, that of "primate" (of Gaul, Germany, etc.) Pseudo-Isidore had wished to raise this position to what one might call a "supermetropolitan." In the tenth century, little remained of this program other than precedence at synods. Nonetheless, politically meaningful rights were derived from the position. In the case of Trier, which, as we have seen, claimed to rank above the metropolitan of Reims, this prerogative was the basis for claims to chairmanship at "Gallic" and "Germanic" synods, at least as long as no papal legate was present. When the archbishop took his seat as "second" after the emperor or king, this precedence greatly promoted his prestige. Even more important, the presiding archbishop could direct and control the course of the synod. As president he had the right to announce his judgment first (*primatus sententiam edicendi*) and to publish the resolutions of the assembly.

Indirectly bound up with the primacy was the right of the primate, as the highest and first ecclesiastical dignitary in a kingdom, to consecrate Otto I. The well-known dispute of the Rhenish archbishops in 936 over the right to consecreate the king seems to have been followed by their attempts to obtain confirmation of primacy from Rome. In the West Frankish kingdom, thanks to better sources, the situation is clearer: here, as early as the ninth century, Reims and Sens had disagreed about the primacy. Silvester II solved the question by confirming the right of Reims to the royal coronation along with the primacy.

One can hardly ascertain how Rome extracted itself from these affairs in face of competing claims: ecclesiastical princes obtained such broad rights that scholars often have great difficulty explaining how these various rights did not cancel each other. For example, on 18 January 975 Archbishop Dietrich of Trier received from Pope Benedict VII confirmation of the primacy of his church, but in March of the same year the pope confirmed the powerful Archbishop Willigis of Mainz in the same position, along with the right of crowning royalty. One must assume an abrupt change of policy in order to understand these two confirmations. And in 981, the same Benedict VII granted Archbishop Giselher of Magdeburg the equal (*aequalis*) rank to the archbishops of Mainz, Trier, and Cologne "in the order of standing and sitting and in the discussion of all ecclesiastical affairs." This grant has correctly been seen as an implicit but total cancellation of primacies.

Perhaps a pope such as a Gregory VII could have established a strong ecclesiastical order on the far side of the Alps. However, the uncertain responses to the problems of rank order also had some general reasons, rooted in the period. The Roman clergy had little feel for problems of canon law in the tenth century, which was a transitional period between the earlier, predominantly episcopal structure of the Church and the later structure of an absolute papal primacy. Under the Empire, the matter of rank was intertwined with the fluctuations between monarchic and oligarchic secular power as well as with personal questions. The position of Mainz was underscored by its nearness to the kingship, while on the other hand the pope could not simply ignore the "historical" foundations of Trier's position. Otto I's dearest wish was to advance the cause of Magdeburg. The final result was a sort of neutralization of the primacy, which devalued it. Burchard of Worms says nothing about the right of primacy; in the eleventh century, Magdeburg, Trier, Mainz, and even Salzburg obtained the same ritual privilege, namely that the archbishop could have a cross carried before him, which suggests that the whole matter of primacy was being borne to its grave.

In Italy of course the pope, as bishop of Rome, exercised the primacy, so there the issue could be only that of the prestigious second place at synods. If the emperor was present, he sat at the pope's right hand; if he was absent, the old argument arose of whether this position should go to the archbishop of Milan or of Ravenna, or to the patriarch of Aquileia. Arles, where the primacy of Gaul was seen as an ancient privilege which had been unjustly forgotten, claimed to hold the second place behind the head of the Roman church. But the path to realizing this claim was blocked for a long time. In 876, Archbishop Ansegis of Sens had been raised to the position of papal vicar and primate in Gaul "and Germany" by Pope John VIII. Sens's vicarate (for Gaul) was renewed in 986 when Reims seemed vanquished from the field of contenders. The papal vicar held first place at synods and served as the intermediate judicial instance in appeals to the pope. Vicarate and primacy were as closely connected to each other as precedence at national assemblies was connected to both of them. In 937, following the dispute among the Rhenish archbishops over the right of consecration, Friedrich of Mainz was named papal vicar for "Germania," that is, Germany east of the Rhine.

Apostolicity and Ecclesiastical Precedence

What has been described in the previous two sections corresponds to the concept of order of the Roman Empire as well as that of the Roman church, which was developing from it. Beside this concept, and originally not in the sense of a competing system, was the attempt to understand ecclesiastical organization in categories drawn from the New Testament and the Acts of the Apostles. Christ's directive to the apostles to go forth and teach all peoples, and, even prior to this, his sending out of the disciples, suggested that so important a task as missionary activity could hardly have been undertaken by chance (confuse): worldwide misisonary activity must therefore have begun and been furthered according to a divinely willed plan. Each apostle must have gone to preach the gospel according to the will of the Holy Spirit in order to teach one or more peoples. Greek, Syriac, and Latin sources explained how this occurred. A text from the beginning of the tenth century explains how the task of converting "all" the peoples of the earth was divided up: Andrew went to Achaia, the apostles Thomas and Bartholomew attended to India, Matthew evangelized Ethiopia, Simon and Judas went into the Persian empire, John went to "Asia" (Asia Minor), Peter and Paul to Rome, Philip to Illyria, while James the Elder and James the Younger remained in Samaria and Judaea.

It was clear that the most important churches, that is, the old patriarchates, must have been founded by apostles. Apparently there were differences in rank among these too, and they compromised on the question of who had first position. This view seems to derive from what one can call "episcopalism." It is found in the canonical collection of Burchard of Worms, while elsewhere the papal *principatus* was derived from the powers of Peter's keys. Constantinople, which was so much more recent in comparison with the Eternal City, had difficulty establishing a rank equal to Rome. For this purpose the apostle Andrew was employed, who was put forth as the founder of the bishopric. In the gospel, Andrew appears as the first to be invited by Christ to be his disciple; it was Andrew who brought his brother Peter to Christ. Thus he had temporal priority and with it a higher rank.

Such tricks of biblical scholarship, of course, could support the interests of ecclesiastical politics only in few cases. Consequently, either the notion of "disciples of the apostles" was emphasized, or the concept of "apostle" was extended to include the disciples, who in turn had a great number of their own largely legendary disciples. As a last resort, one could claim, as happened in Le Mans, that the holy founder of a bishopric had lived in the postapostolic period but that he had been made an apostle in the same manner as had Paul— by God's will.

During the controversy over the right to crown Otto the Great, the archbishop of Trier argued for the primacy of his see on the grounds that it was, in a manner of speaking, founded by Saint Peter. He invoked the Trier legend that this saint had commissioned three of his followers, investing them with his staff, and thus had himself legitimized the apostolicity of the bishopric. There are numerous similar legends with which the antiquity of rank of Gallic bishoprics was supported. They were invented or reworked in order to show the rank of the particular church. Thus Flodoard would write that the first apostle, Peter, had sent Saint Sixtus to Reims as its first bishop and thereby had given that city primacy over all of Gaul. Not only in Sens was there a different view: according to Rodulfus Glaber, Lyons had been since ancient times the bearer of the true light (of faith) to the largest part of Gaul because it was there that the first messenger of the faith had been sent by Saint Polycarp, a disciple of the apostle John. In the second half of the tenth century such legends were particularly numerous in Aquitaine: starting with the tale that Peter had given his staff to Saint Fronto in order to found the church of Péri-gueux and had made him the bishop of his native land, numerous holy Aquitanians were certified as Peter's emissaries. We shall discuss only one of these cases in detail.

The name of a certain Martial is first found in the writings of Gregory of Tours, where he is said to have been a missionary and bishop in Limoges. In the ninth century he was styled a saint and was moved from the third century back to the first as the alleged representative of Saint Peter in Limoges; chronological incongruencies of this sort were frequent, and one challenged them only when the preservation of one's own interests was arousing criticism. In the tenth century, Martial's grave in Limoges became a respected place of pilgrimage and his monastery gained wealth and honors. It was further advanced through a (second) version of his life written by a supposedly contemporary "Aurelian." Here Martial appears as a cousin of Saint Peter who followed Peter to Rome and christianized Gaul from Limoges. Thus he was almost an apostle; the further development of his story can be credited to the fact that, from the ninth century on, missionaries to whole regions were increasingly referred to as apostles.

In 1029 the apostolicity of Martial was solemnly recognized by a synod, apparently against the wishes of the assembled bishops and as a result of the pressure of Duke William V of Aquitaine. The duke wanted to strengthen his lordship over Aquitaine by the foundation of a religious center for his territory. Another circumstance favorable to Martial was the role he had played at the beginning of the Peace of God movement. In 994 the saint was both witness and guarantor for the decrees of a synod in Limoges. There his relics were solemnly displayed and inspected by a crowd of magnates who had hurried there "from all parts of Aquitaine," "together with bishops and an endless mass of people." The director of propaganda for the promotion of Martial was Ademar of Chabannes, who was accused by his opponents of having received money from the monks for his efforts.

The arguments which both sides brought to the discussion are characteristic for this sort of ecclesiastical-historical reflection. Martial was taken from the ranks of the disciples of the apostles and certified as a disciple of Christ (codisciple of Peter). Just as Peter had been delegated to the "Italians" and Andrew to Greece, Martial was sent to Gaul. Only after him came the saints Martin and Hilarius. Martial converted the Aquitanians and founded the churches of

Tours, Poitiers, Clermont, and even, through his emissary Dionysius, Paris. The seventy-two disciples sent forth by Christ were apostles, and Martial was one of them; apostles, moreover, are all who, like Martial, first preach in a region.

Admission to the ranks of the apostles was not sufficient in itself; now it was necessary to determine Martial's rank within their inner order. This order was that of the name order in the litany of the saints. In Limoges, Martial's name was placed in fourteenth place (behind Matthew and Paul but before Mark and Luke). This led to a protest demonstration by an opponent: during the recitation of the litany he shouted out Martial's name in a minor position, among the names of the confessors.

The opponents of the alleged apostle objected to the broadening of the definition of apostle to include all seventy-two disciples and the declaration of their places of burial as apostolic sees. They pointed out that for the diocese of Limoges and its patron, the protomartyr Stephen, the promotion of Martial would result in a reduction in rank, and even Saint Peter would be downgraded by Martial's new position.

Ademar and the supporters of Martial were partly defeated. The saint's apostolicity did not achieve general acceptance until the end of the eleventh century. Had the program succeeded, however, it could have had far-reaching consequences. Martial was now, so to speak, a rival of Saint Stephen, patron of the cathedral, and his monastery began to push the canons and the cathedral aside. Ademar and his colleagues hoped to attract to the monastery of Saint Martial both ecclesiastical prerogatives such as baptisms and secular ones such as the emancipation of serfs. It was hoped that in the future the magnates of the Limousin would have to bring their sons to the cathedral for baptism and that other churches would be used for ordinary baptisms. The greatest number of such baptisms should take place at Saint Martial.

A further effect of the cult of Martial might have been that his monastery, as the "First Church of Gaul," would establish itself at the head of an association of monasteries. This never happened, in part because of the prior existence of Cluny and its "king," Abbot Odilo. In addition there was Fleury with its great influence. According to Gerbert of Aurillac, Fleury held the place of honor among the monasteries of Gaul "because of the veneration of Father Benedict," and as the place where his relics were to be found.

The Abbot Primate

In Gerbert's day, the abbot primate in Gaul was acknowledged to be in Fleury. Here there was no clear order. Nicolas II had confirmed for the abbot of Montecassino that he occupied the highest place among abbots, possibly even for the entire Church, and as such should always be the first to announce his judgment (*sententia*). Alexander II communicated to Fleury that its abbot was "the first of the abbots of Gaul." Previously Gregory V had proclaimed the abbot of Fleury as the primate of Gallic abbots. The diploma is genuine, and it speaks of an *ordo* of secular clergy who have no rights in monasteries. This phrase reflects the influence of Abbot Abbo, who was at that time in Rome and secured the privilege; it was he who had distinguished three *ordines:* the laity, seculars, and monks. In 1007, high ecclesiastics sought to burn the privilege of Gregory V. When an archbishop of Sens and a bishop of Orléans so acted, one can be sure that much more than protocol was at issue.

Matters were never really clarified, however. At Sens, for example, it was believed that its Archbishop Seguin had confirmed the abbot primate of the archdiocese of Sens to the abbot of Saint-Pierre-le-Vif. Seguin was thought to be relying on the supervisory right of the bishop over monasteries. On the other hand, when the situation required it, the abbots themselves could choose the one among them who would be the highest-ranking, as was the case in an assembly of the abbots of the archdiocese of Reims. For the most part, however, it was popes who made pronouncements concerning the "natural" abbot primate.

In Germany, Fulda's abbot was spoken of as the ranking abbot, in the tradition of Saint Boniface. Mainz also appealed to this tradition in order to obtain the title of papal vicar for the archbishop. In 969, Pope John XIII bestowed on the abbot of Fulda the right of "first seat" (*primatus sedendi*). As the bearer of a high honor (*archimandrita*) he was to be respected and his advice was to be sought. This was to be for assemblies in "Gaul" and in "Germany," that is, in the sections of the Ottonian Empire on the left as well as on the right bank of the Rhine. When in 999 the Aquitanian Gerbert, who as pope had taken the name Silvester II, confirmed this right of primacy, he spoke only of "Germania." One can imagine that for him the term Gallia must have had a much wider meaning. That he took this issue seriously enough to concern himself with it personally is significant. In preparing the confirmation, Silvester did not follow the formula of his predecessors John XIII and John XV but devised a new, carefully thought-out formulation.

The "first seat" must not have meant the presidency at synods of abbots, concerning which there exists no documentation from Germany. "Whenever abbots come together," reads the confirmation of John XIII, and by this one should understand above all synods of the German high clergy including both bishops and abbots. The *primatus sedendi* could apply here within the curia of the abbots. Apparently its real meaning lay somewhere between a rather colorless and powerless position of honor and what Silvester II allegedly intended by the insertion of two words, *sive iudicandi,* that is, the power of jurisdiction over other monasteries. At best it may have indicated arbitration, or rather an echo of a prerogative which, in the case of bishops, had real importance. In 969, John XIII interpreted the *primatus sedendi* of the archbishopric of Trier in the following manner: at convocations the archbishop should be the first to announce his decisions. From this question of protocol developed a not unimportant political claim. When the archbishop of Trier or, for the assembled abbots, the abbot of Fulda had announced his juridical opinion, it was much more difficult for the subsequent speakers to plead a contrary position. Thus quite properly the circumstances of the Fulda primacy have been viewed as an echo of the Rhenish archbishops' struggle over the primacy in "Gaul" and in Germany. Fulda, which at that time stood far removed from the efforts of Cluny, had certainly not striven "to become chief and leader of the entire German Benedictine order," as in 1944 the German scholar Konrad Lübeck believed.

The ecclesiastical primacy described above was tied to its own time, and after the tenth century it continued in a much more modest form, as in the title of the abbot of Fulda, who until 1803 styled himself primate of Gaul and Germany. What was timeless was the fact that there had to be a seating order at assemblies and that the order of speakers followed the seating. Little could be accomplished without the designation of a president of an assembly, and, without a specific order, debates and votes could easily degenerate into chaos. These were, and remain, practical necessities; what has become foreign to us today is the belief that the organization of earthly society is necessarily a reflection of the heavenly one. This "conception" of the heavenly hierarchy was accessible not only to visionaries; it could also be presented on a smaller scale in various churches. When the church of the Virgin was to be consecrated in Cambrai, the bishop of the diocese and the abbot of the monastery ordered a multitude of relics, which had been collected for the solemn occasion, arranged as though for an ecclesiastical assembly. As the "president," the principal patron in his reliquary had his place on the *cathedra* of the bishop. He was termed *pontifex summus,* and "holy bishops," represented by their remains, were positioned beside him. Then followed the rest, "that is, the martyrs, confessors and virgins, each according to rank (*ordo*) as was appropriate." Together they formed a circle, in the center of which was probably the main altar of the church. It was a sort of synod of the saints of Cambrai, who had been summoned to this solemn occasion. This circular arrangement was likewise normal at ecclesiastical assemblies.

SEATING ARRANGEMENTS AT RELIGIOUS ASSEMBLIES

The earthly participants in such convocations were seated according to ancient, simple principles of ranking: bishops were arranged in the order of their consecration. How abbots were ordered is hard to ascertain: apparently they were usually arranged according to the date of their *professio* or entry into the monastic life. When bishops and abbots assembled together, the latter were naturally "placed below." An exact seating order of a German general synod held in 1027 in Frankfurt at which the emperor was present has survived. It is interesting to note how the general principles of ranking were harmonized with the specifics of this instance.

The episcopal *cathedra* in the east of the church was occupied, as was his right, by Archbishop Aribo of Mainz, although he was a party in the matter before the synod—it was a dispute concerning Gandersheim. Sitting in the apse of the church indicated the right of spiritual lordship, which was precisely the question in the Gandersheim dispute. In the west choir stood the royal throne of Conrad II, flanked by the seats of the archbishops of Cologne and Magdeburg. Archbishop Pilgrim of Cologne had been consecrated in 1021 and Archbishop Huntfrid of Magdeburg in 1023, so that without fear of protest the former could be seated on the right and the latter on the left of Conrad. Next to each of them sat their suffragan bishops, who were present at the synod, according to the order of their consecration, so that the one who had been consecrated most recently sat the farthest from the emperor. In the east, the archbishop of Mainz was at the center, and next to him on both sides sat his suffragans, again according to the date of their consecration, although in alternating lines: to the right the bishops of Strasbourg (1001), Bamberg (1007), Würzburg (1018), Hildesheim (1022), and Worms (1025); on the left those of Augsburg (1006), Paderborn (1009), Verden (1014), and Halberstadt (1023). The "senior" among them, Werner of Strasbourg, directed the judicial proceedings since the archbishop of Mainz was a party to the dispute, and the "second in seniority," Bruno of Augsburg, was the first to be called as a witness.

In this description we should note that the bishop of Strasbourg "deserved this position (*honor*) because of his primacy," that is to say, there was a sort of "consecration primacy" to which certain rights were attached. The fact that the emperor had his throne in the west may be explained by his function as protector of the Church rather than by his position as a layman. The author of our account seems not to have actually ascribed him to this *ordo* since he mentions that the laity took part in the synod only in the person of Conrad's sword bearer. Moreover, the western end was that part of the church which bore the least prestige, and one would not expect archbishops to sit here. "Proximity to the king," however, certainly made up for that disadvantage. It seems that the king's throne was not placed in the area of the western entrance but near the transept, if for no other reason than for that of acoustics. The north and south transepts were also occupied, so that the assembly was cruciform. In the south, the "better" section, sat bishops from other ecclesiastical provinces: Verdun, Mantua, Oldenburg, Schleswig. In the north choir sat the abbots of Fulda, Hersfeld, Mainz, Bleidenstadt (near Wiesbaden), Schwarzach (on the Rhine) and Würzburg.

This seating arrangement had probably been prepared in the court of the archbishop of Mainz, for he certainly would have been pleased with it. Cologne and Magdeburg played supporting roles while the high clergy of Mainz dominated the scene: they sat before the main altar in a raised sanctuary (*super gradus*), opposite the enthroned emperor. The Mainz clerics had followed canonical rules of order and thereby emphasized their own precedence. It was an excellent piece of work complying with both the canonical rules and those of the seating order of a court banquet: the most prestigious bishops should be in the center, the more important ones should always sit nearer the center than the lesser ones; the second should always have his place on the right and never on the left of the first. We can perceive in such formalism the sense of order shared by high ecclesiastics, who were noblemen too.

In certain situations, principles other than the date of consecration determined seating order. Still, in 1046, at the beginning of the reform period, a general synod was held in Pavia to deal with a dispute over the seating of the bishop of Verona. It was decided that he should sit on the right hand of the patriarch of Aquileia; henceforth at councils and synods the city (*urbs*) of Verona should have the second place (*sedem*) next to Aquileia. One would think it was a question of ranking Roman city gods in a temple rather than an assembly of bishops. In this instance the awakening urban self-consciousness of the northern Italian cities overlapped ecclesiastical tradition. The bishop was the representative of his city—in a new sense an *episcopus civitatis*. Quite naturally, in Italy the question of rank was also related to the traditional hierarchy of late Roman cities, since more was known about ranking in Italy than what could be gleaned in Gaul from the *Notitia Galliarum*. In Italy, disputes over seating order also included conflicts concerning the seat on the right hand of the pope and thus the position of second in the entire Church, or at least of the Church in Italy. Likewise the primacy, of which we have already spoken, was the primacy of an episcopal city, not a personal position of honor such as an appointment as papal vicar.

The ranking of the secular clergy in the tenth and early eleventh centuries is too broad a subject to be presented here in its entirety. The few examples we have presented are sufficient to indicate the large and complex role it played in the thought of the ecclesiastical hierarchy. One might imagine that role to have been quite different in monasticism. Yet even here we find many problems of "internal order."

Monastic Rank Orders

In parallel to the consecration dates of bishops, Saint Benedict had commanded an ordering of his monks according to the dates of their professions. Entry into the monastery was a kind of rebirth; he who had been called at the second hour of the day should be considered "younger" than he who had been called at the first hour. The abbot was authorized to change this order, not on whim but only for good reasons: he would reward good and faithful conduct or he would "downgrade" (*degradaverit*) the lazy. Reward and punishment only had meaning when they were made explicit for the community. When in procession, the brothers walked *secundum ordines,* that is, according to their actual or adjusted order of profession, on their way to the kiss of peace, to communion, or to the chanting of the psalms. They stood in this order during the office. Anyone who came late had to stand as the last. The relations between *maior* and *minor, senior* and *iunior,* were also evident in the obligation of greetings: the younger had to offer his seat to the older and was obliged to remain standing until the older had ordered him to sit. An order of greeting continues today in the military as a training method with one important difference: it is not used among holders of the same rank. In the language of our day we might speak of a high degree of ritualization in social relations, which reaches its zenith in Cluny but had its origins in the Rule of Saint Benedict. Behind this ritualization was the idea that the education and disciplining of the inner man must be accompanied by equally intensive training in outward forms; throughout the Middle Ages and beyond, many clerics thought it right to put the emphasis, in training, on forms of behavior, believing this did not jeopardize the inner, spiritual life. We shall speak later of the "ritualism" of Cluny, which formed the monk's entire existence.

The real problem of ranking within the monastery began when the lay monks, who had been ordered according to the date of their profession, were confronted with the priesthood. According to Benedict, if a priest entered a Benedictine monastery, the abbot could assign him the second place (after his own); if he did not, then the order of profession would apply. A lay monk who had been selected by his abbot for the priesthood, and who had been ordained, was to guard against pride and retain his assigned place based on the order of his profession unless the abbot "advanced" him. Clearly the texts in the Rule of Benedict foresaw a solution for exceptional cases. The situation was quite different when priest monks became increasingly numerous and formed a group within the group. The prestige of the priesthood reached the point that in Cluny the priest monks went first in processions in the choir of the church, followed by the deacons, the subdeacons, the holders of the lesser orders, and finally the lay monks. The group was subdivided into smaller units, each organized according to the date of profession and placed before or after the other groups. Thus even monasticism underwent a process of "hierarchization," and in view of this tendency we may better understand why monks strove for an *ordo* of their own alongside that of the secular clergy.

One might expect public processions to have revealed this order to the laity. Here, however, various practical considerations had to be met, so that even in Cluniac monasteries the principles of rank did not become explicit. The spectators were impressed by the carrying of cult objects as well as by the alteration in groups of persons: Children led the procession, followed by monks according to their *ordo*, and then, either before or after the lay brothers, came the abbot with his crozier.

The principles of order were more explicit in seating arrangements, according to which one could sit "above" or "below" one's neighbor. The order of standing, too, was regulated at least in part, and here we again find the perception that the middle places were the "highest," this time even extended to the *pueri*. These were the children raised in the monastery and destined to become monks. As "literates" (*pueri literati*) they often held a higher place than the *conversi*, lay monks, who had once belonged to secular society. To these two groups were added, as a third group, the literate monks (*cantores*), those who, in consequence of their literacy, could participate in the liturgical chant.

Monastic ranking, then, had greatly changed without abandoning its basic principle. Men who did not fit into it did not have to be sent back into the "world" in any case: monks were needed for managing monastic property on a farm; others may have served as chaplains for bishops or for noblemen; one could become a hermit, at least temporarily, thus removed from the community of monks but remaining under the spiritual direction of the abbot. Eremitic tendencies within the monastery could, on the other hand, place the system itself in doubt: the cofounder of Gorze as a reform monastery, Abbot John I, who had come out of the eremitic tradition, threw himself to the feet of those brethren "who were the lowest in the order of rank," begging their forgiveness, and did not take the place in the choir due to him as first, but took the last. He did so on account of "his humility of heart." This motivation was especially important for one who had once led the life of a wealthy layman. Humility had played an important role in the Rule of Saint Benedict, but in that context it had not come into direct conflict with a strictly established order which John broke through his conduct.

Ranking in the Secular Sphere

In the lay world the principles of order were never as thoroughly developed as in the monastic, and they were seldom committed to writing. They were part of the domain of "custom," which we learn about only by chance from remarks of clerical writers. Here the late Roman ranking system had almost entirely disappeared, and the imperfect institutionalization of public power left much uncertain. Yet this very limitation of formal systems can, from another perspective, be seen as a strength: the instability of the ranking system encouraged the desire to achieve status within the society. It corresponded closely to the continuous transformation of "noble" families, which with every marriage and with the death of their leaders, assumed a different form. We have no idea how far rank differentiation went among those lay groups of the middle strata of society or among the unfree peasantry. To judge from our present-day attitudes, it is not unlikely that even in the peasantry there were differentiations both within and between groups. A hint in this direction may be the fact that in the land records of Freising we can recognize a small group of men belonging to the *familia* of the bishopric who were unfree but nevertheless held a particular place as what might be called "representative witnesses" in legal transactions.

In recent years, numerous studies have demonstrated how rank pervaded the daily activities of the courtly nobility of the modern period. By rank, the king kept the restless nobility occupied; he bound them to himself and defined their social position within the courtly society through approval or disapproval, awards or withdrawals of differentiated forms of favor. Questions of rank and ceremonial appeared extremely important outside the court as well. Here it was not the lord who measured out social prestige but rather the group of social equals, to which ecclesiastics often belonged. It is difficult to determine just how far ecclesiastical censure could change a man's prestige. The effects of excommunication were often quite limited because the social equals of the sinner maintained their solidarity with him.

The reconciliation of a noble family which took place at the synod of Jonquières in 909 had been preceded by a solemn execration of this same family. The formulaic curses that had been pronounced were now made ineffective by invoking the opposite formulas of blessing: May God bless the work of your hands and make you the head (*caput*) not the last (*cauda*), and you should ever be above (*supra*) and never below (*subtus*). Before and after came good wishes for the prosperity of the household and estate. The family's political role was not at issue here, but rather its social position in the region. One notes the uncertainty of worldly social ranking; even a count and his family could fall back to the last position of their *ordo*, either in reality or, at least, in the wishful thinking of the clergy.

Another example, which elucidates both a special problem and the role of ranking in the life of court, is that of Charles of Lorraine. Charles ought to have become king, but the archbishop of Reims reproached him for a mismarriage. How could the "great duke" Hugh Capet stand it, the historian Richer has the archbishop say, if a woman out of a family of his *milites* should become queen and give him orders? How could Hugh give a higher rank than his own (*capiti suo praeponet*) to a woman whose equals, and even her betters (*pares et etiam maiores*), kneel before him and (when he mounts a horse) place their hands (as a support) under his feet?

The social boundaries had to be protected, or else the existence of monarchy itself would be endangered. At the Synod of Limoges, which dealt with the apostolicity of Saint Martial, Abbot Odalrich offered the following hypothesis: if someone should number King Robert, who was present, not among the kings but among the counts subject to him, that person would be regarded either as a peasant (*rusticus*) or as someone wickedly contemptuous of the king. In the first case the king could easily pardon the peasant's simplicity; in the second, he would be angry because of the disrespect shown his person.

A lowering of one's position within a group could occur for various reasons. One reason was an unworthy marriage, which not only reduced the prestige of the individual but was also bad for the entire family, for its *fideles* and "friends." A similar, possibly even more serious misfortune was to overlook disrespect shown by someone else for one's own position. Anyone who allowed another to act toward him with disrespect without a hostile reaction did not deserve his position. The rules of the game, however, held only within the specific group: a peasant could not offend a nobleman.

Kings and queens were raised out of their previous sphere through their elevation; nevertheless they remained in it. This could produce conflict when members of their family or former "friends" did not receive every claim to which they believed they had title. When the king Henry II walked past a row of bishops, all stood except one, Bishop Megingaud of Eichstätt. He justified himself with the words, "I am the elder kinsman (of the king), and both profane and sacred scriptures teach us to honor older relatives." The reason for Megingaud's behavior was not simply his kinship but also the fact that he was being required to take part in the services to the court like all the other bishops; in private, he even called the king a lunatic on this account. Megingaud was, after all, the blood relative and companion (*socius etiam genere*) of Henry, who had made him, as he said, into a poor pastor (instead of especially favoring his kinsman).

A lord could overlook muttering and a casual gesture of displeasure as long as no one drew his attention to it. The situation was more serious in a case such as that of the grandfather of Thietmar of Merseburg, who accused his enemy Duke Hermann, the imperial regent in Saxony, of demonstrating *contemptus* toward the emperor during his absence: Hermann had sat at table "in the midst of the bishops in the place of the emperor," and had slept in his bed. As expected, Otto I was infuriated by the report. The count of Stade was a kinsman of the emperor and therefore regained his favor while the archbishop of Magdeburg was punished for having given Duke Hermann liturgical honors. In the same vein, here is another of Thietmar's stories: In the palace of Werla the table had been set for the sisters of the recently deceased Otto III. But Ekkehard of Meissen, a candidate for the crown, and some others sat down on the carpeted chairs which had been prepared for the princesses and their followers. While Duke Hermann, as the representative of the king in Saxony, could have believed he had the right to do what he did, Ekkehard was clearly usurping the right of the lord. In any event, both situations must have been of real significance in the eyes of contemporaries, or else Thietmar would not have mentioned them.

A good example of how questions of rank excited women as well as men was a dispute in Gandersheim which, according to Thangmar, was sparked by the emperor's daughter Sophia. This princess showed her sensitivity to questions of precedence by refusing to take the veil as a canoness from the bishop of Hildesheim, insisting that it would be unworthy for her to be consecrated by anyone but the archbishop of Mainz.

That women knew or thought they knew what was proper was already in existence in late antiquity. At that time, according to a somewhat mocking report in the *Historia Augusta,* there was a "Women's Senate" which determined such things as how each lady was to dress; to whom she was to give precedence; who among them could travel by carriage; who might mount a horse, who a mule, and who had to be content with a donkey. The *Nibelungenlied*'s account of a dispute between the queens on the way to the minster that led to disastrous consequences could just as easily have occurred in the tenth century.

A new problem of precedence in the sphere of monarchy was created when the Carolingians ceased to be the sole royal family and the eldest brother was no longer assigned a superior position. Regino of Prüm saw the collapse which followed the death of Charles III as a problem of weak leadership: there were capable leaders, but none at that time was so outstanding in relation to the others that they would willingly cede precedence to him.

We have already noted that, in unstable situations, signs of rank and honor are particularly prized. In the period under discussion there were *reges Francorum* to the east and the west of the ancient monarchy. If they wished to accomplish anything together, it was essential that the ever-present questions of rank not be raised. Today, anyone can grasp the idea of equality. At that time it was difficult to imagine it, at least in the upper strata of the population. Where necessary, new forms of representing the idea had to be found. When Charles the Simple and Henry I concluded the Treaty of Bonn in 921, they did it on a ship on the Rhine, thus in no-man's-land between the two realms, and in a form that limited ceremony to a minimum. Still, a written draft of the treaty had to be prepared in which Charles and his bishops were named before Henry and his. This was tolerable for Henry, for unlike Charles he had only recently obtained his kingdom. The document, however, reflects also a certain superiority of the Carolingian king over the Saxon.

At the Synod of Ingelheim in 948, where a conflict over the archbishopric of Reims had created a problem between the two states, the equality of rank of the two kings Otto I and Louis IV had to find an expression meaningful for all present: they sat down at the same moment and next to each other. Louis was nine years younger than Otto and had been crowned shortly before the synod in 936. Did he sit on the right or, as one might expect, on the left of the Saxon, who was his brother-in-law? The sources do not say, although such things were then taken so seriously that they could conceivably lead to murder. The following story was told in France about another meeting between Otto the Great and Louis IV: The two kings had seated themselves on a couch in such a way that Otto sat nearer the head. Duke William Longsword of Normandy had not been invited to the conference and wished to break the friendship between the two kings. He forced his way in and shouted that it was unseemly that the (West Frankish) king should occupy the "lower" place while anyone else held the "higher." Otto is said to have then risen and to have given up his place to Louis, next to whom, nearer the foot of the couch, William seated himself. Otto did not allow the duke to see his anger but he complained to the French magnates about the disregard shown his person. For this reason, so the chronicler alleges, the nobles agreed to kill the Norman.

Whether the entire story is fiction, or only its combination with the anecdote concerning the death plot, is unimportant. What is significant is the fact it was considered possible that a form of contempt (*contemptus*) of this kind should be avenged through blood. Also worthy of attention is the implication that the French king recognized no superior: *rex superiorem non recognoscens*. The king of France had no lord; thus courtly etiquette should not present the appearance that things were otherwise. The establishment of the Ottonian Empire did not lead to a change in the situation; Adalbero of Laon speaks of the "two princes," one who rules as king, the other as emperor.

Two monarchs were seldom present at the same assembly. Normally it was one's own ruler who naturally took first place at his table or in the council. Eating and drinking together were much more important then, as they are at the diplomatic banquets of our own time: they provided virtually the only opportunity to seek proximity to the ruler and to get to be his "familiar." A lord's best way of binding people to himself was to invite them to share his meat and drink. Every lord was enthroned at table as though a king, and the king showed his lordship in like manner. Of course, the lord established the seating arrangement, and the place of highest honor for a guest was to the right of the host. This custom is not specific to the West, and can also be found in the Bible.

He who occupied the head of the table, the *solium*, had the supreme command, the *dominatus*, over the household community. He assigned their social position in the house by giving them seats in a particular order. Thus we must understand a story told in one of the Cambridge Songs: a fraud pretended that he had been in heaven. Archbishop Heriger of Mainz (913–27) asked him what honor God had given him there, that is, where he had been seated. The answer was, "In a corner."

When we want to suggest the powerful position of a courtier, we say he is the ruler's "right hand." In the tenth century he was called "the second after the king" (*secundus a rege*). When the king sat "at his side," he held the key position—an unwritten, nonbureaucratic form of appointment. This appointment could most quickly be canceled when another favorite took the place of the first. If the *secundus a rege* held a powerful position, as did Bishop Gebhard of Eichstätt, one could say that "the king (Henry III) surpassed him only in that he was enthroned on a higher seat."

The second best place was on the left of the lord. On one occasion, both seats next to the king were held for approximately equal positions. Charles the Simple had a favorite named Hagano, who did not come from the high aristocracy. The king seated him on his left, to the anger of Duke Robert, who sat on his right and who later would be a contender for kingship. Both Hagano and Robert sat *pariter,* which was translated "sur le même rang"; Robert declared that it was unworthy that a person from the middle level of society should be made his equal (*sibi aequari*).

We do not know the rank order of the remaining seats. If there was one, it has not survived in written form and it was not a permanent protocol as in modern monarchies. All we know is that three groups could remain in the king's presence: the magnates (*potentes, principes, proceres*), the holders of royal office (for the most part drawn from the first category), and finally those who had acquired the favor of the lord, even when they were from a lower social order. We have just seen an example of the tensions which could result from such a situation.

One might well assume military affairs to have been the second major factor in determining the order of precedence among the laity. That, however, would have required fixed organizational forms and a chain of command such as the Roman Empire had once possessed. Since there were no professional officers in the tenth century, the holders of "civilian" offices and the magnates exercised the power to command, and this confusion made it impossible to use military rank to determine a layman's position. In the conduct of war, ranking was not nearly as unequivocal as was the royal table. For a long time neither the king nor the magnates had exercised the ancient right of "first strike" on the battlefield, it is hardly conceivable that their rank determined the marching order or, rather, the order of riding or travel by carriage—of their columns.

Military considerations did exercise a certain effect in the attempt to bring order into the bonds between the king and the upper strata through feudal attachments. When the magnates or favorites became vassals, a relationship began which, since it was often cemented by the bestowal of a fief, initiated a process of institutionalization and group formation. But this process remained incomplete. Formal social orders, or estates, in the legal sense of the term certainly did not exist in the tenth century. They appear for the first time only in the late eleventh century in some North Italian towns. Likewise, a true feudal hierarchy never developed under the early Capetians in France, since the multiplicity of vassal bonds confused the system. Elsewhere feudalism had even less potential to bring a system into reality. Still, the magnates who held their fiefs directly from the king always had the highest position and sought to make those who were weaker than they their own vassals, thus drawing them down to the position of second-ranking powers. Still others, as for example Atto-Adalbert of Canossa, succeeded in rising from episcopal vassals to margraves with their own vassals, including former counts. From the writings of Rather of Verona we learn that the magnates were willing to receive episcopal properties but refused to do homage to the bishop for them so that they would not lose their rank as direct vassals of the king.

Feudalism tended toward a personal rank ordering. This attempt to achieve an order remained forever unfulfilled. In its pure form it existed only in the heads of theoreticians of a later time, with whom we are not concerned here. It was not possible to establish an order of precedence in the ecclesiastical sphere in all its details, and even less so in the secular area. Yet most people were satisfied to know who their lord was, whether a nobleman, a count, a bishop, or an abbot. Questions of rank within the upper strata concerned the members of those strata alone.

2 &· SOCIAL GESTURES, A CATEGORY OF "CUSTOM"

IN THE YEAR 953, COLOGNE RECEIVED A new archbishop. He was a king's son and the brother of the reigning monarch. Surely he could have ruled at his pleasure; nevertheless Bruno "inquired diligently everywhere in order to determine what he ought to do and upon which traditions (*consuetudines*) he should rely." The word *consuetudo* in this context was used in a very broad sense; it meant the good old Frankish traditions of behavior, law, and administration as well as the regional "customs and usages" in their fixed forms. One expected their observance on the part of the new supreme pastor as part of "what he ought to do."

Maintaining the proper order of precedence was only a small part of the encompassing thought "in orders" which was actualized through actions.

Law and order had to exist. In this "closed" society, emphasis was placed not on the compulsion of law, which was manifested only in extreme circumstances, but rather on the compulsion of order. Anyone who failed to follow the rules of the community thereby either excluded himself from the group or ran up against such opposition of the right-minded majority that to live in their midst became difficult for him. This was more effective than a declaration of infamy, such as was threatened at the synod of Trosly in 909. Either the laity found their control of clerics and ecclesiastical property in accordance with "custom," in which case threats against the abuse had little effect; or they managed to change the *consuetudo* in small, laborious steps in accord with canonical law—only then could an opponent of the clerics lose his "good reputation" within the group and be separated from it by legal means.

If each individual knew "what he ought to do" (*quid agendum sibi esset*), and acted accordingly, it was easier for him to make his weighty decisions as well as to live his daily life. Acting according to the rules of custom tempered spontaneous emotions and placed them under social control. Reactions were formalized and lost their haphazard individual character. This was particularly important for monks. From the circle of Gorze we learn that the humble exercise of the monastic customs (*consuetudines*) leads to a calming of the spirit, which reminds one of the Stoic *apatheia*. This spiritual or "noble" attitude was a mark of the differentiation between social spheres: as noted above, the peasant was forgiven what in higher spheres would have had to be condemned as lack of discipline.

Historians have reproached the Cluniacs for something that was common to virtually all people of the time: that they did not value interiority and that they reduced the essentials of monastic life to ritual and ceremonial, that is, to an outward show. This judgment posits a contrast between spirituality and exterior behavior—between the "quiet little chamber" and an ostentatious, affected piety—which simply did not exist for most Christians. As Arno Borst has said, "There was no distance between form and appearance of ceremonial actions; everyone meant what he did, and anyone who did not participate remained outside. In this way ceremony established community." Only very few social critics of the time understood the nature of hypocrisy.

With such presuppositions, customary conduct and appearance were seldom reproached as mere externalities. Gestures, clothing, and weapons became the transmitters of meaning, "signs" as defined by Augustine: "A sign is something which, in addition to its perceptibility to the senses, suggests another understanding derived from its own nature." That everything had, or could have, so much hidden meaning was not only the opinion of symbolically oriented theologians but also of their secular contemporaries. So in the area of human relations it was natural to allow symbols to speak: someone who knew how to interpret and to employ them possessed a kind of education, and not the least important.

The interpretation had to be clear, at least for members of the group concerned; today it is often difficult to determine what this meaning was. Think, for example, of historians' discussion of the events at Ponthion in the year 754: What did the pope mean when he threw himself to the ground before the king, and what did Pepin mean by extending his hand? The difficulty lies in the fact that relatively few behaviors were repeated with constantly changing meanings. Did Pope Stephen II perform a "commendation," the "subjugation of the Church under the legal protection of the Frankish king" as Johannes Haller believed, or was he making a nontechnical use of a gesture to indicate supplication for help? At the time there must have been no doubt, for a gesture fails in its purpose when it is either misunderstood or not understood at all. The same is true of objects used as "vehicles of meaning," especially those used for such gestures as we have mentioned: here the selection of possible meanings of one and the same thing was large. A staff, for example, could "be" support, a sign of office, or any property or office that was transmitted through it. Gesture and object were bound up together, a fact which allowed for a closer determination of the intention. That the meaning was not always clear to nonparticipants can be seen from various examples. Richer and Thietmar of Merseburg tell the story that after the unfortunate attack on Otto II in 978, the French turned the eagle on the palace at Aix-la-Chapelle in another direction. This gesture was clearly directed against the Germans, that much was clear; but its meaning was understood in two different ways: Thietmar thought that the French had supposedly turned the eagle toward their own kingdom, that is, to the west; according to Richer the bird looked menacingly into the neighboring realm, that is, to the east.

In the political sphere, any detail could become a vehicle for transmitting a meaning. Again in Richer we read about the negotiations of Otto II with Hugh Capet (981); at their departure Otto intentionally left his sword on a chair and asked the duke to pick it up for him. A French bishop noted the danger that Hugh could thus become the emperor's "swordbearer" and snatched it from his hand. This probably apocryphal anecdote should show how much one had to be on one's guard against both friends and enemies in order not to be duped.

Custom and Tradition

We usually distinguish between ritual, ceremonial, and folk custom along the lines of the modern separation between the Church (that is, the clergy), the courtly sphere (later to be imitated by the bourgeoisie), and the "simple folk," or lower classes. In the Middle Ages, gestures associated with these three areas often overlapped, as in coronations. Cluniac ritualism found its lasting effects not in a *rituale*, but rather in written *consuetudines*; unwritten "customs" controlled the everyday life of the laity. We tend to attribute most of these latter to folk custom, but here we must be careful. If riding a hose sidesaddle was said to go against the honor of a man (*honestas virilis*), we see that a sort of collective reputation of the nobles was at issue. "Custom" (*Sitte*) was mainly of concern to the elite. It had a tendency to become fixed and more complex, especially at the king's court; hence, that court acquired increased prestige compared with the courts of the magnates. Custom was often tribal or regional, while ceremonial included arbitrary elements: it could be dismissed and replaced by something else. Thietmar of Merseburg tells us that Otto III took his meals sitting alone at a semicircular table, according to the "Roman custom" (*consuetudo Romanorum*). The notion of "ceremonial" was unknown to him, and what Thietmar took to be a custom of the ancient Romans was actually the outcome of highly developed monarchical propaganda.

The boundaries between ecclesiastical ritual and clerical custom were also fluid. In Cambrai, for example, the newly appointed bishop used to ring the cathedral bell himself in order to announce the assumption of the *episcopium,* which primarily meant episcopal properties. The bell rang at vespers only when the bishop was staying in the city. This unique manifestation of lordship continued as a local tradition throughout the Middle Ages. Nevertheless, the gesture had been invented at a particular time, and the romantic idea that custom dates from time immemorial has long been corrected in historical folklore. What needs to be demonstrated is whether an action is really something new or whether it is something old that has reappeared in a modified form. When Otto II granted the cathedral chapter of Magdeburg the right to free election of the archbishop, he "confirmed" the grant with the gift of a book, which contained his portrait and that of the empress Theophanu. During the Mass after the sermon, the imperial diploma was read and the book was shown to the archbishop. This solemn action closed with the cursing of anyone who might flout the imperial command and with the "Amen! fiat! fiat!" of the congregation. Was the book with the portraits a symbol of the imperial couple's permanent relationship with Magdeburg, and of its lasting "presence" there? Imperial images in the church are a well-known theme of late Roman-Byzantine state symbolism.

Sometimes the symbolism of gestures which certainly were not without meaning can only be guessed at. We have already spoken of the various roles of the staff as a symbol. When the monks of Fleury came out of the church during the Easter procession, staffs were distributed to them, and at the same moment they pulled their cowls over their heads; they had to keep their heads covered as long as they carried their staffs. The gesture may have been intended to indicate the "pilgrimage" of the soul to God, but in any case it provided onlookers with something to see and to think about. What did it mean, to cite another example, when bishops in the year 1033, on behalf of members of the peace movement, "took up a crosier in their name (or: with their aid) and raised it toward heaven, stretched their arms out to God and cried "peace, peace"? We could only speculate, had Rodulfus Glaber not given the authentic explanation that this was "a sign of the eternal covenant" with God. Here the staff assumed the role of expressing of the collective will. The outstretched hands, in retaining their primary meaning as an indication of being unarmed and desiring peace, may also have retained their secondary meaning as the ancient gesture of prayer.

Here we have the suggestion of an innovation. Since there had never before been such a thing as a Peace of God movement, there could not have been any specific symbol for it. Contemporaries controlled and expanded the symbolic language with an ease that is foreign to us. A bishop had sworn before the king that he had been dispossessed of a *villa*, that is, a manor. After an inquiry, a royal agent returned possession of the manor to the bishop by touching the door of its church. The fact that a charter was prepared to confirm the matter certainly made less of an impression on observers. Here is another example: the bishop of Metz was riding to Gorze; in order to show respect for the monastery he dismounted at a wayside cross and walked the rest of the way barefoot. This gesture is timeless and yet could be reinvented again and again. Thietmar of Merseburg was also an "inventor" of this kind. A priest gave him a list of his sins, and Thietmar laid it on the reliquary in the priest's own church to assure the help of the saints in obtaining forgiveness. "I had never heard or seen this done," Thietmar guilelessly added in his account.

It is thus impossible to force custom, constantly evolving and multifaceted as it is, into a coherent system. We can only vaguely describe its extent and the kinds of things it includes. We have taken our examples from the domain of gestures—in the widest sense—and have selected simple physical actions; but words or objects could also be central. More complex events used all three.

SPECIFIC GESTURES: FAVOR AND DISGRACE

As these examples show, such actions were of various kinds; in the realm of gestures, however, certain groups of similar actions keep recurring. One thinks of various postures which signified various things: pride and humility, power and weakness, favor and displeasure, and so forth. In our own times we generally express such things spontaneously; in the tenth century the form of expression was often ritualized, that is, depersonalized and standardized. This was particularly true for monarchs on the one hand and for monks on the other. For both, collective public comportment was more pronounced than for aristocrats and secular clergy.

Henry II once met with Archbishop Heribert of Cologne, who had caused him political troubles, particularly at the beginning of his reign, and hence was in disfavor. A divinely inspired vision showed Henry his fault, but he continued to play the role of the displeased monarch; he assumed with premeditation (*ex industria*) a darkened countenance, and demanded a large sum of money from Heribert. Upon the archbishop's complaints of unjust treatment, the displeased emperor became gracious; he stepped down from his throne, and embraced and kissed the archbishop. The chronicle did not need to mention here what is often reported: the *facies hilaris* of the emperor, who up to that point had been "making a face" and then, so to speak, replaced it by another.

Humiliation

According to the Rule of Saint Benedict, the monk had to practice humility above all virtues. The highest, the twelfth degree, was that which he "not only has in his heart, but also makes manifest by his physical comportment to those who see him." These physical gestures included always keeping one's head bowed and one's eyes toward the ground. He who keeps his head bowed makes himself smaller and indicates his insignificance. An excellent example is provided by a page of Gregory the Great's *Registrum epistolarum* in the city library of Trier, copied around 984. Gregory's scribe is shown smaller than his lord; he stoops low and looks up to his superior. Also bowing as they step forward are the figures of four women who represent the parts of the empire of Otto III. Likewise, the secondary figures of most medieval paintings are small, as they are on Oriental monuments. Rank order must find its graphic expression. In representing the announcement of the good news to the shepherds at Bethlehem, it was natural that the largest and central figure should be the angel; the recipient of the message, a person of rank with red cloak, shirt, decorated trousers, and short boots, was presented in a medium size; and behind him are to be found two smaller figures of barefooted shepherds clothed only in shirts. Obviously an angel of the Lord could hardly address ordinary people directly; the chief shepherd was there to transmit to his people what God had announced through his servant.

Another gesture of self-depreciation is genuflection, which was especially appropriate for servants, who dared not stand before their lord. But even the free fell to their knees before their *senior*. The ritual of commendation, which established vassality, demanded another gesture, the *immixtio manuum;* this was an old ritual of servitude which, at least in a later period, was combined with the entry into vassality. One became another's vassal by placing one's clasped hands within the hands of the lord, a gesture present as early as the eighth century. This gesture may have been combined with genuflection. As far as the members of the imperial church are concerned, tenth-century sources tell us nothing about such a combination, but the accounts are so laconic that genuflection is not to be excluded. If the king sat rather than stood during the ceremony, it would have been unseemly to undergo the ritual of commendation while standing before him.

That in general vassals genuflected before their lords is documented, at least in France, for our period. Certainly members of the elites followed a rule, by no means limited to Europe, that the head of the lesser should never rise above that of the "higher." If the higher stood, the lesser dared not sit, as Saint Benedict had already taught his monks. Mieszko I, a tenth-century Slavic prince, held to this basic custom whenever he met the emperor Otto I.

The most vexing "humiliation" appears to have been connected with prostration. Yet prostration was not seen as humiliating, for it was practiced even by individuals of the highest rank: Pope Stephen II in 754 before King Pepin; Pope Leo VIII before Otto the Great in 964; the archbishop of Mainz at a synod before the bishop of Hildesheim, and the latter before the emperor in 1027. Henry II, for his part, prostrated himself a number of times before the bishops who were discussing the foundation of the bishopric of Bamberg. It was a gesture of humble supplication, not a surrender of one's honor or rank. In 1027 the archbishop of Mainz learned what could happen when prostration was performed in vain: he was derided, but nothing more. In monasticism the transferral of the liturgical *prostratio* to the human sphere appears to have shaped a portion of the language of gestures which, under the Cluniacs, was developed for bridging the hours of silence.

Next in importance to the gesture of humiliation is naturally that of the clasping of folded hands. The literature on this gesture is so complete that we can limit ourselves here to a few general comments.

Dudo of Saint-Quentin recounts that the dying Duke Richard of Normandy was asked who was to be his successor. He designated his son Richard, to whom the other sons (as vassals) "were to give their hands into his in place of their hearts." Here vassalage enforced brotherly love. In this field one often finds the indication of an inner connection, from which Jacques Le Goff infers a "symbolique parentale." The vassals thus became members of the lord's "family." Carlo Guido Mor has extended this hypothesis to the parallels between the faithfulness between spouses and that between lord and vassal. Such parallels are hard to prove, but they are certainly worth considering, as long as the familial obligations and, of course, the kiss of vassality are seen not only from a social point of view but also from an affective one. Rather of Verona once observed that bonds are forged either by fear or by love and then continued, "Why should someone love you to whom you can give nothing?" This may sound cynical, but it is not meant to be. It would be a waste of time to argue whether a child's affection for its parents precedes or results from their efforts to protect, feed, and instruct the child—the two go hand in hand. Likewise, protection and faithfulness in marriage, with a material substratum, are tied together, particularly at a time when individual affection seldom led to marriage but usually only began with it.

Modern ethnological research has shown that individuals need a certain amount of personal space and are angered when someone not connected to them in a special way "gets too close to them." A large personal space surrounded the king. The man to whom he vouchsafed close contact by clasping his folded hands and receiving from him the kiss of vassality was from now on affectively bound to the king. He was "near" him whether or not he entered the royal household. Only later did vassality become a sort of business connection.

The Feudal Kiss and the Kiss of Peace

The feudal kiss seems to have become a part of vassallic gestures already in the tenth century. The earliest German example may be an account from Saint Gall, dated 971: Otto I said to the abbot-elect Notker, "So at last you become mine," took him through the gesture of the clasped hands (to become one of his vassals) and kissed him. Previously Otto had not granted the emissaries of the monastery the kiss of peace or friendship because they opposed his wishes, but finally all received it with the exception of Notker. Otto said that the hour was perhaps yet to come, meaning that he kept open the possibility of making Notker abbot according to the desires of the monks of Saint Gall and giving up his own candidate. Hence it is not clear that the concluding kiss was the "kiss of vassality" rather than a belated kiss of friendship, which had already been completed with the others.

In this instance, the lord kissed the subordinate, although at this time and later the opposite is often described: the vassal would kiss the foot or the knee of his lord. This gesture of subordination was not a fixed element of commendation but initially a more general right of lordship which could also be used with vassals. The gesture is ancient and was practiced in antiquity by defeated enemies. It was no accident that Duke Tassilo of Bavaria had to perform the knee kiss in 787 and that the Norman Duke Rollo apparently did the same in

911. Vassals also had to concern themselves with their lord's feet, as when they helped him mount his saddle, but more often servants did so: the disguised Hugh Capet was recognized because servants, with knees bent, helped him pull off his boots while others massaged his feet.

Thus one can assume that the clasping of hands was the primary feudal gesture, which could be augmented with other requirements of medieval sign language. In the period under examination, the kiss on the mouth can hardly be said to have been among these signs; it could only be given between equals, rather like the kiss on both cheeks exchanged in some countries between politicians, military men, or society women. When kings met in friendship, they kissed each other; this was known both by Richer and by the author of the *Ruodlieb*: the latter tells us that after this ceremony one of the two kings invited his bishops to do the same(?), and then kissed "in order" (*ex ordine*) all the abbots of the other realm. Gerbert of Aurillac speaks of a reconciliation between the Carolingian King Lothair and Hugh Capet in June 985 by saying simply: "On June 18 Duke Hugo kissed the king and the queen."

The kiss of reconciliation was a particular form of the general kiss of peace that was certainly known not only in the liturgy. Since earliest times, when two strangers came together, neutrality was hardly a possibility, and they had to decide immediately between peace and discord. If one gave a kiss of peace, he guaranteed that hostilities would be avoided and that the other would be accorded the hospitality of his house. In monasteries, strangers were received with a kiss. The *pax* of the Benedictine Rule was from the start the implied embracing and kiss on the cheeks between brothers; at Cluny this kiss was passed on to the laity present in the church by one of the brothers. The spiritual peace was to be extended to the entire community.

It was certainly not in the spirit of Saint Benedict that elements of lordship should have been introduced into the Cluniac ceremony of the kiss. At Fruttuaria (Piedmont) in the late eleventh century, and possibly even earlier, the abbot was seen as a person of high rank like the king or a great feudal lord. He could not receive a (fraternal) kiss from anyone; on Holy Thursday during the ceremony of *caritas,* a deacon was to sit beside him at his command and—also at his command—kiss his knee. If a monk had been punished for serious offenses and was to be taken back into the community, he had to kiss the abbot's foot. This was a gesture of subordination which was usually performed to the pope by a bishop some time after his consecration. Fruttuaria was under the influence of Saint-Bénigne of Dijon, whose abbot, William, had introduced a very rigid regimen. The customs of Gorzian monasticism were much closer to the spirit of the Benedictine Rule, for they required the abbot and monks to perform service to the poor, including washing their feet, distributing money and clothing, and even kissing their hands. Christian love of one's neighbor and monastic humility mandated that the normal order of lordship and service be forgotten. Members of the imperial church, as far as is known, practiced only the hand kiss to the king.

Gifts and Praise of the Giver

Distributions of gifts also had a meaning that went beyond their material significance; like the hand kiss, they were signs with a specific meaning. Ethnologists recognize that a gift indicates a positive relation to the receiver. With time this meaning was reduced to what Georges Duby calls "les générosités nécessaires." The element of personal devotion of the inferior and of the favor of the superior was sometimes reactivated, which gave rise to some novel practices. Ekkehard IV of Saint Gall tells the following story: When Conrad II and the empress Gisela were cerebrating Easter at Ingelheim in 1030, Ekkehard was rewarded for his role as choirmaster "as was customary": he was ordered to "look at the feet of the empire (= of the emperor) and he took up the ounces of gold which had been placed there"; the same thing took place before the empress. The Mainz schoolmaster and cantor had to look for his reward in the shoes of the imperial couple, a game which must have made the audience laugh and at the same time brought the "good servant" into intimate contact with the rulers without forgetting the necessary respect. Another story told by Helgaud about the court of Robert the Pious is noteworthy in this respect. One morning Robert ordered that the poor be allowed to enter while he was at breakfast; one of them, who was sitting under the table at the king's feet, ate what the king slipped him. The man saw a golden decoration on the king's robes, cut it off, and ran away—apparently without incurring the king's anger. In a manner of speaking, the king had allowed himself to be plundered, just as Conrad II and Gisela had done.

Royal care of the poor was usually of another sort. Here, its symbolic character was stressed, rather than material help for the lowest levels of the population; feeding and clothing all the poor in the kingdom would have far exceeded the king's means. In the words of

Georges Duby, "ritualized aid to the needy was little more than a symbolic gesture in the normal course of liturgical ceremonial." Robert the Pious, of whom we have spoken, arranged massive feedings of the poor on major feast days; on other days, twelve paupers "whom he particularly loved" accompanied him on his journeys. They marched along "glorifying God and praising the king"—an effective and not particularly expensive form of royal propaganda. The son of Hugh Capet had a lot of catching up to do in face of the Carolingian lordship, and was helped along, among other things, by proximity to monasticism and to what his biographer termed "the holy poor."

As the successor to the Roman system of providing for the unemployed, Merovingian Gaul had continued the *matricula*, a list of people who received assistance from urban and, to some extent, from rural churches. In the ninth century, enrollment was frozen and the *matricularii* no longer included the actual poor. There were usually twelve of them, occasionally eighteen or twenty-four, and they were used in episcopal churches for the ceremony of the washing of the feet on Maundy Thursday. The institution was taken over by secular powers, as in the case of the French royal court. There were also mass meals, which certainly demanded a significant sacrifice for the royal or episcopal resources. Even these latter had a primarily symbolic character since they alleviated hunger only on feast days. Helgaud tells of feeding from three hundred to one thousand poor in royal cities, of one or two hundred loaves of bread which were distributed daily to the poor by the court during Lent, of three hundred poor whom King Robert personally provided with food and money on Maudy Thursday—he did the same for one hundred "poor clerics." That these numbers are not exaggerated is shown by the prayer confraternity formed by the Synod of Dortmund in 1005, according to which the participating bishops were to feed three hundred poor on the occasion of the death of one of the members, and the imperial couple was to spend 1,500 denarii for the repose of the soul of the deceased and to feed the same number of paupers. These amounts fairly describe the financial possibilities of the members; one could hardly expect much more, at least from bishops. In times of famine and the consequent flow of foreigners into the city, the resources of a bishop could hardly suffice to lessen the need.

Liberality (*largitas*) was a universal virtue of rulers; to be generous to the poor was appropriate for a Christian ruler and made him popular. In his daily activities the care of the poor—usually in a ritualized form—had its permanent place. Was there nothing more important for him to do? Would it not have been better to delegate this activity to subordinates? His contemporaries would not have understood these questions. It was an extremely important duty of the ruler to conform to the centuries-old image of the good lord. When this image "fit," people were ready, whenever possible, to follow the decisions and wishes of the king, since they issued forth from a *rex iustus*. The king had no private sphere; his daily activities had to be exemplary for the rest of society, especially in the court; so the time a ruler spent succoring the poor could not be said to be wasted.

Mourning

When the charitable king died, the previously passive role of the poor changed for a short period, and they became the executants of the dirge. In eleventh-century Cologne, and probably as early as the time of Saint Cunibert (died ca. 663), there was an institution clearly rooted in the Frankish *matricula*. It consisted of twelve benefices for the poor in the hospital near the chapel of Saint Loup, four of them ecclesiastical benefices, collectively called "crying benefices" (Schryprouen). A miniature from 1248 shows them all strenuously gesticulating. Even in the eleventh century they had to maintain the deathwatch for dying archbishops. Like the official female mourners in the Orient, the twelve brothers filled an official function: they acted as if they represented the poor who mourned the deceased.

Just as the existence of *matricularii* did not hinder genuine care of the poor, ritual mourners did not monopolize grieving. When Archbishop Walthard of Magdeburg died in Giebichenstein castle in 1012, the funeral cortège was met by the mourning peasantry (*plangens familia*); in one village it encountered the full assembly of the mourning clergy and a great crowd of Jews and orphans to whom he had been "father." The crowd showed their sorrow by their lamentations (*dolorem lamentando manifestat*). In the cathedral were assembled the "friends" of the archbishop (mainly kinsmen in the widest sense) and the *hereditarii* (presumably those who held inheritable property), and they received the body "with hands raised in mourning." The gesture of prayer and of being unarmed can also indicate sorrow; its meaning was made clear by the circumstances of its use.

After Thietmar of Merseburg had described this scene, he thought it appropriate to indicate that he was familiar with the treatment of mourning as found in classical authors: "Who would not have mourned at such a sight?" Sentences such as this are to be found in many authors; where they are used so concretely, however, they should not be dismissed a priori as worthless. A count dies; "There arose the mourning of the vassals (*militum*), the cries of the servants, the frequent wailing of the women"; all this is to be taken quite literally and not, as the editor suggests at this point, as an empty topos. Cries and wailing were a permanent part of the burial ceremony and were only slowly replaced with funerary music.

The burial of the penultimate Carolingian king in 986 was accompanied by both musical and nonmusical mourning. The performance of the singers was hampered by their tears; with great lamentations a cleric carried the crown and the insignia of the dead king in the funeral procession, followed by the mournful (*cum lamentis*) laymen—the royal vassals who led them were, admittedly, constrained merely to showing a sad face. Richer particularly points out that they were arranged according to their rank (*suo ordine*).

The *lamento* of the crownbearer, whom Richer simply describes as a cleric, was no simple wailing but rather a recitation describing the impermanence of all that is earthly. The secular magnates had to show their dignity as persons of a particular social position; immoderate cries of sorrow were more suitable for the lower ranks of society. If a great lord wished to demonstrate his sorrow in an especially striking way, he had to find another means. King Henry III found it by adapting the ritual of penance to the ceremony of mourning. At the death of his mother, Gisela, he dressed as a penitent with bare feet; with arms outstretched in the form of a cross he sank to the ground, moistened the floor (of the church) with his tears, did public penance (*publicam poenitentiam egistis*), and moved everyone present to tears. It may be that he truly felt guilty, as there had been a conflict with his mother. But there were other occasions of what one might call "contrasting ceremonies" during Henry's reign: in this way he emphasized his Christian attitude toward the earthly dignity of kingship.

Penance

The public penance of a sinner included standing barefoot before the door of the church "day and night," unarmed and wearing a woolen garment. Additional disciplinary and dietary requirements depended on the seriousness of the sin for which one had to atone. Servants without any "office" went without belt or shoes; but so too did ascetics in order to show their denial of the "world" and its attractions.

When a king at the zenith of his success, after a victory over an enemy, walked barefoot in a procession and sang "Kyrie eleison," as is recorded of Henry III, it must have made an extraordinary impression on spectators. It was a gesture accessible to a noncleric, as the king was, but it also emphasized the semi-ecclesiastical character of emperorship. In a similar manner Otto III had previously entered the Polish capital of Gnesen, as a pilgrim, although he nevertheless remained emperor.

As with many other gestures, going barefoot could mean various things depending on the circumstances in which it was done. Monks at Fruttuaria participated in the Lenten processions barefoot, or at least in sandals, in order to show exceptional asceticism during this period of preparation; criminals walked barefoot to the gallows as "poor sinners" doing penance for their guilt. It served as a gesture of subordination when a delegation from the besieged city of Tivoli appeared before Otto III, carrying a sword in their right hand, a rod in their left, and almost naked. It meant something else again when, after the death of a saintly bishop of Utrecht, the people of that town walked to the place of his death "barefoot and armed." In tears, they begged the monks and the episcopal vassals the privilege of carrying his body home. For the ceremony at Tivoli we are given the explanation that the citizens of the city freely offered the emperor the choice of punishing them with the sword or with the rod. The citizens of Utrecht both begged and threatened with the force of arms; swordplay almost broke out between them and the bishop's vassals.

Such explanatory comments as have come down to us leave no doubt concerning the meaning of these gestures. In the gesture itself there were possibilities of more subtle differentiations, which could not have been stated by the chroniclers: the people of Tivoli, unlike those of Utrecht, apparently held their swords not by the handle but by the blade; so the weapons were not threatening as "drawn swords" would have been.

The sword in its scabbard was a normal, everyday thing; the "naked sword" in peacetime was primarily a symbol of justice. When, in 1026, a revolt in Ravenna against Conrad II had collapsed, "the surviving inhabitants of Ravenna appeared before the king in hair-shirts, barefoot and carrying naked swords as their law required of conquered people." A similar event took place the following year in Rome where the subjugation to imperial justice was symbolized variously for each social order: the free came barefoot with naked swords, the unfree with a halter around their necks "as though to be hanged." In both cases the attire was that of criminals being led to their execution. The sword signified the sword of justice, which needed no scabbard.

Gestures with Cap, Staff, Scepter, and Lance

Items of clothing and weaponry could also be used gesturally to the extent that ridding oneself of them had a particular meaning. This was true of shoes, of sword belt and sword, sometimes of staff and cap. We are used to seeing people of the early Middle Ages depicted without headgear; only the king, contrary to reality, wears his crown. Actually he too had an everyday headcovering; Charles the Simple, for example, wore a cap (*pilleus*) and probably supported himself with a staff. In Liutprand of Cremona's description, the "king of the Franks," meaning Otto I, in contrast to the long-haired Basileus appears "with a cap on his head" (*pileatus*) and "handsomely trimmed"; that is to say, his hair was cut. At Saint Gall, Otto the Great appeared "with his right hand supported by his staff"; he dropped it in order to judge the reaction of the monks. Just as Charlemagne had dressed in the manner of his people, so the dress of later kings did not differ essentially from that of their contemporaries. They would stand in church with staff and cap; during the reading of the gospel they removed their cap and placed their staff on the floor. Staff and cap or hat had long been a sign of male dignity; in some rural areas this is still the case, while in the urban bourgeoisie the demands of style (walking canes, top hats) come and go. Even monks wore caps with ear flaps (*pillea aurita*).

Originally the hat was a protection against the cold and rain, the staff a support and in emergencies a weapon against wolves or "evil men." Both were incorporated into the system of gestures and acquired a symbolic value—the staff or rod to a great extent and the cap occasionally. As a mark of respect, one took off one's cap to a superior. Once, it seems, the cap came close to symbolizing a royal crown: Richer tells of the lowborn favorite of Charles the Simple who often infuriated the magnates by removing the king's cap and putting it on his own head.

So much has been written about the staff or rod as a component of gestures and as a symbolic object that a very few observations will suffice here. During an epoch that could better be called the "wood age" than the "iron age," it is not surprising that wood should have been used to emphasize various things. The list runs from the simple twig, the *festuca,* to the emissary's staff and the bishop's crosier, to short and long scepters, and to the papal *ferula.* Pope Benedict V had to break his *ferula* and show it to the people when he was deposed in 964. The *festuca* served as the symbol of the conveyance (*cessio*) of a piece of real property, or, more precisely, it "was" the property at that moment, and its transfer brought about the legally binding transaction. The twig and, in a similar manner, a clod of earth served as a small portion of the property being exchanged by its possessor. In the *libri feudorum* of upper Italy and elsewhere, the actual provenance of the twig played a diminishing role; what counted was the gesture of its transferral to the other person, not the specific piece of wood used. At an assembly of royal emissaries of Otto III in 998, the monastery of Saint Vincent of Volturno demanded the return of a *cella,* that is, a priory, from which a Count Rainald had expelled the monks and replaced them with nuns. When the judgment had been pronounced, the count took a twig (*virga*) and, also through verbal explanation (*consona voce*), handed over the property to the abbot of Saint Vincent; the count's agents who had carried out the expulsion order then did the same. In this instance the explanations made by the losing party were reported; elsewhere they are not referred to, but one can assume that such explanations of the symbolic actions were given. It was particularly important in property transactions that the witnesses should be left with no ambiguity.

A staff and even the king's scepter could play the same role. Conrad II returned a farm to the nuns of Obermünster in Regensburg in 1029, explaining in his deed that he had invested the monastery with the farm through his staff "and had left the staff there as eternal witness (of the event)." At the moment of the legal proceeding the staff had personified the farm. Afterwards it did not return to its ordinary role but acquired new meaning as a lasting sign of the imperial decision, and thus was certainly much more than a simple memento. Such a transformation of meaning has become almost entirely alien to us, only to be found in the surrender of the key marking the transfer of a house. The use children make of objects comes closer to it, as for example when a chair becomes first a saddle horse, then an automobile, and then is again simply a seat. In the past, the playful element was not central; what was important was the object's capacity to make invisible occurrences visible and understandable.

The bishop's crosier was first a support, which in the eastern Church has maintained its form of a shepherd's crook; it is indeed the staff of the good shepherd, the *baculus* (*virga*) *pastoralis.* The crosier is the symbol of office in the Roman Church and incorporates this office in various situations: upon the death of a bishop it used to be sent to the emperor and given by the latter to the candidate of his choice. That the action was more important than the object is shown in the case of the imperial chancellor Heribert, who was invested as archbishop of Cologne by Otto III in the presence of Pope Silvester II with the pope's "staff of Saint Peter." During the administration of a bishop, the crosier was the appropriate symbol for various manifestations of his will. Thus Thietmar of Merseburg received from the archbishop of Magdeburg the parish rights over four castles and a village "through his staff," and he carried out a mutual agreement with the bishop of Meissen in the course of which both (temporarily) exchanged crosiers. The return of the crosier could take longer when it served as the security for the maintenance of an agreement. After the negotiations over the foundation of the bishopric of Bamberg, Bishop Henry of Würzburg confirmed an alliance with the king "secretly through the transmission of his crosier." The following story was told of a French bishop: once, while inebriated, the bishop promised an abbacy to a monk; then someone purloined his crosier, and the next morning the new abbot appeared before the now sober prelate to thank him for granting him the office, producing the crosier as evidence of the concession. Nolens volens the bishop had to confirm the grant.

Here too, words must have accompanied the actions, but they are seldom transmitted. At a Roman synod in the year 1001, Pope Silvester II presented the papal *ferula* to bishop Bernward of Hildesheim with an explanation that Bernward's companion Thangmar recorded. The gesture reestablished Bernward's episcopal jurisdiction over the canonry of Gandersheim. In a similar manner in 1007, Archbishop Willigis of Mainz returned the jurisdiction over Gandersheim by handing Bernward his own crosier with the words, "Beloved brother and fellow bishop, I announce my surrender of this church and transmit to you in the sight of Christ, in the sight of our lord king and our fellow bishops, the pastoral staff which I hold in my hands as a sign that henceforth neither I nor any of my successors may advance a pretension or claim in this matter." Thus were the archbishop's words reported, and they could not have been much different in reality. The meaning of symbolic action was explained, and attention was called to its public nature, which was an essential requirement in legal proceedings.

The crosier was part of the official attire of episcopal office; the royal parallel was the scepter, which was used on solemn occasions especially in Italy, where it had been recognized since late antiquity as an imperial *insigne*. Of the two types then in use, the short and the long scepter, the latter became the more important for the tenth century; the shorter one appeared to have first played a role around 900. The *aurea virga* of the French king was once compared to the long staff of a cantor, which certainly served as a support rather than as a signaling device or to mark the beat. The long scepter or a substitute for it could be used as a token, as when Otto the Great, in 967, invested the archbishop of Ravenna with property confiscated from an enemy by means of a gilded staff. A golden scepter served the same emperor in the investiture of the subordinate king Berengar and his son Adalbert. They received the *regnum Italicum* along with the scepter from his hand. However, Otto retained the scepter—this instance was not one in which the *insigne* was permanently transmitted.

The symbolic use of staffs could only be sketched briefly here. It should be noted that military banners also belonged to this category since they were primarily standard lances to which a cloth was attached as a distinguishing sign. During the siege of a castle, if one can believe Thietmar, a count who was one of Henry II's vassals was despoiled of the lance which had served as the symbol of his investiture with a county. "With honeyed words" he tried to recover it from the castle's defenders, but his efforts were in vain. In the end he sadly went away "without his standard and without his fief." One can hardly imagine that the possession of the county depended on the possession of the standard lance; rather, the loss of the fief might have been punishment for the count's carelessness in allowing the standard to be raised in front of his tent without a proper guard. In any case, the lance was clearly a staff of a particular sort, a long-lasting symbol of military command; well into the nineteenth century it was considered shameful to loose one's banner to the enemy. In a charter for the monastery of Gorze Otto II said that on the day of the battle against the Saracens (at Cotrone in 982) a count Conrad had made the emperor the executor of his will "under our banner (*sub fanone nostro*), that is, under the imperial standard and before the entire army." The flag, or rather the banner, as secular and ecclesiastical symbol came into vogue in the tenth century. In Augsburg on Palm Sunday, people carried *cruces et fanones* in the traditional procession, while in Rome they carried *crucem et vexilla,* which should not be confused with the dragon banners also carried in Rome on this occasion. The latter were particularly favored by the Vikings as terrifying battle flags.

Military and religious "battle flags" waved near each other, a situation fostered by the old idea of the *militia Christi*. The processional crosses and church standards were closely connected, for the church standard had a long handle which ended in a cross, and below it, on the arms of the cross, a small cloth banner was hung.

How closely ecclesiastical and military banners were connected to each other in the thought of the time is shown in the quest to find a new form of battle standard. According to the account by Rodulf Glaber, before one of his military expeditions Geoffrey of Anjou attached to his standard lance the seal of Saint Martin, the reparation of whose monastery he had lauded, and with the assistance of his new patron he obtained victory. This was a gesture that never recurred because it came about under very particular conditions—after negotiations with the clergy in the town of Tours then under siege by Geoffrey. For us the account is valuable because it indicates how one could experiment even within the boundaries of the received system of meaning. The whole area of standards was then still in the stage of "developing custom" and not fixed as it is today. Among its peculiarities was the "holy lance," which brought victory through the sacred relics it contained and hence merited genuflection. So much has been written on it that nothing more need be added here.

Gestures with Ecclesiastical Insignia

The presentation of symbols of offices and honors has focused less on the gestures than on the objects and words of these rituals. Royal and imperial dignity had a meaning that was shown during the coronation, but the dignity of ecclesiastical offices also had to be manifested by the transmission of symbols: the ostiarius received the church key, the lector a book, and so forth, to the crosier of the bishop, to which was later added the ring. The papal bestowal of ecclesiastical privileges of honor—for abbots the right to wear the sandals of a bishop and special vestments during the Mass—was accomplished by writing; for the hierarchy this was enough, and in any case the common people understood little of this most highly developed Roman form of hierarchization. It must have appeared conspicuous when, for example, the archbishop of Trier, on the model of the archbishop of Ravenna, was granted the right to a purple saddle cloth and to be preceded by a cross. Such images bring us into the area of "representation" and thus of a subject even less susceptible of exhaustive treatment than that of gestures.

3 ✦ REPRESENTATION AS EVIDENCE OF STATUS

THE "CITIZEN KING" OF THE FRENCH RES-
toration could only have existed in modern
times. If a medieval monarch wished to maintain his reputation and with it his authority, he
constantly had to make clear his position of superiority to the people. He could also lose the
support of the magnates of his kingdom if he
relinquished splendor and glory at his court:
people were not accustomed to separating essence from appearance, nor did they perceive
the latter as "mere appearance," something a
powerful person need not resort to. The representation of the office coincided with the office
itself in such a way that there was hardly any

private sphere for the monarch; even when hunting in the forest he was rarely without a retinue, and these followers expected outstanding performance from him as a sportsman. Traveling incognito had not yet been invented for monarchs, and even their pilgrimages remained, in a sense, affairs of state.

The same was true for the nobleman. He could not devote himself solely to agriculture or, when it was required, to military service. If he did not want to sink to the level of a rich peasant, he had to demonstrate his noble character and outstanding talent in constant competition with his equals. This involved both the manly virtues and the conspicuous expenditures that he could afford. That these expenditures seem somewhat modest in comparison with those which were demanded in the late Middle Ages was the result of the limited material possibilities of the age, not of a different mental attitude.

As far as prelates were concerned, they were secure in their office as long as they enjoyed the favor of their kings and the respect of their subordinates. They too had to represent themselves in order to retain this respect; and they also had to be concerned with a sort of "heavenly representation": magnificent churches and solemn processions had to serve the glory of God, and great attention had to be paid to the glory of the patron or patrons of the city in competition with those of neighboring cities, dioceses, and monasteries. These efforts brought color to the monotony of daily life, led to lasting architectural achievements, and cost an enormous amount of money, for which today people would have found other uses. To attend to the glory of their respective lord was the constant obligation of the subordinates. Only the hermit could withdraw from this obligation. His was another sort of divine praise—extreme renunciation rather than the usual pomp.

RECEPTION

The presentation of the social position of magnates required personal action, material assets, and strict adherence to current custom. Only by these means did one acquire that dignity and respect which could not be obtained merely through actions or generosity. In its general lines, custom remains constant; it is merely refined and elaborated from one age to another. We know how spare the court customs of the Frankish period were in contrast to the later Burgundian or Spanish ceremonial. Even in the tenth century, however, questions of etiquette were a sensitive indicator of worth, easily deflected. Things we consider trivial details, or as occasional minor infractions of current rules, could have great importance. Here is a characteristic story told by Ekkehard IV of Saint Gall: Bishop Salomo of Constance once encountered by chance the king's chamberlains. "He greeted them first and waited in vain for them to return the greeting. When he sent them messengers to settle the affair, they refused to make peace with him." He fled, the chamberlains wanted to imprison him, and finally the king commanded them to make peace.

Bishop Salomo had shown the chamberlains a mark of respect that belonged to them, or rather to their royal lord. Then it was their role to recognize his position as ecclesiastical prince. When they failed to do so, they lowered or destroyed his social prestige; it was a sort of declaration of war, and in vain the bishop sought "to make peace." Behind this conduct, of course, lay some extremely important concerns: it was actually a fight over power in the region of Lake Constance.

Normally, encounters between two magnates were not left to chance—the ceremonial was determined beforehand. When a meeting was prepared in 924 between the West Frankish king and Duke William of Aquitaine on the Loire, which formed the boundary between their territories, messengers went from one side to the other, and it was night before the manner of the meeting was agreed upon. Finally, William allowed himself to be transported across the river, apparently remaining on horseback. Only on the other side did he dismount and go to the king, who was awaiting him on horseback. When the two stood facing each other, or perhaps with the king leaning down from his horse, King Raoul gave the duke the kiss of peace. With that the most important aspect of the conference had been accomplished: the superior rank of the West Frankish king had been recognized, and the two separated, agreeing to meet the next morning to deal with the business at hand in detail. In the form of the meeting the legal content had already come to the fore.

How one was received was so important that even nuances could give rise to disagreements. In Saint Gall, a bishop of Verona complained that upon his arrival an evangelistary of mediocre value had been carried before him and that at the Mass he had been given a silver (rather than a golden) chalice. In this instance the monks had not been at fault; on the other hand, it may have been intentional that Duke William the Great treated a Count Erluin, who had complained about the count of Flanders, "like one of his youngsters." Erluin then went to the Norman Duke William, "who ordered that he should be lodged with honorific display and that all that he needed was to be given to him with great ceremony." Honor is the demonstration of honor; it must be "actualized" in order to exist. Ostensible disregard destroyed social position at a noble court; even apart from other political necessities, anyone to whom such a thing was done had to look for a new setting for his existence and to plan revenge for the insult.

"To meet someone halfway" is today little more than a figure of speech; in the tenth century, one of the most important means of honoring someone was to come out with a great retinue to meet him. Rather than repeating the large body of writing on the topic, we will note here primarily the distinction it presents between the empire and western Europe: under the Ottonians it was a right reserved to the king; in the west it was even permitted to counts. A well-known example is the anger of Otto the Great when the archbishop of Magdeburg used this reserved ceremony for Hermann Billung, guiding the duke by the hand into the cathedral while all the bells were rung. For King Berengar II, who was prepared to accept submission, Otto allowed the court to set out to meet him a mile away from Magdeburg; in other words, he recognized Berengar's kingship, but he dishonored him after the reception by making him wait three days for an audience. On feast days it was Otto's practice to be accompanied in solemn procession to church by the Magdeburg clergy with crosses, reliquaries, and censers. "On the return to his apartments he caused many candles to be carried in front of him and his great following of priests, dukes, and counts."

In France, the count of Chartres could order the monks of a local monastery "to receive him in the monastery with a procession." When in 1027 Count William of Angoulême returned from the Holy Land, the clergy "went out to meet him in white vestments and with many types of (ecclesiastical) ornaments," together with a crowd of laymen, a mile from the city, everyone intoning songs of praise and antiphons "as is the custom." Duke William of Aquitaine was received with a procession "of the entire city" of Limoges in 1021. The monks of the local monastery came with evangelistaries and censers, "just as the duke was always received by them." On this occasion William invested the new bishop with his crosier as was due the lord of a territorial church. "Wherever he went and wherever he held an assembly, one could believe one was before a king rather than a duke."

We are well informed about the lordly *adventus* and the associated *occursus,* the ceremonial meeting. The example we have before us illustrates a dual process: the representation is complemented by what might be designated "recognition," that is, the homage paid by those ruled. Although, since the French Revolution, the meeting of a ruler with the people has tended to be patriarchal and secular in character, in early times the triumphal and sacred aspect was dominant; the *adventus Augusti* and Christ's triumphant entry into Jerusalem on Palm Sunday, inwardly comparable to each other, provided the models. It was not the glorification of the person of the prince but rather the presentation of the context of the entire system. The ruler and his subordinates had constantly to make clear the *existence and form* of the political relations through what might be called the "representation of the state." During the first half of the eleventh century, "processional streets" were apparently laid out in Augsburg, Würzburg, Speyer, and Trier for processions from church to church at festival times. In an age when powers of abstraction were limited, lordly "splendor" and the devotion of subordinates had always to be made visible and thus comprehensible. We see merely as a political event the meeting of Henry II with King Robert of France at Mouzon in 1023 in the presence of many magnates; a chronicler asserts that most of the bishops and dukes "from various regions of origin" appeared here "in order to gaze at the imperial office, which was preceded by such a great reputation." It has been said of that society that every action in the collective existence of people had its value for maintaining prestige; certain actions were particularly suited for this purpose and were therefore developed specifically to exhibit prestige. These would be performed, as in processions, especially in the proximity of liturgical or quasi-liturgical activities.

This sheds light on the meaning of "purely ecclesiastical" processions, as they have been preserved into the present. These also made explicit the rights of lordship—the rights of Christ or of a saint, who, for example, at the time of the translation of his relics, was recognized by the community as their patron and undertook its protection. Moreover, the rights of clerical lordship were recognized in this manner. In 955, the bishop of Verona complained that the ecclesiastics of his city did not attend his synods and "also did not want to come to his processions." They were pledged to obedience; even *in processionis honore,* that is, in the episcopal right of procession, they were subordinate to their diocesan bishop and not directly to the patriarch of Aquileia.

Homage and Obligatory Processions

The disciplinary supervision of the bishop over the clergy of his diocese had to be continually "shown," just as in the Merovingian period, when councils ordered that parish clergy must celebrate major feasts with the bishop under penalty of excommunication or removal from office. It was from these journeys that the obligatory processions of parish clergy and faithful seem to have developed, processions increasingly noted from the tenth century on: Bishop Goderic of Auxerre (918–33) ordered that at Pentecost all (?) of the laity and priests of the diocese were to come together in the cathedral with their parish crosses. In Trier the situation seems to have been similar; in 1072 there was a report of the crowd of pilgrims from surrounding villages who would arrive with their crosses. The right to organize processions always belonged to the bishop, and he could also designate new destinations, especially when establishing pilgrimages for the benefit of monasteries. He certainly had practical reasons, for it would have been inadvisable to gather too large a crowd in the city. Processions to monasteries meant the material support of the monasteries because the participants brought offerings with them— mainly in the form of candle wax—as tribute in recognition of the spiritual lord, the saint of the monastery. Such rights were held by Tournus (949), Bèze (1008), and the monastery of Mettlach (931–41), where these processions, although abolished in 1830, nevertheless survived into the Bismarckian era.

There seem to have been no opposition by the population to these long walks, which is astounding to our modern sensibilities, all the more so since they were associated with payment of a tax. Pilgrimages interrupted the daily routine, broadened horizons, and strengthened the unity of the community; above all, by means of the honor rendered to the spiritual supreme pastor and the saint, they made it possible to ask the protection and assistance of these latter. When we consider the precarious position of the rural population, and not only in years of famine, we can understand their willingness to render to God that which is God's.

So much for the "recognition" of spiritual lordship. Did the trains of pilgrims also serve as "representation" of ecclesiastical prestige? It would so appear when we remember the enthusiasm with which popular spectacles were described in the Middle Ages. Floods of pilgrims brought economic benefits to the episcopal city, they increased its honor, and mass pilgrimages to the saint of a monastery made that saint famous; his renown spread worldwide, and the prestige of a saint was almost identical with that of his monastery.

RETINUES

Pilgrimages were things far outside the sphere of everyday life. But even in everyday life a lord needed numerous people around him both for specific purposes and also to maintain the honor of his house and to provide a spectacle. Without an appropriate number (*multitudo*), in the opinion of Hincmar of Reims, the royal household could not exist purposefully and honorably (*honeste*): people were "the jewels of the palace." Already Jacitus had written that for the Germanic peoples an entourage was an ornament in peacetime, protection in war. The transformation in the use of words such as *ornamentum* and *decus* that has taken place in the past two hundred years is telling: today, a numerous entourage is dismissed as having a purely decorative function; it is considered unnecessary pomp. We have almost forgotten that in earlier times the isolation of a leader indicated his impotence, while the image of power, dignity, and honor was associated with a mass of servants standing by and receiving orders, and horses, which gave them mobility. Of horses we shall say more later.

What we describe as territorial lordship was above all lordship over men—*decus* and *praesidium* appeared more important than economic profits, and could hardly be bought. In Latium, for example, fortified villages were built up according to noneconomic considerations (and sometimes were failures). Their strategic importance and the prestige of populousness (in Italian, *far gente*) seem to have been the main criteria for their location by the nobles of that region. The clergy was not without similar concerns about prestige. Abbo of Fleury's comment in a letter to Abbot Bernard of Beaulieu was appropriate to many prelates: "I know that the noisy host of your kinsmen now surrounds you, the army of vassals (*milites*), the crowd of friends." And secular lords prized the service of "very noble clerics and cowled monks" next to the "noble, unending, and fine" crowd of secular followers.

In this instance, "recognition" was part of representation, not as an action but as praise of what is seen. When Duke Gisulf I of Salerno came from the sea to Terracina with a great entourage to meet with Pope John XII, the Romans accompanying the pope were amazed at the sight of the numerous nobles and the *gloria* of the princes and they said, "Now we have seen more than we had heard." Appearance had surpassed reputation. It was therefore no wonder, according to the simple reasoning of the chronicler, that an alliance should be concluded: the southern Italian prince had made it clear to the Roman urban nobility and especially to the family of Alberich that he was an acceptable partner. One's social rank could in this manner be confirmed and even raised. This is shown in another story, no more to be taken literally than the first, yet characteristic of the thinking of the period. In the house of the Margrave Adalbert (II) of Tuscany, King Louis (III) in 905 saw such a great number of "elegant" vassals and such an entourage that he was taken with envy and said to his people that Adalbert should be designated a king rather than a marquis; he added that this man was only in title (*nomine solummodo*) inferior (that is, ranked below) to himself, Louis. The margrave's wife spread word of this comment, whereupon, we are told, the magnates of Italy became disloyal to the king.

An impressive following of armed men had to surround important persons when they traveled, both as protection against possible attack and for the sake of reputation. One traveled "in a noble manner" (*nobiliter*) and honorably (*honorifice*); one increased one's importance through the number and magnificence of one's following. When a bishop attended a synod, he did well not to select only clergy as his entourage; a "most suitable" (*decentissima*) host of clergy and vassals surrounded Bishop Godehard of Hildesheim when he traveled to a synod at Frankfurt in 1027, where the case of the supremacy of Gandersheim was to be treated.

The existence of a kind of liturgical following can be only mentioned in passing. When a bishop surrounded himself with numerous clerics while celebrating Mass, it was officially done for the glory of God. That other reasons may also have had a role is indicated by synodal decrees enacted against an excessive number of chaplains and deacons on such occasions. There were abbots like the one from the monastery of Saint Martial in Limoges who wished to be equated to a bishop. Hence the second synod of that town, held in 1031, decreed that bishops could employ up to seven deacons in the celebration of solemn feasts, abbots "and other priests" at the most three, to which the abbot of Saint Martial could add a chaplain. The rank and prestige of a prelate was measured even by such apparently insignificant things.

BANQUETS

To follow a lord meant that one did not have to take care of one's food but would receive daily rations and also, in many cases, necessary equipment—clothes, weapons, horses—from his hand. In ideal circumstances the following ate with the lord; the *Waltharius* describes the amount of eating and drinking, the golden vessels, and the tapestries in the royal hall, which provided an attractive background for the one hundred places at table for the vassal following. Eating and drinking played a very important role in traditional society, and not only because there were so often shortages. These activities bound together the men who ate from the same dish and drank from the same cup. The medieval word *companio* signified someone who ate the same bread as oneself; from it is derived the word "companion," as well as the colloquial French *copain* and German *Kumpel*. One was particularly attached to one's lord if he shared out the food himself, which could happen in the smaller courts. Bishop Udalrich of Augsburg did so, as did Mathilda, the widow of Henry I, in her monasteries and among her servants. In familiar circles this was done as a matter of course; in political terms it indicated patriarchal authority. That the coronation banquet of the German kings came at the end of the entire ceremony meant a lessening of its importance in comparison with Germanic tradition, in which according to Islandic sources the "inheritance banquet" introduced the lord's entry into his office in the circle of his followers. Such a practice is by no means exclusively Germanic; one need only remember the promise of Christ that his disciples would eat and drink with him in his kingdom at his table.

A meal at a princely court was to be a feast not only for the stomach but also for the eyes. It entailed both magnificent furnishings and a number of courses, which at the German royal court could be considerable. Above all, the court table represented the "first rank" position of the ruler. Possibly the best illustration of this is an anecdote reported by Liutprand of Cremona: Wido of Spoleto wanted to become the king of the West Franks. His seneschal was to go to Metz in search of "nourishment worthy of a king," and the bishop there "according to the custom of the Franks" provided it abundantly on demand. But the official offered to make a private deal with him: for the price of one horse, he would arrange things so that King Wido would be satisfied with a third of the anticipated expenditures. The bishop answered, "It is unsuitable that we should be ruled by a king who for ten silver coins (drachmas) would be content with a wretched meal." For this reason the Franks abandoned Wido and elected Odo (of Paris) as their king. Those who retold this story thought it possible that the decision for or against a future king could have depended on such considerations. And the same was apparently true of bishops at the Ottonian court: Liutprand of Cremona tells of Byzantine bishops at this court who sat at an unadorned table eating rusk; they were rich in gold but poor in servants and (table) ware. This was just as contrary to the noble style as Liutprand's later report that these bishops even did their own shopping and were their own cooks.

Lordship had to manifest itself externally by means of a quantity of servants and every form of material magnificence, all of which was evidence of political potency—if full treasure chests were sufficient manifestation for the Greek bishops, this was the expression of a "modern" and intellectual concept. The daily common meals alone in a secular or ecclesiastical court would have been inadequate to maintain the lord's prestige. From time to time he had to give stronger emphasis in the form of banquets, which people loved to describe; verbal propaganda extended and embellished the material display. In the celebration of feasts the ecclesiastical magnates did not stand far behind the secular.

A banquet served also for initiation into a society or the establishment of friendly ties between equals. Conviviality promoted a quasi kinship of familial relationship. Two lords had been carrying on a feud; when they were reconciled, friendship was sworn and one invited the other to a *convivium*. There followed a return invitation from the second lord, which the first accepted against the wishes of his vassals, because it would have been contrary to custom (*nefas*) to decline. The second feast lasted three days, and then the host, "cheerfully and amicably" accompanied the guest "with a great following." The situation was similar among ecclesiastics; when Thietmar of Merseberg was received into the dining society of the Magdeburg cathedral canons, the feast continued for two days, all at the expense of his father, the count of Walbeck. In contrast, the union between clerics and vassals of the church of Reims against archbishop Gerbert expressed itself in the fact that no one wanted to eat with him or to attend his liturgical celebrations. In this instance the vassalic following was active and repudiated its lord by breaking off the liturgical and dining community with him. Thus a *coniuratio* functioned in a way similar to an *excommunicatio* pronounced by one's ecclesiastical superiors.

While eating provides relatively brief amusement, the same cannot always be said of drinking. "Long, almost to the first light of dawn, they sat together," goes a report of a drinking bout of a bishop from a rich family with ecclesiastics and laymen. "He devoted himself too much and more than too much to an affair which should have taken place at another time," because when the guests had left or had fallen asleep in their seats, the pious bishop wanted to say the nocturn and, while doing so, suffered a stroke. At least, that is how the affair is recorded by his biographer. Atto of Vercelli's *Polypticum* describes a drinking bout during which music was played through the town, the tavern keepers did all they could to "chase away sobriety," and "indecent laughter" was to be heard above bawdy stories, incentives to even worse. While such worldly things were celebrated with cheerfulness in northern Italy it was reported of a merchant's guild in northern Brabant that its members, so to speak, solemnly celebrated their getting drunk.

Opinion is divided about whether the drinking bouts of such guilds had ritual cultic roots. The relationship is clearer in the so-called *Minnetrinken* (memorial drinking), since *Minne*—which originally meant "memory"—referred to thinking about the other world, essentially similar to the ecclesiastical *caritas* customs in which a cup was drained in honor of a saint. The connections with the Germanic custom go along with those of the classical funerary meal and the Christian *agape:* Christ's last supper with his disciples and the early Christian liturgy are seen as elaborations on the ancient memorial services for the dead. At the same time the Last Supper was a lord's feast.

The extreme form of memorial toasting, leading to drunkenness, was disapproved by the Church in the tradition of Ambrose. The admonitions seem to have been little observed, for Hincmar of Reims, Regino of Prüm, and Burchard of Worms incorporated them into their works. No priest was supposed to get drunk in memory of the dead or on other occasions; he was not to invite or urge others to participate in toasting the souls of the dead or in honor of the saints, nor was he to "drink to excess at the request of others." Drinking on command, even in honor of the dead, is still done occasionally today.

The other, more modest form of memorial drinking was practiced above all in monasteries. In Fleury the monks emptied their cups *in amore patris Benedicti;* at Cluny they drank three times in honor of the Holy Trinity. Christian rulers also followed the practice: Otto I ordered a memorial drink in Regensburg in honor of Saint Emmeram.

When noblemen had agreed to murder the Bohemian duke (and later saint) Wenzeslaus at a banquet, he is said to have invited them to drink in honor of Saint Michael and a Christian hour of death. The idea of inviting one's own murderer to a sort of anticipatory death commemoration suggests a taste for the dramatic.

The purely terrestrial conviviality bound the living together, while the cultic meal enlarged the circle of members to include those in the next world. The celebration of the Lord's Supper, to which Christ continually invites the faithful, became the central part of the Christian liturgy, its location being the house of God. At this mystery the saints had no place. Even when the saint was the theoretical lord of a monastery, the cultic meal with him could not surpass the cultic meal with the "poor souls": offerings were made to the saint and to the souls in the same manner. There were, of course, other symbols of community with the dead, such as dividing their servings at meals among the poor, just as there were other forms of honoring the saints.

TABLE MANNERS

As we have seen, eating and drinking not only served to satisfy basic needs but also established community and confirmed the existing order by representing it visually. Dining communities could also be the occasion for emphasizing manners, especially where excess was likely to occur. Table manners, although always present in a rudimentary form, were significantly advanced during the post-Carolingian period and eventually formed an important part of chivalry.

One element of table etiquette was that on the day of a feast the host had to behave in a warm and friendly way (*hilariter*). Evil people such as Boleslav, the brother of Saint Wenzeslaus, were by nature poorly disposed to friendliness, but at least they had to feign it (*sub hilaritatis specie*). Traditional pleasure in abundant food and drink was at the origin of this cheerfulness. There was also the need for the head of the house to show a positive attitude toward friends, in contrast to the *gravitas*, the dark countenance, which the lord had to show when he was negatively disposed toward someone.

The ascetic tendency that is emphasized in many priestly biographies did not seek to change customs but rather to imbue them with a deeper meaning. When Bruno of Cologne fasted, he was as cheerful as the most cheerful of the participants at his banquets; he thus acted in accord with the biblical injunction, which forbade "ostentatious" fasting. Roswitha of Gandersheim describes a joyful drinking bout which lasted until sleep overtook the participants. The pious duke then happily spent the night in prayer; in other words, he did not take part in the drunkeness (*ebrietas*) of his guests and previously had only joined in the general amusement (*laetitia*) in outward appearance. Before the banquet he had fed the poor, whom he normally fed at his own table with his own hand and thus demonstrated his Christian attitude. This pious gesture appears again in the biography of Queen Mathilda, now extended to the servants: In the monastery, Mathilda ate only after she "had distributed everything" to the nuns; in the secular sphere she treated the sick, as well as her servants, in the same manner. While giving preference to the poor and the sick also accorded with moral practice—he who accepts them, the Bible assures us, accepts Christ—servants were another matter. Whether Mathilda really acted in this manner or whether it was an invention of the hagiographer is less important than the fact that here the hierarchy of command seems to be broken, although elsewhere the common meal had to show who was the lord. We might recall Abbot John of Gorze, who wanted to take not the first but the last seat in the choir during the office; such charming "Franciscan" traits foreshadow much later times, when the hierarchical structure would be called in question.

"Refined manners" were fostered above all by clerics and women. It is certainly no accident that we know about the table manners of another monarch, also a woman—the daughter-in-law of Mathilda. We are told that the empress Adelheid, at a banquet she held for clerics and laymen, held her knife as if she wanted to eat more and thereby prolonged the meal in the interest of the participants. Manners also required that one stopped eating as soon as the lord or lady did so—as was still the custom at the imperial table of the Habsburgs in the twentieth century. It is a pity that information concerning table manners in the tenth century is very scanty. Only by chance do we learn from the Life of Count Gerald of Aurillac that he never forced anyone to drink, occasionally held a breakfast for his guests—normally one fasted until around noon—and never ate anything himself before the third hour of the day. We can assume that patriarchal customs predominated: eating at a long table out of common platters, drinking out of a cup that was passed around. At court, there was occasionally a yearning for entertainment by jugglers and musicians, and we hear that the emperor Conrad I, to the anger of the monks, ordered such entertainers to perform even in the monastery of Saint Gall. In canonical collections priests were forbidden to tell or sing unedifying stories. Nor were they to watch "disgraceful amusements with (exhibitions of) bears and dancers."

The *Ruodlieb,* that informative poem from the second half of the eleventh century, which could have been used at the time as a sort of manual of correct behavior seems to come from another world. Certainly its clerical author idealized the everyday circumstances; nevertheless, the tendency for table manners to become refined and, in part, "privatized" is clear. In Ruodlieb's house, the raised chair of the lord was still to be found, although—perhaps already influenced by the cult of ladies?—he seats his mother in it. There is no common table but various small tables at which the guests sit in pairs. This arrangement was for a family conference to advise on the possibility of a marriage—we can well imagine how difficult it was to establish a rank order among kinsmen—but the same arrangement was used for a banquet to honor the son upon his return home. Ruodlieb had a single *conviva,* his nephew, with whom he shared bread, platter, and cup; his mother's table companion was her jackdaw. The mother directed the servants and sent food and drink to the individual tables. Unlike Queen Mathilda, the lady did not serve her guests or her servants. That the hostess should remain seated rather than run about in order to provide for her guests is still part of "good form" in our own century.

The table community was not abolished but, rather, relaxed in a way that hardly corresponded to daily practice. The case is interesting even as a mere project, as an attempt to abandon traditional forms and to develop a new style. The creation of small groups within the larger group makes one think of ladies paired with gentlemen at table in modern times. Eating alone, as Ruodlieb's mother did, was certainly not desirable, even if Byzantine bishops did it. The emperor never dined alone in Constantinople. When Liutprand had been assigned to one of the lower seats at the "long, but not wide table" of the emperor, Nikephoros Phokas sent him as a gesture of reconciliation a slice of meat from which he himself had eaten. This emperor had once been a general, unpretentious and accustomed to being surrounded by many people.

The *Ruodlieb* speaks of drinking only in connection with the introduction of a novel ceremony. A man of peasant standing entertains a knight; after the meal and the washing of hands, wine is brought out; the host tastes it and offers it to the guest. The latter hands the cup to the lady of the house and only drinks from it after her. At

Ruodlieb's engagement celebration we learn that the servants who carry cushions to the castle's ladies' chambers are given a cup of wine for their service, which, with a bow, they return empty to the cupbearer. Drinking societies were something the poet did not know about or, better, did not with to know about. Chivalrous propriety, the new "civilized" behavior, manifested itself in particular by a moderate use of alcohol.

Here and elsewhere, the novelty in the *Ruodlieb* is a stepping away from earlier custom, substituting something considered better or more elegant. Customs, as long as they are not questioned, are followed by most of the population without reflection; to the ethnologist's question of why comes the reply that they have always been so or that the gods so commanded. Only with the beginning of reflection is free reign given to experimentation, to a kind of a playfulness that has a serious intent: in the words of Johan Huizinga, "It creates order, indeed it *is* order." What remains from the experimentation is a new, more finely structured form of custom with a bow in the direction of ceremony. The complicated rules of the game are no longer accessible to everyone; they confirm group solidarity and separate the group from outsiders. By its style, the *Ruodlieb* belongs to the beginning of a new epoch, which can be recognized precisely in such small matters. These are things that have retained importance up to the present, though we seldom reflect on their origins.

SECULAR MARKS OF STATUS: CLOTHES, JEWELRY, WEAPONS, HORSES

As with social customs, appearance and fashion too have their symbolic value. When we turn to this subject, we must realize that, in contrast to the uniformity encouraged today, both dress and behavior were meant to indicate rank and social position in the tenth century.

In the past century, description of styles of dress constituted an attractive part of what was then called "cultural history," and even today historians seldom go beyond a merely descriptive presentation. It would be useful to have what Georges Duby has called an "archaeology of the marks of social differentiation," which is already being done in one area, that of monastic habits. Clerics were separated from laity primarily by their dress. Rather of Verona could write that one need not ask a person to which *ordo* he belonged when one had seen his dress, his beard, "and the other indications of secular life." Language, custom, and dress together constituted the identity of a people. We must point out a few exceptions in practice to this general principle: even clerics sometimes enjoyed stylish innovations in their dress, and Rodulf Glaber objected to the adoption of Aquitanian styles by the Franks. The reasons are not hard to find. Clerics often remained very attached to worldly things, including fashion in clothes. Aquitanian clothing came to the Franks along with the favorites of Queen Constance—they showed that the regions were beginning to grow together, above all in the area of the courtly high society.

The official clothing of clerics indicated a number of graduated ranks, which in the highest range were regulated by papal bestowal of wearing apparel such as the pallium. Such a graduated ranking may not have existed in the laity; though we know next to nothing about the subtle shadings of dress. The most important point of differentiation between high and low was the bearing of arms; the second most important was the amount spent on clothing. The way clothing was cared for was also significant: one could be dressed poorly but cleanly and honorably and thereby maintain prestige within one's group. There was an official dress for kings, which was similar to the vestments of the priest but was only worn on exceptional occasions. Widukind of Corvey says that Otto the Great always wore native dress and never foreign—that is, Roman—clothing. Royal insignia were now added to this native dress, and the people thought of the king as someone richly clad, wearing a diadem rather than a cap. Secular princes sought to imitate royalty in this area, something which had already begun in the ninth century. Whether there was at this time a tendency toward special dress in the lower ranks is unknown, but quite conceivable. We have already noted how the chief shepherd in a miniature was differentiated from the others by his dress.

It was proper for nobility to distinguish itself from the masses by means of particular qualities, behavior, and dress. The sword was the supreme symbol of social rank and was thus worn even when hardly needed. The quality and the ornamentation of weapons had to correspond to the rank of their bearers; the sword of the Norman Duke William was so well known by his warriors that he could establish peace among them by simply sending it out. When it was brought before plundering troops "as a symbol of his coming" (to hold a punitive court) "they bowed their heads and knelt before the steel." The sword represented the duke's person, and announced his magnificent position: six pounds of gold had been used in making the hilt and in the inlay of the blade.

For such extraordinary objects, words such as "ingenious" and "wonderful" were certainly not inappropriate, and even the sober Liutprand of Cremona could characterize troops as having been "beautifully" provided with weapons. In Catalonia there were collectors of weapons; before the turn of the year 1000, weapons were the only luxury objects possessed by nobles. The Marquis Boso of Tuscany had a sword belt "of wonderful length and width made of gold and sparkling from many precious stones." Making an impression with gold jewelry was a general custom of magnates in Italy, and only precious stones could surpass the usual splendor. The social position of the elite depended on similar displays to such an extent that they could not give them up even in the field. When Marquis Adalbert of Ivrea found himself surrounded by Magyars, he put aside his sword belt, bracelets, and the rest of his usual costly *apparatus* and put on the simple garments of a *miles*. In the north among the Saxons, a golden neck ring (*torquis*) was the most important badge of the noble. The rebellious king's son Thangmar placed it on the altar, along with his weapons, as symbol of surrender. Like gold jewelry, luxurious clothing was not limited to Italy. In the ninth century the magnates of the empire had been decking themselves out apparently according to the imperial model: on feast days—and only then— Charlemagne had worn garments made of cloth threaded with gold, shoes with precious stones, and a cloak with a golden clasp. Toward the end of that century a member of the elite wore a cloak and clasp of the same sort, a costly tunic, possibly interwoven with thread of gold, a belt encrusted with gems, and golden bindings on his legs. "The self-exultation (*elatio*) of expensive garments," the narrator believed, was something that could not be found among other peoples. The Capetian kingdom seems even to have exceeded such luxury. Robert the Pious dressed in a "golden garment" and wore leg bindings (or cloak border) for which six pounds of gold had been required. That Count Gerald wrapped himself in wool or linen even on feast days was seen as worthy of exceptional mention and a sign of his great piety.

Horses, of course, were also one of the symbols of rank and office. Hincmar counted noble horses among *ornamenta* along with clothing and precious metals, and not only for the laity. In order to disgrace a captured bishop, one saddled a cheap horse for him. Part of the asceticism of the holy bishop Adalbert of Prague was that he never rode a purebred, fast horse decorated with gold and silver, but preferred a bridle made of rope "in the peasant manner." By contrast,

Italian bishops are described as seated on "Saxon saddles" with golden reins, the bit made of silver. For the horses of such prelates there was a golden neck decoration, which, when combined with the headgear of (pure) silver, was so heavy that the strongest animals had to be selected to wear it. Some rhetorical exaggeration may be at play here; yet the observation that one should not ride the same noble horse every day but should frequently parade a different one for the benefit of spectators sounds believable.

ECCLESIASTICAL MARKS OF STATUS

The life of a mounted warrior often depended on the quality of a sword and the strength and reliability of a war-horse; for him the cultivation of horses was much more than a pastime, and warriors quite properly were willing to pay dearly for horses. It should have been different for clerics. But they too were under constant obligation to demonstrate their prestige and that of their office, just like secular magnates. Saint Adalbert's humble walk was not understood in his own bishopric of Prague, and a bishop of his kind would probably have been ridiculed in northern Italy. In Verona, the foreign outsider Rather was presented with great difficulties: he could not ride on richly decorated thoroughbred horses and sleep in a gilded bed strewn with silk cushions or sit on a stool with a "Gothic carpet" spread over it. It was hardly because of this, or not only because of it, that he became a moralist. But the effect of his admonitions to his contemporaries would certainly have been greater if they could have been convinced that his asceticism was voluntary.

The *apparatus,* which can only inadequately be translated as "splendor," was an *appareil de l'ostentation* (G. Duby), the sense of which again can scarcely be transmitted with the devalued expression "pomp." What was put on display was not primarily wealth, but the outstanding rank, the differentiation among people. The splendor of the magnates certainly exercised an incentive on the people of lesser status who entered their service: anyone with gold to display could be no miser and must reward service fittingly. This was true also for prelates who had their own vassals: In Italy it was important for a bishop to dispose of a lot of them. Complaints about the dissipation of episcopal properties to the laity point less to the carelessness and incompetence of the higher ecclesiastics than to the fact that they were forced, just like their lay kinsmen, to live beyond their means.

An important part of the social order was the clear distinction among laity, secular clergy, and monks; church fathers and councils had ordered that everyone should wear the clothing of his group. But what was to be done when one was both of high status and a cleric? Should every trace of one's noble birth be hidden for the benefit of one's ecclesiastical office? The biblical injunction to become a new man was not a goal that could be attained by everyone. One often remained what one had been, and willingly if one was a member of a distinguished family. Lofty origins had to be expressed to some extent in one's clothing. There were monks whose habits distinguished them from the mass by the color and quality of the cloth, abbots who avoided wearing the monastic habit altogether, as confirmed by Odo of Cluny, who thundered against those who gloried in their "physical nobility" and lived *secundum carnem* in violation of the apostolic command. In this context, "flesh" meant everything pertaining to this world.

In Odo's opinion, any cleric who wore secular clothing committed a crime. Ancient synods had decreed that such people were to be excluded from the Church. One could not be so absolute in practice, since little differentiated clerical garb for longer journeys from secular. Saint Benedict had prescribed riding breeches for monks who were sent on trips; in Cluny, all the monks were provided with them, for no one could predict which of the monks might need these garments. Some sort of head cover was needed too, and for this the layman's cap was available—Liutprand of Cremona caused displeasure in Byzantium when he arrived so equipped, even though he was in the presence of the emperor. Since priests were repeatedly ordered to wear their stole while on journeys as a sign of their office, we can assume that usually they differed little from others while traveling. Adalbero of Laon's famous satire describing the secular military attire of a monk who was at once a Cluniac and a *miles* caricatured a tendency that was nonetheless real. He wore a fur cap, a split coat, long hose, and a belt, and carried weapons. That he rode a fast horse goes without saying.

Bishop Adalbero must have known what great value was placed in Cluny on the *vestis regularis,* the Cluniac habit, from which there was to be no deviation. His description of a Cluniac as a *miles* according to his clothes and equipment meant that Cluny had separated itself from the true and proper monastic tradition. Adalbero belonged to the powerful comital family which favored Gorze, and it is possible that the difference in the monastic habits of Gorze and Cluny played a role here. In Gorze, one habit was intended for work, the other for the office, both with the cowl prescribed by Saint Benedict for his monks. The Cluniacs, in contrast, wore the two habits one over the other: the wider and longer-sleeved robe, intended for ceremonial, was now the outer garment; the other, simpler one was an undergarment.

The question to what extent these external forms had a symbolic meaning, to which spiritual-religious attitude they corresponded, is certainly legitimate; unfortunately the sources provide no satisfying response. We can surmise that every reform sought to delineate itself through innovations: a difference in monastic habit could be primary; the symbolic meaning—if there was one—may have followed the fact. To wear two garments one over the other was already a well-established custom among the secular clergy. If a priest's chasuble along with his stole and maniple were removed, then he passed as a mere deacon. The Mass vestments were worn only during the office, while the wide cowl was a "liturgical" covering only in the broadest sense; in contrast with the Mass vestments there was no canonical prohibition against using it for other purposes.

White garments were generally regarded as a sign of purity and heavenly glory; they indicated an elevated status and "solemn joy," as was befitting to secular clergy, while the black dress (of the monk) suggested a lowering (*humiliatio*), that is, humility and mourning. Linen garments were appropriate for laity and secular clergy, wool for monks. At Saint Gall, the community was displeased when a noble patron of the monastery, the royal chaplain Salomo—later Bishop of Constance—entered the cloister in linen clothing. It was useless to remind them that the abbot of Saint Gall, the royal archchaplain Grimald, walked around the cloister in similar garb.

Anyone who counted himself among "persons of rank" needed to demonstrate it frequently by his clothing; a noble family may well have seen to it that its ecclesiastical members did not entirely renounce "fitting" appearance. In monasticism the color and fine quality of the cowl served to indicate an elite status, but one still remained within the confines of prescribed dress for different social groups. In the case of the secular clergy, we can assume that there was no fixed boundary separating clerical from lay dress. Rather says explicitly that bishops wore the clothes of the lay elite, and even "barbarian" head-bindings (*redimicula*), to the disgrace of the priestly state. From riding breeches were developed long leg coverings, which were decorated with a fibula and held up by a belt—both of course made of gold, to the anger of the poor. Rather adds that such a person preferred the finest fabrics. He may be stretching the truth a little when he continues, "One can see some who, in place of the cloak, wear a fur, in place of the bishop's miter, wear a Magyar fur cap, and in place of the crosier, carry a scepter."

Rather was a bitter polemicist, as was Adalbero of Laon; but similar things can be read in the works of entirely serious authors—in the letters of Gerbert of Aurillac, for example. This writer once informed the abbot of his home monastery that the archbishop of Reims would send Abbot Gerald of Aurillac a skillfully made (*operosum*) linen *sagum*—that is a Celtic-Germanic cloak fastened with a fibula; another communication concerned a garment with golden filaments (*vestem auro textam*) and a "Phrygian" stole "along with other things of a similar nature." Exaggerated, but by all appearance not entirely incorrect, was Rather's comment concerning his social equals: "We have so accommodated ourselves to worldly custom that it could almost be said that only the shaved chin, tonsure, and celibacy separate bishops from the laity."

Clean-shaven faces and tonsure were important symbols of clerical status, but even they were not entirely beyond question. Here the customs of the eastern and western churches separated, and at a synod in Limoges as late as 1031, reference was made to the Byzantine argument against shaving beards: it contradicted the dignity of man, who—in contrast to woman—was endowed with a beard "as an adornment"; Christ had worn a beard, etc. The other side insisted that Saint Peter was the "founder of this custom" (to be beardless) and that it was essential that clerics should be distinct from the laity even in physical appearance. For the Greeks, tonsure of the entire head was sufficient distinction, while (partial) tonsure (*corona*) and clean-shaven faces were required in the West at least for the holders of ecclesiastical offices. Ten years before the Limoges synod, Duke William of Aquitaine had "elected" a bishop of Langres and ordered clerics to bless the candidate's beard and then to shave it, after which he invested the new bishop in his office with the crosier.

One should not imagine the clerics of the tenth century under normal circumstances as entirely clean-shaven. The Benedictine Rule knew nothing of hair and beard clipping; in the tenth century it was normal to shave every two weeks, at most. The Consuetudines of the Cluniacs required a shave before high feast days. Likewise the secular clergy seem to have cut their hair and beards only on special occasions. It was said of the famous canonist, Bishop Burchard of Worms, that before his death he had his tonsure, *corona,* and beard shaved, put on clean clothes, and held a departing colloquium. When we recall that the Carthusians and Cistercians later reduced the number of days when monks were to shave to six or seven a year, we realize how annoying this duty was for the monks, a duty for which they certainly had no appropriate razor at their disposal.

When a monk had to sacrifice his beard, the "man's adornment," he thereby became neuter. To this neuter state corresponded the long cassock, which reached the ground, and the "womanly" work in the kitchen and garden. The western custom of wearing the beard short, added to the fact that stubble was allowed to grow for weeks or even months before being cut, further blurred the distinction between the clerical and the secular state. On solemn feast days one appeared in the cathedral shaven and dressed in the robes of the priesthood; at least on these days, and at least externally, the injunction "to become a new man" was fulfilled.

CULTIC REPRESENTATION

An ecclesiastical officeholder thus "represented" his office in a building which, as the "house of God," had an exalted representative function of its own. Architecture is uniquely suited to symbolizing ideas. The cathedrals of the Salian period were often likened to "castles of God"; the tower was always a symbol of lordship, only secondarily did it become a bell tower. In the tenth century the tower was a symbol of heavenly or earthly kingship, and only afterwards did the number of towers of nobles increase. The stone church steeple may also have served as a memorial to the bishop who had it built.

A church was always a place of complex and often secret meanings. The learned could be edified by them, the ignorant suspected that something extraordinary was being symbolized. No exegesis of this symbolism was carried out for the people—quite the reverse. Mysterious things occurred particularly at the consecration of a church, when the bishop "wrote" the alphabet on the floor from the left of the eastern end of the building to the right corner of the west end, that is, he traced the letters with his crosier. Whether the origins of this ceremony are Christian or pagan is debated; one could attribute its meaning for believers to the opinion that the alphabet contains all possible prayers and oaths. A learned commentator describes the cruciform manner of the writing as referring to Christ, the four corners as the presentation of the four cardinal points, to which the message of faith incarnated in the alphabet is spread. Such things the average layman could not know; nevertheless, as witness to the ceremony he was certainly convinced that it had a sublime and mysterious meaning.

God is the principle of order in this world, and He has fixed all things according to their measure, number, and weight. Measure and number have always dominated architecture, and what was true for the profane sphere applied all the more to the church as a sort of architectonic praise of God along with the liturgy. Thus the church of Cluny II (948–81), in whose architectural system the number seven and its multiples are often repeated, seemed to glorify the seven gifts of the Holy Spirit. One can assume that the monks were aware of this, were edified by it, and informed theologically educated visitors of it—if these latter had not themselves, through the numbers of altars, columns, windows, etc., already found the key.

Things appear to have changed at the beginning of the eleventh century, at least in part. In Bernward's church of Saint Michael in Hildesheim, in Cluny III, and elsewhere, extremely complex numerical relationships have been discovered whose esoteric nature is beyond question, unless they are purely the result of modern overinterpretation. Such relationships no longer had anything to do with external "representation"; rather, they were supposed to reflect in its highest form the divine wisdom in itself. Along with this system, however, went the simpler and earlier type; bishops such as Bernward of Hildesheim incorporated some popular biblical symbolism within church architecture.

It is unfortunate that we have little written information from the time on the intentions of the architects. An exception is an account, by the monk Arnold of Saint Emmeram in Regensburg, of the construction of that church's crypt in 976 by Abbot Ramwold after the civil war. That the abbot venerated the Holy Trinity and held fast to the four Gospels is represented in the uses of the numbers three and four; the columns which support the crypt are double columns because they signify the dual love of God and of neighbor. The five altars correspond to the five books of Moses as well as to the five senses which one needs to maintain prudence. This is probably an authentic interpretation, though contemporaries may easily have read other "edifying" meanings into the given numerical relationships. The educated who cultivated theology were thus granted a "review" of the house of God that went far beyond admiration of its construction and beauty.

Although the monastery shaped a world for itself, its church was, like that of the bishop, also built for the laity. When in 1001 Abbot William of Volpiano had completed the church of Saint-Bénigne in Dijon, one could look with wonder on its eight towers, three chapels, 120 glass windows and 371 columns; the interior was 100 meters long and 26 meters wide. A layman accustomed to wooden and half-timbered construction must have perceived a structure of this kind as something enormously costly to which no earthly person had a right but only God and the saints. Churches were adorned with artworks whose effects on contemporaries we can only faintly imagine. Whether King Robert the Pious truly wept tears of joy when he saw the newly decorated church of Fleury-sur-Loire after a fire, or whether it was simply an invention of Andreas of Fleury, the story must have been believable to his contemporaries. There were many ways of accomplishing decorative effects—large murals, fully sculptured images of the saints, picture stories in bronze relief, architectural sculpture, and so on. Not only the saints were depicted but also the devil and his followers, representing the disorder of the world. Building and decorating churches was a means of praising God and promoting the Christian religion. Moreover, it increased the honor of the bishop and abbot, and perhaps also the prestige of his family.

In Romanesque churches today we see only the hewn stone and, in exceptional cases, the original murals. We can scarcely imagine the role played by ecclesiastical textiles in the tenth century, especially on feast days but also on normal days. Such things were a luxury even in the homes of the rich, whose furnishings were hardly different from those of poorer people. The walls at Cluny, for example, were adorned with light tapestries made of wool or linen and hung by cords from eyelets, and later, during Lent, the sanctuary of the high altar was separated from the main church by a huge translucent cloth, the "hunger cloth." On Holy Saturday, images of the saints were erected before the main arch (*ante arcum principalem*) in wooden frames. Carpets decorated the church, particularly the choir stalls. Some curtains have survived in the form of trompe l'oeil painting, which can hardly give an impression of the former effect of the space.

The rooms in the monastery were decorated in a similar manner on feast days. That it was a disgrace for an abbey to be without carpets is learned from a letter of Gerbert of Aurillac. When an irregularly installed abbot at Fleury departed, he took with him everything of value that he could transport. The schoolman of the monastery asked the influential Gerbert to appeal to the royal couple for restitution. The monks requested not gold and silver but "that which is a disgrace to do without. We speak of wall tapestries, carpets, and the like." Here we see that even in the reform monastery of Fleury a somewhat worldly sense prevailed of what was *dedecus*. Saint Benedict, whose body was venerated here, had never demonstrated such a predilection for decorative textiles.

The ornamentation of the church needed sufficient light to be admired. If Romanesque churches do not impress us as extremely luminous, it is by comparison with later church buildings. At the time, glass had only just begun to replace the transparent cloth that had previously covered windows. In the tenth century the abbot of Teernsee wrote that his church used to have old pieces of cloth rather than glass windows, and now for the first time sunbeams could shine onto the floor of the church; everyone was delighted with this and all admired "the diversity of the strange craftsmanship." A count had donated painted glass windows. But what were the many-hued circles of sunshine on the floor beside the wonderful sight when the church was shown with a hundred lights! In 1003 there were twenty-two chandeliers in the monastery church of Prüm: one large, one "shaped like a cap," over the main altar "made of gold and decorated with precious stones"; another in front of this altar, with little bells which were probably rung by the air currents rising from the burning candles; seven silver chandeliers and thirteen smaller ones hanging from silvered chains, two of which were of gilded silver, and in their midst a crystal paten. There were also nine lamps, two of gold, and fourteen candlesticks—thirteen of silver, one "large, made of brass, with the figures of lions," which naturally had an edifying meaning.

On feast days, this combined play of lights, shining precious metal, and sparkling stones must have created an effect on its viewers far surpassing that of a modern Christmas tree on children of today. Hearts were to be filled with joy at the birth and the resurrection of the Lord and during the feasts of the saints. Acoustic means also served this end, namely the pealing of bells and sacred singing. That these last two contributed to the celebration of the Mass "with great joy of the heart and voice" was often attested. The opposite mood and deportment was suitable on certain nonliturgical occasions. The bishop of Chartres was threatened by a nobleman; he ordered that the bells, those bringers of joy, should remain silent as a sign of mourning, and that clerics should lower their voices during the celebration of the Mass "in the manner in which one asks for mercy."

The material resources required to accomplish such a truly unearthly impression were enormous. The easiest to procure was the wax for the candles. Dependents brought it to the cathedral or monastery as duty, often as the sole tax (*cerocensuales*). Precious metals and gemstones were mostly donated and not acquired out of the profits of the church in its economic activities. For eliciting gifts, the prestige of the individual church and the fame of its saints were just as important as connections with magnates and their pleasure in the donation of select objects. Helgaud of Fleury wrote that King Robert "took delight in relics, which he ornamented with gold and silver, in ecclesiastical vestments, precious crosses, chalices of fine gold, censers which spread choice odors, and silver cups for the washing of the priest's hands." Helgaud had a particular understanding of such an attitude, being the treasurer of his monastery and a man who did not have precious objects made only for liturgical purposes. He himself had a silver staff with gems and "a shining crystal on the end," which he used as director of the choir.

Writers have often given the impression that the "common people" brought their gold and silver to the monastery. But, with the exception of a few merchants in areas such as Northern Italy or Catalonia, few of the people could ever hope to possess such treasures; such things belonged to kings and princes. Ademar of Chabannes tells us that Henry II had donated to Cluny a portion of his treasure that totaled one hundred pounds of gold: a scepter, an imperial orb, a "golden" imperial garment, a crown, and a crucifix. Such extraordinary objects were not simply hoarded at Cluny but were carried in processions; others were melted down or arrived at the monastery in the form of bars, such as the jewelry of Saracens who had been slain in battle. "According to their custom" they had been loaded with gold and silver when they had fought. Abbot Odilo had a ciborium made above the altar of Saint Peter out of this votive offering. Coins were also melted down, such as the one hundred gold solidi that Theirry II, bishop of Orléans (died 1021) had made into a chalice "because he wanted a remembrance of his name"—a kind of *memoria* that only a member of a wealthy family could afford.

When we seek reasons for such liturgical luxury, thanksgiving for help in this life and in the next come first to mind. A king's son is ill; the mother donates to the cathedral a massive golden crucifix, the father a silver vessel weighing six pounds. Mentioned only in passing and as a matter of course is the fact that the son—Robert the Pious—recovered. Even more common were donations for the salvation of the soul, which could include all sorts of ecclesiastical ornamentation, including carpets and tapestries. Richly decorating the house of God increased its glory and also that of the donor, whose name was mentioned with praise. Another factor was fascination with shining, reflecting, sparkling objects, a fascination that for us today, in a period of a constant superabundance of visual stimulants, has become almost entirely alien. Angilbert called the church of Centula *fulgentissima,* and similar words recur constantly in church inventories. These inventories were not always limited to precious metals. Fleury had a screen with sheets made of Spanish copper, separated from each other by columns; "in addition, eighteen mirrorlike metal plates were fixed in the spaces on the panel." Many altars had front plates made of silver or gold, often ornamented with gems; for the gilding of the front of the main altar of the church of Saint Aignan in Orléans, fifteen pounds of gold were used.

Enjoyment of gleam and glitter was justified through theological explications. The tradition of decorating the church with gold, silver, and gems went back to the apostles, Ademar of Chabannes assures us, and he explains the symbolism: gold indicates spiritual wisdom, silver eloquence, gems are the various virtues. The "Romano-Germanic" pontifical includes a *benedictio crucis metallizatae,* in which the allegorical explanations for brilliance proliferate: gold is the shining of the *splendor* of the second divine person; it reflects the glory of the passion on the cross where the work of salvation shone forth; in the *splendor* of the crystal we glimpse the purification of our lives. Here and in similar places the wood of the cross became the triumphant symbol and sign of the reign of the God-king Christ.

Filling churches with precious objects had another function, and this is often forgotten: it created reserves for times of increased financial need. Although this function cannot be connected directly to the foundation of ecclesiastical luxury, one did have the choice of making donations of precious metal visible to all as art objects or of keeping them in one's own coffers, and the first option was usually preferred. Valuable objects served the needs of representation until they could be used for a more important purpose.

Widukind of Corvey pursued in his writings a rhetorical *deliberatio* of Henry I before the war with the Magyars, which concerned the question whether the treasures of the churches should be "plundered" for tribute to the Magyars, or whether war should be waged against the enemy. Elsewhere, the melting down and selling of church ornaments was resorted to for the satisfaction of everyday needs: we hear, for example, that Robert the Pious had had a golden altar front made for the church of Saint-Aignan in Orléans, but his widow had the gold taken back and used seven pounds of it for the church roof and divided the remainder "among all those to whom she owed it." Church treasures were frequently seized during famines, when the rural population streamed into the episcopal cities looking for help from the "saints," that is, from their relics. In theory, ecclesiastical treasures were to be used, aside from the care of the poor, only for the redemption of prisoners and the enlargement of cemeteries. Nevertheless, bishops returned hoarded precious metals into circulation for purely economic reasons. Books, furs, goldsmiths' products began to change hands in Italy from the late tenth century on as a sort of substitute money, especially for the purchase of land, and ecclesiastical hoards sometimes served the same purpose. Atto of Vercelli wrote that it was meaningless to conserve the church's treasure while outside authorities emptied granaries and wine cellars and thus indemnified themselves for unpaid sums at the expense of the clergy and their servants.

Thus ecclesiastical *apparatus* frequently changed its form, although the change was often more gradual than that of lay magnates. Art objects were not made for generations far in the future but mainly for contemporaries, and were subject to fashions of the time. There was also an ascetic tradition which opposed ecclesiastical pomp; but it did not have the power to change the situation, even when formulated by an Odo of Cluny. Only in the twelfth century, particularly with Bernard of Clairvaux, would the idea of the poverty and simplicity of true Christianity, in contrast to the cult and its trappings, become a reality.

The renunciation of ecclesiastical splendor, which came later, affected only a portion of the churches; moreover, decoration was just one of various means of representing the lordship of the king of heaven: there remained the words of the liturgy, directed by the strictly regulated gestures of the celebrant and his assistants. These words expressed submission to God and supplication for protection and help; they also reflected internal ecclesiastical structures. The Cistercians replaced the former splendor with the pathos of simplicity; they accepted and even heightened the severity of Saint Benedict's rule as well as the rank order in the monastery.

II·FAMILIA

4 FAMILY AND CLAN

MEDIEVALISTS HAVE PAID MUCH LESS AT-
tention to the family than they have to many
other social groups and institutions. However,
one should not point out this lacuna, noted
with regret by Marc Bloch, without admitting
that the situation has improved since the beginning of the 1970s. In France and Italy the history of the family has been undertaken in its
entirety; in Germany, one aspect of it has been
studied in the context of research on the aristocracy, a subject which has interested scholars
since shortly after the end of the Second World
War. The reason that the study of other social
structures continues to dominate medieval his-

tory is to be found in the structure of modern society. While the family still plays an important role, reflection on the family no longer predominates as it did when other social structures, particularly the state, were less developed. For this reason scholars have spoken of the "family mentality" of the early Middle Ages: during this period the family was not simply the center of human behavior but also served as a model for understanding other social units such as the monastic order.

As Claude Lévi-Strauss has observed, "primitive"—actually extremely complex—societies are based on personal relationships among individuals. Even when the population is widely diffused, social ties in such societies consist of "direct relationships," generally modeled on kinship. In such societies it is not biological kinship that plays the greatest role in personal relationships but rather the *concept* of kinship.

Social groups composed on the model of kinship are hence separate from the kindred, and the kindred itself is different from the community living together in a single household. The household may be an extended family under the authority of a patriarch, or it might be a nuclear family composed of a married couple, their children, and possibly one or another of their kin. The household can be even more complex since others besides kin may live together with kin under one roof, but this latter case will be discussed later.

Extended Family versus Nuclear Family

The question of nuclear versus extended family households has been a principal cause of division among medievalists. The first scholars to study the question in the 1930s tended to conclude that the patriarchal extended family household was characteristic of the feudal period and that the nuclear family household belonged to the later, more urbanized period. Ethnographers also attempted to prove that at some time in the past the extended family household had existed in Europe. Marc Bloch believed that in eleventh-century Bavaria "as many as fifty persons" lived together under one roof. Only in the thirteenth century, he believed, did the number of persons constituting a family diminish—the *vastes parentèles* were gradually replaced by something like the modern nuclear family. Bloch's only evidence for such extended Bavarian households is a passage from the *Niederaltaich Annals* which recorded the following events: In Reichenhall, where the monastery had property, two brothers were carrying on a feud with their uncle. With a group of helpers that they had assembled, the brothers killed the uncle and burned "his six sons with their small children and the remaining crowd, differing in sex and age, not less than fifty persons, all together in a single house."

Had these fifty-odd persons been living together in the house, or had they taken refuge there in the face of danger? The words *omnes simul in una domo* seem to suggest that this was an exceptional situation. It is unlikely that there was a single house in the *vicus* of Reichenhall large enough for fifty persons to assemble for reasons other than temporary shelter. Even if one were to suggest that the house was some sort of dormitory for the monastery workers in this area— the site of the best-known Bavarian salt works—one could hardly generalize from this one case. Generalization is particularly unwarranted, for this dubious evidence is all that we have, and one must search far and wide to find other traces of extended family households in the same period. In a region such as Picardy, for example, where evidence appears in greater quantity, the extended family was already in decline by the tenth century. A communal life shared by several generations might make sense when for some reason the division of land through inheritance had to be avoided. As the polyptychs of the period indicate, ecclesiastical estate management normally reckoned one nuclear family household on an individual *mansus,* and merely tolerated circumstances in which two or even three such families worked a single *mansus.* The latter arrangement usually resulted from the division of quasi-inheritable peasant *mansus.* From the perspective of the lord, it was more advantageous to have men in their productive years as economic partners than to demand the contributions of a larger number of people from a patriarch—if indeed such persons existed at a time when life expectation was hardly more than thirty.

Although it can be theorized that, from the eleventh century on, a "new mentality" appeared in Picardy, characterized on the one hand by a quest for financial gain and on the other by what Robert Fossier has termed "a decline of the extended family," this situation can hardly be generalized. The opposite tendency was to be found in Catalonia, where after 1030 it was no longer unusual for four or five brothers and their wives to form one household *à pot et à feu* instead of dividing their inheritance. There and elsewhere, times had become uncertain, so that people crowded together. In Latium, the foundation of fortified villages, the so-called *incastellamento,* brought with it the necessity of grouping together familial units larger than the nuclear family within the protection of the village walls. These units appear to have formed genuine communities sharing both living areas and household responsibilities. A chieftain would assume responsibility for several nuclear families which were related to each other. In other instances a group of brothers would act in unison as the contractual partners of the lord. These were transitional arrangements, which arose from the exigencies of living and working in the new settlements. Such extended family households may have been extremes of household organization rather than the norm, as earlier scholars believed. As far as one can tell without systematic studies of the sort conducted in Latium, similar circumstances seem to have prevailed in other areas of Italy. With the relative abundance of sources, it will surely be possible to reach firmer conclusions about the structure of peasant households in Italy; elsewhere the documentation is too thin for this period. Only for later periods does the quantity and quality of source material improve until, thanks to the Inquisition, it reaches the detail and abundance that we have, for example, concerning one modest Pyrenean village. In his well-known study of Montaillou, E. Le Roy Ladurie concludes, "A single family expands, then becomes a nuclear family again, then expands again, and so forth." It would appear that this summation has general validity and better characterizes the history of the peasant family than earlier, static views.

Thus, the norm was probably a "two-generation family," which included the married couple and their children, possibly enlarged at times with unmarried brothers and sisters, the husband's mother, and grandchildren. All were included as individual persons under the authority of the householder. When the children were grown, the lord could either add them to the ranks of the house servants or give them land on which to found new families—a cellular division of the small family that could continue unhindered as long as there was sufficient land, which was usually the case during this period. That some areas, in spite of this abundance, were overpopulated although they contained unworked farmland is a phenomenon not yet fully understood, but it need not concern us here.

When the lord did not have absolute power to dispose of the land, there arose the problem of who should inherit the pieces of land on which the peasant family felt at home. Particularly in Italy, where, after the Magyar incursions, the population was too small for rebuilding, freed serfs obtained leases which were in theory for limited periods but which in practice often became inheritable. Here and elsewhere, after the father's death, one could avoid dividing the estate by establishing on it a sort of "corporation" composed of nuclear families, provided that it could actually furnish all of them with the means of subsistence. Normally it was more realistic to allot the succession to one son, with the result that the others were forced to move on. The problem of lineage formation in this period is best known in the nobility, but it also arose in the peasantry. The problem was most pressing where the social standing of a family was intimately connected with the possession of a piece of private property. To divide it would have caused the family to sink to a lower status, since under such circumstances the obligations incumbent upon property owners could often no longer be met. The free man who had no means to participate in the military levy and did not appear at the comital *placitum,* or the noble who could not perform his obligations to the king, eliminated himself from his social position. Such a man sank into the peasantry and sooner or later had to put himself under the protection of a lord. In France, where public service played little or no role, vassalic obligations during the protracted period of latent civil war bore down on the lesser nobility in the same way. The *coseigneurie,* inheritance in indivision, could delay for a generation the inevitable: paying off some of the sons with apanages and handing over the allod and fief to the eldest.

COGNATIO

A firm inheritance pattern, which has become increasingly plain since the tenth century, gave a new dimension to the nuclear family. The "lineage" or the "line" continued for generations and had a more or less fixed geographical center—usually a castle—the name of which provided the surname of the family. Had something entirely novel thereby begun, as some now believe? Had the "consciousness of the male line" pushed aside and replaced the earlier, imprecise concept of kindred in the wider and widest sense, which had included or even emphasized the maternal side? The broader grouping of the clan or *Sippe* seemed to fit into the picture of the Carolingian monarchy, whereas "agnatic" connections of lineage and line seemed to belong to the post-Carolingian feudal period.

In reality things are more complex. In post-Carolingian times, *libri memoriales* were written, books intended for the liturgical commemoration of living and dead in monasteries and cathedrals in Germany, France, and Italy. They indicate that the inner unity of kindred could extend far beyond the group we would today consider kin. First and foremost, these groups included "friends," which must be understood not only as political allies but as an expansion of kindred beyond the clan; the principles by which one recognized this wider circle, however, cannot be identified. As the *libri memoriales* and other sources show, around the year 1000 a transformation of family structure and of the concept of family becomes visible, and with it a transition from "cognatic" to "agnatic" groupings. This change did not take place suddenly; it had been long in preparation—first among the aristocracy created under the Carolingians, then among lesser powers such as the chatelains of the Mâconnais and in the Lombard lowlands.

In recent decades a distinction has been made between the increasing actual significance of the agnatically oriented family or lineage and the agnatic conceptual model. The latter was to be found alongside the cognatic model even in the early Middle Ages, though often overshadowed by it; but the agnatic model never entirely prevailed over the cognatic one. Agnatic thought dominated very early where there was something to bequeath in the male line which was essential in establishing the authority of the family. This was especially true of royal dynasties, and likewise of "family monasteries" since the seventh and eighth centuries—for example, in Lorraine and Bavaria. In the declining period of the Carolingian state, the inheritability of offices and fiefs became increasingly important, and agnatic inheritance also endowed the French *seigneurie banale* with a "firm," that is, fortified, center.

Also tenacious was the concept of a wider, more indeterminate personal group, if we can call it a group, since it never had a legal form but existed rather as a sense of solidarity. This group was conceived of differently in different situations: the personal circle in the entries in memorial books differed from that in literary enumerations of kin. Unfortunately we know too little of its practical application, the summoning of family and "friends" in the case of feud or other threatening situations. There were family alliances with the obligation of advice and assistance, *consilium et auxilium*. More important than the alliance, the consciousness of blood relationship engendered the obligation of assistance. This consciousness was founded on the conviction, objectively false, that blood kin were "of one flesh and blood" and hence obligated to strive for the same goals.

The Protean character of this phenomenon, which has been labeled with the German technical term *Sippe* (clan), has defied repeated attempts by legal historians to banish a concept so difficult to define. It belongs less to the realm of law than to the "kinship mores" of the period, if such a term is admissible, and to the resulting mutual obligations. These latter were also mutual in the case of the memorial books, since the living had to pray for the dead and the dead had to intervene before God on behalf of the living. "Friends" could in these instances also be included in the kin, and thus enlarge its circle.

The mutual bonds created moral as well as quasi-legal obligations; in the case of blood revenge, which still existed in the tenth century, these obligations came into conflict both with the current law and with Church teaching. Yet they constituted an attitude which had custom and quasi-religious sentiments on its side. An enumeration of sins in an official source (*Pontificale Romano-Germanicum*) speaks of sinning "in disdain of kinsmen" (*in despectione propinquorum*). Even for Thomas Aquinas, *pietas* was a reason for the support of kin and friends: promoting their welfare would therefore be a virtuous action. One could designate contempt of the (wider) kindred and contempt of the collective social or world order in the same breath and thus make them almost equivalent. While alliances of friendship required an oath in order to stamp their violation as a sin, concord and assistance among kin were part of the "natural order." Aside from the genealogical, moral-legal, and quasi-religious aspects of these bonds, their practical importance in a period of absent or diminished public power is clear.

The dramatic high point of the obligation of aid was the feud; in the daily routine of agrarian existence, one needed cooperation and help when one's own capacities were insufficient—both in this world and in the life to come. Refusal of help was an injury to the entire group; the rise of a member to a place of higher honor had a positive effect on all.

It was in the natural interest of every clan to expand its circle of potential helpers. This was an expensive activity: the sense of belonging together had to be imprinted in the hearts of the members through keeping each other's company, which meant frequent mutual invitations, and hunting or traveling together. In his *Polypticum*, Atto of Vercelli describes how feasts or drinking bouts would provide the occasion for promises of gifts, marriage arrangements, acceptance of godparenthood, and the sealing of sworn alliances.

Feudalism introduced other social bonds, which could enlarge or decrease those of the clan. The obligation of "advice and assistance" predominates in vassality, and it might be more effective to call upon one's vassals or feudal lord than one's kin and friends. In most cases, both groups probably converged. The old "cognatic" sense was not altogether dead. It was revealed, for example, in boasting about one's own clan or about some great hero in one's mother's clan who could not be ignored. The mother's side was often given preference if a famous ancestor was to be found in this part of one's genealogical tree. People were less likely to speak of their paternal kindred as a whole than of one or another ancestor who might elicit respect. When Widukind of Corvey described the ancestry of Queen Mathilda, he first gave the name of her father, then spoke of the deeds of one of the father's brothers, and then jumped back to the family's origins: "And these were from the race of the great Duke Widukind," whose heroic deeds he praised. When Anselm of Besate (on the Ticino) was competing to become chaplain to Henry III, he enumerated his "ecclesiastical ancestors"—first the bishops in his paternal kindred and then those on his mother's side.

Such proofs of outstanding ancestry served as an abridgment of the whole *cognatio;* there were also more complete genealogies such as the one later enumerated by Anselm. At its origin was his grandfather's grandfather, whose name was the only thing he knew about him; he was included because one of his sons was an archbishop, a grandson a bishop. Anselm then speaks of six brothers and two nephews of his great-grandfather; he had something to tell about only one of them, namely, that his ecclesiastical career had been ended by an early death in Jerusalem. We hear of the outstanding marriage of Anselm's great-grandfather: his wife was the daughter of a sister of that Adalbert-Atto who had built the castle of Canossa and had founded the noble family that bore its name. We are then informed of the history of this family as though it were that of close relatives of the author. We learn less about his grandfather and his three brothers, or about his father and his father's five brothers, one of whom was a bishop. Once again, it is his father's marriage that seemed noteworthy to Anselm because his maternal grandfather had one brother who was a bishop and another who was an archbishop.

Thus the kindred itself was less important than the people with whom one wanted to be related. This could change from case to case, and we can imagine how Anselm of Besate could have written a different genealogy, of the famous warriors rather than the famous ecclesiastics who had been among, or close to, his kindred. Certainly he had one or two lay ancestors who had done deeds of martial valor;

but the future chaplain did not want to speak of such things in this particular context.

The accent is quite different in the report of the monk Ademar of Chabannes: his father was the great-nephew of a bishop and the brother of a prior of Saint Martial (Limoges); there was nothing else to tell. Ademar's mother had three brothers, two of whom were valiant commanders (*strenuissimi duces*), of robust physique and martial disposition. The third, who had also been a prior, was a faithful and wise adviser to an abbot. With one of his brother she "very forcefully" protected the borders, just as their father had "very forcefully" protected a castle against King Robert. Here the description of the kindred is extended to two "very gallant princes" (*principes*) in whose service Ademar's uncle had been. Ademar moves elegantly from the kindred to its highly placed "friends." These were among the family's protectors and were spoken of with praise, as was the family. Here as elsewhere, women's role was merely to establish a genealogical tie; at least Ademar tells us the name of his mother, while in Anselm of Besate's account all the women remain anonymous.

Even during the period when agnatic succession was practiced, the fame of noble origins could not dismiss the kindred acquired by marriage. The agnatic principle was also limited by practical considerations. An example is presented by the clan of the counts of Walbeck to which Thietmar of Merseburg belonged. They had two castles and a family monastery as common possessions. There was a tendency to divide into two lines, but in troubled times a division of property would have weakened their collective position.

Royal families too often moved beyond the agnatic structure in their thinking, in spite of the tendency to transmit offices to the eldest sons. Marriage was certainly an essential element of dynastic politics, though it did not always fulfill this end. When Queen Emma was captured in Laon after the death of her husband, she wrote the empress Theophanu: "I too had kindred (*genus*), office (*dignitas*), and the title of queen. Now I am virtually without kindred and without office and am burdened with every humiliation." Earlier she had complained that the accusations against the bishop (Adalbero of Laon) exposed her and her entire *genus* to insult. Her Burgundian kin were far away; her mother, the empress Adelheid, had had to step back behind Theophanu. As a widowed queen, Emma could have directed the regency of her son or retreated under his protection. Since in this case the son opposed his mother, it should have fallen to the kindred to protect the prestige and the material rights of which Emma was deprived. Without kin and without friends, she had become, as she herself wrote, a serving woman (*ancilla*)—she was subjected to foreign protective custody.

What was here called *genus* appears elsewhere as *generatio* and is equivalent to *cognatio*. Kinsmen and vassals had the obligation to avenge an insult or an injustice done to one of them. In such a case we can see the clan in action and can learn something about its composition. Whether it is a matter of the old obligation of blood revenge, which we will now discuss, or of a compromise (*compositio*), is of secondary interest here. We learn the mechanism of revenge, projected back into the seventh century, in a story about a bishop Landibert of Liège. Two brothers had harmed the servants (*famuli*) of the bishop, and his dependents (*clientes*) and kinsmen (*cognati*) resolved to use violence. They fell on the brothers and killed them; the "next of kin" (*proximus affinis*) became "heir" to the obligation of revenge and therefore had to kill the bishop.

The author, of this account, Stephen, amplified his source expertly. He was himself bishop of Liège and probably had to deal with revenge in matters concerning his landholdings just as did his fellow bishop Burchard of Worms, who lost thirty-five servants in one year as a result of such affairs. Burchard ordered that compromise proceedings were to be initiated instead of revenge. The perpetrators were to contract peace with the kin (*proximis*) of the dead and to pay mulct (*wergeld*), a portion of which was to go to the "friends" of the dead. Here we see that such "friendship" included a specific circle of persons who enjoyed rights to indemnities similar to those of close kin.

Matrimonial Politics

We return now to the upper levels of society. Considerations of prestige and material interests went hand in hand with the politics of marriage. There could be no permanent security in a social position once reached; rather, every marriage carried with it an opportunity or a threat. Every marriage was a marriage of a woman into the family of her husband and not the reverse; thus there was no direct reinforcement of military potential. The advantage for the clan lay in the chance to obtain heirs, the dowry of the bride, and the high prestige of her family. Conversely, a poor marriage would bring with it a decrease in both the material and nonmaterial spheres. The ideal marriage pair would be described thus: The man is full of (military) virtue, of good family and bodily proportions, and possesses prudence; the woman is likewise well formed, from a good house (= family), and possesses wealth and good manners.

It was always the business of the *consanguinei et amici* to select a bride. The feudal lord, of course, also had an interest in overseeing and taxing the marriages of his vassals. His own prestige was bound up with that of his vassals, and one of them could easily be led into the sphere of influence of another lord through his wife's kinsmen. The wife did not always become integrated into her husband's family; if she was of higher birth or wealthier than he, she may have looked down on him: "Her noble ancestry and her riches made her proud . . . nothing is more unbearable than a rich wife." The woman so described in the words of Juvenal by the chronicler Alpert of Saint Symphorian in Metz was said to have been responsible for the renewal of a feud between two comital families, connected through a marriage.

The matrimonial politics of the nobility was also that of royalty. Thietmar of Merseburg tells that King Henry I had competed for Hatheburg, the heiress daughter of a count "because of her beauty and the usefulness of her inheritance and riches"; later he felt less love for his wife than for Mathilda, because of her "beauty and property," for which reason he separated from Hatheburg. Beginning with such simple considerations, the motivations for marriage extended from the acquisition of prestige to a complicated balance of power politics between royal houses. That Gerberga, a sister of Otto the Great, had married a West Frankish Carolingian brought the Saxon house, which went back to Widukind through Queen Mathilda, into kinship with Charlemagne. That another sister of Otto had Duke Hugh of France as her husband provided the necessary balance of power; both bore fruit when the one sister became the regent for King Lothair, the other the administrator of the Capetian house, and Otto's brother Brun, thanks to these kin connections, for nine years became "almost as much regent of France as he was duke . . . of Lorraine."

Since the goal of matrimonial politics was to incorporate higher-ranking spouses into the kindred, it was necessary to aim at the pinnacle of the "family of kings" in the Byzantine ruling house. Otto II's desire to marry a princess from the Macedonian dynasty must be seen in light of the contest over the empire, the settlement in southern Italy, and the division of spheres of power between East and West.

Yet another ruler, who was free of such interests, sought a Macedonian princess for his son: it was Hugh Capet, in the years after his coronation. The reason for Hugh's wish lay in the ecclesiastical marriage prohibitions which prevented the young King Robert from finding an equal (*parem*) wife. That the newly minted king of France stood behind his Carolingian predecessors in rank and that a new marriage alliance with the Ottonians would have broken canon law explains the desire to repeat an action in which the Ottonians had succeeded—or at least seemed to have done so.

The descent of Theophanu is somewhat obscure; it could not be used to strengthen the "sanctity" of the dynasty as other princesses had done: Queen Mathilda, the *sancta mater;* Aeda, Oda, and Edgitha, the descendants of Saint Oswald. Theophanu's conflict with Adelheid is well known, and she appears to have been one of those women whose integration into the family of her spouse did not succeed. Outside of official circles she used to be called "the Greek empress" or simply "the Greek." Theophanu remained an outsider in Saxony and also in Italy, where she sought to act as *imperator.* A chronicler of the time tells us the following anecdote, which he heard from Bishop Dietrich of Metz, who had waited with Theophanu in Rossano after the lost battle of Cotrone in 982. At the rumor of defeat, the empress, in "insolent and truly feminine form," had exalted her countrymen, the Greeks, to the skies and had belittled her husband, whose military valor had been so highly praised and who had allowed himself to be so easily defeated.

By means of matrimonial politics it was possible for a social climber to insert himself and his successors into the upper ranks of society. Rodulfus Glaber tells how Otto-William, the son of the rebel Adalbert (and grandson of Berengar II), a foreigner, *licet advena* came to high authority in Burgundy. His mother's second marriage was with Duke Henry of Burgundy; he himself married the count of Mâcon's widow, the sister of a bishop of Langres who supported him. One of his sons became count of Mâcon, the other a count in Burgundy; his eldest daughter married Count Landerich of Nevers, who came to Otto-William's assistance during his rebellion against King Robert II. Another daughter was the wife of Duke William V of Aquitaine, and a third married the count of Provence. Otto-William's son, the count "of Burgundy," was the son-in-law of the duke of Normandy, Richard II. No wonder the well-protected Otto-William became a military and political figure to be reckoned with, who threatened the Burgundian kingdom and against whom even Emperor Henry II was essentially powerless.

Certainly this was an exceptional case: in Otto-William, personal virtues united with illustrious descent from an enemy of the Saxon house which was about to annex the powerless Burgundian kingdom. Moreover, without the Burgundian possessions of his mother, Otto-William would have lacked the springboard he needed in order to begin his rise. A kinship coalition such as his could only be of limited duration; yet it permitted Otto-William's successors to establish themselves in Burgundy and even more: a grandson founded the lineage of the kings of Castille, and one of Otto-William's granddaughters became the wife of Emperor Henry III.

Family connections secured existence mainly where public power had become questionable—for example, in the Mâconnais in post-Carolingian times. Here, in the lists of witnesses to charters, we find larger groups than in earlier periods. Since no one dared to divide inheritance, it served as the unifying bond; the opposite was the case in Ottonian Saxony. There, where women not only inherited but did so even before the father's kin, every death could lead to disputes over succession; conflicts between *cognati* were the rule, unity the exception. In Saxony, as elsewhere, the establishment of kin groups was often a final attempt to end conflicts among interested parties.

The uniting of two clans through marriage could effect naming patterns of descendants, which became an additional means of integration. In the tenth century, it should be noted, the tradition of name variation (Chlodovicus, Chlotharius, etc.) had given way to the tradition of repeating an entire name that had been used by an ancestor. The ancestor was not necessarily taken from the agnatic side. This usage was common in royal or high aristocratic families (Otto I, Otto II, Otto III); the eldest son, who was to receive inheritance, received the name of his father or grandfather. Elsewhere, names from the noble family of the mother were adopted, sometimes in overwhelming proportion. This repetition of a very few first names designated a family to outsiders. Along with these names, other repeatedly used names appear to have been taken from the circle of people with whom one felt connected by kinship or friendship. Through such names we can also recognize the overlapping of kinship groups, though it is not possible to determine the boundaries of such groups on the basis of the names. One must also remember the desire to be related to a famous family, even by the use of foreign names for one's own family; the best-known examples are the Merovingian names among the Carolingians. This practice could also mean the "appropriation" of a kindred, or the revalorization of existing but possibly very tenuous kin ties.

Unfortunately we know almost nothing about women's role in name giving. When the maternal side was emphasized, we may be seeing the wife's influence at work. Such was probably the case of Queen Gerberga, sister of Otto the Great and wife of Louis "d'Outremer" in France; her elder son bore a Carolingian name, Lothair—it could hardly have been otherwise. After the birth of twins, the names selected for them were Charles (he was later Charles of Lower Lorraine) and Henry (he died shortly thereafter). A sister was called Mathilda; thus two of Gerberga's children bore the names of her parents—we know the important role that naming after grandfathers played in early thought.

The concentration on inherited property and inheritable offices and fiefs resulted, as we have already indicated, in the agnatic side's becoming constantly stronger, and led to a certain monotony in naming—possibly one of the reasons for the tradition of giving double names which became established later. In Catalonia lords were already being identified in the last decade of the tenth century by their castle and thus distinguished from each other in a novel manner. The "noble family" in the modern sense began to take the place of the old clan with its complex structure and numerous purposes, although it certainly could not serve all those purposes.

PROHIBITED DEGREES

Until now we have not spoken of the Church's teaching concerning kindred. Marriage among kin was forbidden; anyone who took a woman *de propria cognatione* as wife was to fall under anathema. Of course, only when one knew about the kinship could one be liable to prosecution. The various definitions of the degrees of prohibited kinship are only expressions of the basic principle, interesting as an indication of how far ecclesiastics had drawn the boundaries of possible knowledge of kinship. At the synod of Koblenz in 922 it was extended to the fifth degree of kinship; at the synod of Bourges in 1031 it was to reach to the "sixth or seventh," a formulation whose uncertainty speaks for itself. Burchard of Worms wrote that Isidore (Pseudo-Isidore) had designated the seventh degree because he wanted to extend kinship as far as man was capable of remembering.

That is correct, no doubt, although the intensifying of the prohibition of incest to the seventh degree according to the canonical method of reckoning had already been propagandized by synods in the first half of the ninth century. Only in 1215 was there a return from the seventh to the fourth, in a period in which large kin groups had become rare; the norm was lineages and lines. To appreciate the difficulties which resulted from the ecclesiastical prohibition, we must remember that not only biological kinship but godparenthood and "spiritual kinship" were also impediments to marriage. For example, the family of a godfather and that of the godson were seen as kin, and no marriage could be contracted between them.

Despite such difficulties, the high aristocracy, which stood so much in the spotlight, did try to obey canonical prohibitions, at least as long as no specific reasons made this goodwill impossible. Where such reasons existed, canons were forgotten, and hardly anyone thought this sinful. At a synod in Dortmund in 1005, Henry II complained about the popular view that marriages within the third (canonical) degree were allowed. The famous Hammerstein marriage quarrel concerned a question of marriage within the fourth degree. Bishop Gerald of Cambrai wanted to forbid a marriage between two families because of prohibited kinship, but he "unwillingly" gave up on the advice of his fellow bishops. They referred to the instructions of Gregory the Great for the missionaries in England: that in the interest of the extension of the faith, marriages within the fourth or fifth degree of kinship should be tolerated. The pious King Robert II was married to his cousin Bertha by the archbishop of Bourges; in spite of a papal protest, the marriage continued. They were later separated, not, as it seems, on canonical grounds, and the king remarried.

Just as there was a matrimonial politics, so too there was a sort of "divorce politics," which used canonical prohibitions as its basis, or rather as its alibi. One could support one's policy by referring to these prohibitions in order to repulse opponents. Henry II weakened Duke Hermann II of Swabia by first disputing the marriage of Hermann's daughter with Conrad of Carinthia as uncanonical and then by ruining Hermann's cousin Count Otto of Hammerstein with the same argument.

What had prompted ecclesiastical assemblies of the ninth century to repeat again and again pronouncements whose effects were so grave? It was hardly a general ecclesiastical lust for power; on the other hand, marriage regulations at that time were part of secular law, and the clergy tried to control this domain by canonical means. In ecclesiastical circles, the possibility of inherited biological problems resulting from incest was known, but this is at best only a partial explanation. Quotations from the Bible on which one might base the interdiction could provide no real foundation. What we are seeing, in a broad context, is an extension of the taboo of endogamy well known in folk tradition as well as in classical law. This taboo, whether based in religion or not, fulfilled an important social function. Claude Lévi-Strauss has explained, "exogamy provides the only means for maintaining the group as a group, of avoiding the indefinite fission and segmentation which the practice of consanguineous marriages would bring about. . . . Consanguineous marriages . . . would not take long to 'fragment' the social group into a multitude of families, forming so many closed systems or sealed monads."

It may well have been feared that the ever-present tendency of the empire to become dismembered into separate provinces could go further, to the atomization of the ruling elites, so that the ecclesiastical members of these elites did what they could to check such a process. These are things that cannot be stated with certainty. Ecclesiastical marriage prohibitions in the tenth century did, however, contribute to the introduction of new blood into the upper levels of society. They worked against both provincialization and the exclusion of social mobility from below.

5 &PATRIARCHAL LORDSHIP

FOR ROMAN JURISTS THE WORD *FAMILIA* meant on the one hand the total assets of a person—we must remember that slaves too were considered material property—and on the other hand, in the words of the Roman jurist Ulpian, "a number of persons who by nature or by law are subordinate to one individual." He, the paterfamilias, exercised in his house the right of lordship (*in domo dominium*) over wife and children, over nephews and nieces, over all who lived in his house or who had to live there because they had no other means of existence. The *famuli,* the servants who were likewise subordinated to the absolute authority of the head, also belonged to the *familia*. If the paterfamilias died, his authority went with the inheritance to his sons or to a plurality of heirs who now formed their own *familiae*.

Not only in antiquity but also in the Middle Ages, what Ulpian had laid out clearly and simply was taken to be just as natural and immutable as the course of the sun or the changes of seasons. Nevertheless, the right of the father had been weakened by the fact that he no longer had the power of life and death; he was expected to regard his servant as his brother and to guide his family in a Christian life. Since the distant past, even the father's "subjects" had enjoyed certain free spaces to make their existence bearable. Living together on a farm or a manor decreased the social distance; master and servants recognized the importance of willing cooperation, and the "house" became their common business. Scholars agree that even in the *Odyssey* "the heartfelt participation of the unfree members of the household" was "perceived as having high emotional value." The same was of course true for sons and daughters of the householder and the other members of the family in the strict sense, above all for the mistress of the house. As we shall see she had a limited sphere of command in the house.

FAMILIA *and Family*

In its narrowest sense, which corresponded to *famulus,* the word *familia* was applied to domestic slaves and animals. A wider sense included the totality of the inhabitants, that is, the head of the house, the members of his family, and his servants. In ancient Rome the term was adopted beyond the domestic sphere to designate a collegium of slaves or of free men, such as gladiators, coin makers, and the like. Finally, also in Ulpian, we find an extension to the wider kindred, which did not depend on one paterfamilias but consisted of agnates and cognates and was thus a part of the *gens* or even the *gens* in its entirety. Lacking was the modern usage of the word, that is, the narrow circle of kin exclusive of servants, who rarely form an integral part of the household today.

It has been thought that this modern sense of family was first found in the eleventh and twelfth centuries, "because," as Karl Schmid has pointed out, "in the early Middle Ages *familia* meant primarily the servants." For these centuries our sources concern almost exclusively ecclesiastical domains, in which the term "family" is applied to their occupants and personnel, the *familia* of a monastery, etc. This was also the most important sense in those farming "families" which worked the land in part with their own personnel; alongside the manorial *familia* were a number of peasant *familiae*. A family without servants was the normal situation in areas of small farms, in which the father's authority was of the same sort as found in higher spheres: the unfree farmer ruled in his hut and on his fields—even when they actually belonged to his lord. As a paterfamilias he commanded his wife and children, and perhaps even his unmarried kin. In relatively unusual cases there were also landless or "homeless" serfs (*servi non casati*), that is, people without house or farm. When, for example, the monastery of Werden on the Ruhr received as a donation *tres familias cum rure suo*, and two others that occupied a single unit of land, we can assume that these were "modern" families without servants. True, in descriptions of properties and incomes of ecclesiastical domains, the word *familia* was relatively seldom used, and usually in the extended sense in which the patron saint of the spiritual community was made the paterfamilias.

As we have seen, sources mentioning an ecclesiastical domain speak not only of one *familia* but sometimes of several *familiae*, which have their center of authority in one and the same place. The plural *familiae*, in a concrete sense of the word, seems to have been present before the spiritual concept of the *familia* under the patronage of its saint. Thus, landed serfs (*servi casati*) had been accepted as masters of their houses, their limited authority had been recognized, and they were regarded as economic partners. The obligation to pay taxes lay on all members of the farm household, although the "head of the household" was responsible for the payment. In property records either his name alone appeared or else it was listed first ("A. *cum uxore* B. *et filiis* C., D.").

Only rarely does one find a determination of the work to be performed by the husband, by his wife, and by the couple together. The higher valuation of the man in this context did not have a "patriarchal" but rather an economic basis: his capacity for work was greater than that of a married woman, who was also responsible for raising children and thus owed less tax than a man or an unmarried woman.

Sources do not indicate whether or to what extent sons may have had the right to participate in decisions. The norm was that they should have their own house when they were grown as a basis for a new family. Clearly the son was dependent on the economic conditions: it could be that parents and married children worked a hide together and even had to live together. The detailed records of the monastery of Farfa listed all the members of families who lived and worked together. While both here and in the property enumeration of the monastery of Santa Giulia in Brescia a peasant family averaged five members, there were exceptional cases with ten or even more. These exceptions were often the households of a *scario,* according to some scholars, a sort of agent or steward although there seems to be a close relationship between this word and the *Scharmannen* of Saint Maximin in Trier. Here, *scaram facere* meant doing messenger service for the lord. The *Scharmannen* had significantly more wealth than the other farmers in order to be able to fulfill their mission, a condition which has also been determined concerning the *scariones* of Farfa. One may suppose that the exceptionally large property of these monastery ministerials included more people than usual, and that on the other hand this property was indivisible since it belonged to their office. This may have been the reason that Otolf, a *scario* of Farfa, had living in his house two married sons with their five children—eleven people in all. There must likewise have been exceptional circumstances which explain that in one household, along with a husband and wife, seventeen kinsmen (*nepotes*) are summarily listed. In these very rare cases we may be encountering a three-generational family under the authority of the grandfather, alongside of many nuclear families. We cannot determine how far the authority of a *scario* extended over the kin in his house. When away on business, he seems to have delegated his authority to one or more of his sons.

In nuclear families the head of the house worked the land along with his wife and children, and lived with them in a hut which often contained but a single room. While the physical proximity of the family members was a strong element in bonding, such circumstances were hardly conducive to the expression of intimate emotions. Even in the nascent knightly sphere of the poem *Ruodlieb,* not a single word of emotion is exchanged between mother and son—it was contrary to custom to emphasize such things. This attitude has already been recognized in the Indo-European root of the word "father": it is a term from the realm of legal order. Neither the biological nor the affective aspects were adequate to fix the ancient term for fatherhood. In the New Testament, the father of the house is the *oikodespotes,* the despot or absolute lord over the house in a sense entirely lacking the humorous overtones of "domestic tyrant." This power was exercised in a peasant's hovel as well as in a magnate's palace—aristocratic orders were only slightly different from those of peasants in their essential structure. In practice, however, the multitude of servants made it impossible for all to live under one roof. So the physical unity of the habitation began to weaken although it was never totally dissolved: a landlord's *familia* always contained "familial" elements in the modern sense, as for example when the personal names óf the servants were chosen from the names of the lord and his close kin.

THE HOUSE AND ITS GOVERNOR

We must now consider the various meanings of "house," which, like *familia*, were already in use in antiquity. *Domus* is the place of habitation in both the narrowest and widest senses. One can describe the whole world as the home (*domus*) of mankind; on the other hand, *domus* is almost synonymous with *familia:* it can mean servants, or the nuclear family, or the wider circle of kindred. The word *domus* has even been used for the noble ruling house of later periods; *domus Austriae* means the Habsburgs and their realm. The authority of nobles and kings was understood as "domestic authority"—a subject with which we need not deal. Our concern is the situation within the nuclear family. That we can say something about this only within the upper levels of society is due to the lamentable nature of our sources or, rather, to the limited interest of literate people of that time in the life of the basic stratum of population. Things have changed only partially in this respect.

The terms "house" and "family" were popular but were never clear, simply definable terms, as is the case with many other terms in the period under discussion. In earliest times, people sought to indicate a multitude of phenomena of the external world with few words; later, the increasing vocabulary always lagged behind the constantly increasing differences among these phenomena; even the jurists of our own day have not succeeded in establishing in their field a system of clearly separated, unambiguous terminology. Popular concepts are ciphers whose respective meanings come from the context in which they are used. The meanings overlap, without clear differentiation. Rodulfus Glaber, for example, tells about the house of a noble in which boundary stones used to fly through the air. This was a bad omen for the family that lived there (*illius domus familia*). We believe he is speaking of a household, the nuclear family living in one house, but then we hear about a boundary conflict with neighbors stemming from the couple's rich possessions, which they had received from both of their kindreds. The conflict was fought out by the sons and nephews of the couple in a "war" against the opposing party, in which eleven sons and nephews "from the above-mentioned house" were killed. In its aftermath there was an "innumerable number of killings (of members) of each family," and the feud continued for thirty years. In the course of the report, the "household family" grows into a large feuding association; the meaning of "house" expands from the place of residence to indicate a large number of people. The family association and the obligations resulting from it were originally incorporated in a common residence, and "house" continued to be used for such a community even after its real meaning as a common dwelling had been lost.

All this is a preliminary comment to the question: What do our sources tell us of the structure of the family? We begin with the legal position of the wife.

The Wife in the House

The wife was under the protection and authority of her husband. If a wife wished to prosecute her husband in court, she had to be temporarily freed of his authority. She recovered authority over herself when she no longer lived with her husband, but in that event she was normally returned to her father's authority. In the *Ruodlieb,* the bride is reminded with words and symbols that her infidelity in marriage could cost her her head. The author of the *Ruodlieb,* in semihumorous form, reminds the bride of the right of the betrayed husband over her life, a right which, in popular custom, has not entirely disappeared even to today. The canonist Regino of Prüm repeated without commentary the pronouncement of a Roman jurist that a husband had the right to kill a wife caught in infidelity in his own home. As far as we know, there is no account from the tenth or eleventh century of an actual case in which the killer of his wife went unpunished. As for the unfaithful women of whom Thietmar of Merseburg complained that they were neither mutilated according to the old Saxon custom, nor stoned in accord with the Old Testament, nor beheaded according to the old (Roman) law, "today . . . the liberty to sin . . . prevails everywhere, and thus not only many seduced virgins but many married women too are driven to unfaithfulness even during the lives of their husbands . . . Today there is no longer a harsh penalty for such crimes, and so, I fear, the new style is coming constantly more into practice."

We may even recognize among the "modern youth" of that period subversive trains of thought aiming at equal rights. Such a tendency is at least visible in the *Ruodlieb:* the young woman who was so drastically taught her obligations to remain faithful reminds her future husband that these obligations ought to be mutual: "Tell me why I should show you greater faithfulness than you show me? . . . Far be it from me that I should bind myself in such an agreement." To which the young man responds: "It will be, my love, as you wish," and swears that she would have the right to cut off his head if he should be unfaithful to her.

The clerical author of the poem presents the one-sidedness of the obligation of faithfulness for discussion, hoping that it will have an educational effect in the sense of a moral obligation for the husband as well. Such attempts could be effective in a period when the mutual obligation of faithfulness between lord and vassal stood in the foreground of interpersonal relations. It was probably no accident that women apparently addressed their husbands as *mi senior,* "my feudal lord." The lordship of the husband was thereby maintained, a relationship of mutual trust was indicated, and the social distance between husband and wife was lessened—she was, in a sense, a vassal and could talk with her husband "man to man."

The husband, nonetheless, had the right to repudiate his wife without bothering with an ecclesiastical court; only in the twelfth century did divorce become a matter of church law. Marriage and divorce were understood as transactions between families involving relationships and property. The divorce was complete when the dowry of the wife returned to her kin. Ecclesiastical authorities could be mollified by the argument that the kinship was too close to comply with canonical regulations, and with this argument the prohibition of subsequent marriages was also rendered invalid. The marital life of Robert the Pious was viewed with considerable ill will in Rome, but he was never excommunicated, and serious difficulties overtook him after his divorce from his first wife only because he retained her property.

Varieties of Marriage

A woman lived in her father's house until he handed her over to another "house," that of her husband. Two things were essential in order to establish a fully valid marriage: the public announcement—transactions must be made public—and the transferal of the *dos,* a gift of the bridegroom to the bride; formerly it had been a payment to her kindred. The announcement was guaranteed by this payment and above all by the transferal of the girl from the father in the presence of the family to the bridegroom. A valid marriage, at least in the eyes of the Church in France, could only be contracted with the consent of the father or his representative as "guardian" of the bride. On the other hand, Pope Nicolas I had attempted to place the consent of the couple being married in the center: to him the mutual consent of the spouses was essential to marriage, and without it everything else was without effect. Even here the approval "of the parties in whose authority they (the bride and groom) are" was mentioned; but a great stride had been made toward the self-determination and equality of rights of married persons.

The pope's declaration, however, did not yet bear fruit. Views concerning the presuppositions and nature of marriage were numerous. Even the most ancient traditions were still present. When ecclesiastical lawbooks dealt extensively with bride theft, they were not simply repeating old provisions; Otto the Great had to deal with the matter seriously as a current custom. Along with full, valid marriage there were other forms of union, and there may also have existed the much-discussed *Friedelehe*, a morganatic marriage of the Merovingian and Carolingian period; it is reported only in cases of the elite, and was placed by the clergy on the same level as concubinage and thereby devalued. In the tenth century it seems no longer to have been customary to have concubines; however, if some progress had been made in this area, an ecclesiastical regulation of marriage still lay far in the future. People were satisfied initially when a legal marriage was additionally blessed by a priest. The Roman pontifical reads: "After the woman has been betrothed to the man and according to the law has received her *dos,* she and her husband (*maritus*) should enter the church," where the bishop would pray over them. Thus the marriage had taken place before they entered the church, preferably in front of the church door or—normally—in the house of the bridegroom. When Bishop Udalrich of Augsburg visited his diocese, he would ask the clerics "whether they had excessively taken part in invitations to drink and to banquets, whether they had participated in disputes, in competitions, or in worldly weddings." Parish priests were to avoid such marriage feasts.

In the east, Emperor Leo VI (886–912) had ordered that ecclesiastical blessing should be a condition for the validity of every marriage; the west knew no such compulsion prior to the Council of Trent. A civil marriage without a priest was sufficient, although attempts were made to forbid it; Burchard of Worms prescribed public penance for such marriages. How far this order was put into effect cannot be known. In the ninth century, according to Jonas of Orléans, the ecclesiastical requirement that the marriage couple should be *incorrupti* when they married was the reason for the rarity of (*perraro*) ecclesiastical blessing at Mass. The old requirement of virginity for the bride was the reason that girls of the Saxon nobility were married at the age of thirteen or sooner: at the same age women presented their husbands with their first sons. A breakthrough in favor of the church wedding took place in the twelfth century. From that time on, the official teaching emphasized the sacramental character of marriage and the importance of the couple's consent. Ecclesiastical marriage did not depend on material presuppositions. It was not equated with the foundation of a household by heritage or by the will of a paterfamilias or a lord. The contract was not made between families but between the bride and groom. This radical position, of course, had to compromise with reality, at least in most cases, and much of the former thinking remained alongside of the new positions.

DEVALUATION OF WOMEN

Through the kind of transformations already indicated in the *Ruodlieb,* the status of the wife in her husband's house rose, though it did not achieve equality. The dynamic force in this rise was the clergy, a fact that at first glance seems amazing in light of the low opinion traditional clerics had of women. That opinion was usually founded in the foolish conduct of Eve, the principal example of the instability of female character, supplemented by further reproofs of feminine cunning and malignity. The world of the Old Testament had been a man's world, and little had changed since then. There is documentation on roughly 150,000 persons from the Carolingian and Ottonian periods; barely 10 percent of the names are of women. It thus appears a positive sign that 23.4 percent of the saints living in the first half of the tenth century, and 16.2 percent of those in the second half, are women. One cause of the negative attitude toward women was ecclesiastical celibacy; another had deep roots in paganism: ethnologists have found that women in almost every society, on account of their physiology, are considered unclean, less in the moral than in the magico-religious sphere.

During Lent in 966, Rather of Verona sent the clergy of his diocese a pastoral letter in which among other admonitions he stated,

"No woman should approach the altar or touch the cup of the Lord." It was a sin for any cleric to allow such things. In the confessional questions that Regino addressed to the parish clergy we read that the bishop or his representative asked whether the pastor "had allowed women to approach the altar and whether he had allowed women to touch the cup of the Lord." The basis of such prohibitions was a text written around the middle of the ninth century under the name of Pope Leo IV. Atto of Vercelli also cited this opinion, adding that women should be mindful of the weakness of their sex. Atto never-theless agreed that older pious women might prepare the offerings for the priest and might clean the floor of the church.

Saint Jerome was the leading propagandist for general antifem-inism, although he was surrounded by noble ladies who admired his rough ways. Even this note found its imitators: "O brother, tell me who is not ruined by the impious and perverse thought of women?" The exclamation was made in the context of an old theme, "wife as bad counselor." It was applied to the case of Duke Giselbert of Lor-raine, who was supposedly influenced by his wife Gerberga, sister of Otto the Great, to revolt against the king. Whoever credited women with nothing but evil could see them as the source of every misfor-tune. Who was responsible for the extinction of the ruling line of the Carolingians? The unfaithful wife of Lothar, who poisoned him in 986 and his son Louis in 987. Who was responsible for Count Wil-liam of Angoulême's death after his return from Jerusalem? A "dis-graced woman" had employed evil arts, as three witnesses claimed; that the count before whom the case came did not have the supposed malefactrix tortured but, instead, "spared" her was reported without comment.

One can see an antifeminist tendency in many authors, including historians; it could be used for political purposes, when the truth was mingled with slander that the author had heard or may even have invented. Probably a case in point is Liutprand of Cremona's account of the Roman petticoat government which was ended by the acces-sion of Otto the Great. In modern times, the activities of the family of Theophylact for Rome and for her monasteries have begun to be seen in a positive light; still, Marozia could not have been a saint, even if we now suspect that she became a nun after the papal annul-ment of her marriage with Hugo of Provence. In any case, we must use extreme caution in cases such as this one in which we hear only one side, the other having left no historiographical defense. Such cau-tion has not always been exercised by modern historians, especially in the last century; many comments of modern historians read as though they were of medieval origin.

Historians of recent decades have sometimes adopted the negative attitudes of medieval authors toward women and have thus done many a woman injustice. Such judgments are almost always aimed at married women of the nobility, who are depicted as political intriguers and "wicked advisers." Widows generally appear honorable, and the highest praise is given female servants of God who take their spiritual calling seriously. When one of these latter, like Hrotsvith of Gandersheim, takes up the pen, she has no reason to complain about any lack of honor in the world dominated by men. In conformity with her environment and as expression of spiritual modesty, in the preface to her *Gesta Ottonis* she writes about the weakness and limited knowledge of the female sex. We hear nothing of this weakness in the image of female saints of the "virago" type, in Flodoard, for instance; here we find "women with a manly heart," and even "good advisers." Rather of Verona calls attention to the fact that in the Old Testament tells of women who obtain victory when all the men have been seized by fear, and that since that time the palm of victory has fallen to many women who (in the fight against evil) had forgotten their female weakness.

THE WIFE'S ACTUAL STATUS

Rather than listening only to the negative pronouncements of ecclesiastics, we should attempt to see what freedom of action women were allowed in the confines of the accepted order. It was taken for granted that a woman should remain in second place and thus, as "housewife," should come behind the "master of the house" and be subjugated to his command—unless she was acting in his place during his absence or after his death. Then, as we shall see, she could become the master and could exercise command both within the household and over its external resources. Here and there, a wife would share with her husband the right of permanent codetermination over property, as well as autonomous control over her dowry and her inheritance. On this topic opinions differed by region and could change from generation to generation. Thus in the Mâconnais before the start of the eleventh century, a woman controlled her inheritance herself even within marriage; after that date it was the husband who exercised this duty. Both Roman law and Germanic custom favored personal property for women, even during their marriage; at least some married women were able to act in legal transactions of property. There could be a "community of control," as it was called: a couple's joint control over private property, offices, and fiefs; there were sporadic double investitures in the later tenth century in the western parts of the empire and, later, in France. A woman alone was able to be a feudal tenant: the bishop of Cambrai invested the daughter-in-law of the castellan of that town with a *villa* with the obligation to undertake needlework for him and to persuade her husband to cease his hostile behavior toward the bishop. The legal situation was particularly favorable toward women in Catalonia, either because of the influence of Visigothic law or as the result of the paucity of men: many men had died in battle after the beginning of the Reconquista, the conquest of territory held by the Moors. In Catalonia a married woman had full control over her own property as well as the right of codetermination of her husband's property. Charters of that region note at least the wife's consent, or she appears next to the husband as initiator of the act. When the marquis Boniface of Canossa, for example, took as his first wife a wealthy heiress, she shared his lordship, and joint decisions of the couple are preserved.

Recently it has been observed that in Catalonia, beginning in the tenth century, surnames for women appear which imply praise for their external appearance (Bella, Elegancia, Gradiosa, Miravella) or their virtuous personality (Bona, Fidela, Pura), some even indicating tenderness (Passarella, Torterella, Amada, Carissima, etc.). Here we may be seeing the beginning of the cult of women and courtly love, which found its particular home in nearby southern France and in the sort of vassallic relationship between a (married) woman as "lady" and an (unmarried) man. Even when it was only a game more or less tolerated by the husband, it presupposes a freer position of the woman, who could rise to dominance in the social life of the noble house. Certainly we must distinguish here between the pretty appearance and the harsh realities of life.

The expenditure dedicated to the purposes of "representation" not only of the lord but also of the lady of the house was certainly not a game but a necessity of noble life. Their "lordly" life was eventually the object of clerical criticism and pious warnings: young girls were not to give themselves into the chains of marriage, not (as wives) to take pleasure in the extent of their possessions, not to rejoice in a throng of servants and maids or in the various forms of ornamentation which belonged to (noble) attire. They were not to take pleasure in the troops who served them in various ways—among these may be meant unmarried young noblemen who were the admirers of the lady of the house. Characteristic is a description of the goings-on in a convent that had been occupied by laity: young men—the sons of vassals?—practiced swordplay, female weavers sat at their noisy looms, men assembled, and the lady (*domina*) walked to and fro, accompanied by the host of her handmaids (*pedissequae*). *Domina* and *Dame* are the same word.

This description suggests what the primary duty of a noble lady was in her household: not the care and education of her children and not the "private" cooking, but command over all the maidservants entrusted with these and other tasks—especially spinning and weaving. Her duties were more like those of a department head in a factory than those of today's middle-class housewife. "Women's work" was mainly cloth production and sewing, and the supervision of the workers engaged in it. In addition was the responsibility for a large kitchen operation for the household staff and sometimes also for construction workers hired by the lord for defensive fortifications and so forth.

It generally depended on the woman herself whether she was content within the confines of these duties. The possibility of reaching beyond them was suggested to her by the frequent trips away from home that a man of "elevated position" was compelled to make. Then the wife had to make decisions for him and also control his vassals. We hear of one countess who, during the absence of her husband, built a castle, and of another, who, while her husband was in captivity, followed his instructions that she should defend his castles and under no circumstances should be willing to surrender. In Catalonia, a woman who had taken part in the administration of three counties "ruled" them after the death of her husband in the name of her minor son. Another took part in the conquest of a town, built a tower there, and had the new castellany transferred to her command. During the siege of Merseburg by the Polish duke, women were active in the defense of the upper castle; similar events had already taken place during the Norman invasions.

In times of peace as well, ladies had rights which extended beyond their "house." Not only queens had the right to intervene with their husbands in behalf of petitioners. We have already told of a bishop of Cambrai who wanted the wife of his opponent to support him and thus to neutralize the husband through her. It was primarily ecclesiastics in conflict with laymen who found support in their opponents' wives. In some cases a wife would even work against her husband's will: When the Counts Palatine Erchanger and Bertold had captured Bishop Salomo III of Constance, the bishop was taken to a castle, where Erchanger's wife was staying. She prepared an honorable reception for the prisoner, dined with him, and gave him the hope of imminent release.

An unmarried woman too could play an important political role. Although some of the tribal laws required that she have a guardian, this requirement was not always observed in the Frankish realm; in Saxony, property transactions of single women were quite normal, and single women could be chatelaines. Reinilda, the *domina* of the castle (*urbs*) of Altenbeichlingen, had to promise the king (Henry II) never to marry without his knowledge and advice—a promise which did not prevent a kinsman of Thietmar of Merseburg from carrying her off. In contrast to other cases mentioned by Thietmar, this noble lady was not married according to the desires of her kindred; she was not under the authority of her father. She was "of age" and possessed a "fortified house," which she had probably inherited. That the king had the care of widows and orphans had been the legal foundation for the promise she had had to make him. The king's obligation of protection allowed unmarried women a real area of action within a "man's world." A king, of course, could exercise protection only in those regions where he had power and possessions at his disposal.

Independent ladies were rare in the secular sphere. Although there were many widows in these dangerous times, it was nevertheless by far the best for them to remarry. That women could make second marriages against the will of their sons from their first marriage and even enter a second marriage during the lives of their first husbands indicates a certain freedom of action. Such things took place in the highest ranks of society, which were above criticism. "Lower down" one thought otherwise, at least in Aquitaine, where widows of vassals were apparently perceived as a sort of appurtenance to their fiefs. From the early eleventh century, reference to a contract between the Duke William of Aquitaine with one of his magnates has survived, in which the duke (after the death of a vassal) announced that he would transfer the "honor" and the wife of the deceased to the other party in the agreement, Hugo ("Chiliarchus") of Lusignan.

Little is said about the condition of women in the lower orders. Even here, however, a woman had a specific circle of duties alongside those of her husband; there was man's work and woman's work. When the pious Count Gerald of Aurillac saw a woman behind a plow, he is said to have asked her why she was there. On learning that her husband was ill and that no one else could help, the count provided money so that they could hire a laborer: she ought not to perform man's work (*opus virile*). Women's work was the cultivation of the garden, the care of cattle, participation in the harvest and in the exploitation of woodland, preparing food and drink, and, of course, the *opera textilia*, from harvesting flax to sewing clothes. The peasant's wife was more concerned with the work inside the house than was her husband and had to perform less heavy work than he. After the death of her husband, if there were sons, the woman could take his place; she would be indicated as the holder of a *mansus*. Otherwise a son could take over the farm, establish a family, and have his mother and perhaps other kin living in his house.

Sons

At this point one had to face the problem of younger sons. It was a fortunate occurrence when the lord gave each of them a farm in order to establish a household; in other situations they might be employed in the lord's household, which was apparently seen as a social decline. In this sphere as well as among the nobles there was differentiation in rank: the husband preceded his wife, the elder the younger, the married the single. It was a general custom, which had originated in antiquity, to emphasize the lower rank of those who were without their own household, hence unmarried, by terms that indicated a reduction in age: thus a servant was a "boy" (*puer*), in the same way that a black servant, regardless of age, used to be called a "boy" in the American South. Since the time of Isidore of Seville, boyhood was considered to span the seventh to the fourteenth year; only rarely was the term extended to the age of twenty-eight. Among the Franks, one reached one's majority at the age of twelve or fifteen. The word *puer* could also be used in the elevated strata of society for persons who had no independent personality, as for example the Frankish *pueri regis*, who were certainly not boys but young royal functionaries along the lines of those in the Lex Burgundionum. Later, the word *tiro* was used in a similar manner. The word designated vassals who served their lord in his house as *tirones domus.* They too certainly were not youths or students. Equally significant is the word "housemaid" for female house personnel of any age. Serving women were relegated to the position of maiden as early as the Lex Salica with its *puellae milituniae.*

Interestingly, in the Lex Salica the *puer regis* appears in the context of the death penalty for bride theft. What the head of the clan saw as a crime was seen by the "youth" as a praiseworthy demonstration of courage—a view which, in a cultivated form, was continued in courtly gallantry. Sons without houses of their own formed the restless bands of youth, always ready for military undertakings and uprisings, whose outrageous behavior was constantly written about. When Hugo, the eldest son and co-regent of Robert the Pious, received no lordship of his own, he began, "along with some youths of his age" (he was then seventeen years old), to pursue a feud against his father in which he laid waste his parent's property.

The actions of Liudolf of Swabia were similar: after the second marriage of his father Otto I, he began a rebellion "with the support of evil men and, above all, with that of *iuvenes* from Franconia, Saxony, and Bavaria." In this case it was certainly not only an uprising of seventeen-years-olds. According to Thietmar, Liudolf was alternatively known as Dudo, just as Thangmar was often called Tammo and Henry the Wrangler appears as Hezilo—these were familiar nicknames: Dudo and Tammo probably originated, like mama and papa, in the babbling of small children. We should not assume that it was out of lack of respect for such troublemakers that the historian failed to designate them with their full names. Designation by an abbreviated name was not limited to younger sons; nevertheless, it was appropriate to the social position of the *iuvenes.*

Liudolf had found support among the "youth" of three duchies. Ernst of Swabia collected "a great army of *iuvenes,*" invaded Burgundy with it, and built fortifications with ramparts and moats. Such undertakings could not be completed only with the friends and vassals of a prince; there seems to have existed a kind of military reserve force that sought to be activated and was willing to be commanded by a "young" leader. Military exploits belonged to the life of the youth just as peaceful labor did to men with homes and farms. In the *Waltharius,* the king of the Huns wants to see his faithful follower marry, and he puts at his disposal the means to become established "on the land and in his own house." With courtly thanks the hero declines: as a married man he would have to build houses and engage in agricultural work. As a bachelor he gladly remains day and night in the service of his lord. In the self-perception of this group, its own particular lifestyle—an uncertain military existence—was more highly prized than a "civilian" life. But this does not prevent Walthari from finally marrying his beloved Hiltgund in his homeland and then, after his father's death, ruling the Aquitanians felicitously for thirty years.

For as long as a son stayed in his father's house, he remained under the father's authority. When he became of age, he could enter the following of a lord and hope to be rewarded with an "honor"; or the father could share his inheritance with him, making it possible for him to found his own household; or else the son could succeed his father in his possessions after the latter's death. The "dispatch" of sons by the father could only succeed where sufficient land was available; in Saxony, particularly in its eastern part, there were abundant possibilities. After the death of the father the sons could hold equal portions of the paternal estate, a solution which quickly led to the fragmentation of property; or, in order to avoid fragmentation, there could be an undivided possession by brothers—a system that was always popular in the Mâconnais, for example. Thus one could protect one's social position since the division of property often led to the social decline of its occupants into the peasantry. The negative side of such an undivided possession was that there was no "lord of the manor," and marriage did not lead to the establishment of a household. It could be only a temporary solution to the "overpopulation" of a piece of property. As a member of the second generation one had either to remain a bachelor on one's own soil or to seek one's fortune elsewhere. Among that section of the peasantry where the *mansus* was often de facto inheritable, surviving documents only rarely present situations in which several brothers worked their lands together after the death of their father. In any case one of them was answerable for all before the lord, and one can thus assume that he exercised a certain authority over the others.

Primogeniture offered those in the upper ranks of society a means of holding estates together and protecting their social position. This solution was all the more attractive since a fief, an allod, was indivisible and could not be passed on to a group of brothers. The eldest was the sole authority over the family estate and, as such, usually followed his father without difficulty as the holder of offices and fiefs: in this way a noble clan began to narrow itself into a "house." To avoid division of the inheritance, full marriage (marriage with dowry) was gradually limited to one or two sons, and married daughters were excluded from the family estate. A daughter received movable property as her dowry and could make no further claims against her parents' estate. As far as the younger sons were concerned, their lot could be to enter the priesthood, which required donations to a church or monastery; these donations ended their claims to inheritance. Thus a father or a family council would decide the fate of the younger generation in accord with the general conviction that the collective good of the family had to take precedence over the personal interests of its members.

This common weal was, as it were, incarnate in the head of the family; in order to promote his honor and welfare, all had to work together. This effort extended into the next world, so that many heads of families reduced the family inheritance in order to make generous donations for the salvation of their souls. A historian wishing to chronicle the appreciation of family might reach strange conclusions. A dying Catalan vassal entrusted to his lord the destiny of his horse, his sons, and his wife, in that order. Bishop Adalbero of Laon's famous satire concerning the Cluniacs describes a monk who became a warrior. Arriving home, he jumps from his horse and calls for his superior, his "nourisher," and only then for his son and wife, again in this order. A man's special interest in his horse was understandable; in times of crisis his life depended on the condition of his animal; the son was his heir, the wife had already performed her primary duty by giving birth to the son, and now she stood last in line.

One arranged one's daughters' marriages at a very early age with their formal consent. Sons were raised as clerics from childhood; after they had reached their majority they could—although it rarely happened—leave the ecclesiastical community and return to the world. There was also the possibility for unmarried daughters or widows to remain in the home and live there as nuns; the Romano-Germanic Pontifical includes the words spoken by the bishop on the occasion of the consecration of these so-called "house nuns." With this system, the family was spared the donation to a convent, and, besides, it was more pleasant to stay in the family castle than to live abroad in monastic discipline. The reputation of the clan or lineage was increased by family members of the religious order, and thus all could be content. We shall speak later of nuns and canonesses in ecclesiastical foundations of noble families.

For the superfluous younger sons there was no such possibility to remain in the family. The spirit of the community within Benedictine monasticism was too strong for there to have been "house monks"; the hermit was characterized by radical departure from the established society, and it had become difficult to lead an ascetic existence in the secular world. The value of a monk for his family lay in the prayers he said for them and also in the—usually limited—chance that he might become an abbot and aid his relatives.

Things were better for the secular cleric. Normally literate, proficient in Latin, he could look forward to prebends and positions of honor, perhaps supported by intervenients of high rank. When he received the favor of the king, one could see in him a future archdeacon or bishop. A family had real importance almost only when its members held both secular and ecclesiastical offices and when their private property was supplemented by ecclesiastical and secular benefices. A man in the service of the Church opened wide prospects for the family, and often felt himself their exponent on an advanced position. As a cathedral canon, he could maintain a lordly lifestyle in his own house and with servants; the reformers had great difficulty stopping this practice. The need for representation that we have described above was transferred to the ecclesiastical members of important families, a subject to which we shall return. What belonged to a lordly lifestyle and was prohibited for a cleric were a wife and children: the "house" needed a "housewife."

CLERICAL MARRIAGE AND CHILDREN

The profession of the ecclesiastic without spiritual vocation, the tension between the ancient commandment to celibate life and the fact that the secular clergy were not separated from "the world" (*saeculum*) but had to interact with it, the rigor of the family as ordering principle of life—all these elements together resulted in a truly conflictual situation which cannot be explained simply by reference to "clerical immorality." Current custom placed the unmarried below the married, and male virginity had no value. People were not used to living according to written canons inherited from some distant past, but according to local custom, and custom was not favorable to the celibacy of the secular clergy.

In an encyclical to the clerics of his diocese, Rather of Verona enumerated those days on which they were to abstain from intercourse. In the poem entitled "Unibos" the pastor has an *uxor nobilis* who is once even called "priestess" (*presbiterissa*). Ten wills have survived from Catalan clerics of the tenth century; four of them—one by a bishop of Barcelona and three by priests—made provisions for their wives and children. It was reported that Archbishop Robert of Rouen (990–1037) died leaving a wife and children; Burchart III of Lyons was certainly married, and Archbishop Arnulf of Tours was probably married. These were not "legal" marriages which included a dowry, but they were nevertheless generally recognized, publicly contracted unions which had been designated from the ecclesiastical perspective as concubinage. In 1022, Pope Benedict VIII complained at a synod in Pavia that clerics associated with their women publicly and "with display (*pompatice*) and not with prudence (*caute*)." He said they were more hardheaded than secular transgressors of their marriage vows. Such behavior could only tend to revalorize both the relationships and the women concerned, and to emphasize that these really were marriages, contracted in accordance with custom. The monks of Farfa who had begun a secular life had acted in a similar manner: they did not meet secretly with their concubines but each walked with his beloved in the manner of a lawful union. From Atto of Vercelli we learn that ecclesiastics lived and ate with women, appearing with them in public; they ordered that these women "should supervise their house, the entire service personnel (*cunctae familiae*) and the movable property," they even established them as their heirs.

The attempt of clerics "to run a household" sometimes found support, or at least a certain understanding, among the secular powers. Atto of Vercelli complained that ecclesiastics admonished by their bishop for this reason placed themselves under secular powers and—against church canons and their vassallic oath—served the latter rather than their bishop. When the abbot Hildeprand of Farfa, who along with his monks had entered into a public marriage, appealed to Otto the Great to be reinstated in the monastery, he was refused. The refusal resulted less from his marriage and the dissipation of the monastery's property than from the regular election of his opponent Abbot Johannes. Hildeprand, because of his age, was to retain two pieces of property for his support. We learn from the Chronicle of Farfa that Inga, Hildeprand's wife, was present during the legal proceedings and that she too received a piece of property from the emperor, possibly one of the two named in the deed.

This particular problem could be resolved by compromise because no children were involved; the liquidation of Abbot Campo's lordship, which had supplanted Hildeprand from the property of Farfa, was more difficult, since Campo was married and had distributed many monastic properties among his kin. He was the father of seven daughters and three sons, "all of whom he had provided with dowries from the monastic property." Here we come to the real reasons for the prohibition of marriage—reasons that reformists' polemic suppressed in favor of the ideal ones. For monastic communities, celibacy was a matter of existing or not existing; for the secular clergy, a matter of existing as social order alongside that of secular society; and for the clergy as a whole, a matter of maintaining its material foundation in a period when this nearly always took the form of real property.

The same was true of ecclesiastical offices and income from tithes; they too were in danger of becoming components of family resources with hereditary holders, just like secular fiefs. In extreme cases there could even be clans of ecclesiastics founded on such revenues. The archdeaconate of Pistoia in the tenth and eleventh century developed into an inherited office within one and the same family, and the office was passed from father to son. At first an ecclesiastical dynasty, it later became a secular one, that of the "Arcidiaconi," which continued to hold some of the rights still bound to the religious office. Another example is the cathedral of Arezzo, which owed a quarter of its property and income for the support of its members; "having become rich, they took wives and raised sons with them, and they divided the church among themselves." They hired a monk to look after the church services and sent agents to the church at the times when the faithful were to bring their offerings, so that they could collect them. Later, *custodes* provided the divine services of the church. There was one priest with several sons, among whom was one Salomo, likewise a priest, who held a quarter of the offerings. Salomo divided it among his own sons, among whom one was a cleric, and among his nephews. Salomo's brother, the cleric Andreas, held another quarter, which he left to his two sons, one a cleric and the other a layman. The accounts of the divisions of the custodian's prebends fills more than a full page in print; alongside laymen one always finds clerics—possibly in minor orders and thus not bound to celibacy—and also priests. Thus the priest Johannes could pass down his inheritance to a son, the priest Gerhard, who left it to a cleric, the latter to a layman, all in the direct line.

Such examples do not prove that all clergymen disregarded the injunction to celibacy. Charters of the territory of Farfa, in spite of the sorry situation described above, mention only a few married priests. This does not necessarily indicate adherence to the command of celibacy; it could also be that scribes were loath to record the actual situation. According to secular law, the marriage of priests was not punishable, though we can presume there was constant awareness that ecclesiastical laws had been broken. Clerics knew the canons and did not essentially reject them as guidelines for life, but these regulations were considered impossible to fulfill in all their details. Neither servant nor lord, neither fool nor sage, neither layman nor pope—none of them worries about canon law, said Rather of Verona in rhetorical exaggeration. This was not simply a complaint but also a justification of his own actions, since Rather had left his bishopric and had assumed another in violation of the canonical prohibitions. He had had to besiege Garda castle along with the emperor and thus, like others, had broken the canons against the use of weapons by clerics. When another ecclesiastic in front of this castle had complained about the obligation of military service, Rather had reproached him: just as canon law forbids the bearing of arms, it also forbids intercourse with women.

The laity lived in a similar tension between actuality and obligation, since they were not to kill their enemies, not to marry even distant kin, and not to participate in monetary transactions. Also among the laity were sons from illegitimate unions. They were respectable personages, particularly in ruling houses; even William the Conqueror described himself as a bastard. Priests' sons often seem to have been looked upon in the same manner. To allow them to follow in their father's occupation was forbidden by canon law, but in the eyes of most contemporaries it appeared acceptable. It was only the decretals of the late twelfth and early thirteenth centuries that effected a total devaluation of illegitimate birth of clerics; and the illegitimate members of the secular orders were also looked at askance after the emphasis on the sacramental character of marriage.

On the other hand, Atto of Vercelli has left us a picture of how ecclesiastics could be involved in lawsuits in order to care for their wives and children. Being in a very unstable position, the families of priests could be threatened with extortion by urban petty officials. Married priests could find protection among the powerful against those threatening them and could then become, as Atto said, "weapons of the enemy" (of the bishop). At their protectors' command, such priests were willing to absolve those under excommunication and to excommunicate the enemies of their protectors, to say Masses anywhere and at any time, and to perform baptisms.

The struggle for power required an obedient lower clergy, with whose help the episcopal seat could be brought into the sphere of influence of the family concerned. Political strength, of course, lay elsewhere, above all in the cooperative efforts of secular and ecclesiastical members of a noble clan. We shall later study the widespread involvement of such relationships by focusing on a specific example: Bishop Adalbero II of Metz, who was from the house of the counts of the Ardennes, was related in a sense to all the magnates of his time. In that instance the interests of the bishop, count, and duke went hand in hand, since all three came from the same family.

The biographer of Adalbero II of Metz tells that the bishop had ordained "more than a thousand" priests and, in so doing, "disdained no one," but rather granted ordination to the sons of priests while other bishops had refused them out of pride or stupidity. Adalbero's father, then his mother, and then his brother held the duchy. In addition to this position, the family was anchored in the clergy: they not only occupied the most important episcopal sees of Lorraine but also had their supporters in the lower clergy. In this land, once so restless, peace and order reigned thanks to the competence of the clan. Anyone who, because of the severity of his principles, was unhappy with the kind of order that prevailed, could withdraw to the monastery of Gorze, which Bishop Adalbero I of Metz had established. He too belonged to the family of the counts of the Ardennes.

6 ✿ THE FAMILIAL MODEL

WHERE THE FAMILY WAS THE SOLE FUNC-
tioning principle of common life, it was inevitable that other group formations should be
understood according to its model. By this extension of familial thought, sentiments and
emotions were aroused. Family ties had such
high affective value that they were seen as inde-
structible; transferring this value to nonfamilial
groups could be expected to give them stability.
Dependence was a harsh reality, but it was
made milder when the superior attended to his
inferiors in a "fatherly" manner and when the
latter looked up to the former "as would a
son." Anyone who left his father, mother, and

brothers in order to follow the Lord needed a "new family," and he found it (although incompletely formed) in the monastery: there was a father and brothers, but no mother. In real families the mother was responsible mainly during a child's early years; after that, he was supposed to learn from his father and his older brothers. Thus, in women's convents the head was not called "mother" but "father" (with a feminine suffix, *abbatissa*). The force of this word, said Atto of Vercelli, expresses high esteem in fear and in love, in respect and in dedication.

THE MONASTIC *FAMILIA*

The abbot, according to the Benedictine Rule, acts in the monastery as the representative of Christ. In the monastery, the real paterfamilias is Christ. He calls the shepherds of his flock to account when the sheep bring forth no profit. Later, the patron saint of a monastery was regarded as its real lord, though the heavenly protector was not seen as father to the monks. That position was retained by the abbot. The monastic association was enlarged from below, as first the unfree and then the free too were included in the monastic community, and these laypersons became the *familia* in the narrow sense of the term. This situation favored autocracy, but it was softened through the claims of the Rule to treat subordinates in a familial way: persons placed above them were not to become proud on account of their position; they should not oppress those below them but should command them in the place of a father and in a temperate way. This was true not only for the monks but for the entire "family"; the abbot had become the *pater monasterii*. The monks themselves became the abbot's particular responsibility: he had to educate them; he was their *pater spiritualis*. The mutual control of "brothers" served the same end.

Before speaking further of the monastic "family," we should ask whether it had parallels in other institutions. As far as the bishop was concerned, his position as "father" was more a theoretical than practical one. There was a great distance between this "shepherd" and his flock. He was, rather, a high official, such as the Roman civil service had produced; or he was a *dominus episcopus,* an ecclesiastical lord among secular ones. Ruling over hundreds or thousands of people made it impossible for him to care for them all as a father. The situation on a small farm was quite different: the *Ruodlieb* tells of a young steward who, after the death of his lord, managed the farm for the lord's widow. From then on, "the serving men and women called him father, and for his part he called them his children." A social relationship was seen as a familial one. The Benedictine monastery may have had a similar relationship in times when the number of serving peasantry was so small that the abbot could oversee them as a householder oversees his family.

Along with the father's authority, there was some comradeship in the monastery, but hardly an equalitarian one. We have already seen how great a role concepts of hierarchy played, with the profession date as the criterion of rank. The inequality of the brothers was also emphasized in the manner of address: according to the Rule, no one could address others simply by his name; the inferior had to call an elder *nonnus,* who in turn called the younger *frater.* The word *nonnus* was a colloquial expression with which one acknowledged the respect due to elders. The later spread of the word appears relatively narrow, and it may have survived only by its connection to the Rule. Here the similarity to real families is lacking, for a particular term of address for older brothers is unknown outside the order.

In the tenth century, an abbot could not be "father" to a hundred or more monks, and he could have no personal relationship with the hundreds or thousands of peasants working on the land. What did last was the term *familia,* though in a depersonalized form. One spoke of a *"familia Sancti N.";* the peasants belonged to a heavenly lord. Monastic lordship may have differed from secular lordship in its greater obligation to care for its subjects, but it generally consisted of the same type of landed property. So the term *familia* could be applied to the peasantry of a nobleman.

Within this very large group there was no need for a hierarchical principle; people acknowledged *meliores,* an elite group without fixed limits. We recall that at certain places in the memorial rolls of Farfa, *scariones* with large families were named first, and we identified these with the *Scharmannen* of Prüm, who were pledged to serve as agents of the abbot. A *scario,* though unfree himself, could have serfs under him. In the tenth century there were also freeholders of ecclesiastical fiefs with the obligation "to ride or to fulfill other services" for the head of the monastery. Once it had been required that at least for the "internal services" of the monastery—cellars, laundry, infirmary, etc.—only monks or novices be used, but this was no longer true. Well-to-do persons who had purchased their freedom often became craftsmen in the monastery and overseers of farms.

From the eleventh century onward they were aspiring to an "elevated" lifestyle of a knightly sort.

It is thus not surprising that most scholars have counted a monastery's vassals among its *familia*, as indicated by some of the sources, while others have attributed a narrower meaning to the term. The vassallic relationship certainly bound a "man" to his *senior* in a manner that was understood as a sort of fictive kinship. In the widest sense, a monastery might include an outstanding benefactor among its familiars or its *familia*.

Prestige within the constantly differentiating *familia* was initially based on a person's free or unfree legal condition, though the separation gradually became obscured and the servants were closely assimilated as "dependents." Just as office and property largely determined the prestige of a nobleman, so they did in the humble sphere of monastic servants. Cobblers and blacksmiths were "office holders," ranking above the mass of the landless servants in the monastery. They had this position because in many cases they were granted a piece of land in benefice for their services, which they could cultivate and use as the basis for establishing a family. For the free, there was also the possibility that these prerequisites of a household could be acquired through their family. As we have seen, marriage was viewed less from a religious than from an economic and social perspective. We have also noted that married men had a higher social prestige than did bachelors. By marriage a man became the father of a household and rose from the position of *praebendarius,* a person working for food and lodging, to that of a self-provider who paid his dues. This was true for most of the unfree who had been given a farm, as well as for craftsmen, shepherds, and other office holders in the monastery. A steward in charge of dependents who had their own houses automatically enjoyed greater prestige than they and the possibility of still further advancement.

FAMILIES WITHIN THE *FAMILIA*

In the tradition of Greek and Roman economic practices, the Carolingian economy was geared to freely available labor, in other words, workers not settled on their own farmstead. This requirement was less widespread in the tenth century, but still existed. Thus, besides landed workers (*servi casati*), there were others in the *familia* who seem to have no possibility of founding a family—a situation that appears paradoxical to us today but was then seen as self-evident.

A Roman slave had no chance of marriage; he could only enter cohabitation (*contubernium*) under the supervision of his lord and owner. The unfree servants of the tenth century could contract legally valid marriages with a small *dos,* although the right of the lord was protected: he had to consent to the marriage and could put land at the couple's disposal. What happened when one received neither the lord's permission nor the material possibilities? Did marriage without an economic basis exist? We know next to nothing about this, for house servants (*servi non casati*) are generally passed over in our sources. People who had to produce no specific dues or services were uninteresting for most property records. We can reasonably conclude that the situation was not favorable to marriages among such people. Nor could the lord be interested in married servants. The availability of household servants would be limited: marriage implied the right to live together, since the married couple were not to be separated, which was then the same as a dissolution of the marriage. Further evidence against the existence of legal marriages among house servants is the virtual absence of such unfree servants—with the exception of officeholders—from family groups listed in ecclesiastical charters and property records. First the names of the men were listed and then the names of all the women with their children.

Cinzio Violante has called attention to the fact that the landless unfree could not form a legal family even if a marriage before a priest was guaranteed them: they were counted among movable property, while *servi casati* were part of the real property on which they lived; they belonged to their home (*casa*). There were also landless servants who dwelled within the enclosure of the monastery. These were called *hagustaldi,* unmarried persons. They may have been waiting there until assigned a piece of land, which would make it possible for them to establish a family. More often the domestic servants lived in dormitories, men in one, women with their (small) children in the other. This would certainly not have been seen as antisocial, for the monks too had their dormitories, and even a bishop was used to sleeping in the same room as other ecclesiastics. It must have been seen as an improvement when small bedrooms, rather than a common dormitory, were located right next to the workshops of the various "offices": the infirmary personnel slept in the hospital, the gardeners next to the monastic garden. This division into small units is shown in the copy of the plan of a monastery prepared for Saint Gall. When all the people devoted to the same office slept in one room, we may infer that they had no families.

The relations between house servants' occupations and living arrangements may help to explain something we find in the estate records of the monastery of Farfa. In the Abruzzi mountains the monastery had a farmhouse called Forcone, in which (*infra casam*) craftsmen, gardeners, and a groom lived—in all, twelve "hands" (*homines manuales*), two of them with their wives. In addition there were fifty-five servant women, who seem to have been occupied in textile manufacture. Along with the twelve holders of "offices," a similar number of "male children" are listed, and after the names of the women we find thirteen "female children." Only in seven cases is the name of a child's father noted: it is always that of one of the officeholders. The "fatherless" children are distinguished from each other by their mother's names. In eight cases (of a total of ten) the names are those of women listed above, the presumed textile workers. So we can assume that they had children without being legally married. Only two of the *homines manuales* are listed with their wives; the other officeholders appear to have been bachelors. Among these unmarried men, only two—the smith and the groom—seem to have acknowledged their sons. The gardener had five children with his wife.

The remainder were one small son and four daughters of women who do not appear among the fifty-five textile workers. One can accept a suggestion of Dom Berlière's that orphans or children of mothers who were ill were incorporated into the domestic staff of monasteries. At Forcone, whatever the fate of the mothers may have been, their names were known, and so they certainly numbered among the servant women of the farmstead. It is also possible that one or another of these women had married one of the "housed" servants and had left their child behind in the farmhouse.

This evidence is so limited that we cannot draw general conclusions from it. It does suggest, however, that servants on monastic estates had just as few opportunities to found a family as in the secular sphere, and as is the case today for rural workers. The problem of servants' children produced outside of marriage was probably dealt with in a matter-of-fact way not only at Farfa; this would change partially in later centuries under the influence of the canonical laws of marriage.

In the sphere of the unfree servants, the same problems occur, in exacerbated form, as in the upper levels of society. We have already spoken of the liberal attitude toward bastards and of internal restriction of marriage in the middle levels. Georges Duby provides examples in his examination of fifty rich families in the Mâconnais: of six sons, only two or even one would marry, and the number of grandchildren hardly exceeded that of children. Here we find "'girls' grown old in the circle of the family, and old boys (*vieux garçons*) without ties." They had it better than the weavers at Forcone and at least some of the ministerials working there in the house and the garden. They could not all become monks or nuns, or did not all wish to. Only two *ancillae dei* were to be found in Forcone, pious women who had not taken the veil or entered a spiritual community, unfree women with no "dowry" to give to the monastery. When a peasant's farm was too small to feed all the members of the family, the solution was for some to become servants in the lord's household. They lived within a *familia* without a family. For monks and nuns, an artificial replacement was created for the natural family, a community in which one was united with one's fellows, with people who had come up short in this world and could place their hopes in another world, where the least would be the greatest.

Were there ways to escape from this narrow life cycle? Just as there were monks who left the cloister and nuns who returned to the world, there was no lack of escaped servants. In such a situation the unfree joined the world of outlaws; they sank to the level of the vagrants, along with some of the free who had fallen under the wheel of fortune. By chance we know of one poor man who spent an entire winter with his wife and six children under an overhanging boulder; he was a newcomer and had been unable to find hospitality anywhere. Even if this story was invented, it must have been listened to as if it were possible. A single person could more easily get by as an itinerant worker than a family of eight, even if, as was the case in this story, the family was virtuous and went to the parish church on Sunday.

A large ecclesiastical estate was organized, as we have said, in a manner little different from that of its lay counterpart. Thus the word for its personnel could well penetrate into the secular sphere, and the concept of *familia* can be seen as a basic structure in social history. In both the lay and the ecclesiastical spheres, the familial idea often retreated behind an emphasis on rank and class, resulting in a division between high and low. In the Rule of Canons issued at the Council of Aix-la-Chapelle held in 816, the word *familia* was equated to the term for the lower orders (*viles personae*); one was warned against receiving people of this class into the canonical community, to the exclusion of noblemen. In the same text we learn that a regular canon who had come from a *familia* and had been freed was constantly in danger of being beaten by his superior and could even be returned to the status of an unfree servant. We have no such reports from monasteries, but there too social ranking and a lordlike authority was often strongly in evidence. The image of the father was seldom used, but rather that of the shepherd who pastured his flock.

THE COURTLY *FAMILIA*

In the house (or court) of magnates, the term *familia* was not limited to low-born members of the household, but included servants as well as men of middle- and upper-level groups who served their lord in military, political, and courtly affairs. Their duties were dignified and often merely symbolic; here the stable boy became a marshal. In this atmosphere the lord was seldom perceived as "father"; such a perception occurs most frequently in poetry and rhetorical prose. Thus, for example, the *Waltharius* describes the youths (*adolescentes*) Hagen and Walter as *nutriti* (in a sense, "foster sons") of Attila. It is a term that reappears in the French chansons de geste as *no(u)rri*. When a historian thought it necessary to employ pathos, he could have the magnates of a kingdom swear to the king that they wanted to remain faithful unto death to their father who nourished them in the manner of a family (*familiariter*). Court poets could celebrate the queen as "sweet mother," as one sees in the Cambridge songs. It was customary to describe the king as the father of the Frankish kingdom, or of the fatherland, etc. In Radulf Glaber we hear that the Roman orb was like a house at the service of the emperors (Charlemagne and Louis the Pious), which rejoiced in the successes of the father. Familial metaphors were obligatory for historians who had to describe harmony and peace.

CONFRATERNITIES

Other expressions have more substantive content. Thietmar of Merseburg speaks of *confratres,* not meaning "spiritual brothers" in general but rather the brotherhood in whose community (*fraternitatis consortium*) Thietmar was accepted through a two-day-long banquet which was "great and welcome to all." He was referring to the cathedral chapter of Magdeburg, whose members had to recognize each other as "spiritual brothers" with *caritas*. Thietmar first learned what this meant in a dream, in which a deceased canon reproached him thus: "Why did you not visit me (before my death)? Why did you not sing the psalms and perform the memorial service fixed in (the prayer confraternity of the synod of) Dortmund?" The text of this decree, which Thietmar copied in his work, started with the *decretum* issued not only by Henry II and his wife Kunigunde, but also by three archbishops, and twelve German bishops: When any one of them, thus including both the emperor or empress, should die, the other members of the prayer confraternity and their subordinate ecclesiastics were to celebrate Masses and to sing all psalms ten times for the deceased. In addition, great feasts for the poor must be given, which, with the lighting of candles, were to serve both as memorial for the deceased and as a spiritual aid for his soul. Secular members too were supposed to engage in thankful prayers for the salvation of his soul.

This great display for the salvation of the soul was so organized that the *confratres* themselves had the fewest obligations while their subordinates had to fulfill progressively greater ones: archbishops, bishops, and their cathedral clergy had to celebrate only one Mass, the normal priests three; deacons and those in minor orders had to sing 1,500 psalms each. This was a principle similar to that which charged monastic vassals with insignificant duties and the unfree members of the *familia* with heavy burdens. True, in this case the magnates also had material obligations to fulfill which could not have been expected from the "common people." The king and queen as well as the duke of Saxony had only material duties. The double expansion of the prayer confraternity upward and downward to include both rulers and diocesan clergy was a secondary development; originally the bishops, as *confratres*, had to pray only for each other, and not only when one of them died but also "for the salvation of the living."

The normal form, so to speak, of the prayer confraternity was that of monasteries. Here the monks, bound together as brothers according to the Rule, now bound themselves with others into a *societas et fraternitas*—an expression found later in the request of the novice to be admitted into the monastery. While the term "society" still today designates a group organized for a specific purpose, the word "brotherhood" has been almost lost. It was not burdened with an emotional charge as in the sense of brotherly love; otherwise no one would have thought of leaving the prayers for the brothers to a substitute. Nor did these confraternities form true communities like those of the monks in a monastery. Only the momentous obligation to render assistance, especially in situations of urgency, remained of the familial life. That obligation, in modified form, could be far extended, even to laymen and to the king.

From here it was not a long step to the voluntary association of laymen which, according to Hincmar of Reims, "the common people call a guild or brotherhood." The former term is more often used of associations with secular purposes—sworn bands fighting the Carolingian authorities—and the latter for predominantly religious groups, as in Italy. We have the articles of a brotherhood from Modena, which included over one hundred men and women. They paid money for candles in the cathedral church; the articles make it clear that the eternal life was conceived of as a community of the table.

Spiritual Kinship

In this instance the familial element is weaker than and subordinate to the "social" element. The bonds created by "spiritual kinship" were conceived in a much more concrete manner. One was born again in Christ, and as such one had, alongside one's physical parents, a spiritual father and a spiritual mother (*compater, commater*). The godfather assumed responsibility for the Christian education of the godchild; he was his "nourisher" and *pater spirit(u)alis*. For this reason spiritual kinship could become an impediment to marriage. According to Justinian, nothing else could bring forth so much fatherly love and thus serve as legal ground for prohibition of marriage as a relationship of this kind: through it, two souls are united (*copulatae*) by the agency of God.

That even ecclesiastics had godparents and could be godfathers crossed the two spheres of the ecclesiastical "family life": Might a monk have another "father" besides the abbot, might there be a spiritual "son" of a monk? At an assembly of the abbots of the ecclesiastical province of Reims (972/973) the abbot of Saint-Rémi objected to such monks: to have a son or a daughter was unchaste. Therefore the metropolitan forbade monks to take on godfatherhood. For reformers it seemed no less important to free the monastic community from the ties of godparenthood than from those of biological kinship.

What we see as a secondary meaning of a term could be understood as the primary or spiritual reality, whereas the transitory appeared to be merely an allegory. Similar reasoning is found in the ancient view that a bishop's relationship to his church was a kind of marriage: in the ninth century the Pseudo-Isidorian Decretals pronounced the transfer of a bishop to another diocese as a crime of unchastity and marital infidelity. Although the episcopal ring was a (Roman) emblem of office (*signum pontificalis honoris*) which needed no explanation, at the end of the tenth century the pontifical of Aurillac spoke of a "ring of fidelity (or of faith)" by which the bishop became the trustee of his church; the church is certainly not his own "bride," but that of Christ. It was not until the twelfth century that the bishop's ring became a marriage ring, which the bishop wore "in the place of Christ." Later canonists used the spiritual marriage of a bishop as the basis for defining his position and legal authority.

The Church as the bride of Christ and the Church as the mother of the faithful are two concepts which had been transmitted together since antiquity. It is immaterial that Rome was designated alternately as mother of the Church and mother of the bishops; this metaphor supplemented the concepts of "head" and "pivot point" (*cardo*) without demanding that concrete conclusions be drawn from it. Familial metaphors are frequent in patristic writings as well as in those of later centuries. Thus Hrotsvith of Gandersheim referred to a letter of Saint Jerome when she had the mother of three virgin martyrs explain that her daughters were now the brides of Christ and that she herself had now become the "mother-in-law" of the heavenly king. Familial structures continued even in heaven. It should have aroused no surprise to report that "a translated saint took his kindred along with him." In the year 839, Saint Felicity was translated from Rome to Saxony; in the next generation one of her sons followed and in 1014 half of the bones of three other sons.

FAMILIAL FORMS OF HIERARCHICAL THOUGHT

The conceptual field of the family was also used to emphasize differences in rank. Designation of the bishop or abbot as spiritual "father," secular clergy or monks as "sons" were common forms of address. The "holy father" was accustomed to address even kings as "most beloved son." This was an expression of honor and of quasi-familial relationship. That ecclesiastics of high rank could be addressed as "brother" even by the pope indicates how little this field was a rationally or legally founded system. It is possible, however, that such forms of address represented practical attempts to overcome problems of rank. Such is the case in a (possibly fictitious) account of a meeting between Otto the Great and John XII in February

962: Otto had invited the pope to come to him in the imperial palace. Hastily convened papal officials decided that it would be reasonable that the father should go out to meet the son, upon which John accepted Otto's invitation.

In this instance the "familial" relationship outweighed considerations of rank; the main thing was neither superiority nor inferiority but rather familial unity, community. Thus a delicate problem could be resolved in such a way that the prestige of the weaker vis-à-vis the stronger could be salvaged. The story may be a kind of instructional anecdote, demonstrating how to solve a difficult problem. Anecdotes of this type occur frequently in courtly literature.

We shall not speak here of the *familia sancti Petri* or papal familiars, for these terms only begin to play an important role in the late Middle Ages, even though Saint Boniface had wanted to acquire *familiaritas* with the pope. We will only touch briefly on the "family of kings," because there is a well-known article on the subject by Franz Dölger. He refers to Byzantium and the Byzantine custom of recognizing Carolingian monarchs and their successors as "brothers." The custom was accepted in the west but not developed further. Why was this? As Arno Borst suggested, "there was no family of kings, because in the western Middle Ages there was no recognized father; the emperor was no more the accepted father than was the pope." Indeed, we have seen that in the application of familial thought such completeness was not always necessary. Rather, we might point to the fact that European princes were actually related to each other in a manner which competed with the system of spiritual kinship. Ottonians, Rudolfings, late Carolingians, and Capetians were cousins, or uncles and nephews, or in-laws—it would have seemed strange if they had called each other "brother." How long the Byzantine custom reflected courtly thought is shown by a curious example from the events leading to the Crimean War: the new French emperor Napoleon III complained to Czar Nicolas I that the czar denied him the title of brother and simply gave him that of friend.

It has been correctly noted that familial structures in the early Middle Ages were the most important framework for thought and actions; those things which went beyond it were often expressed in "familial" aspects. Much more than today, people lived in and with their family; hence the family was the most important category for understanding one's environment. What has changed since then can be measured, among other ways, by considering that nepotism has changed from a practical virtue to a term of abuse and that we speak of overcrowding when more than two persons must live in a single room. In the past one lived, so to speak, in the plural, and this was true not only of peasants but also of the lord. The plan of Saint Gall shows a spacious house intended for the abbot; yet nine beds are drawn in his bedroom. This was not an ascetic decision; it was simply a matter of wanting one's people at hand, even at night. We set no great store on eating in a crowded dining room, and even less on spending the night in a common bedroom. In the tenth century it was a punishment to make a monk dine alone. Family, *familia*, and kin provided what remains today of greatest importance to children: human proximity and security.

III·NOBILITAS

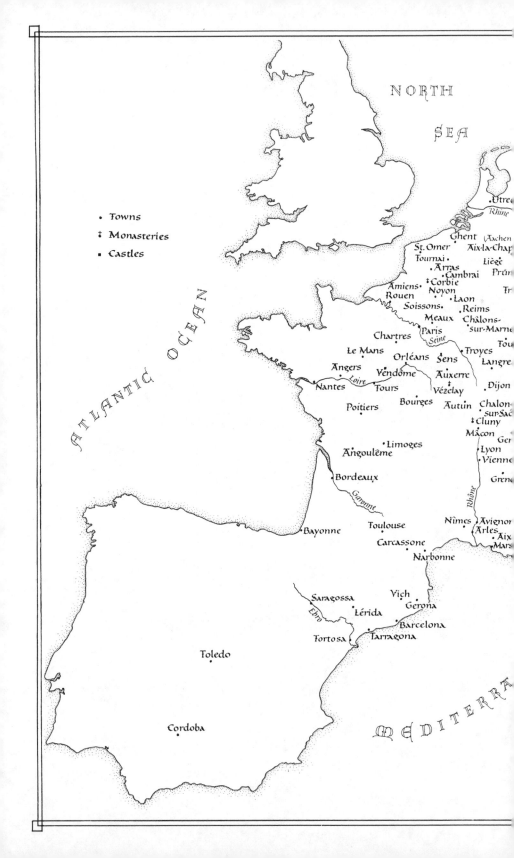

BALTIC SEA

Hamburg
Bremen
Verden
Havelberg
Minden
Brandenburg
Weser
Osnabrück
Münster
Paderborn
Magdeburg
Merseburg
Dortmund
Cologne
Bonn
Coblenz
Frankfurt
Fulda
Schweinfurt
Würzburg
Bamberg
Worms
Lorsch
Erfurt
Meissen
Prague
Strasbourg
Ulm
Eichstätt
Freising
Augsburg
Danube
Passau
Salzburg
Constance
Basel
St. Gallen
Rhine

Kingdom of Denmark
March of the Billungs
North March
Kingdom of England
Duchy of Saxony
March of Meissen
Duchy of Normandy
Duchy of Lower Lorraine
Duchy of Franconia
Duchy of Bohemia
Duchy of Upper Lorraine
Duchy of Bavaria
County of Anjou
County of Blois
Duchy of Burgundy
Duchy of Aquitaine
Kingdom of Burgundy
Duchy of Carinthia
Kingdom of Hungary
Kingdom of Castille
K. of Navarre
Duchy of Gascony
Lombardy
Romagna
Tuscany
Spoleto
Benevento
County of Toulouse
Duchy of Barcelona
Salerno

Trent
Belluno
Bergamo
Verona
Ivera
Milan
Vercelli
Cremona
Mantua
Venice
Pavia
Po
Parma
Modena
Genoa
Bologna
Ravenna
Lucca
Florence
Pisa
Arezzo
Siena
Perugia
Spoleto
Tiber
Rome
Monte Cassino
Bari
Naples

ADRIATIC SEA

0   50   100   Miles
0   50   100   Kms

· FRED O. CALDO · MCMXC ·

7 ❧ THE NOBLE

WHILE KINGSHIP AND FEUDALISM WERE AT the center of German scholarly interest only a few decades ago, by the 1980s the focal point had become the study of the nobility. Much has been written about the existence and nature of the nobility, its origins in the Carolingian period, and the position of its members in the tenth century as holders of offices and privileges. Was there actually a nobility in the tenth century? Some legal historians and legally oriented social historians have denied it insofar as nobility is defined as a class (or rank) which possessed certain privileges by reason of birth and which was closed to lower levels of society.

The closure from below comes to light in the later Middle Ages; in the tenth century it is found only in specific regions.

Before the twelfth century, then, we may speak of a "developing nobility," or an aristocracy. That there was an upper stratum that exercised lordship can be denied only if "lordship" is understood as free and unlimited dominion. Every medieval lordship was limited; it was placed under God and under the law, and even the unfree were therefore not entirely without rights. Whether the term "lordship" can be applied to all the members of a familial structured stratum called nobility although lordship was exercised only by one or the other of its sixteen members is another question. Marc Bloch denied the existence of nobility as a legal "class" during the "first feudal period," but accepted its existence as a *classe sociale*. Such a view is not supported by the sources: they provide ambiguous information concerning the question of whether a legitimate son of a castellan (*seigneur châtelain*) in France who had no claim to inherit the castle could be regarded as noble. This ambiguity is connected with the contemporary use of the word *nobilis*, which we shall discuss below.

Our investigation touches this complex of problems only tangentially. While most scholars strive for conceptual clarity, our task is to seek medieval "popular understandings" in all the richness of their connotations and in all their vagueness. Not being the product of an intellectualism which has excluded emotions, they touch the deeper levels of the personality. Many of these concepts are ideals specific to a particular social stratum. Fame and honor cannot be sought by servants, since they lack the prerequisites. In what follows we will deal with the content of words that appear in the sources under the collective term *noblis*. First, we must briefly discuss the word *noblis* itself.

Noble and *Nobilis*

Nobilis is usually translated as "noble" (*adelig*). This is correct as long as one understands the term in its oldest and widest sense. In the great German dictionary published by the brothers Grimm, of which the first volume appeared in 1854, nobility (*Adel*) is "an advantage of rank and race . . . , hence dignity and sublimity"; noble (*adelig*) means "nobly born, from the nobility . . . ; more properly however we separate from the mere advantage of social status that of the inner man . . . ; a person of high rank is hence not automatically noble." The authors quote in this context expressions such as "nobility of soul" and the proverb, "Nobility is found in the heart, not in the blood."

Since the Enlightenment, the "mere" advantages of high status have ranked far below the nonmaterial qualities that indicate nobility, in a manner that had been fostered in the Middle Ages by ecclesiastical tradition: God does not recognize earthly advantages; he recognizes no distinction between noble and commoner. Heavenly glory puts earthly nobility in the shade; earthly nobility was created not by nature but by ambition. Through sin, the lord becomes a servant; through righteousness, the servant becomes a lord.

Thus two things must be differentiated: *nobilitas carnis* (noble blood), and spiritual nobility, *animi mores*. Did a man of noble ancestry have expectations of spiritual nobility? Under the influence of ecclesiastical critics no one dared to assert this explicitly. Still, many sources proclaimed both in one individual as though this was self-evident. Later, in the thirteenth century, an author wrote an entire treatise on spiritual nobility. With scholastic thoroughness he differentiated between men who unknowingly possessed spiritual nobility, those who knew of this nobility but failed to transform the knowledge into action, and finally those who were "fully noble" since they united in themselves possession and knowledge, and *nobilitas animi* determined their entire activities. Thus it was not sufficient to possess the two other forms of nobility: the physical kind (ancestry and noble appearance), and the *nobilitas fortune,* under which the author placed lordship (*dominium*), fame, and riches.

Full nobility includes the entire person; it is the "noble nature" as opposed to the legal historian's understanding of the term, which is restricted to ancestry and lordship. He who did not act "nobly" lost the right to the epithet *nobilis;* inversely, many had the right to it who could not boast of any ancient forefathers. All of these expressions concern individuals, while "noble" in the modern sense focuses on families. Further, "being noble" is susceptible of gradation—something other than higher or lower rank in the nobility. In the charters of the Mâconnais, as in the writings of the chronicler Rodulfus Glaber—and not only there—*nobilis,* in Georges Duby's formulation, is "a comparative": one person is "nobler" than another. For an earlier period the opinion was held that "the gradation that is reflected in the progression from '*nobilis–nobilior–nobilissimus*' is to be understood as levels of a higher or lower noble quality," in which nobility is judged according to the noble birth. If *praenobiles* or *nobilissimi* appear next to *nobiles* in many sources, these are social qualifications which neither have nor need to have any ranking character. Such epithets are often affected by a certain inflation, so that we must deal cautiously with them. In the book of miracles of Sainte Foy of Conques, for example, *nobiles* from various counties are presented, although the author could not have been aware of the position of these men's kindred in their own region. People from the fairly broad middle stratum (*mediocres*) are seldom mentioned, and one has the impression that the sources present society in black and white. In Catalonia around the year 1000, two entirely separate "classes" can be said to have existed. The members of the one were designated as *maximi, maiores,* or *nobiles,* while the others were presented as *minimi, minores,* or *inferiores.* Not only people could be *nobiles:* authors liked this word so much that one author played on it for rhetorical effect: in the same sentence *nobilis* was applied to the king, a castle, and a monastery. If we recall that in later centuries one could even write of a *nobilissima vina* (a noble vintage), we see in what direction this word was leading, both then and on into the nineteenth century. It has finally come into common use, without any deeper meaning.

We can hardly translate *nobile castrum* as "castle of the nobility," or *nobilis abbatia* as "monastery of the nobility," or *nobilis vir* as "nobleman" in the strict sense. This *mot passe-partout* (as Marc Bloch calls it) can nearly always be rendered as "noble," in the sense of the German word *edel,* but this is not much help. Once again we must fill the empty husk of this word with the different meanings it once had in people's understanding. We shall not speak of the nobility of this or of any century, nor of an upper social stratum, but rather of the image or images that people had of the "noble man," of the high qualities of outstanding persons (and families). Strictly speaking, this was the concept of the ecclesiastic who held the stilus, but we can believe that the picture was shared by other groups of society. It was certainly valid within the upper strata, from which the nobleman (in the strict sense) was recruited. What was at first a hazy image was solidified, at the time of the formation of social ranks, into the ideal of a social order and a principle for the conduct of one's life.

The Essence of Nobility

"Nobility of spirit" could only be developed within a nobly built body. The ideal image of the noble was that he was "handsome" or "of elegant stature." To this was added a behavior which was "seemly" and "attractive," not "repulsive," since the lord formed the center of a great circle of people. As an officeholder too, he had every reason to make friends with his subordinates. He had to be able to rely on his people as could Duke Eberhard of Franconia, of whom Widukind wrote that his vassals had stood by him, through every outrage, because Eberhard was "of bright disposition, affable toward inferiors, lavish in his generosity." The words *affabilis* and *incundus* recur frequently as indicators of quality in the personalities of leaders. We think of a courtly style of life when Bishop Thietmar describes his predecessor as "wise in council, amusing in social gatherings." Later, chivalry tried to reduce human emotions by the virtue of *mesure* or *mâze*, that is, appropriate reactions. Such an attitude is already apparent in the observation that Queen Mathilda never mourned or laughed "beyond measure" (*ultra modum*). A count is praised because his speech was moderated by *mediocritas* and *discretio*. Everything had to take place within the confines of custom and to conform to that *decet* frequently encountered in proverbs. Everyone was to control himself and to watch over the comportment of others.

The cultivation of manners in daily life created the expectation that a noble would also behave properly in war. Here several changes had occurred. True, the original type of hero who "with his own hand" slew "an unbelievable number" of enemies had not disappeared. But a more important type had emerged—one who in critical situations could keep calm, give an example to others, and accomplish objectives through disciplined activity. Indeed, military activity was called *disciplina militaris*. Disordered crowds which fought wildly had no military value. When Vikings arrived at the monastery of Prüm, the "ignoble populace" (*ignobile vulgus*) met them and were slaughtered "like cattle" because *disciplina militaris* was alien to them. The popular militia had lost its value; what was needed was small, militarily powerful contingents of nobles.

For the Romans, *virtus*, virility, was above all military prowess, and the greatest of all virtues. To this *virtus* were added other "virtues"; only slowly did they take a form satisfying to philosophers. Both for the Romans and for the Germans, war was certainly not "the father of all things"; yet through it one was put to the most serious test. More easily in war than in any civilian activity, one could recognize qualities that appeared essential and were widely praised: even monastic schoolboys were glad to hear and write about military deeds. Through them one earned "immortal" fame; without them, life was tedious and prosaic.

The desire for fame is seen today as the yearning of an immature personality; it is certainly not as necessary as it once was for young warriors. They had to demonstrate their "nobility" and could do so—as long as they had neither wealth nor office to control—only through military ability. The quest for proving themselves often consumed them. When Duke Hermann accomplished great military exploits in Saxony, his success so angered Ekkart, the son of Liudolf, "that he swore to accomplish still greater ones or to depart this life." He showed in an exaggerated manner what was actually a necessity for the "noble": to measure one's self against others and to surpass them when possible, an assignment undertaken today only by athletes. There was no prize and no fixed ranking; nevertheless respect carried great weight. People flocked to a famous man; he qualified for offices and fiefs, his voice was heard by the great, and his daughters had better marriage opportunities. Things should be seen in this context, just as fame in warfare cannot be considered in isolation from other forms of testing. Epics—the *Waltharius* and later the chansons de geste—offer only a small slice of the noble life, and that in exaggerated, one-sided form. If there were people who strove above all to wound or kill others in an honorable manner, such heroes were hardly a model for the nobleman. His aims were broader.

Another test of nobility was "practical knowledge (*scientia*), the administration of everything which pertains to the house." It was the knowledge of a wealthy farmer who did not work the land himself but who understood something of all the various activities and agricultural necessities. It could not have been easy to pass scrutiny under the eyes of "specialists" and to surpass them. Farming and cattle raising were considered of prime importance; followed by the control of servants and mastery of the "various crafts which are necessary for the diverse sorts of equipment." A man had to know how to build a mill, how to operate an oven, a wine press, etc., without material loss. There was still no nobility "without crops and land," and well into the modern period people in this position ranked behind those with property who resided on their estates. Even today the landed gentry enhance their prestige when they concern themselves with their estates, however unimportant such a concern may be from a material perspective.

Is this work? We learn from medieval sources that work is more something for servants than for the free, and that in no circumstance should peasants be idle, while outstanding warriors who later entered monasteries should have to do there the work of servants. It does not follow that idleness was a privilege of warriors and clerics. *Labor* referred to primitive, "servile" manual labor, not work in general; the *laboratores* mentioned in Italian royal charters and elsewhere were agricultural workers. The work of servants was contrasted both with idleness and, at the opposite pole, with the achievements of skilled artisans, and with administrative activities of all kinds. For "intellectual work" there was no special term. The landed warrior whose property did not adequately support him could least afford idleness: he entered the service of a magnate, who assigned him military or other duties. It was up to the lord whether to allow his man to sit idle; the basic military rule that troops should never be unoccupied was probably already in force. The goal of such a person was in any case to improve his material situation through activities. For younger sons who otherwise had no means of establishing a house, this was even truer.

THE *HONOR*: OFFICE, LAND, PEOPLE

When Ademar of Chabannes describes an esteemed person, he speaks of his rich paternal inheritance, the *honor,* meaning his (proprietary) churches and estates; to this, Ademar adds the "great troops of vassals (militum) who hold fiefs from him." The *honor* was originally an office; then the office with all that belonged to it, such as the comital estates; and now—not only for Ademar—the whole complex of riches. The word, which in its primary meaning designated the honor and prestige of an outstanding person, underwent this transformation for good reason: the material existence and social value of the holder depended on the possession of the office, fiefs, and, of course, inherited property. The *honor* of a king consisted of office and dignities as well as the respect he enjoyed, the deference paid him by subordinates. Honor had to be constantly expressed in gestures of respect, it had to be "celebrated."

For the Champagne region it has been shown that the word *nobilis* is usually connected with the nobility's characteristic wealth. Today the two terms are not considered to belong together. They have even been transformed: spiritual nobles in the modern sense need no pomp, and modern wealth is rather an abstract power residing in industrial or commercial property and partnerships, not primarily in "visible riches" in the framework of a necessary representation. This value was measured by the number of followers and size of the *familia* as well as by military qualities—excellent horses, weapons, and fortifications. Display did not fulfill its purpose unless the lord demonstrated generosity always and everywhere. He had to spend when necessary, and he had to do so abundantly. Thrift, the later bourgeois virtue, was a disgrace for the elite. To accumulate goods for times of emergency was acceptable—the granary was opened for the poor when crops failed—but everything else should return to the people. It was not normal to hoard money in this rural society, and anyone who did acquire it usually sought to transform it into something impressive.

Noble manners and noble metal, outside the daily experience of average people, fired their imagination and appeared connected to each other in a deeper sense. The clerical recipient of a versified saint's life wrote to the author that the poem was like a heavenly treasure: just as bright silver smiles upon the sevenfold bright gold, the author had in nobly (*nobiliter*) conprehended the noble life of the noble Rictrud in noble words. Gold and silver were indications of social differentiation and only secondarily of material value. The clarity (*claritas*) of precious metal and its luster symbolized noble manners and had "symbolic character": the public display of gold and silver in the secular world implied rank.

In a rural society, wealth often had to take modest forms. Burchard of Worms noted that a rich person had to pay penalties only twice as high as the penalties of a poor person and about seven times as high as those of a "very poor person"; income is not estimated as very high. Wealth primarily meant possessing a quantity of (not very intensively worked) land and control over the people who lived off this land. There was little agricultural surplus and few means to sell it at a profit. The situation was different where flourishing commerce and craftwork led to the creation of working capital. We learn of luxuries for the prominent, particularly from Italian sources, along with evidence of a significant monetized economy. From Rome, a tenth-century chronicler tells us that "Queen Money" bestowed nobility and beauty there. Elsewhere, the path to a certain material comfort had only just been embarked on. At the beginning of the eleventh century, the castles in Catalonia were still cramped and poorly furnished, hardly better or even worse than the houses of peasants; the only luxuries were weapons and fine horses, which were both symbols of rank and military necessities.

Anyone who wished to increase his prestige needed more people and hence more cultivated land; uncultivated land brought little revenue, and the lord could best use it for hunting. Even more important than a populous *familia* was the command of numerous vassals. In troubled times, vassals could exercise pressure on neighboring powers or maintain a balance of power with them; in times of peace they increased the political power of their own lord at the royal or ducal court—the lord could put this military potential at his disposition and thereby secure his candidacy for new fiefs. It was popular to lure away one or the other of the vassals of weaker lords with promises or sometimes with force. The victims of this political ploy were often ecclesiastical lordships. At Cambrai, after the death of its bishop in 1012, the castellan launched a sort of coup d'etat, depriving the indigenous vassals of their fiefs and replacing them with foreigners. In the view of the chronicler, this was not simply a struggle for power; the castellan was acting "in order to make himself thereby respected and to spread the fame of a good opinion (concerning himself) even as far as the barbarians."

The hunt also numbered among the indicators of wealth, but it was not the exclusive privilege of the lord; not until the twelfth century was hunting forbidden to commoners. Among all the occupations of noblemen, only hunting was called an amusement. Moreover, it served as a military exercise and a social activity. A lord would invite guests, hold conferences with them, and go hunting with them much as diplomats do today. If this was idleness, it was nonetheless one of its most exhausting forms.

As there was plenty of land to be cultivated, a lord was less concerned with increasing its productivity than with increasing the number of people who lived on his estates. The number of servants indicated social rank; by it, one distinguished between *pauper* and *potens*. On the other hand, the lord was not to be a nouveau riche. Normally, riches were inherited, the powerful man was "rich in paternal inheritance," as the name of bishop Udalrich of Augsburg was interpreted. Wealth alone was insufficient, of course; one needed personal merit too in order to be respected, and a number of vassalic followers. Seldom did these followers form a closed group when treating with their lord; solidarity appeared only when they were defending or expanding the prestige and position of their lord. The vassals of the Saxon margrave almost took the bishop of Halberstadt prisoner because he had confiscated a hunting falcon of one of the margrave's clerics; they considered this act an insult to their lord, and to the whole group.

Honor did not concern simply the individual; its violation led to a chain reaction, and if the king had not intervened, as was the case in the above situation, a feud would have been imminent. Ecclesiastics reproached the attitude of secular lords as arrogance, although without success even in difficult times. It was merely outward appearance; in fact, they were often afraid of a decrease in the fragile social prestige. Part of its fragility lay in the suspicion with which anyone who succeeded too much was regarded. Envy was to be found even within the family: there was fear of appearing inferior to a more fortunate brother. The inclination to fight with all possible means for position made itself felt. Rather of Verona indicated that in Northern Italy, even among cathedral canons, only a very powerful, rich, and "wild" man had a chance of winning a position as high as that of bishop. Certainly there were peace-loving, prudent magnates who looked to the general welfare; they could guarantee peace in their region in cooperation with central authority as long as this cooperative effort continued to function. If the ruler was absent, however, either because of Germano-Italian politics or if there were two rival dynasties such as in France, then "wild" powers outside of central authority could contest their rank and power differences almost unhindered. Such a contest took place under Otto III on the lower Rhine, where two families and their allies fought over precedence and *potentatus.* In the background stood the imperial court on one hand, and the archbishop of Cologne on the other. In Franconia at the beginning of the century there had been a famous feud between the Babenberg family and the Conradines, which was conducted with "unquenchable hatred" and had been triggered by a contest between the two families over their respective renown. Both parties prized their *nobilitas carnis,* the great number of their kin, the extent of their seignorial estates; and soon it came to murder and bloodshed.

Pedigree

This all sounds very "old Germanic." The panegyric on one's own greatness existed among the Anglo-Saxons as a ritualized custom. In antiquity, the panegyric not on oneself but on others was cultivated; this too required reference to ancestors. The whole thing was disapproved by Christian moralists. A tenth-century author explained to his readers that a genealogical tree is like a real tree whose branches are already dry. The tree is admired not for its branches but for its roots, which are still fresh. He who admires roots in this fashion shows that he belongs to those who only know things of the flesh (worldly things). And nobility of blood disappears like smoke. For

Christians, only their own acts matter, not those of their forefathers. There are plenty of instances in which God raised up a shepherd or a fisherman to rule, while destroying power and nobility.

We are accustomed to explaining the term "noble" by the noble family tree, that is the sum of noble ancestors, rather as in the old Habsburg monarchy one needed a sufficient number of noble quarterings to receive particular court offices or endowments. Such was not the case in the tenth century, since the concept of nobility was not yet formalized. It was only those ancestors which one could admire that mattered: they formed a portion of one's personal fame. In this sense the stereotypical forms of praising a person's ancestry are to be understood. Isidore of Seville contended that a person is noble who has "a name" and whose family (*genus*) "is known"—and thus, we can add, is worth being known. We are reminded of the dialogue between Normans, reported by Dudo of Saint Quentin. They asked each other "questions about their ancestry, prominence, and the esteem they enjoyed from others." The esteem of one's fellows constituted a person's worth, and it also incorporated the "value" of ancestors who lived on in that person. The living "represented" their ancestors with their own qualities; thus it could justifiably be said that the designation *noblis, nobilissimus* referred primarily to the ancestors' fame.

We saw in part 1 that tenth-century authors selected from among their ancestors and kinsmen quite subjectively. They most often chose holders of ecclesiastical and worldly office, war heroes, shrewd advisers, pilgrims to Jerusalem, rich heirs from famous families—a mix of people whose only common quality was fame or reputation.

Speaking of noble ancestry implied the sum of such persons. There were various ways of bringing together a sum of persons into the kind of unity that we today call a clan. One way derived from evidence that the group was a *nobilis prosapia*, a *genus* that "was known." In any case, we must remain conscious of the difference between then and now in this area: today a noble has a specific number of ancestors, calculated from the moment of ennoblement (nobility of the robe, *Briefadel*) or from the recognizable beginning of a noble style of life (nobility of the sword, *Uradel*). At that time a royal chancellery did not have the right to grant patents of nobility; *nobilis* was anyone so designated by his contemporaries. A distant parallel to this situation was that of saints, who were recognized as such by the faithful without need of papal permission. This was true, for example, of Bruno, archbishop of Cologne and brother of Otto the Great, who even to this day is venerated in his diocese as a saint. His biographer Ruotger said that "his exploits are still fresh in memory, and none of his people to whom truth and faith are sacred will ever cease to speak of him." Such formulations would have applied equally well to worldly nobility. How important fame or reputation was for the elite of this period was can be seen in the fact that this term was used in the giving of names, as in the case of Hrotsvitha of Gandersheim, whose name means "strong in (or by) fame."

We have already spoken of the rhetorical element in the lives of saints and have shown that the popular term *noblis* called for an expansion and had a comparative and a superlative degree. One must be particularly careful with such generalized expressions; "noble origins" can atrophy into a commonplace. Ruotger rhetorically exaggerated the particularly distinguished ancestry of the emperor's brother Bruno: "His great-grandparents and their great-grandparents (*attavorum eius attavi*) were all of the highest nobility (*nobilissimi*) from time immemorial. Anyone who was not outstanding or who became degenerate could hardly find a place in his clan (*stirpe*). But he (Bruno) excelled them all in every respect." Yet this example suggests that the author intended to describe an exception, that is, that the "stirps" of a noble was not normally composed only of outstanding members, and that one or another might be recognized as unworthy (*degener*). Further, it indicates that the fame of ancestry was not alone sufficient; an individual must have his own deeds in order to prove *nobilitas*. Probably not only a criminal would be considered *degener*, but anyone who was devoid of any achievements.

It was congruent with the self-perception of the period that not only clans and individuals but an entire tribe could be acknowledged as having noble ancestry. One traced one's origins either to an outstanding *stirps*—the Franks, for example, could be seen as the descendants of the Trojan kings—or to a famous tribe: according to Widukind, the Saxons were either Vikings, or Greeks from the army of Alexander the Great; whichever the case might be, he continued, they were without doubt an ancient and noble people. The fame of these ancestors reflected on the entire Saxon people and thus on each of its members.

The virtues and deeds of a clan or a people were sometimes seen as a sort of aura, which German scholars call *Heil* (*Konigsheil*, *Sippenheil*, and so on). It was a matter of good luck and prosperity, detached from rational causes: everything went well with members of such clans, and so it was good for everybody to be around them. Such concepts were to be found not only in Germanic tribes; they lived on wherever archaic thought was not altered by rationalism. So the Saxon Widukind was convinced of the notorious luck of some clans, especially that of the royal family. One finds a similar concept in the Normans; Dudo of Saint-Quentin reproduces a dialogue in which a West-Frankish count asks a Norman, "What good luck, what fortune, what abilities (or means) do you have and did the founders of your race possess?" The question of the *origo* was also asked and answered by Widukind. As we have seen, he referred not to a single mythical progenitor from whom this aura of prosperity descended, but rather to a group of men favored by destiny and whose deeds "were known."

In the Frankish area, such things receded behind others, and we have already suggested that the senatorial nobility in Gaul transmitted ancient Roman virtues to the Early Middle Ages. Modified by Christianity, these virtues retained their value among the high ecclesiastics of the Frankish kingdom and entered the vitae of bishops of the Merovingian period. When these men's noble origins and noble nature were described, their *nobilitas* was presented in the form of both stoic and Christian-eremitic comportment, without entirely excluding the various other elements. For the laity there was not yet an independent Christian lay ethic. Though directed to the Bible, the laity tended to adhere to the customs of their region and tribe. The nature and particularities of later chivalry are debated, but it is clear that a new ethos of Christian knighthood began to develop in the eleventh century.

SPIRITUAL CARES

Before the eleventh century, anyone wishing to lead an especially Christian life had to embrace monastic ideals, as Louis the Pious and the Aquitanian mirrors of princes had done. An individual ethic was at play here, without reference to origin and clan, in stark contrast to the martial *virtus* of the heroic epic. We can assume that monasticism had very little interior effect on the elite, since it would have constantly led to conflicts. The monastic hagiography of the period has only rarely transmitted images of magnates who either lived or who were supposed to have lived according to such ideals. The only examples are Otto III as described by Brun of Querfurt, King Robert the Pious by Helgaud of Fleury, and Count Gerald of Aurillac in the *vita* written by Abbot Odo of Cluny. It goes without saying that the personality of the emperor was very imperfectly understood when presented in this manner, and the same is true of King Robert. There remains the count of Aurillac, who "devoted himself to a monastic life (*religionis proposito*) in secular dress," wore a secret tonsure, never touched his sword, etc. If Odo of Cluny hoped thus to create a generally valid ideal, he hardly succeeded; in any case we know of nothing of the kind. Piety could only become a true lifestyle in old age, if one managed to reach such an age that permitted contemplation of the next life. What Odo of Cluny actually accomplished was that a part of his own kindred entered the order, as well as the "famous robber" Aimoin, leader of forty bandits, who entered the monastery on Odo's advice.

Generally, a middle way between worldly obligations and spiritual concerns was sought through endowing churches. The idea of purchasing salvation with land was often expressed rather bluntly by the use of biblical citations, but it was not such a simple matter for people of the time. What was sought was spiritual assistance through *oratores* charged primarily with the obligation of prayer. The laity had to be responsible for their support by means of contributions. Since a pious donation was usually bound to an obligation to pray for specific persons, it was a kind of neighborly assistance: the monk had a primary obligation to save his own soul; his spiritual obligation, however, allowed him to seek the same for his less pious fellow humans. One might believe that his prayer had particular power when made on behalf of kinspersons and friends.

Those who could afford it were wise to found a monastery, since the founder and his family stood first in rank among the beneficiaries of prayers. One could also have oneself buried in a monastery, preferably close to the altar. A monastery could provide a childless couple with "spiritual descendants" and a prolific couple with means of support for sons or daughters. The altars and the graves of ancestors were the center of gravity in the continuing transformation of a clan's property and formation. Canonical pronouncements required that properties donated to the monastery be transferred to the bishop, but was it not frivolous thus to weaken the family wealth? Many monasteries would never have been endowed had this obligation actually been observed. When, around the turn of the year 1000, a particularly large number of monasteries were founded in northern Italy, the primary reason was a need to provide for spiritual protection within the growing aristocracy, facilitated by the increasing material means. People needed intercessors against the evil in this and in the next world. The development was even more rapid in Saxony, where, between 919 and 1024, thirty-six religious houses for women were founded. In many parts of the former Frankish kingdom, the heyday of such foundations was already past; many came into the hands of bishops or large abbeys, or fell into royal possession, which resulted in decreasing interest of the former founding families.

One is tempted to perceive the spiritual remembrance of the dead in the same way that remembrance is important for the historian: as a prophylactic against oblivion. Sometimes such tendencies really existed: the life of Saint Odilia states that a man brought the saint three young trees with the request that she plant them in the earth. Upon seeing them, later kinspersons were to remember him. Secular remembrance of this kind and religious commemoration operated at two entirely different levels, yet could be found side by side: Bishop Udalrich of Augsburg lived on in the memory of the people through minstrels and was nevertheless a canonized saint. As such he no longer needed intercessory prayers; quite to the contrary, he was invoked as intercessor for the living. Udalrich's predecessor Adalbero was in a more difficult position; he appeared to a cathedral canon, asking him to see to it that the established intercessory prayers were performed for him assidously. If the canons should be negligent in them, they would have to render account for it before God. A hermit in Africa was reported to have said that the importance of the Cluny monastery for Christendom lay in the fact that it was the best place for freeing souls from the domination of the devil.

Cluny provided spiritual assistance to the living and the dead by remembering them during the Mass, by frequent appealing to the saints in prayer, and by toasting them. Prayer, liturgical offering for the "poor souls," and the so-called *caritas* drinking—in all three activities, ancient, pre-Christian concepts played a role. Also present was the desire to associate oneself with the spirits of the departed in a particular way, ideally to become related to them. This idea was not inappropriate for Christians of this period, because one could certainly have a noncanonized saint, revered by popular opinion, as a kinsman. When miracles took place on the grave of an abbot or a monk from the founder's family, everything possible was done to give him the highest honor. The same was true, of course, for saintly bishops: In 982 the brothers Folquin and Regenwala came from Lorraine to the monastery of Saint-Bertin in order to be present at the elevation of the remains of Bishop Folquin of Thérouanne, who had been a brother of their grandfather. Folquin, a son of the above-mentioned

Folquin, served as a monk of Saint-Bertin, and he commemorated this event in his chronicle.

Even if they were not saints, one needed kin in heaven where one hoped eventually to be received and aided by them. It would have been a bad situation if one of the kin had not won eternal rest with God. To avoid such an eventuality required copious intercessory prayers.

In Cluny, all the bells were rung when Mass was celebrated on the first Monday of Lent for the dead kin of the monks and the associates of the monastery. Afterwards, in the refectory, the monks received in their memory (*pro illorum defunctorum amore*) more food and drink than usual. A similar celebration occurred for the commemoration of benefactors of the monastery on the anniversary of their death. Members of various clans were here assembled into a "fictive kindred," which included the living along with the dead. The spiritual community of prayer grew constantly, as did the community of the table: when a monk died at Cluny, his rations were given to a pauper, who was supposed to pray for the deceased monk. Elsewhere, things were done in less systematic a fashion, but the basic idea was the same. Thus, after the death of a monk in Reichenau around 1016, a Mass was celebrated for him every day for one month, and a large number of paupers were fed.

There were also prayer confraternities of secular clerics, which included an aristocratic element. For example, three German archbishops and a dozen imperial bishops bound themselves at the synod of Dortmund, which we have already spoken of. The emperor and empress were included in the confraternity. At the death of the archbishop of Bremen, a prominent member of the group, Henry II expressed regret, but then immediately announced his joy that he now had an intermediary (in heaven). The dead archbishop had received much assistance from the living members of the group; now he had to return it, first of all in the interest of the king.

When Thietmar inserted reports of important people into his chronicle, he did so not to enhance their reputation but rather for spiritual purposes. As a German scholar put it, "It is the intervention of the dead that Thietmar anticipates as payment for his form of commemoration." The same was true for the author's six confessions of sin in his work; they were to encourage the reader to pray for him. Thietmar's concern for a memorial has even been seen as "a central motivation of his historical writing," a sort of "pastoral care through obligation for commemoration and intercessory prayer." If this is so, it was true of a very small circle of persons whom Thietmar describes or who would read his book. Besides them, there were other clerics who were "bound together with him in a confraternity." As Thietmar tells us, he hoped to see God eventually, not by virtue of his works but rather through the aid of these brothers. He may have done little good in this world; nevertheless, he was always mindful of the dead—whose complementary assistance could not be withheld.

Scholars debate Thietmar's part in the "Merseburger Necrology" which contains names of many ecclesiastical and lay magnates; its source has been thought to have been a lost "royal necrology," which arose from familial notations of the Liudolfing and the Saxon dynasty. A necrology commemorated the dead according to the date of their death, so that everyone could pray for them on this date. The other type of commemoration was the "memorial book," which presented lists of the living and the dead in their natural contexts of convents, clans, etc. Although this is a difficult group of sources for historians, it made things easier for contemporaries, who could use the books to remember cumulatively all the persons recorded in them. In the Carolingian period an attempt was made to arrange memorial books by strata: either preceding or following the monastic community came the members of the royal family, bishops, abbots, priests, laity. Family and clan groups soon came to predominate; in the words of Karl Schmid, "The basic entries in the memorial books were overgrown with entries of natural communities." The first type, the necrology, achieved universal acceptance in the course of the eleventh century, and it would be too simplistic to explain this transformation with "the growth of individualism" in the period. Rather, it was related to the monks' greater accuracy in fulfilling their obligations. In Cluny, where more than ten thousand dead had to be recorded, it became the rule to enter them according to the date of their death.

The organized process of commemoration was supplemented by literary commemoration; here it was left to chance who should be invited to offer prayers for the dead. The shortest form of such prayers are the tomb inscriptions in a more or less refined Latin form and as such intended for the elite. Most of the ones that we have were transmitted not on monuments but in manuscript form. Let us consider just one of them, probably referring to Count Kunibert of Lomello. At its conclusion the reader is asked to beseech God for the salvation of the deceased. Intermediaries should ask the Heavenly King for grace. The text is also characteristic in another way: it shows how official mourning for the dead had a fixed literary form. Its statement that not only the people followed this custom but even the elite (*proceres*) wept for him (*fleverunt*) may be considered a mere topos. We also see some new accents in the image of the nobility in that Kunibert belonged to the urban nobility, and his son was appointed count of the city in Pavia. Nothing is said of the military virtues of the deceased; *virtus* is used here as a term in connection with the protection of the rights of the burgers. The world was beginning to change. We hear of Kunibert's generosity; it was still a virtue, but nothing is said of vassals. The emphasis on the truthfulness of the count is new. It applies only to friends, however, which may surprise the modern reader. We shall see below that cunning behavior had its admirers. The city was less a place of powerful military actions than of clever transactions.

FIDELITY, VASSALAGE, FEUDALISM

Such statements are based on the conceptual horizon that must now be discussed: *fides, fidelis*. These concepts are often discussed in connection with feudalism, and can be dealt with briefly here. *Fides* designated faith in God and fidelity to an earthly lord. One could be a *fidelis* of Christ, of an earthly king, or of a member of the elite. Faithfulness is a two-sided attitude as a (new) covenant with God or an engagement with men with whom one is not naturally related. It is never a relationship between equals; The partners are distinct in rank. A new human bond is created beside that of kinship and "friendship," or of the patriarchal power over servants, or of the military-political obligation of obedience to the king or his officer. Fidelity is something like all of these and yet different.

A new period in the history of fidelity began when, in 858, Charles the Bald and his *fideles* swore oaths to each other. King and magnates of his kingdom stood almost on the same level when he swore, as "faithful king" (*fidelis rex*), to take his faithful men into his protection. Just as important is the definition of the obligation of his men: through their office and with their person the *fidelis* would be a helper (*adiutor*) of the king, without deceit or seduction (*dolositate aut seductione*), with advice and aid (*consilio et auxilio*). Likewise the lord would protect his *fidelis* without falsity and in righteousness, would allow "honors" to come to him (or would honor him—*honorabo*), and would show him "mercy" so far as was allowable. Above all, this meant carrying out requests and granting favors.

The power struggle in the form of courtly intrigues, the art of disinformation and diverting supporters—all this was to be replaced by truthfulness and assistance, as later the count of Lomello practiced with his friends. How that was to take place was first explained in such a context in 858. The *fidelis* is an adviser; he informs his *senior* according to his best knowledge and advises appropriate measures. Secondly, he has an active part in their execution. He gives his support to all actions of his lord. On all levels, moral, political, military, and financial, his fate is bound together with that of his senior partner.

To be a *fidelis* was not the privilege of the elite, but it required, as can be seen, disposable means. When Charlemagne ordered his subordinates to swear an oath of fidelity to him as king, his command was directed to servants as well, but only those who held as *honor* fiefs and offices (*ministeria*), or who held an *honor* as vassals with horses and weapons. This meant principally the unfree holders of monastic "offices," the beginning of the ministerials. We must keep this in mind when we read the essentially negative definition of the obligations of fidelity in Fulbert of Chartres: everything one must not do because doing it might harm the lord is here fully explained; only briefly Fulbert adds that the *fidelis* must also provide advice and aid. Some scholars have extracted from this text the negative character of the obligations of fidelity. The reason Fulbert emphasized the negative was probably to be found in the person to whom he addressed his advice: he had been invited to give his opinion by Duke William "the Great" of Aquitaine, who was a very harsh lord for his followers. The duke had said to Hugo Chiliarchus of Lusignan, "You are so much my creature (*tantum ex me tu es*) that I could order you to make a peasant your lord, and you would have to do it . . . You are mine that you might do my will." Alongside the tendency toward equality between lord and man was an opposite tendency, an assertion of the lord's absolute rights. Fulbert could not hope to temper such despotism; but at least he did not give the duke new reasons for his conduct. Around this time, fidelity had lost much of its ethical nature, and not only because of its connection with the fief. These were uncertain times in France, and so this form of covenant was strained even beyond the sphere of fiefs; it was formalized and misused. Every day one swore, so to speak, to act faithfully. Under such circumstances, all that could be expected from an oath was some sort of truce. Churchmen complained that it was impossible to fulfill as many oaths as they had sworn.

Some have thought that counsel and aid derived from the property received by the vassal, not from the oath of fidelity, and have based this opinion on Fulbert. This was not Fulbert's meaning, and it could hardly be true of the magnates who had sworn to give counsel and aid to their king. When, for example, Archbishop Arnulf of Reims sent the Frankish kings Hugh and Robert his written expression of faithfulness along with promises of counsel and aid, it became a political act which was certainly not derived from royal fiefs of the church of Reims. Had it been, the solemn form would have been inappropriate. The archbishop spoke of his own salvation in the face of God and the heavenly host, and the signatures of the clergy he declared as "signs of salvation or of condemnation." Such words do not fit in an essentially profane contract.

Here the oath was intended to regain the weight it had held at the beginning of feudalism. The oath of the archbishop to the two kings was not a sign of "friendship between unequals"; nor was it servile subjection under an almighty lord. Most relationships of fidelity moved between the two extreme positions. Even Duke William of Aquitaine, who had brutally reminded a vassal of his nothingness, could—when the political situation favored it—say to the same vassal: if you will follow my wishes (in renouncing a marriage) "then you will be the first among all my friends with the exception of my son." Following the request, the vassal stepped back from the marriage, supposedly "because of his love and faithfulness (to the duke)." We see from the duke's actions that marriage was not an affair between individuals but concerned two families, that of the vassal and that of the *senior*. These two men were not alone but rather had kin to whom they were related in social connections. Shortly after 840, a concerned mother had admonished her son that he should fear, love, and honor the kindred of his lord and should show them veneration (*obsequium*). This advice probably seemed old-fashioned, but it does indicate that the relationship had not yet become merely a rational or even a commercial affair.

Recent research has made it clear that both vassality and feudalism were of less significance than had been previously thought. From about 930, the magnates of the Mâconnais were no longer designated as vassals but were now called *fideles* of the king; their duties were not specified, and the king had no judicial authority over them. In parts of southern France there was supposedly no vassality at all; in Picardy it did exist, but there the fief played no role. Belief in a pyramidal form of feudal society in France was shown to be unfounded some time ago, and it is generally questioned whether the tenth century should be considered an *époque féodale* at all. We know that in Germany, where the Carolingian order continued into the Ottonian period, feudalism had been incorporated into these institutions but had not really changed them. The situation was at least partially different in Italy, where a greater differentiation developed within the elite, which also manifested itself in categories of vassals. There the close connection between personal and material elements, between vassality and fief, only appeared in the second quarter of the eleventh century, though vassality had formed an important aspect of social valuation even before that time. A social climber was characterized primarily by his vassalic position. We hear, for example, that Adalbert (Atto) of Canossa made the jump from an episcopal vassal to a lord over vassals with comital origins.

In summary, personal factors still took precedence over material ones in the tenth century, such that personal and above all familial relationships were still the foundation of traditional societies. One expressed oneself in a quasi-familial manner when one spoke of a *senior* rather than of a *dominus*. Nevertheless, in vocabulary and hence in the value accorded to institutions there was regional variation, especially in the Germanic countries. In Salzburg tenth-century sources the word *knechtlich*, "servile" (*servilis*) was used for vassalic relations. Since German lacked a formulation parallel to the Romance *senior-seigneur-signore,* the word *Herr* was used, rendered either as *dominus* or as *senior* in Latin texts. German wives spoke of their husbands as their *senior* or their *Herr,* as did chaplains of their bishop. We must not overemphasize regional differences; but a kind of West Frankish form of feudal relationship did exist, which was understood as a mutual contractual relationship, in contrast to the feudal bonds of the Carolingian and even the Ottonian empires. There one was more "conservative" than in the west.

The physical substratum of feudalism had, among other effects, the very important one of holding the family together, often through several generations. While personal property could be divided, the fief had to remain whole, and a fixed pattern of inheritance naturally developed between the two. Allods were given to the church for the salvation of their owners; normally the fief was not included in such donations. On the other hand, inherited property, in parallel to the fief, can likewise be seen as subject to obligations even after a transfer of ownership. In this way the allod was not actually alienated from the family by being donated to a possessory church of this family.

The full development of feudalism in the central regions of the

Frankish kingdom, particularly between the Rhine and the Loire, offered the magnates of the region important opportunities, while elsewhere office and allod remained in the foreground, as in Saxony, central Italy, Aquitaine, and Catalonia. Difficult circumstances in the west encouraged the development of multiple vassality, which in Germany remained the exception. The weight of the vassalic relationship shifted from the human to the economic, from a spontaneous union to technical complexities and a mechanistic order of military service. The "second feudal age" had begun.

8 ❧ THE KING

"EVEN MONARCHY IS, IN ITS ESSENCE, EN-
hanced nobility; the king is the 'first nobleman'
of a 'crowned republic.'" These words of Heinrich Mitteis can be illustrated by Widukind's
justification of the change of dynasties in 919,
after the death of King Conrad I: Fortune (*fortuna*) and very noble customs (*nobilissimi
mores*) were Henry I's portion, and so the
Saxon was elected. A noble clan with outstanding ancestors, personal virtues, riches, and success qualified for kingship, and these qualifications were solemnly recognized by the
governing stratum through the election of the
German kings. Most western European histori-

ans have long viewed medieval history largely from the perspective of monarchy, failing to grasp the obvious roots of monarchy in the nobility. Some have thought that the king might have been a model for the nobleman, or that monarchy and aristocracy followed parallel paths. Certainly monarchy and courtly life had an educational effect on the leading classes, but this was incidental. An example: we know that Charlemagne used to dress as a Frankish noble, and only under his successors did the most important people in the kingdom begin to dress in imitation of regal costume. Except on feast days, Otto the Great always wore native dress in consciousness of the roots from which he thought his government should never too far remove itself.

Kingship and Nobility

Such things appear secondary, but they were extremely important in a period during which an abstract concept of the state had first to be learned. Until then the king "embodied" the kingdom; he was, so to speak, the quintessence of all the nobles who belonged to it. To this end, physical perfection played a great role, for the behavior of the ruler had to correspond in every detail to the native customs; his decisions had to have at least the appearance of having been prepared by "good advisers" from the circle of the ruling elite. On the other hand, the king enjoyed liberties that today would be considered inappropriate in rulers, such as ruling by means of nepotism and favoritism. Indeed, an encomium of Conrad II actually praised the emperor for seeking "with all his power as far as it was possible to support the affairs of his kin and friends no less than his own." Such concern for one's familiars was entirely in accord with the values of the nobility.

Kingship of course was the most important of those institutions which transcended familial and party concepts. It was supposed to serve the common peace, if not always the common good. There might be opposition between the monarch and aristocratic families, which held similar duties through royal commission. Many kept peace in their lands without the king and thus rose to the position of *principes* in these areas. Without the defense provided by clan and "friends," such achievements were seldom possible; the holder of an office from the king expected his kinsmen and "friends" to employ all their means to accomplish their public duties. The king and his family ruled together with the magnates and their families or clans. At least this was the ideal: the role played by internal conflicts both within the royal family and within aristocratic families need not be discussed. It was complained of but accepted as divine judgment. The ruler was often criticized for employing individuals who were not backed by a respected family.

Where the monarchy was still intact, it played an active part in the continuous transformations within the upper strata. In spite of the inheritability of offices, new counts had to be named by the king upon entering their office; the Italian expeditions opened here a wide field of possibilities. The king's favor played a role in the west too, but here, in a monarchy which was largely based on negotiations with the magnates, this favor was narrowly limited. The new kings Hugh Capet and Robert had to tolerate the fact that noblemen denied their legitimacy and with it their authority to appoint counts.

King and royal court worked as a model for the aristocracy, though in differing degrees according to their "nearness to the king" and the strength of the monarchy. In the ninth century this closeness was so important that for the highest stratum of lords the court was the social forum. Many ideas spread from the court, including perhaps the custom of giving children the name of their parents, which became customary among the elite in the tenth century. At that time the aristocracy might be seen as an emanation of kingship. The magnates of the West lived as if they were Carolingians.

In Saxony, the Liudolfings (later known as the Ottonians) began as one noble clan among others. They had first to impart to their fellows the essential fear of royal punishment. The expansion of the dynasty beyond its tribal territory and the introduction into the royal family of foreign princesses instead of the daughters of local magnates made clear the distance between ranks, indeed the chasm which was being formed. It was a great learning process: on the part of the Ottonians the growth into a superregional, Carolingian, and European mission; on the part of the noble clans the duty to recognize a king who was hardly still a Saxon as their lord and the bearer of their political identity. This was especially true in times of crisis. Through civil war, some, if not all, learned that "it was better to perish with a *rex iustus* than to conquer unjustly with one's own kin." This sentence, formulated by Liutprand of Cremona, was new for most of the Saxons.

For the magnates of other regions such an understanding was still more difficult. Arnulf, son of the Bavarian duke Arnulf "the Bad," was incorporated into the royal family by the marriage of his sister with Henry, brother of Otto the Great; he received from the king the office of count palatine in Bavaria. All this occurred in spite of the fact that he had taken part in the fight against Otto in 937/38. When Henry rushed to help his royal brother in the revolt of Liudolf in 953, Arnulf was entrusted with the defense of Bavaria. He joined the rebels and laid Augsburg to waste. He perished under siege in Ratisbon, a man who had never been inwardly reconciled with the Saxon monarchy. His son warned the Hungarians of the arrival of the royal army but nevertheless was not harmed after the battle of the Lechfeld, and only his participation in the revolt of Henry the Garrulous brought him into custody. He may even have been Bavarian count palatine like his father until 976.

The story of the life of count palatine Arnulf indicates that opposition to the monarchy could not find its expression in separatism, but rather required a position of power which only the monarchy could give. Further, as this case indicates, one did not always have the simple choice between the royal house and one's own family; Arnulf could have justified himself with the fact that his brother-in-law Henry, as well as Liudolf, was defending valid claims within the royal family. This internal opposition could not be fully separated from the external; kindreds created the crossover. To fight for the *rex iustus*, even against kin, was a fine goal. First, however, one had to be brought to total conviction that the king was indeed in the right.

Certain nobles and those of the king's sons who remained without inheritance opposed the royal lordship and the indivision of the kingdom. Centrifugal forces had always existed, and monarchy required ideological protection against them. Where the concept of the state was hardly developed, raison d'état could offer little help; even more incomprehensible would have been the modern historical perspective that the king acted in the interest of historical development. What contemporaries did understand and take very seriously was the sacral foundation of kingship.

The most impressive means to this was the Aix-la-Chapelle consecration of Otto the Great, the "elect of God," by two archbishops. Secondary coronations on the days of the principal Christian feasts manifested the religious background of the dynasty, as did ostentatious visits to churches and other evidence of royal piety. The same was true of the Capetian monarchy, which in its second generation would emphasize such things even more strongly. The life of Robert "the Pious" is stylized exactly like a saint's *vita,* and has been seen as having been designed for future liturgical readings for the anniversary of the royal saint's death. What we have here are written reflections, influenced at least in part by tradition, of the new divine right of kings; it was a propaganda disseminated through ecclesiastical circles whose effects are difficult to evaluate. In general, this propaganda had a delayed effect, applying to an already deceased king. It was more important that the imperial dress should be similar to that of ecclesiastics, that the sacred lance was in the possession of the German dynasty, and that—at least according to current views of historians—from Otto III onward the king could also be a cathedral canon. The king was neither an ecclesiastic nor a simple layman; he stood between or above the two spheres. In the Aix-la-Chapelle Liuthar evangelary (ca. 990), the emperor is enthroned in a mandorla between the symbols of the evangelists; above him is suspended the hands of God, its fingers appearing to touch his head. Aix-la-Chapelle, either then or at least in the Staufen period, was a location of royal canons. The mandorla was a form of the nimbus which was appropriate above all for the image of Christ. Later biblical citations relative to Christ were used for the king; in Ottonian times this occurred only in isolated cases. Occasionally Otto I was called "holy" or "very holy" (*sanctissimus*) by Liutprand, something that was not necessarily a Byzantine reminiscence.

SACRED KINGSHIP

This leads us back to the literary sources that German historians have repeatedly investigated with respect to the sanctity or the "luck" (*Heil*) of the king. A distinction would be made here between accounts of ostentatiously pious acts according to the perception of the duties of the *vicarius Christi*, and an ancient stratum of thought originating in belief in a hero's particular gift, or charisma, or "luck." That this is not a uniquely Germanic but a more general phenomenon is no longer debated; in its application to kingship it can also be found, for example, in the Old Testament. In any case, we must retain the term "luck" (*Heil*) and not use it interchangeably with "sanctity" (*Heiligkeit*) just as *sacer* does not mean *sanctus*. The saint had usually undergone afflictions, while someone with luck succeeded in everything. It must have been tempting to enter the service of such a man, and all the more so when he was king.

These characteristics come out strongly in Widukind of Corvey, but not at all in Thietmar of Merseburg, who emphasizes that the king was given special divine direction. We have evidence here of a simple Christianity similar to that portrayed in the evangelary illustration showing the hand of God over the emperor. The pre-Christian power of luck was sometimes modified into the Christian divine will: the king lost military luck (*prosperitas belli*) from the moment he did his mother a wrong; God had removed his hand from him.

In France after the decline of the Carolingian monarchy, frequent attempts were made to place the sacral side of monarchy before the eyes of the people. Less than two months after the coronation of Otto the Great in Aix-la-Chapelle, on 19 June 936, Louis IV, having returned to his homeland from exile, was crowned by the archbishop of Reims in Laon in the presence of twenty bishops. At that moment a monk at the Baume monastery had a vision of Saint Martin, who told him that he had come expressly from Rome because his presence at the celebration was essential. The then fifteen-year-old king and his successors seem to have done little on their own to demonstrate the sacral side of their kingship. While Otto the Great often fasted and then "went under the crown," crown wearing among the West Frankish kings was little practiced.

The development of the Capetian royal mystique began with Helgaud of Fleury and his famous statement that divine grace had transmitted the power of healing to the hand of Robert II: when he touched the wounded and made the sign of the cross over them, their pain and illness vanished. Later, Philip I was said to have cured scrofula, and even into the Restoration period his successors appeared as *rois thaumaturges*. Marc Bloch assumed that this succession of healing kings had begun with Robert, but this remains uncertain. What we do have is a *vita*, or saint's life, and the miraculous cures that belong to it: King Robert, for example, was said to have returned sight to a blind man. This remained entirely within the Christian sphere; more traditional images of the luck of the king were hinted at by a statement of Richer's concerning Hugh Capet. While the archbishop's electoral discourse and Hugo's oath on the occasion of his elevation are composed entirely of realpolitik, Richer says that at the beginning of his rule the new king ordered everything "with fortunate success"; and in response to his luck (*ut beatitudini suae responderet*), raised (*levatus*) through many successes (*multo successu rerum secundarum*), he devoted himself to great piety.

Pre-Christian perceptions of the favor and luck of outstanding men appear in tenth-century authors partly in ancient, partly in Christian form; we cannot say how far such references are mere rhetoric and how far they represent a popular belief in the special powers of certain men. These interpretations are not mutually exclusive, and it is possible that literary topoi kept ancient conceptions alive or revived them. A good example of this is the combining of praise of the king with the idea of paradise.

In Isaiah we read that in the kingdom of the Messiah "the wolf shall dwell with the lamb, and the leopard shall lie down with the kid" (11:6). Around the Lord, only peace can prevail, just as clear weather (*serenitas*) surrounds the king. In the Hellenistic period, writers described a "paradise" of this kind; it was further concretized in Charlemagne's zoological garden at Aix-la-Chapelle: "And if you wish," Walahfrid Strabo told the king, "lions will spring happily . . . tigers will come, and domesticated snakes, and will share in the common pasturage of the cattle and sheep; all the animals will exist together in peace." We must recognize of course that pleasure in the contemplation of wild animals, especially exotic ones, was equally responsible for the establishment of royal zoos. Yet it cannot be denied that an antique topos transmitted by writing found concrete form here and repeatedly prompted authors to present the greatness of the king in this manner.

There were Byzantine precedents for such concepts. Liutprand of Cremona tells us that the Eastern emperor asked him whether Otto the Great had a zoological park; he could answer in the affirmative. According to Widukind, the emperor received animals from emissaries of the Romans, Greeks, and Saracens that were previously unknown in Saxony: lions, camels, apes, and ostrichs. Indeed, two lions arrived as gifts from Hugh the Great in France, and the Polish duke Mieszko presented a camel to the sixteen-year-old Otto III. There were zoological parks at many important palaces, including Pavia, and Italian magnates such as Marquis Boniface of Canossa kept lions—certainly as symbols of their power, in imitation of royal zoos.

To characterize more clearly the sacral and generally "numinous" references to kingship, we might say that they express its otherness, its distance from the mass of ecclesiastical and secular magnates. For us, this is royal propaganda, but for the people of the Middle Ages it was evidence of the proper, divinely willed order. The new dynasties, drawn from the regional nobility, were now raised above them: one had to approach the king with respect. He was thus best understood as a person filled with fortune or with the sanctity of his office, to which he had been appointed by God.

In troubled times it was essential to portray the ruler as inviolable and to make any oath sworn to him of such lofty import that to break it was sacrilege. This was the purpose of the synod of Hohenaltheim in 916, following the oathbreaking and military actions of the count palatine Erchanger against Conrad I and Bishop Salomo of Constance. The king was *christus domini,* like the bishop an anointed of the Lord; the biblical admonition "Do not disturb my anointed ones" applied to him. Erchanger and his captains were condemned to monastic imprisonment "because they had sinned and had attempted to raise their hands against the anointed of the Lord, the king, their lord."

From this same principle we can better understand that the king's command was exempt from criticism. Like the bishop, he had received God's grace in his office; as long as he did not fall away from God and become a tyrant, he could only act rightly and in accord with the divine order. That he worked in accord with this order, that it was part of his office, was constantly proclaimed in the preambles to his charters: the king was saying, in effect, "I act within the scope of the commission of the Christian king, I act for the salvation of men, and so I am no sinner; I bring about thereby protection of the church and the good of the state." Royal charters were supposed to be read in church and were translated into the vernacular for the lower classes. They furnished an important medium for the self-presentation of the king, no less significant than coronation rituals performed on Christian holidays. People were accustomed to believing what was shown them and what they heard; only rarely were they conscious of a rift between reality and appearance.

Administering the Kingdom

Modern administration is usually exercised through a more or less anonymous, regular apparatus without respect to a person's social rank. This apparatus is unremitting and ubiquitous in its operation, whereas the king and his few officials could intervene only where they were present themselves or where they might be summoned in times of emergency. They worked on an ad hoc basis to preserve the peace, whereas the modern state has a wider scope, namely the common weal. Individual activities predominated: one brought one's cause before the king, who settled it, with or without advisers; one requested privileges as *fidelis* and received them personally—as bishop, abbot or layman—announced by a royal charter even when the gift concerned an institution. Obviously such administration could hardly reach the general population and was virtually limited to the elite. Anyone who was counted among the unfree, in other words the majority of the population, did not live in the domain of this public activity, but rather within the *familia* of his lord. The king's general orders concerning fair treatment of subordinates applied to the unfree; they were published to all lords, but their effects could hardly be controlled. This rudimentary character of public (that is, royal) administration had its advantages in a period when central government was collapsing: it prevented the outbreak of anarchy, and the majority of the population only encountered the decline of central administration when local feuds were no longer settled by the king.

That the decline was very strong in the west, while the Ottonian monarchy in the east managed to overcome crises, may be attributed in part to the royal obligation of generosity. For centuries the Carolingians had had to reward their followers with fiefs while their own possessions were not being sufficiently enriched. In the east, the Ottonians profited from the chance to conquer new territories; moreover, the magnates were not in a position to organize independent lordships. People remained more conservative, and the established form of lordship was here, in the words of Jean Lemarignier, a "neo-Carolingian kingship." The west, where more local and more intensive forms under aristocratic leadership controlled the field, almost ended up without a monarchy. Would the same have occurred in Italy if it had not come under Ottonian control? Hardly, for before the Ottonians arrived, in spite of all symptoms of disintegration, the "Italian" kings had held fast to a hegemony over the region's magnates.

THE EMPEROR

There is a massive, and controversial, literature on the Italian politics of the Ottonians and their imperial dignity. The overwhelming opinion today is that their Italian expeditions were not a monocausal phenomenon and can be neither praised nor condemned. The empire of Otto the Great was seen on the one hand in its non-Roman hegemonic context and, on the other, as the renewal of the Carolingian Empire ideologically centered at Rome. The two ideas or, rather, groups of ideas are not mutually exclusive; both could have existed side by side even before 962. Charlemagne's contemporaries who drafted charters and his court intellectuals held different opinions about the character of the empire. Agreement about the means of winning the imperial crown was indispensable, but not about its theoretical foundations.

While ideal figure of the king was derived from that of the noble-man and the royal figure in turn became the model for the aristocracy, the imperial nature was by no means fixed and was open to various interpretations. The emperor as military commander, as supreme king, as defender of Christendom and of the Roman Church—these were possible forms. Others—the imperial architect, the learned theologian or philosopher—receded in this period. When Thietmar wrote that Otto I had founded the "city" of Magdeburg—it was ac-tually the monastery of Saint-Maurice—he was not attempting to present him as a "city-building emperor" (*poliouchos basileus*) of the Hellenistic-Roman stamp. It was simply part of the general praise of the ruler, similar to the way in which Helgaud of Fleury presented the ecclesiastical construction and reconstruction projects in the time of Robert II as if they were the works of Robert himself. Classical topoi were used, in the tradition of the "Carolingian Renaissance."

In spite of the former equality in rank between east and west, the Ottonian Empire established the unambiguous dominance of the German monarchy. Not surprisingly, the king of France was occa-sionally moved into the "imperial" sphere, but it should be noted that the word *imperator* (ruler, or commander) was used for his function in a nontechnical sense. The position of emperor was almost implied when Robert II was presented as "Augustus"; on the other hand, Adalbero of Laon rejoiced that the "empire" (*imperium*) had been defeated by kings: wherever possible he sought to place empire and kingship on the same political level. The king of France was a ruler of a special sort, not a "normal" king, as was evidenced in various ways, including the name of Augustus. In the twelfth century, names and terms reminiscent of antiquity were again employed, although the French royal mystique under the direction of Saint-Denis had already taken a different path. In literary glorifications of kings it was natural to borrow descriptions from the world of the ancient Roman Empire. That this was not only a literary exercise is shown in the concretiza-tion of "Augustus" in the name of the French heir to the throne, Philip II Augustus.

QUALITIES OF THE RULER

The enumeration of royal virtues recalled certain classical phrases in praise of the emperor. It coincided, at least partially, with the image that had been created of the nobleman as a human being, exemplary for his family, and as a holder of public duties. Virtues such as the *clementia Caesaris* or the *pietas Augusti* had originally been reactions to a political situation in the form of prudent restraint; Julius Caesar had renounced punishment of his conquered enemies. Even in the imperial period these virtues were so generalized that they could apply to medieval kings, and not only to them. Hrotsvitha made no essential differentiation between the virtues of the king and those of members of his family: the *summa nobilitas* is at home in the ruler's clan and expresses itself, as she suggested, in the name of the Empress Adelheid. Next to the image of the noble is that of the Christian ruler, as reflected in the writings of ecclesiastical authors; as early as the ninth century it had been applied to kings by synods and in "mirrors of princes."

The king had to manifest his high nobility in his outward appearance too. Although Robert the Pious is presented by his biographer as a saint of humble demeanor, Helgaud had nevertheless to emphasize the aristocratic appearance (*corporis elegantiam*) of the king, his above-average height, his respectable beard (that is to say, a beard in the style of magnates), and the manner in which he wore his crown: from these things it could be recognized, as Helgaud says, that he descended from grandparents and great-grandparents of royal blood. Many authors—Regino, for example, more than once—had emphasized the attractiveness of Carolingian princes. Robert was not one of these; as far as royal ancestors were concerned, the only one mentioned was his grandmother Hathui, daughter of the German king Henry I; once more the female line served to demonstrate a family's preeminence. For Robert this was a delicate matter because his second wife Bertha was herself a great-grandaughter of Henry I and therefore related to Robert in the third degree. That this risky marriage, which the pope had tried to break up, had been undertaken was probably because of Bertha's Carolingian origins: her grandfather was Louis IV. Helgaud sought to foster the fame of the Capetian kings further by speaking of their Italian, perhaps even Roman origins.

The king was member of a family of ancient renown, and he remained bound to this family after his coronation. We have seen that even Thomas Aquinas located the Christian virtue of *pietas* in the relationship to one's kin; he said that one sinned if one forgot them. When a king benefited his family, he engaged in what historians would later call "the politics of family power" (*Hausmachtpolitik*). Such actions could be performed without harshness to those concerned, according to the principle of *do ut des*. When Otto the Great was rounding off the properties of his family in the middle Elbe region, the Hersfeld monks remained quiet although they were threatened by this action; the emperor had granted a privilege of immunity to the monastery, and Hersfeld now enjoyed a position similar to that of Fulda, at the expense of the diocesan bishop. On the other hand, difficulties arose when Otto did not accede to family members' demands because to do so would have weakened the central power. Such reactions show that family interests were secondary; royal duties came first.

Besides the family there were "friends," whose interests the king had to take into account. According to Widukind, Otto I did not refuse them anything and was faithful to them in a "superhuman manner." The term "friend of the king" seems to have held a middle place between his kindred (in the broad sense) and the kingdom's ruling stratum, which was subject to him. In the ninth century we encounter the *amicitia regis,* in which something of a rank order can be recognized: there was a "first among the friends of the king." Here there is no question of an equal partnership; the king is superior to the "friends" who have sworn faithfulness to him and have therefore received favor and presents from his hands. In the tenth century, although no study of this form of alliance has been undertaken, things may not have been very different. Here we must be very cautious, since vassality had already overlaid more archaic forms.

We are now in the realm of "practical" royal virtues, which for the most part are similar to those of the nobles. Generosity toward one's friends and toward all those who stand in the king's grace was one of these virtues; Liutprand of Cremona lists it among the virtues of King Hugo of Italy. Here generosity did not refer to the magnates of the kingdom, but implied concern for the poor and for the Church; the same meaning is found in Helgaud of Fleury. From the viewpoint of clerics it was more important that the king should relieve the bishops of the care of the poor, at least in part, and that he should provide for the clergy, than that he should endow his worldly allies.

Liutprand further praises Hugo's wisdom and his love of "philosophers," virtues in which the king for a time remained almost alone. That Otto the Great learned to read books late in his life and that Otto II was present at a learned disputation might be pointed to as distant parallels. Still, things had not yet reached the point where an illiterate king could be described as a crowned ass, as the saying went in the twelfth century. Next to Hugo's wisdom Liutprand enumerated the king's daring, strength, and cunning (*calliditas*), and with these he was by no means alone: Regino, for example, praised Louis the German in a similar manner. These were certainly not Christian virtues; the story was told that the Franks had elected Clovis their king because he possessed these virtues as well as a gift for making wise suggestions in council. In war, cunning was an excellent supplement to physical strength and military courage. We shall have to show how such terms as *ingenium* (cunning) could be evaluated positively. Today such characteristics would not be considered virtues; and even then there were authors who praised a very different kind of kingly comportment—unpretentiousness and simplicity of bearing, that *simplicitas* which has always been evaluated positively in the Christian sphere. The term was also used in describing royal virtues, as for Louis II "the Stammerer" and his son Charles "the Simple." The unpretentious and peace-loving prince was a creature not admired by some eleventh-century writers; thus Charles was characterized as a stupid, simpleminded king.

Wisdom appears in the *Ruodlieb* as a late addition to royal virtues, although the first Carolingian mirror of princes had promoted it. The term *sapientia* or *sophia* approached the stoic ideal on the one hand and, on the other, included literate education; Robert the Pious was described as *sapientissimus litterarum*. Generally, however, the term "wise" was used of a person with practical common sense, who could give good advice in bad circumstances. "Cleverness in counsel" (or "in council") was something generally demanded of noblemen and especially of vassals. Whether this sort of wisdom took the form of simple Christian virtue or of military cunning depended on the case in hand.

What was constant was the commonplace, or rule of conduct, concerning the duality of the royal attitude: the king is mild toward the good, harsh toward the evil. We are reminded of the old oath formula, "to be a friend to your friends, an enemy to your enemies," though the division of one's world into these two groups was now tinged with political morality. An enemy was anyone who set himself against royal lordship and thus against the "state." He was the recipient of royal *terror*, just as the compliant received royal grace and favor. Crimes against the king were sins (*peccata*). Political and religious morality were thus closely associated, just as the word *fides* designated both Christian faith and the vassal's faithfulness. We recall that the synod of Hohenaltheim launched an anathema against all who wished to undertake anything against the king, and condemned a magnate along with his followers because they had "sinned" against the king.

As long as it was not normal to see the state as "transpersonal," the person of the king needed every possible protection. His deposition or premature death could throw the commonwealth into a serious crisis. The fact that kings lived in danger had to be taken seriously by anyone who strove for the royal dignity, as was pointed out in the epitaph of the Carolingian Louis IV. Kings were not even secure in peace; their lives could be threatened even in holy places. While in Rome, Otto I was said to have ordered his sword bearer to hold his sword over his head while he was praying at the tombs of the apostles. The king himself had to be a valiant warrior, a model for all those who fought for him. A king fighting in the center of the battle must have drawn the full force of the enemy attack and thus was in primary danger. No doubt, his actual place even then was on the "commander's hill."

THE KING AT WAR

Raison d'état could not yet entirely destroy the old concept of the commander at the forefront of battle. Widukind, for example, writes that in the battle of Lechfeld Otto I drove his horse against the enemy as leader of the fifth or "royal" squadron. Thus he was "fulfilling the duties of both the most valiant of warriors and the most excellent commander." That he carried the sacred lance and was protected by a mass of hand-picked warriors "as though surrounded by a wall" indicated that leadership at the forefront was becoming symbolic. Nevertheless, it was still dangerous.

It appears that battling troops wanted to know that the king was in their midst, more because of his luck-bringing presence than his individual ability as a warrior. This is very clear in a story told by Regino. A Breton king was ill; he wanted to stir up his men to battle, and so he gave them his military standard and promised them victory. When they still did not want to move forward without him, he had himself "set before the battle lines of the enemy" on a stretcher, and thus his army achieved victory. The military standard lacked the charismatic power that issued from the king's person. The sacred lance was another matter, at least in part. At the battle of Lechfeld it enhanced the king's presence, and once before it had had to replace his presence. In March 939 a portion of Otto's army had been attacked by the Lotharingians when crossing the Rhine, while he was with the other contingent of troops. Widukind excuses Otto's continued absence by saying that no ships were available—one would have been enough. Liutprand tells us that in this instance Otto prayed before the sacred lance, a prayer which led to victory. In a well-thought-out manner, Otto is here compared to Moses, who by his prayers aided the army in victory against the Amalekites. Neither author mentions that it would have been extremely unwise for Otto to have put his life in jeopardy by intervening personally in this situation. In order to show that the prowess of the royal family was not in question, Liutprand adds that Otto's brother Henry killed a good number of enemies in this battle and was wounded in the arm.

In the civil war of 923, the West Frankish (anti-)king Robert died at Soissons, pierced through by the lances of the supporters of the Carolingian Charles (the "Simple"); his son Hugo the Great saved the field for the dukes of Francia and the later Capetians. It is worth noting how Richer embroiders on Flodoard's account, in which he juxtaposes two principles. On one side stood the Carolingian, who wanted to fight but was "convinced" by the clergy and commanders to remain on the sidelines in order not to put the dynasty in danger; he exhorted the warriors to action and then watched the battle from a nearby mountain. On the other side, the usurper Robert moved hither and thither, raging against the enemy. At first he was unrecognized but then, when asked who he was, he identified himself. Fifty supporters of the Carolingians who had sworn to kill him went after him and felled him with their lances. The battle ended in victory for the legitimate party according to Richer, and in the direction of political reason, in contrast to the old heroic ideal focused on the king.

Richer also tells us how Hugh Capet justified his request that his son Robert be made co-regent: war with the infidels in Spain was approaching, and there had to be two kings so that the army might have a commander should one of them be killed. Otherwise the land would experience great unrest after the death of the sole ruler. These were excellent reasons in a period when lordship was interpreted in personal terms. The reasons for the destruction of the royal palace in Pavia are known: faithfulness and possessions end with a person's death, and if there is no longer a king, one has the right to destroy his house. Rodulf Glaber correctly observed that the Vikings were especially violent toward the Frankish realm when the king had died. After the death of the East Frankish king Louis III in 882, the Norsemen were said to have been beside themselves with joy and no longer to have thought about war but only about booty. Personal relationships were essential in battle; there was no real discipline within a military unit; rather, all acted according to the model of their commander. Not only the Magyars despaired of success in their fight for an Augsburg city gate after their leader was killed. Elsewhere, after the "loss of their head," a French contingent in confusion (*errore*) and mourning renounced certain victory over an isolated band of Vikings. Sometimes an army "went home" after the death of its leader.

The battle of Soissons, mentioned above, is also enlightening in this regard. If King Robert had had the possibility of raising his son Hugo to co-regent before his death, Hugo would probably have been victor because the Lotharingian troops had left the Carolingians in the lurch. Hugo's military success in the battle was not used to the full. It is said specifically that because of the death of the king, the vanquished were not pursued. It was not Hugo who was named the new anti-king against Charles the Simple but the Burgundian Raoul (Rudolf). It was possible to exclude the deceased king's son from succession by election even though he had demonstrated his military qualification. The only real guarantee for the continued rule of the king's family was, as has been said, co-regency. The election of a three-year-old child as co-regent with Otto II saved the throne for the Saxon dynasty in 983.

At least to some extent the validity of royal privileges was bound up with dynastic continuity. The rights of the clergy generally remained inviolable. When the holder of privileges was a secular person, however, it was not clear whether the successor in the kingdom felt bound by the decrees of his predecessor. The son of the deceased could raise the fewest problems in this regard; he was bound by the obligation of piety to carry out his father's will. The young king did not always carry this piety so far as to make his father's friends and advisers his own. Nevertheless, the leading individuals at least had some chance of maintaining their position at court, whereas an outsider on the throne would favor his own people over those of his predecessor.

The constant peril to the king and the vicissitudes of his reign were part of the *miseriae regum*. Awareness that these travails could not be overcome by one's own strength diminished the arrogance and deepened the religious sense of many rulers. It had led ancient emperors to stoic philosophy; now there was the monastic-ascetic lifestyle, which in truth the king could lead only in specific situations and not throughout his entire reign. This was true for Otto III and for Robert

II of France, whose "constant humility" was praised by his biographer. Robert depended on people from the middle and lower levels of society and, as emphasized by Rodulf Glaber, on monks. Wipo's characterization of Conrad II as "a man of great humility," wise, honest, and generous, seems to have a different intent; it refers to the simplicity and affability of the king—who had himself fought the Slavs like a private soldier until he stood hip-deep in swamp water. Henry III practiced public rituals of penance, as we have already noted. Thietmar suggested that Henry I had "preferred the pains of a journey on foot to traveling on horseback during a pilgrimage to Rome" in order to gain forgiveness for a sin—a story which, as it seems fabulous, tells us nothing about the king himself, but does show us that such a preference was deemed possible.

ADVISERS

For ecclesiastical historiographers, humility belonged in the catalogue of a ruler's virtues, and people seem to have desired a symbolic gesture of this sort as early as the royal coronation. The pontifical of Mainz (ca. 960) prescribes that the elected should "stretch out in a cross-shaped form," that is, with extended arms and face to the floor. The clergy, as part of its duty, endeavored to moderate the aristocratic pride of the king. If a king presented himself as scornful of earthly vanities, he could use this attitude to his advantage by removing from the magnates their monopoly on distinguished offices. Robert attempted, as Louis the Pious had already done, to raise persons of low birth into the high clergy. He thus evoked the anger of the magnates (*primates*), who despised the humble or lowborn (*humiles*) and would elect proud men (*superbos*) like themselves. Since the same terms had to be used for humility and for low birth, such phrases could make the perspective of the king comprehensible to the reader.

Humility was appropriate for dignitaries of the church, but it was no prerequisite for being a secular adviser to the king. Chroniclers therefore had an easier time of rejecting the promotion of "humble" advisers. Here the monopoly of the elite on forming the king's entourage seems to have been maintained as their due. Advising the king was primarily the job of the vassals: "council and aid" were their obligation. Various possibilities were hidden behind this formula, ranging from advice "on demand" to the permanent activity of the *consiliarii regis* who are found in the diplomas of the Italian kings and, coming from the most powerful families of the kingdom, sometimes played a leading role in the court. In France, Hugo of Francia was said to have made his homage to the recalled King Louis conditional on the agreement that the latter swear to follow Hugo's advice. The perils which arose from such an attitude on the part of the magnates were the primary reason that kings sought support elsewhere. According to Brun of Querfurt, Otto II followed the "childish advice" of his Byzantine wife and rejected that of the magnates. Charles the Simple was abandoned by almost all of the counts of Francia because he did not want to abandon his adviser Hagano, who had come from the middle level of society. Charles had to flee, and Robert was made anti-king. The greatest anger was reserved for kings who promoted not only non-nobles but even women to administrative roles, as did Zwentibold (895–900) in Lorraine. He was therefore "hated by all" and abandoned by the magnates.

Equally condemnable was a king who chose no advisers at all and ruled at his own will (*ad suum arbitrium*). In this case even his own kin might oppose him, and he could be expelled "as if he intended to establish tyranny." The aversion against individual initiatives that were not controlled and "advised" by others is characteristic of a "closed society," which tended to conformity and mutual control of its members. Richer says of the last Carolingian king, Louis V, that he wore foreign rather than native dress and in the manner of a youth concerned himself with frivolities. The reason, Richer adds, was that Louis had no instructor in the customs of his ancestry (*morum informatorem*). Such a prince was considered degenerate (*degener*) and therefore excluded himself from lordship.

A king who was a model in his virtues and advised by wise men was adequate to all that the laity expected of him. The clergy expected still more, as was most fully expressed at the synod of Trosly in 909: the ruler had above all "to rule himself," that is, to conquer his passions and to foster good habits. This formula went back to the Hellenistic mirrors of princes, and beyond Xenophon to Persia and India. The clergy had to obey the king, and the king must obey the clergy according to the nature of the issue at hand. Furious (*terribilis*) toward the evil, worthy of love (*amabilis*) toward the good, the king had to raise up the oppressed, console the poor, serve as protector for widows and orphans. The expectations went still further, in the tradition of classical literature and the Church Fathers. The Romans had given the emperor Octavian Augustus a dedicatory shield on which, next to military prowess (*virtus*), his principal virtues were depicted as *clementia, iustitia, pietas,* and the bishops at Trosly proclaimed that their king should rule "piously, justly, and mercifully." Conversely whoever ruled impiously, unjustly, and cruelly was not a king but a tyrant. Quotations from the Bible and from the Church Fathers substantiated this proclamation. Finally the synod quoted a seventh-century Irish treatise which had been disseminated under the name of Cyprian.

This treatise, which was important for the "political theory" of the early Middle Ages, explained what the rule of an unjust king meant for his kingdom. Not only would there be war, but also crop failures, infant mortality, livestock epidemics, tempests, and frequent thunderbolts. In contrast, under a just ruler there was peace in air and on the sea, the fertility of the fields, etc. The ancient idea of an intimate connection between the world of men and the universe, of a cosmic order which could be disturbed through disorder in the human sphere, of the intermediary role of the king between the earthly and supernatural worlds, was very common in troubled times. Civil war had ended only a few years before the synod of Trosly, and the inhabitants of northern and western France had almost become accustomed to the continual plundering by Viking expeditions.

THE QUEEN

While the bishops in Trosly dealt extensively with the king, they remained silent about the queen. We have heard about the disinclination in ecclesiastical circles to give too positive an appreciation to female intelligence. Nevertheless, there was much here to talk about. The wife, as we have seen, had her own sphere of activity in the "house," and this was true of the royal household too. It was also possible for her to make political decisions for her absent or deceased husband. Queens did all of this in great measure. The designation *regina* meant more than simply the wife of the king; *imperatrix augusta* was more than an empty honorific title. Full power certainly belonged only to men, and the *domina* never reached the position of the *dominus*. But occasionally the term *domina dux* was used. Judith, who ruled for her son Duke Henry of Bavaria, was so called in 965 — she was a "duke," as was Henry. And in Italy, in 990, Theophanu was not only called "by the grace of God, Empress (and) Augusta," but even "Theophanius, by the grace of God, Emperor (and) Augustus." Women could exercise full power only when they were regarded as men.

Did the queen hold the same position as a co-regent? Was she in the full sense a "joint ruler"? This question has been answered in the affirmative because in Italy the queen was designated as *consors regni* and thus as "fellow of the lordship" of the king, and the same term was used for a co-regent. Yet to speak of "original rights of sovereignty," equal for each of the royal spouses, would be an exaggeration. We have seen how difficult it was for the thought of that period to deal with the problem of the equality of crowned heads; equality between a man and a woman would have been even more unlikely, since the sphere of political action of a wife was only that which she had received from her husband or which was created by a crisis that required her to act. It depended, of course, on the individual queen, how far she could or would fill this sphere. After the death of Otto II, the Byzantine Theophanu did so to the limits of her potential; we have no evidence of her previous involvement in government, though she was described as the "co-emperor" of Otto and *consors* in the empire.

Within the sphere of the queen's given duties was intercession with the king. Petitioners bound themselves to her, especially clerics; representing their affairs was a form of advisory duty. Whether a royal charter was delivered on the intervention of, at the request of, or, more rarely, on the advice of the queen was merely a question of terminology. Not only charters but narrative sources praise the virtues in queens. The dying King Henry I thanked his wife Mathilda for calming him when he was angry and for giving him useful advice. Wipo listed the advisers of Conrad II and went on to say, "more than all of these was his beloved wife Gisela strong in wisdom and council." It is no accident that the above-cited sources come from Germany, while contemporary historians in the west had little appreciation for such things. In France, the frequent interventions of Hemma, from 966 the wife of king Lothar, found no such praise.

As a "housewife" the queen was responsible at least in part for the direction of the court and the royal household. In the late ninth century it was her responsibility to supervise the "honesty" of the palace (*honestas palatii*). This duty implied less the supervision of the morals than concern with the proper and clean appearance of the buildings and the behavior of the servants. She was also responsible for royal ornament (*ornamentum regale*), that is, all of the decorations the royal prestige required: tapestries, tableware, and the like. Finally, she had to provide the necessary gifts to vassals with the exception of food and horses. The chamberlain, under the queen's direction, was responsible for the practical details of these activities. The queen thus exercised authority not only over servants but also over free persons, in this case over one of the powerful functionaries of the palace administration. The chamberlain was in charge of the royal treasury, higher in rank that the seneschal, cupbearer, and marshal. Even in Charlemagne's time, chamberlains were sometimes entrusted with high offices: they served the king as commander of an army, as royal ambassador, or as a member of the royal court of justice.

Odorannus of Sens maintained that Queen Constance, wife of Robert the Pious, received from her husband authority over all royal properties and privileges. In any case, it was Constance who gave Odorannus gold to have a reliquary made in his monastery for the relics of Saint Savinianus. In the French court, the queen may have been entrusted with supervision of the use and storage of material goods. In Robert's *vita*, Constance was presented as the counterpart of her husband, who allowed himself to be robbed while she could not stand the theft of valuable objects—a golden garment border, the silver plating of the royal lance, a silver candlestick.

In Germany, with its "peripatetic kingship," the queen seems to have been responsible at least at times for the transfer of the royal household and its technical problems. In the collection of correspondence from Tegernsee there is a letter, unfortunately incomplete, from the empress Adelheid in which she gives directions for the reception of the royal court in Würzburg. At the time she was writing, she was probably still regent for Otto III. Since the Carolingian epoch, the queen had had her own court personnel, and she claimed the right to hospitality for that personnel when she was separated from her husband, as for example on an Italian expedition; likewise the royal palaces were at her disposal. We happen to know that Kunigunda, the wife of the emperor Henry II, had her own chamberlain and a cupbearer; in most cases we know very little or nothing about the queen's staff in this period.

We have seen the importance of representation for the social position of the elite; the queen could not be an exception. Hemma, daughter of the empress Adelheid and widow of the penultimate Carolingian king in France, complained after her downfall that she had commanded thousands of men and now did not even control lowly domestic servants (*vernaculos comites*). Such words say nothing about the character of the queen; they certainly apply less to her political influence than to her social position. After Hemma's liberation this position did not improve: from being a widowed queen she became an ex-queen.

As a widow, a queen either ruled for her minor son or lived under the control of the new king, a control which extended to her expenses and finances. Her own son could exhibit a certain harshness in this situation, as was shown in the well-known conflict between Otto I and his mother. That conflict was not over the number of her following but concerned her attachment to monasteries. That a widowed queen needed a following and "lordly" clothing (*herilia vestimenta*) was universally acknowledged. The pious Mathilda would wear two valuable arm rings (*armillae*) until the death of her husband; afterwards she wore only "a little gold" as ornament, and a linen outer garment that was distinct from mourning garb (*ligubri veste*). Although the biographer presented the queen beside her husband on official occasions "adorned with precious stones and silk," more appropriate to her as a widow was a simpler, though still royal, lifestyle. This lifestyle was normally financed by her wedding portion, the *dotales regiones*. In the conflict with her son, Mathilda had to surrender these regions and go into a convent.

Around the year 1000, there was a Saxon tradition according to which Mathilda (in 936) had used all her influence to enable her younger son Henry rather than Otto I to be made king. The real reason for the later conflict between Otto and his mother may have been her attempt at that time to intervene in a situation crucial for the kingdom. Such activities were always risky, even from the point of view of public opinion. As we have seen, medieval historiographers seldom praised and often condemned the political influence of women. Yet anecdotes were recounted that gave female cleverness its due. According to Liutprand, Berta—the daughter of King Lothar of Italy—claimed that by means of her political experience (*scientia sua*) she would make her husband either a king or an ass. Hugo the Great of Francia was said to have asked his sister Emma, wife of the Burgundian Duke Rudolf, whom she would elect king. Her answer was that she would rather kiss the knee of her husband that that of her brother; Hugo then "allowed Rudolf to occupy the royal throne." The response was presented as shrewd, although a woman was unlikely to find herself in the position of completing a vassalic oath with a kiss on the knee. The anecdote implied not only that this woman was greatly influential, but also that she thought like a man. Although Liutprand reported all the evil about the elder Theodora in Rome, he did praise her for obtaining political control of the city "in a masculine way." As for Queen Emma, she did not swear a vassalic oath but demanded one—from the guardian of a castle. To be sure, she did so on behalf of her husband and not for herself. A few years earlier, when Rudolf was making for Burgundy, he "left the defense of the city of Laon" to the queen, in conjunction with the local count.

There were countesses with military skill, and there were queens who "took the place of their husbands" in this area. Willa, the wife of Berengar, fortified an island on a small lake in northern Italy; she was besieged there by Otto I for almost two months. At last Otto secured her a safe withdrawal. A queen was accepted as commander in circumstances of crisis if she could gain the trust of the military commanders. She also was accepted as regent following the capture or death of her husband if her child had been named as his successor. On the other hand, an ongoing reign by a woman was entirely abnormal. What Liutprand tells about the *monarchia* of the elder Theodora in Rome is exaggerated. When he suggests that the marchioness Hermengard of Ivrea had held control of all of (Upper) Italy after the death of her husband, Liutprand obviously intends to be satirical, as is shown by the story of how Hermengard had reached this position.

In Germany, Adelheid and Theophanu held key political positions as did the queens Hemma, widow of Lothar (d. 986), and Constance (after the death of Robert in 1031). They defended their positions with varying degrees of success. If no heir was in place, as was the case following Henry II's death in 1024, his widow either could work on the strengthening (*corroboratio*) of the new royal regime, or she could try to undermine it. Empress Kunigunda chose the first route: delivering to Konrad II the imperial insignia, "she supported him in his rule in as far as female authority made it possible." During the eight weeks prior to Conrad's election, Kunigunda had continued to rule the empire "with the advice of her brothers" and thus, in the words of Wipo, she aided the *res publica* as much as she could. To this end she certainly needed no male guardianship, for Theophanu and Adelheid could rule without it. It was a sort of interim familial rule, and legally the function of the brothers did not go beyond giving counsel. The empress assumed the place of her husband and his not yet designated successor.

Theophanu and Adelheid ruled for a minor; after the death of Lothar in 987 Queen Hemma had the magnates swear fidelity both to the nineteen-year-old King Louis and to herself. She herself directed foreign policy, which was now entirely changed. Now the future of the kingdom in the west as well as that in the east lay in female hands. In the last year of Lothar's life a "conference of ladies" (*colloquium dominarum*) is said to have taken place in Metz, that is, a conference between the two empresses and Duchess Beatrix of Upper Lorraine, Duke Henry of Bavaria, and other magnates. At this time Hemma wrote to her mother Adelheid that the empress was the "mother of all kingdoms" and that her advice would be fully followed by her daughter; a personal meeting was planned. When Louis V began to rule in a petulant manner and proceeded against his mother, the political landscape was changed once again, and the ground was laid for the Capetians' reign.

In this instance the son not only moved against his mother but accused her of marital infidelity. In a contrasting instance, it seems that in 1033 Queen Constance wanted to depose her unbeloved son King Henry and replace him with his brother Robert. The intrigue failed and Constance died in 1034. The power of a queen's personality was very important for her prestige and political position; yet she remained a substitute for the king, not an equal competitor. Theophanu and Adelheid were recognized as long as the king was still a minor; Hemma and Constance were doomed to failure because they opposed a mature king.

We can conclude, then, that a queen held a political and military position which was not expressly defined but which was in practice sufficiently well delineated. She was a sort of junior partner, who in emergencies could fulfill the duties of her senior, but usually concerned herself with matters of her own scope. Male lordship, a postulate of medieval reflections on order, was preserved; yet administration did not rest on one person alone. The queen had two sorts of rights and duties, those which had been delegated to her and those which belonged naturally to her. She was above all concerned with the continuity of rule, something which, in a period of very deficient institutionalization, was crucial. Although chroniclers usually took note only of the major events in a queen's life, this was because of the nature of the times. Their accounts certainly did not do justice to the role many women played in the governance of the realm and in the wider field of interpersonal relations at court. But we are better informed about queens than we are about any other women, except for the few who were honored as saints.

9 &THE BISHOP

In 1910, Aloys Schulte published *The Nobility and the German Church in the Middle Ages,* a book that commands high respect even today. Schulte demonstrated that before the Concordat of Worms very few persons born unfree were raised to episcopal office by Carolingian and German rulers. Two such cases occurred in the ninth century, four or five in the reign of Henry II. Only in the thirteenth century would free commoners appear as bishops. Thus Schulte could argue that "for all the centuries of the Middle Ages since Charlemagne, it was virtually the rule for nobles to be seen as the most appropriate candidates for episcopal office." This conclusion remains undisputed. Only a few years ago Jane Martindale studied a series of bishops and abbots, especially from France, who were designated as *nobiles,* and found only a "small group of exceptions." Here, however, a methodological question arises, namely, whether the authors, being clerics, intended to present a realistic image of bishops' social situations. It is more likely that they were following a literary tradition which reached back into the Merovingian period in which the bishop was described not only as "noble" but also as "handsome," and to which a third quality was added, that of wealth. Such statements were significant because they indicated that the bishop fulfilled all of the requirements of the common image of nobility.

ORIGIN AND KINDRED

As far as social reality is concerned, there is no doubt that a bishop born unfree, and freed only as a cleric, could not obtain the authority that he needed in his office. Even in antiquity freedmen were distinct from fully free men throughout their lives; Thegan rightly wrote in his famous invective against Archbishop Ebo of Reims: "He (Emperor Louis the Pious) made you free, not noble, for that is impossible." The noble needed free persons as ancestors, and some of them had to have distinguished themselves. The period's strongly delineated concept of rank was contradicted when social advancement did not take place step by step, generation by generation. It was evil indeed when "the highest princes of the church were recruited from the lowest of servants." Thegan did not consider this contradictory to his idea of hierarchy but believed there were practical reasons for his disapproval: people who were accustomed to serving as he says, become quarrelsome and arrogant when raised to high office. They want above all to be praised—we would say they had difficulty establishing interpersonal relationships because of a lack of natural self-confidence. They overcompensated and became aggressive. We are not told whether the conduct of those around them promoted this attitude. One can imagine an attitude of thinly veiled arrogance on the part of a "noble" when he had to obey the commands of a "non-noble." Thegan correctly recognized that the family of the new bishop could also lead to problems. Should one continue to treat them as domestics? Thegan complained that men who had risen to become bishops tried to turn their families into free people and wanted the daughters to marry nobles and the sons to study so that they could despise and mock "noble elders" (*senes nobiles*) for their ignorance. Disruption of the normal social order naturally brought with it behavioral problems.

The extreme case, in which an unfree person became bishop or archbishop was, as we have said, very rare. But it does demonstrate with great clarity the difficulties which even free persons could have when they held positions which, according to the view of the elite, were reserved for themselves. When Otto II made his chancellor Willigis archbishop of Mainz, "many persons" opposed the appointment because of the candidate's lowly origins (*ob vilitatem . . . generis*). His mother was a free woman, but she was described as "poor" (*paupercula*). This implied that she did not belong to the elite, one of whose characteristic was wealth as the presupposition of an exalted lifestyle. A "poor" person was one who lacked support, in terms both of material means (*opes*) and of kinsmen and noble blood (*sanguine fretus*) with which to further his career. This was written by one who should have known, Bishop Fulbert of Chartres. He described himself as a poor person who had risen from the mire. Fulbert may have been a fellow student of Robert the Pious in Reims. In any case, the king called him to the bishopric of Chartres. This was an important position of support for the crown in the context of a political program which purposely raised common people to such positions. With great sarcasm Adalbero of Laon, representative of the proud aristocratic elite, advised King Robert to make shepherds and sailors bishops while their episcopal brethren, who came from the earlier period, should walk naked behind the plow. In this manner Robert created willing helpers. His actions could be justified on other grounds, of course, as Rodulf Glaber shows: the king hated the proud and loved the humble; he took care that independent bishoprics had competent pastors, even if they were of very lowly origin. This seemed better to him, Rodulf continues, than to select a man who was noble and who reflected worldly splendor.

The famous Gerbert of Aurillac, later Pope Silvester II, called himself in a memoir a needy exile who was supported neither by a renowned family (*genere*) nor by wealth, who nevertheless (in his election as archbishop of Reims) was preferred over many well-to-do persons conspicuous by the nobility of their kindred. We always find the same things, wealth and kinship, cited in connection with episcopal election. We can assume that what was required was the ability to make presents to the right people and to have kinsmen as lobbyists. A man was "poor" if he had neither or if he came from a distant country, from which no help could be expected. Whether Gerbert's family was wealthy in Aquitaine or not played no role in Reims or in Bobbio. Besides, Gerbert had entered the monastery of Saint-Gerald in Aurillac at a very early age, and this monastery was his real home. Later on, his former connections with friends and distant relatives were for Gerbert but a shadowy memory.

The wealth of a bishop also brought advantages to his subordinates. Adalbero II of Metz, whose very important family we have already heard about, fulfilled the heavy and almost annual obligation of service in the imperial army for himself and his men by cash payments. These payments, according to his biographer, were drawn only to a small, almost insignificant degree, from taxes. Most of the money came from the income from his family's inherited estates. Adalbero's *vita* also indicates the mixing of personal income with that of the bishopric: the bishop spared neither when it was necessary to use it to assist the poor, widows, and monasteries. Not every well-born bishop was so generous, but all had the possibility of doing so. The poor had to rely on themselves and also had to care for their kinsmen. Even the history of the papacy reflects this situation. In 985 the son of a priest from Rome became Pope John XV under the influence of the Crescentii. He was hated by the clergy of the city "because he divided up among his kindred everything that he had and everything he was able to acquire." The only detail known is that he raised his nephew to duke of Ariccia.

In many cases the payments from family wealth and the donations from episcopal property or offices to kinsmen were a political necessity. Emperor Henry II depended even more on the support of the clergy than had his predecessors. He asked Thietmar whether he was prepared, as future bishop of Merseburg, to aid his bishopric with a portion of his own wealth. In the same year Henry II gave the poorly endowed bishopric of Paderborn to Meinwerk, "who was as suited for it through his noble origins as he was through the quantity of his estates." He expressed the desire that the new bishop might take pity on the poverty of his diocese and come to its assistance. When such a person from an outstanding family endowed his kin with episcopal property, this could have a positive effect on the diocese: The kinsmen too might reach into their own pockets when it was necessary. But above all they were loyal vassals, on whom the bishop could rely in wartime—something of major importance in the service of the empire, and even more so in the civil-war atmosphere in France.

Diocesan monasteries also often profited from the wealth of the episcopal family. Many were founded with its property or gifts from it. The opposite was also the case. Bishops—and not only those with poor relatives—often bestowed monastic property on their kinsmen to the monastery's disadvantage. It was reported of Adalbero I of Metz that he had brothers whom he could not enfeoff because the episcopal estates had already been given out by his predecessors. Hence he sought an opportunity to transmit something to these kinsmen. When Adalbero was to restore property to the monastery of Gorze, which had reverted to him upon the death of its incumbent, one of his brothers demanded it instead. The result was a conflict, which the bishop ended with these words to his kinsmen: "You protest in vain. If I had given half of the bishopric's property to these monks, I wouldn't take away a single foot of it because of one of you."

In Laon an Irishman named Malcalanus wrote a treatise which dealt with the problem of the episcopal kindred. Malcalanus had been educated in the reform monastery of Gorze and had been commissioned by Bishop Rorico of Laon to transform a house of canons in reduced circumstances into a Benedictine monastery. This canonry's estates were held by episcopal vassals, and their restitution was a vital question for Malcalanus and his monks. One means of accomplishing this was writing the treatise in the form of a dialogue in which he set himself, under the pseudonym of Theophilus, against Bishop Rorico (Eutitius). We are told that it was this bishop's kindred who held the episcopal estates. Eutitius explains that episcopal estates are the property of God, but if it is permissible for the bishop to use them for the support of himself, then why not also for the support of his relatives? Episcopal wealth ought to be dedicated to the support of the poor, so why not also for the (poor) kin?

This was the reflection of a popular view and not "sophistry," as the reformer Theophilus-Malcalanus asserted. His dialectical education colors his view that the immediate necessities of life (*cibum et vestitum*) are due to kinsmen as well as to the poor, but not immovable property (*predia et possessiones*). The bishop apparently accepts this, because he asks, "And what should be done with the possessions which have already been given out contrary to this differentiation?" Theophilus desists from passing judgment and leaves it up to God, the supreme judge. The time was not yet ripe (around 962) for a radical solution to such problems. Friendly persuasion seemed better and promised more success than heated polemic.

This dialogue expended and deepened a position which in more summary form had already been pronounced by Carolingian synods: No bishop was to give (*condonare*) episcopal property to his kin. If his family was poor, he could care for them as he cared for other paupers, but he could not rob his church on their behalf. Of course, the reality was not so simple: property which came to the family as fief, precarium, or, in Italy, through a rental contract was not a donation in the legal sense. In this manner, perhaps, bishops had kept open the possibility of harmonizing the canonical directive with reality. Synodal decrees certainly cannot be used to justify the statement that "prelates considered church property a source of spoils." Such a judgment indicates how alien to modern authors were the concepts under which bishops of that time acted and how the black-and-white depictions of the polemical writings from the period of the investiture contest have influenced the thought of historians.

The secular clergy took their name from the fact that, unlike monks, they had not left the *saeculum*, the world. They continued to live in this natural environment, which meant first of all within the family. Even in late antiquity, ecclesiastical office and family were often perceived as one, and there was a de facto tradition of inheritable episcopal sees. This had less to do with the Germanization of the Church than with the fact that the state had receded into the background and, with it, ecclesiastical organization, so that the latter was no longer the only, or the dominant, form of life for its functionaries. In Gaul the families of the senatorial nobility were the pillar of the regional church, and in the Frankish kingdom of the Carolingians a writer like Thegan was only expressing what was the general opinion of the elite.

FAMILIAL POLITICS AND FAMILY-BASED GOVERNMENT

We have a good example of how it was taken for granted in the early tenth century that the kindred should serve the bishop and that he in return should support them. It is presented by a man of high morality and exemplary lifestyle: Udalrich of Augsburg, who was later canonized. He was descended from a comital family which was related to the house of the Burchardings in Swabia. Duke Burchard "and other kinsmen" presented the young Udalrich to King Henry I. Because of his knowledge and—something actually mentioned first—his commanding appearance (*herilitatem staturae*), Udalrich was taken on by the king as a vassal and the kinsmen introduced him into his episcopal city. In the civil war, Udalrich entrenched himself with his followers in the castle of Schwabmünchen; his brother Dietpald brought reinforcements, and later perished in the battle of the Lechfeld along with other of Udalrich's kinsmen. Dietpald's son Riwin received from the king the "countships" of the family with their castles. In the interest of a continuation of the ecclesiastical lordship in Augsburg, Udalrich gradually introduced another nephew, Adalbero, into that lordship. Adalbero became commander of the episcopal vassals, then the representative of the bishop in court service. He received the oath of fidelity from the bishop's familiars, and finally even carried the episcopal crosier. This was too much. At a synod, Udalrich's fellow bishops inveighed against him and accused him of heresy. Because the bishop was not alarmed by these threats, the other bishops sought to convince him by pointing out the effects of his example: others would demand similar things for their nephews and clergy. Admitting they were right, Udalrich was satisfied with the promise that after his death Adalbero would be elected bishop in his place.

This instance was one of a small circle of episcopal kinsmen: involved were Duke Burchart, a brother, and two nephews of Udalrich. But there were cases of wider clans and their political operations. An excellent example is provided by the counts of the Ardennes, who, after the death of their ancestor Wigerich (who died between 916 and 919), began a great rise supported by the Saxon imperial house. The name given the members destined for ecclesiastical orders was Adalbero; the place where they were educated and awaited appointment was the cathedral chapter of Metz. The famous Adalbero of Laon for example had belonged to this chapter during his youth. The case we shall describe here is not his but that of his rather unimportant uncle, Adalbero II of Metz (984–1005). In contrast to the bishop of Laon, he led a calm life in the center of kin connections. As we have seen, Adalbero of Metz was rich enough to be able to buy his way out of his military service obligations. His father was Frederic, duke of Upper Lorraine. When the latter died in 978, his widow controlled the duchy; then Adalbero's brother Dietrich became duke. The mother, a daughter of Hugh the Great from the later Capetian family, saw to it that Adalbero could give up his position as bishop of Verdun for the more important one of Metz. This went against canonical regulations, which did not allow such transferrals. A similarly named cousin of Adalbero II was archbishop of Reims (969–989). Another had to be satisfied with a position as provost. His nephews had it better, among them the above-mentioned Adalbero of Laon, bishop Adalbero of Verdun (984–991), and, later, Adalbero III, the subsequent bishop of Metz, who was still a child at the time of his elevation in 1005, possibly no more than five years old. By that time the counts of the Ardennes could no longer retain their central position in Metz; a Luxemburger, brother of the empress Kunigunda, usurped the see.

Adalbero II of Metz was a cousin of Queen Kunigunda, and therefore during his lifetime remained undisturbed. He was of Carolingian ancestry, a cousin—although in the second degree—of both Otto III and Henry II, a nephew of Hugh Capet and thus cousin of King Robert II. His enemies called him a drunkard, dull-witted (*hebes*) or mad (*vecors*). But he must have possessed martial virtues given the number of castles which, according to his biographer, he had besieged and whose surrender he had effected. The holders of these castles were said to have harmed the episcopal *familia;* so Adalbero had not acted on personal grounds. This one certainly should believe; what he did was for the benefit of his office and his family, whose bulwark this bishopric was.

We can suppose that the middle and lower strata in the diocese of Metz knew better times under Adalbero than they would have under a bishop "without family," who could only call his own vassals to assist against expansionist secular lords. First of all one had to look to the preservation of peace, and only then could one consider other matters. On the other hand, family politics during the period of civil war could result in the means of a bishopric being used for apparently destabilizing purposes. It was also bad for the entire diocese when a family lordship of this kind was broken, something that usually happened with the assistance of the emperor. We have already spoken of the period after Adalbero II and the Luxemburger's coup.

There are also examples of how much the lack of assistance by one's kin could alter the political situation. The archbishop of Reims, Heriveus (900–922), had been an energetic and active lord, destroying castles which harmed the episcopal *familia,* and standing firmly at the side of the Carolingian king during the war with the Robertines. When he died, the situation altered dramatically: King Robert installed Seulf, the archdeacon of Reims, as archbishop. This man had "no family" of his own, and he had serious conflicts with his predecessor's family—a brother and a nephew—on behalf of the fiefs that they held from the episcopal estate. Since Seulf could not succeed alone, he had to rely on the assistance of another comital family, which finally became the winner in the conflict: Count Heribert of

Vermandois got Seulf to promise that Heribert's son Hugo should succeed him in the archbishopric. After the early death of the archbishop—apparently by poisoning—the comital family was installed in Reims, at which time the ecclesiastical historian Flodoard lost his fiefs. In his account, Flodoard repeats the justification by which this uncanonical procedure of consecrating the not-yet five-year-old Hugo was defended: In this way the archbishopric would not be divided among outsiders (*extraneas personas*). The bishop of Soissons was to take care of spiritual matters while the secular affairs were to be "directed and controlled" according to the will of count Heribert. For the individuals directly affected by it this replacement was a disaster, but for the majority of the population it was better than the anarchy which might have resulted in the dismemberment of the *episcopatus* of Reims (in the sense of its estates) and thus might have led to the decline of the city. No reformer rose up against the arrangement that a layman should rule the archbishopric and that, in Auguste Dumas's phrase, "the Church was in the hands of the laity."

Bishop Abbo of Soissons, who exercised the *spiritualia* of the archdiocese for Heribert, was "closely tied" to the latter. One could also describe him as the puppet for the count. This is suggested even more strongly by the fact that Abbo's successor was an exile, Bishop Ulrich of Aix, who had fled the Saracens. Heribert gave him a Reims abbey and a single canonical prebend to support himself, which could almost be described as an employee's salary. The count's indirect control was intended to continue under the pontificate of Heribert's son Hugo. This did not happen because his conflict with the king resulted in a long-lasting reversal in his fortunes.

The means by which laymen might seize control of power within a diocese were numerous. In Milan in 983, for example, an inconspicuous means was chosen—the investiture of major vassals with fiefs from ecclesiastical property. To keep the people quiet, a portion of these fiefs was further bestowed on lesser fief holders. This left the clergy of Milan, who had previously held these fiefs, with nothing. As an example of another form of dependence, in the eastern Pyrenees around the year 1000, bishops were actual vassals of the counts of Cerdaña and Besalù. There were still other routes to power: it has been assumed that Boso of Provence and Rudolf I of Burgundy had allowed themselves to be made kings in order to become lords of the bishoprics in their regions. Later on, the kingdom of Burgundy was very weak; it was actually ruled by the magnates. So Thietmar could write that the Burgundian bishops "served the magnates as they would serve their king, and thus they enjoyed peace." Whether the legal foundation of this maintenance of peace was their advocacy (*Edelvogtei*) was a secondary question. In Germany, the heyday of inheritable advocacy of the noble (*Erbvogtei*) would begin after the death of Henry III; in France, bishops whose sees were outside of royal control had to be satisfied when they found highly ranked protectors. The bishop of Autun placed himself under the Burgundian duke, the bishop of Le Mans under the count of Anjou. When magnates did not elevate one of their own to the episcopacy, they were particularly careful to arrange that suitable candidates should be elected, especially those who were prepared to pay a high price for their election out of ecclesiastical property.

It is certainly true that ecclesiastical property and offices were "usurped" by laymen. In each case, however one should attempt to determine if the weakness of episcopal power and resources did not justify in the eyes of contemporaries the subordination to powerful families. Much rarer than such domination were protests against them. Other bishops besides Thietmar of Merseburg thought as realistically as he, and they were apparently content when in hard times they could nevertheless carry on a tolerable existence. On the other hand, there were bishops who had acquired comital powers either by delegation or usurpation of comital rights, especially in cases in which continuity of holders was broken. They served as subsidiary supports of continuity when secular power failed. The Church was not in the hands of the laity, nor was the laity in the hands of the Church; rather, within the elite was found an intimate relationship between the wielders of spiritual and secular power. This relationship did not harmonize well with canonical law, but it harmonized well with the dynamic principles of royal lordship and of the noble family.

Monarchy and great families were not so much antagonists as partners that needed each other. It would be difficult to demonstrate that the aristocrats of France had excluded the king from a great portion of the kingdom; rather, they held it for him where he was not present. In areas of limited royal power, kings had helped establish great families in such positions, and this was certainly not against the interest of the monarchy. An example is Ansfried, a nephew of the count of Toxandria, once a valiant warrior, who after the death of his wife lived in pious retirement. Against his will, Otto III made him bishop of Utrecht (995), "by force" as a chronicler reported. The author included in his work a poem which applauded rather than condemned this strange change of profession.

There were regions in Europe of dominant episcopal power and others of dominant secular lordships, such as the east German colonial regions and the Loire valley. As the great families competed for control of a region, the dominant place was won by those who could hold the key position in it. In order to maintain this position it was important to occupy the complementary position; that is, a bishopric needed a comital office and vice versa. Where such positions did not exist, attempts were made to create them. Catalan counts concerned themselves with the establishment of dioceses whose territories corresponded to their own administrative districts. They were successful; in 956, the bishopric of Roda was founded for the counts of Ribagorça, in 1016, the bishopric of Besalù was founded for a son of that region's count, while the count of the Cerdaña had to purchase the episcopal dignity of that area. Episcopal and comital justice more and more resembled each other, and both were designated with similar terms: *comitatus* referred primarily to the properties and profitable rights of the count, just as *episcopatus* usually designated the properties of the office rather than the bishopric itself. For this reason it is inaccurate to speak of the sale or inheritance of a bishopric. When, for example, the viscount William of Béziers left that city to his daughter along with "the *episcopatus* and the rights (*honor*) belonging to the city," what was meant was the episcopal properties that he held. Control over the episcopal property entailed having an important influence on the episcopal election. Juridically this power is hard to assess. While such matters have often disturbed historians, recently they have been seen as essentially harmless: the disposal of the episcopal *honor* has been explained as simple supervision, which may sometimes have been abused. It is correct from a formal perspective that in Lorraine in the tenth century no layman was lord of a bishopric and that laymen were merely made the advocates of episcopal property. On the other hand, we have seen how Adalbero II of Metz became bishop and how the counts of the Ardennes actually controlled the bishopric until they were replaced by their Luxemburger cousins.

Episcopal Appointments

Elsewhere, the control of important families over episcopal property and episcopal appointments was overt. The counts of Barcelona were lords of three bishoprics; they had the right to nominate and invest the bishop-elect, for which they received a "gift" in gold or silver proportionate to the "worth" of the bishopric. People were satisfied with the fact that from a formal viewpoint all was in order since an "election" was carried out by the clergy and people of the diocese. Before the period of the investiture contest, people generally understood canonical election less in the sense of freedom than in the concept that a member of the local clergy should be elected. The electors had long been restricted to the circle of the elite. Where the king did not set the tone, a member of the aristocracy usually directed the electoral assembly. The right to revise and to approve the election belonged to the metropolitan and two of his subordinate bishops. The king frequently took the place of the metropolitan, and the bishops were seldom consulted. Fulbert of Chartres complained in a letter that one of the favorites of the count of Troyes had usurped the "house and property of the bishop of Meaux" without royal command and without the agreement of the bishops after promises and a cash payment to the count.

The election of their pastor had originally been the prerogative of the Christian community. A practical supplement was a right of public supervision, an examination of the bishop-elect from administrative and political perspectives. The more the social sphere of episcopal activity increased, the more important became his suitability in this sphere; testing it and excluding incompetents were the duties of the political authorities: king, duke, count, and "people" in the sense of the leading strata. Brun of Querfurt tells us, as if it were a normal procedure, that after the death of Bishop Thietmar of Prague (981) the duke and the magnates (*maior populus*) met to elect his successor. There were various opinions, but finally they all raised their hands and filled the air with shouts—Adalbert, who would later become a saint; was elected.

It was in this manner that Saxons viewed an episcopal election in a region in which there was hardly a cathedral chapter. Elsewhere, in the west Frankish regions, one could ignore the secular magnates almost entirely and speak only of royal consent. In the civil war, the bishops had control of the ecclesiastical province of Reims, and they believed they had found the ideal candidate in Arnulf. A significant factor in Arnulf's "political suitability" was his Carolingian ancestry, as was Adalbert's descent from the Slawniking clan. These were things that only the magnates could judge, ecclesiastical or secular or both, but in no case could the Christian people of the diocese do so as a whole.

It was possible to reduce the number of electors to the cathedral chapter where the general interests of magnates did not come into play. It goes without saying that there were a great many such elections that fulfilled the will of leading powers and could not be called true elections in the modern sense. Kings and magnates frequently thought they could exercise the right of appointment without bothering with a pseudo-canonical detour. Such a case was the "election" in 1020 by Duke William of Aquitaine of a bishop of Limoges, which triggered a conflict among the local magnates over the right of appointment. Another conflict had occurred a few years before. After the death of the archbishop of Magdeburg, Henry II ordered that there be no election of a successor but merely an indication of the consensus of the chapter. At which Thietmar of Merseburg declared to the members of the chapter: "My lord may request what he wants. You however should protect yourselves from the loss of your rights . . . ," and called for the election by the chapter to proceed. The simplest procedure, followed especially under Otto III, was to send a representative to the court with the crosier of the deceased bishop in order to explore the will of the king and to carry out an election in accord with it. Thus one avoided the danger of losing royal favor by taking canonical rights too literally—something that could have very serious consequences.

In 979 Otto II had granted the clergy of Magdeburg the special right (*ius speciale*) of free election of the archbishop. This played a role in the above-mentioned statement of Thietmar of Merseburg, who was a member of the Magdeburg cathedral chapter. Election was a right which, as we have said, had not been given to all the churches in the kingdom. The standard case was what had been done before the privilege of 979 for Magdeburg: with papal approval the monarch appointed an administrator (*provisorem praefecit*) for the cathedral clergy. The right of royal appointment was as venerable as that of canonical election. The Christian emperors in late antiquity had appointed the institutional authorities, both clerical and lay. With their coronation the Frankish kings acquired little more than a claim to lordship, and they had to try to materialize this power by the appointment of their own agents. In a time of a rudimentary development of public institutions this meant to nominate specific individuals for generic duties. On the other hand, a bishop elected by the clergy regarded himself as carrying a mandate from them rather than as serving as agent (*provisor*) of the king, and a subsequent investiture at the king's court could but little change this perception. In the Ottonian period the emperors needed bishops still more than in the

Frankish period. Perhaps one should not look to the concept of the "proprietary church" in order to understand the investiture with the episcopal crosier which now came into fashion. The bishop had to be the king's man, his *fidelis*, and not an *episcopus civitatis*, who was only subsequently bound to the king. If there could be electoral privileges, these were to be demonstrations of royal favor and not statements of self-evident rights.

From the Gregorian perspective such actions were abuses, but the papacy of the tenth century took the situation for granted. What it most desired was the restriction of the right of naming bishops to the kings alone. The ancient custom (*prisca consuetudo*) should be observed: that only the king had the right to transfer a bishopric to a cleric, and that episcopal consecration be tied to royal permission. Maintenance of the existing order was especially important in difficult times, and to this end the bishop was an important, perhaps even the crucial, factor. Whenever an archbishop or a duke had "his" bishops, the empire was threatened along with the imperial church.

We can again cite Thietmar of Merseburg, who reflected the general view when he wrote that emperors and kings filled bishoprics as the representatives of Christ; Christ had installed them as princes, and it would be senseless for bishops to be subordinated to lesser powers. "In spite of this I have learned that many bishops are under the lordship of dukes and, what is still worse, suffer serious limitations from counts; they are allowed to do only what is useful to those lovers of this world (*seculi amatoribus*)." The spiritually legitimated royal authority was contrasted with the "world"; it was viewed as fundamentally "good," and occasional criticisms of specific occurrences could not change this opinion. Thietmar's general recognition of royal power stood alongside his resistance to royal command in the exceptional situation of the Magdeburg election, where he knew himself to be in the right. What he could not know was that it was a fundamental principle of Henry II's government to eliminate the right of election wherever he could. The empire's churches had now to bear a still greater burden than before and required obedient servants of the emperor. Even in the Ottonian period, theory and practice had not always coincided. In 981, for example, Othric, the archbishop elect of Magdeburg, was not confirmed by the emperor. In extreme cases it was thought possible that a king might direct coercive measures against the *familia* of a bishop who did not side with his candidate in an election.

As early as the Carolingian period, the functions of lay and ecclesiastical officeholders had come to resemble each other, and feudal law contributed to the assimilation. Under the Ottonians this development received a further impetus which, while founded in the Carolingian tradition, went beyond it. Historians have described the process by which the Church was absorbed into the apparatus of the state. The king tried to loosen the ties binding regional churches to their dukes. Feudal forms of investiture and the right of appointment were part of this program. The emperor served as a court of appeals for refractory clerics alongside the synods competent for such cases. Clerics could appeal to him as well as to their bishop, and not only the latter but the king exercised a coercive power designed to enforce obedience to religious vows. There was no clear delimination of competency; society was accustomed to the involvement of the king in the domain of both secular and religious affairs.

This involvement was generally accepted because proximity to the king carried favor, and a lessening of the mutual relationships had its disadvantages. When Rather of Verona wished to present himself to his readers as "original," as one who lived in a manner different from that of his fellow bishops, he recounted all that he did *not* do for the emperor and also what he did *not* request of him. On the one hand were *servitia* (material supply), military and court duties, and on the other appeals to the king, the request for favors, and intervention on behalf of Rather's own supporters. Leo of Vercelli, in a humorous aphorism, summarized what most people wanted of the ruler: he was to make them very rich and lay their enemies at their feet.

Such a comment presumes of course that the king had the power to do this and that both parties profited from the symbiosis. Rather's reserved comportment corresponded to the circumstances of a time during which an unstable ruler demanded much without being able to provide anything. From prison Rather complained to King Hugo, "Ecclesiastical property is like fire, you cannot give it away, you cannot eat it, you cannot drink it." In contrast, under Ottonian lordship being a "court bishop," as Leo of Vercelli termed Otto III's episcopal supporters, yielded rich rewards. Leo's expectation that he would receive similar treatment from Henry II, however, was premature. The time was past when a powerful ecclesiastical position could be handed out with a single humorous line, as Otto had done in his famous letter to Heribert of Cologne, his "Archilogothete," (chancellor) in 998: "Otto, Emperor only by the grace of God, (declares) to Heribert the archilogoteta his grace, and (gives him) Cologne and one foot of Pallium (= the expectancy of the archiepiscopal pallium)." In this ironic manner Otto had presented the absolutist course of Ottonian ecclesiastical lordship to one who had been his faithful follower since his early youth. Likewise it anticipates the modern, written form of appointment, a "decree" appearing in place of a verbal pronouncement of the royal will. Elsewhere, and in this case for the public too, the traditional oral and symbolic forms were preserved. The major emphasis was placed on the investiture. Heribert, who as chaplain was already a royal vassal, possibly commended himself once more into the protection of the emperor.

The bishops of imperial Italy, who were not foreigners as was Rather, mostly came from important families of episcopal vassals which had benefited from the sale of royal honors, especially under Berengar II. Thus there was no opposition between episcopacy and nobility, and hardly any concerning the decision of Otto I to make the bishops his supporters against the magnates. The construction of an Italian "Imperial Church" on the German model may not have been the goal of Ottonian policy but, rather, simply a balance to the existing powers and a support of their rivalries. Certainly in many instances a spontaneous alliance developed with northern Italian bishops, and their support by the emperor was beyond question. All in all, the ecclesiastical hierarchy of Italy had neither the advantages of their German counterparts nor the full complement of obligations born by these latter. Military service and material support were obligations in both regions, but the duties of the German prelates were more important than those of the Italian. They were still heavier to bear when Henry II took the reins of power.

In France there was nothing that could be compared with the Ottonian imperial church. Although historians have counted nineteen "royal bishoprics" during the reign of Robert the Pious, one must remember that many of them had been filled by the king not by free choice but under political pressure. The opposite was possible, too, of course: the candidate could be designated by the king's intervention, even though there is no mention, in the sources, of the royal appointment. At the court of Robert the Pious, bishops were predominant until the last years of Robert's reign. We know, however—and not only from the complaints of Adalbero of Laon—that the king liked to promote humble individuals who were dependent on him, especially monks. The new dynasty was not sure of the aristocratic families, which still had connections to the Carolingians and across the border to the east. Faithful cooperation between kings and bishops, from which both sides profited, was a characteristic of the imperial church; it therefore had to endure the brunt of the Gregorian movement.

THE BISHOP AS LORD

In the name of his lord, Bruno of Cologne directed a successful policy of creating bishops from the court chapel personnel or from the clergy of his own diocese. A precondition was that the will of the emperor and of his Duke Bruno be attended to and carried out. This policy required the material basis for a successful pontificate. If a bishop was in need, the emperor had to help him or face the possibility that the bishop would appeal to one of the important families and thus be drawn into its political system.

The king of France could not offer such preconditions. When King Lothair had besieged and conquered Verdun after the death of Otto II, the city was to receive a new bishop called Hugo. After his installation he received a report on the material situation of the bishopric and learned that the episcopal manors had been destroyed. He "soon mounted his horse and rode back. When he had ridden off, our people elected one of our own without royal appointment (*sine regio dono*), Adalbero, the son of the very noble Duchess Beatrix." This person was Adalbero II, later bishop of Metz, of whose manifold family connections we have already spoken. Verdun was still in French hands, but even under the subsequent Ottonian government little changed for the bishopric and the city—peace was achieved under the protection of the most powerful family of the realm. The episcopal manors probably were reconstructed at the expense of the family of the counts and dukes. While Hugo, being a foreigner, had asked "from what he was to live," Adalbero had no such problem.

Thus there were good reasons for enumerating not only noble ancestry but also wealth among the virtues of a bishop. He who is counted among the rich, as Rather of Verona said, is seen as the wiser; he who has more estates (*massutior*, from *massa, mansus*) will be more celebrated. He who is seen as thrifty is despised; parsimony is reproved even when it is attributed to monks. On the other hand, everyone praises generosity. The existence of a bishop who is not rich in specie (*pecuniosus*) seems without foundation.

The catalogue of praiseworthy virtues in bishops was similar to that of the nobility. Here, as there, critical voices such as Rather's were sometimes raised against excessively worldly appraisals of such qualities. Even Rather did not despise earthly riches entirely; we know that in his later years he had accumulated enough money to buy a monastery. Contemporaries spoke against noble pride mainly when they wanted to describe the life of a member of the middle level of society. Thus Aimoin of Fleury, in his *vita* of the abbot Abbo, explained that the latter was not full of pride because of the noble blood of his ancestors. Nevertheless, Aimoin says, he came from a family which had been free for as far back as human memory reached. Some mention of ancestors was essential, and even modest origins could honor ecclesiastics, provided of course that they did not come from the ranks of the unfree.

The self-perception of bishops was in many ways a "familial perception." An example is Udalrich of Augsburg, who had served his uncle as (episcopal) chamberlain but did not wish to serve his uncle's successor because he was not highborn. Another count's son, Bishop Burchard of Worms, has been described as having "impressive self-assurance"; in the words of Horst Fuhrmann, "he was not among those medieval authors who avoided giving their names in their work." Ademar of Chabannes named himself as the author of his historical work although he was a monk, and he did so in the context of enumerating his important kinsmen, both clerical and secular.

It would clearly be incorrect to see bishops of this period merely as exponents of their families. The office of bishop was much more of an institution than was that of count, and it could not be totally subsumed into individuals or families. Whoever held it had above all to be united with his ecclesiastics and his episcopal colleagues. If he was of noble origins, his family and social equals were added to these groups. Even a man such as Thietmar of Merseburg demonstrated a certain distancing from noble interpretations of law and from the aristocratic idea of honor. Spiritual community with the clergy did not yet mean with the entire Church, and rarely with the entire empire, but it often meant community with ecclesiastical province. Conflicts between the different spheres of life were not unheard of. Bishop Balderich of Liège, for example, made important donations from his allodial property to the churches and monasteries of his city in spite of the danger that his numerous family might thereby be left in distress. Not every bishop was concerned with the needs of his family, but each remained bound by the concepts and customs of his social group. The primary motivations of the episcopal rank remained very close to that of secular elites. The two *vitae* of Adalbert of Prague refer to these motives. They demonstrate that harmony ruled between Adalbert's office as bishop on the one hand, and his noble personality, his wealth, his deeds, and his private life on the other.

There were episcopal "courts," just as there were secular magnates' courts. This was true not only of the most important prelates. Even the bishop of Carcassonne spoke—as did a Capetian king—of his chamberlain, his steward, his seneschal, and his cellarer. It was a matter of rank, in the same way as the number of one's following bespoke one's social status. Bishops frequently demanded oaths of fidelity from their clergy, thus making them similar to a vassalic following. This practice was not even entirely alien to monasticism. Odilo of Cluny always had a great following of monks with him; he created the impression of contrast to the magnates of this world, but remained bound to their concepts.

A courtly retinue had its center in the community of the table. For the spiritual significance of the episcopal office it was sufficient if this community consisted of the cathedral chapter and perhaps a few of the ecclesiastical dignitaries of the city. But in addition there were frequently ecclesiastical and lay travelers to entertain, which increased the prestige of the episcopal court. It may have been for reasons of this sort that such care was accorded to episcopal vineyards. After the fellowship of the table came the fellowship of the cup, which provided an opportunity for necessary bargains and transactions. A "noble" ecclesiastic at the court of the bishop of Orléans, for example, negotiated with the latter concerning the bestowal on him of the office of abbot in one of the monasteries of the city. Official consultations could even be conducted in the bishop's bedroom. He did not rest alone but even at night was usually surrounded by clerics. The personal, informal governing style of secular lords had its parallel in the episcopal sphere.

The bishop's lordship was also clear in his role as both recipient and giver of gifts. The former was a sign of homage or of goodwill; the latter showed his grace to others. We have previously been reminded that the meaning of a gift could lie in its social value, as symbol of the connection with others; the symbolic value predominated here. When bishops visited each other, they returned home with gifts from their host. It was a means of showing respect which at the same time honored the giver as an indication of his generosity and prosperity. It was different from the priest's "gift" to his bishop when he arrived at a synod, or the assessment that he was sometimes required to pay, which was entirely opposed to the canon laws and therefore forbidden. In the secular sphere, presents of this kind had some parallels in the gifts of magnates to the king as well as in the *dona* or *exemia* of peasant landholders to the abbot, provost, or pastor. The devotional and ritual character of these gifts has been noted; only when the traditional gift became a tribute payment, when the *porcus donativus* became a simple *porcus,* did the presentation assume a primarily financial character. Nevertheless, the relations between governor and governed were made clear through such duties.

Traditional gift giving indicated social ties from "below" to "above" or—when there were sufficient means available—in the opposite direction. This latter was possible only for the highest level of ecclesiastical functionaries. In Rome, every newly ordained priest in the diocese received ecclesiastical vestments from the pope as a gift along with gold or silver, wine, grain, and oil. Similarly Archbishop Heriveus of Reims, as the nephew of the count, could disperse wealth from his abundance: he returned feudal properties to the church; all that was needed was there in superabundance: the granaries were full, "and also," wrote the chronicler, "he gave me and the other ecclesiastics, canons, monks, and nuns many possessions."

In such a portrait, spiritual matters in the narrow sense have a very limited place; but the portrait was a true one. Concern for material security, in everyone's eyes, was a precondition for all other concerns and often constituted more of the bishop's work than did the spiritual.

The obligations of the newly consecrated bishop of Liège are summarized by Rather: "I was enthroned, I presided (over an assembly), I began to do what had to be done, I led my military host against the enemies of the emperor (Otto I). I returned, I received him who had consecrated me (Bruno of Cologne), I served him, gave him gifts . . . , accompanied him on his journey home as a most devoted servant (*famulatissime*) as far as Maastricht. . . . I turned around, traveled through the diocese, conferred with the most important clerics and laity about what was to be done, in order to do justice to everyone." It was at this point that Rather's conflict with his environment began. Others, like him, could find little peace when they had to serve in turn the emperor, the archbishop, the clergy, and the laity of their towns.

The daily routine could be a string of vexations. When Rather, in Verona, called for one of his clerics or servants who failed to appear, he ordered him seized by force by his lowest agents, the *baculares* (stick-bearing beadles). Bishop Adalbero I of Metz argued with the abbot of Gorze over a servant of the monastery who administered some property for Metz; a detailed presentation of the dispute was preserved in Gorze. Finally, we are told, Adalbero restored to the monastery a manor that his brother had received in fief from Gorze. This caused a conflict between the monks and an episcopal administrator of the manor conerning a quantity of grain stored there. Rather asserted that it was the bishop's duty to know how many persons subject to the tithe, how many peasant tenures, how many bushels of grain, and how much wine was needed to support a particular number of clerics. He believed it was an ignorant shepherd who did not know where pasturage for his sheep was to be found.

Secular Activities within the City

Not only the clergy but also the members of the episcopal *familia* had to be taken care of. When thirty-five of these were murdered or killed in one year in Worms, this was "a great disgrace to our church," as Bishop Burchard correctly wrote. Little could be done from the pastoral perspective, because the perpetrators "bragged about their deeds and were proud of them rather than indicating any remorse." We can assume that these deaths often were the result of blood feuds. A steward named by the bishop functioned as judge, but he could accomplish little: blood justice belonged to the count in the county of Worms, who was a member of a family which was hostile to the bishop. Moreover, frequent use of the death penalty would have greatly reduced the *familia*. The only recourse was to punishments "of hide and hair" (that is, birching and hair shaving) and an attempt to prevent the continuation of conflicts between hostile clans. Burchard had regularized this and much else in his famous "court law" (*Hofrecht*) for the territory of his city. As a final provision he established penalties for anyone who "conferred (*consiliatus est*) about his feudal lord, the bishop, with the latter's enemies," that is, for anyone who assisted in a conspiracy against "the episcopal estates (*honorem*) or against the well-being of the bishop." Burchard did this although the contest for lordship over the city had been settled and the unique "good" member of the family of his enemies was preparing to ascend the royal throne as king Conrad II.

Like a secular lord, the bishop was expected to temper the harshness of justice with mercy, when appropriate. Both justice and mercy were ancient Roman virtues which were expected of the lord and his agents. They were part of a centuries-old literary tradition and something of the old concept of office continued to exist. Like the king, the ideal bishop was supposed to be feared for his sternness and loved for his kindness. He was supposed to temper with clemency his authority to punish. In everyday business with its quarrels and divergent interests it must have been difficult indeed to maintain such an attitude.

Even more than secular lords, bishops had to serve as building commissioners. They had as many castles to construct as secular lords, and were frequently responsible for the construction of their city walls as well. In Italy the burghers often lacked the money for such work, while the counts lacked interest, so that the responsibility fell to the bishop. In Rhenish towns this was already the situation in the ninth century; we have the written order of Bishop Thiedlach of Worms (891–914). The walls under construction were divided into segments for the different social groups of burghers who had to do this heavy work. Stone walls provided more security than simple earthen walls and wooden palisades. Hence the population increased, and the fortified zone received its own separate legal jurisdiction. Naturally, a solidly walled city raised the prestige of its bishop.

Bishops who undertook the construction of new churches or restored existing ones had always won praise. In the tenth century, bishops began to build great cathedrals: Notker of Liège constructed a cathedral ninety meters long, twenty meters longer than that city's modern cathedral, and almost as wide. In the eleventh century—and certainly not, as Rodulf Glaber suggested, in connection with millenarian tendencies—a veritable frenzy of episcopal construction was embarked on, to which we owe such great accomplishments as the cathedrals of the Salian dynasty, but which had dubious effects on the prosperity of episcopal cities. The costs of such construction were more easily afforded by important monasteries to which gifts flowed from all sides. Small bishoprics like Eichstätt were severly afflicted with building fever: under bishop Heribert (from 1021), as we learn from a later source (ca. 1080), the old buildings began to be torn down and new ones were built. Heribert's predecessors had been content with modest structures; but he and his successors built either new churches and palaces or new castles. People forced to work on them were reduced to poverty. Instead of doing important agricultural labor, they were forced to spend almost all of their time building stone walls; nonetheless, the traditional tribute payments were demanded by the bishop with extraordinary harshness.

When Thietmar wrote about the life of a bishop, he never forgot to praise—as the noblest undertaking—the construction or renovation of his cathedral church. The consecration of the cathedral was a sort of festival convocation of the royal episcopacy as well as of the secular magnates. As early as 992, at Halberstadt, three archbishops, sixteen bishops, and "all the magnates (*primates*) of Saxony" had come. That virtually the entire royal church was present at the consecration of the Bamberg cathedral is hardly surprising. Thirty-six bishops assisted and in addition "an unbelievable crowd of clerics and laity" were there assembled; many who had been in disfavor with the king returned to his grace.

Construction increased the prestige of the bishop not only vis-à-vis the king and his episcopal colleagues but also with those strata from which the episcopal vassals were recruited. To accept ecclesiastical fiefs was no humiliation even for counts, but those who had to do military service under a lord did it most willingly for one who reigned in a "lordly" manner. The distribution of ecclesiastical property to *milites* was certainly necessary in unsettled times; moreover, vassals were needed for royal service as the kernel of the episcopal contingent. Some bishops passed out too much of their property, either by dividing it among kinsmen or for reasons of representation: the size of the secular following raised both the prestige and the political and military value of a bishop. It was said of the bishop Heribert of Auxerre (971–996) that "he made gifts to his vassals (*militibus*) more than was proper, so that the counts Odo of Chartres and Heribert of Trécon obeyed him because of the fiefs that he had given them." This fact should be noted with some reserve: we are dealing here with multiple vassality. All the same, each count had entered a relationship which required that he coordinate his political program with the bishop of Auxerre.

Secular Activities in Feudal and Royal Service

Heribert of Auxerre was the feudal lord of two counts; his successor Hugo was himself count of Chalon-sur Saône. As the only son of the count of that city the bishop undertook the exercise of comital rights "at the command of the king." This was not unusual in France; Charles the Simple had bestowed comital rights on the bishop of Noyon, King Raoul gave such rights to the bishop of Le Puy, and Louis IV had given the *comitatus Remensis* to Archbishop Artold of Reims. In this manner the king avoided the inheritability of the comital office and could oversee the exercise of the bishop's comital duties through his own agents. Where both the ecclesiastical and the secular office were united in one hand, competition between the two functionaries was avoided, a competition which often resulted in the division into "episcopal city" and "comital city." It was best for the population if the ecclesiastical lord of the city had unlimited power so that, if need be, he could safeguard the keys to the city gates under his pillow at night, as Archbishop Arnulf of Reims was said to have done. The bishop was also the lord of the city in cases when a weak count, in order not to be entirely excluded, entered episcopal vassalage.

Often, and not only in France, a distinction seems to have been made between the *comitatus* in the narrow sense, that is the properties and valuable rights, and the full authority in the county along with judicial rights. Even for Reims it is not entirely clear that the archbishop exercised authority over the county in this full sense. In troubled times, primacy in the city was the decisive factor. In northern Italy, too, this part often fell to the bishop. Pavia was burned by the Hungarians, Genoa was destroyed, but we hear nothing about the counts of those regions. In those situations the bishops appeared as leaders of the defense, and subsequently countship further lost its importance. On the other hand, Rather of Verona could not prevail against the count; we are told of a rivalry between bishop and count in Parma in 962. The situation differed from region to region.

In Germany, sometimes the exercise of the comital or ducal office by a bishop was thought to be scandalous. We learn this from the famous letter in which the archbishop William of Mainz complained to the pope Agapet II (955) of a measure until then unheard-of: Otto the Great had entrusted Bruno, archbishop of Cologne, with a duchy, namely Lorraine. Even for supporters the affair was not deemed appropriate. In the same context William criticized an episcopal countship which had not previously existed in Germany. He may have been sensitized to the issue by the situation sometimes found in France. In Germany the bestowal of comital rights on bishops first became normal under Otto III. Early cases of this sort concerned borderlands such as the dioceses of Liège and Hildesheim. Here Bishop Bernward had built the Mundburg castle for protection against the Slavs and held comital rights around it from Otto. As this emperor was frequently absent from Germany, such a concentration of rights was necessary.

When the emperor extended his claims against the military and financial power of the imperial church, as was already begun under

Otto II, he had to loosen the reins and be more generous in his awarding of fiefs. We have little information about a direct relationship between military service and donations, but the emperor's policy toward the hierarchy must have played a major role in this context. In France, military aid was often made directly dependent on the promise of donations by the king. Such things, if they existed in Germany, were concealed. For a secret arrangement with the emperor we have one clue: the enrollment list of heavily armored cavalrymen for the Italian war of 981. Here we are told that the bishop of Liège was to provide sixty cavalrymen; two years later he received, through the good offices of Otto II, the revenue from the market taxes in Visé for "his faithfulness abroad (*extra*) and at home (*domique*) and his devotion in the exercise of his vassalic obligations (*nostrae fidelitatis executionem*)." Two years later Bishop Notker appeared at court once again and was granted the comital rights in the county of Huy. In the charter was noted that he had been "in all things a true executor of the vassalic obligations to his lord." This was the first such grant during the regency of Otto III.

Imperial service in Italy and elsewhere made it necessary for bishops to have a powerful vassalic following. Only a few of them could afford to contribute money instead of the military service owed. Adalbero II of Metz could, because he was the son of a wealthy family. But even his biographer complained of the "almost intolerable" extent of "gifts" which the bishop had to pay the court. As to military power, a full assessment of the total available troops is difficult to make, and the amount that ecclesiastics contributed to their support is not easily determined since we do not know which bishops replaced military service with payments. This is equally true in the above-quoted list of armored horsemen who reinforced the army in 981, who were drawn from areas that had previously contributed none or only a few. It is clear, however, that of all the troops called into service in 981, three-quarters came from the contingent of the higher clergy.

Such a figure probably cannot be generalized. In France, where the political situation was quite different, the later Carolingians had to depend almost exclusively on the service of bishops. They no longer had any direct secular vassals who obeyed them. During the Hungarian invasion of 919, Archbishop Heriveus of Reims was the only one who responded to the royal appeal for assistance, allegedly with fifteen hundred armed troops. And as late as the middle of the eleventh century a French chronicler wrote that the major part of the resources (*facultates*) of the realm were to be found in the hands of the bishops and abbots.

The weight of military service fell heavily on bishoprics. What could happen when episcopal troops were once again called into combat is described by a (not strictly contemporary) author: In 1018 Duke Gottfried of Lower Lorraine had to muster troops at the command of Henry II against the insurrection of the count of (West) Friesland. Bishop Balderich of Liège excused his absence from the proposed expedition on account of illness and the fact that in previous wars he had provided the requested service. The duke angrily accused him of infidelity and insubordination (*contemptus*) and suggested that the reason the bishop did not want to join in the expedition was that some of the enemies were his kinsmen; in his heart he was a traitor and indifferent toward the prosperity of the empire.

Balderich was forced to give his contingent marching orders. He died soon afterwards, allegedly on the same day that the royal army suffered a severe defeat at Vlaardingen in Holland. In 1046 one of his successors showed little interest in appearing with his army in Holland for embarcation. He turned back, which resulted in a complaint to the emperor that cost Bishop Wazo a fine of 300 pounds of silver. He had lost the emperor's favor and was not even offered a seat when he came to court.

The military authority of the emperor was not without its limits. Vis-à-vis clerics, at least, he had only financial and moral means of coercion. It lowered the bishop's reputation when he had to have ecclesiastical ornaments melted down in order to pay the fine, and it was shameful for him to be treated not as a lord and one of God's anointed but as a servant. One can suppose that this loss of honor also fell, at least indirectly, on the bishop's clan.

If bishops did not always willingly place their *fideles ecclesiae,* their episcopal vassals, at the disposition of the emperor, it was also because they had other obligations to fulfill. The vassals had to protect episcopal peace in the diocese and thereby to serve the needs of regional and local politics. Archbishop Heriveus, who fought for the king in 919 against the Hungarians, constructed castles which secured episcopal lordship in the area of Reims; he besieged "with his men" the castle of a count who had often harmed the *familia* of Reims and had entrenched himself in Reims's territory. This type of territorial politics with military means would later become typical in France. It was characterized by the construction of castles and "countercastles," reprisals in the form of devastations and constantly expanding alliances. What Friedrich Prinz calls "a regionally expansionist episcopal lordship which used its military power for its own ends" was virtually the norm in unsettled areas. Thus bishops had to call upon the assistance of their "friends," kin as well as vassals, to thwart a secular magnate who had seized an episcopal castle.

THE ARMED BISHOP

Such a task could hardly be accomplished by a simple command. The bishop himself had to be present and to intervene if necessary, and so he had to carry at least defensive weapons. That bishops should play an active role in battle was generally accepted, at least in the case of war against non-Christians. In the year 1010 the bishops of Barcelona, Gerona, and Vich were killed in battle on the Guadiaro river along with a single count. Surely they did not allow themselves to be slaughtered without putting up armed resistance. In 951 a bishop of Urgel bequeathed to his kin a fire-tempered sword (*spatha ignea*), a spear, three helmets, and a shield. Pope John X may have been in full armor when—as he boasted—he put "himself and his body" in jeopardy to hunt down Saracens.

Were these military activities exceptional cases, justified by the extreme circumstances of the wars against the Italian and Spanish Saracens? It is a fact that bishops bore arms and used them in local conflicts as well. One example is Bishop Berengar of Cambrai, a foreigner, who had many enemies among the inhabitants of his city. He carried out a successful feud against them in revenge for their having once closed the city gates against him. He sent his supporters a wagonload of the lances of his slain or captured enemies in order to glorify his victory. He himself drove two of his enemies through the fields outside the city, spurring on his horse and hunting them down "so that his lance almost touched their shoulders," until they reached a monastery. The martial activities of Pope John XII are still better known. Luitprand of Cremona, in the presence of the emperor and of "all the Romans," accused the pope of setting out against the emperor, "his sword girded, with shield, helmet, and cuirass." Only the Tiber, which separated him from the (imperial) army, prevented his being taken captive in this costume.

Liutprand's description shows the aversion of many clerics to such practices, which, indeed, in part led to the pope's depositon in 963. Around the middle of the century it was felt necessary to reflect on the problem of episcopal military actions. These had long been tolerated although they could not be reconciled with canon law. Ruotger provided an answer to the question of why a bishop, in this case Bruno of Cologne, "would be involved in political affairs and would occupy himself with dangerous military activities when he should only be concerned with the care of souls." Bruno, Ruotger continues, acted in this manner in order to protect the peace; and, moreover, such activities were not novel. Anyone objecting to Bruno's attitude was among "those who do not comprehend the divine order of the universe." Traces of the same conflict of attitudes can be found in France. While Flodoard, writing in 948, dispassionately described the role of Lotharingian bishops in the siege of Mouzon Castle, at the end of the century Richer spoke only of the activities of the royal army in this siege.

Ecclesiastical historians also found it helpful to rework an old topos from the life of Saint Martin of Tours by Sulpicius Severus: Bishops like Udalrich of Augsburg rode into the midst of the battle; spears flew past them, stones crashed all around, but the bishops remained unharmed, protected not by armor but by their liturgical robes. Given the negative effect of the death of a commander on soldiers' morale, we may assume that ecclesiastical princes acted so incautiously only on rare occasions. It was another thing to use a priest or deacon for an equally dangerous service without weapons: clerics were used as flag bearers in battles in the eastern areas of the empire.

Still, voices were frequently raised in opposition to clerical military service. Understandably, the most common critics were Italian bishops, who were heavily burdened by obligations of imperial service. Many examples of this sort could be quoted. We have chosen a statement by Rather of Verona, complaining about the practical morality of his cathedral chapter. Its members believed that some forbidden activities such as dicing, drinking, falkoning, and hunting belonged to the sphere of venal sins. The least of such sins, they thought, would be military service for one's lord. They justified this position on the grounds that a vassal who refused to perform military service broke his feudal oath. While dire penalties were prescribed for oathbreaking, none were for military service. Wasn't it better for a priest to fight in armor than to break a solemn oath?

Falkoning and hunting were privileges of lords, gambling presupposes property, and wine costs money; such activities belonged to the lifestyle of nobles and prosperous burghers. What was appropriate for the laity could not be a serious sin for secular priests, and so military service was pardoned. Monastic circles often opposed military service. Adalbero I of Metz, the reformer of the monastery of Gorze in 933, wanted to give the monastery only as much property as necessary so that the abbot would not find himself in the situation of giving out fiefs to vassals whom he would have to lead on military expeditions. He was not to perform any *servitium,* but only to concern himself with serving his brothers and the monastic life (*religioni*).

The king was interested in the number and military power of the higher clergy's vassals; in many cases the clergy shared that interest. The enfeoffed estates were not alienated from property of the church; rather, military and political goals now replaced economic ones. Whatever was left outside of enfeoffing and leasing had to satisfy many different purposes: the episcopal court, the cathedral chapter, church construction, care of the poor, reception of guests, and, especially in Italy, the supplying of military detachments passing through the diocese. Without large donations from the faithful, above all for the care of the poor and for church construction, this remainder was very often insufficient. Donations depended on many factors: the general economic situation, the renown enjoyed by the patrons of the diocese, the prestige of the bishop, and his familial connections. If he had come from a different region and had made enemies of the cathedral chapter like Rather of Verona, then his attempts at reform earned nothing but invective and complaints. Rather had improved his own finances by confiscating the benefices of clerics who abused him openly. Another complaint against him was the poor condition of the episcopal palace in Verona. It was in this way that the bishop had freed himself of the "guests" he was forced to house there. They were for the most part German emissaries and military commanders in transit. To care for the poor he ordered clerics to invite them to share their own meals. One-quarter of the episcopal income was earmarked for the poor and for travelers. It was certainly too little. Clearly, care of the poor never reached the level of real social service. In this connection Rather cited a text of Saint Jerome to the effect that neither the wealth of Darius nor the treasure of Croesus could satisfy all the world's poor. When a bishop such as Wazo of Liège cared for the city's population during a famine in an exemplary manner, he did so in part out of his own property (*de suo*).

It was easy for Wazo's biographer to praise his generosity and to compare it with the parsimony of other bishops. The author employed the topos of envious people who were astounded at the fame and virtue of someone less powerful than they. In this sphere, *liberalitas* was not exactly the same as it was for the laity: clerics were expected primarily to look after the poor and travelers rather than their own vassals; a total donation to the latter of episcopal property seemed extremely questionable. A century earlier, episcopal hospitality included both gifts to transient royal vassals and food for members of the middle strata of society (*liberi mediocres vel nobiliores*). The reality had probably changed but little; biographers, however, placed different emphasis on the facts.

Pastoral Duties

Unlike secular lords, bishops were not simply to be models for others through their actions; they were also responsible for the Christian education of their clerics. Spiritual readings at the bishop's table were not yet in use, as though in a monastery, where readings were seen as the most important aspect of common meals. Sometimes there was a sharp contrast between the pleasures of the table and the spiritual nourishment of the clergy. Bishop Megingaud of Eichstätt (989–1014) was criticized for often breaking off the liturgical singing so that he could get to the dinner table more quickly.

The bishop was duty-bound to teach, primarily through his sermons. In fact, he was the foremost Christian preacher in his city. Latin sermons, of course, were directed to the clergy, and only few laymen understood anything of them. The question of preaching to the laity had been raised earlier. Bishop Notker of Liège was praised for preaching to the people in their own language and to the clergy in Latin and thus for having offered "the children milk, and the strong solid nourishment." This nourishment was particularly solid in that Latin sermons were prepared in written form, while vernacular sermons seem to have been given extemporaneously. For this reason we have hardly any traces of them.

We know little about the extent to which bishops concerned themselves with missionary and pastoral activities within their dioceses. The detailed description of the activities of Udalrich of Augsburg includes information about the content of his sermons, but only of those delivered in Latin. His role in episcopal courts in the diocese seems to have been more important; he had to impose penalties and not only admonitions, for misconduct. On visitations Udalrich called together the "wise and trustworthy" and ordered them under oath to say what had taken place "against justice and law."

This ecclesiastical parallel to the comital court had little to do with "internal evangelization." At least in part, the situation was different for clerics in the episcopal court, "whether they were from lower free status or high nobility." Not only did they receive food and drink, but the bishop also let them be instructed (*docere praecepit*). The parish clergy, on the other hand, who had been drawn in part from the non-free, seem to have been provided with only the usual visitation questions.

The means by which the Christianity of the cathedral clergy was fostered conformed to the period. It was said of Bishop Walpoto of Liège that he greatly prized fasts and vigils and was always pleased when he found one of the clergy keeping vigil in the church. He esteemed such clergy highly and honored them with gifts. It could be that the reasons for these vigils were not always religious, for the bishop's preferences were certainly known.

The most vivid means of educating clergy and laity were the sacraments and the liturgy. When Udalrich of Augsburg continued performing confirmations until late into the night while on his visitations, he thereby came into intimate contact with the masses. The people thronged into the cathedral for important festivals and took part in the divine office. Udalrich's biographer devoted much space to the manner in which the bishop celebrated Lent and Easter. Such liturgies were also a presentation of the divinely ordained order, with the bishop in the center and his clergy serving him. His actions were also vital to daily liturgies. It was the bishop's responsibility to ward off the various evils that diabolical forces might inflict on the faithful. From this period we still possess the liturgies for the benediction of a monastic smoke house and for protection against the rotting of grain as well as special blessings for the staffs carried by pilgrims and for the travel bags of those who either wanted to or were required to journey to Rome.

An essential ritual was that of the dedication of a church, described in a treatise probably by Remigius of Auxerre. The bishop knocked with his crosier thrice on the church door, which was then opened to him. After a prayer offered by the clergy he began to "write" letters with his crosier on the floor of the church, in alphabetic order from one corner to the one diagonally across from it, as we saw above. This ritual must have been very impressive for onlookers, whether or not they understood its deeper meaning. Next followed the blessing of water with a mixture of salt and ashes: the water was a symbol of the Christian people, the salt represented the

Christian teaching, the ashes the passion of Christ. Everything had a deeper meaning—every gesture, every step, the painting of crosses on the walls of the church, and other rites which might be amplified according to local traditions. In our own day such symbolism is little appreciated, even by Catholic clergy. Some scholars have attempted to identify ritual aggression in such ceremonies.

At the risk of eliciting opposition, we must say that the liturgical and ritual duties of the bishop were often more important for the faithful than verbal pastoral care. Take, for example, a person who, because of a sinful deed, was required by his pastor to undertake a pilgrimage to Rome. He probably trod the long and dangerous route with a lighter step if he was carrying a pilgrim's staff blessed by his bishop. That the church was a sacred and immune space open only to peaceful men and women was evident to everyone who had taken part in the consecration of a church or to whom the secret rituals had been described. An integral part of liturgy is the conviction that it is important and meaningful. This conviction was mutually shared by clergy and people.

For clerics, instruction by their pastor and liturgical duties were probably less effective than the pastor's living example of spiritual virtues. It is difficult to determine how far we can believe the accounts of the harsh asceticism or quasi-monastic life of some bishops. These biographies were frequently written by monks on the model of previous holy ascetics, and their purpose was more edification than history. The descriptions were sometimes exaggerated, but they must not be dismissed. When we read of a bishop who used to wear a hairshirt or even practiced self-flagellation, we must ask to what extent such practices were related to monastic ascetic circles such as that of Gorze. Although such activities were normally practiced in secret, word of them must have circulated.

A more important example for the clergy was the bishop's participation in the "hours," common prayers at fixed intervals of the day. Without them, the community of cathedral canons and every other community was threatened with disintegration. Participation or nonparticipation at the "hours" determined the choice between an active and a contemplative life. Bishops had so much to do that the most pious of them could not always share in the celebration of the canonical hours. Even so holy a man as Wazo of Liège could participate fully only during Lent; at other times he was present in the choir for the hours only in the morning and evening. And this was in spite of his otherwise very pious life: it had been almost impossible to force him to accept canonical election to the episcopacy. He had dedicated himself to self-mortification, and during Lent he drank beer or even water, instead of wine, a practice seen as harsh asceticism.

Seldom were bishops saints. If they were not, the battle against their specific weaknesses could have an effect on the surrounding community. Such was the case of Walpoto of Liège, who was a gourmand. His corpulence was, according to the excuse made by his biographer, the result of the mass of his bones; he ate relatively little for his size. This man was an example for all voracious clerics: when at table, he took plates with the best portions as though he wanted to eat them himself, but he gave them to the poor. He accused himself of gluttony. So human could a bishop show himself to those who sat at table with him. For the masses he had to remain a representative of his office and protect his dignity, even when his girth interfered.

Public Dying

A bishop always had to be a model for clergy and people, especially in his last, most difficult hours. A public life demanded a public death, which is presented in bishops' *vitae* in a ritualized form. First, the bishop was said to know of his impending death. Bruno of Cologne would not allow himself to be dissuaded of this premonition by his companions. He prepared his will, called for two bishops who happened to be in Cologne, and carried on an edifying conversation with them. He received the Eucharist, and only then was he ready to die. The author of the *vita* noted with wonder that Bruno "remained for no less than five days in the same weakened physical condition and the same fervor of spirit." Finally he awakened from unconsciousness and summoned a circle of high dignitaries, with whom he had a second edifying conversation. The archbishop died around midnight to the "singing of psalms, prayers, and deep sobbing of those present."

The edifying character of the *vita* is very clear in the two conversations, which were naturally as fictional as the usual speech before the beginning of a battle in the biographies of laymen. The authors constantly attempted to make the actual events—the details of which were orally transmitted—conform to the model prescribed for the death of an ecclesiastical magnate. Abbots, too, were expected to follow such customs. Abbot John of Gorze sent messengers to summon five abbots, the officers of the cathedral chapter, and "a number of lesser persons (*minorum*)." They approached his bed one after the other, he kissed each, delivered a sermon on the sorrows of this world and the joys of the next, dismissed the crowd, called the abbots to him—and lived another four days, which the chronicler excused by saying: "What difference does it make to the elect who aspire to eternal life if they must sometimes die with such difficulty (*dure*)?"

The ritualization of death has both Christian and non-Christian classical precedents. Death provided both a real and a literary opportunity to show how much the spirit, or faith, is superior to this world and its vanities. The stoic uttered his last words to like-minded friends; the saint combined sermon and example, as he had in his life. True, not everyone played out this role to the full. The biographer of Saint Udalrich, for example, wrote that in the saint's last hours he greatly desired to see his nephew, Count Richwin, who was at the imperial court. Once long before he had laid down to die, but to his regret death had not come, and his later biographer consoled the bishop with the thought that other men also had to meet with this misfortune. An author better trained in hagiography might have omitted the episode.

The fourteenth canon of the provincial synod of Trosly (909) describes what happened following the bishop's death: "Among our people an evil custom has appeared whereby immediately after the death of a bishop the property of the church is invaded by the magnates (*a potentioribus*), as if it had been the personal property of the bishop. But even if it had been, this would be against all law." Atto of Vercelli wrote that in the interlude before the installation of a new bishop the ecclesiastical functionaries were supposed to keep the episcopal patrimony together, but laymen broke into granaries and cellars, robbers made themselves at home in church properties. One of Henry II's charters complained that such customs were normal in Italy and that recently (in 1007) the bishopric of Cremona had fallen victim to them. One lay magnate broke into the (cathedral) church, another usurped the property of the cathedral chapter (*abbatiam*), and a vassal of the deceased bishop declared that he was ready to swear that his late lord had given these to him.

In Germany such practices were unusual except in unstable borderlands. Thanks to the thorough chronicle of Cambrai we know that there as soon as word reached the city that bishop Erluin had died abroad, the castellan Walter seized the city, oppressed the citizens, broke into the episcopal palace and the houses of the cathedral canons, and took the bishop's horses from their stalls. In a privilege of 996 for Cambrai, Pope Gregory V had forbidden the plundering of the property of the bishop or of a priest after his death. The reason for this prohibition was the occupation of the bishopric by Charles of Lower Lorraine while Otto II was occupied with a campaign against the Slavs and could not name a new bishop. Charles had his wife's bed set up in the bishop's bedroom, entertained guests at the expense of the episcopal treasury, and sold ecclesiastical benefices. He behaved as a robber (*raptor*) although he should have served as a protector (*tutor, observator*) of the bishopric.

Here we see how thin the line could be between legal and illegal exercise of power in an orphaned bishopric. The bishop of Cambrai had been unable to establish himself in the city against his vassals and had died in exile. At the same time the West Frankish king Lothair threatened to capture the city, since he had already taken Arras. The local magnates therefore called on the duke of Lower Lorraine to serve as protector until the installation of a new bishop after the return of the emperor—an altogether appropriate move since Charles was an imperial vassal and was antagonistic toward his royal brother. The duke, in the name of his imperial lord, certainly had the right to temporary exploitation of the episcopal wealth. Who could blame him if he went still further? We hear nothing of any censure by the emperor upon his return, and seventeen years went by, 979–96, before Gregory V issued his privilege for Cambrai. This privilege did not prevent the castellan Walter in 1012 from acting as a "robber." He apparently had a certain right on his side, which he grossly abused.

A dying bishop usually divided up his personal possessions because a will was likely to remain a dead letter; such directives issued by a dead bishop often lacked authority and found no consent. For someone like Bruno of Cologne it might have been sufficient to leave written directions, which were actually carried out. His is the only written will that is reproduced in full in his *vita*. Elsewhere we are told about gifts to family members gathered around the bed of dying bishops. Adalbero II of Metz, as we have heard, was stricken far from his city. As soon as he could speak again, he began to make donations from his possessions. He continued doing so in Metz, where he was brought, "so that he would not hold back anything that belonged to him. If anything nevertheless remained, it was not the result of his carelessness but due to the avarice of his kinsmen." The ducal and comital family had made important resources available to Adalbero during his time in office. Now it was concerned that pious donations for his soul should not be too extravagant. The fact that Abbot Constantine, in these paragraphs of his *vita* of Adalbero, used terms of gentle criticism rather than speaking of "robbers" was the result of two circumstances: first, Constantine's monastery was the burial place of the bishops, and second, the abbot was himself a member of this same widespead clan.

When there was no written will but only an oral directive made by the dying bishop, some legal ambiguity was possible. We are told that after the death of a great prelate, a vassal could claim that he had been given this or that property by the deceased. Bishops were obliged to die publicly; but in a situation full of emotion and hasty improvisation, legal testimony of witnesses remained an uncertain thing.

Ecclesiastical institutions are essentially "transpersonal"; bishoprics and episcopal property continue to exist even in the absence of a bishop. We can hardly speak of an incomplete development in the episcopal sphere; yet its institutional character was incompletely perceived by the contemporaries. We shall see how serious the crisis of the state could be after the death of the king, how armies scattered after the death of their leaders—something of the same mentality affected people's attitude toward spiritual pastors. A bishop was the minister of the sacraments, a preacher and the proclaimer of liturgical worship; in addition, so far as was possible, he was a living model of Christian virtues. But in the minds of contemporaries he was above all a lord, one of those magnates to whom one was subordinated.

10 WORLDLY CLERICS

As we have seen, the social position of the elite and their "noble" character was measured by their appearance. Such indications included an imposing stature, appropriate clothing, ornamented bridle and weapons, and a noble horse. In much the same manner, the higher clergy emphasized their rank as well as their connection with a family that made such things both possible and necessary. There was no specific clothing to indicate the social position of the secular clergy outside of liturgical vestments, and so it was natural that the position of prelates would be indicated in a similar manner. No bishop or chapter provost praised a life of poverty, none followed the ideal of the twelve grades of monastic humility. A person who wished to be recognized as a lord had to dress as one. Of course there were some modifications. Clerics did not usually carry weapons, they avoided excessive pomp, and their mounts were not war-horses. The pope rode a white palfrey when he traveled through his city surrounded by chanting crowds of its inhabitants.

SECULARS

Clerics were not supposed to own hunting dogs or falcons. How seldom these rules were obeyed is indicated by how often they were repeated. Bishop Gunzo of Eichstätt, for example, who loved hunting "to excess" (*ultra modum*), exchanged a manse for a hunting preserve "near Hungary," which made no payment to the bishopric. We gave two examples of a situation that may have been common: an ecclesiastic appearing in public with a falcon on his fist. Although hunting was permitted on workdays, it must have been seen as a violation of divine law to disturb holy days with it and provoke God's punishment. Once, when a priest tried to celebrate Mass after returning from the hunt on a Sunday, he found that the only sound that he could make was that which he used to call his hounds. Another clerical hunting enthusiast lost his mind and was only cured by entering the Cluny monastery.

Hunting was not yet exclusively a noble privilege but, as a sport which was preparation for war, it was an activity of the upper strata of society, in contrast to the peasant population's quest for fresh meat. There was a military purpose to other pastimes also, including chess, which became popular during the tenth century and was even enjoyed in monasteries. A monastic text on chess justifies preoccupation with this game with the argument that it involves no cheating and that no player (*certator*) intended treachery. In this, the author continued, it differed from "the corrupting game of dicing"—we know only too well how much this game was enjoyed by clerics. On the chessboard, according to the author, the white and red "people" (*populus*) stand across from each other with their kings and their counts, who have the king's ear—the counts were our bishops. Our rook was a marquis (*bigis seu rochus*). There was also the knight (*eques*) and the mass of peasant footsoldiers or pawns (*pedites, ruris agmina*). When the battle begins, the peasants go forward first and have to fight: they are forbidden to retreat. When a piece is taken, the author of the chess treatise speaks of the serious wounds it has received and of its fall. All in all, the game was presented as "terrible war" (*horrida bella*) and as the killing of the opponents. Only the king did not die—an idea inherent in the political philosophy of the game.

Not on the chessboard, but in stark reality, the royal army was composed in large part of clerics or of their vassals. As the king's vassal the bishop was obliged to participate in royal military expeditions with his men. Often enough this was against the interest of his kinsmen and to their detriment. One might imagine that only lay vassals were involved, but French and Italian bishops required vassalic services of their clerics. The death of a bishop meant that they had to renew the bonds of vassality with his successor. If the latter came from the opposing party, this often meant the ruin of the episcopal vassals. The historian Flodoard received a fief from an archbishop of Reims, but his successor took it back and had him imprisoned because he had questioned the legality of the new archbishop's election. There were even bishops who only ordained clerics who swore oaths of fidelity. When the bishop's party failed and power changed hands, it was a good idea to forget this oath.

If a cleric did not bend to the will of his bishop, he could be ordered to do penance or, worse, "the bishop's favor together with all his fiefs" could be taken from him. Everybody thought in secular categories, including the parish clergy. Church property was seen as a benefice (*beneficium*), for which one owed the owner service. In addition, the view was widely shared that in rural and parish churches one should differentiate between the altar and the rest of the church. The altar belonged to the saint and thus to the bishop who acted for him, while the church and the church property belonged to a secular or religious lord. The donations of the faithful, as Abbo of Fleury explained, benefited the horses and hounds of laymen more than travelers, widows, and orphans or the upkeep of the church itself.

In one French diocese, the number of churches with incomes—in other words excluding simple chapels—was said to be a thousand, but this probably meant simply a great number. Where the clergy were so numerous, they could hardly lead a lordly life. The questions that bishops asked during diocesan visitations included, according to Regino, whether the church possessed a chalice and Mass vestments, and whether they had been pawned to a tavernkeeper or merchant. It was possible for a poor cleric to buy property for others, serving as their cover, or to practice usury, or serve as the steward of his lord (*sui senioris*).

According to the canons, only a free man could become a priest, but this requirement could be circumvented or ignored. Just as there were "proprietary churches" belonging to laymen, there were "proprietary priests," unfree men from the lord's *familia*. This was not always a case of churches that had fallen into the "power of the laity." Lay persons frequently built or restored oratories and commanded their bondsmen to be ordained priests to serve them. Rural pastoral care was often made possible through such foundations when bishops did not have the means to organize such activities, so there was little protest against the system. Once a synod opposed the bestowal of proprietary churches by their owners without the accord of the bishop. There were also to be no arbitrary dismissals and retention of the estates of deceased priests. The synod said nothing of their free or unfree condition, nothing about their education in a cathedral or monastic school. They may have "studied" with a local cleric, at least when the church was not the proprietary church of a monastery. Monks were not allowed to staff parish churches, and turned over the pastoral care of their churches to secular clergy.

Clerics who had a flare for business could also do well if they had no property. In northern Italy it was common for bishops to hand over parish churches to powerful laymen, or to lease churches to clerics, who in turn handed them over to laymen. These laymen thereby obtained episcopal property and could inexpensively comply with the obligation to provide divine services. Atto of Vercelli complained about clerics who came to churches with nothing and grew rich through church benefices. As long as they were needy they presented themselves as chaste, but when they became prosperous they took concubines (*meretrices*). The concubines adorned themselves, churches were plundered, and the poor were tormented (by demands for payments). In the early tenth century almost half of all parish churches in the diocese of Lucca were in the hands of laity in spite of the general prohibition against giving laymen such churches as fiefs. The scarcity of workers and above all the necessity of maintaining a numerous vassalic following here caused a difficult situation. It was certainly not typical for the whole of Italy.

In the symbiosis between the higher clergy and the secular elite, the latter often gave more than they received. Such questions as arose were concerned less with ownership or use in itself than with protection and, connected with it, lordship, with vassality and the size of one's following, especially for royal service. In a *Grundherrschaft,* or territorial lordship, men were usually more important than the territory itself. The military-political value of property could greatly exceed the economic profit. And even if we take "the Church" to mean the clergy, we must still distinguish between the ecclesiastical elite and the common clerics who served in parish churches, performed duties as scribes or stewards for secular lords, worked their land with the help of a few servants, and often attempted to establish families. Only service to their lords offered the possibility of expanding the narrow horizons of this semipeasant existence. Prelates seldom came from this lower stratum of clergy. And yet these poorly educated rural churchmen, burdened with so many bad habits, were the fundamental element of Christendom. Most of what our sources say about them is negative. Their positive contribution can only be supposed; it escapes our knowledge as does so much about the middle and lower levels of society.

What a bishop required was more than these very ordinary men could offer him. For the protection of his city, for royal service, and to be assured of important donations, his connections with the secular elite were essential. These connections were provided mainly by the cathedral clergy.

Clerical dignities and prebends were very attractive for younger sons from such families. Of course, the lifestyle and activities of these people could undo that which their background had led the bishop to expect from them. When Rather came to Verona, the priests and deacons had largely divided up the possessions of the church among themselves, to the detriment of the bishop and those holding lesser clerical orders. They did this "in order to be lords over the others" and "as means to provide wives for their sons, husbands for their daughters, as well as to buy vineyards and fields for them." Rather wanted to reestablish the canonical arrangement in which the income of the bishopric was to be divided into four equal parts, one-quarter for the bishop, one-quarter for the clergy, and the rest for the poor and for church construction. He wanted to undertake the division himself so that he could maintain supervision and control of gifts made to the cathedral chapter. The donations to the chapter outweighed all other forms of revenue and were usually protected from the bishop's grasp. People were usually more willing to make donations to a chapter or to its individual members than to a bishop. This was in part the result of kinship connections and can in part be explained by the opinion that prayers for the salvation of one's soul were better entrusted to a community than to an individual.

THE CATHEDRAL CHAPTER

Rather's attempt to reform the cathedral chapter of Verona already floundered over the preliminary question of the division of prebends. Many other attempts to correct conditions had likewise failed, whether they concerned the higher or the lower clergy. There had once even been an attempt to reform the entire secular clergy. Full of the optimism which characterized the early years of the reign of Louis the Pious, reformers in the Aix-la-Chapelle synod of 816 had thought they could order a strict common life for all the secular clergy. This so-called rule of Aix-la-Chapelle was a whole book of excerpts from Christian authors and canons from early Church councils. It could not be applied to the rural clergy of parish churches without separating them from the rest of the population and threatening their economic underpinnings. It was more successful with that portion of the secular clergy which had previously seen common life as a more or less realizable ideal. In the tenth century an attempt was made to tighten the reins, especially in cathedrals, and thus to renew the common life of the chapter. In Reims, Archbishop Adalbero (969–89) reorganized the common life of his cathedral canons and made it stricter by introducing such monastic practices as partial silence. Adalbero was a kinsman of Adalbero I of Metz, who had restored Gorze. There and elsewhere in Lorraine a stricter life was introduced, as for example in Liège and Aix-la-Chapelle. Here the canons of the Church of the Virgin complained to Otto I in 966 that they no longer would follow the customs of Gorze and no longer would recognize a monk from that monastery as their superior. In Bremen, until 1013, the cathedral canons lived "in the vestments of canons but bound by the rule of monks." There were complaints in Trier against this quasi-monastic life just as there had been in Aix-la-Chapelle. Under Henry II, Hildesheim was offered to the canons in Bamberg and elsewhere as the model of semimonastic life. Such reforms developed later in Italy, where the transfer of cathedral churches from the suburbs into the city helped the development of a common life.

This reform generally took place against the will of those concerned and in the name of higher values which were not always of a spiritual nature. Henry II encouraged the Hildesheim model also out of concern for the estates of the cathedral minster, which were royal property. If the canons lived "according to the manner of laymen," they were tempted to transfer their prebends to wives and children or to more distant kinsmen. The common life prevented the establishment of families and strengthened the institutional character of the minster, which often was called a *monasterium*. The very word "minster," used to designate the cathedral community, derives from the word *monasterium*.

CANONS AND CANONESSES

Canons

After the year 1000, the authority of the "Rule of Aix-la-Chapelle" of 816 increased in all areas of the Ottonian empire. This rule was already influenced by monasticism, but not yet characterized by that rigor which would have been intolerable for secular clergy. During the tenth century there were frequent dramatic expulsions of "worldly" canons and their forcible replacement by monks. Later, however, the extremes of lay and quasi-monastic life found a middle course, and occasionally canons were even introduced in place of monks. In some instances this practice may have been due to the personal preference or interests of the bishop; in others it was connected with the respective structures of a monastery and a canonical community. The monastery was normally the center of a major economic system, whereas a canonical community better fitted the conditions of urban life and did not require a complex administration. The rising appreciation of the lifestyle connected with the Rule of Aix-la-Chapelle also played a part.

Anyone who lived according to that rule remained a lord and exercised his rights of lordship over his servants, his house, and his prebend. This facilitated the willing entry of sons from important families into such circles. Individuals without these family connections could also do well here. As a scholast of the cathedral chapter of Reims, Gerbert of Aurillac had not only his prebend but also urban houses and even proprietary churches, "which he had acquired through free and legitimate donations in accord with the customs of the region." His properties came "from many people" and were in part rewards for the good services of the multitalented scholast. Another cathedral scholar, designated as *dydascalus* (schoolmaster), was Herward, chaplain and notary to Otto I and Otto II, and thus mostly active in court. He held the prebend of a schoolmaster in the minster of Aschaffenburg, though an assistant usually tended to these duties. The students of the cathedral school lived in his Aschaffenburg house, and Herward had to defray their living expenses out of the income from their prebends. Thus the master was the director of a boarding school and was responsible also for school uniforms: "Only the schoolmaster may give them (the students) their cloak, furs, sheepskin coats, stockings, and shoes."

From the Aschaffenburg records we learn that there were whole "canonical clans." The assistant teacher quarreled with the minster cantor, and the fight ended in the death of an innocent bystander, a student who was the nephew of the cantor. Both clans of the opponents now became involved. The chapter sacristan, who was the father of the cantor, "and many of the other clerics who were their blood relatives along with their lay friends" besieged the teacher "in one of the towers of the church in order to kill him." Only on the following day was the chapter's advocate able to free the beleaguered teacher, dispel the armed besiegers (*milites,* minster vassals?), and seize their goods. The cantor was removed by the archbishop and a synod (976), tonsured, and sent to a monastery for penance. The clan that had revolted retained their canonries, "but they were reduced to the lowest place and permanently lost their voting rights" (in the chapter). In the future there were no longer to be fathers and sons simultaneously among the Aschaffenburg canons, and the maximum number of members of a single clan who could henceforth be canons at the same time was fixed at three.

What was not corrected at this synod was the frequent absence of Herward, the master of the cathedral school, without which the violence might well never have taken place. Quite the opposite: at the same synod it was determined that he would have the right to "go on educational trips for two, three, or more years for the glory of God and of the minster, during which time he might retain his income," and such trips would be in addition to his annual vacation (*annuam licentiam*). This was a lifestyle that many modern university professors would willingly adopt.

The events in Aschaffenburg, as fortuitous as they were, nevertheless found a lasting echo in the decrees of 976. Through them we have a detailed description that is extremely important for an understanding of the internal life of a canonical chapter in the period when common life had been almost entirely abandoned. Many questions remain open, among them the matter of the clan which was so powerful within the chapter. Aschaffenburg was probably founded not by the clan but by duke Liudolf of Swabia. It is not known whether the family formed such an intimate relationship with the chapter out of primarily idealistic or material considerations. In this and similar cases, both probably played a role: interest in a spiritual center for the clan or family whose prayers would assist deceased members, and the economic value of the property. In its simplest and most attractive form, a prebend consisted of landed property. In France, for example, prebends could be passed down from uncle to nephew, and ultimately be reckoned among the family's allods. In a minster, not only young men were in good hands but older ones as well, such as the sacristan of Aschaffenburg who had probably become a cleric after being widowed and who lived alongside of his son the cantor.

Material reasons were secondary, however, when Count Fulk of Anjou, father of Count Geoffrey Grisegonelle, accepted the habit of a canon at Saint Martin of Tours and chanted psalms, thus making himself an object of ridicule to the magnates of the region. Likewise the position of the German king as *frater* of the canons, whatever its actual sense, was certainly not based on financial considerations. Otto III doubled the prebends of the Aix-la-Chapelle church of the Virgin and certainly became one of the *fratres* here for ideal rather than practical reasons.

Shortly after the year 1000 the Rule of Aix-la-Chapelle took on new importance, undoubtedly because of its moderation. Monastic features persisted, but they took second place in a lifestyle that nobles too could accept. Here the essential was not humility but obedience, not poverty but moderation in the use of earthly possessions. Canons dressed not in wool, like monks, but in linen like everyone else, although of course canons were supposed to value morals more than fine clothing. If a layman was accustomed to walking with a stick or a staff, the same seems to have been allowed for canons: their rule forbade staffs only during prayers in the choir. Canons ate meat as did the laity and secular clergy. If the minster farms could not provide enough meat, the bishop could be required to give them sufficient land for their own cattle herds. Wine was supposed to flow generously at all meals whenever possible, although one was expected to be moderate in its use. If wine was short, occasionally beer had to do. Canons had their own houses, as we have already heard. The rule tolerated this practice, insisting only that a wall should encircle the minster quarter and that the canons should not allow women to visit them within this boundary. Common meals were not explicitly required; the only remaining requirement of the common life was the celebration of the canonical hours in the choir. The Aschaffenburg document of 976 provides an idea of what this might have looked like in the tenth century: The schoolmaster was not obligated to take an active part in liturgical celebrations even on the highest feast days. He was only expected to read a text with his senior students on the eve of these feasts days. Whether he was excused from choir duty is not recorded, although his extraordinary dispensation from liturgical duties might suggest that he was. There may have been no canonical hours celebrated at all.

Only important families could keep on placing bishops and abbots from their kin, thereby anchoring their position in the spiritual sphere as well as the secular. At a somewhat lower level a similar function could be filled by canons. For canons, more than for bishops, there were differences in reputation and also in the economic importance of prebends. The officials of cathedral chapters were the richest, followed by the cathedral canons, who often numbered only twelve. For a bishop to increase the number of prebends was considered meritorious, although he often did so with insufficient funds. Such imprudence was one of the reasons why the lifestyle of the prebendaries often left something to be desired. Upon his installation in 1021 in the small bishopric of Eichstätt, Bishop Heribert found seventy canons and expelled twenty of them on a single day. To the rest he gave parishes. Elsewhere, bishops seem to have attached the distribution of canonical prebends to the donations of property made by families of postulants. Whenever Bishop Wazo of Liège was offered such an arrangement, he answered that he did not need such oblations.

Differences in rank and social position were much more marked among canons than among monks. Since late antiquity, there had been a ranking of provinces and of episcopal cities; now this ranking was extended to that one of titular saints and of the prestige of the bishop. Moreover, there was a rank ordering among canons based on their status as priests, deacons, or subdeacons. According to the Rule of Aix-la-Chapelle, for example, deacons were allowed to sit in the presence of priests only on their "command" and subdeacons had to stand when deacons were nearby. In Rather's day, there was a separation into the wealthy and the poor, with the prebends reserved to those of higher orders. Although such conditions did not foster institutional unity, they were what people were used to in the secular sphere. One received much respect only when there were others who received less respect. Saint Benedict had not demanded universal equality among his followers. To many of them, such equality would have seemed an unnecessarily severe requirement.

Canonesses

Most of what has been said concerning canons was also true of canonesses. "To eat well and to dress well were the essentials of the aristocratic style to which canonesses were accustomed." Uta, a niece of the empress Kunigunda of Luxemburg, wanted to be "the last to choir service, the first to the table." Benedict of Aniane's so-called "Rule of Aix-la-Chapelle for women" sought to modify such attitudes. The Rule did not fully differentiate between nuns and canonesses, and the boundaries remained fluid. According to the Rule, canonesses could keep their own private property but had to ensure that after they entered the canonry their property would be administered by a kinsman. Common dormitories and common tables in the refectory were required except for the ill and the elderly. At table, the noblewomen were not to put themselves before the non-noble (*se praeferant*), and all were to receive the same food: three pounds of bread and three pounds of wine a day, and, in areas without wine, one pound of wine and two pounds of beer. If a canonry was poor, only the number of women who could be provided with this daily drink ration were to be taken into the community. They were dressed in woolens and linen; like nuns they had to live within a strict enclosure. On the other hand, canonesses could retain female servants within this enclosure. As in male canonries, there were schools in which young women were educated by canonesses.

All of this was in accord with the intentions of the original Rule of Aix-la-Chapelle. The reality was often very different. As late as 1280 it was considered legitimate for canonesses to live without a common life, without regard to the rule, and without vows. Above all, they had the possibility of leaving the canonry to marry.

Scholars have debated whether only those girls who had been placed in the canonry for their education, but not as *religieuses* in the narrow sense, could marry. But this opinion contradicts parallels with canons; many families whose sons had been serving in spiritual life would decide to restore them to secular pursuits when the need arose. There were not only canonesses but also nuns who married or, rather, were married. We do not know whether a perpetual vow was involved when a daughter from a renowned family entered a house of canonesses, and it is quite possible that there was no conflict of conscience when a temporary bond to the institution was loosened.

In Lorraine and Saxony, especially, monasteries and canonical cloisters for women flourished. In Saxony there were twenty-six new foundations of this kind in the tenth and early eleventh centuries. Superfluous daughters of noble families were deposited in them, as was done by the Liudolfings in Gandersheim, for example. This canonry provides the best example of the problems which might result from such a policy. The difficulties were heightened by the conflict between the small bishopric of Hildesheim and the all-powerful archbishop of Mainz over the question of the exemption of the canonry. Ottonian princesses and noble daughters considered it humiliating when the Hildesheim bishop rather than the archbishop of Mainz celebrated the liturgy and exercised other church functions in Gandersheim.

A portion of the *vita* of Bishop Bernward of Hildesheim is contemporary and was written by the Hildesheim cathedral scholar Thangmar. As an eyewitness he described the "Gandersheim conflict" and the attitudes of the principal parties: highborn young canonesses, to whom too much freedom was given, relaxed the canonry's discipline. "And even Sophia (the sister of Otto III), against the forceful opposition of (the abbess) Gerburg, and on the urging of archbishop Willigis, went to the imperial court. Here she remained a year or two and traveled the path of an undisciplined life, which provided the occasion for various rumors."

Sophia had taken no vows, but at the time of her reception had sworn to be "subordinate and obedient to" the bishop of Hildesheim. He had presided together with Willigis of Mainz over her taking the veil—an unusual procedure, which already suggested the Gandersheim conflict and indicated its deeper causes. Bernward had risen to the position of Otto III's tutor, and this was regarded with displeasure by a court clique to which both Willigis of Mainz and Sophia belonged. After the temporary departure of Sophia from the religious life, Willigis and she took part in the Roman expedition of Otto III, and both were frequent intervenients in imperial charters. Sophia, as presumptive successor of the ailing abbess Gerburg, was the driving force when a scandal broke out at the consecration of the new Gandersheim church. The canonesses threw the offertory gifts at the feet of Bishop Bernward during the Mass with "wild curses" and "unbelievable fury."

In the days before this scandal, Sophia had been "constantly at the side" of the archbishop and had "lived with him." In later years, as abbess of Gandersheim, she experienced similar disobedience from two of her subordinates. Against her will they fled to Mainz, where they entered another religious community. Bishop Godehard of Hildesheim sent them a letter demanding that they return. They tore up the letter before the eyes of the messenger and warned him that he had better go home quickly if he valued his life.

Only women who knew that their clans stood behind them could dare such arrogance and take such liberties. These canonesses were daughters of the palatine count Ezzo and Mathilda, a sister of Otto III and of Sophia. Their high birth guaranteed them freedom in Gandersheim, and they were not bound to their place of study. "In accord with ancient custom" they despised the bishop of Hildesheim as an "inferior" (*inferiorem*) and, through pride, abandoned the "norm of holy conduct." Even before their flight they had come to Mainz as dinner guests of the archbishop, and they lived for a period "in a rather familiar way with him," something that Sophia, certainly mindful of her own conduct, allowed to happen. When her two nieces were again invited to Mainz by the archbishop, she assigned them—perhaps in suspicion of what was to come—an official escort—vassals, clerics, and servants. These were dismissed by the young women in Mainz and sent back to Hildesheim. Probably to indicate that they intended to lead an honorable life far from the country, the two entered a female convent in Mainz under the direction of the archbishop's sister. They were joined by three other canonesses who had left Gandersheim on the pretense of visiting kin.

Abbess Sophia was successful in obtaining the return of the fugitives after a complaint was lodged with the emperor. They were to spend the rest of their lives in Gandersheim as nuns, that is, cloistered more strictly than before, in order to prevent another escape. After a few months, however, they were carried off by "unknown persons" and secretly taken to Mainz, where they remained with the knowledge of the archbishop. All evidence suggests that the kin of the five restless nuns had planned and carried out the affair. It was in the interests of the clans to make possible for their superfluous daughters an existence that corresponded to their rank and honor. One of Sophia's nieces later died in Mainz; another became abbess in the institution in which she had not wanted to be canoness—in Gandersheim.

We have described the actions of the Gandersheim ladies in detail because they indicate that, as in Aschaffenburg, a very powerful secular element could insert itself into a female canonry too. The systematic psychic training that Benedict of Nursia had demanded of his monks and had summarized in his Rule could not be replaced by the pages of patristic citations in the Aix-la-Chapelle rules of Benedict of Aniane. This second Benedict organized the spiritual life rather than making it more profound.

The importance of the canonical tradition for the Carolingian and post-Carolingian periods remained great. It constituted the organized core of the secular clergy from which many ecclesiastical dignitaries were recruited, and it contributed to the self-awareness of the secular clergy vis-à-vis the monks and the laity. Whereas monks and nuns had to renounce their ties to the "world," life in a canonry required no such a renunciation. On the contrary, when living in a respected canonry one was a respected member of one's family. Also involved were the protection and accumulation of prebends which belonged to the family and, of course, the salvation of the family members. In this domain, monasticism was a strong competitor, and we must remember that in Ireland the family monastery was the only type of clerical life and had, at a very early date, completely driven the secular clergy from the field. It is unlikely that the monastic life would have been as pervasive on the Continent, even without the canonry. Yet monks might have achieved the high standing they enjoy in the Eastern Church, with the secular clergy becoming little-respected parish priests. There were tendencies in that direction. For the laity too, the high prestige of monasteries and the "holiness" of their inhabitants could become dangerous. Important families like the Supponids in northern Italy, for example, disappeared from history after making enormous donations to monasteries. It was different with contributions to a cathedral, a canonry, or individual canons: these did not entirely alienate the property from the family. Often they even strengthened its influence.

Monasticism and the Laity

We must keep all of this in mind when considering the relationship between monasticism and the laity. The division between the two spheres was an effort which frequently remained incomplete. Those who felt it most were the young people, who were supposed to find their "father" and "brothers" in their monastery rather than in their families. That a *nutritus* might miss his family is the premise of the poem of the "Ecbasis captivi," and the theme appears elsewhere as well. Rather of Verona, infuriated by monks' kinsmen who, as he wrote, tried to alienate their affection to the cloister, advised monks how to repulse such kinsmen. On the other hand, Ekkehard IV of Saint Gall remembered with nostalgia the good old times when pious laymen took part in processions wearing the cowl, sat at the monastic table, and sometimes offended against the rule, a fact which created a jovial mood among the brethren; Ekkehard was anything but a reformer. Cluniacs had less sympathy for such a comfortable association and used to chastise monks who preferred "frequent visits with kinsmen and friends to the common life with their brothers." There was a dual danger: that clans might remove their members from the monastery, and that the monastery might become "familiarized." John of Gorze was accused of settling his mother in the monastery "better than she was at home," and of turning the cloister into a *geneceum,* a residence for women. He had brought along the servants of his household (*familiam domus suae*), who "served the monastery along with the mother." The situation benefited the monastery, for John endowed it with his entire familial property. One can see that even for such strict spirits as John was, not all personal ties to the former household had been broken. Nor was nepotism alien to reformers: Odilo of Cluny's nephew and namesake received the monastery of Novalese (which had been removed to Breme). He reformed it so thoroughly that Conrad II had to intervene.

Lay Abbots, Feudalism, Advocacy

Families that supported monasteries or canonries did not always renounce their rights. People surrendered family foundations reluctantly because—quite apart from economic interests—such foundations could hold a clan together and form its center. A good example is the Saxon priory Walbeck, founded by the grandfather of Thietmar of Merseburg. Thietmar's uncle held one-half of the priory's property and Thietmar himself the other half, finally becoming prior after paying off his predecessor. This caused Thietmar some remorse, as did a request which he unfortunately did not refuse his brother, namely that his brother's recently deceased wife be buried in the tomb of the first Walbeck prior.

Except for such improprieties, proprietary monasteries and canonries in Germany seldom had any complaints about their lords. Rougher custom prevailed elsewhere, as in Catalonia, where a count spoke of "his" monastery and described the monks as "his servants in things spiritual and temporal." It was acceptable for a magnate to make his sister the abbess, but not for his mistress to hold this position. The next step in this direction was the governance by lay abbots who ruled their monasteries as "count and abbot," as "abbot-count" (*abbicomes*), "archabbot" (*archiabbas*), "abbot and lord" (*senior*) or simply as the "lord" (*dominus, dominator*) of the monastery. The title of lay "archabbot" arose in an exceptional situation. In Angers there was a monastery and a house of canons. In both, Count Fulk I of Anjou was abbot (929/30). Later, Fulk III granted the monks one of their own number as abbot, while the canons were governed by a lay abbot. Both were and remained subordinate to the count, who was called "archabbot of the two abbots."

Such things were an outrage to reformers of all periods. Irrespective of canonical thought, it was undesirable for an abbot of a monastery not to be a "father to the monks" and their leader in spiritual matters, but merely an administrator of the institution and its properties. On the other hand, there were situations in which only a powerful person could protect the monastery against external threats and, when necessary, force its internal solidarity. Duke William I of Aquitaine, later the founder of Cluny, explained in a charter of 898 for Saint Julien in Brioude that he had been entrusted with the abbatial office by royal donation, "so that the place might be more secure in all things." Only a magnate like Count Baldwin of Flanders had the means to protect the monastery of Saint-Bertin by a rampart with a gallery (*ambitum castelli*). He might well not have done so if he had not been the lay abbot of the monastery. After Baldwin left the office of abbot to his son, the latter became a benefactor of the monastery in another manner: as he lay dying, he gave it his golden cup, his sword belt for the fashioning of a chalice, and armillae for its paten. Saint-Bertin received further valuable donations from the counts of Flanders. The only concession demanded by the "abbot-count" was that the cloister be opened to his wife so that she might pray at the tomb of the saint.

The existence of lay abbots cannot always be attributed to greed for ecclesiastical property, but neither can one attribute it only to piety. There could be other grounds as well: In his correspondence, Viscount Fulk I of Anjou was called count presumably because he was the lay abbot of Saint-Aubin. Since the consecration of the bishop of Angers took place in this monastery, Fulk had a decisive influence on the nomination of the bishops. Saint-Aubin was a royal abbey, so Fulk exercised a royal prerogative. That Giselbert of Lorraine could style himself "by the grace of God count, marquis, and abbot" certainly raised his prestige. Such designations being a constant source of irritation to reformers, a lay abbot could increase his prestige by initiating reform himself and restoring the canonically proper situation. Not in every such case, however, did the former lay abbot actually resign all of his influence over the monastery and over the election of its head. Around the middle of the tenth century, it became increasingly common for powerful families to have abbots as well as monastic property under their control, especially in areas where the king had little or no power.

In this way, although in a purely formal manner, the scandal of laymen ruling as abbots was removed—laymen who were not even well informed of the context of Saint Benedict's Rule. They lived among the monks "with their wives, sons, daughters, with vassals (*militibus*) and hunting dogs." The most complete description of such a situation was written by the monk Letald of Saint-Mesmin in Micy. His abbot was expelled by a lay steward of the bishop of Orléans. The brothers had to look on, while rooms were being used as horse stables. There was a falconry, a dog kennel, a fencing area for the youth. Weaving looms clattered, and the steward's wife (*domina*) went about with her entourage of serving women.

In order to maintain control of a monastery, some monks had a kinsman enter monastic life and then had him elected abbot. Count Geoffrey "Grisegonelle" of Anjou tried this with four abbeys at the same time. He wanted his brother Wido to be their abbot. Later, Wido confessed in a charter: "I have undertaken military service for Christ, taking on the burden of monasticism. However, I have not followed the monastic rule as would be fitting (because worldly preoccupations prevented me from so doing). . . . Instead of doing all that I could for the monasteries under my care, I took much (of their property) from them and left them to fall into ruin." One of these four monasteries was that of Saint-Aubin mentioned above. When it had finished playing its role as stepping stone for the rise of the counts of Anjou, it went to a vassal (*fidelis*) of the abbot count Geoffrey "Grisegonelle" as part of the family property which could be disposed of freely. In 966 the monastery was reformed and a monk was "placed in charge"—which meant that there was still no question of a free election, an idea that existed only as a future program. Previously monks and canons may have lived together in Saint-Aubin; now it became exclusively monastic. Only in 1036 would the monks themselves be able to elect their abbot for the first time.

The most significant difference between a lay abbot and a monastic abbot could be the latter's renouncing secular court and secular dress. One man held on to worldly dress though he had sworn an oath to the king to become a monk when he had received the abbey of Saint-Martial in Limoges. "He ruled the monastery for many years, not in the manner of a monk but rather in that of a canon, dressing as a layman." Not until three days before his death did he assume the monastic habit and thereby absolve himself of guilt for having broken his oath to King Lothar.

In most cases it was the wealth of the monastery created by donations from laymen that led laymen to assume control over a monastery. The restructuring of the Carolingian order required these changes, which in some cases appear to have been the most important ones. Hugo the Great, the head of what later would be the French royal family, was lay abbot of Saint-Martin of Tours, Marmoutier, Saint-Germain d'Auxerre, Saint-Denis, Morienval, Saint-Riquier (where a lay abbot, Angilbert, had ruled as early as Charlemagne's time), Saint-Valéry, and probably of Saint-Aignan in Orléans, Saint-Germain des Prés, and Saint-Maur-des-Fossés. The last two Carolingians held only the monasteries of Saint-Vaast and Saint-Amand, but that does not mean they were much poorer than their rivals. There were still important royal estates to which the Capetians had nothing to compare; to these, the economic power of the monasteries provided a balance, and the direct lordship over important vassals tipped the scales in their favor.

The main reason there were so many lay abbots in France was the political and military insecurity caused by Norman invasions and civil war. Free election of abbots was a fine thing, but it lost its value if there was no one present to protect the monastery or canonry. The Burgundian monastery of Vézelay enjoyed papal protection but nonetheless had to be ceded to the count of Nevers at the end of the ninth century. The count built a castle near the church; he installed guards and received from the monastery a "gift," which soon became a tax. The count retained his influence even when the monastery was reformed by Cluny. He was needed as a counterweight to the demands of the diocesan bishop. Roman freedom was replaced by "Cluniac servitude" on the one hand and "comital tyranny," as the chronicler of Vézelay puts it, on the other.

This tyranny was tolerated by monastic reform, and Vézelay was not the only monastery in which monks were unhappy with the cautious reactions of the Cluniacs in the face of stark reality. The lords of a monastery had the choice either to content themselves with a merely formal protection of continuing rights or to exercise their power unrestrained. In Saint-Aubin (Angers), leadership of the monastery changed six times between 966 and 1027. In five cases, the count of Anjou issued a charter installing the new abbot "without prejudice to the will of the monks." Never did their will diverge from that of the count. It could have been otherwise. The count of Chartres learned from one of the monks of his cathedral monastery that the abbot was dying. He quickly designated this monk as the new abbot and invested him later with the abbot's crosier. All protests remained in vain against this authoritarian procedure, which had taken place while the previous abbot was still alive.

From the perspective of customary secular law, such actions appeared thoroughly legitimate. Since Carolingian capitularies had used technical terms relating to enfeoffment not only for secular property but also for monasteries, we can assume that people were hardly aware of a distinction between the two spheres. In the eastern and southern parts of the former Frankish empire the Ottonians could exercise the right of investiture comparable to feudal investiture; a count could do the same in the west. He could also give a monastery, whose lord he was, to another "in fief," and the recipient could subenfeoff it. It was not impossible for this vassal to appoint an abbot. This abbot, having virtually unlimited authority over the monastery's possessions, was expected to produce a profit for the purposes of the secular lord. A person enfeoffed with monastic property likewise expected to profit from it. It may have been that the lower the lord's rank, the heavier was the burden on the monastery. Even without subenfeoffing the situation could be difficult. We are told of many monasteries and canonries which had once flourished but had been given to vassals (*milites*) and had subsequently declined.

Monasteries subject to a monarch were not much better off. Under Emperor Henry II, as we have seen, the obligations of imperial churches greatly increased. Along with spiritual reform, as a sort of indirect secularization of ecclesiastical property and the property of the monastic community, the abbot could give the monks only what was essential for their maintenance; the rest could be claimed by the abbot, not for himself but for the king, and could be distributed by the ruler as vassalic fiefs in return for king's service. In the west, Abbo of Fleury complained about those *doctores* and *rectores* who established improper laws which allowed them to misdirect church property. Instead of the support of the poor it was used for the support of vassals. The justification presented was that the endowment (*dos*) of a church had been meant for the maintenance only of its altar and for nothing else. The altar could be maintained with very little income, and the rest—so it was argued—did not belong to the ecclesiastical authorities but to "some other lord."

Later, exploitation of ecclesiastical property was often accomplished under the title of advocacy. In the tenth century "seigneurial advocacy" (*Herrenvogtei*) began to appear here and there, and the free election of a advocate, which had been guaranteed the monasteries in their foundation charters, was in such cases merely hypothetical. Kings, as in Bavaria, gave the advocacy to members of important families, and the monks were constrained to confirm this procedure. We can well imagine that founding families had no intention of separating themselves from their foundations by the guarantee of free election of advocate. They often exercised a kind of protective advocacy (Schutzvogtei). It could also be that the monks themselves stressed their dependence on a seigneurial advocate because they needed his good favor. In the monastery of Sant Andrea of Exalada, for example, the monks appealed to the count Milo of Carcassonne as their "helper, protector, and enricher (*ditator*)" and urged him "to defend, to protect, and when necessary to discipline his servants the monks."

The harsher and more insecure the times, the more monks had to depend on such protectors. On the other hand, there were complaints about advocates who stole church property, attacked monks, reduced peasants to poverty, and posed as lords. When enemies withdrew, so the monks complained, the advocates took what remained, so that the monasteries were left either in ruins or in desperate poverty. We should not always take such tirades at their face value. We know from many sources, as for example the Tegernsee letter collection, that specific words such as "robber," "invader," or "plunderer" did not always mean exactly what they seemed to. "Robber" for example covered a wide variety of meanings. It could include upright and honorable laymen. In a small, poor monastery in the area of Cambrai, for example, an armed robber named Aldo was pursuing his criminal activities inside the secluded part of the monastery. The count (of Mons) was summoned but did nothing "because he was himself a robber and was accustomed to wish other robbers well." The robber in the cloister was probably the monastery's advocate who knew better than to enter the monastery unarmed when he had to deal with the monks. Perhaps the monks wanted to prevent him from giving any orders inside the monastery.

WARFARE

In those areas in which the king still actually ruled, monasteries were sometimes caught between his demands and the desires of other powers. Such demands were often military in nature and did not only concern monastic vassals. Gerbert of Aurillac, as abbot of Bobbio, was personally answerable for the imperial military obligations of the monastery. After the death of Otto II he saw that the alternative to constructing castles, assembling military contingents, and the like was to place himself "under the yoke of tyranny." He chose a third way: he left the monastery in which "there remained for him nothing more than the abbot's crosier and the apostolic blessing." Even the abbot of the reforming monastery of Fleury-sur-Loire had to protect his institution militarily. A castle had been built by an enemy in the center of Berry and thus in the sphere of interest of Fleury. The abbot "captured it, destroyed it, and razed it."

Many examples indicate the extent to which monastic existence was intertwined with military activities. This was true mainly in the marginal areas of Christendom, where resources were often lacking. Under Sancho II, king of Navarra (970–94), "the region's monks, because of the paucity of troops, had to take up arms." When the Hungarians approached the monastery of Saint Gall, Abbot Engelbert had a "castle" erected at a strategically important point and equipped with hastily manufactured arms. He wore a cuirass (it was only made of felt) under his cowl and ordered the brothers to do the same. The Hungarians pillaged the monastery but did not attack the fortification. During a small skirmish the monastic personnel captured a Hungarian, who was later baptized. In the monastery of Farfa, not only did the monks survive a siege by the Saracens, but the abbot "ordered them to be pursued for a considerable distance, so that many of them were killed."

Military analogies for religious life appear in the Bible as well as in the Rule of Saint Benedict with its quasi-military lifestyle. Benedict's prologue speaks of the "strong and splendidly shining weapon of obedience" which anyone who wishes to serve as soldier of Christ (*militaturus*) must grasp. Such words were perceived as rhetorical images intended to aid in understanding reality, but the war against heathens brought image and reality together. In his poem, Adalbero of Laon could speak of an alleged war against the Saracens fought by the Cluniacs under "King Odilo." The spirit of the epoch was exaggerated and caricatured in the poem. A military spirit was manifested not only in these preludes to the Crusades. In Cluny and Fleury the monks fought for the sake of monasticism on all fronts, above all against the bishops. Adalbero of Laon was not the only one to describe this fight in military terms. Odo of Cluny saw Saint Benedict of Nursia as the "duke of monks," and Odo's successor Odilo would be praised by Abbo of Fleury as "the standard bearer of all monks (*totius religionis*)."

In a century when monasteries resembled castles or fortified towns with their city towers, we should hardly be surprised if things in the political or educational spheres were also seen from a military perspective. An educated man such as Gerbert of Aurillac used such language. Alongside the "spiritual weapons" of the monks, he explained, there were the "weapons of the school," books and other things which cathedral students should carry with them on journeys. The chess poem from the monastery of Einsiedeln of which we have already spoken may have been a school exercise. It shows the clerics' pleasure in describing a battle that was neither as bloody nor as graphically depicted as that in the *Waltharius* poem. Youths required to grasp the stylus rather than the sword or lance needed at least an imaginary replacement for the deeds of valor which they would never accomplish.

In general it is unclear whether clerics really carried weapons only in extreme circumstances. Even at the beginning of the peace movement, southern French bishops considered it necessary to repeat the prohibition against clerics' carrying weapons. But in 1023, too, there must have been secular and regular clergy who were armed. In that year laymen swore that they would not attack secular clergy or monks who carried no "worldly weapons, . . . or anyone who went around with them (weapons) but who carried no spear or shield." There must have been a meaning to the differentiation between those who were entirely unarmed and those who carried only a sword. Clerics traveling in insecure areas presumably carried weapons to protect themselves against robbers but not against fully armed professional warriors. Thus, clerics conformed at least in part to the prohibition against bearing arms.

Monks were supposed to live outside the "world" in a protected realm which allowed them to fight their passions with "spiritual weapons" and thus climb the twelve steps of humility. This protected realm did not always exist. Wartime destroyed it most, but even in times of peace the fighting between conflicting interest groups, the "militant" style of competition between families and cliques, penetrated monastic existence. Contemporary writings constantly bemoaned the situation, and we should not simply reject this testimony. It was no simple topos and made good sense when, in 909, the synod of Trosly launched a call to arms against pride and jealousy, the followers of hate and discord. If Benedict had considered pride the greatest threat to monks it was true *a fortiori* in the tenth century. The chronicles give many examples, but few are as striking as that which took place in Lobbes. After ninety years without an abbot, the monastery received one who was summoned to reform it. This abbot, Erluin, was of low birth, for which the monks reproached him, lived in constant conflict with him, and finally decided to punish him. Three young monks, proud of their noble birth, attacked the abbot in the monastic dormitory with the consent of their kinsmen and blinded him.

Not only "secularized" communities were concerned with rank and honor. In the monastery of Fleury-sur-Loire the biographer of Abbot Gauzlinus recorded that "in order to embellish the nobility of his ancestry by signs of his energy, he ordered a tower of squared stone to be built in the western area of the monastery." The stone came from afar by ship. When asked what sort of construction project he was undertaking, Gauzlinus answered, "One which will serve as a model to all of Gaul." It was appropriate to the character of this man that he was portrayed as an archangel with flaming sword fighting for the glory of this monastery: "As commander of his units (*cuneis*) of noblemen (*procerum*), he held the law in his right hand, and in his left he wielded the flaming sword of glory. He rivaled the deeds of that Maccabee who through warfare expanded the land of his forefathers. In the same way he (Gauzlinus) looked after the expansion (*ampliationem*) of his monastery, with similar intent."

ABBOT AND BISHOP

Gauzlinus, perhaps the illegitimate son of a noble, later rose to the position of archbishop of Bourges. His predecessor Abbot Abbo of Fleury (988–1004) had appropriated the spirit of the Maccabees in his long conflict with his bishop Arnulf of Orléans over the exemption of his monastery. Pope Gregory V had finally confirmed the exemption as well as the right of the abbot to precedence over all the abbots of Gaul. The abbots of Fleury, it was said, wanted to serve only the king and not the power of the bishop, which the bishop exercised excessively. When the bishop of Orléans ordered the vineyards of the monastery occupied, Abbo countered by arranging a procession with the relics of the monastery's saints. When, later, Bishop Fulk of Orléans wanted to come to Fleury against the will of Abbot Gauzlinus, he ran up against the monastery's dependents in a village. Shouting the name of Saint Benedict, they attacked the bishop's people, beating many of them "almost to death." The chronicler triumphantly declared that the bishop had been "defeated and put to flight" in this manner without indicating whether it had been a spontaneous reaction or the product of a conspiracy. Not surprisingly, on the bishop's side the position of Gauzlinus was described as *superbia*. *Superbia,* or arrogance, was the sin of Satan, who refused to serve God.

Other bishops used the weapon of morality against unruly abbots. The bishop of Cambrai maintained that the lascivious lifestyle of the abbot of Saint-Vaast was, along with his distaste for episcopal admonitions, the real reason that the monks of Arras wanted to be free of episcopal control. Moreover, he claimed, "everyone who wishes to cast off the episcopal yoke refuses to bear the yoke of Christ." But were these not yokes of different sorts?

Saint Benedict, whose relics were venerated in Fleury, would have been astounded to hear that his monks were obliged to submit to the episcopal yoke. In his Rule the bishop appears only twice; he should have a certain power of supervision over morals in the monastery. From this role developed a certain coercive power, and bishops attempted to transform the right to supervise the election of the abbot into the right of naming abbots. The king often exercised this right in Germany, but there were also episcopal abbeys, and since the ninth century it was normal for a monastery to be subject either to the king or to a bishop. Disobedience could have the same effect in either case. A bishop of Perugia threatened an abbot thus: "If the abbot contradicts me in anything, either I force him to do penance, or, when I am not in a position to do that, I withdraw my favor and all my fiefs." His justification was that "the monastery belongs to my episcopal property (*episcopatus*)." Not only in the royal court did the loss of favor bring with it a threat to the material position of the person concerned. Customs from the secular sphere were considered appropriate for ecclesiastical property and its holders as well.

In western Europe these customs included the vassalic oaths that abbots and ecclesiastics who held property of the king or of a bishop had to swear. A bishop could even make the oath of fealty a condition for the benediction of an abbot. In the case of Gauzlinus of Fleury, Bishop Fulbert of Chartres suggested a compromise: if the abbot were satisfied with the canonical submission to the bishop of his diocese, the bishop would "out of fraternal love of the king set aside the oaths and everything that belongs to secular law."

Tension between a monasticism that understood itself as a specific *ordo* and the bishops it did not wish to "serve" was not universal. Cluny generally maintained good relations with bishops, and in Ottonian Germany opposition to the dominant role of monarchy could not develop very far. That there was a "monastic party" in the court of Robert the Pious to which, for a time, he gave all his favor, was an exceptional situation and led to no decisive weakening of the episcopacy. For our investigation, the conflict between the two groups is not important in itself. What needs to be shown is the mentality—on both sides—that led to such struggles. On each side a lordship ruled, which demanded its rightful place and fought for it by means of law and, when necessary, with force.

IV·RELIGIO

11 &HERMITS AND REFORMERS

THE LATIN WORD *RELIGIO* DENOTES BIND-
ing or being bound: people bind themselves to
something supernatural and are in turn bound
by this entity. Thus in antiquity a place, a day,
or an action was put under particular commands and prohibitions—it became taboo.
Along with its general meaning, the word *religio* was used in the early Christian period to
describe people who had entirely subordinated
their lives to religious goals and had left their
former environment on the way to salvation
and sanctification. At a time when there were
few unbelievers, *religiosus* rarely referred to
laypersons who were religious and thus pious,

but was generally used of clerics, especially monks. Even today the French use the phrase *entrer en religion* to mean joining a religious order. In German, *Religiosen* are "persons who have professed vows in an order or a religious congregation." When the archbishop of Reims wrote to the abbot of Cluny about *religiosos vestri ordinis,* he did not mean just those Cluniacs who were pious but all those who belonged to the order. Very often *religio* meant living according to the Rule of Saint Benedict—the law circumscribing the lifestyle of those bound to God, to the abbot's bidding, to a place, and to a strictly organized daily routine.

THE EREMITIC TRADITION

The binding of the *religiosus* resulted from his or her separation from "this world." An ancient but still-extant secondary tradition of living as a *religiosus* was the eremitic life. In this tradition, separation was stressed almost to the point of pathos: there had been prophets who lived in the wilderness on locusts and wild honey, and there were Christian hermits in the tradition of the desert saint Anthony. Translated into the West, the *religiosus* was a hermit who lived in the wasteland, in forests, or in the swamps of the Po valley. Wild animals did not harm him—we wonder how during the plague of wolves in the early tenth century such northern Italian hermits could have survived. Yet, during that century their number increased, so that it could be seen not as a dark age but as a golden age: "Golden, I tell you, is the century which nourished so many citizens of the heavenly Jerusalem amid the wild animals of mountains and forests." Hermits were said to have become so numerous that they "could not all live there" in the mountains and forests but had to come together and accept a common life in a monastery.

The progression from an individual practitioner of this alternative lifestyle to hermit community and, finally, to monasticism has been repeated more than once in history. It was a progression that Saint Benedict himself made. On the other hand, monks sometimes separated themselves from common life as they sought a more perfect way of life than that of the Benedictines. Such hermits were tolerated by Benedict himself, as long as they obeyed the commands of an abbot, who continued to control their spiritual life from afar. There were also totally isolated individuals, who sought their altogether personal lifestyle. Neither Saint Benedict's condemning them as cranks nor the admonitions of later critics could change them.

While monks were guaranteed a modest but sufficient material life, the hermit deliberately placed himself in an extreme situation. He lived in the wilderness; no one saw to his nourishment, his clothing, his shelter from cold and damp. To enter a monastery meant to exchange one's accustomed form of social existence for another, strongly controlled one, which offered protection and sustenance through solidarity. Hermits, in the words of Benedict, fought alone, in contrast to the "fraternal order of battle." The hermit risked everything. Extreme precariousness, extreme flight from the world—even the monastery was a place of multiple activities—and possibly absolute solitude was the basis for the ascetic's sanctity. Freed from all or almost all bonds, he wished to belong totally to God.

In a monastery, temporary solitude was a serious punishment, and continual solitude was something the people of the tenth century hardly could bear. A person lacking a neighbor to talk to did not always take God as his new partner. Too often in solitude there were demons or even the devil himself to be fought with. Subjugated nature rebelled and the "world" returned in the form of evil spirits. The battle with them did not always end as described in saints' lives.

People often departed from this extremely individual form of spiritual life. In moments of danger, it was good to be able to call on other hermits, with whom one could pray and seek advice. The eremitic community provided a certain control through others as well as the possibility of methodical progress; it also spurred religious fervor. Saint Romuald, the leader of a community of ascetics, wrote for its use a treatise "On the Battle against Demons," containing practical advice. He was known as "the father of the reasonable (that is, of reasonably living) hermits, who live according to a law"—the way back to monastic life had begun. Nevertheless, such communities distanced themselves from the Benedictine Rule in external matters too. "All walked about barefoot, all were unkempt, pale, and content with extreme want of all things. Some had shut themselves (into a cell) and seemed to have died to the world as if they had already lain down in the grave." No wonder a greater percentage of members of these communities became saints than from the other areas of monasticism. The lone spiritual warrior was an almost perfect counterpart of the nobleman—he represented an utter denial of the noble's lifestyle, yet was bound to the noble in the awareness that he belonged to an elite.

If such a comment seems extreme, we should remember that at one time even the eremitic community of Saint Romuald—the only one about which we are well informed—experienced a rather worldly disturbance. Romuald struck one of his students, who took his revenge by accusing the saint of homosexual acts. Everyone ran to the spot, and there was a clamor for the lecherous old man to be hanged or burned alive in his hut. The student, who was "of noble birth," later became bishop of Nocera.

The eremitic community that time did not carry out the threat and only imposed a spiritual punishment on Romuald: he was not to perform the Mass. The hermits were in the wilderness and therefore in an area devoid of a lord. So they formed their own court just as if they were a secular clan outside of the public sphere. Similar procedures exist today, not only in non-European countries, as the easiest means of protecting the honor and reputation of the group. It may be that Peter Damian, Romuald's biographer, invented the story although he explicitly attributed it to the testimony of the saint himself. If fiction, it must have been conceivable to contemporary readers that lynch mob justice could occur even among God's warriors.

The community of hermits was essentially lordless; it had no abbot with the power to command but only a spiritual adviser. Nor did the hermits care about the labor that Saint Benedict obliged his followers to perform in the manner of the apostles. Each could nourish himself as he wished, either by gathering chestnuts or by catching fish by hand in a brook. Many, and this was particularly important in cold areas, received gifts from lay people who were happy to care for holy men. Life in the high Apennines, in the French Massif Central, or in the Bavarian Forest (where the hermit Gunter, count of Käfernburg-Schwarzburg, lived) would not always have been possible without such support. Hermits were not tied to a particular place. Romuald himself did not always follow the exhortations to *stabilitas* that he preached. "Gunter the Hermit" gave up his life with a group of hermits from time to time in order to preach to the Czechs and Liutizi, and was even guest in the court of King Stephen (the Saint) of Hungary.

The attitudes of contemporaries toward the eremitic tradition varied greatly and ranged from shy respect to physical rejection. Important people tried to experiment with them. "Otto (III) forcibly drew Romuald from his hermitage and made him abbot of (Saint Apollinare in) Classe." Here Romuald found "his rest and purity" threatened and "threw away his abbot's staff in the presence of the emperor." Previously, Archbishop Bruno of Cologne had attempted to end the unrestrained life of hermits by enclosing them in cells near a monastery or church so that they could be protected and controlled by the local clergy. Unrestrained, "acephalous" hermits were also fought with propaganda. There was the figure of the ridiculous hermit who behaves like a rough, crude peasant. In the Argonne, for example, a certain Lantpert lived, "fully a peasant (*rusticanus*) in his manners and in his learning," so that many could not help laughing when they saw him. He was stiff with filth, went about naked, and had no particular schedule and peculiar eating habits. Another ascetic of unfree origins was Heimerad or Heimo, who had been ordained a priest in the service of a noble lady and then undertook pilgrimages to Rome and Jerusalem. Upon his return, he wished to become a monk in Hersfeld, but he got into a quarrel with his abbot and brothers, was beaten, and wandered away. When Heimo came before the bishop of Paderborn with his pale face and his poor clothing, the bishop asked, "Where did this devil come from?" It was noticed that he had liturgical books with him from which he said Masses. The bishop looked over them, had them thrown into the fire, and had their owner beaten, reputedly on the command of the empress Kunigunda. Was she angry that Heimo, in his strife with the Hersfeld monks, had claimed to be a brother of the emperor? Was this assertion an outsider's answer to frequent mocking of his lowly origins and boorish character? One might also ask whether ascetics of low birth, in contrast to those of higher origins, were viewed with mistrust by the clergy. That is unlikely. Here, as usual, people were opposed to anyone who stood out from the norm. Later, Bishop Meinwerk of Paderborn regretted his too hastily formed opinion of Heimo.

The ascetic with his unusual lifestyle and appearance could be seen either as a heroic solitary warrior against evil or as a Don Quixote, possibly even as a cunning fraud. It was better, most thought, not to try to stand out but to remain in the military formation (*acies*) of which Saint Benedict had spoken to his followers. Both groups, monks and hermits, were striving to defeat the "old Adam," and to abandon egotism in order to place God in the center of their being. A "new man" was to be "put on" like a piece of clothing (Col. 3:9–10). The monk did this gradually "because in all things, even the good, excess is a vice." In external appearance neither beautiful dress nor rags are the right clothing; in all things one must hold to the mean.

Such moderation was foreign to the eremitic tradition. They wanted to reach their goals quickly and full of fervor. We must remember that for a very long time the model of the martyrs who had offered their lives for the faith had been the highest ideal and had been presented as such. In the tenth century, virtually the only hope for martyrdom was in the East or in Spain. The eremitic life offered an alternative to this total self-sacrifice. More moderate clerics enjoyed the following story, which apparently entered the West from Byzantium. An abbot named John (Johannes Kolobos) went naked into the wilderness in order to become an angel. After a week he returned hungry and disillusioned.

People were skeptical about anyone whose external appearance proclaimed too loudly, or replaced, internal perfection. Hypocrites were condemned for pretending (*praetendunt*) to evidence the model (*formam*) of sanctity. They might appear to the people as genuine saints, which was dangerous in a period when the notion of sanctity was not yet officially defined.

Churchmen attempted to remove the term "saint" from the living and to use it only to honor those dead of whom miracles were told at their tombs. Likewise the clergy did not want to leave the determination of sanctity to the people but rather to have it declared by their own authority. The recognition of the cult of saints was now proclaimed by bishops and synods, and in the year 993 Pope John XV celebrated the canonization of Bishop Udalrich of Augsburg. No one yet imagined that the papacy would later reserve to itself the exclusive right to make such decisions. For Bishop Udalrich it was intended as a particular honor that he should be so proclaimed by the highest of his episcopal brethren. Nevertheless, until well into the late Middle Ages there were noncanonized popular saints, both living and dead, whom the clergy regarded with distrust.

Saints always were a small minority in—or, rather, above—Christian society. Many hermits, a fair number of bishops, relatively few monks, and very few laypersons were recognized as saints—no wonder, since laypersons were either churlish or military. Odo of Cluny had attempted to show the noble laity a means of becoming saints. The authors of *vitae*, often monks, were both devoted to the Benedictine ideal and indebted to an ancient literary tradition. Some things in the *vitae* remind us of the eastern wilderness saints of antiquity, bound to the pre-Christian (and Christian) idea of the man of

God (*theios anēr*), who was a miracle worker. Most, however, consisted mainly of a listing of pious virtues and actions: prayer, vigils, fasts, humility, chastity, charity, etc. The list was similar for clerics and for laity. The secular duties of bishops fitted into this catalogue well. They were time-consuming, so that bishops often had to work nights on their "private" sanctification. A magnate such as Count Gerald of Aurillac was portrayed in his concerns for justice and law and as a man who refused to be the vassal of two different lords. He went to war but took care that no one was killed.

Monastic Reform

The battle of the desert saints with demons and the asceticism on the verge of self-destruction seem here to have been replaced by small daily efforts which led step by step to *aedificatio* the construction of a new personality. The permanent contribution of Benedict of Nursia was to have brought such actions into a collective order. Every Benedictine abbot had the duty to establish the "foundations of the monastic life," and by means of virtues to "cause spiritual mansions to be built," which he "covered with the ornament of wisdom." Such comparisons seem forced to us, and "edification" has lost its original meaning. At the time, it indicated not only plans and constructive activity, but also the amount of sweat the monk invested in it.

Monks followed a preestablished plan, while the acephalous hermit (without spiritual direction) "wanted to follow what seemed best to him." Such a plan could also be different from that which Benedict had drawn for the majority of western monks. There was the extreme collectivism of the Egyptian peasant's son and former soldier Pachomius; it could have taken the place of the extreme individualism of eastern ascetics and miracle workers. For Pachomius's followers the monastery was a walled citadel, and monks marched to their manual labor to the sound of trumpets. Pachomius based everything on obedience, as was clearly manifest in the detailed schedule and precise functioning of the system. Benedict's Rule also "regularized" life, but only in the most important matters. Other things could be established along the general lines provided in the Rule. This was a possible field of action for reformers. If things were turned over to a born organizer like Benedict of Aniane, monastic customs (*consuetudines*) would be unified and increased. When such things were pushed still further, they resembled a military exercise. In Cluny the result was a daily schedule that was complex and emphasized liturgy. This style has been termed "ritualism." From the eleventh century, thick volumes of *consuetudines* have come down to us, prescribing what was to be done in monasteries when praying, singing, kneeling, bowing, holding vigil, and participating in processions. Related to these directives was the strict uniformity of the monastic habit. Benedict of Aniane had already specified the appropriate length of monk's robes and similar matters.

In recent years, research on Cluny has progressed considerably. While previously the term "Cluniac" had been used to designate every form of monastic reform in the tenth century, an opposition between "Gorze and Cluny" has become the new point of departure for a reinterpretation of the sources by Kassius Hallinger. Since then, some scholars have softened the harsh contours of both phenomena and blurred the distinction. The "imperial monasticism" of the Gorze type and the Cluniac reform of a "western" sort had the same roots and the same goal, control of the junglelike growth of lifestyles through strict organization. One must wonder when and where the term "ritualism" is appropriate: with the phenomena of the eleventh or even the tenth century, or in the rules of the ninth century? If in the latter, Benedict of Aniane is not the only relevant figure. Angilbert, lay abbot of the great monastery of Centula (Saint-Riquier), divided his monks into groups and night shifts to maintain a perpetual divine praise. In the reform of the tenth century, ninth-century tendencies were revived and expanded. Cluny was not alone in its expansion of the liturgical work of monks, but it does present the most impressive example of liturgical increase in comparison with previous periods. Even under Abbot Odo, Cluniac monks, unless they were assigned other specific duties, were expected to recite 138 psalms a day, more than three times as many as in previous times. This was possible because the psalms could be recited along with other, nonliturgical occupations. At times, especially on feast days and during winter, the private prayer life was entirely subordinated to this continuing obligation of psalm recital. For the manual labor that Benedict of Nursia had directed his monks to perform, Cluny had a great supply of servants and workers, so that the monks' involvement was more symbolic than real.

Along with this liturgical expansion came an increasing complexity of liturgical rituals and the apparatus associated with them—curtains, cushions, carpets, and draperies, which had to be placed, or hung, and removed. Equally important was a strictly organized system of gestures. In addition to bows, prostrations, embraces, and genuflections there was—and not only in Cluny but also in Saint Gall—a well-developed sign language, which could be used at times when silence was required. The signs could be used for entirely mundane purposes: "As a sign for a cheese, press the hands together as though one were pressing a cheese." "As sign for a layman, hold the chin with one hand, for a beard, because in the old days people of this kind did not shave their chins."

There were regulations for all normal occurrences, even for the emotions. On Good Friday in Fruttuaria (and Cluny), the monks were free at the end of the psalms for reading and prayer, which were to be combined "with tears." This was not only a Cluniac tradition. Romuald of Ravenna could shed tears "at will" and even the tempest-tested Bishop Udalrich of Augsburg wept as he preached on the Lord's passion and thereby moved many of his listeners to tears. The tenth century was an age not of sentimentality but of routine spiritual practices. Thietmar of Merseburg counted the ability to weep at the proper time, as during the Mass, among the virtues worthy of being imitated. Such weeping was an ascetic skill which indicated that the will could control the body. Hence the quantity of tears was also important, whether, as Widukind described, the weeper's habit became wet from his tears or, as with Abbot Odilo of Cluny, the floor ran with tears as though a wave had washed over it.

To the directives by which the course of the day was complicated and controlled were added special directions on dress. We spoke earlier about variations in monastic dress. Such variations, however, did not always accompany a specific part of the general reform movement. One could wear a narrower or a wider cowl, or a wide one over the narrow one, as was the Cluniac custom. The wider garment hid the outline of the body, and the fullness of the material indicated the wealth of the monastery. The wide cowl was more favored in Gaul than in central Europe, where narrower forms were more common. The narrow cowl was ideal for work, the wider one for liturgy; those who wore both stayed warm and indicated that they belonged to the *oratores*, the worshipers. They also showed that they had been received into the fullness of the monastic life: in Cluny, novices did not wear the narrow cowl.

Care was taken to ensure that the monk's cowl had the right color. A synod held at Reims ordered that no one should wear a garment that contained admixtures of white or drab wool or wool that had its natural (dark) color. The cowl had to be dyed black. The character of the uniform was also lost when monks favored a (dark) blue color. Odo of Cluny had objected to this preference; he told the story of a monk who could find no rest after his death because Saint Benedict did not recognize him as one of his own. The saint said that someone wearing a blue cowl had to be a member of another order.

Here we see that external things were considered as making the difference between the reformed monk and the nonreformed, more "worldly" one. Clothes make the man; in other words, they designate the lifestyle whose expression they are. A monk in a narrow-waisted cowl with flattering sleeves made from fine material "looks from behind like a whore." Who needs pointed shoes, polished by servants until they gleam? By such clothes one indicates his inner attachment to worldly men and will behave like them.

The same is true of "ritualism." Any student of ethnology knows that rituals, like other functions, separate groups from each other. Only those who know and practice the rituals are recognized as members. To be bound to a system of rituals does not seem a hardship. Quite the opposite, such an obligation calms the insecure, who willingly renounce their freedom of action. Insecurity reigns when the traditional orders appear too weak and the world goes in new directions. Strong, reforming abbots certainly played the major role in restructuring the monastic lifestyle. There must have been a need for a detailed elaboration of the *consuetudo;* otherwise they could have accomplished little. In contrast, there were always individuals and whole communities that refused reform. Comfortable living may have been behind their refusal, as well as the idea that the old way was best and that change brought confusion. When Otto III planned to suppress the monastery of S. Paolo fuori le mura of Rome and sought to establish canons there, Saint Paul, so we are told, appeared to him in a dream and warned him, "It serves nothing to eliminate or to change the kind of living (*propositum*) of a religious order. This is true even when the *ordo* has become somewhat depraved. Everyone has to be judged according to that order to which he first dedicated his life to God." Nevertheless the saint added a short general statement that amendments are allowed.

We may distinguish between reforms that corresponded to genuine needs of the religious, or at least to a part of them, and the more or less forcible imposition of a new style of life from above. We must not always see these changes from the perspective of the reformer and assume that only chaos and immorality prevailed beforehand. Sometimes the better order became an enemy of the good one, at least in the eyes of those whom the reformers wanted to force to adopt a new *consuetudo.* Many saw in such attempts the threat of penetration by foreigners, as did the monks of Fleury when Odo of Cluny entered their monastery with a large entourage. It was said that they armed themselves with swords and shields and occupied the roofs of the monastic buildings in order to protect themselves against the invasion. Other clerics, like Thietmar of Merseburg, reacted more temperately; Thietmar did not conform personally to the militant western form of monastic reform. The new lifestyle (*nova conversatio*), he explained, is worthy of praise, but its adherents are not always what they seem to be. Thietmar's ideal was *mediocritas,* the moderate use of food and drink and a warm heart. Who benefited from that which was denied the fasting wearers of the double cowl (*diploide indutis*)? It might have helped their own monastery, but it is also possible that "everything was sent elsewhere (*extrinsecus*)." This suggests that Cluniac monasteries had material obligations resulting from the association of those monasteries under the direction of Cluny.

REFORMERS AND CONSERVATIVES

In every age the majority of people are content with the real circumstances of life, with their own inadequacies, and with outward irritations; it is the minority that protests against such circumstances. Members of this minority are criticized as do-gooders and as unrealistic idealists. What Kassius Hallinger has called the "antisecular protest" was present with the birth of monasticism, and it was renewed within the order when monastic communities were given over entirely into the hands of realists. To this extent, reformers were correct in emphasizing that they wanted only to reestablish the "earlier condition," the living according the Rule (of Benedict of Nursia). On the other hand, every such movement carried within itself its own particular rules and started with different preconditions.

What Benedict of Aniane intended was a part of the general tendency to organize and assimilate disparate elements within the Frankish state. The Cluniacs were supported by laypersons who lived in a region free of royal government: they sought to establish an outward and an inward order as balance to all the disturbances of their epoch. Zealots for spiritual concerns thus had a free hand, but they did not everywhere find understanding. "And there began" wrote Widukind of Corvey, "a hard persecution of monks because some bishops preferred to have a small number of admirable monks than a large number of indifferent ones." Reforms seldom took hold entirely without bishops; indeed, many bishops seized the initiative, as did William of Mainz and Adalbero I of Metz. Often the result was the expulsion of monks who did not want to abandon their previous lifestyle, and only later did bishops attempt to establish a common life for both groups. "We do not condemn the good who are forced to live among pseudomonks or under evil superiors . . . , as Saint Gregory said, 'No one is truly good who refuses to tolerate the bad,' and the bad are all the more to be tolerated if they are the majority."

Odo of Cluny would hardly have understood such words and would never have accepted them. For him the world was in desperate straits, all had gone mad, no true order was still observed. An energetic idealist could not accept such a situation. John of Gorze wanted to enter a monastery at the beginning of his career, but "there was no monastery on this side of the Alps and hardly any in Italy of which it could be said that life was led according to the Rule with fervor." Possibly this statement is correct, if the Rule of Benedict is taken as an absolute law to which no modifications can be made. For centuries it had been different, and the abbot had had the right to decide what was best for the lives of his community. Monks lived according to a "mixed rule" based on various sources. It was considered permissible to pass over the injunctions of Benedict for practical reasons, including human weakness. The monks were to be spared injunctions that were too harsh.

So opinions diverged: some held fast to the continuation of the law according to which they had first entered the monastery; others appealed to the will of the order's founder and endeavored to bring everyone into line with a single way of life. *Una consuetudo* became the battle cry, as it had been for Benedict of Aniane. The reformers considered themselves a new spiritual aristocracy and dismissed as ignorant sinners those who defended a more relaxed life. This had nothing to do with social divisions. The unreformed or unreformable monks were sometimes characterized as "the more refined and noble" (*subtiliores et nobiliores*), sometimes as *agrestes monachos,* that is, as rustic and thus ignorant, crude brothers. During the early period at Cluny a relatively high proportion of the monks were from a free peasant background, and only in the course of the eleventh century did members of the aristocracy become predominant among the monastic population. The self-consciousness of reforming monasticism did not need this social support. Cluniac instructions indicate that in memorial prayers for the dead, right after the name of

King Conrad (of Burgundy, 937–93) the names of deceased Cluniac monks were recited, and only then followed the name of Duke Henry (of Burgundy, died 1002). In the necrology the names of deceased monks were to come first, and only after them that of the dead king.

Anyone who had proposed a higher goal (*propositum*) than that of the average religious could live as a hermit or could enter the rectified society of a reformed monastery. In the name of a stricter life according to the Rule, new practices could be introduced which were really opposed to it: Pope Leo VII abolished the duty of *stabilitas loci* in favor of Fleury, which was ruled by Odilo of Cluny, by allowing monks to leave their monasteries in order to flock to that "leader of monks" (*ducem monachorum*). They could do this if they had no possibility of leading a life in poverty. Absence of poverty was not really the reason, however. The pope simply cited it as the most striking characteristic of the lax lifestyle. At the same time, Fleury was to receive complete exemption from episcopal authority and to possess an abbot elected by the "wiser portion" of the monks. The *pars sanioris consilii* was an ancient notion. What was new was that this portion had the deciding vote even when it formed an extremely small (*minima*) group within the community. This was a total break, mitigated only by the right to leave, which was accorded anyone who found the new form of life too difficult (*onerosa*). What difficulties and burdens the new form of life entailed we do not learn from this charter or from others, and seldom from contemporary chronicles. Only modern research into the *consuetudines* has shed some light.

In the privilege of Leo VII for Fleury, the lax monks were given permission to leave the monastery "so that they would not disturb the others." These monks probably took the position that it was the reformers who had brought disturbance into the community. Conservative defense was often harsh. We are told of libelous attacks against the reformers and of "acephalous" monks who had driven out their abbot. In one place a whole community left town and a great crowd of people accompanied them a long distance in tears. The community refused the invitation of the abbot-count to negotiate, and the monks found a new home in England.

A monastery clearly showed itself in need of reform when plans were laid to murder the abbot or Cluniacs who had been sent to institute reform. Reforming Cluniacs sometimes had to retreat from "occupied" monasteries, or expeditions against unruly communities were hopeless from the beginning. When, as in the case of Vézelay, even the diocesan bishop stood on the opposite side, the kind of tension existed that Adalbero of Laon was later to describe in his satire on the militant monks and their "king" Odilo.

Was all this more of a departure from the rule of Saint Benedict than a fulfillment? The question is not easy to answer. Authoritarian and repressive tendencies are found in every collectively structured lifestyle. Cluny disseminated these tendencies and increased them. Soon the abbot found himself at the head of a whole league of monasteries, including all their servants and their militant supporters. Benedictine mildness had not always reigned, even in the earliest period of the order; so the Rule included corporal punishment. It was limited to three groups: children, youths, and "those with less understanding of how great the punishment of exclusion from the community (*excommunicatio*) is." This sort of punishment was not extended with time. At Cluny there was a birch for children, and in the old *consuetudines* from Gorze we are told of a four-finger-wide whip used as an instrument of punishment for serious offenses. In the Rule, these primitive means of discipline were to be used only as subsidiary means beside psychological discipline. Force was largely replaced by a tradition of obedience and by the precise functioning of a complicated system of behavior and duties. Ritualism was the heart of this system.

Whatever Benedict of Nursia might have thought of his Cluniac followers, they were convinced that in their style of life they held the key to heaven. To whoever followed the *consuetudines* of Cluny, "the secrets of heaven" would be revealed; "he will be pleasing to God and agreeable (*dulcis*) to men. Whoever breaks or abandons them will be abandoned by God and hated by the world." Odo of Cluny had seen the madness of the ways of his age and had urged for a life "beyond" the world—the life of the *professores sublimis propositi*, those "who confessed to having a supernatural goal in life." A reform movement inspired by such ideas could not agree to compromises. It had to exhort, to persuade, and to attempt to break resistance with rigor.

Thus we can understand how difficult, even impossible, it must have been for two wholly different groups to live together in one monastery. Those who remained loyal to their former *propositum* and who would not accept the increased obligations were a constant source of annoyance for the stricter ones, and their very existence disturbed the inner peace of these latter. The reformers reproached them for following their own will and for paying little attention to the "work of obedience" described in the preface of the Benedictine

Rule. True, according to the Rule the monks should obey primarily the wisdom of their abbot, whereas obedience had here become impersonal and a part of a complex canon of behavior. We must recognize that private initiative and private prayer were possible in reformed monasteries, but for monks of the reformed group they were rather marginal aspects of their daily life.

Modern intellectuals are nonconformists, seldom satisfied with living in homogeneous groups. We may assume a similar thinking among those hermits who sought their own lifestyles. Was the rejection of community a form of asceticism for them, or was it an absolute necessity in view of the imperfect *propositum* of their companions? If we can sleep in a private room rather than a dormitory, we prefer the private room, and we are quite content when our food is brought to us there. In the old Gorze *consuetudines*, both sleeping and eating alone were punishments for serious offenses, along with standing outside the church door during the office. To be left alone was a punishment considered so harsh that consolers (*consolatores*) were designated by the abbot. They had to comfort those who had been temporarily expelled from the community. Such punishments were explicitly compared to episcopal excommunication: the guilty individual was "separated from the mass of the faithful." Gorze was not alone with such regulations; they were also to be found in Cluniac monasteries. One may say that they corresponded fully to the spirit of the Benedictine Rule.

Where solitude was seen as a punishment, living with a community was seen as a positive experience; the more collective the life, the more homogeneous was the group. We may call this situation an intensification of what Benedict of Nursia had wanted, but it was an intensification that Benedict would probably have seen as exaggerated. What had been innovative in early monasticism was now simply the old tradition. Strong, enthusiastic people could not be satisfied with it. Even if they did not become hermits, they often joined the Gorze reform, which had been influenced by the eremitic tradition. But they could also elect the lifestyle of Cluny, which was opposed to eremitism but was connected to it by the harshness of its demands.

RITUALISM

Many adjusted to the Cluniac style, and perhaps many learned to appreciate the positive side of monastic industriousness. Simpler spirits were probably satisfied with a naive and playful element inherent in "ritualism"—an element sometimes expressed openly. What a joy when on feast days dozens, or even hundreds, of candles were burned, or when the cellarer rang his little bell, or when new shoes were hung from strings in the chapter room, "strictly arranged according to rank." On the other hand, one's reputation increased for knowing all the details of the *consuetudines* and for teaching them to others. Such details included knowing that three carpets were laid down for the Palm Sunday procession and that the kneelers were to be separated from each other by one foot; that after the priest and the other ministers had thrown themselves down on the carpets and had stood up again, the carpets on either side had to be picked up immediately while the middle one remained. Exemplary behavior was rewarded, as the prologue to the *liber tramitis* shows. One might even rise to the office of prior, who enjoyed a higher position in the rank order but had little authority. Those who took pleasure in supervising others and noting their mistakes found a wide domain of activities thanks to the obligation to denounce incorrect behavior to the authorities.

The industriousness of such a form of monastic existence makes it difficult to speak of a contemplative lifestyle. The modern term *Leistungsgesellschaft* (performance-oriented society), though still inadequate, would be more appropriate, for it implies the importance of competition, which was highly developed. This brings to mind a story told by Rodulf Glaber. Abbot Odilo of Cluny complained that jealousy raged not only among the worldly but also among monks. When Rodulf renewed the inscriptions of the altars in his monastery, it may have been a monk from Cluny who infected the abbot and some of the brothers "with the poison of jealousy" so that they destroyed his work. Perhaps they justifiably found the work shoddy; perhaps, according to the Cluniac view, one ought not begin such a project without the abbot's permission. This is more likely, for Rodulf spoke of the request made by the brothers that he do the work. He had attempted to distinguish himself and was bitterly disappointed. In so highly structured an organization, only the completion of established norms was prized; competition should occur only in this field, not in private initiatives. But it was in collective activities that the jealousy arose of which Odilo complained. Rodulf Glaber meant something other, envy of creative work.

Communal activity was a binding force; yet it could lead to division by the "poison of jealousy" toward one's neighbor. The experiment of a ritualistic lifestyle had its natural limits. Although it did not create a "new man," it aided those who were striving to form a new Christian personality. After Benedict of Nursia and Benedict of Aniane, the reform movement of the tenth century was the third great attempt to reach a goal that one could only approach to a certain degree. We know from Ekkehard IV of Saint Gall that factions, envy, and slander could be found in a conservative monastery. We may doubt that the daily life in a reformed monastery totally differed from this picture. The "old man" could not be entirely expelled any more than he could be by later reforms. To conclude that the reforms failed, however, would be incorrect.

12 ❧ MONASTIC LIFE

BENEDICT OF NURSIA INTENDED THAT THE
monastery should present an indivisible unity
and an example of continuing communal life.
All should be of one heart and one soul, as the
apostolic community had been depicted. The
reality was usually different, concerning both
the *stabilitas loci* and the various groups with
various ways of life within the monastery. The
more numerous the members, the more difficult it was to establish an interpersonal bond
among them.

The Burgundian Rodulf Glaber was taken
into the monastery of Saint-Léger in Champeaux around the age of twelve, left there not

entirely of his own accord, and found haven first in Moutier-Saint-Jean in the diocese of Auxerre and then in the monastery of Saint-Germain in Auxerre. There he experienced the conflict concerning the altar inscriptions mentioned in chapter 11 above. Later we find him in the Bèze monastery and then in the respected monastery of Saint-Bénigne at Dijon. The abbot of that monastery, William of Volpiano, took him along on a trip to Italy. After the death of his patron, Rodulf moved to Cluny, where he completed his historical work at the request of Abbot Odilo. William was an important reformer who had been trained in Cluny. Neither he nor Odilo was bothered by the unsettled life of this man. They were accustomed to placing and transplanting monks in different monasteries for the purpose of reform, and we have already seen that the papal privilege for Fleury allowed that monastery to accept reform-minded monks even without the approval of their abbots. Rodulf himself wrote that foreign monks were always accepted with respect in Saint-Germain.

We also hear of the departure of whole monastic communities, such as that of Chartres in 1004. The *vitae* of saintly monks often give the impression of instability. Outside the sphere of reform, we are told, for example, in the life of a monk from Saint Gall named Tutilo, that he was "a man who loved to travel and who knew all of the lands and cities for far around," and had been sent as far away as Mainz to purchase cloth.

According to the Rule of Benedict, anyone who, upon returning from a trip, told his brothers of his travels was to be punished. This was a requirement which later left no trace and was hardly ever followed. Benedict of Nursia also thought that traveling monks would stay in his monastery and would desire "a fixed location" there, that is, that they would enter his community. One could even try to convince exemplary monks to stay, since "everywhere one serves the same lord, fights for the same king." This sentence from the Rule could also justify moving from Benedict's monastery to another. In any case, even at that time *stabilitas* was not seen as a strict law. On the other hand, a change of residence was to be an exception and should not lead to a fluctuation of the monastic personnel.

GROUP FORMATION: *NUTRITI* AND *CONVERSI*

Monks coming from abroad had to fit into a distinction that was made in the everyday life of the monastery between those who had served from childhood and those who had taken the vows late in life, that is, between *nutriti* and *conversi* (in the old sense of persons who joined the community after adulthood). Here, people who were accustomed to following the direction of others interacted with noble or freeborn men who had lived a secular life before entering the monastery. On the one hand there were monks who had been educated in the monastery's "internal school," on the other those who were barely literate and knew no Latin. Relatively few of the great abbots but almost all of the monastic historians came from the former group. In everyday life the *nutriti* apparently formed a core group, which took a reserved attitude toward the latecomers. The opposition was obvious in many ways, particularly in a speech by an enemy of Ademar of Chabannes in the debate on Martial of Limoges. Benedict, prior of the monastery of San Michele della Chiusa (near Susa in the Piedmont), said in his clumsy Latin that he was the nephew of the abbot of that monastery and was his designated successor. If there had been no wicked monks, namely *conversi* with their churlish ways, he would long since have been abbot. This man, who behaved as a learned monk, was thus rejected by the *conversi* of his monastery. It is likely that these included influential people.

The entry of young monks, or rather the oblation (*oblatio*) of children to the saint, took place very early. Rather (of Verona) was brought to the monastery of Lobbes as a small child (*puerulus*) "along with bread and wine as an offering." William of Dijon had been given by his parents to a monastery near Vercelli at the age of seven. Thanks to his exceptional parentage he was looked after by a trustworthy woman who lived near the monastery, and there he was occasionally allowed to spend the night. Since children were not always baptized as infants, an unbaptized son might be given to a monastery by his father.

For the family it was reassuring if one of their members was a pious intercessor in a monastery. This was still more true of sick children, who in a monastery were nearer to God and out of the family's way. Gerald of Aurillac, later considered a saint, was often ill in childhood; so he was allowed to study. "Although little suited for worldly affairs, he was suitable for an ecclesiastical office." Saint Adalbert of Prague and others were said to have recovered their health after entering the monastery. In Cluny the number of *pueri oblati* was limited to six in the late eleventh century. Apparently this was to prevent the abuse whereby families with numerous offspring offered some of them, especially their blind, deformed, or leprous children, to the monastery, "not to do God's will, but only to avoid the burden of their education and support."

While those who entered the monastery later, even those in clerical orders, had to spend a period as novices, in Cluny children were immediately given the scapular cowl and thus made full members of the community. After achieving their majority—that is, at an "appropriate age," usually fifteen years—the young monk had to show, by placing his charter of profession on the altar himself, that he wanted to belong to the community. The *consuetudines* did not provide for a situation in which a monk would request to leave at this time. Apparently such things hardly ever happened. If they did, the monastery would have had the unpleasant task of returning property that the parents had donated at the time of the oblation. In the ninth century, a situation of this kind, involving Gottschalk in the monastery of Fulda, had caused a scandal. Although the monastery immediately granted him his freedom, it did not wish to return his family property. A synod of Ingelheim in 948 ordered that children who had been brought to the monastery could no longer return to secular status. Of course this went against the intention of the Rule, and the promises of the monk in his charter of profession—*stabilitas loci,* moral conduct, and obedience—became mere formalities. A report of the Frankfurt synod of 1027 shows that the 948 order was being followed: A man named Gebhard was ordered to return to monastic status because he had fled from a Würzburg monastery when he was a child. It was of no help that he was a stepbrother of the emperor who was present at this assembly.

Along with sick children, old people, in monastic habit, awaited death in monasteries. That could take a long time or could be as fast as in the case of Count Odo I of Chartres, who fell ill, became a monk, and died, all in four days. At the critical moment when a sinful man stood before the tribunal of God, he needed helpers, and he found them if he was a monk. According to custom at Gorze, all the bells were rung and everyone hurried to the church to pray for a dying brother. The same was supposed to take place at the death of the king or other magnates, especially when the dying individual had been accepted into the prayer confraternity of the monastery. True, it was some time before word of their death reached the monastery. Perhaps judgment of the soul of the deceased had already taken place? In any case, dying in the monastery guaranteed that intercessary prayers would be offered at the proper time. Here one could die in peace.

This kind of death did not always occur as desired. Count Albert of Vermandois became ill, had himself tonsured, and took the cowl. Then he recovered and had to listen to the reproaches of his family, who considered it stupidity to have entered the monastery. So he "exchanged the cowl for the warrior's clothing," for which he experienced the punishment of God. The count fell ill once more, and this time he really did die.

Abbots were pleased when magnates wanted to end their lives in their monastery, for material reasons and also because such choices demonstrated the reputation of the community. For spiritual life, the presence of a pious outsider whose social status had to be taken into account was rather a burden. For example, Duke William III of Aquitaine, count of Poitou, whose daughter was later the wife of Hugh Capet, went to Saint-Maixent then back to Saint-Cyprian in Poitiers, where he died in 963. Was he really one monk among many, or had the monastery become a sort of court for him? It would have taken a great strength of will on both sides to make a duke conform to the Rule in every detail. Even the ascetically strict monastery of Gorze gave special treatment to a rich man of noble family who brought with him "a burden of gold and silver and other furniture (*supellectilem*) in great abundance." Because he was an important person (*ampla persona*), he was treated more gently than the others and honored more than they.

The ideal situation, and a real advantage for the monastery, was that young men should decide of their own free will and with full awareness to enter the community. Romuald entered the monastery at the age of twenty as penance for a violent crime committed by his father. Odo of Cluny became a monk at thirty. Both became very important for the monastic life of their epoch. For adult monks it was more difficult than for *pueri oblati* to separate themselves entirely from their families. Such attachments could result in a monk's being followed into the monastery by his family. John, a son of free parents, entered Gorze and convinced his two brothers to do the same. The mother, a widow and thus independent, later moved "with some of the people from her *familia*" to a place near the monastery and occupied herself as a servant (*serviens*) to the monks. In conjunction with her own servants she looked after the clothing of the Gorze convent. While an advantage for Gorze, this activity was considered questionable by some monks.

If we examine the most important groups of which the convent was composed, we find the monks raised in the monastery forming the nucleus of its tradition, in full possession of spiritual education but without the worldly experience of latecomers. We can assume that the attitude of men like Rather of Verona vis-à-vis the realities of existence had its source in their background as *nutriti*. Apart from the *nutriti* and the latecomers there were arrivals from other monasteries: reformed monks, or restless souls with disciplinary problems. In addition there would be people of genuine late vocation, experienced in the world and thus capable of assuming positions of leadership after acquiring the necessary instruction and training. A strong hand was needed to lead such different kinds of people toward a common goal. One means to this end was the full occupation of all members through prescribed daily work.

PRIEST MONKS AND CRIMINALS

The Rule of Benedict dedicated a whole chapter to priest monks. At the time it was written, they were few in number and were selected by the abbot; Benedict ordered strict punishments for those priests who fancied themselves something special. In the tenth century things were different: priests formed a large minority or even a majority of the community, and many monks held minor orders as well. It is probably true that priest monks—like the former *pueri oblati,* with whom they were often identical—considered themselves the real notables of the monastery. This process of intellectualization pushed the simple *conversi* ever more to the periphery. Noble birth may have provided a certain balance to this elite, but a "boorish" monk, possibly from an unfree family that had taken refuge in the monastery, was not much respected. In the *consuetudines* the *conversi,* often in contrast to the *cantores* and the *pueri,* were charged with responsibilities marginal to the liturgical life. They carried candlesticks or the aspersorium and were allowed to swing the censer. A monk became more and more similar to a lay brother without profession, "who is not a monk but a tonsured layman."

Another sort of marginality resulted from the fact that monasteries could be a refuge for criminals, who could not be thrown out when they sought asylum with signs of penitence. No one was surprised at a story told by Regino that one day (in 746) the former mayor of the palace, Karlmann, after his resignation, went incognito to Montecassino, knocked on the door of the monastery, and requested a meeting with the abbot. Karlmann told him that he was a killer and asked with all signs of penitence to be allowed to choose that monastery as his place of penance. The second synod of Limoges in 1031 had to deal with the question of whether someone who had committed a murder and had then become a monk should be allowed to be ordained. The synod considered the case of a cleric who had murdered a bishop. Since he was taken in nowhere else, he was offered the possibility of penance in Cluny. Abbot Odilo inquired in Rome how to treat the man and was told that the sinner could neither be ordained nor receive communion. We cannot doubt that Abbot Odilo wanted to see this penitent criminal fully integrated into the monastic community. We do not know if many of the brothers found his presence in the dormitory and in the refectory sinister or even threatening. The fact that the pope imposed limitations may have prevented Cluny from becoming an asylum for more clerical criminals. Previously, Abbot Odo had brought a "very famous robber" (*insignissimus latro*) to Cluny, who was given the position of assistant to the cellarer and carried out his duties with one hand "while holding the psalter in the other." In this case the young man became a monk after a period of testing. Apparently he came from a good family and could have been one of those "younger sons" who either would not or could not wait to be released from their father's authority.

Monasteries Great and Small

The communal life of men of such different origins and education created problems about which we know little. The situation was easier in small communities than in large ones, of course. We usually think of monasticism in connection with large abbeys rather than small dependent houses (*cellae, cellulae*). These small institutions were further differentiated into those with a dozen monks and those with even fewer. The average community—if we take into consideration the large ones (*monasteria*), the middle-sized (*coenobia*), and the small (*cellae, cellulae*)—must have included around thirty monks. At the time of new foundations and new settlements this was the number most frequently mentioned, along with the number twelve. Understandably, there were more small monasteries than middle-sized or large ones. The same image is presented in the (questionable) modern lists of houses associated with Cluny, or involved in the Cluniac reform.

Small communities were subject to the discipline of an abbot of a larger monastery and thus experienced temporary control. The lifestyle might be strenuous, as we may suppose it was in the twelve "cells" of William of Dijon's monastery of Saint-Bénigne. In other cases the life of so small a group might have led in other, more relaxed directions. Such "cells" were often established on small properties of a monastery, sometimes because the donor of the property had requested that monks pray at that place for his soul. Possibly their presence was a guarantee against alienation, and in order to better oversee the exploitation of the property. When one of the large monasteries had too many members, founding of a "cell" was also a means of reducing the number of inhabitants. It is more likely that "boorish" monks who were experienced in agriculture would be sent to these cells than those who were important for the liturgy and spiritual level of the mother house.

At the other extreme stood the great monasteries. At one time there had been 300 monks in Corbie and in Centula-Saint-Riquier, 150 in Saint-Denis, 120 in Saint-Germain-des-Prés. There were 300 monks at Aniane under the great abbot Benedict, but after his departure the monastery quickly became insignificant. Centula had Abbot Angilbert to thank for its size, Corbie a cousin of Charlemagne's, Wala. Benedict of Aniane had all of the convents in the subkingdom of Aquitaine handed over to his monastery. Family connections with Charlemagne and the wealth of the highest elites, or the great personal influence on the young king, had caused this extraordinary growth. Elsewhere, less than one-half of that population was achieved. The cause was not a deficiency in rural property. That of the monastery of Saint-Germain-des-Prés, with around 30,000 hectars, was enormous. Nevertheless the number of monks was relatively small.

In the Ottonian period, proximity to the monarchy was lacking, as were the economic underpinnings for such communities. Huge monastic lordships had been replaced by smaller units. In the protocol concerning the election of Abbot Odilo of Cluny in 994, the names of 76 monks are listed, and the dormitory at Cluny contained at the most 100 beds, possibly only 64 (the second number might be too low). The Carolingian plan of a monastery in Saint Gall indicates 77 beds in the dormitory. In addition there were 8 in the abbot's house, 5 in the gatehouse, 2 in the living quarters of the external school, and 3 for the hospice personnel. Officers and monastic officials too may have been housed in these locations, and perhaps also their servants and those of the abbot. With a dozen novices, this could add up to as many as 110 religious. The plan came, according to all indications, from Reichenau. By the year 940—that is, four generations after the copying of the plan—this monastery housed the abbot and 95 monks. The decline in number since the Carolingian period was less here than in many other communities.

Cluny, then, was not an exceptionally large monastery in the tenth century. We know this to be so, even if the often cited number of 64 monks who received books to read during Lent is not much to go on. In the German monastery of Prüm there were said to be 186 religious, 100 of them priests, in the second half of the tenth century. This is unusual, for even a large monastery such as Farfa had only half as many monks. In contrast to the Carolingian period there were no monasteries with as many as 300 monks. The elites had become poorer, and what the chronicler of Saint-Géry in Cambrai described was true of many communities: "Once there had been a greater number of brothers (in the monastery), now want had caused a reduction in number to 50." In some cases there was a catastrophic drop, as in Hirsau in 988 when the number of monks fell from 72 to 12 because of an epidemic. The monastery of Bèze burned down in the year 937 for the fifth time, this time by arson, for which a Hungarian detachment was responsible. For fifty-one years it was impossible to reestablish the earlier standard (*statum*). Even without data on numbers, this is an impressive example of the situation at that time.

Monastic Buildings: The Role of Fire and Light

War and pestilence threatened only at specific times, the danger of fire was constant. It was, so to speak, a daily occurrence for a burning candle could set the bed straw on fire at night. This even happened once to some craftsmen who were working for the monastery as foundrymen and had learned to deal with fire. In the monk's dormitory a candle had to burn constantly according to the Rule, a command with a practical purpose. There were "eternal" lights for religious reasons, too. At Fleury, three candles burned day and night: one in the church, one by the tomb of Saint Benedict, one in the crypt oratory. Candles were the most dangerous form of lighting, but there was more than enough wax: Dependents were burdened with wax payments to ecclesiastical lords throughout the Middle Ages. The greatest danger was that of fire in the church. The transition to building with stone for this practical reason began first with church construction; fortifications and city walls came afterwards. However, even stone churches promised no absolute security: the cathedral church of Chartres burned in 962, its replacement in 1020, and the renewed church, in part, in 1030 before its dedication.

In the secular sphere as well, people seem to have seen fire as an unavoidable danger, yet failed to do everything possible to reduce their risk. We know that walled fireplaces and Roman floor heating were not entirely forgotten. Nonetheless, a fireplace, in which logs were burned, was normally built in the middle of a room. The smoke exited through an opening in the ceiling, over which a small roof was erected as protection against rain and snow. This sort of heating is known from prehistoric finds, was still in use in English university colleges at the end of the Middle Ages, and existed in peasant dwellings as late as 1770. On the Saint Gall plan, where other forms of heating were used as well, the open fireplace in the center of the room was employed for the servants' buildings, for the "external school," and for the guest house, in which important persons were housed. No doubt the monks wanted students and distinguished visitors to feel at home. The cost of fuel was merely the food and clothing of the servants who brought it from the forest, and thus was minimal.

Although people enjoyed gathering around the open fire in a large room, in small bedrooms the corner fireplace with semicircular chimney was the favorite form of heating. This was probably used at Reichenau (according to the Saint Gall copy) in the abbot's bedroom and also in the rooms intended for important guests. The disadvantage of this sort of heating was, as we still know today, that it heated the room unevenly. It may have been for this reason that the abbot's bed stood nearest the fireplace. For monks and novices, who had to spend many hours in the church, a warming room with floor heating had been prepared in Reichenau. Above the monks' warming room and at least indirectly heated by it lay their dormitory. Floor heating was also found in other monasteries and palaces, such as Werla (in Saxony), built between 920 and 930.

Such luxury seems to have been the exception in smaller monasteries and "cells." In any case it was a hard life for those who did not tolerate cold, but few or no such people seem to have survived to adulthood. By comparison with servants, monks were better off: they wore underwear and a cowl which reached almost to the floor. They had furs and not only regular shoes but night footwear as well. Peasants, on the other hand, to judge from contemporary illustrations, went barefoot and wore only short tunics. They protected their feet as well as they could by wrapping them in rags. One wonders how people could survive for thirty or even forty years in such conditions, but the answer is simple: their ancestors had lived like that since time immemorial and even less comfortably than in the tenth century.

We know from an ancient description of the Cluniac buildings, and in part also from the excavations conducted by the Medieval Academy of America, that there was a monastic building tradition extending from the plan of Saint Gall, through the reform of Benedict of Aniane, to Cluny. The description begins with the monastery's church, which also corresponds to the chronological development of the buildings. The church is "Cluny II," the work of Abbot Maiolus, dedicated in 981. His successor Odilo replaced the wooden roof with a stone vault, a daring construction which greatly increased the fire protection of the building.

William of Dijon did the same for his church of Saint-Bénigne at Dijon, and it is assumed that he introduced Lombard construction forms—and probably experts as well—into Burgundy. The description of Cluny II says nothing about this important improvement. Instead, it tells us that the church had 160 glass windows. This is certainly either an exaggeration or a later scribal error. But even if there were only 60, they must have been marveled at as an unheard-of luxury. And there were more windows of this kind: 97 in the dormitory alone, all as high as a man holding up his arm, and two and one-half feet wide. This was nothing essentially novel, since already in the ninth century churches such as those in Reichenau had glass windows, even glass pictures. In a poor monastery in the late tenth century, window openings were still covered with cloth, which admitted little light. We mentioned earlier how the monks in Tegernsee were delighted by the "extraordinary work" of stained glass windows.

In the Saint Gall plan one can see that the scriptorium had windows. For most of the other buildings, people were content with the light that came from the smoke opening in the roof. There were some windows in the rooms for important persons. Here the new construction of Odilo could be regarded as "modern," for he had procured the entry of light and sun. The concern for baths and toilets also suggested modernity. One would not have expected to find, next to the house for noble guests with 70 beds, that 70 toilets had been installed, which apparently corresponded to the standard of courtly comfort. The monks of the Saint Gall plan had had to manage with a total of 9 toilets next to the dormitory. In Cluny there were 45 in the corresponding space, each with its own window. One can imagine that each had two users, so that there was a total of 90 monks in the cloister dormitory. Perhaps they showed their latrines to visitors with pride. Decorum and hygiene were two of the bases of the Cluniac system.

The Cloister and the Outside World

Since Odilo built a guest house for 70 persons, he must have been thinking of royal visits. In two rooms, 40 men and 30 women could be accommodated. Accompanying personnel were given less comfort. They had to sleep and eat in a *solarium* over the horse stables, which meant in the open air, protected only by a roof. Here only the horses had separate stalls; their grooms had to arrange themselves as they wished. One must add that no one traveled in winter without urgent reasons.

There was a third group of travelers: those who came without horses and—it went without saying—received food and drink as alms. The description of the monastic buildings of Cluny reflects the usual dichotomy when it names nobles and "countesses" on one side and simple pedestrians on the other. A person traveling without being able to command horses and servants was, in the best case, a pilgrim, but he was more likely to be one of the crowd of tramps who had been set adrift by war or personal guilt. The borders between the two groups were indistinct: pilgrims often had to do penance for some crime; beggars wandered under the guise of pilgrims.

The description of the monastic buildings stops short with the dimensions of a house whose purpose is unknown. We learn nothing about many other important structures, such as the external school, nothing about the workshops of craftsmen except for those of the tailors, the goldsmiths, and the glaziers. Perhaps the whole complex was still under construction. The fact that the optative mood, "it should be built" (*construatur*), is used in the second section would support this hypothesis. In any case, the concept of the description was followed, since the excavations have not indicated any significant departures from it.

The organization of large monasteries demanded great skill on the part of the monastic officers and much discipline on the part of their inhabitants. There were large secular complexes too, which cannot be fully compared with the great monasteries; a royal court or a magnate's court, oriented toward the outside world, presented almost entirely material problems, while a monastery had both material and spiritual needs. In the monastic sphere, silence and composure were to reign, and secular guests and the care of the poor in the hospice were to be separated from it. Moreover, the monastery was the center of a complicated agricultural operation with mills, wine presses, and the personnel who worked the lord's reserve (*terra indominicata*). Finally, there were monasteries which served as centers for the veneration of saints by the common people. In the monastery of Sainte Foy (Fides) in Conques, monks as well as "educated laypersons" maintained vigils. The chanting of the psalms was disturbed one day by the noise and singing of peasant pilgrims. The church door was closed, but the pilgrims raised such a hue and cry that it had to be opened again. The pilgrims crowded into the church, so that the monks had hardly any room.

When important visitors came, they desired social contact with the monastic officers. For this reason there was sometimes a special table and kitchen for the abbot. The poor were cared for separately. In Fleury, as a reminder of the old institution of the *matricula*, there was a house for twelve paupers, who were lodged here permanently. The building had its own bakery and kitchen. The novitiate also formed a separate living circle. In Cluny each novice had his own protector or guard (*custodia*) during his first year and could speak only with him. Novices had their own house and special care. This was also true of the inmates of the hospital. In most of the monasteries there were, as in the Carolingian plan of Saint Gall, various kitchens as evidence of the various groups: monks, perhaps abbot (and guests), novices, the sick, important guests (those who arrived on horseback), the poor, pilgrims, etc. The secular monastic personnel did not form a specific group in the sense of having their own dining arrangements, since they probably took care of themselves in their own houses nearby.

Benedict of Nursia had instructed his monks to receive foreigners as though they were Christ himself, and he prescribed a specific ritual of reception. He had hardly imagined that there would be whole cavalcades of important men and women. This was not changed by any reform, either in Burgundy or, still less, in the lands of royal ecclesiastical lordship. Monks sometimes sighed under the burden of such quartering of guests, but they did not consider eliminating it. They did complain about the burden of caring for the poor, a responsibility more appropriate for the secular clergy than for monks.

The Benedictine Rule had prescribed a special table for the abbot because he was always to dine with his male guests. Therefore the monk's table had its own supervisor. In Reichenau and in Cluny things were different, and the abbot and monks dined together in the refectory where laypersons were not allowed. Cluny had no abbot's house because the abbot slept among the monks. This was a symbolic return to the "familial model" without, however, eliminating the very marked lordly position of the abbot that was characteristic of Cluny. Neither here nor in smaller monasteries could the abbot spend much time in the role of father to the monks, for he was primarily the top administrator of a complex, multifarious institution. When the monk Wigo of Tegernsee was elected abbot provisor of the monastery of Feuchtwangen, he opened his heart in a letter to a hermit about the unaccustomed duties his new office had brought with it. All the brothers were either sick or excused by their manifold duties, so that Wigo could hardly catch his breath. "All the keys of the monastery hang on my belt. In addition I must look to the observance of the Rule, provide for necessary food, supervise the kitchen, sometimes take charge of the refectory (as *refectorius*), and I must constantly be at the service of all who live in the monastery and of guests who pass through it."

Nevertheless, an abbot had reason to be content when daily life went on in this manner. There could be significant economic problems, especially in years of bad harvests when an abbot had to write letters to magnates begging for grain, or when there were disputes over monastic possessions. Many holders of monastic offices seem to have been overburdened, like Wigo. In some monasteries, for example, the responsibilities of the cellarer expanded to include all storerooms, so that he was responsible for the distribution of shoes and even for the decoration of the cloister on feast days.

We know that in liturgical matters nothing was arbitrary or left to chance. So monks took written directions seriously, a "modern" tendency. In Cluny, bulletin boards displayed the schedule of the monk's kitchen duties, the schedule of celebrants of Masses for the dead, etc. Monks had to live according to a preestablished plan with precisely apportioned times, while the laity distinguished only between day and night, hours of work and hours of rest.

CONTEMPLATION AND PRAYER

This active existence was difficult to reconcile with the requirement that monks needed calm for spiritual contemplation, a stillness that the hermit sought in isolation. A great silence had surrounded God— and the "divine" emperor—since late antiquity, and in silence one had to approach God. Moreover, controlling one's tongue at certain times was a disciplinary exercise that was not easy in the midst of so many activities. There was therefore a wide variety of punishments, from loss of wine rations to beatings, for those who violated the times of silence. Since one could use a kind of sign language during these periods, the form rather than the purpose of this exercise was observed. Inward composure, not a strong point in tenth-century piety, was nurtured by external aids. In the monastery's cloister, the capitals confronted the monk with a stone gallery of symbols, which assisted him in achieving conviction: the temptation of Christ by the devil; Samson's fight with the lion (a symbol of evil); the tree of the world with its two opposed branches. The arcades of cloister formed the monks' spiritual home, especially for those who were illiterate. The literate too could here find silence and an aid to meditation.

Meditation and prayer were intended to help monks save their own souls. But the threat of judgment hung over the dead too. Therefore all had to help, concentrating on particular individuals so as to raise the chances of success. This activity too represented a triumph of organization. If we can believe Rodulf Glaber, the system of prayer for the dead was the real source of Cluny's fame, extending as far as Africa. On that continent a merchant from Marseille had learned from a hermit that in the domain of intercessionary prayer Cluny was far more successful than any other institution in the Roman Christian world. Hardly a day passed, the hermit continued, when no soul was freed from the power of the evil spirits through the Masses celebrated in Cluny.

Prayers of all religious were good, but the best were those offered in the Mass by priest monks. This was the main reason it was important to have such monks in the monastery, many more than necessary for the liturgical needs of the community itself. The number of priests was also important in negotiations with other monasteries with a view to entering prayer brotherhoods. Hence the organization of praying for souls grew even greater. Hundreds of deceased Christians were prayed for in the Mass, then thousands, and finally all. It was at Cluny that the feast of All Souls was conceptualized as an obligation for all priests to celebrate Mass on one specific day for all of the dead. Besides this, priest monks had to celebrate a special commemoration, four times a year, of every brother with whom they were bound in a *societas,* as though they were monks of Cluny. Commemoration of the dead was found everywhere, but nowhere was it developed so intensively, systematically, and with such economic consequences as in Cluny and in its priories. If a monk died, his name and date of death were entered in the memorial book. On the anniversary of his death, a pauper who was to pray for his soul received a special ration of food appropriate to a monk. This fine thought, scrupulously executed, brought the monasteries increasing burdens. By the twelfth century it had developed so far that care of the poor on the anniversaries of the dead was as expensive as care of the monks themselves. The practice contributed to the decline of the reformed communities.

We indicated above that in Gorze and the monasteries reformed by it the brothers were supposed to be present when one of them died. At the same time, bells were rung with all possible force as an alarm, and not in gradual crescendo as before Mass. The immediate "attack" of all the monks was required in Cluniac monasteries too. They were to run to the dying brother as fast as they could and simultaneously sing the Credo. This was to be done even when they were at table. Reformed monks did not live lives of pleasure, but they died like kings.

WORK

Their spiritual duties had already separated Benedict of Nursia's monks from the surrounding rural population. Yet they still had to perform physical work. In order to avoid idleness they had to perform four hours of manual labor per day during six months of the year. This work could be done in the fields, but only where it was necessary, as in poor monasteries or during harvest season. In fact, Benedict's command usually involved kitchen work or gardening, and only rarely did a particularly strict abbot require his monks to participate in agricultural work or even help in the fields himself. From the east came the story, already mentioned, of an abbot who attempted to become an angel. We can now further relate that after he returned, he was brought back to his senses by shame, and he began to work in the monastery's garden. Physical labor could have some spiritual purpose; a real necessity it was not, at least in most cases. Monasteries almost always had sufficient servants to do that kind of work.

Hence, in reformed monasteries, too, manual work became a traditional gesture. It was seldom mentioned in the *consuetudines* of the earlier period, and then only as a part of what is called "ritualism." According to the Benedictine Rule, the brother's work should begin the first hour of the day. In Cluny this canonical hour was celebrated first; then the monks had to sing seven psalms and a litany and to assist in the early Mass. When they finally went to work, the work was accompanied by the singing of further psalms and the recital of sacred texts. We could also, of course, put it the other way around, and say that this spiritual activity was accompanied by traditional gestures such as working in the monastery's garden. Writing and decorating books was considered a part of physical labor.

Although Adalhard, a cousin of Charlemagne's, absolved the noble-born monks of Corbie from physical labor, this act cannot be interpreted as a purposeful rejection of work. Theologically such a rejection could not be justified, for Adam—the father of all mankind—was compelled to earn his bread by the sweat of his brow as fruit of his sin. "They are true monks if they live from the work of their hands like our fathers and the apostles"; this sentence in the Rule of Benedict could not be put aside. It required no ideological or social prejudices to regard physical labor as inconvenient and to wish to replace it by more important work: the obligation to save souls could not be done through service in the kitchen and garden. Monks saw these things as traditional, but rather secondary duties and accomplished them with the assistance of servants.

There is little in the sources to support Jacques Le Goff's opinion that monks regarded work as penance, since they saw themselves as sinners. Penance for personal guilt was imposed in the Benedictine Rule by separation from the community. The effects of Adam's original sin could not be removed or diminished by the community's manual work. For hermits and sometimes for secular clergy under the influence of hermits, iron chains, hair shirts, and such things served as means of individual penance. The Rule contains none of this, nor do the *consuetudines* of those reformers who stood outside of the influence of eremitism.

This brings us to a consideration of the attitude of monasticism toward things of the flesh. Of course, sexual asceticism was required; it was made simpler by the lack of women in monastic life. Homosexual temptations were occasionally reported. The public nature of the communal life provided some protection against such things, since everyone could observe everyone else. Written comments by monks showing their aversion to the human body were in the tradition of earlier patristic texts. Monasticism still had eremitism as its neighbor, which often continued the attitudes of the desert fathers taking the field against both their flesh and the devil. The Benedictine Rule and the *consuetudines* indicate hardly anything of such tendencies. The life of a monk was hard, but no harder than that of a Roman soldier.

He too had to obey orders rather than follow his own will, he was not always able to sleep during the night, and his conduct was always under the control of others. Benedict did not intend to harm his monks with his Rule. "We shall build a school of service to the Lord, in which we hope that nothing will be commanded that is harsh or burdensome."

As in the military sphere he "who wishes to serve (*militaturus*) Christ, the true king," should receive whatever he needs to remain healthy and able to carry out his duties: enough to eat, appropriate clothing, a bath. We must remember that many people did not have, or had not always had, such amenities. When members of the middle strata of society entered a monastery, they retained their previous standard of living rather than stepping down. One exchanged the bonds to one's family for those to the monastic community, the activities of this world and their dangers for an almost certain place in heaven. Living outside of an ordered community would have been a lot harder; individualists were few in that epoch. As for the family of the religious, it received both intercessary prayers and increased prestige. It was important that the monastery in which its member now lived was of good repute.

MONASTIC FARE

Of course, much was different in the monk's life from that which he had known in the world. There was little room for independent activity. Monks had to obey the Rule, the *consuetudines*, and the commands of the abbot as long as they seemed reasonable. They gave up life in the open air and the taste of meat. Periods of fasting were hard, feast meals rich. At one time, prehistoric hunting had produced an oscillation between hunger and a superabundance of meat; then agriculture had introduced a certain balance, which was only disturbed by poor crops and, to a lesser extent, by Christian rules of fasting. For the monks, fasts were long, and they longed for them to be over. A tendency toward gluttony occasionally manifested itself in the monastery. Discipline apparently failed more often in this sector than in others. The enumeration of the seven deadly sins was sometimes extended to gluttony and drunkenness.

The prohibition against eating meat, not explained by Benedict, did not extend to fowl, which, however, was used mainly in the diet of the sick. Animal protein was supplied chiefly by eggs and cheese. During Lent, fish appeared as nearly the only food yielding animal protein. The menu in the monastery of Lobbes does not seem to have offered much variety. From that monastery we have a record of the duties of one of its properties; it had to supply the monastery for one month in a year with the following foods: fish every Monday and Thursday, cheese and eggs every Tuesday, cheese or eggs on the other weekdays. In addition, the monastery cellarer provided fish on four weekdays from his supplies. There were also legumes, vegetables, and—except on fast days—lard. It is not surprising that there were monks, as Odo of Cluny says, whose appetite for meat led them to unholy activities.

The monastery of Lobbes, from which this menu has come down to us, had twelve manors and was thus well supplied. Here animal protein could play as great a role as in the meat consumption of the upper levels of lay society. In Lobbes we also have evidence of the "higher" cuisine of secular custom in the generous use of spices. These did not come all from the kitchen garden; some, such as pepper, which was treasured everywhere, had to be purchased at a high price from merchants. This was also true of the spices used in wines. In this manner the tickling of the palate that the prohibition of meat was supposed to have excluded crept back in. We may wonder whether, at least in the secular world, the motive of representation did not also play a role in culinary matters: among many ways of showing one's superiority to the masses was the extravagant preparation of meals. Already at the court of Charlemagne, the *cibi pigmentati* had been praised by one of his poets. We read in the *Ruodlieb* poem that one did not pepper bad wine but rather the best.

There were other monasteries in which supplies were more meager. When the bishop of Orléans had seized most of the properties of the monastery of Saint-Mesmin in Micy in order to give them to his vassals, the monks' daily ration was "a small bread and a handful of vegetables, seldom any wine." In Tegernsee monks complained that even on the highest feast days they had only rye bread, which "fills the stomach but leaves one empty." The troops that had to march into Hungary had consumed almost everything. When the economic basis was small, there was always a fear that the monastic elite would provide themselves with a greater proportion of food than that allotted to the rest. For a time this was the situation even in Saint Gall. Some of the brothers lived from their own labor and the charitable donations of their kindred. In this time of distress, all sorts of food, including meat, were welcome. The special cuisine of the abbot could become a stumbling block, and so Abbot John of Gorze was praised for ordering that he should not have any better food prepared for himself than for the monks, that he should eat the same bread, and that he should not drink any better wine than that which he set before the monks. When such things were so greatly emphasized, they were probably unusual and even against custom, since "nobler" food was allotted to the lord, and also to the abbot, as an expression of his position.

On average, the monastic diet must have been generous in quantity but not so much in quality. For the ninth century, historians have attempted to determine the precise weight of the food consumed in certain monasteries and have come up with the following amounts: between 1.5 and 2 kilograms of bread per day, 70–110 grams of cheese, and 123–230 grams of legumes, for each monk. That is more than a modern person could eat, and it may be that the figures are too high. Characteristic are the high percentages of bread and legumes that are to be found in many records. The food of ecclesiastics seems to have differed little from that of the monastic *familia*, which received additional rations of meat or bacon but possibly less cheese. Someone engaged in physical labor all day could manage such portions better than clerics. That monks did not always maintain an ascetic figure is natural. It was not considered bad.

That beans and peas were cultivated in the tenth century not only in gardens but in field areas north of the Alps is said to have been one of the causes of an explosive rise in population at that time. In the late eleventh century—and probably earlier—beans were on the menu every day in Cluny, or a vegetable soup or a bean or vegetable dish on choice. Some have even thought that the word *fabae* (beans) must have been used to designate all vegetables, "because surely one cannot suppose that beans were served every day."

At one time monasteries were founded near rivers or lakes because their fish resources were made available to the monks. By the tenth century these resources could no longer be relied on, even in large lakes. In Saint Gall there were hardly enough fish for the table of the abbot. Their price was so high that a single fish dinner cost the same as a man's normal meals for an entire week. Raising fish in ponds offered only a partial solution and seems not to have been common. During strict fasts, fish were forbidden as well as cheese and eggs, so that only plant proteins were available. Bread and beans were the plainest fare that one could receive in a monastery, but in Saint Gall in times of crisis even these foodstuffs were not always available. In the late eleventh century the eighteen *praebendarii* (official paupers) each received one pound of bread a day, beans four times a week, and vegetables three times a week. On the thirty-five feast days of the year they got meat instead of beans. They were given wine every day—next to bread it was the most important foodstuff.

Fortunately, Benedict of Nursia had written only about food for fasts, not for feasts. Their meals could compensate for Lenten fares, at least in wealthier monasteries. There it was normal to serve at least three warm plates instead of the two prescribed by Benedict. Moreover, an increasing number of days were declared feasts with two meals, although Benedict had prescribed only one daily meal for Lent and for the winter months. Eating between meals was forbidden, but drinking the amount of wine allowed by the Rule was possible at any time. Thus it became customary for brothers to gather for a drink in the refectory. That the normal drinking ration was not always all that was consumed can be explained by the *caritas* drink, the ritual drinking rounds to the honor of the saints. On particularly hard days—during Holy Week, for example—the *mixtum* was allowed as well as the *caritas* drinks. The *mixtum* was originally diluted wine, but then became a late breakfast of bread and wine; the sick, the elderly, and children received it too. Our present-day custom of beginning the day with breakfast was not common in the Middle Ages even among the laity. The first hours of the day were spent on an empty stomach.

We know that in Cluny and elsewhere, children drank wine, just as they do today in countries where Romance languages are spoken, and they had their own small cups (*vascula*) for this purpose. The measure of wine that Benedict prescribed for his monks, the *hemina*, was and is the object of much discussion. In the earliest period it seems to have been little more than half a pint. Later it grew, but we don't know by how much. Some have reckoned it at a pint or even more. Still, it did not always quench the brothers' thirst. For example, the reforming abbot Gauzlin of Fleury held an edifying discussion with one of his protégés late into the night. The protégé grew thirsty, and both monks went down to the closed monastic cellar. Without a key, only with the power of prayer, Gauzlin opened the locked door so that the monk could quench his thirst. The idea that under certain circumstances even water might have had the same effect seems not to have occurred to the two monks, as they were absorbed with their conversation. Later *consuetudines* contain recommendations on how to combat the evening's thirst; so this seems to have been a general problem.

In wine-growing regions, even monks of strict observance could sincerely believe that water was bad for their health. Monks from Gorze complained about this to John, their model abbot, and were amazed at his ascetic strength, such that he was able to go two days without food or drink. John of Gorze was born on the Moselle and had given the monastery "a splendid number of vineyards." No wonder that in his earlier days, as he himself recounted, he fell ill from drinking water. He could not stand this sort of drink, for he was accustomed to "continual drinking of wine." When he had to make do with water for one day, he refused all nourishment.

Ecclesiastics, especially monks, practiced viticulture and introduced it into regions where it had not previously existed. Sacramental wine was a necessity, and at the same time a Roman tradition was continued. From Benedict's reluctant acceptance of wine rations, these became an integral part of monastic life. They helped the weak over the hard path and could also be used by the abbot as an educating device: removal of the wine ration was a punishment that no one willingly incurred. Here and elsewhere we see the middle course between strictness and permissiveness that is a characteristic of Benedictine monasticism. Eremitism had taken a stand against this lifestyle without finding many adherents in monastic communities. Abbot John of Gorze, who was influenced by this sort of free asceticism, amazed his monks, but they did not emulate him. It was a habit of John's never to bathe except after a serious illness. By contrast, we learn from the Gorze *consuetudines* that on the five major feasts of the year the brothers were to take a bath. While five may seem few, it probably corresponded to what was normal for free laypersons.

Was this moderation of the severity of the lifestyle only intended to increase the number of candidates for monasticism? Such a consideration was certainly an element in Benedict's thinking and in the directives of later monastic customs. The essential idea seems to have been that the brothers' energy should not be totally expended in the battle against the flesh. It is an entirely undramatic concept: the small steps leading to salvation from God's damnation. Spiritual athletics were replaced by the "construction" of a new personality in constant self-control and under the supervision of others. Thus every brother, even if not exceptionally talented for the monastic profession, could accomplish something in this direction. Few saints were to be found in the monastery; yet the monks did constitute an army of simple soldiers of Christ. They made a far greater imprint on their age than did the lone spiritual warriors of the eastern variety.

13 EDUCATION AND SCHOOLING IN THE MONASTERY

For us, education means either the general formation of personality or a special professional training. The only legitimate goal of monastic education was *edificatio,* which meant that the individual's psyche had to be built up, reformed, with the specific goal of re-modeling him into a monk. The monk was supposed to become "another person" and had to learn what was necessary to that end. His education took place primarily in the com-munal life with the abbot and brothers and only secondarily with books. This principle, which underlay a kind of spiritual professional school, was antithetical to the humanistic ideal. The "inner school" of the monastery formed monks, while the "external school"—if there was one—provided a basic course of study for laypersons, who here acquired some knowledge of Latin literacy.

THE PURPOSE OF EDUCATION

Although the openness of monasticism to culture has been much emphasized, the monastic rules say nothing about schooling. Saint Benedict was dealing with people whose mother tongue was still Latin and who could already read. Later, assistance was needed to acquire these skills. The number of students was small: the plan preserved in Saint Gall shows space for a dozen oblates and novices in the inner school, and there may have been about two dozen in the external school. At Cluny, it was determined later on that there should be no more than six *pueri* in the monastery at the same time, and that two teachers should be assigned to them.

The educational program was extremely limited in comparison with that of today. It might seem that an ideal student-teacher ratio had been established in such monasteries as Cluny. But things were far from idyllic. Latin had to be taught—with inadequate pedagogical methods—so that it could form the basis of reading, and at the same time it was the language of instruction. This was necessary because there were almost no translations into the vernacular and because many concepts of Christian-classical literature had no counterparts in vernaculars. These intellectual gymnastics found their culmination in the study of dialectic, and linguistic skill was to be supplemented through rhetoric.

Strict drilling and the teacher's rod made school an ascetic activity which was fully integrated into the existence of the monastic student. The amount of knowledge acquired remained small because it was less important than the development of qualities and ways of thought needed by monks. This development too was an endeavor designated by the words "teach" and "learn" (*docere, studere*). From classical pedagogy, monastic education had taken over the idea of the value of the teacher's personal example as well as the imitation of important men of the past (*imitatio maiorum*). Imitation dominated moral and intellectual life to an almost inconceivable degree. It reached the point that Benedict of Nursia established the principle, of great consequence, as it turned out, that a monk was not to do anything for which there was no model either in the Rule or among the elders (*seniores*). The term "elders" included both older brothers in the monastery and spiritual or literary models from earlier times. Already in the Roman Republic there had been "examples" of different virtues; now there was the reading (*lectio*) from saints' *vitae*. Literary models were found especially among Church Fathers, who were also moral and spiritual exemplars. Unfortunately, such models were also to be found among pagan authors, about whom we shall speak presently. The essential examples, however, were the living ones that the young monk had at his side.

ANCIENT AND MODERN PATTERNS

Abbo, later to become abbot of Fleury, began his study of the liberal arts in the monastery, where he "clung to the side of the old monks." At many times of the day he was with his fellow classmates too, but he "was closer to the elders." Here we are told in greater detail what was expressed in the old topos of the "youth as old man": the metaphor was supposed to explain that even a young person could reach the high moral and intellectual qualities of elders. This concept led the Middle Ages to a lack of originality that is often deplored by modern readers. It was not the development of individual personality, the so-called self-realization of today, but a merging into the general tradition of Christian authors and a rethinking of their ideas. Personal contributions were not necessary, and often they raised the suspicion that the author who made them was looking to make a name for himself. There are many examples showing how people guarded themselves against the reproach of bringing something new with the argument that they were only copying the ancients. The monk Aimoin of Fleury-sur-Loire defended himself in the dedication of his historical work against the possible complaint of critics that he had usurped the words of his predecessors. "I do not deny it, I am not ashamed of it, and I will continue to do it. I have the example of good (authors) before me, and I believe that I am allowed to do what they did." Yet it is clear from such words that the strict elimination of all "private" opinions was not to everyone's taste. Communities varied in their interpretation of the monastic lifestyle, and strictness and consistency did not reign everywhere. Even more liberal were the views in the circle of Archbishop Bruno of Cologne, the leader of the "Ottonian renaissance" north of the Alps.

While monks of the strict observance saw "new ideas"—that is, those without precedent among the ancients—as dangerous, Bruno's biographer tells us that "together with learned men of all languages he constantly examined with the greatest care what was new and important in the historians, orators, poets, and philosophers." This statement is undercut by the fact that it was a quotation from classical literature: the greatest pleasure of the Greeks was to hear or discover new things. In the political sphere, novelty had a negative ring, even for Bruno.

Thus, in episcopal circles, novelty was not always and everywhere rejected. Bishop Adalbold of Utrecht gave a basic defense of this position. People generally honor what is old in writings (*in scriptis*) and reject what is new. But even the old was once new, and therefore the new precedes the old. Hence it is foolish to scorn that which precedes and to cherish that which follows. This was a dialectical game with the chronological and hierarchical meanings of the term *praecedere*. Adalbold asserted that he did not wish to attack the old but only to secure an equal place beside it for the new. This was easier said than done.

Procuring Books

Even without the well-known rejection of unknown ideas and without the perception that modern authors were dwarfs standing on the shoulders of giants, it would have been impossible adequately to disseminate the new. There were practical reasons for this. In our time new books are generally recommended and read; the older ones remain—at least for the most part—unused in libraries. In the tenth century people worked with manuscripts that were decades or centuries old. It was possible for some, by exchanges between monasteries, to acquire and copy the writings of contemporaries, but only at the cost of great effort. To purchase books was possible only for the wealthy. Catalonia, a region from which a rich store of charters has survived, provides some comparative values of manuscripts. In 1004, two liturgical books, a (partial) missal and a lectionary, were worth a horse. In 1011, a single volume was worth, on the average, two ounces of gold. In Germany, books were probably even more expensive. One of Liudolf of Swabia's men exchanged a manuscript that he had obtained as booty during the plundering of Augsburg for a horse "that he liked a lot." A learned Italian ecclesiastic who wanted to impress people claimed that he had brought with him to Germany "almost a hundred" books, an extremely unusual number. The famous abbot Adso of Montierender, in contrast, left only twenty-three volumes on his death in 933. The "royal daughter" Ida gave Salzburg thirteen volumes, a nun from the royal family endowed the monastery of Benediktbeuern with twenty books. In 984, a bishop of Cremona found sixty-four manuscripts in his cathedral library and contributed an additional thirty-one from his own collection. Even in Catalonia, despite its growing prosperity, the stock of books was modest. The cathedral library of Vich, about which we have some information, had to give books to parish clergy and received important donations from secular magnates in order to purchase what was absolutely necessary. This cathedral library, which had had only ten manuscripts in 908, had sixty-five by 971.

These figures correspond to the average size of monastic libraries in the tenth century. The few great monasteries that had five hundred or more volumes were quite exceptional. Scholarship in the modern sense, or in the sense of scholasticism, was impossible under such conditions. Scholastic activities were far from the intentions of Saint Benedict, although in his time there were still booksellers in Rome. Books were expensive objects for the rich, and the new form of monasticism had to be free of the goods of this world. Thus Benedict required of his students the same attitude toward literary culture that had been developed in Christian lay circles, that is, an intensive study of sacred texts. Monks were not required to read many books—just one a year. At the beginning of Lent, the books from the monastic library at Cluny were placed on a carpet. The librarian read out the names of each brother. Each returned the book that he had had the previous year and received a new one. Of course, not every book was suited to such an intensive reading.

What was needed was, as said, a "professional" training, mostly by the example of others. It could be achieved with only a few books. An idea of such a limitation is given in the *vita* of the well-known canonist and bishop of Worms, Burchard. He ordered his sister, the future abbess of a canonry, to "learn" (*discere*) the following books: the rule of canonesses, a calendar of feasts (*computus*), saints' lives, the *Dialogues* of Pope Gregory the Great, and "other books which correspond to this life(style)." The *Dialogues* of Gregory were the most common professional reading. Besides such spiritual texts, an abbess had to know the organization of the liturgical calendar adapted for her community, she had to know the rules of her community, and she had to direct the "reconstruction" of the soul on its way to God both for herself and for her subordinates.

Such a program was hardly suited to transmit the literary inheritance of antiquity and to preserve the educational values of the west. Yet we know by what strange detours this transmission occurred. That there should be a minimum of literary education available was essential to protect the clergy from sinking into illiteracy. A purely religious education could have taken place without the written word, as in the lay world, where practical knowledge was more important for the upper levels of society than were reading and writing, which few could do. A warrior, a man in public life, and a lord over far-flung estates neither could nor wished to be a pen-pusher. He could learn little from books. The noble style of the tenth century was similar in this respect to that of Homeric Greece.

Among some of the clergy, literacy was equally lacking. Abbot William of Dijon established "external" schools in the monasteries under his control because knowledge of reading and liturgical singing, especially among parish clergy, had declined or disappeared in the area. At synods, Abbo of Fleury wrote, one seldom saw an open book. In monasteries there were monks who "could not write." If the comment referred to inability to do calligraphy, which played a great role in Greek monasticism and also among the followers of Saint Nilus, it was not that serious. But many monks could not even manage a signature and had to find others to sign for them.

Saint Benedict had required that his monks read books. His Rule does not mention writing or copying texts. In the following centuries, monks realized that they had to prepare almost all the texts that they needed in the monastery themselves. This work never ended because of the catastrophes that befell monastic libraries. Even in times of peace, fire posed a constant danger. In wartime, many manuscripts were dispersed or seized as booty. Along with the copying of whole volumes there were summaries of their most important contents and the tedious collection of maxims from various sources. Odo of Cluny collected the sayings of several Church Fathers at the request of a bishop who had to do without books while traveling and performing military service. Anthologies and summaries of texts from earlier times were an important part of monastic libraries. Since monks had to transcribe the books they used for teaching, they felt free to rework, abridge, or expand them. Such revision was performed on the works of famous authors, including the oft-commentaried *Ars grammatica* of Donatus. The idea of intellectual property would hardly have been understood in the tenth century. The only text for which something of the sort existed was sacred scripture: it alone was safe from alteration.

THE HERITAGE OF CLASSICAL EDUCATION

The function of grammar had changed greatly since late antiquity. Even in countries where Romance languages were spoken, grammar had become a textbook for a foreign language rather than a vehicle for transmitting the rules for use of ones' mother tongue. The grammars transmitted from antiquity were ill suited to such a use, and, indeed, never had fully achieved their purposes. It was impossible to create a real textbook for teaching syntax, and style had to be learned from reading outstanding authors. In late antiquity, the "pedagogue" taught reading and writing, and the *grammaticus* dealt with grammatical problems in the form of a dialogue and then introduced the reader to classical authors. Classical poets were particularly important, as their writings had become a sacred heritage for pagans, much as the New Testament was for Christians.

What were pagan authors doing in the monastery? The question was often asked, but opposition to these authors rarely succeeded. The fact was that sacred scripture, as well as the psalter which was so essential for monasticism, were transmitted in Latin, and Latin was one of the three sacred languages. Monks submitted to the necessity of copying Latin books, considering it an ascetic activity. By writing, one "learned" what one had written better than simply by reading it. Above all, one learned Latin style. We might well ask why a monk should write with good style. Wasn't it enough if he could make himself understood in everyday Latin?

It was not enough, because in the choir, in the refectory, and in the chapter room, monks had to be able to read Latin texts that reflected something of the polished style of Roman intellectuals. They had to make this style, which already appears in the Pauline epistles, their own in order to avoid harsh criticism. It was said admiringly of the later saint Udalrich that while he was being educated at Saint Gall he performed the refectory readings flawlessly, although the elder monks thought it a capital offense if one missed a single punctuation mark. The value of Latin as an educational tool was recognized and built into the professional monastic training. A novice had to be disciplinable (*disciplinabilis*). Whether or not he really was, became evident in grammar classes. It was not mere pedantry when even a bishop became personally involved in the teaching of discipline. In the monastery of Fleury it was thought that the weakness of the flesh had to be fought with various weapons: with prayers, with fasts, and with written lessons, "especially dictation exercises" (*dictandi exercitia*).

Thus the classical school system, at least in its elementary level, regained something of the meaning that it had once had on a private basis. With this study, along with linguistic forms and expressions, the contents of classical and patristic works were also acquired in considerable measure. One "learned" not only edifying books but also books that transmitted classical learning and poetry. Poetics were usually included in the area of science, and poetry was especially useful in intellectual training because of its difficulty. Christian "poets" of late antiquity had introduced the apparatus of encyclopedic learning into poetic writings. In the Carolingian and post-Carolingian periods, poets continued to write in the same manner. Learning was fused with the goal of religious formation, and young people in particular could draw attention to their abilities by "poetic" productions. Such activities increased or reestablished one's reputation. The latter was particularly important for one monk who, because of a misdeed, was incarcerated by the bishop of Eichstätt. While in jail he wrote a liturgical poem on the life of Saint Walpurg, sang it out loud, and hence was released.

Writing poetry was learned in school. The eighty-odd school poems that Ekkehard IV had to write for his teacher Notker in Saint Gall show how diligently it was practiced. We can understand how the Latin word *dictare* gave rise to the German word *dichten* (to write poetry) when we are told, for example, that the young Otloh of Saint Emmeram was more experienced in writing poems than in writing prose. Ekkehard had collected his own poems and had used them to train his students. Teachers could not limit themselves to their own productions, nor could they only use Christian texts. The highest and most perfect form of poetry was found in pagan works. Monks attempted to use them for models without succumbing to their content, which was questionable or at least not did not promote Christian values. The biographer of Bruno, archbishop of Cologne and patron of the "Ottonian renaissance," tells us that Bruno, unlike others, had used the comic poets as authorities "only in the compilation of words," not in their content. We know however that this was not always the case. In the cathedral school of Rouen around the year 1000, someone wrote a *Satira contra Iezabel* whose content is thoroughly obscene from beginning to end. This satire was written after the model of stories about loves of Jupiter. This sort of literature was more easily excused than the opinion of a cleric named Vilgard, who was condemned by the archbishop of Ravenna as a heretic because he placed the ancient poets above all that was Christian. It was said that there were even more people like him in Italy who "met their end by fire and the sword." Apparently the life of an enthusiastic classicist was dangerous in the tenth century.

It is not surprising, then, that the monks in Cluny were warned of the danger of poets. The great abbot Odo was said to have seen in a dream a large urn full of snakes. The urn signified the *liber Virgilii*, the content the "teaching of the poets" (*doctrinam poetarum*). We read in the *vita* of the later abbot Maiolus of Cluny that he had refused to read the works of poets. The trick of despoiling the poets only in a formal sense and learning style from them without being affected by the magic of the ancient world was beyond the ability of most clerics. Usually they attempted to forge a middle way: The classics were read but with a suspicion that was befitting monks. They railed against the lies of the Greeks, citing Juvenal in this context. When an author took the field against pagan texts, we are not always sure whether he did so out of personal conviction or in order to follow the established tradition of his peers.

To master the classical form of poetry and of artistic prose was a fine reward for all the misery of the school lessons. Here monks had a certain freedom for personal development and here too was that lightheartedness that young people need in their lives. A playful element sometimes asserted itself; style became artistry. Monks were proud of learning and proud also that they could understand artfully constructed sentences. Besides the "high" poetry a simpler form took hold: on the model of the satirists, epigrams and animal fables began to be composed, and Hrotsvitha of Gandersheim sought a sort of "poetic antidote" to Terence's comedies. That the pagan *praeses* Dulcitius lies in wait for Christian virgins, comes into the kitchen and, deluded by God, kisses pots and pans must have occupied the imagination of the young Gandersheim canonesses in a harmless way.

PRIDE IN KNOWLEDGE

We may well imagine that these cultural activities provided a certain relief from a total orientation toward the spiritual goal. They served as a safety valve and at the same time, like any game, as a means of improving skills. If there was a danger in such things, it was less in the secular spirit of classical authors than in the learned vanity to which knowledge of them might lead. We are constantly reminded that literary knowledge leads to the foolishness consisting of the vain pursuit of glory, and that empty eloquence and (pagan) philosophy lead to arrogance and pride. For monks, such an attitude was particularly bad since according to the will of Benedict they were bound to climb all the steps of humility. Error of this nature, no doubt, was seldom recognized by the offender himself because people believed that in the literary sphere other rules applied, as in play, which was usually competitive.

Thus, the monk Froumund could describe himself with false modesty as humble and untalented in order to express unpleasant truths to a Würzburg abbot, "the most learned of the learned": namely, that a certain letter could not have come from him because it was so poorly written. The same Froumund wrote a poem of four lines in which he used ten Greek words. To make it comprehensible, he had himself added translations below the Greek. An alleged knowledge of Greek was shown not only by widely traveled Italians such as Liutprand of Cremona but also by clerics north of the Alps. How far one might go can be seen in a poem about Adam and Christ in which Greek words appear, almost certainly taken from a glossary and from the poems of John the Scot. Ekkehard IV had advised his brethren, "Get into the habit of decorating your style with splendid words," and he left them a versified introduction to doing so. In a cruder form this practice was a continuation of something that had begun in ancient Rome. Roman authors had imitated the Greeks and created a writing more artificial than spontaneous. In the tenth century this was done as though authors knew not only Latin but also Greek and, where possible, Hebrew, the third "sacred" language.

Thus, a kind of intellectual elite appeared to exist. This supposition sometimes had practical consequences, since such people's "scholarship" assisted their rise to abbot or even bishop. The term *scientia* referred to philology and literature and, even more, to ecclesiastical expertise. It was not by chance that bishops were pictured holding the crosier and a book, the latter probably thought of as a pontifical or a collection of canons. Nevertheless, the monk Rather was said to have become bishop of Verona because of his piety (*religio*) and because of his knowledge of the "liberal arts." He was more at home in classical literature than in Christian, which probably accounts for his success in Italy at the court of King Hugo. Things were similar in the circle of Bruno of Cologne, whose preference for heathen literature was defended by his biographer, Ruotger. Ruotger himself had a good classical education and seldom quoted the Church Fathers.

When one of these men described his relationship to those around him, he did so with indulgent derision. This is how Rather described how people in Verona thought of him: If he could, he would sit with his books all day long. He hated crowds, loved solitude, did not play, and was unmoved by hunting dogs and falcons. Anselm of Besate, a "modern" satirist, described the primary objection to his work: his writing was superfluous, for there were already so many books that reading them was a great annoyance. Everyone knew that Anselm liked solitude, and so, since he was not a hermit, he must have been a magician.

Wandering Scholars

The spirit of sharp-tongued literacy led away from the bonds of the monastic life, and not only in a metaphoric sense. The monastic school was usually nothing more than an elementary school, and anyone wishing to follow the educational program of antiquity—the "seven liberal arts"—had to become a wanderer. If such a person had an understanding abbot, he was given the chance and the money to do so. It was not cheap. In Limoges, the nephew of the abbot of Clusa, about whom we have already heard, said that his uncle had already given more than two thousand gold pieces for his education "in many places in Lombardy and in France." He was of course exaggerating. With that much money one could have established an entirely different sort of ecclesiastical career. But we know from other sources that education abroad was not inexpensive. For example, as a young monk, Abbo of Fleury had to study music with a cleric in Orléans "for much money and in secret because of envy." Previously he had been sent to Paris and Reims, where he had been instructed in philosophy and, less than he had wanted, in astronomy. So monks in search of education turned into traveling scholars. What would Saint Benedict have thought?

The years during which monk Abbo wandered about did not harm his reputation. He became the most important abbot of his monastery and later was venerated as a saint. Anyone who had studied became a teacher wherever people were willing to listen to him, and Abbo traveled as far as England as a teacher before he was given the abbacy in Fleury. Others remained abroad, as did Huothilbert, a monk from Mettlach. In the early tenth century he crisscrossed northern France, Aquitaine, and the Basque region, "teaching and learning." Then he settled down in Navarre, surrounded by a host of students from all over Spain. A successful teacher brought his monastery respect, students, and money, the last sometimes in great quantity. When Abbo returned home to Fleury, he gave the monastery "many treasures, gold bracelets (*armillae*) and necklaces (*torques*), ecclesiastical vestments, a golden cup, and much silver money."

Although Benedict had criticized wandering monks, the master-scholar tradition in many cases resulted in weakening the bonds to one's cloister, the *stabilitas loci*. Normally a runaway monk had little chance of being received into another monastery. The situation was different for someone with outstanding abilities, such as Rodulf Glaber. When Rodulf was driven from the monastery of Saint-Léger in Champeaux, his brethren knew that he would always find lodging somewhere because of his literary knowledge, "and this proved very often to be true." He enjoyed changing monasteries; yet he was welcomed into them, at least initially. Here we glimpse something of the independent existence of a man of letters such as would eventually be possible at court. Education in the humanistic sense once more became valuable in itself, at least among a numerically small group of ecclesiastics. The Carolingian renaissance had cleared a path which even in difficult times and in the face of rigorist tendencies would never again be entirely blocked. Had it been otherwise, the situation might have been much worse in the west than it was in Byzantium, in spite of the intransigence of eastern monasticism. In the east, the cultural life of the metropolis lived on, something which could not exist in the West until late in the modern period. Slowly and with interruptions, circles formed which cherished a renaissance of culture. As deficient as the schooling of the tenth century certainly was, it nevertheless established a basis for that development.

The Liberal Arts

The *artes liberales,* which we have not yet discussed as a whole, initially were considered worthy of study by free men precisely because these studies did *not* bring in money. Far below them stood the *artes* of Roman craftwork. Yet proficiency in literary Latin, rhetoric, and dialectic were very useful to a secular career in late antiquity, and they were also important for a bishop when he was preaching to learned audiences. For simple monks they provided purely intellectual training without any practical purpose. Instruction in the liberal arts focused attention on form in a period which tended toward formlessness. Being largely formal disciplines, the liberal arts supplemented the formation (*edificatio*) of the Christian psyche. The process of civilization had not yet eliminated "wild" thinking, it had to be conquered anew in every novice. Civilizing and "edification" went hand in hand. Thus Gerbert of Aurillac, writing about geometry, could say that it led one to wonder at the power and the ineffable wisdom of the Creator and to praise him, the Creator who ordered all things by measure, number, and weight.

Gerbert's importance for the teaching of the *artes,* however, seems to have been overstated. We have a detailed description of his teaching from his student Richer. In essence it coincides with things which had been taught in the cathedral school of Speyer. It was an accepted rhetorical practice to present a person in such a light that his predecessors were cast into darkness. Ruotger described Bruno of Cologne as having "brought back to life the long forgotten seven liberal arts." Richer used similar language: In Italy music and astronomy had been entirely unknown before Gerbert, and Gerbert had "made them known everywhere." What both authors meant was that Bruno and Gerbert, each in his own manner, had significantly raised the level of instruction.

Both had insisted that their students actually speak Latin, and good Latin at that. Gerbert had introduced the classical authors, who had traditionally been connected with the study of grammar, into the study of rhetoric, and not without reason. Like prose, classical poetry made use of the rhetorical figures and of all the other artistic means that a beginning rhetor had to learn. Here we see great distance between life in antiquity, which was always in official communication with listeners, and the monastic life. In the monastery school a student could still conduct disputations in the classical manner, but after he had finished his studies a monk needed a correct, but in no way artistic, style. The situation was different for urban clergy only as long as they could still find people who appreciated their art. No one ventured the opinion that a preacher could save souls by rhetoric; so what use would rhetoric be for the urban clergy?

From Cicero, through Marius Victorinus, to Alcuin and beyond, scholars emphasized the civilizing effect of artistic speech. Christian authors since Gregory the Great had posited an intimate connection between "right living" and "right speaking." As Gerbert put it, "I have always connected the quest for a good life and the quest for a good manner of speaking (*studium bene dicendi*)." Although it was said in the manner of Cicero, this remark probably reflects Gerbert's own opinion. The good deserves the beautiful, substance needs a worthy form, and the two together form a human ideal that reached from Hellas to the chamber of the Reims schoolmaster. Gerbert felt himself surrounded by barbarians—he was bound up with the Mediterranean world and as a southerner worked easily in a discipline which, it was said, one learned either quickly or not at all.

Beauty of form sometimes acquired a value of its own; clerics produced art for art's sake. The cathedral canons in Liège laughed when a simply written saint's *vita* was read to them. A monk in Soissons complimented another in Saint-Amand with the extravagant statement that there was nothing more Latinate, nothing more beautiful, nothing sweeter than his style. "O fortunate Gaul, that has at its disposal such a scholar!" Abbot Gauzlin of Fleury, from a cathedra on the Capitoline hill, delivered an address on the cultural history of the city using "sophistic" tools, that is, rhetoric and dialectic.

In his lectures, Gerbert "rushed" through dialectic, taught rhetoric, and then sent his Reims students to a "sophist," or dialectician. In the battle of words they needed to learn to use both these arts in such a way that no one would notice they were being used. That, according to Richer, was the greatest achievement of the orator. A dialectically organized speech demanded extraordinary concentration and the kind of formal logic that was largely alien to the early Middle Ages. When two clerics so armed disputed with each other, the result was an artistic pleasure both for them and for their audience. Uneducated listeners would be lost and confused. It was a game which excluded those who didn't know the rules. The cornerstone was being laid for the progressive intellectualization of thought leading to scholasticism, which also relied on the dialectical method. Many students remained lost in the externals and learned nothing other than tricks with which one could confuse an opponent.

It was difficult to combine these artistic skills with the goals of the monastic life. The antagonistic element in dialectic was alien to the brotherly behavior and humility that was expected of monks. Still, there were attempts to find "edifying" uses of dialectic. How one might perform this was explained in a long school poem: "I am what I was not, what I was I am not . . . What is a man? Something laughable" (*risibile,* that is, he is capable of laughing)." Various are the qualities of men, one thing they all have in common, that they must die."

Anselm of Besate saw grammar, rhetoric, and dialectic as heavenly beings who embraced him, crying, "The young man is ours!" For him, education ended with the *trivium,* and thus it usually was. The second half of the educational program, the *quadrivium,* was taught only in a few schools and often only in part. As already said, it is not true that two of its disciplines were unknown in Italy before the arrival of Gerbert. Anyone who wanted instruction in arithmetic, geometry, astronomy, and music had to seek the "workplaces of wisdom" in various regions, as Abbo of Fleury had done. He found that even in Paris and Reims too little could be learned about music (or, rather, music theory), and so he went to Orléans.

The character of abstract presentation of a formal order was still more in evidence in the *quadrivium* than in the *trivium.* Thinking through these forms and orders disciplined the scholar and led him beyond them to intellectual understanding of the subject matter. The harmony of the classical cosmos became clear and offered a view of its creator. Joseph Navari has attributed the mathematical studies of Gerbert of Aurillac to his longing for order in a disorderly world. These studies also had an edifying function since they led back to the formal orders established by the creator.

The theoretical study of numbers was called arithmetic, in contrast to the practical use of numbers. Gerbert had cultivated this discipline too and had learned the Arabic systems of calculation with which one could quickly multiply and divide. Of prime importance, however, was number theory. It offered another, more modern route to insight into the creation than did the earlier number symbolism. That earlier system could invoke the Bible and the Church Fathers, but it remained without limits and open to every subjective explanation. Number symbolism contained residual "wild" concepts, which contradicted a higher notion of science. Gerbert was not the only one to see a relationship between number theory and religion. Hrotsvitha of Gandersheim had Wisdom (Sapientia) appear in a play to teach the pagan emperor Hadrian the basics of number theory. By this means she informs him of the creator, citing the biblical text concerning measure, number, and weight as the principles of the divine organization of the world.

Measure and number also defined geometry, which no longer had a practical meaning. Even Gerbert's apparent advice on how to measure fields simply consisted of classical reminiscences. In the tenth century the classical techniques of land surveying were no longer practiced. Even in late antiquity, sons from good families who studied the *artes* were not practitioners of such techniques. For them, geometry was a formal discipline of general value for intellectual training. Monks could use it for the same reasons. As in all other elements of the *quadrivium,* there was no danger here that reading the ancient and very difficult texts might lead to inappropriate ideas.

The situation seems at first to have been different for astronomy, which was suspiciously close to astrology. It had the practical purpose of transmitting the basics for calculating the Christian feast days. Furthermore, the stars, when visible, could be used for calculating the times of night prayers for monks. In fact this use was rare and the dates of movable feasts were calculated not for a monastery but for all of Christendom. Here again, the theoretical elements of astronomy were the most important. And astronomy presented a richer field for edification than any other discipline. Reflecting on the starry sky was sufficient for simple souls. Gerbert sought to "research" the heavens with instruments—a pedagogical activity which aroused great interest among students. Richer enthusiastically described the discoveries that one could make by using these instruments with the teacher or even alone.

Since choral singing was a major activity for many monks, they were naturally interested in music theory. In debating the value of the "new music"—which conservatives termed monstrosity and barbarity—music theory could have provided arguments for both supporters and opponents. *Musica* (music theory) and *cantus* (performance) were, however, two entirely different things, which were kept separate and were rarely combined. Singers had nothing to do with the true music of the heavenly spheres, which could not be heard by the human ear. The audible proportions that were studied with a monochord were but pale reflections of the harmony of the heavenly spheres. In music theory one learned a discipline close to mathematics, and once again one found edification in evidence of the divine origins of the tonal orders.

When we read the texts that discuss these four disciplines, we can understand why the *quadrivium* was not offered to (or imposed on) all students in the monastery. First of all, these texts seem extremely dry and difficult for anyone without an enthusiastic teacher at his side. This subject matter found its way into the educational curriculum of the Middle Ages only because a unified program had been constructed in late antiquity from the various disciplines constituting the *artes liberales,* and no one dared to give up that unity. Great efforts were made to master the material; whether the religious results were worthwhile for individual edification remains questionable.

One thing is certain: The *artes* kept Latin literacy alive and formed the intellect of students who would otherwise have remained helpless in the area of formal abstract thinking. This education was anything but universal and did not prepare students for independent thought. It was based on late, "Alexandrian" classical learning—and that only in a radically summary form. In the west, however, people were long unable to replace this system with one of their own. Since the *artes* concerned only a thin stratum of clerics, they did not deform the "Germanic soul" or the "western spirit." People learned and practiced thinking and expression of thought—these facts were more important than the content of the educational material. We must again remember that the Rule of Benedict says nothing about what we call education. In the generations after Benedict, when the cultural level was dropping, it was not self-evident that a modest sort of general education would develop in monasteries. A pious illiteracy might have reigned, like that of many hermits. Monastic schools and the study of the *artes liberales* thus served a valuable function.

v·VULGUS

14 POPULAR BELIEFS

ALL WE KNOW ABOUT THE VAST MAJORITY
of the laity in the tenth century is what clerics
thought worth knowing. Modern historians
must deal with a "silent majority," for their
tenth-century counterparts rarely drew attention to the lower orders of society. The politically responsible stratum was composed of the
free, but within this group now were respected
only those who were economically free and
could serve as well-armed warriors. Servants
did not belong to the "people"; they were chat-
tels belonging to a "house" and could make no
independent decisions. Hence we know almost
nothing of the common people's opinions and

little of their actions, though we do know something of their sufferings: famine, the destructions of war, infectious diseases. Only in miracle stories were individuals described, and as objects of religious care they were depicted in their religious attitudes, customs, and superstitions. Since the time of the great polyptychs had almost passed, and the huge estates were in decline, our understanding of the economic existence of the rural population is much less clear than we might wish. Political history can be written as the history of the elite, because that is how it was written in the tenth century. For the common people we must painstakingly construct a mosaic for which many of the stones are missing and others give no indication of where they belong in the overall picture. The poor state of the social history of the period is less the result of historians' attitudes than of the basic preconditions for work in the area.

INBELLE VULGUS AND VULGUS INDOCTUM

Even today, words such as "boorish" and "vulgar" reveal the vast distance between the elites and the mass (*vulgus*), the populace (*populus*) who neither knew noble customs nor were militarily or politically useful. Their inability to participate in disciplined military actions was especially noticeable in times of troubles. During the siege of a town by the Normans, the militarily incompetent mass (*inbelle vulgus*) was depicted as capable of nothing more than uttering sounds (*mugitus,* lowing) like animals and raising their hands to heaven. True, the clergy (*oratores*) did not belong to the warriors (*bellatores*) either, but their support of warfare was extremely important. Chroniclers could not decide whether victories were due more to their prayers or to the actions of warriors.

The "unarmed people" (*inerme vulgus*) was already so termed in 826, that is, at the beginning of the Norman incursions. The expression occurs in the writings of Odo of Cluny. The one thing that the majority of the population could be useful for was their physical labor. They were *laboratores,* workers. In many sources, "work" meant the same as "plowing," so important was agriculture to the thought of the tenth century. Warfare was increasingly entrusted to well-armed and trained professional soldiers, who willingly distanced themselves from the masses of the people.

In antiquity the elite had not separated themselves from the rest of society through military ability but through education. On one hand was rusticity and ignorance, on the other the outstanding individual who dedicated his whole life to all-round education. This was no longer an option for anyone, and hardly anyone had an interest in it because of the numerous duties that even the nobleman had to fulfill, in his own sphere as well as in royal service. For these duties one needed education as well, though practical knowledge and skills took precedence over literate abilities. In this, magnates were in a situation similar to that of peasants, who could not manage agricultural life without broad practical knowledge.

Given the rare appearance of heresies, the clergy could forgo an intensive theological education of the laity. More important was the teaching of Christian morality, a summary of commands and, above all, of prohibitions. This continued the Old Testament tradition: the Ten Commandments were largely prohibitions. When Rather of Verona appealed to his flock, he exhorted them, in addition to such negative statements, to fear God and to pray to the saints. Furthermore, the Christian had to meet his financial obligations to the clergy and look after the poor. That is, he had to pay his tithes and give alms. Within the family he was taught to respect marital love and fidelity, to look to the education of his sons (not of all his children), and to perform works of mercy such as visiting the sick, burying the dead, etc. One hears nothing of Christian love of God and neighbor. Spirituality was poorly developed in the tenth century even among clerics, and people were comfortable with concrete, defined commandments. Pierre Riché was not entirely wrong to compare pastors of this period to rural policemen.

Preaching to the laity was supplemented and sometimes even replaced by images, which had a direct effect on the faithful. One thinks of Bernward's famous bronze doors at Saint Michael's in Hildesheim, of the statue of Saint Fides in Conques, of the frescoes in the church of Saint George at Oberzell on the island of Reichenau. A series of images visually presented salvation history or the *historia* of a saint. Presenting the text in images meant that most things that were not concrete and visible had to be omitted, and so an important portion of sacred scripture was not covered. Most of the Bible became "biblical history," which in turn became a collection of exemplary stories. As for symbols and allegories, laypersons understood little of them, though of course the meaning of such things as a cross or a tree of life was clear enough to them.

This picture-book Christianity also was presented by songs and recitals outside of the ecclesiastical sphere. In France there were players who sang of "the deeds of princes and the lives of saints"; the *chansons de geste* may have had their origin in such performances—for example, a sort of Song of Roland as edifying chant. Studies of oral poetry have shown that in societies in which literacy is restricted or entirely lacking, people have a great capacity for memory. In the tenth century, recitals were free renderings, not verbatim recitations. What mattered was the forming of their content; recitation was a poetic paraphrase. For such performances, easily conceivable subjects, especially series of events, worked best. The clergy was accustomed to partially reshaping sacred texts. It could justify such actions with the proverb that one cannot climb a mountain without making detours.

Certainly, attempts were made to give depth to the rather two-dimensional style of preaching. Some of those listening to a bishop's sermons might be expected to understand a little more. Thus Udalrich of Augsburg in his sermons described the heavenly Jerusalem with its twelve cornerstones, which were various precious stones, and he explained the allegorical meaning of each. "The third cornerstone is chalcedony, meaning the fire of inner love," and so forth. It is unlikely that this sermon was meant as a sermon to the laity; rather, it was a Latin sermon for the clergy. Preaching to the common people was primarily the duty of the priest, with the limitation that he was to do so "according to the measure of his knowledge." For such preaching the celebration of the Mass in the parish on Sundays and feast days was the appropriate occasion. These sermons were not written down, but one can imagine that obedience to the religious commandments generally formed the major theme. Ordinary clerics could not be expected to preach in a manner barely mastered even by bishops.

We should avoid painting too dark a picture of the ignorance of the clergy and laity. Since a profane general education was not yet considered universally desirable, religious education was hardly an essential of life. People were satisfied with a knowledge of religious activities and of the limits of what was permitted. This was true not only of the western laity but also of the laity of the much better educated Byzantine world. Byzantine merchants, large landowners, and the like, especially in the provinces, were known to be "free of theology."

DISBELIEF AND SUPERSTITION

There is some evidence of disbelief in the laity. Though sparse, this evidence does raise the question of whether medieval belief differed from the way in which it usually is seen. In the tenth century, disbelief existed in both the rural and the urban spheres. After the defeat of Bishop Balderich of Liège, people in his city said that not providence but chance ruled the world. When a priest in the diocese of Utrecht admonished the population of a village to observe the obligation to receive the sacraments at Easter, one of his hearers answered that they would rather drink a mug of beer than the cup of the Lord. The speaker was the village mayor and spoke for the whole community. Are we to see this response as the continued existence of West Frisian paganism? More likely it was a sort of practical lack of faith, which we think of as "modern" and which expresses itself in negativism. True, in other sources it is easy to discover pagan traditions under a thin veneer of a more or less enforced Christianity. We know that Rollo, the recently baptized duke of the Normans, sacrificed prisoners to the gods; that the people from the Fallersleben area avoided churches and clerics, venerated household gods, practiced a sort of cult to Wotan, and so forth.

Atto of Vercelli seems to consider unbelievers as a particular type of lower social stratum when he tells us that the devil has developed various methods of leading mankind astray. The devil tempts the powerful to rob, encourages the clever to deceive, leads the strong to pride, and fosters disbelief among fools and rustics. Atto adds that superstitions are spread in this manner.

We have here another instance of something we keep encountering: the fact that in the tenth century the age of popular religion, characterized by the continuity of pagan concepts, had not yet ended. This continuity was particularly visible in Italy and the south of France. It also occurred in Germanic lands, though in less developed form than the surviving beliefs of antiquity. Since some medieval German authors also record southern concepts, classical and Germanic traditions are sometimes impossible to separate. People and their styles of life had so little changed since antiquity that religious thought and needs could be expressed in the same way as in the past.

This general continuity is of very long duration. Some scholars have even spoken of a "pre-Indo-European archaic mentality" in the Middle Ages. Along with traditions reaching into prehistory, one must also pay attention to mentalities of non-European peoples and not shy away from ethnological parallels which only a few decades ago many scholars rejected. European civilization has not managed to sever its connections with "savage thought." Since Lévy-Bruhl we must realize that even in our thought logical elements stand alongside illogical (or prelogical), the reasonable next to the irrational. Only the extent of each of the two areas is different. The affectively experienced environment now retreats behind that observed through reason.

Religious conceptions of so-called primitive peoples correspond to their "lived" environment as well as to their innate thought. Instruction by missionaries seldom has the power totally to change these preexisting ways of understanding the world. The same was true of the popular beliefs of the tenth century. Christian aspects were grafted onto people's natural religious understanding of their environment, and the Christian and popular elements tolerated each other quite well, too well for the taste of the clergy, who sought to establish a strict division between belief and superstition. This opposition was expressed in accord with the spirit of the time: magical practices were forbidden, but their efficacy was never contested.

People in the tenth century experienced the phenomena of their environment very intensely, phenomena whose interrelation and true nature necessarily remained unknown to them. The human environment had its friendly and pleasant traits. On the other hand, there was much that was sinister and threatening, and this side of nature dominated popular thinking. It would have been impossible for the clergy to suggest to the common people the ideas of hell and the devil if such ideas did not overlap pre-Christian conceptions. When the clerics emphasized these things—something they did less often than people like to believe today—they did so in part for instructional purposes and in part because they themselves were formed by ancient notions. Evil spirits had always existed, only now they were understood as the agents of the devil, who was presented in the image of a lord before whom the hellish servants prostrated themselves.

Although belief in a single God had been accepted, this God was imagined as a somewhat sinister and threatening figure. When we examine the themes of early medieval frescoes, we find that the presentation of Christ in majesty was the most frequent. Unlike Gothic images of Christ, "this iconography had the sense of a *mysterium,* of a terrifying and hidden God." The image of God and of the heavenly king Christ conformed to the contemporary concept of rank and had concrete human models. It was far more difficult to make people believe in divine love and in the suffering and humiliated Christ. Odo of Cluny had attempted to convey that side of Christology.

GOD AND DIVINE JUDGMENTS

God was the highest lord, and the average person had no more to do with him than he did with the king. People did not address their wishes to the highest court but to a lesser authority. A processional hymn from Strasbourg expresses the idea that no one can pass through the gates of heaven, and so Mary is asked to bring the petitions of the faithful "to the seat of heaven." Usually, however, it was local saints that were entrusted with the charge of intervening to the extent that they could not fulfill requests themselves. The saint was a notable, whom one approached with respect and in a formal manner. Alongside the image of the divine majesty were many "majestic" cult images of the saints. People spoke of *maiestas* or, when the images were gold-plated statues, of *aurea maiestas.* Shortly after the year 1000, a synod was held in Rodez to which the "saints" from monasteries and cloisters were brought—that is, their statues or reliquaries. Present were "the golden majesty of Saint Marius" and of Amandus, the golden shrine of Saint Saturninus, the golden image of the mother of God, and, finally, "the golden majesty of Saint Fides," the famous and still-extant Sainte-Foy de Conques. It was a sort of heavenly court assembly held in the open under tents.

People experienced God himself in terms of his ruling of the world, in a continuing direct influence on the human sphere, inscrutable in its nature and unlimited, in contrast to earthly lordship. Timely recognition of signs announcing God's anger was important. The human race, wrote Rodulf Glaber, would long ago have been destroyed as punishment for its sinfulness, had God not worked miracles as danger signs, in addition to natural omens and admonitions by men of foresight. All unusual events could be omens, there was was always a reason for warning, and the announced punishment could always be found in the large circle of human troubles. God's relationship to humans was above all that of the supreme judge to the successors of Adam, who continued to fall into sin ever since Adam's fall.

This Old Testament understanding of God was not the only one, but it was easier to grasp than the idea of divine love, for which there was no earthly parallel. People who worked the land were accustomed to paying attention to heavenly signs. The fact that God sent these signs showed that there was a meaning behind them. Making note of such things and explaining them was the favorite activity of clerical chroniclers and sometimes became a literary habit. Again Rodulf Glaber provides a good example. He compiled a list of all the accidents, illnesses, famines, and even the deaths of prominent people in the years before the year 1000 in order to present the meaning of his time in the proper light. Richer, although he knew the reason for an eclipse of the moon, nonetheless explained the darkening of the moon as a warning of an influenza epidemic. In one monastery, Christ on a crucifix was seen to have wept shortly after a wolf entered the cathedral church of the town; in the following year(!) the city caught fire. The citizens had certainly not spent the whole time between these events awaiting a catastrophe. Still, there was always insecurity about the future, a basic pessimism. On the other hand, people seem to have awaited almost with indifference what might have been avoided by acts of repentance. There is no indication that anyone really changed his lifestyle because of indications of impending catastrophe. Rather, there are numerous complaints by clerical historians that such warnings hardened men in their sins. Conscience was a collective rather than a private affair. People rarely dealt with God as individuals: only at Easter by receiving the eucharist, and in preparations for death.

In exceptional cases, people on trial had to deal with God through oaths and ordeals. Oaths were not always taken as seriously as we might think; swearing was much abused. In contrast, the ordeal was seen as a very serious undertaking. It was the last means of establishing guilt or innocence when all other means failed. When assertion opposed assertion, when oaths and sworn testimony were not possible, an emergency situation was intentionally induced: duel or ordeal by fire or water. Since God was a just God, he had to save the innocent from danger and thereby settle the case. In this manner God provided legal help to everybody, even to the unfree and the "dishonorable people" who were not allowed to exonerate themselves from an accusation by oath. The ordeal by cold water had already existed in ancient Babylonia. Behind the ordeal stood a pre-Christian belief, especially a belief in the gods of the elements. Their purity ought not to be soiled by a guilty person; the water would reject this man's body. Besides, the elements were seen as executors of heavenly commands: "God manifests his will through signs and through the elements."

When the wife of Emperor Charles III was accused of marital infidelity, she offered to prove her innocence either in a duel or through the ordeal by glowing plowshares, "because she was a pious woman." Here free will was noted, but such tests were often forcefully imposed. As late as 1694, a couple who were accused of poisoning and magic were forced to undergo the ordeal by cold water, after which the French parlement abolished this venerable popular custom. There were still "witch baths" in Holland in 1823 and in Pomerania in 1836.

In ordeals based on the elements, it may have been that innocent parties acted differently from the guilty and thus passed the test. The same should have been, but was not always, true of the duel. Many people were rational enough to recognize the weakness of such proceedings. Thus Atto of Vercelli wrote: "Often, as it appeared, the innocent are defeated and the guilty are victorious." The duel was not provided for in canonical law, and many churchmen did not like it, at least in the Romance-speaking regions. The spoken formulas accompanying ordeals can be seen in connection with magic spells. Secular authorities in Italy, however, did not want to abandon what they considered a convenient means of discovering truth. Moreover, it could be used on persons who could not manage martial activities. The weak and the sick, and even kings, could arrange for substitutes. In such cases the powerful had the advantage over the poor in that the latter could not hire a professional fighter to take their place. Liutprand of Cremona told how King Hugo of Italy nominated an experienced young fighter in his own place; nevertheless, the substitute was beaten. Liutprand in this context cited the psalmist, "God is the judge and just is his judgment." Otto I allowed the legal duel and the use of substitutes in Italy. In Saxony, Otto had previously allowed a question of inheritance to be settled "between gladiators," as Widukind writes in his quasi-antique style.

THE DEVIL AND DEMONS

Faith in one true God had diminished the belief in numerous gods and spirits, and, likewise, belief in the devil as a part of Christian doctrine had somewhat changed the image of the evil powers. The numerous following of Satan, which included nature spirits and pagan gods, corresponded negatively to God and the saints. Satan's group seldom played an important role in popular belief. The host of saints, some closely connected to Christ, and others responsible for specific needs, had no counterparts among the demons. The evil powers remained largely anonymous. The essential was that people knew who had sent them.

The devil seldom appeared in person. Those who did see him, of course, were most often the pious people who were preoccupied with the struggle against him. What they observed was his ability to transform his shape and the craftiness with which he sought to trick believers. This could only happen when they themselves gave him a point of entry. A hermit in Niederaltaich named Tammo, who was possessed by pride, believed that he had seen Christ, who ordered him to wear (episcopal) sandals at Mass. It was obviously the devil that he had actually seen, who had known the hermit's secret desire and used it for his own purposes.

As we have said, the devil appeared in person mainly to hermits or in monasteries. In such events the lives of the desert fathers and the hermits who had defeated Satan in hand-to-hand combat continued to have their effect. Anyone who took himself and his psychic work seriously needed an evil counterpart. A monk in the monastery of Waulsort was ordered to perform kitchen duty. In so doing he hurt his hand, or, better, the devil intervened and did it. Often his presence remained unknown because he worked invisibly. In case of fire in a monastery, for example, the devil alone was the arsonist. His external appearance, when he manifested himself, was a paragon of ugliness—he no longer bore any resemblance to Hrotsvitha's majestic king of hell. He wore dirty clothes, had the teeth of a dog and a goat's beard. While he did not cut a ridiculous figure, he did seem less terrible. He could be despised like a social outsider.

The imagination of the secular clergy too was confronted with this image. It was more common for them to see the devil as a nonanthropomorphic power of destruction. Flodoard described how Saint Remigius threw himself toward a fire in Reims (*se flammis obiecit*), called out the name of Christ, and made the sign of the cross. The fire, "so to speak, began to flee." The saint followed it until it fled through the open city gate. A new method of fighting fires was developed by some priests in Germany. They tossed the *corporale,* the small cloth on which the consecrated host was placed, into the flames. A synod in Seligenstadt forbade this practice, threatening with anathema the "extremely stupid priests" who engaged in it. Clerics could not always know whether they were dealing with Satan personally, as when Arnold of Saint Emmeram saw a dragon-shaped cloud flying over the Pannonian plains. This "horrible enemy," which, in contrast to the images created by painters, lacked wings and legs, was either the devil himself "or one of his friends." We are reminded of the use of the word "friends" in the sense of an expanded clan.

The devil had not always shown himself alone, even to the desert saints. His assistants often took the form of animals, since these were familiar to hermits, and went to work to turn the holy man aside from his path. Hideous ravens and vultures often sat beside Saint Romuald of Ravenna in his cell. There were evil spirits (*iniqui spiritus*), which tended to take on various forms, including that of an Ethiopian. The saint spoke with them, without of course converting either of them. Laymen were also not free of such apparitions. King Louis IV (d'Outremer) was once riding from Laon toward Reims. A demon in the form of a wolf ran before him. The king followed him, fell from his horse, and died from the injury he incurred.

Was this "popular belief"? Most such incidents concerned clerics, and the accounts were always formulated by clerics. We can nevertheless answer the question with a qualified yes if we consider the sources in comparison with late antiquity, the Bible, and the evidence of ethnology. Some of the desert saints may have been intellectuals, but they were exceedingly popular figures. Their Christianity was not that of the philosophically influenced fathers of the Church. The Old and New Testaments as well as so-called primitive peoples knew of evil spirits and their exorcism. Every Christian was asked, when he was taken into the Church, whether he renounced Satan and all his works and associates. He or his godparents answered, "I do renounce them." The dialogue, which took place in the vernacular when necessary, could not have failed to impress those present. It was more an acknowledgment of that which seemed self-evident than a real choice between masters. This was no confrontation with a terrifying figure, unknown in pagan times. What was new was the devil's name and his position over the other evil spirits; both could be learned by catechumens without presenting any great surprise.

Prayers and blessings served both at baptism and elsewhere as preventives, paralyzing Satan and the evil spirits before they could carry out their work. The powers of evil played no major role in the liturgical sphere. Liturgy more frequently emphasized the positive. Thus the Holy Spirit was mentioned much more often than evil spirits. An exception was demoniacal possession and its cure, both fully in the biblical tradition. Much liturgical effort was expended to exorcise the *daemonium* and to expel the "unclean spirit" from the head, hair, shoulders, and all the individual parts of the body of the possessed. The most important of these were then individually blessed. As follow-up treatment and precautionary measures against subsequent contact with evil spirits, the formerly possessed was told that he had to fast, to wash only with holy water; he must not watch a killing—were they so common?—or look at a corpse. The series of directives, along with belief in the wholesome effects of the ritual may have contributed to the disappearance of the symptoms of psychological disorder. Sometimes curing it was simpler. Although Saint Ursmar had to conduct a formal exorcism of a nun in Maubeuge, he learned—from the evil spirit itself—that for a girl of secular status it was sufficient to strike her three times with his crosier.

Just as the devil rarely appears in person, so we have few accounts of hell as a place of eternal suffering. Adso of Montierender, who also gave information about the Antichrist, described this place in detail, allegedly after the report of a pagan king's son who had been resurrected by a saint. The southern type of hell can be distinguished from the northern type. In Adso the two are found together, with fire, heat, and snakes, but on the other side is eternal cold, the image of horror for northern peoples.

Purgatory was first conceived as a place in the twelfth century. Arnold of Saint Emmeram (in Regensburg) already knew of a temporary punishment for the dead which should have been accomplished on earth. He told of two such sinners who had to break stones in a pit. One of them had unjustly acquired property. His heirs returned the property at his request, and he was redeemed.

Gods and Spirits

There were plenty of dismal places of other kinds. If we leave the realm of Christian representations and turn to the pre-Christian, we find "graves" (cultic sites) of former gods. The heathen gods, stripped of their original nature, continued to exist. According to Atto of Vercelli, Mars and Janus were "perverse and unfortunate men" whose statues are inhabited by demons because of their sins. Generally the heathen gods remained more than human; they were demons, as they had been at the time of the apologists. Saint Paul said that what the heathens sacrifice is offered to demons and not to God. While the pious implore the saints, the evil could call on the help of the old gods. Even a pope was accused of so doing. No one considered it unbelievable when witnesses testified at the trial of John XII that he had called on the assistance of "Jupiter, Venus, and the other demons," while playing dice.

It was similar with the Germanic gods. In the Saxon baptismal prayer the person to be baptized rejected not only the devil but Thor, Wotan, and Saxnot (*Thuner ende Uuôden ende Saxnôte*). Widukind shows that there could be a real syncretism. He tells us that the Danes had long been Christian and adds that they continued to venerate their old heathen gods as well as Christ. Memory of the pagan gods had not disappeared even among the Franks. When a storm destroyed the church and vineyard on Montmartre near Paris in 944, people believed that it had been done by the hooves of ghost horses. Some had seen "demons, who appeared as riders"—a clear reference to the "wild hunt," Wotan's ghost army. The belief that a wolf or wolves swallow the moon and thereby cause darkness or moon's waning is not exclusively Germanic but is found among various other peoples.

Nature gods survived, mostly without a name, in local cults as tree or forest spirits. When speaking of them, the sources often cite old synodal decrees from the Mediterranean world. If phenomena of this kind had not been known to Regino of Prüm or Burchard of Worms and their contemporaries, they would probably have omitted them from their canonical collections. Outside of these texts, one finds scattered statements about such cults in narrative sources. Folklorists are familiar with tree cults. They existed into the nineteenth century in Livonia, where it was believed that ancestors or (after lightning strikes) the thunder god lived in sacred trees.

Thus, when Burchard, in his *Decretum,* describes people praying at trees, springs, and rocks, offering lights or torches, bread and other *oblationes*—a word used in Christian cult—he is probably telling the truth. Arnold of Saint Emmeram speaks of peasants who, in their stupidity, believe it a sin to cut down trees "at which the heathens used to perform their auguries (*auguriari solebant*)." Here we find only partial understanding concerning customs that belong to the past. Adso of Montierender was better informed. He described the foundation of a monastery in the Merovingian period as though there had been no conflict between popular belief and Christian teaching. Deep in the forest the saint asked shepherds for an "advantageous" place, and they indicated a beech tree under which they often saw lights that had not been lit by human hands. "We believe that this is of God." The Christianization of such things goes on in one of the rare testimonies from a layperson of this period, the vision of Flo-thilde. An old man took her to a place with a "very beautiful tree" and told her that it was the "place of Saint Mauritius." He com-manded the girl to pray here. In tune with the illogic of the fever-induced dream, the prayer had to be directed to two other saints.

Along with nature spirits and of the same rank, so to speak, were spirits of the dead, who were usually bound to one place, that of their burial. They were uncanny, their power was limited to the night, but they were not necessarily evil. The Christian bishop Thietmar of Merseburg has left us a great number of ghost stories, apparently in order to make believable the resurrection of the dead. At midnight the dead celebrate a sort of liturgy in the cemetery; they are seen bringing gifts or heard singing. When one of the living bothers them, they may throw him out or even burn him to ashes. Many a person who has seen ghosts has died soon afterwards, or else terrible things have happened to him. Night sounds are often heard: wood being chopped, voices, or noises of other sorts. Most are blamed on the evil Enemy. He can be escaped by means of prayers, holy water, and the sign of the cross. Thietmar must have enjoyed telling these stories, and he certainly didn't tell them purely for the pious reasons he ad-duces as justification. They were a part of Thietmar's vision of the world, just as they had been for his heathen forefathers.

Far and wide it was believed that the dead normally were "at rest" in the grave but actually were alive. This idea even influenced legal concepts: the tomb of the ancestors played a role in the south of France, for example, where one could carry out an emancipation either in a church or "before the body of the closest dead relative." It was logical to prevent any kind of action by someone's "living corpse" by burning it. That was the proper sort of death for magi-cians and heretics, and possibly also for sacred persons whom one wanted out of the way. Otto III proscribed a man who had killed Bishop Peter of Vercelli and had burned his body. On the other hand one could call someone out of his grave, talk with him, and reproach him with his evil deeds. According to Liutprand, this is what a pope did in the trial of the corpse of his predecessor Formosus. The body was finally thrown into the city sewer, the Tiber. It was a humiliating burial and not a precautionary measure. Pope Formosus was accused of having usurped the papal throne and so was not considered one of the sacred persons, who were untouchable.

The opinion that the deceased was present in the grave and there-fore could become active became important for the cult of relics and saints. It was equally important that there were saints who had charisma that made them the best opponents of all that was evil. When speaking of charisma, historians usually mean royal charisma, sometimes the much-debated family charisma. These are but small aspects of a much more general kind of belief—that the lives of men are determined by powers which work on them or within them. Objects too could be endowed with such power, though here we are dealing primarily with human creatures and only secondarily with the remains of their earthly existence, their relics. People were not simply passive in the working of such powers but could attempt to influence them. The power of saints could be directed to the pious and to his concerns through prayers and donations. A life pleasing to God, so clerics declared, is essential for such power to be invoked. Human wickedness called forth the anger of God and with it war, pestilence and bad harvests. Good actions were rewarded with peace and fertility of the fields. Rodulf Glaber believed that the peace movement of the year 1033 had resulted in such a good harvest that the grain had a minimal price.

The people were unwilling to seek the roots of misfortune in society and its actions as a whole, and were much more eager to make one individual or group responsible. Blame was often laid on the unjust ruler or, as early as the tenth century, on the Jews, whose cultic practices were greatly mistrusted. Above all, it was essential to avoid magicians, which accorded with clergy's warning against practicing or allowing the practice of black magic. Even a hermit from the east, the Trier recluse Simeon, came under suspicion in this regard. He was blamed for heavy rains, although he was not accused of having caused them himself by magic. It was said that because of his crimes the world was threatened with flooding as a divine punishment. So people smashed the windows of the formerly most revered man and wanted to stone him.

NATURAL PHENOMENA

Mankind was surrounded by mysterious and wonderful things; it was a sign of a sober mind simply to register them—which is what many chroniclers did. On the other hand, it was also their duty to promote edification. A cleric always had to refer to God and to the supernatural. In a monastery in the city of Capua moisture appeared on marble, a phenomenon that might also have been noted elsewhere. Since this occurred on the main altar of the church, it was seen as "a wondrous sign." The natural site of wonders was, of course, the sky, with its cloud formations, eclipses of the sun and moon, northern lights, etc. Here nothing was impossible; the weeping, crucified Christ could appear in the firmament. A monk was waiting one night for a boat to carry him across a river. He looked up and saw a star, which left its place and wandered away, stopped, and then returned to its original place. This happened by "divine power," certainly the best explanation at the time. Uncanny phenomena often had something to do with the devil. While shooting stars seemed harmless, meteorites were "so hard and horrible" that they were believed to have come from some place in the underworld (*de infernalibus locis*). Flodoard reported that, in 944, fire balls had flown through the sky in Germany, setting houses on fire. They could be driven off with holy water, candles, and episcopal blessings.

Narrations of this kind were usually followed by edifying explanations. The monk who watched the movement of the star was receiving a message from God that his trip would go well. Diabolical phenomena could be driven off by the power of exorcism. Though exorcism is a Christian practice, pre-Christian traditions underlie it. In the Orient, in antiquity, the heavens were searched for premonitions of earthly events. The fire balls were repelled (*repellebantur*) by rituals; so they were not simply things but demonic beings. Observing nature in an enlightened epoch may be linked with feeling and sentimentality, but when the mechanism of the apparitions was unknown and people felt under their power, the predominant emotion was fear of disaster. In that earlier time, moreover, the ability to experience emotions was much greater than today. In our time we are so inundated with stimulations that a sensual impression rarely arouses emotion. We wander unmoved through exhibitions of religious art; in the tenth century people "lived" every object. A chasuble decorated with an illustration of death could be so "unbelievably horrifying" to all who saw it that for several days they could "only think about death." Ethnologists speak of a double reality—the one we experience in our "normal" world and another, separate reality that arouses feelings, thus a world more felt and lived than simply known. This second reality is particularly connected with the supernatural. The mysterious, the awesome, is constantly encountered by so-called "primitive" peoples. It is found in the representation of God in the Old Testament and in medieval frescoes which the laity could see in churches until in the Gothic period, when other elements were emphasized.

Historical writing hovered between the two spheres. Witches cannot cause eclipses of the sun, Thietmar of Merseburg tells us, because the moon causes this phenomenon. Nonetheless, he connected the eclipse of 990, to which he was referring, with the death of the empress Theophanu. Rodulf Glaber wonders whether a comet is a new star or an old one to which God gave more light; but this is something that only God in his wisdom knows. It is likely, however, Rodulf continues, that shortly after the appearance of such a sign "something wonderful and terrible" will happen. Here and elsewhere, such views reverberated in the literate sphere. There are Latin treatises on the omens of tempests, the so-called thunder prognostications. *Libri tonirurales* of this kind were already known in the Etrurian period. After a rain of blood, King Robert of France asked scholars the meaning of this phenomenon. Two responses survive, offered by Gauzlin, abbot of Fleury, and bishop Fulbert of Chartres. The bishop, referring to authors in whose works descriptions of such events are to be found, predicted that a public misfortune would come which, however, through the penitence of the sinners could be avoided. The abbot was more concrete: a rain of blood meant war or civil war. This seems to have been a common view at the time, regardless of social or educational status, as can be seen from the king's letter, the answers to which confirm what was certainly believed in the royal court.

White and Black Magic

To know the future, especially to be able to protect oneself from coming misfortune, had always been a major desire. To this end, there were means allowed by the church, namely, observation of marvelous events either within one's own circle of activity or as signs of the elements (*portentuosa elementorum signa*), and the pronouncements of "very wise people." These sages apparently preferred to be questioned by prominent individuals than by common people. We are told, for example, of the prophecy that a recluse gave to Udalrich of Augsburg, and even a pope was said to have predicted the future for this bishop. To foresee important events, the common people had to try other means, such as the (ecclesiastically condemned) pagan *auguria*. These required that one sit on the roof of one's hut, for example, or at a crossroads. Prodigies described by classical authors are found in the Middle Ages both in historiography and in hagiography.

Here one appears to stand on Christian terrain, without fear of condemnation. For example, the best place to found a monastery was discovered by observing the flight of a white dove. In the prodigies it was God himself, who by his own will sent a sign to men. But there were ways, so to speak, of forcing God to provide hints: they involved magical and therefore forbidden practices. Forcing demons to furnish information was even more dangerous. A man sitting on the roof of his hut on New Year's Eve was working against the will of the evil spirits and so had to protect himself against them by drawing a magic circle around himself with his sword or knife. Demons could be questioned at a crossroads, and here one had to protect oneself against them by sitting on an ox hide.

Even bishops could not always wait for signs and prophecies when they needed to predict coming events. A man such as Thietmar knew the canon law too well to look for them with forbidden rites, so he prayed to God that his future might be opened to him. The provost of Walbeck appeared to him in a dream and referred him to the number five. Did this means days, weeks, or months? Thietmar found out five months later when he became bishop. A dream figure had fulfilled the wish and had done what a Christian had to renounce.

White and black magic were so firmly anchored in the Mediterranean world and among the Germanic peoples that it would have been a miracle if they had left no traces in Christian customs. This is a wide field and we can offer only a few examples here. In an official liturgical handbook, next to curses for devils and ghosts we find a method by which bishops could discover a thief. A piece of barley bread, which had to be stale, and a piece of equally dry goat cheese were inscribed with the words *Pater noster.* The bishop then had a description of the stolen objects drawn up, along with a list of the possible thieves. In the presence of the suspects, an exorcism and a benediction were performed. The exorcism sought to intimidate the evil spirits that might inhabit the bread and cheese. The benediction was intended to prevent a thief from swallowing part of them. We can well imagine how, after all of the preparations and in the presence of the incomprehensible Latin formulas, a guilty conscience would have constricted the throat of the thief when he was required to swallow a piece of dry bread and dry cheese with everyone watching.

Was this a lie detection test, based on psychological know-how, for which the liturgy was mobilized in an almost cynical manner? We are disposed to answer yes. The clerical inventor of the test would have probably denied it vehemently, insisting that it was a truly divine ordeal in an entirely harmless form. God protects the innocent and gives him the strength to pass the test. Obviously it was easier to eat the bread and cheese than to walk unharmed on glowing plowshares. Nevertheless, even today in certain parts of the world there are said to be people in religious rapture who are unharmed by the effects of burning embers.

An ordeal, even in a harmless form, provided a drama for the laity who were present. Its incomprehensibility and apparent danger reminded them of magical rites. Hence the effect of the ordeal: it was transferred into the sphere of the second, "affective" reality, mentioned above. This sphere appeared in paraliturgical customs and in so-called superstition, which included everything that seemed superfluous and harmful. Many such practices were older than Christianity and belonged to the earliest forms of religion. Some survived because they were seen as merely incidental, or as old customs that no one wished to change. For example, the leg bands with little bells hanging from them, worn by the men in the *Ruodlieb,* were charms against magic. These charms cannot be derived from symbols of lordship or from the bells on the fringe of the high priest's robe as described in the Old Testament. Their use was certainly a very common practice, which needed no biblical justification. Small bells were seen even on the official clothing of popes and emperors. Bells are indicated for Pope Sergius III (904–11), and for the Ottonians. The apotropaic character of these objects is clear in the Cluniac sphere. In petitionary processions for a good harvest, banners were carried which were hung with bells.

Protection against demons was also expected from practices of positive, "white" magic intended to increase fertility. Local saints, in the form of their relics, were frequently carried across the fields. In 940, a written order for a monastic procession declared that carrying the local saint around was a substitution for the ancient Arval procession. This is certainly the result of learned reading: the Arval Brethren had existed in ancient Rome, not in the Teutoburger forest, though the Brethren did have to promote agrarian fertility by their good offices. Our source followed a general tendency to replace pagan traditions by Christian ones and did so also where such traditions had never existed.

More suspect than this agrarian fertility cult were the various customs of herdsmen. Herdsmen followed an archaic lifestyle, with traditional ways of curing or protecting cattle, of "blessing" plants and conducting rituals with them. All of this was an abomination to the clergy, and the herdsmen's incantations were termed "diabolical chants." Still, this was white magic, while black magic was used either to do harm or for other godless purposes. The Roman state had regarded magic as a crime. Yet ceremonies and formulas which cannot be explained simply as literary reminiscences survived in the Mediterranean area. Some scholars have spoken of a "kind of liturgy" in which even the censer played a role. It is a pity that the most complete description of tenth-century magical practices appears in a treatise by Anselm of Besate that combines an extremely high intellectual level with contempt for a personal enemy of the author. He could only have achieved his purpose if his contemporaries considered his description plausible, and so he probably deviated little from existing practices. There are other sources which are beyond suspicion. We know from a Hebrew text the central role played by a "revenge doll" in a case in Le Mans in 992. In the synagogue in that town, a converted Jew "found" a buried wax image of Count Hugo III of Maine. He claimed that his former co-confessionals had constantly pierced holes in the doll in the hope that they would thereby kill the count. The latter ordered a judicial duel in order to determine the truth of the accusation. This shows that the situation was taken seriously and not considered out of the ordinary. That as late as the first half of the eleventh century a whole treatise would be written against necromancy had certainly practical reasons. People were quick to suspect magic in situations when an unusual death occurred. Some apparently knew how to use this predisposition of popular opinion for political purposes. The leader of the monastic party in the French royal court, abbot Abbo of Fleury, was accused of magic and had to swear to the kings Hugo and Robert that he had no experience in this art.

Our sources, written by clerics, do not claim that clerics sold themselves to the devil in order to be able to perform magic. Nevertheless, the borders between white and black magic were hazy; so one could try to use the old rites and practices for positive ends. Weather magicians, known as *defensores,* "defenders" (or "advocates"), demanded contributions for "protecting" a community. This probably meant that they would desist from using their powers to harm it. On the other hand, one could call upon clergymen to pronounce a powerful weather blessing. The blessing might include an abjuration of the devil: the cleric would make the sign of the cross over the clouds of heaven, he would use the last words of Christ on the cross and magical incantations, and would curse a Jewish weather demon named Mermeunt. Since clerics could not always be there at the right time, there was blessed salt and water especially against the power of the devil and evil spirits as well as against storms.

A favorite material for magical blessings was chrism, a mixture of balsam and olive oil which plays a role in the Catholic liturgy during various kinds of consecrations. A bishop of Kolobrzeg (in Poland) cleansed the sea of the demons that dwelled in it by throwing in a stone anointed with this holy oil (*chrismate*) and sprinkled with holy water. Chrism was consecrated by bishops and kept in the episcopal church, but sometimes it came into the hands of others, who tried to use it for various purposes. One could drink it before a judicial ordeal in order to influence its outcome, that is, to pass in spite of one's guilt. Rodulf Glaber describes in all sincerity how chrism worked in various situations, provided of course that the faith of the user was above suspicion. For example, it was "raised" against fires—either the fire was extinguished or it receded and continued to burn elsewhere; the sick were cured by chrism; and so forth.

Since both clerics and laymen lived in the midst of emergencies and dangers, it was reassuring for them to have some kind of instant remedy at hand without having to make the detour of petitionary prayers to God and the saints. Hence the frequent use of amulets, which in Christianized form were widely used by common people as well as by lay and ecclesiastical magnates. The most famous was Charlemagne's talisman, two disks of rock crystal enclosing a particle of the true cross. Such talismans were worn around the neck. A cleric, leaning out of a boat, once lost an amulet with a particle of the true cross in the water. This accident filled his fellow travelers with sorrow; previously they had felt confident, but now they were worried about their journey.

Confidence was particularly important in battle in order to have a calm hand and to improve one's chances of survival. Before the men from the monastery of Fleury went into battle, they were given what was called an *eulogiae:* bread and wine over which a blessing had been said. The warriors were thereby made so confident that they believed that "certainly through this nourishment they would conquer in battle and would be immune to death as they performed the service of the honorable confessor Benedict. And their hope did not deceive them."

Different factors were at work here: the power of the blessed material, like that of chrism; the similarity to the eucharist; and, finally, the protection of their patron saint. Familiar, material things were involved, things that could be grasped. It would have been still better to bring relics into battle, but few people had a breast-reliquary; the *eulogiae* served as a substitute.

SAINTS AND RELICS

Relics were first of all bones of saints; secondly, they could be other remains of the saints' existence; and thirdly they could be any object that had come into contact with items in either of the first two classes. Only through this expansion of the notion could the need for relics be to some extent met. The need began even during the life of the holy person. The saint himself sometimes took care to provide for it.

The great hermit Romuald, when his followers were leaving for distant regions, gave them small gifts as "benedictions"—an apple, for example. These had the power to heal illness. Even the water in which Romuald bathed restored the sick to health. Understandably, people soon tried to obtain relics in the narrower sense from this saint. When Romuald left Gaul, the inhabitants of the region were said to have attempted to kill him in order to retain his body "for the protection of the country."

The variety of things that could be done with bones is shown in the case of the saint Hugo of Anzy-le-Duc, who died in 940. His bones were washed with wine and balsam, and the mixture was given to the sick, who came from far and near. After two or three days they were well.

We should not simply discount such stories as the inventions of hagiographers and therefore unworthy of attention. Obviously we must take an extremely critical position with respect to the miraculous cures in view of the fact that many symptoms disappear, either temporarily or permanently, through the faith of the patient. The practices which led to such a result may in individual cases have been invented, but they operated in an ancient tradition of popular beliefs that were well known to all readers of these stories. Little had changed since the time of Gregory of Tours. Such beliefs survived among clerics, even bishops, for various reasons. For one, the border between what was permitted and what was forbidden in this sphere had never been defined in terms of Christian doctrine. Only during the Reformation and the Enlightenment would many things previously accepted as part of popular customs be labeled superstition.

The veneration of saints, too, was circumscribed by no clear limit. During Charlemagne's time, the difference between two types of veneration had been emphasized, the one appropriate only for God and the other for saints. This learned difference had little practical effect. It would have carried more weight if bishops had controlled the proliferation of cults. A saint was anyone who was venerated by the local inhabitants as such. There were living and dead saints, and both acquired their reputation among the people through their power of performing miracles. Canonization needed the framework of a strongly legalistic system of church institutions. Only within such a legal system could one hold a judicial inquiry into the totality of the belief, life, and reputation (*fides, mores, fama, sanctitatis*) of the person so venerated. Only then was it possible, if still exceptional, to have saints without miracles.

The cult of saints flourished not just because of the lack of ecclesiastical regulations. Interference with local saints would have provoked a storm of indignation in the region concerned and a loss of income for its cult center. The population lived in a plurality of cult units, similar to those of the pagan period, with the difference that there was now a sort of head unit, Christendom. In popular understanding, this larger concept played a minor role by comparison with local loyalties. Things would only begin to change with the crusades. The internal bond to the incomprehensible triune God consisted more in respect or fear than in the spontaneous love and devotion that was given to the local saint. Thus, Rather of Verona demanded from the people that they should fear God but pray to the saints. God was everywhere, even *corporaliter* in the Mass; yet people avoided his sacramental presence in the eucharist and preferred to do with eulogies. The Lord of the heavens was not to be burdened with the requests of the ordinary people. They trusted more in their saints, whose remains were close by. There were cults without corporal relics, such as those of Mary and Peter, though objects said to have been in contact with the two saints were still venerated. The absence of relics here was compensated for by the biblical stories with their vivid personal traits.

In visions and elsewhere, heaven was conceived of as a place where the saints were. On the other side—and this can also be seen in biblical texts—the dead, whether saintly or not, lay in their graves awaiting the Last Judgment. The notion of the dead reposing in the grave was the older and generally stronger concept; it offered something both local and concrete. People felt themselves protected in the vicinity of the protective lord, even when he was lying in his grave. The saint rested there like a living person, at any moment ready to act when called upon. Romuald of Ravenna was said to have seen Saint Apollinaris stepping out one night of the crypt of his church, in which he had been buried. Dressed in sacerdotal vestments, a golden censer in his hand, he incensed the altar "and when he had done this, he returned there from whence he had come." When Adelheid, the mother of King Robert of France, gave liturgical vestments to a church, she donated them to the titular saint: "She made a chasuble for the holy bishop Martin, and she sent to her best friend—after the Lord God—namely Saint Dionysius, a chasuble of the same kind." True, a priest wore these vestments during the Mass, but they belonged to the saint's wardrobe.

Decay is a penalty for sin. One of the ways saints were recognized was the good condition of their bodies when their graves were opened. Their holiness was made clear when their bodies emanated a pleasing fragrance. This detail is found so frequently that it can almost be seen as a fixed element of such accounts. There is a traditional manner of presenting this event, complete with a description of how sweet the fragrance seemed to those present, and how they concluded that it must be something heavenly. When a saint appeared in a vision, a "very pleasant odor" might remain after his departure indicating that it was not a dream and had nothing to do with a diabolic trick. Demons could only leave behind an extremely unpleasant stench, especially the smell of sulphur, of course.

The fact that the bodies of the saints were not simply corpses was a precondition for their involvement in human activities. This was true, for example, of the law. "The saint, over whose relics and on whose altar oaths were sworn, was himself a legal subject. He lived and had a legal personality in the sense of civil law." In Rome, rulers made donations or contracted obligations not with the pope but with Saint Peter, who passed on the gift or the obligation to his earthly vicar. The practice of making donations of land not to a bishop, abbot, chapter, or monastery but to the titular saint had advantages for both sides. "The landed property of the saint" (*terra sancti N.*) was under his supernatural protection, and he had to be friendly to the donor. Nowhere do we find any indication of the weakness of such concepts. For example, since many churches in Gaul, especially in Burgundy, had Saint Peter as their patron, these churches would have been part of Saint Peter's property, the *patrimonium Petri,* which the pope controlled. And what about churches with double patronage? Pious laypersons never considered such problems; and the clergy, as the actual administrators of the property, did not theorize either.

Double patronage is often found where relics of the main patron were not present. Here the secondary patrons helped out, since these were usually "lesser" saints whose remains were available.

As we have already seen, a saint was obligated to protect the goods given him and not only them alone. The fate of an episcopal city was connected to its heavenly patron, a fact that every besieger had to reckon with. Poitiers would probably have been captured in 955 by Hugh the Great if a storm had not caused serious injuries in his camp. It was believed that Saint Hilarius was indicating his anger by this storm, and so the siege was raised. The relics housed in the besieged town were often carried along or around the walls, drawing a sort of magical circle, which the enemy was not supposed to cross. This had already taken place in 885 during the siege of Paris by the Normans. The deliverance of the town was ascribed, of course, to Saint Germain and Saint Geneviève. Even before the siege a Norman commander was said to have told his king that on the Franks' side the dead were more powerful than the living. He was referring to the city patron, who allegedly beat him with his staff. Saints who thrashed were not unusual.

The saint was the lord and acted according to his position. Unlike an earthly lord, he could punish the guilty with sudden death. Supernatural beings have always been unpredictable; anyone who sees them risks dying shortly thereafter. Thus, saints were approached with fear, but they were no longer respected if they did not fulfill their obligations toward the faithful. When a craftsman working on the tower of the monastery of Saint Mary of Cambrai fell, his fellows fumed against the patron, saying, "Why should we be part of Mary's following (*obsequium*) if she allowed her servant to fall?"

If the common people spoke in this way, it could not be different with magnates when their trust was betrayed. When Fulk Nerra of Anjou captured and burned the town of Saumur in 1025, he shouted to the saint there, "Saint Florentius, let yourself be burned. I will build you a better home in Angers." But when the relics of the saint were brought to Angers, the transportation down the Loire caused unexpected difficulty. Fulk called the saint an impious rustic lout who did not want to come to the big city and sent the relics back to Saumur.

By an insult, the dignity of the one insulted was called in question. The saint could thus be persuaded to do what was desired. "Humiliation of saints" could be effected in a literal sense by putting their relics on the ground while praying. This could actually be an effective weapon. When the advocate of a monastery in Noyon so oppressed a *villa* that the people wanted to leave it, not only did he come under episcopal ban but he was also execrated by the monks. "They even took the bodies of the saints from their seats (the altars) and put them on the ground." Terrified (*perterritus*), the advocate gave in, and the result was a settlement.

Thus, in the thought of the time the saint was an active personality endowed with human impulses, but was still supernatural. The bonds to him were strong because of the power that he could wield for the good or ill of people in this world and in the next. If asked who his superior was, a tenth-century peasant would hardly have named in the first instance his landlord or the king but rather a saint or saints because they had the most to say about his fate. Still, we must not forget another component of the cult of relics, which might be called "depersonalization." The body of the saint, or a part of it, represented the heavenly patron and "was" that person himself. On the other hand, relics remained things, which distinguished themselves by extraordinary effects. They did not simply represent the saint, they could also replace him in many ways. When the personal momentum receded, people often sought to increase the effectiveness of relics by increasing their number.

"So help me God and these holy relics!" When king Charles III ("the Simple") made this oath on the Rhine to the German king Henry I, it was a confirmation and not a call for the help of a saint. The Gospels might have been used for this purpose. There was probably a considerable number of transportable reliquaries present. The thought that the plurality of relics increased their power and the honor of the church in which they were guarded appears frequently. These could, of course, only be partial relics or contact relics. For the eight altars of Bamberg Cathedral there were for example not just eight but 132 relics, including a piece of Peter's chains, blood of Saint Paul, a piece of the sudarium of Christ, the head of Saint Damian, as well as whole skeletons or individual bones of many other saints.

Thus Bamberg Cathedral was a sort of relic museum, and it was not the only one. Even in the Carolingian period, and especially in the late Middle Ages and until well into the modern period, relics were a favorite object of high-ranking collectors, and people thought about how to acquire very rare pieces which would particularly impress visitors. As in Saint Michael in Hildesheim, relics in Magdeburg Cathedral were enclosed in the capitals, according to Thietmar of Merseburg. This could certainly add to the fame and prestige of a church and the sacredness of its interior. It was a different matter if the church merely contained a few altars with relics, or if the relics were suspended above the faithful and, as it were, radiated down on visitors. The best analogy for a twentieth-century student approaching tenth-century concepts would be the nuclear physics—in which we of today put our faith. In small doses the rays from relics could produce healing. Those rays could come from the ground on which the body of a saint had rested during the transfer of his remains. Too strong a dose of such power could be deadly, however.

The faithful tended to mix the personal and the impersonal components of the cult of saints and relics in their thought and actions. People who wore talismans trusted in the saint as protector and in the apotropaic force of the relic it contained. When the pious beloved of the count Lantbert of Liège learned that he had to go into battle, she bound precious relics onto the buckle that fastened his shirt, "so that he might survive the dangers of battle through their merit (*per earum merita*)." In fact, he was invulnerable until in the heat of swordplay he lost the relics, which were tied in a white cloth. "Immediately the count lost his power (*viribus destitutus*)." He was wounded and died of his wounds. This was, of course, an abbreviated way of describing the event because only saints, not relics, could have merits and use them to help others. In any case, the effect seemed to occur automatically and stopped as soon as the packet fell to the earth. No saints were named to whose power the temporary protection was attributed. One can imagine the confusion which the count felt when he lost his talisman—that moment of carelessness may have been enough to bring him to his death.

Relics were, above all, objects of attraction for believers and therefore became factors of economic prosperity. From the end of the seventh century, physical relics were increasingly divided up. Even the smallest portions were called "the body" of the saint, and it was believed that the saint's entire power was to be found in them. As a result, cultic sites constantly increased and became sources of revenue. According to Flodoard, the canons of Reims were forced by a famine to move to an estate they owned on the Rhine. They took their relics with them, and soon the people from the surrounding areas began to make pilgrimages to them, bringing gifts. The provost of Bonn complained about this practice to the archbishop of Cologne, probably because of the consequent reduction in donations to his canonry. A pilgrimage site might quickly develop, complete with miraculous cures, as so often happened in small communities. When it was believed that the priory church of Juziers in the Vexin owned some hairs from the apostle Peter's beard, over 170 blind and lame were said to have been cured there, as well as all the possessed, who were brought there from far around. Certainly not all of them were poor, and so the cures must have been very important to the priory.

In addition to the small, local pilgrimages for the healthy and the sick, large pilgrimage centers with international importance could develop rapidly. The archbishop of Sens claimed that in the church of Saint Stephen in that city the "insignia of ancient sanctuaries" had been found, including a portion of the rod with which Moses had struck water from the rock. It was easy to give the "discovery" wide publicity. Pilgrims soon arrived, not only from France, but also from Italy and England. As a result, the city of Sens became very rich.

Relic frauds and relic thefts led to no basic change in religious devotion in this area. Frequently, as in the case of the abbot of Bonn, opponents contested the authenticity of relics. Around 930, the abbot of Bobbio sent "the saints" of his monastery to the royal court of Pavia as a protest against the actions of a vassal of the northern Italian count Samson in a dispute over possessions. The vassal indignantly said that these relics "were all horse and donkey bones." Material interests could greatly decrease belief. Miraculous cures as such were seldom doubted, although they were occasionally ascribed to evil spirits who were thereby leading people into temptation.

At a higher intellectual level, clerics cautiously attempted to direct the attention of the faithful to what was central to the faith. Miracles are the work not of saints but of God, who can use human beings for this purpose. The altar is the place on which the mystery of the transsubstantiation into the body and blood of Christ is accomplished; a saint has no business there; in other words, reliquaries should be removed from the altars on which they stood. Admitting that miracles were necessary for the unbelievers in the time of the early Church, some asked: What need is there for them now when there is no people, no mountain, no valley, not even a distant island, to which faith in Christ has not been extended? Christ said of John the Baptist that there was none greater than he; yet John performed no miracles. A saint who leads a "miraculous," that is, a very pious, life is no less to be honored than a miracle worker.

Words like these had little effect. Popular belief was centered on the saints and their miracles, not on Christ or on exemplary living. This sort of piety was normal, and we are not surprised at what Odo of Cluny tells about the reaction of men when a fire broke out in the basilica of Saint Martin of Tours. At the time, Odo says, some people became weak in faith. He is referring not to faith in God but rather to faith in Saint Martin. In former times, he adds, the saint had performed many miracles, and now he had failed. The clergy frequently supported such thinking instead of recommending caution, as the Church Fathers had done. This attitude may be excusable, as clerics were bound by the thinking of their time. They often followed their own interests, which were not necessarily material interests. Among the populace and the clergy alike, local patriotism tended to prefer the familiar to the foreign and thus sought to secure a higher standing for the local patron than for other saints. People were delighted when Saint Remigius in Reims cured a girl who had in vain undertaken a pilgrimage to the tomb of Saint Peter in Rome. Many stories of the same nature were told.

Popular concepts were held by clergy and nobility, too, especially among the laity right up to the king himself. At the command of King Boso, a free-standing statute of Saint Mauritius was created in Vienne between 879 and 887, with the relics of the saint enclosed in it. This may not have been the oldest "anthropomorphic" reliquary; the oldest parts of the still existing statue of Sainte Foy (Fides) in Conques appear to date from this period. In those West Frankish regions which had suffered the least by the invasions, similar statutes could be found, with gold or silver plate encasing a wooden body. To give her a face, Sainte Foy was adorned with the gold mask of a late Roman emperor. In the tenth century this fashion in sculpture spread as far as Fulda (ca. 979), Essen (ca. 1000), and beyond into southern England.

These ostentatious statues with their precious contents made a strong impression and encouraged pilgrimage. The opposing voices that have come down to us are scarce. An Arabic envoy who traveled to Fulda spoke of a "silvered idol"—how else could he have seen it?—and the cathedral scholast Bernard of Angers could not warm to something he considered superstitious, a devotion to ancient gods or demons, a perverse thing contrary to Christianity. It was reported that the reliquary bust of Saint Mauritius that King Boso had donated used to be "adorned by little golden bells all around it." They rang only when the reliquary was removed from its place and carried about. We have already seen how "majesties" of this kind encountered each other at an ecclesiastical assembly. Good use was certainly made of the journey, for the saints could be paraded in front of the people. Relics had long been employed in processions, a form of lordly *adventus* of great solemnity. The golden bells on the statue of Mauritius would have clearly distinguished themselves from the bells on the Cluniac processional banners. Not only could gold, the lordly metal, be seen on reliquaries, but it could be heard as well.

In the Gothic period these massive reliquaries would become outmoded and would be replaced by others, in which the relics could be seen. Another object of visual worship was the monstrance, in which the body of the Lord could be looked upon. The human, childlike, or suffering Christ was brought into that proximity to the faithful which they needed in order to have real contact with the supernatural.

Whatever we may think about the cult of saints and its abuses, in a period of very superficial Christianization it did fulfill an important function. If God had been far away in heaven, and only the devil had walked on earth near men, their life would have been even harder than it was. In need of the succor and proximity of the saints, people willingly put their trust in local patrons, who were a part of their own small, rustic world.

15 & PEASANT EXISTENCE

THE LATIN SOURCES OF THE TENTH CEN-
tury rarely paid attention to the manner in
which the peasant population spent its days.
From pictures, we are familiar with the man
standing in the field, barefoot and clad in a
loose shirt, working the land. What did he do
in winter? He put aside the rake and plow and
took up a hatchet, for there was much work to
be done with wood. He always needed more
fuel, fences had to be renewed, the wooden
roof of the shed in which his livestock was kept
may have needed repairs, or similar work
might be needed in his own dwelling. His hut
consisted of a single room, or living room, win-

dowless, with a high roof in which an opening let in some light and out of which the smoke from the open fire place was supposed to exit. (Sometimes the space was divided, adding one or two small rooms, apparently for storage.) That the roof opening did not always work can be seen in the existence of "smoke kitchens" (in Austria: *Rauchkuchl*) in the alpine regions until modern times. From the poem *Unibos* we learn that the poor peasant who could only call a single ox his own lived in a "smoke-filled house." In the course of the story the hero crept into the straw which lay heaped up in it. He probably slept there, since beds required bedding, which he certainly could not afford.

In the manor with its workshops, textiles were produced, but work in that area offered little comfort for the laborers. The best conditions, even during the Carolingian period, seem to have been found on royal domains and large ecclesiastical estates. In Annappes, seventeen small houses were built "within the court, with the same number of bedrooms (*cameris*), and adjoining extra rooms (*appendiciis*) in good condition." In Centula (Saint-Riquier), next to the artisans' "village," there was a similar complex for the general laborers. This sort of accommodation was expensive, and the workers were not always at hand, when needed. In the tenth century, small houses for servants were sometimes found in the precincts of the monastery, but collective lodgings for a large number of people were much more common. Since these lodgings too contained straw, which a candle could set on fire, the inhabitants, unlike monks, apparently lacked bed linens.

Wood, because it was easy to work with, was the obvious construction material. The peasant houses built of stone on the shores of the Mediterranean were less the result of greater prosperity than of a lack of wood in those areas. Wood had an additional advantage: wooden houses could move around, like those in the Russian folktale of the witch Baba Jaga. Even without her magic, it was easy to take wooden huts apart and set them up elsewhere.

DOMESTIC ANIMALS

Domestic animals were part of the familial community. They lived in the house, were under the protection of the father of the family, and sometimes had personal names. There was a sort of rank order of species, probably according to their material value. Individual characteristics were remarked on, at least in the sphere of poetry. In the

Ruodlieb there is an intelligent dog and a talking jackdaw. In the Cambridge songs, the "faithful" dying donkey calls for her master. We see here, on the one hand, the close symbiosis of men and animals and, on the other, an echo of pagan times and the use of animals as oracles. In Thietmar's time, the Liutizi still had sacred horses and horse oracles. Such instances, noted in Frankish sources from the eighth century as superstition, no longer appear in tenth-century sources. Animals had now entered the Christian sphere. The peasant girl Flothilde saw a "very white horse" trampling demons in the city moat of Reims. In another fever-induced dream, after fleeing from armed men she saw a white dog wagging its tail, but she was afraid of it and ran on. In saint's lives, the animals of the forest often take refuge with hermits. Where these men live, the peace of paradise reigns. Other pious men transferred their sanctity, as it were, to the mounts which served them. Or a saint would bring a dead mule back to life, which then expressed its thanks to God by braying before the church.

As we have seen, horses played a role in the imagination. For most peasants, horses were much too expensive to use for agricultural work. Historians have attempted to determine how many days of paid work or how many pigs corresponded to the price of a horse. The prices appear to have been very high. Horses were used mainly for war and thus had to be "fiery," that is excitable, rather than plow horses. For this end it was essential that they be fed with oats. Oats could only be grown successfully in special types of soil—certain fields in Picardy, for example, which belonged to the knightly elite. This explains the high price of such horses. Horses were also used as mounts for messengers and overseers of large estates, or as pack animals for those who bought or sold goods for their lords at the market. Here too the price of the animals played no great role. A peasant had to be quite well off to be able to keep a horse. It went without saying that he was not allowed to ride it except in the service of his lord.

It is a commonplace among medievalists that horses were not used for agriculture. This belief is undermined by two literary sources that speak of mares. In the *Ruodlieb* the advice is given not to rent out a pregnant mare to a neighbor for harrowing (*ad occandum*) because she might lose her foal. The poem about the crafty peasant Unibos says that his mare (*equa*) was accustomed to tillage. The allusion is not entirely clear, since for the most part the text speaks of a *iumentum*, that is, a beast of burden, especially a mule. Until the death of his only ox, the man nicknamed Unibos could only hitch this one animal behind his plow. Were mares used only for light work such as harrowing and as breeding stock? Surely they were not as expensive as stallions.

In the south, where meadows were rare and high-priced, mules could be used as warhorses and were considered such in mountainous areas. Donkeys, hinnies, and mules frequently took the place of horses in other functions as well. From the tenth century on, there were buffalo in Italy, which withstood the climate in the hot regions on the coast better than cattle. Even here, oxen were still needed as draught animals, especially for plowing. They were usually used in pairs because of their limited energy and size: they were only about three feet high and, until the modern age, weighed hardly more than hogs, which, like oxen, were not fed very well. A good ox was expensive; in the Cluniac region in the tenth century it cost nearly as much as a hectare of land. In the same region, before the Second World War, a hectare cost ten times more than an ox or a cow. In spite of their poor quality, cattle had a high price in relation to the limited purchasing power of the peasants. For this reason, and for lack of systematic pasturage, cattle were not raised for meat.

Anyone who could afford it plowed with oxen, and may have had four or even six harnessed to the plow when working heavy soil. The many who could not afford oxen had to work the soil with a hoe and, of course, had an even lower yield than those with plows. The prehistoric tradition of hoeing continued alongside of plowing, which sometimes was in danger of being given up entirely in certain areas. After one of the frequent poor harvests, Bishop Wazo of Liège gave the more impoverished of his peasants money so that they could resist the temptation to sell their cattle and thereby endanger the cultivation of the region.

FARM IMPLEMENTS

We know less about the plow, or rather about the various types of plows, than we would like. Essentially, there were two types: the shallow plow, which merely broke the soil and was only good for light soil, and the heavy plow, ideally with wheels. The latter had three different parts for working the soil: a vertical knife (coulter), the horizontal plowshare, and the moldboard, which pushed the clod of earth to the side. This implement required great power, but it allowed heavy soil to become farmland. It was still necessary to turn the clods.

For this, the shallow plow was tipped up. The asymetrical construction of the heavy plow was better suited to this purpose.

The real problem lay not in the invention or improvement of technical equipment but rather in the preconditions for their preparation and use. The heavy plow in heavy soil required more than two oxen. It also required more iron than the shallow plow—at least two pieces—but little iron was available. The same problem arose with horseshoes. What seems to be the earliest evidence of horseshoes comes from the Waltharius, that is, out of the elite world, which could afford them. For most people, the Iron Age had not yet begun.

We must not lay too much weight on the silence of our sources. Nevertheless it seems to be no accident that from the beginning of the tenth century until around 1060, for all of Europe, we have only five charters, two chronicles, and one income record giving evidence of iron production. Iron implements were seldom attested in rural circles. Consider the famous inventory of the royal *fiscus* of Annappes, which produced around 2,500 hectoliters of farm produce. There the total inventory of metal tools was one hatchet, two axes, two shovels, two scythes, and two sickles. All the other tools were of wood. The shallow plow, which had developed from the hook plow, was first made of wood, but was then strengthened with a sheet metal casing. We must bear this in mind when we read of the extremely poor yields. We can also judge how expensive warfare was when every arrowhead was an object of value, and even at the end of the eleventh century a shod horse was worth about twice an unshod one.

In an age of mass-produced iron and iron products we can no longer understand why finding a horseshoe was once considered good luck. It is hard to establish how iron was produced and worked. In the Saxon royal palaces, archaeologists have found a single dugout house of 3.8 meters broad and 4.1 meters long, in which a lump of workable iron was discovered that suggests the work of a smith around the year 1000. A small workshop of this kind was typical of the iron foundries of the period, with furnaces no larger than 40 centimeters in diameter. The problems of providing air to larger ovens had not yet been solved. In order to obtain 700 grams of iron, 10 kilograms of iron ore and 12 kilograms of charcoal were needed, filling the oven, which was hardly higher than a man. Neither the miner nor the charcoal maker could do much with draft animals—they needed manpower. The charcoal and ore may have been brought down from the mountains to the nearest furnace on the backs of men.

Iron products could be acquired only under the lord's aegis and were used primarily for the purposes of large estates. Those who had no iron ore nearby had to import the expensive raw material, often from far away, and certainly at a greatly increased price. The work of the smith was generally connected to farming, as in Prüm, where the smith had to farm his own piece of land. In this manner he could provide for himself even when he had no iron.

Pasture and Forest

Which fields were cultivated depended on many circumstances: the kind of implement, the quantity and power of draught animals, the type of soil and its location—far away or nearby, flat or hilly. Mountainous terrain north of the Alps remained mostly forested. In the Mediterranean regions, soil exhaustion had returned the land to scrub; sheep grazing did further damage. Cattle husbandry was generally modest, while sheep and hogs were numerous. In the records of the monastery of Saint Giulia in Brescia in the early tenth century, sheep made up 50% of all the animals; next were pigs (30%), then cows (8%), and finally goats (4%). In the Bergamo area, which is more mountainous, sheep made up 74% and pigs only 21% of the livestock, with cattle (3%) and goats (2%) again playing a minor role. It is mentioned that pigs were fattened on beechnuts and acorns in the forest. Little is said about fowl. In manorial rolls they were not counted, but it was simply noted how many geese, chickens, and eggs were owed the lord. We read in saints' lives that the *aves domesticae,* the domestic animals of the poor, were often stolen from their proprietor.

We usually speak of "farming and animal husbandry" although even today there are regions in which livestock raising dominates and farming provides only a supplement to the diet. In our day this is true almost exclusively of mountainous areas; we think of farming as grain growing. In the tenth century, even in flat country such as the Po Valley in Italy, there were lordly estates whose center was forest pasture, while the cultivation of grain was a secondary occupation left to the dependent peasants. For Italy, a change in the eleventh and twelfth centuries has been postulated: earlier, there had been balance between forest and pasture economy on the one hand, farming on the other. Then the scales tipped in favor of farming. The great deforestation and consequent expansion of arable land may well have prompted similar activity north of the Alps.

The cultivation of vegetables was a third source of food. Some scholars place great emphasis on vegetables in the peasant diet. This is particularly true of Italy, and there is evidence that it was true of the North too. The documents from Gorze, for example, distinguish between *mansus* and *sors*, the former probably referring to fenced land as opposed to pasture, untilled land, etc. What we generally consider the entire economic base of the peasant, his *mansus*, would thus be synonymous with that portion of it which was most intensively cultivated and had the greatest importance for the peasant economy. Be it as it may, scholarship should deal with this problem more intensely than has often been done in textbooks on medieval economy.

In large portions of Europe, pasturage and forest played a more important role before the great expansion of arable land than would later be the case. We must not be content with this observation. The question of why this expansion had not begun earlier remains open. Neither the lack of people nor the lack of technical means provides a sufficient explanation. The situation in both domains improved between the tenth and twelfth centuries, without dramatic change at any specific moment. At some time or another, differing from region to region, clearing land was perceived as preferable to using it in the old way. The transformation of peasant existence went a step further within the context of its extremely long-term development. It was the path from hunter-gatherers of the paleolithic toward modern farm economy.

Field and garden work are the most intensive types of agriculture but not the easiest. Grazing animals take care of themselves; the herdsman has only to keep them together and to protect them from predators. Wild game are trapped in snares, bees collect honey, many trees in the forest provide edible fruits—why should one give up such things and clear the forest as long as one gets enough from it? True, the question is presented here too simply; hunters and herdsmen lead an ideal life only in bucolic poems. Game, honey, fruit, and mushrooms provide a varied diet, but this needs to be supplemented, at least by field crops. When there was no famine, a natural balance could be established between the two food complexes. Forest dwellers and herdsmen were bound into an agricultural system and could not live merely as individualists. Either they had taken over a *mansus* to work, or they were fed at least in part by a lord for their service as hunters or shepherds.

The forest provided the peasant mainly with fodder for animals and with wood. It has been calculated that in Germany in the tenth century, in contrast to later periods, about 32% of the trees were oak and 36% beech; deciduous trees accounted for 81% of the forest. The foliage gave winter bedding for the cattle, which were kept in stalls only for a short time even in Germany. In the fall, pigs were fed with acorns and beechnuts; so they grew fat in the forest. Earlier, they lived on young sprouts, forest fruits, mushrooms, etc. December was the month for slaughter. Large estates had huge herds of pigs with many thousands of animals. But pigs were also an important source of food for ordinary people. In the south, thousands of sheep and pigs similarly roamed across the brushwoods.

Wood was used least for houses and stables; it was used far more for fences, which protected most fields and gardens from grazing animals, and for making fire. For the sake of convenience—to keep the transportation routes short and to avoid the hard work of cutting down trees—deciduous trees were "put on the pole" whenever possible, that is, cut at shoulder height and the top portion taken home. When the peasant returned after about seven years, the tree had grown new shoots, which provided fresh wood. This "low forest" too had to be encircled by a fence so that it would not be damaged by grazing animals.

Alongside agriculture, a kind of forestry was engaged in that today can be seen almost exclusively in the remaining forested land of southern Europe. It might long have continued to be sufficient for farmers' needs. But there were major consumers in towns, monasteries, and secular estates who needed huge quantities of wood. In one year the monastery of Prüm alone used 96 cartloads of building timber, 25,000 shingles, 17,600 pickets, and about 15,000 cartloads of firewood. When we recall that many castles in the west were built entirely or largely of wood, it is no wonder that measures against excessive deforestation had to be taken as early as 1100. In France, at the beginning of the twelfth century, nobles tried to restrict peasant hunting. The age of "forestation" had begun; that is, forest preserves were created for the purpose of the noble hunt.

By this time, the expansion of arable land had already begun. With less forest, fewer wild animals, and more people, peasants faced the hardest work of all, which consisted not so much in burning trees down as in digging out the roots and removing stones. In the tenth century, such activities are mentioned only occasionally; on some sites, either population increase or soil exhaustion forced clearance. Along with such deforestation, what might be called "creeping clearance" appeared, especially in the south. Peasants removed useless wood from the forest and left useful trees, primarily fruit-bearing trees and, secondarily, deciduous trees. If leaves were not needed for bedding down cattle, only fruit trees were left standing; thus the *silva fructuosa* came into being. One could choose whether to leave only wild fruit trees or, in the south, chestnuts. The forest had been transformed into a fruit or chestnut orchard (*castanetum*), into which other cultivated plants could be introduced.

Since forests were measured by the number of pigs that could be fed by them (*silva ad* CCCC *porcos*), they were considered economically valuable territory and not wasteland. This duality derives from the old Roman opposition between *ager* and *saltus* that still appears in modern maps of medieval landscapes. Where woods are shown as green, one must wonder whether tall forests or low woods, grazing woods or wood gardens, are meant. The question can seldom be answered, and so we may have to stay with the unified green. But we must not forget that the reality was much more differentiated than maps can show. To indicate settled land, on the other hand, we should reckon a portion of the forest in with the cultivated territory. The meager, tubelike shapes of settled land that are often found in maps of medieval central Europe should be replaced by a considerably wider zone of cultivation.

Grazing woods can be seen as areas of extensive cultivation in contrast to the intensive field and garden areas. The clearing of these woods must have had a negative effect on animal husbandry. Bread and legumes increased, roast pork decreased. Here too, to think that forest or scrub, along with fields and gardens, covered the whole landscape would be an oversimplification. There were still empty areas, even in flat regions, alongside others extremely densely settled. The reason was only in part a material one. From the ninth century in the area around Paris, we have an account of statements made by dependents of a monastery who were to be resettled on new land. They said that they were too poor in cattle and tools for this move. Familial bonds played a role here, of course. When we look at individual cases, it is often hard to see why certain regions and their soils appeared so unattractive. On the other hand, even in the ninth century, long before the great expansion of arable land, there were some areas in which deforestation took place. These were as different as Catalonia and what would later be Austria.

After the invasions and emigrations, resettlement in Western Europe was accompanied by a slow, almost imperceptible increase in agriculture at the expense of forests and brushland. Population increase has been viewed as one reason for this expansion. The process needed organization, which could only come from above. An important role was played by secular lords seeking new sources of support for their diminished economic position. Forests were cleared in Germany as well, at least after the turn of the year 1000, resulting in more dairy farms in the green regions of northwest and south Germany. At the same time, moors and swamps began to be drained. Drainage and irrigation were major problems in Italy. There were still forests in the Po Valley and in Catalonia. There the steady expansion of arable land had begun in Carolingian times, not at the expense of the forest but largely through the draining and terracing of land. In Catalonia, the land drained by a peasant became his own property. People cultivated land, sold it at a higher price, and then repeated the procedure elsewhere. Nowhere else was there such a businesslike process of land reclamation. This was a frontier region with all the possibilities and dangers of such an area.

Elsewhere, the tiring work of land clearing was encouraged by lords by demanding fewer payments and services than usual. If a lord demanded too much of his peasants, there was a risk that they might depart, regardless of the prohibitions against leaving. Such departures had already occurred at the time of the Edict of Pîtres (862), and in the following generations they became a major problem. Attempts to prevent peasants from leaving an area were as unsuccessful as attempts to prohibit other lords from accepting them elsewhere. Lords gladly allowed foreign "guests" (*hospites*) to cut back the forests where locals were either unwilling or unable to do so.

Farming: Grain, Wine, and Legumes

With the increase of agriculture and the decreasing importance of forests as sources of food, a new age was being ushered in, in which bread and legumes would form the primary foodstuffs. We have testimony of the central role of bread—in the *Ruodlieb,* for example. The peasant gives his servant a quarter loaf of bread each morning and evening as his proper pay. Ruodlieb wants to improve the quality of the bread and to prepare dishes using flour and herbs, for which he needs milk, fat, and salt. This project promises to reduce the monotony in food without significant expenditures. Nothing is said about meat, vegetables, fruit, honey, etc. A foreign king, no less, gives Ruodlieb loaves of bread to take on his trip as thanks for services rendered, bread which turns out later to contain treasure. Along with bread, it was wine or, where wine could not be cultivated, beer that formed the basic foods of the populace. For Catalonia—and not only for this region—a dearth of wine was like a famine. When people had to withdraw into the mountains, threatened by the Moors, they planted grain in the mountains above Andorra, and in Llès (1,470 meters above sea level) they planted vines. Almost a third of the arable land around the town of Bergamo was planted with vineyards. One must be cautious in citing such figures, for mixed cultivation was common: grapevines grew like ivy on fruit trees, and the surrounding earth could be planted with herbs, which had relatively shallow roots. Viticulture did not diminish agriculture, because vines were usually grown on terrain that was unsuitable or, at least, not ideal for grain cultivation.

Is it proper to speak, as Michel Rouche does, of a "civilization of bread and wine, in which the quantity of food substituted for quality and variety"? Phrased so generally, this description is incorrect. Many examples support it, but others contradict it. It is unnecessary to point out that in the tenth century the "daily bread" was often equated with daily food, and one expressed the quality of the food by emphasizing the quality of the bread. We have already heard how the monks in Tegernsee complained that even on feast days they received rye bread. To be sure, bread formed an extremely high portion of the diet in places where a fairly large group of people had to be fed together. The peasant on his manse could find additional foods, which would have been unavailable for many people.

Bread and wine had the advantage of being easily apportioned and thereby established the basic unity of the meal, the "iron ration" to which other foods were normally added. The common life of clerics, and of peasants in general, needed such units, as we can see from the *Ruodlieb*. In that work, no menu is given for the *familia*, and other sources too are silent about what was actually eaten. Generally, the additional dishes were smaller than the large bread portion that is mentioned in the *Ruodlieb* and in ecclesiastical texts.

As we have already said concerning monastic diet, not only bread but also legumes provided an inexpensive way of filling the stomach. Perhaps we should speak of a "civilization of bread, wine, and beans." Leguminous plants have been much emphasized, since they— together with the three-field system of agriculture—were seen to have been responsible for an "agricultural revolution." The introduction of the heavy plow and of the three-field system north of the Alps is said to have been "the most important event in the history of Europe in the Early Middle Ages." As a consequence of the new agricultural system, "the center of European culture moved from the shores of the Mediterranean to the heavy soils of the North, where it has since remained." The three-field system made possible the field cultivation of legumes, and these supplemented cereal foods with the necessary proteins. The number of crops that could be raised with the new methods and their supplementation by proteins provide a far-reaching explanation of the following phenomena: an increase in population north of the Alps; the growth and multiplication of cities; the growth of industrial production; and a new intellectual upswing.

This is the thesis of Lynn White, Jr. The three-field system, however, was not introduced everywhere in Europe north of the Alps. From the ninth century on we find it on large, wealthy estates, mainly the royal and ecclesiastical estates of the Ile de France, northern Gaul, and the Rhineland. Of the situation elsewhere, especially of lands given to peasants for cultivation, we know nothing. We can only surmise that there was a wide range of agrarian systems, just as there was in northern Italy. The two-field system was probably from time to time used at Prüm, one of the largest estate complexes. As for the yields, we shall see how short they often were, an as yet unsolved research problem.

In the framework of the three-field system, the cultivation of peas and beans was possible alongside spring cereals, above all barley. How much this possibility was exploited we can only guess at. In poor monasteries without major landholdings, life was, as we have seen, literally "full of beans." The availability of legumes certainly did not result in a population increase. The growth of cities took place principally in Italy, where there was no three-field system. The whole issue therefore remains in doubt.

Legumes had always been cultivated in gardens, which played an important but elusive role in peasant economy. The products of gardens appear very seldom among peasant duties. In general we are less informed about peasant economy than about that of their lords. Moreover, the material available for an investigation of agricultural yields is limited to a few, largely ecclesiastical lordships. While economic returns were not always the major factor for their owners, a peasant could survive only if he produced enough for himself and his family. Actual numbers are available, as we have said, only for large estates, and here again grain cultivation predominates.

The yield figures that have been calculated are rather strange. Georges Duby reached depressing results, which he read as indicating that the economy was a constant fight for survival. Charlemagne had concerned himself with the improvement of agricultural conditions; yet what are we to think when the ratios of sowing to yield in the royal domain of Annappes were as low as 1:1.8 or even 1:1? If one had to sow almost as much grain as one harvested, how could the population stay alive? Other sources, such as those of the monastery of Saint Giulia (Brescia) seem to confirm the findings. Here the results were negative—less than 1:1.

Duby has suggested that these figures may have represented years of poor harvest. Poor harvests were common; we are told of harvests that yielded a mere fraction of the grain that had been sown. It is possible that the food for the agricultural personnel was not reckoned into the yield figures from Annappes and Saint Giulia, and that these are merely the net returns for the lord. It has also been thought that the figures are deceptive because they are the yields from the lord's reserve, while the peasants on their own lots probably did better since the compulsory service for their lords was probably performed unwillingly and thus with little intensity. Duby himself has pointed to the importance of supplementing grain production by other activities, especially animal husbandry. The scarcity of the sources is somewhat alleviated by a document from the monastery of Saint Thomas of Reggio Emilia. Here we find locally differing yields between 1:1.7 and 1:3.3. Scholars have also sought to determine the per capita grain consumption, with conclusions between 70 and 118 kilograms a year. This is certainly too little, even for a region such as Italy where gardens must have made an important contribution. There are question marks where we would like concrete conclusions. If we had even a small percentage of the information that we have for the political history of the period, we could achieve much better results.

Whether the peasant's life was a struggle for survival, and what the relative consumption of bread and wine was, cannot be stated with any certainty. The very terminology betrays this haziness. What, for example, is "woodland," or "field," or "pasturage"? With our modern understanding of these terms, it is hard to reach firm conclusions when we find in tenth-century sources such items as "a wood with mast for 30 pigs, and from it comes a payment of 40 bushels of oats." We know something more about the organization of large-scale estates, although here too all is not clear.

Large Estates and Small Landholdings

The huge royal or ecclesiastical lordships of the Carolingian times were, in theory, a rational and organizationally perfect structure in the tradition of the Roman art of administration. A *fiscus* of this kind had as center the lord's manor and a number of small estates that served the local administrators and exercised delegated economic functions. These *villae* were, like the manor, surrounded by reserved lands on which serfs had to work in order to receive food and shelter. Around the lord's reserve were found, at least in theory, the land of the peasant manses (*mansi*). The manse was usually the amount of land a peasant family needed for its support. Manses could be held by wholly or partially free men or by servants, possibly with servants of their own. In addition to their work on their manse, the holders were subject to forced labor, especially at harvest time, on the lord's reserve. Furthermore, they had to pay taxes to the steward or directly to the lord. The payments in kind were mostly consumed by the numerous personnel at the lord's manor. What remained in the granaries and smokehouses was reserved for times of emergency, such as a visit from the king or the bishop with his entourage. If a monastic community was numerous, the *villae* might be obligated in turn to supply its needs. Although commerce in agricultural products north of the Alps played a very limited role, the estates were neither self-sufficient nor motivated entirely by economics. The king, the nobleman, and the saint with his earthly representatives had to subordinate economic prosperity to political, religious, and, at least in times of famine, social assistance.

Thus in a very summary manner we can sketch the basis of the Frankish estate organization, alongside of which many smaller units existed that we know little about, because we lack sources. For free smallholders it was difficult, especially during bad years, to avoid being absorbed into the large estates. When the owner of a few hectares of land had eaten his seed grain, a *fiscus* like Jumièges with 4,800 hectares or Annappes with 2,000 (as well as three manors with 200–300 hectares) still had enough to provide help. This was usually done at the cost of subordination to the large estate.

Like any process of concentration, this too had its limits. The system was, like the Carolingian state, cumbersome and not as efficient as it might have been. Vast areas, poorly populated and poorly worked, a rudimentary administration, and enormous political duties had contributed to this situation. While the great estates in the Ile-de-

France were made virtually "all of a piece," elsewhere, particularly in Germany and Italy, they consisted of scattered properties which were difficult to exploit economically and to oversee. Thus they were in some danger of being alienated. On the other hand, there could be too many people established on the lord's manor, making a large estate top-heavy and consuming its surpluses. Beyond the organizational and economic level lay dangers rooted in the fact that large estates were increasingly used for political purposes and suffered from the general unrest of the period. Hence, the peasants had to take on more and more direct and indirect burdens, and they were affected both directly and indirectly by warfare. Actual as well as juridical differentiation occurred, just as population growth differentiated rural existence. The manse could be now either too large or too small for the support of a family, and the peasant world included both "rich" and "poor." Moreover, the lord had to strengthen and reward his political and military supporters by giving them property or by granting it in such forms of benefice that it amounted to alienation. Perspective became confused: the land still belonged to the lord; the income went to another; the legal rights might be exercised by a third. For the lord, the military returns of a large estate were often more interesting than its economic productivity. The vassals were political factors; the grain and the wine were not. Therefore, in some cases the lord's reserve lost its importance, and partly independent peasants were more useful than a mass of serfs who had to be supervised and directed.

The disintegration of the Carolingian manorial system, advancing in the Frankish regions, had already occurred in Italy. There was often only a small lordly reserve and this not in a contiguous unit but scattered. Here and there, peasants had ceased to do compulsory services. Various explanations have been offered: population growth, political confusion, and the greater importance of towns and markets. The peasant, under little supervision, took his produce to the nearest market rather than to the storehouses of the lord's manor. The decline of servitude, greater circulation of goods and persons, lessening of payments and services to the lord—all of this might have led to the greatest prosperity one could imagine. Noneconomic factors prevented such a blossoming. In Italy, the general situation was poor both in the period of the Hungarian invasions and during the so-called national kingdom with its often changing balance of power. Under the Ottonians, the peace so badly needed by the great estates was only temporary. Where lordly control retreated, it was often replaced not by freedom but by new oppression. We cannot suppose that vassals and other petty authorities who took the place of the magnates treated their peasants more mildly than their predecessors had done. Quite the opposite: the old saying that a distant lord was a good lord, and better than one who ruled and oversaw everything from nearby, proved to be true. Given the scarcity of sources it is not easy to observe these changes in detail. Research in Italian agrarian history has long lagged behind that of the Italian communes and still has some catching up to do. Efforts made in this direction have had very positive results.

The decline of the manorial system and the large estates in northern France and in the border regions is usually considered to have begun in the tenth and eleventh centuries. It would be strange if the confusions and catastrophes of the ninth century had not already left their traces. Indeed, research has uncovered evidence of dissolution as early as the reign of Louis the Pious (814–40). In Picardy, while everything was under control in the comital residence, there was little interest in maintaining order in the border areas. Yet the old system continued through the tenth century. Especially in the Vermandois, the proximity of the king and his city of Laon seems to have had an effect. We must differentiate among regions and bear in mind that legal measures taken in the ninth century already indicate resistance to the beginnings of disintegration.

Germany experienced fewer external and internal convulsions than France and Italy did, and so the Carolingian system could better survive. This was true also of agricultural organization. Sources are so rare that we must resort to evidence from later centuries. In Bavaria, the manorial economy survived with some modifications until the beginning of the twelfth century. For Prüm, thanks to a thirteenth-century annotated copy of an inventory from 893, Dieter Hägermann could write: "The monastic economy in 1222 maintained essentially the same economic objectives and centers of control that had been conveyed to the abbacy in the eighth and ninth centuries . . . One cannot speak of the disintegration of the manorial system" but, rather, of its modification. As for the population of Frankish estates, Widukind tells us that the Hungarians captured the *familiae* of one lord, named Ernst, which numbered "over a thousand." If one supposes only four persons per family, this figure gives a total of more than four thousand. Obviously such figures should be approached with skepticism. The economic role of the half-free or entirely free peasants of the time in Central Europe is obscure, although it appears to have been strong in Saxony.

Here and elsewhere we hear of smallholders mainly in their dealings with ecclesiastical lordships. For example the abbot of Gorze was said not to have practiced usury but merely to have demanded back what he had lent. His loans must have been made to economically weak landholders outside of the monastic *familia*. From the abbot they received grain, wine, salt, clothing, and even silver, which was turned over to a mint and made possible the purchase of necessities at a market. The close bonds of such people to a monastery may have been advantageous for the monastery, leading perhaps to the donation of land. The extraordinary expansion of ecclesiastical properties has been explained in various ways, and we cannot determine how far other motives in addition to purely religious ones come into question. That such motives existed is certain. Cluny has been incisively described as a "social institution for impoverished peasants."

When the divisions of inherited land made their economic exploitation unprofitable, they often were given to the monastery with the obligation to support of the donor. Instances of "self-conveyance" are found, often of widows, who transferred themselves and their property to a monastery and thereby solved all their economic problems. Most of the people who transferred their property in return for rents in kind—food, wine, clothing—lived in the monastery, whether in a guesthouse or in their own hut; some settled on an estate or in the surroundings of a *cella*. It is unlikely that peasants enjoyed the activity in a large monastery. They might have preferred to make themselves useful in a small community rather than among the crowds of servants and craftsmen and the comings and goings of visitors in a large monastic center. There were, of course, good reasons for them to entrust themselves to a wealthy and respected monastery. Rich monasteries thus became still richer, and poor ones remained poor. A donor had an interest in seeing that the monastery or convent was maintained in good condition and was in no danger of disappearing. All of this should be studied more closely in its total context, as far as the sources permit. This is possible mainly in cases in which abundant private charters accompany narrative sources. In Germany such charters are usually lacking, and elsewhere the transformations of the structures of lordship rather than everyday social relations are the focus of research.

Some structural transformations had nothing to do with religious motivation. They indicate that too static an image of the structures of order would be incorrect. We have to refer to research which deals with *incastellamento*, an untranslatable term, and the French banal lordship (*seigneurie banale*). Both had great importance for the history of lordship and just as much for that of the subordinate population. We will speak briefly here only about the second aspect of these two institutions.

INCASTELLAMENTO

We begin with a countryside studied by Pierre Toubert in an outstanding monograph on southern and eastern Latium, better known as Roman Campagna, Maritima, and Sabina. Here, *incastellamento* can be described as "the foundation of small lordships on the basis of fortified villages." It was the extreme form of what elsewhere, often following preexisting defenses, led to smaller and more intensive kinds of lordship. This process occurred primarily in northern Italy but also in its Greek south. Research into both areas has been intense and has produced unexpected results.

It has long been known that in France and Italy a network of fortifications arose that were constructed, it was thought, because of the danger of attack by foreign peoples. "When there was no longer that danger . . . (the castles) protected their feudal lords against their neighbors and against their prince." The castle became a means of transforming seigneurial control. According to their military function, new administrative units were founded which took the place of the Carolingian organization.

Today the situation is seen differently, particularly in central Italy. There, the tenth century saw a great number of new defenses, which were not castles but rather walled villages whose center was a tower or a fortified house (*rocca castri, domus maior castri*). The lord or his representative lived in it; the lord may have been a lay usurper of ecclesiastical land. *Castrum* did not mean a castle but a fortified village, usually a new place of habitation for the rural population. There were also some existing villages, which were now walled. The impetus always came from a lord; an initiative of peasant communities played no recognizable role in the affair. The fortified village usually lay on a high point, often around an existing church. People lived in narrow wood or stone houses, which were built like the walls according to the will of the (secular or ecclesiastical) lord. Where there were free people, the power of the lord was initially limited. How far he exercised indirect pressure to effectuate the move to the new settlement and the transformation of property rights must remain unknown. Whenever these fortified villages were founded, charters were drawn up which, from the start, established the obligations of those settled there. Around the new centers, intensively cultivated areas developed; clearing was done according to the lord's directions within the new colony's territory. The boundaries and inner structure of this territory likewise were specified by the lords. From about 1010, the lords also exercised legal authority in the villages and thereby increased their power of command, even where this right was derived from an ecclesiastical overlord.

Thus the main aspect of what has been called the *révolution castrale* in Latium was the concentration of widely scattered population in central, fortified settlements under the command of a lord who had his tower there. Such a development cannot be explained, at least in this region, by the threat of invasion. Toubert has shown that after the battle near Mount Garigliano (915) the threat of the Saracens was past, and that the process of *incastellamento* first began in the 920s. The beginning was made by great families like that of Theophylactus and by ecclesiastical lords. From them, as one chronicler wrote, "after the end of the destruction and persecution" a new configuration of relationships emerged. The later Hungarian attacks (927, 937, 942) had no great influence on this process, of which there had already been some signs in the Carolingian period. In short, external threat was not the reason for the new situation found in this region after 920.

Toubert's impressive work is unassailable. We must ask, however, if there is really no bridge between Toubert's results and the earlier theories. If we examine northern Italy, where new concentrations frequently developed around existing fortifications, we can imagine that the military side of the *incastellamento* may also have played a role in Latium. To build stone houses, walls, and cisterns on a ridge in the Sabine mountains involved tremendous labor, which went far beyond the measure of compulsory services according to the current leases. Such a task could not be accomplished solely by pressure from above. And in times of peace it would not have been in the leaseholders' interest either. They lived more freely in the midst of the decaying Carolingian system than under the control of the nearby lord of a fortified village. It would have been another matter if general insecurity reigned, either in times of war or under the influence of destruction that was still seen and experienced. After 915, no one in peasant society could judge whether the Saracens would return. True, there were reports about the devastation of Tuscany by the Hungarians and about the consequences of the fight for the throne, questions that might be reflected in local factions and feuds. So it was probably not so much the military reality of invasion but the climate created by invasion and the decomposition of the Carolingian empire that encouraged the population to move into new settlements.

There were other factors such as the increase in population noted by Toubert. The preconditions of *incastellamento* included broad unification of the legal status of the peasant population. The old bondage, which had long been in retreat, had almost no place in the reconstruction phase. One could no longer send slaves into ravaged areas but had to depend instead on voluntary cooperative work from lessees, who received desirable contracts. There were people who did not have to pay the traditional one-half of their harvest but owed only one-sixth of their grain and one-third of their wine. Furthermore, the old system had apparently become uneconomical through continuous divisions of land, so that a process of concentration, along with renunciation of distant parcels of land, was entirely in the interests of the peasants. It was a simpler and more comprehensible world that the peasant entered when he was "incastellated." Neighborly help and common economic activities were made easier; a *consuetudo loci* ruled life in a confined area. One could feel more secure in terms of the external world and could probably also find solidarity against unjust actions of the lord. For this security one had to pay: there was the risk that the new foundation would fail; one had to provide guard duty and to maintain the walls. These peasants entered new bonds, the consequences of which they could hardly foresee.

Seen in a general context, the tendency of *incastellamento* to split into small lordships outside of public institutions can be deplored. On the other hand, the intensification of social and political order on a local basis, which led to a new epoch, can be praised. In Latium, there was an early and intensive start to the changes that would appear a little later in other countries.

Among indications of this general process were the increase of the number of castles and the formation of small local jurisdictions in the place of large comital ones. The two processes did not necessarily go hand in hand, however: castles were not always the centers of legal districts. Fortified villages such as those of Latium were rare in northern Italy; there were some settlements on mountain ridges, but few were walled. Towns and castles in the north had already offered refuge in the period of the invasions. Where new fortifications were established near the older centers of regional and parish communities, people may have feared future feuds or wars. Legal titles played a limited role in a period when one was glad to have any protector. Royal charters mention the invasion of heathens and those of "evil Christians" (*mali christiani*) in one breath. As soon as the heathens stopped raiding, there were further civil wars and feuds. People who had the right of refuge in a castle were obligated to perform labor services and guard duty. Some have seen this duty as an opportunity for upward mobility for lower-class people who, as guards, became professional soldiers (*milites castrenses*). Purely rural conditions did not always predominate. In larger settlements, commerce and financing could raise social positions, as could free craftwork. The word *burgus*, once used for the small Roman castle, evolved into *Burg*, "castle," in Germanic languages, while in Romance languages it normally came to designate an unprotected settlement, whether close to or away from a fortification.

The term *incastellamento* has also been applied to northern Italy, but we must understand that it meant something different from what it meant in Latium. It was certainly no "revolution" when the majority of castles came into being by means of walling manorial villages (*curtes*). New forms could progressively supplement and replace the old. Small, new estates nested, as it were, into the old, large ones, and only in the course of the eleventh century did the new lords gather together the fragmented rights over the peasant population so that one could speak of local control. The older units, which had been formed from "public" rights, could coexist peacefully with the new ones, which were built *de facto* from parts of estates of the ancient type. An older manor or unwalled manorial village became the center of the new estate. Peasants too could own small fractions of castles, as around Bergamo. These were probably founded in the form made of associations, in times of trouble. What connected these northern Italian castles to those of the Sabina mountains was the fact that neither were primarily military buildings inhabited by the lord or his representative; they were, rather, walled villages, *curtes*. There were also refuge fortifications, which mainly served the local population and had purely defensive purposes. We have already noted that the jurisdictional districts belonging to the new lordships were still developing.

Castellanies in France

In France, we must distinguish between regions of transition from the old to the new forms of lordship, on the one hand, and, on the other, territories that had been laid to waste and that needed entirely new organization. This reconstruction began in Provence after the expulsion of the Saracens by Count William I. He divided the region among his military supporters. Of Grenoble, we are told that the bishop of that town found "few inhabitants" in his diocese. He reorganized it by giving castles and estates to foreign warriors, who then demanded payments and compulsory services in a seignioral manner but in the bishop's name. In most cases, as far as we can see, some connections with the earlier structures remained. In Picardy, counts and bishops were essentially the builders of castles, while the attempts of lesser lords to do the same often failed. Here too, small seigniories of castle-owners were formed, usually in cooperation with the counts. In Poitou, one castle was actually owned and controlled by monks. The count later gave his approval with the condition that the castle be considered a comital fief. It was one of many cases of legalization after the fact. By such means, a certain continuity was regained. For the peasant population it was inconsequential that the power of their lord might be derived from the "public" (that is royal) sphere. What mattered to them was the new distribution of land. Whether the land had been usurped or not was a question which would become of interest to scholars only many centuries later.

Almost nowhere did the seignorial territory of bishops and counts remain intact. In the old county of the Mâconnais, the count was now limited to the city of Mâcon and its immediate surroundings. Starting in the late tenth century, five or six castellanies appeared in the area, which were soon independent of the count and could be inherited. In the Maine, too, castles of this kind were established with their own little courts and vassals. In Poitou, a new social stratum of viscounts and castellans held "sovereign" rights of lordship.

Historians have spoken of the disintegration of lordships, of "real confusion" and "dissipation of authority." One should also see the positive side of the situation, however. This process resulted in the intensification of the economic and social solidarity in small units as well as in considerable "modernization" and, perhaps, rationalization by comparison with outmoded Carolingian institutions. In short, the way toward the late medieval agrarian society had begun.

Certainly the reproach of dissipation and confusion is not without foundation. The new forces had first to find their basis and their equilibrium; the small seigniories had little time to consolidate in a politically unstable environment. Viscounts and castellans sought to hold their ground against counts and their own neighbors. At the same time they were involved as partisans and vassals in a complicated power struggle among political groups.

These struggles had practical effects on the peasant population, who had to perform forced labor constructing the new fortifications which, in emergencies, went far beyond their normal labor obligations. Construction was simplified somewhat by the techniques used. To build defenses of stone, which generally had to be transported from far away, would have been impracticable and have taken too long. Small castles were built of wood and earth and, to an increasing degree, in accord with the concept known since the mid-tenth century and possibly since the ninth century—the *motte* (*agger, dunio*), a tower on a mound surrounded by a palisade and protected by a ditch, or moat. A wooden tower, of course, was in danger of fire in peacetime as well as in war. Preexisting stone towers were sometimes strengthened militarily by heaping up and reinforcing the artificial hill.

How much time and how many people were required to build a wooden *motte?* To answer this question, historians examined the calculations of French military engineers from around the year 1900. At that time, using modern steel equipment, a tower 12 to 15 meters high on a mound 30 meters in diameter, surrounded by a ditch three meters deep, could be constructed on good terrain by 100 men in 20 days. A palisade fence was added, which required much less time and personnel; 4 men could prepare 40 posts a day, and 3 men could construct 12 meters of palisade a day.

Even though work went much more slowly nine hundred years earlier, these numbers are valuable. They indicate that the construction of castles did not seriously, or for long periods, interrupt agricultural work. The work probably gave the participants a sense of security, which nevertheless could be deceptive. If one group fortified a place, then their potential or actual opponents probably did the same in their own territory, and the danger increased instead of decreasing. With castles and "countercastles," lords carried on a sort of castle politics, and attacking the outlying fortifications of hostile neighbors could become a military necessity. The defenders of these castles were usually professional soldiers. During wartime, the rural population suffered for the most part economically, through the wanton destruction about which we will speak later. Since wooden defense towers were again and again destroyed by fire, stone *donjons* began to be constructed at the end of the tenth century. Not until the twelfth century did stone towers generally replace wooden ones.

While castles played a long-lasting role, their number was not as great as one might think, even in France, the castle region par excellence. In the Mâconnais, around the year 1000, there were sixteen, and there were no more than that into the twelfth century. In the Maine, around 1050, there were eleven; fifteen years later there were already sixty-two. The regional development varies, but most regions show increasing numbers of castles, due to divisions of family property through inheritance, and to the expansion of agriculture. Lorraine represents a transitional area between France and Germany, where things were quite different; in Lorraine, few castles were used before the year 1,000. Secular functionaries, whose positions were controlled by the powerful families, resided there, in good Carolingian style, in palaces or *villae*.

Peasantry and Castles in Germany

For the East Frankish–German region, numerous studies of castles have appeared in recent decades, and archaeology has focused on this topic. Scholars have studied the various forms and functions of castles as well as the relationship between castles and the development of cities and territories. Although most of these studies have not gone beyond the confines of territorial history, the topic should be treated in the context of Europe as a whole, as has been done for the castles of Henry I. For the earlier period the sources are extremely scarce, in comparison with those of Italy and France. Thus, for the castle system of Henry I we have a few literary accounts, but it is almost impossible to connect these to charters and archaeological sites. The theory that the East Germanic castle system goes back to Henry remains a hypothesis of constitutional historians. To answer the question of how far castles influenced the lifestyles of the peasant population, information is scarce.

The most important evidence is an often cited but variously interpreted statement of Widukind of Corvey. Widukind spoke of peasants ordered to military service (*agrarii milites*). Henry I obligated every ninth such peasant, in his so-called castle directive, to reside in one of the "castles" (*urbes*). There the peasant had to provide for the lodging of the other eight and to store a third of the harvest. Assemblies and feasts were to take place in the castles as they were being built, and the construction was to continue day and night in order to be prepared for war against the enemy (the Hungarians).

Was this an *incastellamento?* Certainly not. Nevertheless it is worth examining the factors which might have contributed to such a development. Widukind says that the people should learn during peacetime what they needed to do against the enemy in times of emergency. This means forced labor, but it could also be taken as a slogan for assembling the population in the fortified locations. In this case, the ninth peasant warrior was then joined by the eight others, who had been responsible for sending him, and they all lived together in the fortification and were supplied from what had been stored up there. But what would have happened if the Hungarians had kept returning? Eventually, as many people as possible might have lived in the fortification and worked the fields outside as best they could. Such a continuing situation would probably have led to a transformation in land tenure through the abandonment of distant land and the intensive working of areas close to the "castle." From refuges, these castles would in time have become temporary settlements, which might have persisted after the danger had ceased.

In Germany, always unlike Italy, planning was done by the king. The castle, and later the city, of Meissen was founded by the king. His palace of Werla, like the monasteries of Corvey and Hersfeld, received major fortifications which could protect a large population. Theoretically, only the king had the right to build castles, although in regions where the aristocrats dominated the "subordinate" powers built fortifications without royal directives. This is how the castles of the counts of Schweinfurt originated in East Franconia, and others in the Bavarian Nordgau. Although the counts were agents of the king, they revolted against Henry II. The revolt ended in 1003 with the burning of a castle by its possessor, and the main castle of Schweinfurt narrowly escaped the same fate. As we have seen, wood and earth could be the main building materials even for comital castles. We know that Creussen, one of the four main castles of the Schweinfurts, had relatively large dimensions: it was 140 meters long and 130 meters broad; so it could hold a great number of people. The castle guard had their houses within the outer wall. Ten landholdings for the guard, also belonging to the castle, were later in possession of members of the lower nobility. These guardsmen remind one of the *milites castri (castrenses)* in northern Italy and France. They suggest that free persons had a chance to rise above peasant status and become lesser "lords." In front of the castle of Creussen were a number of small watchtowers, or guard castles, of which nine are still perceptible. This castle system, however, had no influence on the structure of lordship. Everything remained in the Carolingian tradition; there were large estates and an extensive reserve around the lord's castle.

The guard castles in upper Franconia and in the neighboring regions had the form of a hill with a walled tower erected on it. These artificial hills, *mottes* with one or two rings of walls, were found in valleys, on ridges, and on mountainsides. They were the precursors of small manors with radiating agricultural areas and a farmhouse. Their holders were obligated to military service; they could either rise into the lower nobility or sink back into the peasantry, to which their families seem to have originally belonged.

There is much controversy in the research involving *mottes*. The form is found in various regions, especially on the lower Rhine; perhaps it spread east from there. Solid evidence of them goes back only to the eleventh century. Small castles in the form of round walls had already existed in Saxony in the ninth century, and it is not clear whether and to what extent they were built in connection with comital or seigneurial residences. It is not possible to prove that they were centers of small noble lordships which developed from divisions of inheritance. The Ottonian *burgward* castles (ban castles) in the region east of the Elbe with their ban-districts served the military purposes of the king, not the consolidation of noble lordships. Saxon inheritance law prevented consolidation, for it led to the disintegration of the rights of property. In the uncertain atmosphere of opposing rivalries among the lesser nobility, the free peasantry managed to survive, since their families appear to have been much more cohesive than those of the upper strata.

With these few suggestions we have tried to show the various ways in which the history of castles and estates in Germany is connected with the life of peasant population. We find no major similarity to *incastellamento* or the French *seigneuries banales*. We cannot even affirm that in Central Europe things remained entirely Carolingian, while elsewhere things were changing. There remains the hope that archaeology will yield new evidence, though this discipline, thus far, has proved unable to make up for the lack of written sources.

16 STRATIFICATION
AND MOBILITY

IN THE PRECEDING DISCUSSION WE HAVE
used the term "peasant" in a broad sense. It
can continue to serve as a collective term for
the rural population, but it is now time to differentiate among groups within this stratum.
We have already indicated that only in the eleventh century did a peasantry composed of free
and unfree begin to separate itself from other
social groups, in particular from professional
warriors (*bellatores*). Previously the German
word *Bauer* (peasant, or farmer) had meant the
neighbor and companion in a settlement,
whether rural or not. The word was seldom
used in our modern sense of "farmer"; it

seemed unnecessary, since the agricultural activity of a peasant was not significant for him; what mattered was his freedom and his right to bear arms, or his servitude and lack of weapons. The changing perception of the term "peasantry" rested on various factors: a certain leveling of the lower strata, especially in Italy; their more marked distance to the upper strata; also (as it seems to some scholars) a stronger attachment to the soil with the intensification of agriculture at the cost of herding. The peasant had—or is supposed to have had—no time for warfare. The old concepts of freedom and servitude were becoming vaguer and now often meant little. There was an intermediate state recognized but not defined by contemporaries.

Free and Unfree Peasantry

In periods of crisis and reconstruction, one asked less about the legal than the economic status of people. Personal rights and obligations begot obligations that were connected with the soil. When an unfree person was placed on a manse in the Carolingian period, the manse remained "unfree" (*mansus servilis, casa colonicia*) in the tenth century, and its occupant had to perform the corresponding services and payments even if he was a free person. Conversely, an unfree person could receive a "free" manse. Both could be designated with the general term "peasant." Around Bergamo and elsewhere, there were *massarii*, people who worked the land, of whom some were unfree but others fully free.

In the evaluation of this rural population by the members of the elite, we see a certain ambivalence. Although the elite kept their distance, they could not help recognizing something positive about the rural folk. This corresponded to the dual position of late antiquity— the pride in nobility and loyalty to Rome on the one hand, and the praise of the rural population in contrast with corrupt urban civilization on the other. Both appeared in Christian literature, supplemented by edifying admonitions: what mattered was not ancestry and wealth but, rather, personal modesty and simplicity of behavior. In hagiography one could refer to the peasant origins of an important person as long as he was of free parentage. The beginnings of the devaluation of freedom through economic conditions is reflected in the way occupation was indicated first, as when it was said of Saint Maximinus that he was the son of a man who, although a peasant (*rusticus*), was nevertheless (*tamen*) from a free family.

Here unconsciously the distancing of the upper strata from peasant existence played a role. Adalbero of Laon has emphasized this distance very strongly when he wrote that the peasant was lazy, deformed (*deformis*), and evil (*turpis*). Elsewhere he praised peasant work: with his efforts the servant nourishes his lord. Here there is no longer a question of rural freedom. The opposition between high and low, that is king and bishops on one hand, servants on the other, is made very explicit. It was exceptional for Adalbero to express his compassion for the burdened lower orders, and almost nowhere else was the positive function of the peasantry for the existence of lords so much emphasized. This has been noted frequently in recent years. Christian pity and pure objectivity hardly fit into the picture that we have of this bishop. In part, such tendencies can be explained by the nature of the poem in which the statement appears. This poem makes abundant use of paradox; one hears things that are quite different from what one expects and is thus stimulated to reflection. The pointed criticism of Cluniac monasticism is embedded in a general criticism of Adalbero's times, and part of the criticism is directed against the pride of the leaders of society. Kings and bishops should remain aware of the dependent nature of their positions.

It is natural that this population group, which was in the process of formation should have been evaluated in different manners by its contemporaries. On the one hand, the word *rusticus* was almost an insult; on the other, one could say that "all vassals (*milites*) and rustics (*rustici*)" of a bishopric had to assemble in order to advise the bishop. One can imagine among these latter not only free peasants but also "landed servants" (*servi casati*).

Since the majority of the population was involved in agriculture, the term *rusticus* had little meaning aside from the pejorative. Another term, closer to lived experience, was used for the middle and lower levels of society—not solely of peasants, though it usually implied them. This expression, "the poor" (*paupores*), referred not only to material poverty but also to those who had no seignorial rights. Powerful people were never alone: they were protected against injuries which others might do to them. This was the primary basis of their social prestige. Material resources, without which a powerful person could have no following and no friends, obviously contributed to prestige. Servants were less often described as "poor" than were free persons. While servants had no place in public life, the free were expected to participate actively in public duties. Only persons of property could perform full military service, and they would go to war more willingly when the fields back home were being tended by subordinates. The poor was without means (*inops*) when he lacked enough land and necessities of life—food, clothing, tools, weapons—either for himself or, if he wished, to place others in his service. "Poor" and "alone" were already associated concepts in the Old Testament.

Concepts such as poverty can be given no absolute value. As with all attempts of the Middle Ages to connect social realities through pairs of contrasting terms, we must not place too much weight on these categories. They designate the top and bottom ranks of a social scale without mentioning the middle. Moreover, "poor" is always a relative term. The *Ruodlieb,* for example, presents in literary style the wealth of a village. When a count, so we are told, would come to the village with one hundred armed men, he would be received (and housed) in a fitting manner. The question of whether there was a rich man here who could receive Ruodlieb and his companion was considered irrelevant: anyone who could not show sufficient hospitality to the two travelers and their horses was thought of as poor.

From the perspective of the powerful, even wealthy peasants were probably seen as "poor." From this perspective there were "poor" nobles, although they were certainly better off than one of the peasants depicted in the *Ruodlieb.* One was "poor" or "rich" (or "powerful") above all in comparison to the other members of one's social group. "Poverty" meant lack of prestige within this stratum, which included "those of a certain importance" (*alcuius momenti*) and others whom one could disregard. If they were not subordinate to a lord, they were more vulnerable to attack than people of higher status. In this sense the "poor" consisted of small landholders as well as single women, orphans, those deprived of their freedom, and travelers without an entourage. Yet this term could also be used to designate all the members of a very large group without differentiation. For the clergy of the synod of Charroux (989), the poor were identical to the peasantry as a whole. Here we see the multiplicity of meanings of a true "popular term."

We have previously mentioned that the prestige of the nobility depended on various factors, among which wealth was important but not the principal consideration. The lower orders, however, were frequently threatened with real want, both in times of war and in years of poor harvests. A pauper quickly became a person in need (*egenus*), who in turn became a wandering beggar. We should not assume there was social prestige among the elites but not among the common people. Little notice was taken of them, and so there are only few direct suggestions of the judgments by which the lower orders evaluated their members. One factor, certainly, was personal accomplishment, which was expressed mainly in material things. A person who was economically successful was respected and might become "rich," as the peasant mentioned in the *Ruodlieb* was described. In the poem *Unibos*, a man was scorned because he did not have the two cattle he needed to plow his fields. We hear that at the monastery of Saint-Maur-des Fossés there were "cart manses" (*mansus carroperarii*) and manses of people who had no carts (*mansus manoperarii*). We can well imagine that the possession of a cart raised one's social esteem, especially when it was drawn by horses (*m. paraveredorum* in Saint-Germain-des-Prés). Peasants who had servants probably enjoyed greater social prestige than those who had only members of their own family as laborers. An unfree person could also have servants, something that must have introduced further social differentiations within his own circle. In Alpine stockyards even today, dairy maids are considered superior to women who tend pigs, and the latter are considered superior to women who tend poultry. Each has her appropriate place at the table, insofar as there are still common meals.

On the medieval estate, the exercise of an office entailed a higher social position. For these early ministerials the office was not their main occupation. They had to cultivate their own manse and also work as smith, or as miller, or at other similar tasks. If these secondary services developed into the main activity of a peasant, he would become a smith (of the monastery, for example) or a miller, and would feed his pigs with the waste bran. Some of the pigs had to be given to the lord. On large estates the steward, that is, the administrator of a *villa* and the collector of payments in kind, was occupied with his obligations on a full-time basis. Since he could provide for his family from these tasks, he did not need his own manse. The *maior* or steward rose above the social sphere from which he came. He rode on horseback, as did those horsemen who served as messengers across the region. We lack concrete evidence about the social stratification of these people, but Ludolf Kuchenbuch has surmised that a rank order existed: first was the steward, then the miller, the smith, the foresters, and finally the herdsmen. The image of the shepherds of Bethlehem that we discussed in the context of social orders shows that there were also "superior herdsmen."

An unfree man could become a steward and, through this office, gain higher prestige than many free persons who were economically dependent on a manor and its functions. We should not, however, ignore the old division into free and unfree, even though these categories played a lesser role in tenth-century thinking than in that of earlier periods. We must also remember that the sources of the ninth and tenth centuries generally concern large estates and that the agrarian activity of lesser independent people which must have formed an important sector of rural economy remains almost entirely in obscurity. Regional differences played an important role too. In Saxony there seem to have been more free, in Bavaria more unfree. In contrast to the great seigneuries of the west Frankish realm, in southern France there were many small and middling allodial estates. In the Narbonne area services of dependent peasants were less important than in the north, and in this region there were no slaves after the year 1000. The nature of the countryside may have played a role in the preservation of personal property in the south and in its new acquisition. New allods were acquired, for example, through "half-cultivation" (*complant*) in Catalonia: a peasant cleared and worked another's land and after a specified period received half of the cultivated land as his own.

Half-cultivation was used particularly in viticulture, which did not require things normally available only to landlords: seed, oxen, and plows. Viticulture and gardening were a support for independents, and for the lesser grades of dependents they apparently furnished some protection against sinking still further.

In Italy, the unfree, the half-free, and the free were no longer differentiated within an estate but were designated collectively as land tenants (*manentes*). This shows a certain leveling, not necessarily a leveling down. It could bring the unfree a better position, which might lead to freedom. We know that in periods of reconstruction, when individual initiative was needed, the number of servants and slaves declined sharply.

In the tenth century, freely owned, inherited property was less in danger of being absorbed into large estates than it had been in the ninth. On the other hand, problems could arise when the right of inheritance provided for "equal divisions." Such divisions began in the Mâconnais around 980 and led to a transformation of the social scene. "Allods" are difficult to discuss, for the term was also used for possessions not entirely free of obligations. In such cases the term indicated that the property had long been in the family and was not a new acquisition. To overemphasize the opposition between tenure and inheritance probably misses the real situation in many cases. A tenant on a large piece of land, whose obligations to the lord were not excessive, often lived better than the owner of an allod that was too small or was becoming too small for his family. In this latter situation, one had good reason to emphasize one's freedom rather than one's economic status. Legal and social history see the loss of freedom as a decline; from the economic perspective, however, that loss can be tied to the improvement of one's situation. Great lordships did not only pressure small independent farmsteads; they could also be attractive. It was good to live under the crosier, as the saying was. It meant both the desired protection and material security.

As a compromise, some held leased land along with allods and thus remained free although they were simultaneously obligated to the landlord. This "free" person was a "man" (*homo*)—the same term used to designate a vassal—who was usually characterized as not completely free. A person might be leased a "free" manse or an "unfree" one (*mansus servilis*); and in the latter case he was pulled down, at least indirectly, to the status of a servant. Free and unfree people lived side by side in the same village—the settlement community had no influence on legal status but contributed indirectly to rendering it less important, since other things seemed more relevant than these inherited terms. There were also, as in northern Italy, communal organizations of free persons who looked after their common interests without living together. They gathered in the church square and made agreements concerning such matters as common pasturage. These assemblies often provided a collective defense against large estates that might threaten small freeholders. In the Po Valley, for example, a peasant commune of this sort was organized against Saint Benedetto di Polirone, a monastery belonging to the count of Canossa.

Tenants and the Partially Free

Of the various forms of land contracts we will discuss only one, which had great importance for many parts of Italy. We are speaking of the *libellus* (*libellaria*). This was essentially a limited-duration lease, which ran for one or more generations. While in Germany and France the most common form of contract was valid only for the lessee's lifetime, many *libelli* were actually inheritable leases which often became the property of the lessee's family. The number of *libelli* from the tenth century is so great that they cannot be entirely surveyed. Various kinds of contracts were cast in this form: large property transactions of the elite, small peasant leases, direct and indirect contracts, which meant that even townspeople could rent property and could make arrangements, mainly in the form of (sub)libelli, for the working of the land by other people.

Most such contracts appear to have concerned ecclesiastical land, whose alienation was forbidden by canon law. Churches and monasteries owned large amounts of land, which often needed clearing or draining. The lessee was obligated to yield to the lessor a certain amount of the products from the land. The first such products were derived from hunting and gathering. Control by the owner—and not only in these regions—often seems to have been lacking. Many of the payments probably remained only on paper (or parchment), but they were of little import after the devastation of the early tenth century. Now landlords were apparently happy to find peasants who would work the fallow lands. One didn't ask them if they were freemen or servants—times of need made a new law. In Friuli, landlords were even content to have Slavs work for them. On the one hand, it was a matter of generating future revenues. On the other, any means was acceptable to prevent disorganization in the new settlement and to revalidate past rights of possession. Leo Marsicanus tells us that the abbot of Montecassino gave out numerous libelli. He did this to acquire money for rebuilding the daughter monastery Villetta Barrea, which had been destroyed by the Saracens. He also wanted to clarify for the future which properties belonged to his monastery. In this instance the payments had to be made immediately.

When an abbot needed liquid capital for larger investments, he offered a form of the libellus that provided for a large payment at the beginning of the contract and then, for the rest of its term, small sums that symbolically acknowledged the monastery's ownership. This type of contract may also have played a role in incastellamento. The procedure came near to the (forbidden) sale of church lands. Some held large estates by libellus contracts and later merged them into their family property. As to the peasantry, constant payment of low sums was a better choice for ecclesiastical landlords than letting secular lords undertake the resettlement of church land and making the settlers dependent on them. There were other regions, such as the Bergamo area, which the Hungarians had not devastated, in which the libellus played a much more limited role.

Those who simply paid money for the leased property, rather than payments in kind and services, emerged in a sense from the lord's control and belonged to a "free-floating" stratum similar to property owners (possessores). The process intensified as depreciation of money lowered the value of the payments. In this manner—through indirect contracts—craftsmen, merchants, priests, and urban judges acquired land. To prevent this sort of alienation of ecclesiastical property, the clergy ordered that the lessee had to work the land himself or to receive it in fief with all of the duties tied to vassality. The latter practice could also lead to alienation and could be the same as a sale. In Germany, a synod opposed the practice of investing free persons with lands which once had been given to churches for the souls of the dead.

Generally speaking, the tenth century was a period of various and sometimes contradictory developments in the middle strata of society. Attractive land leases, especially in Italy, contrasted sharply with the situation in the Mâconnais, for example, whose inheritance rules we have discussed. The legal status of these strata deteriorated, however, as free and unfree persons were treated with greater equality before the courts of justice. This shift resulted from new forms of lordship and from the peace movement. Those that German scholars call *Minderfreie* (not completely free persons)—the mixed group of people who were dependent in one form or another—also established a foothold in rather conservative regions such as Bavaria. A stratum was now found, as had been the case elsewhere long before, consisting of payers of tribute, *censuales;* some were poor people who had subordinated themselves to ecclesiastical lords for protection and support, and some were wealthy people who thus received ecclesiastical land in addition to their own property. The *census,* or payment, that they made in money or in kind sometimes included compulsory labor, which only very poor free men actually performed. "And there is one free man who has commended himself, who does two day's (work) each week." Our knowledge of this stratum almost exclusively pertains to ecclesiastical *censuales* because of the lack of sources from secular estates.

THE POOR

Did people under the protection of ecclesiastical institutions feel more secure because they were protected by spiritual weapons? Was one closer to heaven when one donated oneself to a church, as was done mainly by single women? We should not forget the part played by the granary, which in times of need the clergy had to open to the poor. Every poor harvest could leave small property holders and independent peasants in severe need. It is hard to judge how often major famine struck in the tenth century, because the sources are so poor and those that exist may intentionally exaggerate. The ever-present possibility of starvation could lead people to give up their independence. We need not assume "constant hunger," or believe Rodulf Glaber when he spoke of cannibalism, in order to understand that people's thinking was determined by the fear of future catastrophes.

Many people were reduced to begging by reason of war or crop failure, and also because in such hard times there was no one who wanted them as *censuales* or servants. Free and unfree wandered the roads in a freedom they would gladly have exchanged for a dependent position. Not only great catastrophes but also local misfortunes could have serious effects on those they concerned. Records from the poor monastery of Tegernsee tell of an area of approximately 60 yokes whose seed corn did not sprout because of cold and frost. The monastic *familia* of this region scattered "and wandered from place to place" looking for food, which their monastery could not give them. The craftsmen there needed food and clothing, and so it was impossible to support outsiders.

Some people who had seen better times could not accept the new situation. Rather tells of poor from the urban society of Italy whose pride was greater than that of the rich. We must distinguish between two types of poor: on the one hand, those who continued to live in the circle of their family and were supported by them, and, on the other, the vagrant poor. It was easier for a poor person to be proud when he lived among the wealthy, and thus easier in a town than in the countryside, especially in times of need. A pauper could remain a free person among the free, even when he would not or could not work. If he left this environment and wandered about, he was without protection and became an outlaw. Our present-day idea of human rights was unknown. Anyone who made a free or partially free person his servant against that person's will had to be punished by worldly authorities but not by ecclesiastical sanctions. We know nothing of the effectiveness of such royal commands.

The clergy's attitude toward the group they described as poor, perhaps a tenth of the whole population, varied greatly. It ranged from a kind of enthusiasm to concealed rejection. Odilo of Cluny wrote that Empress Adelheid, after the example of the Patriarch Abraham, did not doubt that God lived among the poor, "and she worshiped them in humility (*humiliter adoravit*)." On the other hand, Thietmar of Merseburg spoke of the insolence of the servants, and of a woman who was poor "and good in spite of it." When speaking of the great and the small, the rich and the poor, ecclesiastical authors generally took the side of the latter. A typical account was that of the conflict between a "noble and rich man" with poor holders of small plots of land: He wanted to plow their land under. His victims appealed to the saint of their monastery, who caused such a storm that instead of pulling the plow the cattle were thrown through the air.

This case concerned a monastic *villa* held by the rich man, who wanted to enlarge the reserve at the cost of the peasant leases. When some obvious injustice befell a common person, especially on monastic property, he had the saint or saints as protectors. In the case at hand, the concerned persons assembled on the fields at their accustomed eating place and prayed to the saint. Thus they expressed "public opinion," which could be an effective means of protest. Even kings could not ignore such demonstrations. After King Henry II had begun to have the estates of Duke Hermann of Swabia devastated, he broke off the action, "overcome by the cries of the poor," and returned to Franconia.

We should interpret such expressions less as an emotional cry of woe than as a protest against injustice. Whether poor or servants, partially free or free, the common people had the obligation and the right to go about their work in peace in the narrow confines of their divinely planned existence. Servants had no political rights, but they had a place in the Christian community. The word "servant" was not an insult but merely designated a social order, and every social order had received its rights from God. Bishop Ekkehard of Schleswig, for example, after fleeing from his diocese, which had been destroyed by "barbarians," vowed: "Since I have no episcopal see, I declare myself the servant of Saint Mary and of the church of Hildesheim, and I will be useful to this holy place insofar as I am able." It was a sort of "self-donation." Such acts were common particularly in Flanders for free women, from the tenth century onwards.

When a free woman gave herself to a monastery in this manner, she lost some of her rights. For example, she now needed permission to marry. Her economic burden was not great, as it consisted of a small head tax and other payments to her protector. She was quite different from the servant without a holding. He had to put his full power at the service of his lord, even when the latter was a servant with a holding (*servus casatus*). This labor obligation was accepted by the Church and formed one of the fundamentals of ecclesiastical and secular lordships. In the examination of penitents, the lord was asked whether he "loved" his subordinates, and the servant, whether he was loyal to the lord and worked for him "as hard as he could."

SERVANTS AND SLAVES

The line of demarcation between owning property and owning nothing, between relatively free activity and complete subordination to an authority, had no name. It ran through the middle of servitude at the point at which a family's community life ended and a dormitory or a workshop became the living quarters. The tenth-century form of agriculture needed labor which could be freely applied as well as compulsory services, and it needed both male and female artisans, women mainly in weaving. Obviously not all the children of servants with holdings could receive manses. When they came to the manor, they were at the disposal of the lord or his steward. If one wishes to use the modern term "proletariat," one must add that this proletariat was not considered a single stratum or class. This group seems to have been fairly small at the time of the dissolution of the old manorial system. Even in the ninth century there were relatively few such people in the large monasteries. At Saint Bertin (877) there were 112; at Corbie there were servants with no holdings and clerical recruits (*clerici, pulsantes*), about 150 in all, out of a total population of about 450.

The agricultural and artisanal labor pool bore less resemblance to modern labor than to the slaves of antiquity and the slaves that were bought and sold in the Middle Ages. It is nevertheless inappropriate to mix the terms "servant" and "slave," as is often done. The obligations of servants with holdings were, at least from the tenth century on, normally fixed by customary law. Within their manor they could bequeath land, appear as witnesses in court proceedings (as documents from many regions attest), and even bring action against their lord, as happened in Burgundy. This was not possible for purchased slaves. In Bavaria, where in contrast to other regions the number of servants grew in the tenth century, there were *servi proprii*, body servants, who were not only witnesses to charters but affirmed the legal acts of their bishop. It was a smooth transition from such elevated servants to the ministerials of the eleventh century. We must not allow ourselves to be lost in the vague medieval terminology of servitude. Nor should we be confused by the fact that servants, both male and female, could be given or sold. Donations to churches usually took place along with the transferral of the manse on which the peasant family lived. In such cases only the identity of the recipient of services and dues changed, not the life of the family. For servants without holdings, sale or donation was a different matter. These people lived close to the condition of slaves if not actually in it.

The commonest kind of purchased slave was a prisoner of war or someone brought by slave merchants from the margins of Europe. Normally such a slave was a Moslem or a heathen, who would slowly find a place in Christian society. The integration would be formally effected by his conversion to Christianity. An alien who was not a Jew and thus not under royal protection had the fewest rights of all. There was no precise term for this person, since *mancipium* could also be used for servants of higher status, and *servus* meant any unfree person. One such slave was a girl named Maura ("the Moor"); another was named Christina ("the Christian") "or however she is called." After her conversion, while remaining in a condition near to slavery, she could accede to the better position of unfree servant, for she was a part of the monastery's *familia*. As such, she was not entirely without rights. That the monastic ministerials would be drawn from the house servants indicates how little these people were "slaves."

Ecclesiastical lordships could not be administered according to purely economic considerations. It was forbidden to sell or otherwise to alienate property belonging to the saint. Selling some of the servants, which often happened, was equivalent to selling equipment. A few clerics, at least, were not content with a simple prohibition of slave trade but expressed moral objections to treating people like cattle. Only exchange, property for property, people for people, was allowed. Killing slaves or servants was forbidden: it was *homicidium,* a term which included manslaughter and murder. The sale of a Christian *mancipium* was sometimes equated to this crime.

The purchase of slaves required considerable means and paid off only in times of severe labor shortage. Both existed primarily in Italy, with Genoa, Venice, and Bari playing a major role in this commerce. In Byzantine Apulia, the abbot of a monastery (San Benedetto di Conversano) managed to acquire from the secular authority in Bari permanent exemption from sales tax (*pretium commercii*) when purchasing slaves. He probably cited in his request the sorry state of his monastery after the Saracen period. Churches seldom received slaves as gifts, and then most frequently when these were prisoners of war who cost the giver nothing. After the citizens of Narbonne had successfully defended themselves against a Saracen attack, they could richly equip themselves with human wares. One portion of this booty "they kept to serve (themselves)," another was sold, and twenty select men "of enormous physical build" they sent as a gift to Saint Martial in Limoges.

When manpower was in short supply in a part of Italy, it could be increased through the purchase of slaves, through the settlement of Slavs, and above all through the concession of attractive leases. Leasing meant replacing dependent by independent work, exchanging uncontrolled for fixed obligations and services. Scholars are not agreed on whether lords had an interest in making servants without holdings into half-free *coloni* or if this development took place against their will. In Catalonia too the reconquest and resettlement brought with it problems similar to those of Italy. Escaped slaves (or servants) were promised their freedom, even if they were runaways from other lordships in the region. It is no wonder that in the second half of the tenth century there were very few slaves, and those that existed did almost no heavy labor here but were used as personal servants and chambermaids. The "Moor" was already beginning to be the showpiece in the retinue of servants with whom magnates liked to surround themselves until the end of the ancien régime.

In central Europe, in spite of the Normans and Hungarians, the demand for labor was never so great that it had to be filled with purchased slaves and refugees. The number of servants without holdings probably decreased along with the number of large estates of the Carolingian type. The need was filled by the younger sons and daughters of servants settled on holdings. There were also, of course, certain contrary developments. In any case, one could afford to free some unfree servants, partly for economic reasons but for religious reasons as well. We should not overestimate the role played by manumission. More important was the slow and increasing transformation which led from unlimited services to duties limited by customary law, from total lack of property to the exploitation of a plot in the lord's land and to one's own manse. Often such processes can only be suspected, not demonstrated from the fragmentary sources.

We have been discussing persons with and without landholdings as though there were no transitional state between them. No one should imagine that the acquisition of a manse had to mean financial security for a family. "Limited" poverty often simply replaced "unlimited." The house of the lord or his steward did not always offer shelter and food for the growing numbers of children. This seems to have been one of the primary reasons for the wandering laborers, even outside of war zones. The chronicles hardly make note of them, but they do appear in miracle stories; one such story tells of a wanderer who works on a Friday and is punished for it by a saint. In the *Ruodlieb* a well-mannered young man comes to a peasant and asks him for bread and makes himself useful until he is taken on as a servant. Has he run away from his lord? That would not fit the picture here. In poor harvest years, especially, people had to leave the *familia* and take to the road. Many went to the towns to find work, not only in Italy. Others found work through *incastellamento* or with peasants who had become wealthy enough to afford servants of their own.

SOCIAL ADVANCEMENT

Historians have spoken of an "aristocracy of the unfree," such as that which formed in the Mâconnais in the eleventh century and made donations to Cluny from its lands. At a synod in Pavia in 1022, Henry II and Pope Benedict VIII turned their attention to the abusive practice whereby unfree tenants who belonged to ecclesiastical lordships were acquiring property by means of charters (*scriptiones*) "through the hands of a free man." What seems to have been at issue was the *libellus*, from whose attractive leasing terms unfree peasants too wanted to profit. The owner of such a quasi-property was almost entirely independent of his ecclesiastical lord and was not always prepared to accept the lord's directives. His position was that of a lessee with limited obligations like those of most free men. All of this presupposed that the "puppet" remained in the background.

As already noted, the period of wars and the destruction wrought by them had helped dissolve the ancient seignorial relationships. Not only in Italy were runaway or scattered servants engaged as free persons for the purposes of regional reconstruction. In individual cases such runaways could even rise higher. If we can believe an account from Fleury, a former servant who had fled to Burgundy became a warrior with a noble lifestyle, acquiring a charger, hunting dogs, and falcons. He was finally discovered, lost a judicially imposed duel, and had to return to servitude.

A second, legal way was available to servants to improve their social position. They could receive their freedom from ecclesiastical lordships. We have seen how such an arrangement could interest both parties in the period of the decline of large estates. Otto III expressly forbade the clergy to make such manumissions. Servants who did not pay their head tax as acknowledgment of their dependence were to lose half of their lands. Why manumissions had taken place was explained in the preamble to the document, in a manner which protected the image of the clergy. The reasons were, the emperor says, the uncertainty of the legal situation, absence of evidence, and the failure to pay the head tax. Later, Otto III became more explicit: In a criminal manner (*pro adulterio,* injuring the spiritual bond between bishop and church), Bishop Ingo of Vercelli had alienated from his bishopric church property along with its male and female servants. All of such "exchange contracts" were to be void, and the servants who had received their freedom in this forbidden manner were to be returned to their former status. The author of the imperial diploma was Bishop Leo of Vercelli, adviser and logothete to Otto III. He was a man whose bishopric had been badly injured and who wanted to restore law and order there and elsewhere. So Leo prepared a synodal directive for Henry II and Benedict VIII, published in Pavia in 1022, which was designed to prevent the purchase of property by unfree persons.

It is doubtful that prohibitions of this sort really changed things. Perhaps because of them, attempts to secure freedom were better camouflaged. At first people were quite open about it, as when men from the monastery of Saint Ambrogio in Milan frankly claimed at a court session of King Berengar that they were lesser free persons (*aldii*). They were found by the court to be servants of the monastery. Later people had to resort to tricks (*ingenium*). For example, servants were released from the ecclesiastical lordship through a contract of exchange; or they withdrew from it by means of a *libellus;* they attempted to secure freedom, at least for their sons, by arranging for them to marry free women or to become priests. Simple manumissions continued, however, probably for the purposes of *incastellamento.*

According to canon law, priests had to be freemen, and so clerics had to be freed before their ordination. This rule could not always be followed. It was in the interest of some lords to have a "proprietary priest," subject to their authority, to serve their proprietary church. There were members of the higher clergy who had proprietary clerics, even close to ecclesiastical centers. At the synod of Pavia already mentioned, Pope Benedict VIII issued directives concerning the sons of clerics of every degree who belonged to the *familia* of a church: "Since they are servants and must so remain, they should never be allowed to leave the servitude of the church (to which they belong)."

Even Leo of Vercelli, the author or coauthor of this directive, did not attempt to apply canon law to this practical situation.

In rare cases one could even become bishop without manumission. When Henry II had run up against the opposition of the bishop of Eichstätt concerning the boundaries of the diocese of Bamberg, he used the bishop's death as an opportunity to raise Gunzo, the sacristan of the Bamberg church and therefore an interested party, to the bishopric of Eichstätt. Gunzo was a servant (*servilis persona*), and his successor Walter also belonged to this milieu. Could one be at once the lord of a church and its servant? We should remember that the saint was really the supreme power in a church, and the bishop was his "servant." In another case the problem could not be so easily resolved: Bishop Durandus of Liège was the servant of his subordinate, the cathedral provost. The result was a ceremony in which each promised to obey the other.

When unfree persons rose into a sphere normally reserved to the nobility, clerical historiographers often were indignant. Concerning a bishop who had the king to thank for his office, German authors had to be more cautious. They passed over the situation with the commonplace that true nobility is a question of virtue. This was also used to justify a situation in which the son of an unfree ministerial from the *familia* of the monastery of Niederaltaich became bishop of Hildesheim. We never hear of manumission when this bishop Godehard is discussed.

The problem remained that an important element of the priesthood was freedom from secular coercion. Regino cites a Spanish synod which established that when a person was manumitted for spiritual service, his former lord could retain no authority over him. If he did retain it, the usual symbolic action (*manumissio*) was to be insufficient to establish the presumption (of freedom) for the clerical order. Good and proper as this may have seemed, it would have been impossible in this manner to raise the necessary number of clerical personnel. So the German clergy followed a realistic course at the synod of Hohenaltheim in 916: if a lord gave his servant the possibility of acquiring a literate education, freed him, requested that the bishop ordain him, and provided the ordained priest food and clothing, then this man must not refuse to serve his lord by reason of his freedom. If he did, he would be excluded from the ecclesiastical community until he renounced his stubborn behavior. If he remained obstinate, he was to be summoned by the bishop, stripped of his clerical position, and compelled to be a servant to his previous lord, as before. Anyone who sheltered such a miscreant was to be excommunicated, even if he were a bishop or count.

Such stipulations did not eliminate the problem. In order to initiate such a process, a complaint by the lord was necessary. If the lord could not determine the location of his cleric or did not want a conflict with his protector, the situation remained unchanged. A synod in Goslar in 1019 indicated what uncertainties reigned in the practical attitude toward such complaints. Bishop Bernward of Hildesheim, apparently without referring to a specific case, asked what was to be done with a servant who had been designated for a priestly career and, as a cleric, had married in order to have descendants who would no longer be subject to his lord. The synod did not know how to deal with the situation until the emperor took it in hand. He suggested that the synod declare that such a man and his children were to be subject "to the yoke of servitude." When a free woman married a servant, she followed "the worse hand" and, with her children, became part of the *familia*. In the case cited above, however, the problem lay in the free status of the priest, who was also a servant of his lord. It was a real dilemma, as long as the tradition of proprietary churches remained and the marriage of parish clergy was not impossible.

It is hard to judge whether such proceedings were protection against a real danger for the personal position and property of ecclesiastical lordships, or whether they were isolated cases which were overemphasized. The "pronouncement of Pope Benedict" in the resolutions of the synod of Pavia, apparently written by Leo of Vercelli, is highly rhetorical and is therefore to be evaluated with care. It states that all the sons of servants of ecclesiastical lordships attempt to acquire freedom through clerical orders and that by this means "some churches have become poor in servants (*pauperes sunt in familiis*)," so that paid workers (*pretio servientes*) had to be engaged, causing the churches to fall into financial difficulties. What could move a bishop or abbot to admit such a thing? Was it necessary to have so many rural priests, or was it difficult for pious reasons to refuse those who wished to become clerics? If we take this account seriously, it seems to point in another direction. It says that priests not only despoiled church property for their sons but they also provided that these sons would become *milites* of nobles, "so that they would not seem to have become freemen unlawfully." Such arrangements may not always have been undesirable to a particular bishop or abbot when it was a matter of his own faction in troubled times, or when kinsmen were involved. Obligations of episcopal vassals to imperial service may also have played a role. But these are only speculations.

An easier route to freedom than the path through the clergy was the rise through a *ministerium* within the estate. The early, unfree ministerials were only used in limited numbers, as craftsmen, messengers, administrators, and sometimes also as *milites*. Even artisanal work raised prestige, and when a servant received a horse—as a mounted messenger, as an escort to a transport of goods, or, more particularly, as a steward who collected the payments of the *familia*—he had risen above his former condition. In Saint Gall there were *maiores locorum* who acted like persons capable of military service, even like noblemen. They had hounds for deer hunts, concerned themselves only with hunting and with their (peasant) tenures, carried polished shields and other weapons, and "learned to blow horns with a different sound from that of normal peasants (*villani*)." All these things seem to have been part of lordly existence.

Such behavior was certainly exceptional, made possible by the weak administration of the abbot of the time. Further, imitation of a lifestyle hardly resulted in an actual rise into the elite of the society. The steward did not become a lord. Such a rise took several generations and required, at least in many regions of Europe, a detour through urban life. Rather of Verona presented the imaginary family tree of the son of a count, whose great-great grandfather had been a *miles*. "Who was the father of this *miles*? Was he a fortune teller, a baker, a masseur or a bird catcher, a fishmonger or a pot maker, a tailor or a chicken merchant, a muleteer or a teamster, a horseman (*eques*) or a peasant (*agricola*), a servant or a free man? Who remembers now?"

This list includes a series of low-status urban occupations. The alternatives that follow have to do with riding, carting, and, finally, the peasantry. The legal position of such people was left open—in the urban sphere it was not important. The holder of a *libellus* could move into town and leave the actual farming to a subcontractor. A servant could leave his lord and be accepted in town, or he could go to a town on the order of his lord as a ministerial. We can well imagine that Bishop Rather himself counted messengers and carters of peasant origin among his subordinates. Sons of such people who lived in town and in the free atmosphere that went with it could use their parent's money to acquire the weapons they needed to enter military service, which held out many possibilities for further upward mobility.

"When Adam delved and Eve did spin, where were then the gentlemen?" Long after Rather, critics of the nobility pointed to agriculture and artisanship as the points of origins for great families. Slowly the terms "servitude" and "freedom" acquired revolutionary pathos. When the modern autocratic monarchy arose, its subjects were both former groups of people, free and unfree; they both felt subjugated by the authoritarian regime. Now freedom became a catalogue of political rights, or the desire for liberation from all authority, anarchy. Such movements were entirely alien to the people of the tenth century. In that epoch, it was not the lower strata that shook the fundaments of society; the powers of disintegration were of another sort, which will be discussed in the following chapters. Those who sought to break the bonds of their social position or, more often, to elude them were not revolutionaries. Some were failures without any positive political concept; most were merely social climbers. They remained entirely within the obligations of their time but sought to diminish them for themselves. Their efforts succeeded best in towns, in which the bourgeoisie was slowly being formed. Much later this class would itself become an elite, successor to the old nobility.

VI·CONFUSIO

17❧DISORDER AND PUBLIC COERCION

CHRISTIANS VIEWED EXTERNAL AND IN-
ternal conflicts, the destinies of peoples and the
contradictory impulses of the inner man, as the
battle between good and evil or, in theological
terms, as the will of God, which also allows
evil. Neither the grace and goodness of God
nor the wickedness of the devil stood in the
foreground of reflection in the tenth century.
The major focus was on order, in which God
and his human image could be seen. Was this
emphasis on order the continuation of the classical idea of the macrocosm and the microcosm
of the soul? Only incidentally. It was, rather, a
parallel to those rigorous principles in which

many early civilizations found support and security.

Order and disorder were important themes for men and for society. They were established along general lines by religion, as were good and evil, but in their details they were open to more individual interpretation. Good was often, in the thought of historiographers, what corresponded to their hopes or to the position of their party. Whatever disturbed the peace, such as reform of the clerical way of life, was not good. Order meant preserving of the old, or condemning it in the struggle for something new that was conceived of as a return to the original norm. Disorder and confusion were created by political opponents and their partner, the devil. The war or feud of one's own party was a battle for what was true and pleasing to God.

LAMENTS OVER GENERAL DISORDER

On one thing all agreed: order had to reign, and a fixed law had to govern mankind. Later, Thomas Aquinas would formulate it in simple terms: "Chaos reigns where there is complexity without order." Satan was also called Belial, and this name was explained as meaning "without a yoke." Rather of Verona remembered this and wrote further that every social order had to bear its yoke, that is, its law: the laity, the secular clergy, and the monks. The protectors of law and order were princes and the secular clergy; they had to render an account to God for their actions. But what actually happened? An Irishman said it very clearly to a Frankish bishop: Among you, right is confounded (*confunditur*) by the princes and priests; they abrogate the law and exchange right for wrong. As early as 909, the bishops of the synod of Trosly had complained about the oppression of the weak, of robbery and destruction. Men are like the predatory fish in the sea, which see their fellows only as prey. Everyone does what is pleasing to him instead of paying attention to (divine) precepts. Hence, the (political, social, moral, and religious) order (*ordo*) is confused and desecrated. Monks were convinced that chaos in the world was the result of the disorder in the human soul. Fraud, robbery, and crime of every sort reigned throughout the world. From this disorder came the fury of the sword, pestilence and starvation. Yet people did not change. God's goodness had still postponed the Day of Judgment, and only because of this, hell had not yet swallowed up mankind.

Is this the empty topos of the condemnation of the present times, long familiar and well suited to clerical authors? As noncombatants they observed the results of violent altercations without being able to gain anything by them. Patristic literature, which was still extensively used as a stylistic pattern, gave a typology of negative attitudes to contemporary situations. The Last Judgment did not seem very far ahead, a conviction that had been stated even in charters for many generations. People who wrote such things operated the bounds of common sense and expressed the evidence of their Christian attitude. How far they were inwardly affected or stirred by these themes is another question. If it could be reasonably answered by historians, the answer would differ from case to case.

One conclusion can be reached: people were ready to take individual events as a motive for general statements and to see bad situations and actions as worldwide catastrophes and proof of the thoroughly evil nature of mankind. For example, scholars today agree that the invasions of the Hungarians and of the Normans cut veritable highways of destruction through the lands in which they occurred, alongside of which, except for the migrations of refugees caused by these invasions, neighboring areas escaped unharmed. Other regions remained entirely in peace. Still, in the accounts of the synodal acts of Trosly, we read: "The cities are depopulated, the monasteries are destroyed or burned, the fields have become deserts." This is rhetoric, and yet it is more: genuine shock at the fury of war could be expressed in the old forms. People who lived in the midst of such turbulent events had no time for the refined observations in which we can indulge a thousand years later.

Where emotions reign, one tends to depict things in black and white without intermediate shade, such as is seen in tenth-century historiography. In these writings and in charters we constantly encounter "evil" or "perverse" people, "bad Christians," who used ruse and force against donations to churches. These people could be robbers, but also secular holders of rights or claims with which the author did not agree. Whenever something novel threatened their own viewpoint and their own quiet, people were quick to see general confusion breaking out over Christendom. For Bishop Gerald of Cambrai, the "Peace of God" movement was an example. He said it was the responsibility of kings to suppress uprisings; if clerics took it on, the Christian world order would be thrown into confusion. When the monastery of Saint Gall was to be reformed, the monk Ekkehard IV considered this a *perturbatio*.

Words used to show how the Evil One carried out his destructive work were suited, by their ambivalent nature, to increase confusion. The same terms were used for something positive and something neg-

ative. Examples are cunning and deception. Today, too, certain strat-
agems are allowed in war, although actions of the same sort would
be considered fraud in peacetime. Force is a legitimate means of the
government, but in the hands of evildoers it is detestable. For simple
souls in the tenth century, as we have said, fraud and violence were
what one's opponents did. True, anyone thinking more deeply about
it suspected that in uncertain times the value system was in question
and laws could be misused by both parties. Emotions were to remain
outside all such reflections, but in practice this was difficult to accomplish. "To take part in public life," wrote Gerbert of Aurillac, "is
madness today. Divine and human law are confused because of the
enormous greed of excessively evil men, and only what passion and
force can extort in the manner of brutes is considered as one's right."
Gerbert had just had to give up his monastery of Bobbio; it was flight
from a hopeless political and juridical situation. Others who still held
their positions may have regarded their epoch in a similar or even
more negative manner, but perhaps for political reasons they dressed
them in literary garments. Adalbero of Laon depicted in his famous
poem a world gone mad. The order was not only confused, it had
been turned upside down. The author commented that the old norms
no longer held, that a new time had dawned. "The laws are dissolv-
ing, all peace is evaporating, the customs of men are changing, and
the order is changing as well." Superficial listeners at court may have
laughed at the absurdities described in Adalbero's tale. Those who
bore political responsibility must have shuddered at his depictions.
Only once did black humor of this kind become reality, when a deposed pope was led through the city riding backwards on a donkey,
his clothing turned inside out. Here too, horror predominated: the
delinquent's tongue had been cut off and his eyes put out. It was a
wild act of revenge in the form of a judicial atonement, and thus itself
an expression of the world turned upside down.

A generation earlier, Bishop Atto of Vercelli had elaborated a sort
of mechanics of evil in history. It appeared in a Latin which was en-
coded to the point of incomprehensibility because the times were
dangerous and not everyone was supposed to know Atto's thoughts
about the ephemeral Italian kingdom and its supporters. The basis
for all political confusion, Atto says, is the usurpation of power.
Whoever has thus acquired it is caught in a vicious circle. Whatever
he does results in a worse situation, and whoever takes the power
from him suffers the same fate. This text has been described as a mirror of public life in the period and as an early predecessor of Machia-

velli's *The Prince.* Unlike Machiavelli, Atto did not come to terms with the situation of his time. Although he too was entangled in the great political game, he remained loyal to the norms of Christianity. His treatise shows the internal conflict between reality and moral obligations, which seemed to him insoluble.

EMOTIONALITY AND PANIC

Examples of extraordinary sensitivity to the sufferings of the period do not in themselves mean much, for there have always been just as many thick-skinned people. We can conclude, however, that the "emotionality" of the period was such that people were more easily stirred up than we are. Some have attributed this trait to the insecure living conditions of a period in which nature had not been fully conquered. Such an explanation should apply above all to the peasantry, which at the time had few means of self-expression. Bishops were little affected by these matters. There is also a general idea that this epoch belonged to an unfixed, immature stage of humanity. This stage was accompanied by the imperfect institutionalization of secular authority along with some uncertainties in the ecclesiastical sphere. For individual security one generally had to rely on one's own two eyes, and one's life expectancy was short. Thus we can understand the intensity of life and experience in this period and the almost unreflected haste of many actions.

What we mean can best be shown through examples. The abbot of Cluny exercised a hierarchical authority over reformed monasteries, but it was a personal authority, not established by law. After the death of Abbot Maiolus, monasteries began to fall away from the mother house, believing themselves free of it. As mentioned earlier, there was often plundering when a bishop died, and the same sort of things could happen in monasteries. The destruction of the palace of Pavia after the death of Henry II is notorious. According to Wipo, it took place in accordance with "the custom of people to act immediately in a new situation." Does this mean that there might have been the normal plundering but that the Pavese people went too far when they carried off building materials "down to the foundation stone"? They defended themselves by saying that they had remained faithful to the emperor until his death and that it would be wrong to blame them because they had taken "his house." They received, as an answer, the metaphor of the unsinkable ship of state, which must have meant nothing to many of them. As we know, the personal or transpersonal nature of royal property was connected to the personal or transpersonal sense of the state. The idea of the state replaced the concrete and easy understanding of royal government with an abstraction.

"Out of sight, out of mind." Wipo recalled this saying when he reminded his king to let himself be seen in the countryside. Lordship still had its "familiar" aspect and needed visual contact; it was felt rather than understood as a fact. Hence the bitter disappointment when a lord acted improperly, and the extraordinary perplexity at unclear governance. When there was no leader, the followers were without direction. Armies often reacted in panic at the loss of their commander, even when they were made up of competent warriors. The defeat of an imperial army by the Frisians in 1018 was entirely due to psychological uncertainty. Warriors accustomed to fighting on horseback were loaded onto ships. When they had disembarked and formed battle lines, they were commanded to withdraw and reform because it was noticed too late that the field had been interlaced with trenches. Someone began to shout in the hindermost lines that the commander of the army was fleeing, and that it was each man for himself. "They all fled and were so possessed by fear that they threw themselves into the river without hostile pressure (*nemine urgente*) in order to reach the ships." Many drowned, ships sank, and on the shore the remaining warriors, petrified by fear, "motionless as rocks," were easily cut down by the Frisians.

Prowess and an inclination to panic were not mutually exclusive, and piety did not help much in unusual situations. Panic broke out in the cathedral of Ratisbon when a storm shook the roof and stirred up a cloud of dust in the church. "The people were terrified and, what is worse, were even mentally deranged." Rumors circulated of a major fire or even a revolt in the town. Almost everyone fled the church, leaving Bishop Wolfgang, who was in the middle of his sermon, with a few sensible persons (*sensati*) who stayed behind. Along with such plausible accounts there were others, of course, which indicate what was at least considered possible. We are told that in 968 an eclipse of the sun so terrified members of the German army in Calabria that some hid under wine barrels, others under overturned carts or crates. The bishop of Liège attempted to explain to the troops the natural aspect of the eclipse and complained about the foolishness of so many valorous warriors. He said that people who were so terrified would not terrify the enemy in whose midst they were.

All three cases show a false evaluation of the particular unusual circumstance. If the commander turns his horse, he intends to flee; when a storm can be heard in church, it is mistaken for a tumult; when the sun darkens, it is a threat of evil from above, just as in former times people thought a dragon was devouring the sun. Each of these cases indicates a powerful imagination which goes beyond the bounds of reason. Even if some kept their heads in a panic situation, they lost control of their fellows. Panic reactions are the products of momentary fear as against cowardice, which is the permanent desire to escape danger. Flight on account of instantaneous and overwhelming fear is very similar to another phenomenon, which is usually seen as the opposite of panic: furious assault. This reaction too involves an emotional fear of the enemy's power or of one's own failure, leading to the exertion of all of one's strength.

Reflections on natural phenomena were often stamped by horror at the evil in the world. Thus the desire for order had a higher priority than in a "rational" period. There is an emotional component of the quest for order, especially in an age when the Antichrist and the Last Judgment seem to be at hand. Longing for the divinely ordered state may lead to attempts to restore it by violent means, and doing justice can degenerate to cruel retaliation. Rational considerations may give way to aggression and assault in the political arena as well. On the other hand, we can understand how deep the joy must have been for disturbed souls in finding a sphere in which all was "in order," as with the Cluniacs. The overemphasis on ritual had a sense. The principle of order in feudalism may have been more attractive than is suggested by the generally negative image of "feudal anarchy." Where no royal authority ruled, many a layman found firm ground in feudalism and, hence, reassurance from the fear of being crushed by the wheel of fortune.

Conflicting Norms

Church law was a primary factor in the attainment of order, or should have been. We have heard several times of the chasm between canonical prohibitions and reality. These gaps were lamented by many authors, who did not ask what had caused them. They extended from power politics and family interests to the averting of material crisis, from the games of the "rich" to the "poor" in clerical garb. They existed for the archbishop, who simultaneously held four bishoprics against canonical prohibitions, and priests or deacons of Catalonia, who were moneylenders. Did they do this out of greed, or did they lack other income for their daily support? Moreover, canonical prohibitions were not at all unified, so that the genuine could not easily be distinguished from the false. Ecclesiastics may have noticed, as Abbo of Fleury expressed it, that "what is prescribed by one ecclesiastical synod is proscribed by another."

There was another gray zone in ecclesiastical law, aside from forgeries. As serious an author as Burchard of Worms knowingly gave false information on the origins of secular legal texts and represented individual decisions of one or another bishop as though they were conciliar resolutions or papal decrees. Texts by Carolingian authors appear in his writings under the names of Augustine or Basil. Such disguises were means "to effect the reestablishment of the old order by correcting the laws." Either these corrections actually corresponded to the old order, which was seen as the ideal, or the hoped-for situation was attributed to the good old days and to their authorities with potent names. The literary condemnation of modern times had its counterpart in juridical writings, which criticized the attempt to establish new laws and deplored the way modern authors undervalued the ancients.

In some respects, the "good old ways" were nearer to the desired situation than were the modern ones, precisely because certain current problems had been absent or only marginal in earlier times. That was true of the secular duties and obligations of the clergy, and of the influence of the laity on the clergy. Outsiders like Rudolf Glaber could see this mixed sphere in simple colors as the playground of the greed and corruption of kings and prelates. Others who saw simony at work everywhere spoke in a similar vein and strove to separate the two spheres. No one can deny that prelates were subject to very worldly impulses. On the other hand, no modern historians would see their actions simply as unreflected and overpowering greed like that "of a child or a savage" in cases that certainly involved complex moral motivations.

Secular and ecclesiastical law, both incomplete in the sense of modern systems, so intersected each other that no one could respect both at all times. Customary law and tradition (*consuetudo*) were by far the most important factors in the life of laymen and often of clerics. Ecclesiastical prohibitions found their limits in this lifestyle. No one in Christendom, Rather said, from the lowest to the highest, from the most ignorant to those who fancied themselves the wisest, from laymen to the pope himself, bothered himself about the canons. And this in a period when religion was everywhere of overriding importance! There must have been at least some situations of true *aporia*, intensified by the agitation of social competition. "Laws are silent in the presence of arms," said Gerbert of Aurillac in his defense before the ecclesiastical assembly of Mouzon (995). "If someone deviates a bit from the holy canons, it is not out of wickedness but out of necessity." The entire population lived in a state of dichotomy, as Rather had said. The great as well as the small might be uncertain as to what was right. Obviously, the comfortable or lucrative path was more often chosen than the fulfilling of difficult prescriptions.

In the diocesis of Vercelli, the peasantry were accustomed to celebrate Friday as a holiday, as it was the day of Christ's death. So they had to do no work two days a week. Bishop Atto had hard words for this custom: they ought to do their work rather than hang around and talk nonsense. On the other hand, Friday was a fast-day and—as Atto himself said—a day of mourning. Could one work hard when fasting and mourning? Custom seems to have been negative on this point.

On a higher level, that of monasticism, the requirements of the Rule went against care of one's own family. Since such concerns were a virtue, why should monks do otherwise? If it belonged to a man's role not to remain a "youth" but to establish a family, was not this obligation more important than those of the long-dead founder of the order? If secular clergy could own property and Byzantine monks could retain some control over it, was not total poverty an extreme requirement? The monks of Farfa who lived with their wives on monastic property had certainly not meditated on such questions. Things that rigorists called debauchery could also be seen as a return to the life of secular people, and this life had its approved order. Here two normative systems were in conflict. One could understand monks who chose the easier way instead of the harsh path of monastic virtue.

Conversely, it was also possible that people undertook hard and even dangerous things in order to obey demands of custom that conflicted with their office. German bishops saw no contradiction in military service as duty owed their lords or as a moral proof of loyalty. There was also compliance with the demands of primitive norms of ancient times, although both ecclesiastical and secular authorities rejected them. This was true especially of the obligation of members of a clan to avenge the murder of one of their number. In the Carolingian period, traces of the vendetta were found even among the upper clergy; during the tenth century it persisted among the common people. When priests acted as confessors, they had to ask whether penitents had "killed to avenge their kindred." Even Burchard of Worms allowed his *familia* blood revenge; he only wanted to limit it to the next of kin. The obligation of revenge for members of the upper classes was no longer universal, but still traces of such attitudes and actions can be found.

Liutprand repeats a story which must have seemed believable, namely that King Lambert of Italy fell victim to revenge at the hands of a count's son. Rodulf Glaber reports, without comment, that the grandfather of the reforming abbot William of Dijon, a Swabian warrior, took revenge and had to emigrate to Italy. At issue was a man's honor, the violation of which could only be washed away with blood. This was an attitude which continued even into our own century in the nobility and above all in the officer corps of European armies. The honor of one's class demanded what was forbidden by the state. In the intervening centuries the manner in which blood revenge was practiced had been refined. The duel was ritualized even in its most minute details.

Revenge and feuding served to reestablish violated rights, which are elements of the objective system of law. The right of feuding had been preserved especially where the king's power was weak, and all that could be hoped for was to reduce the number of feuds. Revenge and feud could merge into each other; they often were two sides of the same coin. Since 1006 a bitter feud had been waged between two comital families and their followers on the lower Rhine. When the leader of one party, the Billung Count Wichman, was murdered, the bishop of Münster assembled the inhabitants of the region and their neighbors (*conprovinciales et affines*) "to avenge this deed," and together they laid siege to a castle, whose surroundings were laid waste by fire and sword.

SECULAR MEANS OF COERCION

Legal punishment was supposed to be impartial and humane and thus did not satisfy the passions as did revenge and feuding. The upper strata were normally exempt from physical punishment and execution. Only later did government return to the use of blood justice for this class. Ordinary people were sentenced to whipping, had their heads shorn, or were literally branded as criminals. Such punishments did not decrease the labor force, of which the lord was constantly in need. In the ecclesiastical sphere, only nonphysical punishments were available. It is not surprising that they did not always satisfy the offended kin of a murder victim. The *lex talionis* (an eye for an eye and a tooth for a tooth) seemed appropriate. Even Immanuel Kant defended its use in cases of premeditated murder. People's sense of justice was offended when the wealthy could escape punishment in secular courts by paying fines, and even ecclesiastical penalties could be paid in money. The less well-off could decrease their penalties at least in part by reciting psalms and other prayers. In times of peace, order could be preserved to some extent with such measures, but not when there was feuding among rival kindred or interest groups. This was especially true in the kingless territories of France, where a telling event illustrated the principle of *lex talionis* and the duty of revenge. Eblus, the bishop of Limoges, learned that the chorepiscopus Benedict, whom he had wanted as his successor, had for that reason been blinded by count Elias I of Périgord, thus making him unfit for the office. "And therefore Eblus was filled with a very great and unbearable pain until the day of his death." The count of Poitiers advised that Elias too should be blinded. Elias escaped, however, went to Rome as a pilgrim, and died shortly thereafter. The affair could have ended there, but emotional excess claimed another victim. Count William of Poitiers had Elias's brother imprisoned and blinded "as revenge (*in ultionem*) for the chorepiscopus Benedict." The brother was certainly innocent personally but, as kinsman of the offender, was a fitting victim for accomplishing the obligation of revenge. Wherever no one was looking out for the order of the state, customs reemerged from times when there was no state.

EXCOMMUNICATION, ANATHEMA, INTERDICT

In kingless countries, the clergy had to function as forces of order. This was no light obligation since they were themselves often drawn into conflicting groups and formed part of the rival parties. We are told that the laity could ravage each other by robbery and fire only because the bishops were divided and whatever hurt the one was good for the other. When one bishop repelled a person, another received him. Since monks had no ecclesiastical power over the laity, they had to limit themselves to impressive but juridically irrelevant rituals. Enemies could be cursed but not excommunicated; the populace could be denied entrance into the church, but an abbot could not impose an interdict on a locality. At Saint Martin of Tours, the canons closed all but one of the doors of the church with thorns and placed their reliquaries on the church floor in order to display their need for assistance to the people and to pressure the saints to aid them.

Spiritual punishments always depended on the good will of the offender and of the Christian community. Personal penance, most often fasting on bread and water or making a pilgrimage, could be performed in a very lax manner. Public sins were to be expiated through a public punishment under the control of the community. The punishment could not be replaced by payment. It was intended primarily to dishonor the individual and to lower his social prestige. Everyone could see the sinner standing outside the church door and appearing last in processions. When this punishment was not effective, the sinner was excommunicated. The community was expected to cooperate by boycotting the excommunicate. Since people rarely received the sacraments, exclusion from them was not as hard to bear as exclusion from the Christian community, which left the sinner on his own without "friends" and neighborly assistance. Excommunication really worked, and it is no wonder that it was employed with increasing frequency. When the number of excommunicates rose, the boycott diminished, and churchmen had to find other means to raise its efficacy.

Simple excommunication could be increased to solemn excommunication—anathema. In earlier times such a complete and ritually enacted exclusion from the community was almost exclusively reserved for heretics. The fact that they had separated themselves from the Church needed to be made clear to all in order to create a sort of *cordon sanitaire* around them. If they continued to be tolerated and supported, or if the situation developed into a public separation of a community from the ecclesiastical authorities, the final resource was interdict. When a church, a settlement, or even a whole diocese remained without divine services and sacraments, innocent people were among those affected. They were expected to pressure the guilty to bring about a change in their attitude and thus lead to the lifting of the sanctions.

This coercive measure, originally conceived as a self-purge of the community from rebels and other sinners, was used increasingly by public authorities for various purposes. Charles the Bald had ordered that a counterfeiter should suffer, along with the secular penalty(the loss of a hand), public ecclesiastical punishment imposed by his bishop. This indicated the close relationship between the altar and the throne. The reason given by the bishop was that a counterfeiter was a despoiler of the Church (*sacrilegus*) and a despoiler of the poor. In Germany, excommunication later became a direct consequence of outlawry. The coercive authority of the king and his representative, the count, shifted into the proximity of the bishop's authority. Both issued commands under penalty of punishment, and each complemented the other. In France, excommunication served as the most important means for the establishment of episcopal lordship. This was true not only for exterior policy but also for the treatment of vassals. Bishop Fulbert of Chartres wrote to his vassals in Vendôme: "I call upon you in the name of God, in the name of Saint Mary, and in our own name, that you come to us in the approaching Easter season either to perform your services or to submit your fiefs to a proper accounting. If you do not do this, I shall excommunicate you for your disloyalty. I shall forbid you to hear Mass, to receive Communion, and to receive a (Christian) burial. I shall even place the castle of Vendôme and its territory under anathema so that no Mass can be celebrated and no one can be buried there . . . May God convert you, my sons."

Later, Bishop Fulbert wrote to King Robert of France to complain about the viscount Geoffrey. The viscount, said Fulbert, feared neither God nor the king. Recently he had rebuilt a castle that Robert had destroyed. The pain of the bishop was so great over this manner of behaving that he celebrated the divine liturgy in a quiet voice instead of in loud jubilation. The king, he continued, should order the castle destroyed once again. If he does not, "lasting confusion (*confusio*) will reign in our city" (which was threatened by the castle), for Fulbert would forbid the celebration of the Mass in his entire diocese. In conclusion he wrote that he hoped that he would never be in the position of declaring, as a fugitive, that the king had been unable to protect him.

Today we tend to see this mixture of politico-military interests and unctuous discourse as the expression of a cynical, purely pragmatic frame of mind. This was not at all the case. According to the testimony of the apostles, all authority came from God and every person was subject to one of his representatives. He who opposed one of them opposed God himself. If this was true of secular authorities, so much more was it true of bishops. We know from the history of the investiture controversy with what perplexity, and for how long, people tried to deal with the problem of separating the religious from the nonreligious sphere of the bishop. His word was the word of

God—not only in questions of faith and morals. Rebellion remained rebellion, even when it was over feudal issues, and it could be countered with spiritual weapons.

Opposition to the use of excommunication as a punishment was expressed occasionally, especially by anyone who feared that he himself might be inflicted with it. During the episcopal conflict in Reims, Gerbert of Aurillac wrote that if a person who took his own life or the life of another was called a murderer, then the same could be said of one who took eternal life from his fellow human beings. In this case he meant papal excommunication. Nevertheless, the clergy was justified to a degree, in taking the law into their own hands in the face of the limited effectiveness of the usual penitential system and the lack of security against aggression. Bishop Fulbert too saw himself as already fugitive in spirit. If the episcopal lordship in the city should collapse and the episcopal estates should be destroyed, a crisis would arise in the spiritual domain too. It was the bishop's duty to prevent this.

Granting all of these circumstances, the objection remained that an ultimate and extreme means of repression and discipline was being used for routine purposes and thus was becoming progressively less effective. For example, when ecclesiastical property was usurped by laymen, it was insufficient to excommunicate the perpetrator. Even papal excommunication lost its effectiveness: "Because these things occur so often, they are less and less noticed by the stubborn. They abandon the fear of God and attach themselves to worldly justice, they seek lords to protect them, they build castles, and through (ecclesiastical) punishment they grow worse" instead of better.

Even when excommunication was obviously being abused, those affected were expected to obey the sentence. At the second synod of Limoges (1031) the question was asked whether an innocent, unjustly excommunicated person had to accept his sentence. The answer was affirmative in keeping with the decision of Gregory the Great: Just or unjust, whether the party was guilty or innocent, the excommunication was valid. The synod ignored the fact that this means of coercion had become widespread. A pastor once ordered his community to attend two Masses on Sunday instead of one, and he excommunicated a physician who complained about it. The account of this affair is accompanied by complaints about degenerate people (*degeneres homunciones*) who believed that they could disdain excommunication.

Some difficult cases developed into general scandals, such as that of the castellan Walter of Cambrai, who was excommunicated because of his actions against the city's bishop Gerald. Walter was murdered as he prayed outside the door of the church that he was not allowed to enter. As he lay dying, he indicated repentance and the desire for reconciliation, but the bishop nonetheless denied him a Christian burial. (Strictly speaking, this was correct, since the excommunication had not been lifted.) Walter's widow then ordered the area around Cambrai ravaged. Finally the count of Flanders and the archbishop of Rouen arranged for the castellan's body to be transported to the monastery of Saint-Amand, and, after absolution, the deceased was buried there.

The less these episcopal sentences were in conformity with canon law, the more they provoked the indignation of the laity. Rather wrote, "The reason that they care so little about our excommunications and absolutions is that they know, as far as they can understand it, that we too are excommunicated through the holy canons and that no one who is himself bound can bind or absolve others on his own." In a town such as Verona, the weakness of the episcopal position must have been better known than in predominantly rural dioceses north of the Alps. But even in rural areas there were cases similar to that of Cambrai, mentioned above. Everyone there could see that church law was being manipulated by its wielders. Bishop Gerhard excommunicated "robber" laymen, and the archdeacons of the bishopric of Liège absolved them in return for gifts of land or money. In his long letter of complaint, the bishop hinted that the archdeacons were justifying such actions by the need for investment in their districts.

The more frequently a sentence of excommunication was delivered, the more people were drawn against their will into an uncanonical situation. Everyone was expected to avoid contact with the excommunicate; in urban situations this was often impossible. Automatic excommunication threatened anyone who took part in a meal or an assembly at which an excommunicate was present, even if participation was for entirely peaceful purposes. Abbo of Fleury confronted his kings Hugh and Robert with this fact when he admonished them, "Cleanse your kingdom from the evil of excommunication." Abbo continued that there was hardly anyone in the kingdom who was not excommunicate for having been in contact with another excommunicate.

For the severing of bonds to family, neighbors and friends, and for the boycott to become reality, a simple order by church authorities was too little. A similar situation arose in the Jewish communities, where some people shared their meals with those who had been excluded from the community and even did business with them. In order to raise the efficacy of excommunication, old Christian curse formulas used against heretics were repeated, and new ones were invented which must have struck terror in the populace. Against the murderers of Archbishop Fulk of Reims (900), the clergy recited such prayers as: "May they be cursed in the town and cursed in the fields, cursed be their granaries, their mortal remains, the fruit of their bodies and that of their fields, their cattle and flocks. May all be cursed who enter or exit their houses . . . May they render up their bowels in the latrine like the perfidious Arius." Such terrifying images of the agrarian world and the history of heretics were followed by references to the curses of Moses, the Apostles, and the Church Fathers. A most impressive ceremony followed the verbal anathema pronounced by the assembled bishops: they held tapers in their hands, which were extinguished with the explanation, "Just as these tapers fall from our hands to the earth and are extinguished, so shall your light be extinguished in all eternity."

If the sinner repented, the solemn anathema was lifted with equal solemnity. A synodal pronouncement was not always sufficient. In some cases, the curse, possibly on the specific request of the individual concerned, was annulled by an opposing blessing: "May you be blessed in the town and blessed in the fields, blessed be the fruit of your body and the fruit of your fields and vineyards . . ." Blessings or curses were the alternatives for an unstable humanity in a period filled with excitement and danger. The language of the clergy contained threats and curses even where hardly appropriate. A prayer confraternity of Roman clerics served the purpose of celebrating Masses for deceased members. "May whoever does not obey this be bound by the chains of anathema and separated from the kingdom of God," read marble tablets in some churches of Rome announcing the agreement. The oaths of fealty sworn by the archbishop Arnulf of Reims to the kings Hugo and Robert included these words: "Should I depart from this oath, may all my blessings be turned into curses, may my days be shortened, may my bishopric be given to another, may my friends depart from me and become my eternal enemies."

In charters that were drawn mainly for rational, juridical purposes, the punishments of hell were depicted with relish in the framework of the "spiritual penalty formula," which presented the grue-some details as they lived in the popular imagination. Charters were sometimes read in church during religious services. Frequently scribes went too far, as in the diploma in the name of Pope John XIII for Arles, which was a forgery. Here anathema was pronounced against all those who did not follow the papal will. Like Dathan and Abiron (in the Old Testament) they were to disappear from the earth. Like Judas they were to suffer the torments of hell by eternal fire and worms that never die. God was to send them plague, want, fever, cold and heat, ulcers, scabs, madness, blindness, and, in turn, the fatal disease of Arius. They were to be cursed in sleeping and cursed in waking, in eating and drinking, in hunger and thirst—the enumeration could go on and on. The author knew nothing of the rules of rhetoric, which stipulate that speaking too long in a pathetic vein may effect the opposite reaction from that which is intended.

ANTICLERICALISM, ARELIGIOSITY

When anathema was pronounced not on a specific person but on an unspecified group of people who might at some time begin to act unjustly, it lost some of its desired impact. People became somewhat accustomed to such formulas, just as they seem to have done, increasingly, to interdict during the tenth century. The bishop of Orléans had placed the city under interdict, but King Robert nonetheless announced a court diet to be held there at Christmas. This was a blow directed against the bishop, who was having a conflict with the pious king. Fulbert of Chartres, who had to support his fellow bishop, wrote to Robert II that it was inappropriate that at such a holy time the royal court should be without religious services. For himself, Fulbert had an elegant solution to the problem. If the king did not change his mind, Fulbert would stay in a monastery near Orléans and celebrate Christmas there. What might the citizens of Orléans have thought of the effectiveness of an interdict that was circumvented or ignored by the highest clergy?

Obviously, anticlerical remarks seldom appear in ecclesiastical historiography. Yet Thietmar notes, concerning Otto II's military expedition against the Danes, that "during this expedition the first expressions of wicked mockery of the clergy were heard. Wicked people use them even today . . . Many do not really mean their ridicule, but it still remains a hateful sin." The peasant girl Flothilde had a good opinion of ecclesiastical dignitaries. In a vision she saw many people who had been sent to hell and still more who had been saved from it. Among the latter were high-ranking persons (*maiores*): archdeacons, priors, judges, stewards, and deans. But the same girl also spoke of things she had surely heard about from her acquaintances. She spoke of priests who lived with women and who were unworthy to touch the relics of the saints; priests did not know a single letter of what they read (in the liturgy). In her village, people probably had a high opinion of the dignitaries they saw only occasionally, while the parish clergy were observed very closely.

It meant little that the soldiers ridiculed the clerics who marched with them, or that peasants were not happy with their pastors. The situation was more serious when laity came into conflict with clerics, feeling this as their duty. Bishop Gerhard of Cambrai, the immovable defender of the interests of his position, believed that there were some people who clamored against the Church from earliest childhood until their death, and that excommunication had no effect on them. There must have been real bitterness toward the clergy—an attitude which, under the influence of misfortune, could lead people to partial or full disbelief. We have already spoken of the citizens of Liège who disavowed divine providence after the defeat of the episcopal lord of their city. Everything, they contended, takes place by chance. Many people maligned Count Ansfried of Brabant, who in later life was named a bishop and led a strictly ascetic life. One of his flock expanded his criticism to questions of faith, and ventured in the alehouse that the human soul was nothing and disappears with the last breath.

Another comment, which went still further, Rather himself claimed to have recently heard from the mouth of a bishop. The writings about hell fire, the bishop said, were all misleading. The Gospels had been written on sheepskin, and so one reads such things on sheepskin. According to Rather, this meant that "in the Gospels, truth and falsehood can be told." In those days a bishop in northern Italy could only hold his position by committing sins. Rather himself was not entirely free of sin, though he loved to reprimand others for their sinfulness. Was his opponent in this debate just bluffing, hoping to silence him, or had the bishop elaborated his own version of Christianity?

In light of such statements, perhaps we should not always regard such things as simple "rhetorical elements" or as survivals of Germanic pagan thought. The number of such comments is noticeable in the writings of Gerbert of Aurillac. One, in particular, is relevant to their evaluation because it deals with the relationship of *fortuna* to faith in God. "Some things happen by the will of God, others by blind chance." Here God is not the absolute lord and guide of the world but rather a divine being (*divinitas*). He shares the direction of the world with the impersonal power of chance. Thus one can assume that incomprehensible events which appear incompatible with God's goodness derive from this latter power. Gerbert had received the monastery of Bobbio through the free will of the emperor, but chance had wanted things differently and he had been forced to give it up. That Hugh Capet became king was supposed to be regarded as the will of God. Yet Gerbert wrote that *fortuna* had given him to the Franks as their leader. His comment was certainly well thought out and represented a sublime position to take on the rise of a new dynasty.

Concerning the religious attitude of the Byzantine historian Procopius, a contemporary of Justinian, Karl Krumbacher has written: "He did not notice, or at least did not mention the fact, that antiquity's *Tyche* (Fortune) could not be reconciled with Christianity." Procopius spoke at times of God, at times of the divine being (*theion;* Gerbert wrote the Latin equivalent, *divinitas*), and at other times of the goddess Tyche. Gerbert's terminology reminds us of the reserved attitude of the Byzantine, although no literary relationship existed between the two. Pagan antiquity played virtually no role in his writing except as a literary model—Gerbert took from it what corresponded to his own thought. Archbishop Adalbero of Reims, in whose name Gerbert wrote letters, must have approved of his opinions. The two were not alone. For example the priest Gerhard spoke in his letters to Archbishop Friederich of Mainz in several places of deceitful Fortuna and her wheel of fortune. Thietmar of Merseburg recounted that the indecisive result of a skirmish between Danes and Angles was attributed by both sides to chance. On this the bishop commented, "We, however, are forbidden by Sacred Scripture to believe that anything is done by fate or chance." Thietmar did not say that such an opinion was unreasonable; he simply bowed to authority in a problem on which he apparently had reflected. He could also have cited Jerome and Augustine, who considered it necessary to combat their contemporaries' belief in Fortuna.

These examples suggest that people in the Middle Ages were not simply continuing a literary tradition when they spoke of Fortuna. At least in part, such expressions reflect a timeless way of thinking. One can believe in God, or one can doubt that events have a meaning, and this was equally true in the Middle Ages. In rare instances it led not only to doubt but to despair and to the extreme of suicide.

Still, most sources were too laconic to provide a glimpse into the souls of people who had grown skeptical. Gerbert limited himself to hints, and Rather's self-revelations in his confessional dialogue did not lack a touch of the theatrical. Readers were supposed to notice the conscientiousness with which the author decried even smallest misdemeanors and how he drew upon himself all of the evil circulating within the clergy. He was not prone to gloomy speculations, but he did have a lively imagination, and we can believe him when he says that it was not the desire for heaven but the fear of hell that determined his actions. Despair (*desperatio*) was marginal to his catalogue of sins. It was enumerated along with its opposite, presumption, and the other vices. A genuine depiction of doubt, both of the existence of an all-powerful God and of the truth of biblical revelation, first appeared later than the period of our study. Its author was the monk Otloh of Saint Emmeram in Ratisbon, who lived between 1010 and 1070. He noted a contradiction between the pious discourse and impious actions of his contemporaries and transferred this to the authors of the books of the Bible. Might not everything in the Bible about God and the Christian religion be lies and delusion? If, as was taught, the statements in the Bible had a spiritual meaning deeper than their literal meaning, could they be taken literally at all? Paul had written, "The letter kills, the spirit (that is, the meaning) gives life."

It is possible, even probable, that people a couple of generations earlier had had similar independent thoughts, without committing them to writing. Otloh did write about his doubts, because he had later conquered his skepticism. Only for this reason could his writings survive, classified as edifying reading for his brethren. If this monk had developed his theses otherwise and disseminated them in another manner, he would have entered the history of the Church as a heretic.

For many centuries, very few heretics appeared in Europe. Evidence of them becomes more frequent following the millennium, and it is debated to what extent heresies were an eastern import or, rather, original products derived from reflection on opinions such as those discussed above. One thing is certain: not only the political unrest of the period contributed to the critical examination of Church teaching and the growing independence from it; another factor was the gap between reality and ideal and the competition between varying normative systems. Sociology describes this as "anomie," a concept which has recently entered historical literature. Old orders had lost their vitality and the new had not yet appeared, so that there was room for "wild" thinking and actions.

THE SEARCH FOR FAITH: JUDAIZERS AND HERETICS

Openness to the Jewish community provided a sort of transitional zone to heresy. Jewish scholars could provide alternative answers to a cleric's questions of doubt, as well as an alternative lifestyle based on a strong, fixed legal structure. The Christian clergy's relations with the world of Judaism ranged from cooperative business ventures to theological disputations. A Jewish physician and expert on the Old Testament who was respected at the court of Conrad II was said to have been defeated by bishop Wazo of Liège in a theological debate.

As early as the ninth century there had been the sensational case of the conversion to Judaism of a court cleric of Louis the Pious. Agobard of Lyon complained of Judaizers who, without daring to convert, preferred to listen to rabbis than to Christian preachers, followed Jewish dietary rules, and kept the sabbath. Under Henry II, probably in 1012, a cleric who had belonged to the court of duke Conrad (of Carinthia) announced publicly his adherence to the Jewish faith. The result was a short expulsion of the largest German Jewish community, that of Mainz. We also have reports, admittedly uncertain, about Judaizers. Just as one of the weapons of political propaganda was to impugn the morals of one's opponents, one could accuse them of heresy in a strict or a general sense, and also of sympathy for Judaism.

Heresy is known to us only through the writings of its opponents, which are imprecise and often adorned by imagination. So it means little when we hear, in one case, of a relationship between the Monforte heresy and Judaism. It was characteristic of all these religious quests that they did not yet adhere to any existing heterodox community but were, rather, spontaneous (though some may have resulted from an "awakening" by foreign missionaries).

Some have seen these heresies as a socioeconomic movement of rising urban strata. In fact, accounts of heretics are found among various social groups, high and low, and among both clergy and laity. The first contemporary account concerns a peasant from Champagne named Leutard who taught other rural folk, "since the peasants are so credulous." A short time later we read in the same author of a heresy in Orléans whose leaders were two ecclesiastics "who were by origin and knowledge honored among the clergy." The trial of this sect took place before the king and not without reason: the sect, which had already existed for some time and had undertaken missions as far as Rouen, included among its members a confidant of Robert the Pious and the confessor of his wife, Constance. That learned theologians of such high rank could have been "baptized by a peasant (*rustico*), who believed he could work miracles" and distributed a powder made of dead children, certainly suggests a confused account, mixing two different cases. During a visitation in 1025, a group of people was discovered who, in accord with the Gospel, wanted to live by the work of their hands and who told of a man from Italy, who, along with others (craftsmen?) had come into the region. These people understood no Latin, since the text of their excommunication had to be translated for them into the vernacular. On the other hand, around thirty freeholders assembled along with the countess on the above-mentioned castle of Monforte d'Alba (near Asti) in a spiritual renewal. This vivid image indicates that heresy was a general phenomenon and not just a problem of one social group.

The rare accounts of the teachings and life of these heretical groups can hardly be reduced to a common denominator, although such a reduction has occasionally been attempted in the search for a relationship between them and the eastern Bogomils. Their teachings were usually negative; that is, they rejected a part of the Catholic creed or interpreted it in a different way; the heretics nevertheless felt themselves Christians and shared a strong ascetic tendency. It was a spiritualization of piety and a free form of grouping on the periphery of the hierarchy, both characteristics reminiscent of the eremitic movement. If people were prepared to go to the stake for "pure doctrine," it must have had vital power. Heretics and hermits removed themselves from the entanglement and disorder of secular life, from which sensitive souls have always suffered. Hermits sought solitude while most heretics found a new basis for spiritual existence in this world.

18 · LIES AND DECEIT

WHAT IS TRUTH? WHAT WE CONSIDER IT to be is not always the same as that depicted in medieval poetry, edifying literature, or even legal-historical records. Adalbero of Laon has his king say: "It is wrong to call true what is not true. Fables are no equivalent of truth and do not pretend to be true." To which the bishop answers, "Look, I have spoken the truth. You know that the truth has not been violated. Know that things did not happen (as I have written them) but that everything could have happened thus." In a context of this kind we would speak of verisimilitude or the "inner truth"—of a poem, for example. The idea that simple truth is that which corresponds to reality was affirmed a thousand years ago with the modification by theologians that there were several types or levels of reality. The highest reality is God. The least reality is the external appearance of things. Not only the books of the Bible have a *sensus anagogicus,* a meaning which refers to God along with a literal and symbolic meaning. Truth is that which leads to God. Many falsificators meant to serve heaven, as did authors of saints' lives when they recounted miracles without having reliable witnesses for them. On the other hand forgeries and lies received harsh verdicts. As in the case of legal and other norms, contradictory attitudes could coexist in people's minds, usually without causing any concern.

Letald of Saint Mesmin in Micy wrote the life of Saint Julian based on evidence of which he said, "Much is found in the *Acta* of the above-mentioned father that one finds written in the same sense and almost in the same words in the acts of the martyrs Saint Clemens and Dionysius as well as in the life of the holy Confessor Furcaeus." This did not at all lead him to reflect on the value of such sources in general. He wrote that he was not certain which of the *vitae* deserved more belief, but that in any case he believed in the merits of Saint Julian. Only truth pleases God. Letald rejected those who wished to serve the reputation of a saint by lying and invention. He contended that just as the saints themselves cannot have been liars, one should not tell lies about them.

LITERARY TRUTH AND FICTION

We should not doubt the honesty of this author, although his assurance that he is telling the truth and nothing but the truth is an old topos. Similar assertions by another author appear more questionable. We have already spoken of Saint Martial of Limoges and his propagandist Ademar of Chabannes. What Ademar claimed went beyond edifying invention. His polemic aimed to convince people that there were numerous manuscripts of the life of Martial in Gaul, Spain, England, and Italy. (In reality there was only one, and it was hardly a generation old.) Since the text was so widely disseminated, "what devil would have dared to write a lie" about the apostolic rank of the saint? Who would have believed it? Ademar affirmed that this was the truth and that he believed in the *vita* as he did in the holy gospels. His apparent fervor may well have indicated a bad conscience.

Another intermediate area was that of the lie made in jest, which the wise recognize as such, while the foolish are taken in by it, thus demonstrating their simplemindedness. This sort of lie was common in the world of entertainers in order to amuse their audiences. But it was also present in ecclesiastical schools for *pueruli*, twelve- or fourteen-year-old students learning Latin. In the earliest extant poem of this sort, we are told of a clever man who cheats even the king in this manner. Other longer, often almost obscene poems of this genre were intended for adults. The *Modus Liebinc* tells of a woman who lied that the snow had made her pregnant, and of the husband, who countered her lie by claiming that the African sun had melted her child—he had sold it into slavery. We also hear in the frequently mentioned poem *Unibos* of the cunning lies of a peasant. The fact that all of these stories are transmitted in Latin indicates that the genre also found a home in educated circles.

In the second strophe of *Unibos* we learn that this poem was presented at "the table of a great prince." Since the parish clergy is criticized, the poem may have been the product of young "clerics" who were singing the praises of cleverness—a virtue particularly important at court.

Duping, and being duped, was already an old tradition in Roman mimic art and comedy. There were no obstacles in presenting such things to the Saxon canonesses of Gandersheim if the dupes were heathens. So the princess Constantia, who had dedicated herself to God, could devise the ruse by which the general Gallicanus was to be tricked out of the reward for his service—her hand in marriage. That the setting of this comedy was the imperial court, and that courtly life of Ottonian times saw many intrigues, may have increased the effectiveness of the play. At Gandersheim, girls were educated for the life they would lead later, not only in a convent but at court or elsewhere.

Playful familiarity with lies and deception contributed to cleverness, or wiles in the struggle of life. It was not without reason that Benedict of Nursia had expressed the desire that monks returning to the monastery from a trip should not share their experiences "in the world" with their brethren. Such reports might undermine religious edification, resulting in the dissolution (*destructio*) of spiritual values. In spite of this prohibition, monastic historiography is full of anecdotes and accounts of secular wiliness, perfidy, and intrigue. Many authors must have acquired their knowledge of these from the stories told by their brethren. Appropriate disapproval of such events was seldom expressed.

Cunning

Ekkehard IV of Saint Gall tells the following story of Bishop Salomo of Constance and Archbishop Hatto of Mainz, who were friends. "Both were great jokers, and so there was a wonderful rule in their friendship. Each tried, whenever he could, to fool the other by tricks in words and deeds." By a trick, Hatto obtained a golden drinking cup from his friend's possession. Later, Salomo took advantage of Hatto's absence to spread the rumor of the latter's death so that he could dispose of Hatto's episcopal property, and ordered the cup melted down for a reliquary. The charm of this and other anecdotes for contemporaries lay mostly in the fact that the trickster formally appeared to be in the right. The dupe remained not only disadvantaged but ridiculed until he could avenge himself in a similar manner.

What in this case was a game, a measuring of forces with an eye to public approval, could turn to very serious actions with grave consequences. Otto of Freising had read of one of Archbishop Hatto's tricks that was "still today being transmitted by the uneducated populace at inns and resting places and at courts." It was toward the end of a serious feud caused by the Frankish counts of Babenberg (Bamberg) that Count Adalbert had entrenched himself in his castle. Hatto lured him out of it, promising safe escort. After a short ride together, Hatto persuaded Adalbert to return for breakfast in the castle. With this, the escort had come to an end, and when the two departed again, Hatto could deliver Adalbert to the king. "Adalbert reminded the bishop of his oath, and the bishop answered that he had kept his promise and had escorted him safe and sound to his castle." Adalbert was, Otto wrote, of simple disposition in the manner of the magnates of his own day. So he noticed the deception (*dolum*) too late. He was executed in 906.

Some magnates tried to exonerate the king and the archbishop. It was contended that Adalbert had surrendered with the crafty intention of launching a new revolt after the dissolution of the royal army, and that he was beheaded for this reason. Deception was imputed to the deceived, and a predetermined intention to commit a crime was postulated and punished with death before it could be carried out. This version of the affair was not accepted by public opinion. Adalbert remained alive in popular memory as a victim of shameful treatment.

Where was the line between permissible, praiseworthy deception and scandalous fraud? Even the concept of military deception did not exonerate everything that people did to their enemies, as the story of Adalbert attests. On the other hand, the necessities of the time constantly presented situations in which lies and fraud seemed the only way out. Every statement could have a hidden meaning, every negotiation could be carried out with fraudulent intentions. In important affairs, therefore, the honesty of promises had to be secured by means of the mutual renunciation of fraudulent actions. Thereby immoral but formally correct acts became fraud and oath breaking. This solution was hit upon early, and was practiced particularly in the realm of treaties. The oath of fealty of a count to the bishop of Gerona in 1034 can serve as an example: "From now on I, Roger, will be true to you, bishop Peter, with proper faithfulness, without deception (or cunning) as a man should be to his lord, without any conscious deception (of the lord)."

The word "cunning" (*calliditas*) was nearly always used in the tenth century with a positive connotation. The Saxon Thietmar was praised by Widukind of Corvey for his good advice and because "he outdid many mortals by his innate cunning." The same was true of the untranslatable word *ingenium*, which meant neither ingenuity nor genius but, rather, an innate set of human characteristics including various individual virtues such as strength of character, intellectual ability, and, of course, cunning. Their evaluation is complex. Otto III, in his well-known letter to his teacher Gerbert, expressed the desire that the latter would awaken in him the *ingenium* of the Greeks, which in this context referred especially to scholarship. Likewise, in various directives, including some of Otto III's, we find a condemnation of the *(malum) ingenium* of those who circumvent laws and commands. Enfranchisements, for example, were revoked if they had been effected through trickery. In Provençal, the word *engan*, which meant both "cleverness" and "trickery," was also used for a machine of war, hence the modern term *ingénieur* (engineer), one who builds machines.

To clerical authors this middle ground between good and evil appeared quite attractive. We have already spoken of Ekkehard IV, who told of an alleged plan devised by King Conrad of Burgundy to defeat simultaneously the Saracens and the Magyars. Full of noble trickery, *nobili astutia*, he was said to have stirred up both peoples against each other and promised both that he would give them military assistance. Ekkehard describes with delight how "Satan's chosen warriors and sons" attacked each other and how the survivors were defeated by the Burgundians and sold into slavery—an understandable wish-fulfillment without any historical foundation. Thietmar of Merseburg and Richer of Saint Rémi are fond of describing the deception of enemies by disguises. They were used not only by spies and assault detachments but also by nobles. Rodulf Glaber tells how the Bretons, before a battle with the supporters of Fulk Nerra, dug a trench, covered it with branches, and, during the battle, lured their enemies into it by simulating a retreat. Rodulf judged this "very clever" of the Bretons, that "clever people." Still, he called it disgraceful fraud, since he was on the side of the enemy.

Clerics were often aware that deceitful acts could not be their practice. The martial chess game at Einsiedeln was justified by the comment that chess included no trickery or artifice. True, the players had to keep the rules. In doing so, one could nevertheless lead one's opponent into various traps, in the Breton manner. Descriptions of bishops often emphasize their lack of duplicity and mental reservations, for which we could conclude that this lack was not self-evident. Clerics urged that the conduct of war not be based on deception. In military conflicts only God was to decide, not human cleverness. When military ruses or fraud were employed, they were sometimes excused by reference to the inequality between the military strength of the opposing forces.

Experience in warfare was listed among the "good arts," along with rhetorical skill and the art of advising. This latter term had a positive and a negative side. Again we must cite Archbishop Hatto of Mainz. According to Widukind he had a piercing intellect, and it was difficult to say which was greater, the positive (political) or the negative (moral) quality of his advice (*melior consilio foret an peior*). The word used here and elsewhere, *consilium*, meant more than advice given others. It included diplomatic or political affairs, and the art of intrigue, for Widukind connects the above-cited words in a reference to the trick which cost count Adalbert his life. Widukind tells another story of how Hatto of Mainz, "with his usual art (*arte solita*)," strove for the death of the Saxon duke Henry (later king Henry II). The duke was warned not to appear at a banquet at which a murder would be attempted, and Hatto "realized that an end had been put to his machinations." Hatto died soon after, sad and ill, and there were some who believed he had been struck by lightning. Widukind carefully refrained from making the kind of moral judgment of the facts he recounted that one might expect from a historian. Nor was he the only one to do so.

Certain historians sharply condemned the unchristian actions of magnates. Some who have the highest offices, wrote Alpert of Metz, carry on against Christian justice in a way that even the common people could not do. Virtues have become vices; not honesty and faith, but the quest for fame and power prevails. All humanity and decency have been forgotten. Just as Tacitus portrayed the Germanic peoples of his time as models, Rodulf Glaber praised the half-heathen Normans, their loyalty, the way their magnates preserved the peace in Normandy, their honesty in business dealings. Criticism of an epoch is more effective when a contrary image can be offered, either of the "good old days" or, still better, one from the present. The author of the *Ruodlieb* chose a third way. An inhabitant of the kingdom of the dwarfs explains that falsehood does not exist there. If things were different, says the dwarf, "we could not be so old and healthy. Among your kind, people only speak with lying hearts and for that reason you do not live to a ripe old age. The age of a person is in proportion to his truthfulness."

Loyalty and Disloyalty

Nusquam tuta fides: Gerbert used this Vergilian citation to justify his desire to deal with the bishop of Pavia over conflicts concerning Bobbio property in writing only, and not in a meeting (*colloquium*). It was not the usual complaint about the decadence of the present but a position with practical consequences. Since the use of letters was inconvenient for both parties, there must have been concrete reasons to use them. In unquiet and insecure times, great caution was required even in dealing with members of the clergy. The great reform abbot Abbo of Fleury himself was described by a royal scribe as having "lost truth." Abbo denied the accusation with a remarkable comment. God alone is good; all creation is changeable, and therefore the words that creatures speak are changeable also. The comment is a form of syllogism which could be used to justify a change of opinion, or worse.

Among the laity, in times of political unrest one could seldom afford sincerity and faithfulness. One need only read Dudo of Saint Quentin, whose history of the Normans constantly tells of treachery, ambushes, and broken treaties. The victims of these acts were usually Normans, especially the duke. Liutprand of Cremona complains about similar behavior in the Mediterranean world and quotes a

Greek saying about the Marquis of Iverea: the length of his sword was in inverse proportion to his loyalty. Atto of Vercelli, as much a realist as a moralist, characterized the undermining of bonds of fealty as a tool of political intrigue and as a possible means of rising in one's career. From Saxony, Widukind and Thietmar tell of dirty tricks used not only in struggles against foreign enemies but also against rival nobles. One had a bad opinion particularly of one's neighbors: the Saxons willingly believed that the Byzantines were capable of every vice. According to Liutprand, the emperor Nicephoros Phocas was similar to Odysseus in his perjuries and lies. He might have found even worse comparisons in the Bible.

Survival in such an environment was certainly not easy, either for the great or for their masses of helpers and advisers. A highly educated man dedicated to scholarship, like Gerbert of Aurillac, appears in an ambivalent moral light when we read the letters he composed for others. For Duke Charles of Lower Lorraine, he composed a polemical letter to bishop Dietrich of Metz. At the same time he wrote a letter of praise dedicated to the same bishop and termed him an "ornament of the Roman Empire." He claimed to have modified the tone of the attack in Charles's letter by making an inexact translation out of affection for the bishop. Gerbert clearly found himself in a difficult situation. That he had only a mitigating influence on Charles's text is questionable given its literary quality. Gerbert probably collected his letters himself, and his pleasure in artistic accomplishment may have outweighed his concern that readers might appreciate his strength of character less after having read the correspondence.

More than eighty (or 50 percent) of the letters in Gerbert's collection were written on demand and thus under the mask (*ex persona*) of others. Others were written in his own name but on behalf of the archbishop of Reims or other magnates. Applying this talent to playing the role of others did not cause Gerbert to lose his own personality, though he had to make great concessions. Given the poverty from which he had risen in Aquitaine, we must not blame him for his desire for material security. Now he had houses in Reims which he had commissioned and many servants. He had received churches as gifts, held archiepiscopal fiefs, and, after his retreat from Bobbio, he kept "the best portion of his household furniture" in Italy. All these acquisitions were constantly threatened by changes in politics. We can nonetheless see that Gerbert followed a consistent political line, whether from conviction, from gratitude to the emperor who had given him Bobbio, or from political intelligence. His attachment had its natural boundaries, however. Abandoned by the imperial government, Gerbert recalled his fidelity up to that time and indicated that he might have to give it up. He had lost Bobbio and had not received so much as a single manse as compensation. How long, he wondered, should he remain faithful to the emperor?

In the context of feudal law, the question was entirely appropriate. A response soon became necessary. Charles of Lower Lorraine came to Reims. Gerbert's enemies controlled the town, and the only alternatives were flight or abandoning the imperial party. "We cannot oppose fleeting Fortuna, and the deity does not tell me in which harbor she offers me safety." Thus Gerbert did homage to the Carolingian.

This event has been described as "the most puzzling moment in Gerbert's life," and later he bitterly reproached himself for it. "People consider me fortunate," he wrote, "because I survived the change in power. But I consider myself unfortunate. I seek worldly things, I find them, complete them, and am, so to speak, a leader in crimes." Shortly afterwards he changed parties again, which brought him closer to his early position. He went to Hugh and Robert at the royal court of Senlis. The lack of a sure place of refuge, mentioned above, explains why Gerbert had not done so immediately. It was probably only now that the two kings offered him a material basis, which made it possible for Gerbert to give way to his conscience. Now he was in a safe port, and as a philosopher he quoted Cicero's famous words about the useful and the honest (Cicero had put the *honestum* before the *utile*) to which he had directed his thoughts. A great sorrow, he wrote, had left him.

In the case of Gerbert we have focused on the detailed reflections of a man confronted with the problem of political disloyalty. Gerbert's was a very sensitive nature. Still, we can assume that most of the vassals in this epoch suffered from conflictual situations. We can even say that Gerbert had it easier than most of them. He was a loner and did not have to weigh the interests of his family against those of his feudal lord. In the period of tension between east and west and of latent or open civil war, it was particularly difficult to solve these problems.

Some of the letters Gerbert prepared offer good examples of conflictual situations. His patron, Archbishop Adalbero of Reims, was accused of infidelity and treason. Adalbero's nephew had received the bishopric of Verdun from Otto III, and the archbishop had participated in his consecration without royal permission. Both were members of the family of the counts of the Ardennes, who sided with the Ottonians in their fight over Lorraine. Should the archbishop have separated himself from his family in order to show his fidelity to the king of France? He asserted that he wished to do so but he had first to obey the divine law. "Because only few people in these times have foreseen the will (of God), we are charged with infidelity or some other crime when we pay attention to the law of the Lord. So we are caught between the hammer and the anvil, with little hope to escape without damage to body and soul."

We can believe the archbishop that this was a real conflict of conscience. Such cases seem to have found the understanding of contemporaries, while infidelity for one's own benefit or for subjective reasons were more strongly condemned. This was true of Lorraine, in any case, where a relative of Adalbero of Reims, Bishop Dietrich of Metz, allied himself after the death of Otto II with Duke Henry (the Quarrelsome) of Bavaria out of aversion for the empress Theophanu. It was said that everyone who heard of this treason, from the lowest to the highest, abhorred the crime. The report that Dietrich died of sorrow over his sin is the naive cliché of a chronicler.

OATH BREAKING AND PERJURY

Where the balance of power between two parties was as fluid as in France during the second half of the tenth century, it was best to remain on good terms with both parties. This course was facilitated by the institution of double vassality. As a count of Troyes or Chartres, one could survive only if one were a vassal both of King Lothar and of his opponent, Duke Hugh Capet. Double vassality usually developed from situations other than politics. Indirectly it was connected with factionalism: lords needed more vassals than they could properly provide for. Vassals needed a second lord in order to have enough to live on, and they provided only specifically delineated services to each lord. The importance of fealty was weakened, a phenomenon which involved both great and small vassals and gave them room for political maneuvering. In Italy, according to Liutprand, people wanted two lords "in order to restrain the one through fear of the other." Fidelity became a rationally calculated factor of political and military conflicts, even without double vassality. From the sum of feudal bargains—fiefs for vassalic obligations—parties developed with which one could oppose other parties. With such a development the feudal oath lost much of its sacral nature. We must not forget that the oath is "a self-imposed curse. The oath taker stakes his salvation on the veracity of his word." In a penitential which circulated under the name of bishop Fulbert of Chartres, the spiritual punishment for oath breaking was as high as that for murder or sodomy. The penitential collection of Regino of Prüm places the penance for clerics at two years of excommunication, which also means prohibition of exercising their office during this period. "If I were to assign the penance prescribed for oath breaking, which of you could I then permit to celebrate Mass?" asked Rather of Verona of the priests of his city. He wrote that members of his clergy had remarked that they knew perfectly well they had promised upon oath many things they could never do. Oaths had become the small change of everyday life, both for clerics and still more for the laity at every social level. What everybody did was often done without reflection, just as perjury is more or less tolerated today in certain regions. When Duke Hugh of Francia had sworn two contradictory oaths, he ordered a magnate who was well known for his finagling to free him of his obligations through some sort of formal sophistry (*aliquo sophismate*). We are not told whether the duke's conscience bothered him when making this arrangement. Merchants engaged in trade with England were known for their incessant perjury.

The peasant girl Flothilde received the commission from Saint Peter and the Virgin in her fever-induced dream to instruct the count of her region that he should forbid the inhabitants of his territory from swearing oaths too frequently and, above all, to forbid swearing by the love of God. People were constantly pledging the salvation of their souls or other valuable goods. At the synod of Trosly the assembled bishops complained that people were fearlessly swearing by God and all the saints, by relics of the saints, by their own souls or by those of their parents and friends. Thus, the bishops said, people did not greatly value their salvation or that of their loved ones. Oath swearing was a bad habit, but it was also a matter of coercion. For forced oaths the synod of Hohenaltheim lowered the ecclesiastical penalty for perjury. In place of seven years of penance, those who had perjured themselves "out of some necessity" were obligated to only three. Like the fathers at the synod of Trosly, Abbo attacked the error that false oaths were either minor sins or no sins at all. He nevertheless differentiated sharply between freely sworn and forced oaths, and he compared the latter to forced baptism: there was to be no external compulsion in religious affairs. The person who forced someone to swear an oath, not the one who had been forced into perjury, was to be condemned.

Forced oaths were primarily judicial oaths, the normal means of uncovering truth. Later, Henry III forbade ecclesiastics, at least, to swear judicial oaths, a prohibition which did not exclude the normal oaths to secular and ecclesiastical superiors. As early as 967, the Italian magnates petitioned the emperor to alter the legal practice of their land so that deception by means of perjury in legal proceedings could be eliminated. This was the result of a specific case concerning an impeachment of charters whose authenticity was established by means of oaths. When a forger swore to the authenticity of the charters, he won the disputed property—"a detestable custom" by which the wrongdoer acquired a material gain and subjected his soul to eternal loss. It was decided that the contesting party should be given the choice between the oath of his opponent and a judicial duel. Elsewhere too, for example in the collection of Burchard of Worms, the judicial duel began to displace the oath in ever greater proportion. A method of proof that appears irrational from a modern perspective was being replaced by an even more irrational method. While the fear of the loss of salvation led people in some cases to speak the truth, now the judgment was left to God alone because of the supposition that God had to help the innocent. The innocent party may well have fought with more sangfroid and judgment, but physical ability and practice were of paramount importance. So one often relied on a substitute to fight the duel.

People sought to prevent the devaluation of oaths by arranging that the spiritual self-damage to the perjurer would be spelled out in great detail in his own words. The result was various forms of potential self-malediction, either by one's own free will or by compulsion. When the Carolingian Arnulf wanted to become archbishop of Reims, the new king Hugh extracted from him a written statement of "anathema by self-malediction" should he be unfaithful. The assembled bishops further demanded that Arnulf should take up the body of Christ at the Mass, repeating his oaths of fidelity and self-curse.

A few bishops had reservations on this point. They believed it was contrary to faith to force someone to receive the eucharist and to swear an oath on it. The affair ended to the satisfaction of those who had counseled caution. Troops of the Carolingian party entered Reims, and Richer maintains they could do so in consequence of a secret understanding reached with the archbishop. This prelate was said to have ordered that the keys to the city doors, which were kept under his pillow, be stolen and given to the followers of Charles of Lower Lorraine. Thus he was formally innocent of breaking his oath to the king.

What appears to us as pure fraud may have been a final attempt of the Carolingian party to expel the usurper Hugh Capet from power and to reestablish the divinely willed control of the legitimate dynasty. If forced oaths were unlawful, one did not have to keep them. People complained that under such circumstances the honesty of one's fellow humans could no longer be trusted, and that important social structures were breaking down, but they could do nothing to change the situation.

Deceit and the Family

If no public help was available during periods of civil war or weak regencies, one would expect that at least the clan and "friends" would have stuck together. It appears that people differentiated between perfidy to outsiders and perfidy to members of their own circles. Infidelity among kin was often designated as such. When the wife of a count secretly sent word to Bishop Wazo of Liège that he should come with armed men to capture her husband, Wazo was said to have answered that a wife had never yet betrayed her husband with impunity, because this clearly contradicted human nature. The woman had stated that she hoped her actions would prevent infidelity on the part of the count, who, though the emperor's vassal, had sworn a pact with one of the latter's enemies. We see here a detail of the game of political intrigue in which the magnates were so often involved. The bishop's answer speaks of the possibility that the countess was only pretending to betray her husband. Was the count attempting to escape his obligations to his partner, and thus to remain faithful to the emperor?

Lies and treachery have often poisoned relationships among close family members, especially during conflicts over inheritance. Ademar of Chabannes describes a particularly vicious case. Two brothers were fighting with a third brother over the possession of a castle. Count William of Angoulême forced them to swear peace on the relics of Saint Eparchius. In spite of this oath, the two invited the third brother to dinner, captured him afterward in his sleep, blinded him, and cut out his tongue. The count revoked their fiefs after he had besieged and destroyed their castle. The affair was told in the sober style of the chronicler, with no other comment than that the evil deed took place during Holy Week. This must have significantly increased the horror of clerical readers.

The many disputes in the Ottonian family are well known. They more often resulted in open rebellion than in covert intrigues. Thietmar of Merseburg, two generations later, tells of preparations for the deposition of Otto I which, while not credible, indicate what was considered possible. Thietmar relates that Bruno of Cologne, in spite of his wisdom, was convinced by bad advisers to return to his royal brother evil deeds for good. Mindless of his kinship and his oaths to Otto I, the archbishop wanted to hand over the kingdom to Duke Hugh (of France) who was "very unfaithful." Bruno had had a crown made, together with insignia and a robe (*instrumentis regalibus*), in order to crown Hugh during the feast of Easter. Then, Thietmar continues, he changed his mind but still wanted to keep his promise. A good adviser suggested the way out: Bruno should go to the coronation but simulate an accidental slip so that the crown would "be smashed." No sooner said than done, and the duke left Cologne uncrowned. This may have been an example of a common anecdote, an *exemplum* of cunning advice on how one could formally keep one's word and actually not have to do so. Obviously it is difficult to smash a crown or to believe that an archbishop of Cologne could have agreed to crown a foreigner without previous election. Recently it has been suggested that the story had a kernel of truth. In this case it could have been an attempt to elevate a French anti-king in Lorraine, or an action of duke Giselbert of Lorraine, the stepson in law of Otto I, on behalf of Louis IV of France. Even if it is entirely fictional, there remain the words of a son of Otto the Great in reference to his own family: "It is unspeakable, and one cannot tell without tears of the betrayal in which the father betrays the son, the son the father, a brother another brother, like Cain and Abel, and one kinsman the other. All order and every kindred is despised (*Omnis ordo omnisque cognatio detestatur*)."

19 ✒ILLEGITIMATE POWER

LEGITIMATE FORCE WAS ACCEPTED AS THE
natural means to reestablish order where other
means had failed. It ranged from the birching,
in the home and school, to the wheel and the
gallows, and to just war, the definition of
which people did not much worry about. In
cases of orderly assumption of control, the legitimacy of force had to manifest itself. Whenever possible its exercise was a public performance. People saw that all was functioning
properly and thereby were dissuaded from disorderly behavior. The reestablishment of the
divine order was celebrated. Ritual elements
were found not only in justice but also in war-

fare. In some cases the analogy to legal actions went so far that the opening of hostilities was announced like a court diet, or a battlefield was mutually agreed upon.

War and Feud

In its essence, war was and always had been aggression, in forms also practiced by individuals. According to ancient custom, and much like a barroom brawl, hostilities might begin with depreciating the enemy and praising one's own qualities. Boasting and insulting by the opponents took place before battle. Exchanging heated words was customary. Then, when the warriors were sufficiently stirred up, the violence began, announced by a "terrible" war cry. Aggression was unleashed, yet the army was expected to fight in an "orderly" manner and not to thrash about wildly. It was difficult to maintain a balance between discipline and passion, and by this balance the experienced warrior was distinguished from the masses.

The ritualization of war did not usually go beyond such details. Declarations of war were so rare in the period that they seem not to have been expected. True, in many cases preparations for war must have been known of by the enemy and thus replaced the declaration of a state of war. Practical reasons may also have played a role. Sending a delegation to the enemy risked having its members taken hostage. In the smaller arena of feud, the peace movement established the essentials of an order and a certain limitation of hostilities. The modern theory of the protection of noncombatants took the form of immunity for certain persons and of the partial rejection of scorched-earth tactics. Further, there were places of peace, mainly churches and monasteries. There was no mention of an obligation to announce a feud or to agree on the place of combat.

As for the difference between war and feud, we must forget the modern idea that warfare is the business of the sovereign state and feud was a feudal abuse. Considered realistically, the difference was mainly one of scale, which in turn required different behavior. A party fighting pitched battles put all its money on one turn of the card. Small skirmishes indicated the limited forces of the persons conducting the feud, as did the systematic damages on the enemy's territory. Both left open the possibility of peace without a decisive victory or total defeat. What peasant swarms or mounted squads could accomplish was the continuation of political pressure by other means and, often, a strategy of attrition. Such a war was the destruction of things rather than the killing of people. This was not only true of feudal powers. When King Louis IV besieged Reims in May of 945, the cornfields in the area were systematically laid waste, villages were wrecked "and partially burned," and even churches were damaged. The king's decision to use Normans for these actions probably effected the unusual degree of damages.

Hrotsvitha of Gandersheim correctly noted that the civil wars between Otto I and his brother had harmed the people (*plebem*) more than foreign wars had. Since foreign wars were carried out in foreign lands, they had a greater effect on the middle and upper levels of society. Civil war and feuds could result in general impoverishment and lead to famine. When Henry II crossed the Metz area in his feud against his Luxemburg kinsmen, eight hundred members of the cathedral *familia* left without permission "because of hunger and other troubles." Others were given permission to leave by estate managers.

Louis IV used "Christian" Normans as auxiliaries, while Henry II used pagan Slavs against his brother-in-law, the bishop of Metz. The Slavs not only destroyed the surroundings of the city but also a monastery in the area. Henceforth such actions were forbidden, and the king paid for the damages out of his own pocket. Here too one can attribute the high level of destruction to foreigners. Lothar I had already used pagans against his brothers. The destruction of churches was not unique to non-Christians. After the election of Henry II, which was not recognized in Swabia, "a mob of accursed Alemanni, always ready to loot, rushed into the cathedral of Saint Mary (in Strasbourg) without the duke's knowledge . . . , pillaged the entire church treasury, and—their worst crime—set fire to the house of God." Even this was a way of conducting a feud, and not mere pillage. In times of need the church treasure was the war chest, and a bishop who lacked one could accomplish little. For many years afterwards, much of the bishopric's financial power had to be dedicated to making up for the loss.

Not only military necessity but individual interest too played a role. Only what could not be carried off was destroyed. Easily transportable booty included expensive furnishings as well as people, who could later be freed for ransom. Recruited troops seldom received wages. Instead, they signed up in return for the promise of spoils. This was very likely true of the Normans, who were called upon for help by French kings and magnates in disparate situations. Both pay and booty were abundant in 1010, when the general of a rebel faction in Islamic Spain enlisted Catalans to plunder Cordoba. Shortly afterwards they were defeated by Berber reenforcements. Many of them drowned in the Guadiaro River because they were overloaded with booty. Yet enough of the riches taken from Cordoba remained for Ermencol I, count of Urgel, to be able to send Saint Peter's in Rome 100 ounces of gold, a fabulous sum at the time.

When Christians entered Islamic service and heathen Slavs were used against Christians, the argument of the "just war" vanished. War became simply a means of conducting power politics or economic speculation. Since it involved great risk, it must have offered the possibility of high returns. The Hungarians thought so, and— after their settlement in Normandy in 911—so did the Normans. Valuables could be found in large quantities mainly in episcopal cities and in a few monasteries, and so the pillagers often had to content themselves with human booty. When the Hungarians laid waste the area of Capua in 937, "they took many of our people hostage. For their ransom we paid a great amount of money," noted the chronicler of Montecassino. Such accounts are common.

Means of Repression

It would not have been so bad if the Hungarians and Normans were the only ones who took hostages. According to Widukind, after the heathen Saxons had won a battle against the Thuringians, they killed all of their adult captives and kept those not yet grown (*inpuberes*) as booty. In the Christian period, Henry I—and not only he—acted in the traditional manner of his tribe when he invaded Slavic lands and ordered similar treatment for the population. Heathens had no place in the Christian order and could be dealt with as those "barbarians" had been who lived outside of the civilized world of ancient Rome. Even Conrad II had "a great number of captured heathens" blinded and maimed because they were said to have mutilated a statue of Christ. Not only Byzantines but western communities in Italy too had their captives mutilated although they were Christians. These were acts of revenge, which were also supposed to inspire fear and to intimidate the enemy. The fact that these acts could incite the opponents to commit similar deeds was taken for granted, as with blood vengeance.

In the ancient Orient such gruesome acts had had a quasi-ritual character. In the more or less Christian West, they did not become general. When they are described, they are presented as isolated instances which one would rather ascribe to the frenzy of licentious soldiery than to the orders of the commander. We may wonder to what extent they were the result of yielding to the desires of troops that had lost their inner balance of discipline and emotion. The killing of enemies in battle already contradicted Christian teaching. When killing or mutilation were extended to prisoners, the limits had long been passed.

Alongside such peripheral phenomena, the very center of Christendom harbored tendencies toward disintegration. Discipline and order were sometimes minimal. Liutprand depicts the disunity within the army that confronted the Hungarians in northern Italy: many hoped for the death of their neighbors and did not stand by them in battle. Thus both fell together. The "neighbor" (*proximis*) was at once the person who stood next in a line of battle and a member of one's clan, and so we can understand what Liutprand meant when he wrote that the reason for such unsupportive behavior was the desire to rule alone. It must have been still worse to fight in a civil war when the summons to duty had not taken into account relationships with members of the opposing troops. This may have been one reason why Hugh Capet avoided a decisive battle when he faced the army of Charles of Lower Lorraine, which was much inferior in number. Richer reports that the king had qualms of conscience about the injustice of his cause. The other reason may have been that the troops felt they should not deprive the last Carolingian of his life and property after taking his kingdom. The two armies stood facing each other for a while, and then Hugh ordered a retreat while Charles entrenched himself in Laon. For a third time he was besieged there by Hugh, and again the local population suffered under the besiegers' pillaging.

The recurring dream of the peasant girl Flothilde a few decades earlier—that she was being chased by armed men who threatened to throw her into a well—may have reflected a general anxiety in times of war. In any case, throwing people into wells was a simple way to make wells unusable. Houses and fields (at harvest time) likewise were easy to destroy if one had a fire starter handy. According to Adalbero of Laon, mounted warriors carried these on their belt. They consisted of flint, steel, and dry oak rod. Destruction had its natural limits, however. The effectiveness of mounted warriors depended on the availability of fodder for their horses, for one could not rely on the animal's foraging wherever camp was struck. In winter months, the much-abused population could breathe more easily and rebuild their cottages. It was noted as exceptional when warfare took place during winter. Further, it seems that troops ordered to destroy a district did not always go to the limits. For the most part, they themselves came from the segment of the population that was entirely bound up with agriculture, and their hearts were not always in the work of destruction. In this context, destruction has been described as having been carried out "with more ostentation than efficiency." Moreover, destroying vineyards and fruit trees was hard work and required the proper tools. As to dwellings, in southern lands dismantling whole stone structures instead of simply burning their roofs would have been an even harder assignment. Warriors have seldom considered themselves laborers; cavalrymen prefer a quick engagement followed by a quick disappearance. They had orders to carry out, but their interest lay elsewhere, at least in part—with livestock, which they could drive off and sell, with booty, and with captives, of whom we have already spoken. In the course of the great feud among the nobility in the Rhineland, people bemoaned the fact that the troops fighting on one side frequently had to decamp and could earn only limited "wages," which meant principally booty. This was seen as a disadvantage to the "righteous cause" of the party.

One could certainly fight because one was convinced of one's right and not simply out of economic considerations. Justice was usually not seen in the abstract, as an objective norm, but as a remedy for a subjective right that had been violated. The subject could be one's own person, a family member, a lord, or the *familia,* including friends and neighbors. There was no need for the ancient, deeply rooted obligation of revenge in order to prepare for military action. After a true revenge expedition, no vineyards or fruit trees were left standing. Torture, mutilation, and killing of the "enemy" population took place. Destruction and terror practiced against the innocent was sometimes based on an attempt by the weaker party to win the respect of the opposing party by extreme means. A bishop of Como deposed by Berengar II acted in just such a manner. Liutprand included among his acts the depopulation of the region, cutting down vineyards and trees, and blinding many people. The same bishop was reproached by Atto of Vercelli for protecting himself by armed force, avenging himself by raids and destruction, enriching himself with booty, and spreading fear by killing and mutilation. Atto regarded behavior of this kind as the domain of evil spirits rather than of Christian bishops.

The more unjust and oppressive such acts were, the more they elicited similar counteractions. It was no longer a matter of a few horsemen but of the collective revenge of the rural population under the command of their ecclesiastical or secular commanders. Such activities, at least where there was no judge, provoked acts of counter-terror, so that more and more people became involved. The escalating violence might continue for years. A prolonged feud occurred on the Lower Rhine: the Wichmann factions, centered on the right bank of the Rhine, fought under Henry II against the Balderich clan on the left. The conflict may have been fanned by regional feeling, "Gallia" against "Germania." More modest conflicts were pursued over specific subjects, such as the possession of a monastic *villa* in Burgundy between the family of a castellan and the *milites* of Auxerre. What apparently began as a legal process became a "war" during the grape harvest, with many dead on both sides. Eleven sons and nephews of the castellan were killed, and there followed "innumerable deaths for thirty years and longer." Possibly the chronicler exaggerated, but there were other cases of vendetta from generation to generation. The castellan and his *familia*—that is, his family, the servants of the household, and the peasantry—were all involved. We are told that the *familia* avenged itself "by the killing of enemies."

It was not anarchy that prevailed but the order and social obligations transmitted from a period preceding statehood. Clerics had remarkably little trouble in making the terminology of blood feud their own. While remarkable for the modern reader, that ability was less so in an age in which revenge, retaliation, and punishment could be expressed with the same words. We speak of war in the context of states, of feuds in the context of the old nobility, and of blood revenge as a marginal phenomenon of the lower classes in southern Europe. In the tenth century a feud was practically a war of one group against another in which vengeance played a role. We should not use the term "anarchy" of a time in which peace was the norm. Neither "private warfare" nor conflicts between different systems of order are limited to the so-called feudal period, and the outdated term "feudal anarchy" should finally disappear.

Theoretically, feuds could take place only in situations of lawlessness. Where no legal solution could be expected, especially in areas lacking any central authority, people naturally looked to self-help. Yet even today in many countries the common people distrust anything involving lawcourts. They try to conclude things peacefully or by force, without bothering the authorities. The result is often unequivocal. If the decision is accepted by those involved, the affair is settled. But where the parties' awareness of being in the right or their sense of their own prestige prevent such a solution, a lasting enmity may begin. Hostility may not manifest itself right away. A person may wait for a favorable opportunity to pay back the offense.

One might suppose that only laity held such attitudes, and that churchmen would speak words of peace. We have already described a situation in which the opposite was true. We will add one notable comment because it was made by a man whom we usually regard as particularly intellectual. Gerbert of Aurillac, while awaiting a decision on his fate in the episcopal conflict of Reims, wrote: "A fight with weapons is more tolerable than a legal battle." He had already spoken of those who sought to use the law (*legibus*) to wreak vengeance (*ulcisci*), which they had been unable to achieve by force. Gerbert ascribed this strategy to his enemies, but in the following sentence affirmed it for himself: he was prepared to "fight out" a legal contest.

For the upper classes, the "legal feud" existed throughout the Middle Ages and into the modern period. It was merged with Christian teachings insofar as it served to reestablish the justice desired by God and functioned as a sort of trial by ordeal. The requirements that no one should be killed in the feud and that any resulting damages should be made good remained purely theoretical and were part of the contradictory mentality to which people had long become accustomed. Besides, there was no authority to determine which party was in the right. One was inclined to consider oneself in the right even when it was a matter of extending possessions, winning new vassals, and raising one's prestige.

This "right" was often a pure formality, allowing people to pursue under the appearance of legitimacy the politics of power, which inevitably led to open confrontation. A good means to this end was the construction of castles on one's own property but at strategic locations that could be dangerous to one's opponents. Bishop Balderich of Liège (1008–18) built the castle of Huguard (now Tirlemont) on his allodial property only twenty kilometers from Louvain. Unsurprisingly, the count of that town saw the construction as reason for a feud. He was excommunicated. In the ensuing battle, the bishop's men were defeated. It was a case of self-help because a continuing threat to the town would have damaged trade and thereby the existence of the citizens. Elsewhere, questions of prestige played a major role. How these questions were resolved had material consequences too. In the Lower Rhine confrontation mentioned above, Wichmann built a castle against the party of Balderich because "the location was ideal for the acquisition of the office of count." On the other hand, Balderich thought he would lose much of his dignity and power through its construction. Even Cluny was threatened for a time by a castle which had been erected by one of the counts of Mâcon "against the monastery."

Historians have spoken of constructing "defensive" and "offensive" castles as the two means of carrying out "castle politics." There are numerous examples of a historiography eager for sensations. It sounds plausible when we are told that a count's son built a castle against the city of Cambrai and undertook raids from the castle in order to force the inhabitants of the area as well as the citizens of Cambrai to pay him tribute. A second castle erected even closer to Cambrai was meant to increase the pressure. The bishop destroyed it when it was nearly completed. During the uprising that Ernst of Swabia, stepson of Conrad II, undertook with an "army of youths," Ernst sought to build a fortress near Solothurn and repeated this attempt above Zürich. He clearly intended to exercise pressure and to prepare for the subjugation of the population.

Both of these cases are different from that of Cambrai, where the appearance of legitimacy was retained since the castles were built on the count's property. By contrast, in war, or in a warlike operation involving rival camps, no one was concerned with legal niceties. Perhaps the role of armed politics was to avoid the outbreak of direct hostilities by preserving the appearance of legality. It was a game with high stakes, which could be lost through a military reaction since the bishop or count who destroyed an offensive castle greatly increased his own prestige and was honored with high praise. We can assume that the prestige of the loser decreased.

What has been termed "castle politics" was determined by the concept of consolidating existing rights; it served to expand control by quasi-pacific measures. Richer tells that a count of Troyes strongly desired to obtain possession of the royal castle of Dijon. He did this "because he believed that if he could acquire the castle from him (the king), he could bring the best portion of Burgundy under his control." By this time, territorial history was already being dominated by the struggle for castles. That struggle was the primary content of a toilsome arrangement between lords in Aquitaine; it was the thread running through Abbot Hugo of Farfa's account of his efforts to reclaim his monastery's property. The struggle was accentuated by the appearance of newer forms of construction, which made it more difficult to take castles by storm. With not only earth and palisade defenses but a stone tower, one could withstand a long siege. The peasants were doubly burdened in such cases. First they had to carry the stone and work it, and later they suffered under a long siege. The assailants laid waste all possible resources "so that they could not be used by the people in the castle." Hostilities sometimes broke out between one tower and the next within a single city. These could go on for a long time, especially in France, where there was frequent conflict between bishop and count. In Amiens in 950, the Capetian Hugh the Great and his warriors were admitted into the tower held by Bishop Reinbald. Hugh besieged the other tower, held by the followers of count Arnulf.

In France, feuds and civil wars merged into each other; in either case they were likely to be conflicts over rights claimed by one of the parties or individuals. Nothing could be accomplished by legal means. Things should have been different under the control of an apparently strong monarchy, such as that enjoyed by Otto I in Germany. But there were feuds even in Saxony, the center of his power. The Saxon nobility would not put aside the good old custom of feuding when the king attempted to eliminate it. In 938, at the court held in the palace of Steele (near Essen), "even those who claimed that they had not acted against royal power but had simply avenged injustices that had befallen their kinsmen were convicted as disturbers of the peace." The sentence declared that they had disregarded the king's order, but since the accused had not appeared, the king postponed execution of their penalties and later pardoned them. "But this restraint led to even more pernicious acts, for many unjust deeds were begun by the perpetrators: killings, perjury, depopulation, arson. People in those times made little distinction between right and wrong, between sacredness (of oaths) and perjury." Widukind's words suggest that things improved later, but no basic change took place.

HOMICIDE

In "just feuds," lay custom allowed killings as in a royal military expedition (*bellum publicum*). It was more honorable to kill an opponent in open combat than to draw him into an ambush and thus into a militarily disadvantageous position. Still, the latter was a military tactic often described in feuds. The final and most radical tactic was the silent assassination of an opponent. We call this murder, but the tenth century used the word *homicidium* to include murder, manslaughter, and unintentional homicide. Free men who had committed one of these three crimes were usually fined. Only later would corporal punishment be extended to the middle and upper social strata. The unfree did not always face the death penalty either, especially in cases of revenge.

The fact that murder and killing were not daily occurrences can be ascribed only in part to Christian religion and ecclesiastical penance. The killer and his kin had to reckon with the vengeance of the victim's clan. Besides this, there was the judgment of public opinion. If negative, it could entail the destruction of social existence; the perpetrator had to flee and thus lose his property. If people were convinced of the justice of the deed because it had reestablished the proper order of things, they would sympathize with the perpetrator. For example, the marquis Borrell of Barcelona, illicitly, as all could see, effected in Rome the reestablishment of the archbishopric of Tarragona in order to strengthen his regional lordship. At the same time the bishopric of Gerona, which was held by an opponent of the marquis, was supposed to be placed under the control of the new archbishop. The bishops of Catalonia, previously only nominally dependent on the archbishop of Narbonne, thereby received a lord, but not for long. In the same year, the archbishop was murdered. With this murder the earlier situation was reestablished. No feud with all its bloodshed could have attained this goal.

While hardly anyone felt compelled to react to the killing of the archbishop, in the Lower Rhine feud the head of one faction, count Balderich, was generally suspected of having murdered his opponent Wichmann during his return from a banquet, and so "all agreed that they hated him." Balderich barely escaped an attempt at revenge. Authors constantly expressed indignation at monks who killed their abbot, even if the deed was done to resolve the question of a monastery's reform. After Abbo of Fleury perished from a lance blow on a reforming expedition in Gascony at the monastery of Saint-Réole—the particulars remain obscure—a circular was quickly prepared in his monastery to prevent suspicion falling on anyone. It announced that lucky Abbo, by the sword of the Basques, had become a companion of the holy martyrs. Murders of ecclesiastical and secular magnates were usually carried out not by their principal opponents but by their subordinates, so that the guilt remained in doubt. This was the case in the murder of Wichmann, in that of Archbishop Fulk of Reims by a vassal of Count Baldwin of Flanders, and in many other cases. Murder by poisoning was often suspected, though it seems that most of these suspicions were fantasy.

Some historians have lamented "the moral savagery which reveals itself in such acts." This observation is inadequate. Rarely, it would appear, did people lightly undertake acts for which they risked eternal hell fire. Rather, there were questions of honor, or of property that people believed they were entitled to. Simple greed or pugnacity were seldom the motives for murder, at least in the middle and upper strata of society; among "reasonable" killings are to be included those by monks who did not want to allow their lives to be reformed or who had been offended by their abbot.

Murder and manslaughter in the monastery were seen as particularly evil because people there were supposed to devote their thoughts and efforts to things not of this world. But in public opinion, and under ecclesiastical influence, homicide by laymen was also judged harshly, and the perpetrators were believed to be destined for hell or for purgatorial fire. Around 900, possibly in Provence, the report of a vision was drawn up which served political purposes but also showed a very negative opinion of the ecclesiastical hierarchy and the secular magnates of the late Carolingian kingdom. Archbishops and bishops stood in ponds of boiling pitch, sulphur, and lead because in life they had sown discord and had "loved" killing and robbing. "Innumerable souls of vassals (*hominum*) and magnates (*principum*)" of the late Carolingian family suffered on fiery mountains. They, together with Charles III, had taken part in battles, killings, and robberies "out of earthly greed." The visionary was hailed with a cry that could be a motto for the age, "The mighty will suffer mighty torments."

ROBBERS AND SO-CALLED ROBBERS

The vision just described was concerned with the ecclesiastical prohibition against killing in warfare. What is normally called robbery is given another name when done during wartime. The suggestion that archbishops and bishops "loved" robbery seems strange to us. But this was no isolated case. We are constantly told that nobles followed such pursuits. It was suggested that it might be monastic tradition to call lay perpetrators of violent acts *latrones* and their violent acquisition of property *latrocinium*. There were cases in which an "unjust" feud was so described. Twice we are told in Richer of forts which the king besieged and had destroyed because robbery expeditions and plundering were launched from them. In the first case, the "small" people among the besieged were released, and only the chief of the *latrones* was brought before the king. He was supposed to be beheaded—riffraff were hanged—and obtained royal grace at the request of the archbishop of Reims in return for an oath "from now on to rob no more." In the second case, too, an oath (which later in Germany would have been called an *Urfehde*) was sufficient.

There are some excellent but, in these matters, entirely misleading sources. One of the most impressive cases occurs in the *vita* of Bishop Burchard of Worms by one of his clerics. Duke Otto and his son Conrad owned a fortress with towers in Worms, in which, we are told, robbers and thieves and anyone who opposed the bishop found refuge. The result was mutilations and killing "on both sides." The text had already described Worms in the time when Burchard became bishop: the town was suited not for human habitation but for wild beasts, especially wolves. Walls and moats had been leveled, which allowed wild animals to enter the town, as well as robbers, who favored the place as extremely well suited to their crimes. If a citizen did not do their will, they attacked him at night, took all that he had, and left him dead or half-dead. So the citizens left the town and fortified themselves without until Burchard had built a new wall.

This not altogether credible story served to establish what the reader had no doubt already expected, that feuds within a city could only be conducted successfully when each party had its stronghold in it. The city castle of Worms and the territory surrounding the town was in the hands of a family later called the Salians, the coming dynasty. They were counts of the Wormsgau. Their leader was Otto, duke of Carinthia, a grandson of Otto I and son of duke Conrad (the Red). Members of this noble family and their servants were the "robbers" of which the bishop's *vita* spoke. The situation in the city of Worms was similar to that found in many French towns: feuds started up between bishop and count; with time, they often led to a division into *ville comtale* and *ville épiscopale*. At Worms, things would be settled otherwise: After a time of feuds between the two parties, Burchard supported the election of Henry II on condition that he should be the sole lord of the city. The new king kept his word, and the bishop destroyed the count's fortress.

In modern law, "robbery" is defined by statute, and in specific cases a court determines whether it has been committed. In the Middle Ages, "robbery" was a popular term, both richer in connotation and less specific than in our day. The word "robber" designated both the professional criminal and anyone, even of high status, who was guilty of unjust and forceable removal of goods. That the goods had been removed illegally did not necessarily have to be established. A subjective opinion was sufficient. Clerical historians voiced that opinion, and people understood what was meant. Otto of Carinthia and his family, among them the younger Conrad, the opposing candidate in the election of Conrad II, had done wrong. The bishop and those he protected had done right. As for the "wolves," they were part of the *coloratio,* the rhetorical decoration of an account that one learned at school.

There was no lack of real robbers and robber bands. They were not clearly distinct from the groups of evildoers described above. Who were the militarily competent and valiant "thieves and robbers" that Henry I armed and encouraged to commit "robberies" against the Slavs? Some historians have argued that they were lesser royal vassals and freemen, while earlier writers had described them as an "army of criminals." In Saxony, as late as 1017, professional warriors were engaged to fight judicial duels against robbers, who were hanged only after they had been defeated. These were free men or men who claimed to be free.

In Italy, Berengar I constructed castles against Magyars and "evil Christians," who have been seen either as local functionaries with their armed retainers or as "magnates and their lieutenants no longer reined in by royal command." The monastic history of Farfa speaks of "petty Christian robbers" (*latrunculi christiani*) who had begun their crimes out of need. Their actions have been ascribed to an "endemic banditry" as opposed to professional criminality. Such terms reflect the deep crisis of the early tenth-century Italian countryside. Was the rural population responding to the fights between magnates and the ineffectiveness of royal control? The question cannot be answered with any certainty.

Elsewhere, peasants revolted, as in Normandy under Duke Richard II concerning seigneurial rights over forests and fishing. In Frisia some of the population withdrew into a forest area, where they constructed new settlements. These colonists "joined with robbers and gravely damaged the business of merchants. Later on they were subjugated by robbers, who allotted land to each peasant for clearing." Robbers in the modern sense would hardly have acted as landlords. From the community of colonists a new elite arose, which was responsible for defense, land divisions, judicial matters, and the collection of tolls. The use of the term "robber" to describe this elite indicates that this was a new creation outside of traditional lordship.

Peasants sometimes had to deal with real robbers when they were forced into vagrancy. Odo of Cluny tells of one who, "out of fear," became a member of a band that was making the forest an unsafe place to live. Vassals of count Gerald of Aurillac captured and blinded the whole band, including this peasant, who was innocent. Later he wandered on to the Toulouse area and was there supported by the pious count. On the other hand, hungry people may have received food from such ruffians and—willingly or not—remained with them. That robbers felt at home in the forest led people to associate the forest with robbers. A gorge made a good hiding place, too, as the Waltharius shows. It was wise to pass through such places in a group and, if possible, armed. When a monk from Saint Gall went through a forest "which was advantageous for robbers," he took two servants with him, one of whom carried a shield and a lance. Together, the three of them put two "very bold" robbers to flight.

The two robbers had apparently wanted to take the monk's horses, since a monk would have had little else of value. Rodulf Glaber mentions the "rarely heard" fact, in connection with a famine, that people were sometimes "attacked in order to be cut up and devoured." Here we must be careful. This practice was described as part of the terrors which happened before the year 1033, that is, the millennium of the passion of Christ, and the chronicler did what he could to report the most gruesome details. We are told that people offered travelers a night's lodging, strangled them, and devoured them; that people lured children for the same reason by offering them an apple; that in the county of Mâcon, in the Cluny area, a man who lived in the forest collected the heads of people who had been eaten—a total of forty-nine. The story reminds one of Hansel and Gretel. Like the witch in that fairy tale, the man was burned at the stake after a couple he had imprisoned denounced him. Ademar of Chabannes, promoter of the cult of Saint Martial, allegedly or actually a visionary and, like Rodulf, given to flights of imagination, also described cannibalism during a famine. It was supposed to have taken place in 915, that is, a century before he composed his history. It is not impossible that such things happened during periods of need. But the kind of events talked about by the common people and repeated by the two chroniclers probably had more to do with sensationalism than with the truth.

We see here the eternal battle between order and disorder, cops and robbers—a battle with whose vicissitudes people were fascinated as long as they themselves did not become victims of such events. Impressive punishments followed extraordinary crimes, at least in the sphere of the lower social strata. To see someone hanged was something to be remembered all one's life. The fact that an innocent old man was once executed instead of the criminal was noted by Rodulf Glaber without a sign of disapproval. Nevertheless, people were convinced of the deterrent effects of drastic punishments. Dudo of Saint Quentin stated that the recently baptized duke Rollo had had a couple of thieves hanged, and that since that time no one in Normandy had dared to rob or steal. "And so the land was quiet and at peace, delivered of thieves and robbers, and free of all uprisings."

Peace and quiet are rarely achieved by exemplary punishments. These actions, carried out by subordinate agencies, could be seen as arbitrary and could elicit counteractions. In the rare cases when the king himself acted, the punishments for crimes committed by members of the upper orders could be extremely harsh. Instead of the usual fines, the death penalty might be imposed. During the transition from the old Carolingian forms to more modern ones, and above all in areas in which the royal command had little force, new means of keeping the peace were needed.

The Peace of God

Anyone able to protect his own rights or those of other persons by his own means had to be persuaded not to use unnecessary violence. Objective criteria for what constituted a legitimate feud were lacking, and no court could make a decision on this subject in a specific case. Thus the right to use force had to be limited generally, and supervision of that right was exercised by the higher clergy rather than by the king. Barbara Rosenwein has spoken of the "ritualization of aggression" in the context of devastation and pillage. In 975, bishop Wido of Le Puy extracted from the *milites* and free peasants of his diocese an agreement to keep the peace, to respect the property of the church and of the "poor," and to return all that they had taken by violence. The yielding of what these people saw as their "right" was elicited by military pressure: an army was prepared to move against anyone who refused the oath and the surrender of hostages.

This is not the place to retell the history of the Peace of God, later extended to the Truce of God (*treuga Dei*), the periodic suspension of warfare. Both endeavors were religiously motivated and secured, and not only negatively by means of excommunication and curses. Saints, physically present in their relics, were expected to watch over the peace, which was understood as a sort of treaty with God. During Lent and on Sundays, an armed Christian should be simply a Christian and thus unarmed. The restriction of permitted feuding promoted other activities—war against pagans and the crusades.

The weakness of the new arrangements was pointed out by the German imperial bishop Gerhard of Cambrai. Keeping the peace, he wrote, was the right of kings, a right which could not be appropriated by bishops without creating confusion in Christendom (*aecclesiae statum confundi*). Further, he added, forced oaths were a new source of sin (leading to perjury and oath breaking)—we have seen how widespread such practices had become. Bishop Gerhard did not mention what was probably the main reason for his concern. He was in the process of recovering property that the advocate of the city and the castle of Cambrai had alienated. Refraining from using force in this instance meant renouncing episcopal rights. Ultimately the bishop had to make this renunciation in order not to be denounced as an enemy of the peace.

The clergy's introduction of a new means of enforcing the peace—by arousing and manipulating the emotions of the masses—has generally been seen as a positive innovation. If we can believe Rodulf Glaber, "all were so inflamed that they raised up the crosier, via the hands of the bishop, toward heaven and cried with one voice 'Peace, peace.' This was intended as the sign of an eternal covenant that they had contracted with God." In light of the psychological phenomena of the future crusades, the response seems fully believable. All special interests were overcome by the common desire, which had been fostered and articulated by the bishops. It was a sort of mass oath, which the chronicler compared to the covenant between God and his chosen people. The enthusiasm of the masses may have exercised some moral pressure on the powerful. Still, it was insufficient to divert wrongful force onto the path of peace. Soon force was opposed to force in a new form, the so-called "peace militia." Here enthusiastic peasants were ranged against militarily experienced middle strata, with sometimes catastrophic results.

The Peace of God could not remove the antinomy which formed part of the time. Yet the movement did exert some influence in spite of its deficiencies. Here and there the territorial law of later periods was determined by its principles. We find traces of them in the statutes of French towns, where many people lived together in close quarters and where feuds and blood revenge would have had terrible results, leading to anarchy. In rural society, on the other hand, despite all that has been said, the majority of people led relatively quiet lives. We should not adopt the view of most historiographers of the time, who preferred to describe the sensational—violence and misfortune above all—and considered peaceful existence unworthy of note.

EPILOGUE: A LOOK INTO

THE FUTURE OF THE PAST

Much changed around the middle of the eleventh century. There was not so much a break with tradition as a shift of emphasis, which did not occur everywhere simultaneously or to the same extent. This shift has been rediscovered by scholars again and again and cannot be regarded as merely an element of received opinion.

Much has been written about the reform movement that led to Gregorianism. "The more recent scholarship sees something of a spiritual turning point in the mid-eleventh century. Influential monastic circles began to criticize the laity's lordship over churches." In the second half of this century, many matters previously the concern of the Italian bishops began to be brought to the papal see. For France, Marc Bloch saw the decades after 1050 as the beginning of the "second feudal age" and called particular attention to the increase in population. This demographic growth led to the expansion of arable land from the middle of the eleventh century on, and stimulated urban life, commerce, and manufacture. Since Bloch, others have made further observations in this direction, going so far as to perceive a mid-century transformation in aesthetic ideals. Around 1060, in Anjou and probably elsewhere, respect for the old Carolingian institutions disappeared. Counts could no longer control castellans. Many specific observations of the same kind form the basis for generalizations about the break with the past.

We should not overdramatize such observations. The current of history sometimes flows slowly, then picks up speed, but violent breaks when everything changes are very rare. The assertion that there could never have been a revolution in the Middle Ages is correct if we are using this term in its modern sense. But at one time "revolution" meant a reversion to the divinely ordered state of things, which is the goal of every reform. A simple return to the past has never been possible, of course. The new has always been hidden in the "old," to which people look back.

Today we can no longer believe with Marc Bloch that there was an "economic revolution of the second feudal age." Rather, a certain change became apparent, which led to a general transformation, for instance in the Mâconnais in the decades before and after the year 1200. The desire for canonical election of abbots or for the separation of the clergy from the laity and the subordination of the latter to the former was not revolutionary. These things had long been desired and understood as a return to the original state of affairs. Still, we can recognize some sharp shifts in emphasis. Demands that had previously been considered utopian were now taken very seriously, and people were prepared to fight for them. What had appeared to many as internal affairs of the clergy now became concerns of the laity.

In many fields of action the accents were placed differently and in a more modern spirit—a process that would continue throughout the Middle Ages. We have little evidence, for this period, of the conceptual purism of scholasticism, or of true intellectualism, but developments pointed in that direction. Intellectuals like Rather of Verona, who termed himself a fool (*phreneticus*), were still rare; but gradually the number of people more interested in book learning than in everyday things increased. Rather wrote that he fled to the library and to the "judgments of the forefathers" (*priscorum iudicia*), instead of chasing after money with his contemporaries and winning a crowd of friends. The most important judgments of the forefathers were the canons, of whose violation Rather sternly accused his contemporaries.

The gap widened between pragmatists and ideologues, adherents to accepted custom and defenders of the ancient written law—they all decried "the world turned upside down." First it was individual bishops who went beyond complaints and began what has been called "episcopal reform." Then bishops and educated monks closed ranks to bring the papacy to the true path. The "Lothringian reformists" led the way to Gregorianism.

Reforming zeal soon overstepped the bounds of what was practically attainable. Humbert of Silva Candida, complaining about noncanonical occupation of church positions, contended that such activities sprang from a false understanding of the Holy Spirit and were therefore heresy. This was not entirely new and had been stated from time to time since Gregory the Great (590–604). Now thinkers insisted on intellectualizing a moral theme and drawing practical consequences from it. The Simoniac was not simply following an old tradition. He was a heretic and therefore could exercise no office. All ordinations received from Simoniacs were invalid and had to be repeated. Others deemed this opinion "insanity" because the whole of Christendom would be thrown into confusion if everyone could voice the suspicion that the official actions of this or that ecclesiastic were invalid. A dangerous weapon against the clergy had been forged, which did not spare even the papacy. Canonists soon sought to defuse the issue: simony was a practical heresy, and this sin did not diminish power of consecration or the consecrations received. It was a solution that led back to the firm ground of reality, just as the Concordat of Worms would do later. The problem of Simoniac orders and that of lay investiture were both solved in a modern spirit, by taking an ancient and simplistic conception and subjecting it to distinctions.

These intellectual changes were accompanied by changes in the social sphere, less obvious and incompletely documented in Marc Bloch's emphasis on the phenomena of demographic increase and expansion of the arable land was founded on isolated observations. So he could assume rather than prove the course of general development. It is not even certain that the expansion of the arable must be dependent on a population increase. The vigorous growth of urban life may likewise have other explanations. Since the sources are so sparse, we may never have a close-up view and thus achieve a more complex image. So the old generalizations continue to hold. In the urban sphere, we have yet to see citizens in the full sense with their urban liberties; rather, we find a mixture of various sorts of people. In Augsburg, for example, and similarly in Italian towns, noblemen with their vassals, merchants—free or unfree—and humble serfs lived side by side. The city was intimately related to its agricultural surroundings and was in no way a world unto itself. Only in time it would become a social melting pot. Already before this time, symbiosis within the city walls was strong between citizens and noblemen, in contrast to Italian cities, with their antagonism between "nobility" and "people" (*populo*).

Respected men from noble families were soon differentiated from wealthy merchants or craftsmen, whose prestige constantly increased. As early as the tenth century there was said to have been a butcher who preferred his full freedom to accepting a fief. City nobles and patricians had their towers facing each other, and they sat on the same urban boards, while rural nobles continued to pursue a truly lordly life in the old style. In the eleventh century, cities and seignorial castles developed separately from each other, and the intermediary form of the "*incastellamento* castle" soon passed its prime. Around the year 1000, Notker of Saint Gall already knew the difference between town commune (*purclich*) and rural commune (*gebûrlich*). From the eleventh century on, in Italy, Catalonia, and elsewhere, many nobles lived in towns, probably for economic reasons. It was easier to grow richer there than in strictly rural areas.

The urban community was able to defend itself, first by virtue of the episcopal and comital vassals who lived in it, and then progressively by its own strength. In northern Italy the emphasis began to shift in this domain. People spoke less of episcopal vassals (*milites episcopi*) than of town vassals (*milites Novarienses,* etc.). The bishop's palace could become the town hall (*domus civitatis*). When the situation demanded it, merchants and tradesmen could fight bravely, perhaps with the desire not to take second place behind professional warriors. In one account their knightly arms were emphasized. Merchants and master artisans could certainly afford expensive weapons, perhaps more easily than many lesser rural landholders.

These occasional warriors were not *milites.* We have generally translated that word as "vassal," and must note here that it was a broad, imprecise term encompassing large groups. People now judged others less according to their freedom or servitude than according to their profession. One group worked the land and were therefore peasants; the other protected the peace with arms and were therefore *milites,* warriors. This profession, long observed by the clergy with mistrust, was reevaluated positively in the eleventh century even before the crusades. One spoke of a *militia christiana*—a term which later designated Christian chivalry. The *milites* were not a social category and even less a special circle of people within the nobility. Terms become differentiated more slowly in the social than in the legal sphere.

The cavalryman outranks the foot soldier in martial ability and in prestige. An Arab said that just one armored (mounted) warrior of the Polish prince Mieszko I was worth a hundred others, that is, foot soldiers. From the twelfth century, and perhaps earlier, the word *miles* was translated by the prestige-laden term "knight" (*Ritter*), while the generic term *eques,* "rider," designated an "ordinary" horseman, with or without weapons. These non-noble, low-ranking members of the *familia* served as escorts for the overland transport of goods. When there was a shortage of manpower, they could be used for military service. In Romance-language areas the analogous term was *cabalarius,* and it is worth noting that the later term for knightly status (*chevalier, cavaliere*) was derived from it. What united chivalry and cavalry was service to a lord. The man of the people fulfilled his service because he had to. For the noble, a vassal's service to his lord was a moral obligation, and even more so was service in the cause of Christianity or, better, for Christ the Lord.

In the 1930s it was suggested that, after the reform of monasticism and of the papacy, "lay knighthood was also reformed." In this form, the statement is unacceptable, but it is worth amending it. Aristocracy began to concentrate itself in a Christian nobility with a broad base in knighthood, just as the reformed monks were a fundamental unit within the clergy. The influence of Cluny on papal reform is debated, and the bond between the Cluniacs and mounted warriors asserted by Adalbero of Laon may be a bad joke. But the monk Hildebrand, as Pope Gregory VII, did try to assemble around himself a knighthood of Saint Peter (*militia S. Petri*), which was both a spiritual and a military following. Gregory's desire to see vassalic relations to the holy see established throughout Europe ran along the same lines. If every bishop had vassals in his diocese, why should the universal papacy in the West do without them?

The trees of papal reform did not grow to the heavens, and Christian chivalry likewise remained an incompletely realized ideal. We should consider not so much the results of the two movements as the new upsurge of energy that led to them. They were a sort of intellectual expansion of the arable after long periods of traditional modes of thought. For this reason historians have concerned themselves far more with the late eleventh and twelfth centuries than with the tenth and early eleventh. Ambitious projects and dramatic actions of the past make more interesting reading than the everyday life of the past with its limitations and its mundane existence in the framework of imperfect systems. More substantial than the high points, however, when we take a global view, are the terrain and the roots from which our modern history has sprung.

BIBLIOGRAPHY AND NOTES

Additional reference to the sources and many supplementary quotations can be found in the notes to the German edition.

PRIMARY SOURCES
Abbreviations

MGH   *Monumenta Germaniae Historica*
SS   *MGH Scriptores*. 34 vols. Hannover, 1826–1980
SSRG *MGH Scriptores rerum Germanicarum in usum scholarum*. 63 vols. Hannover, 1871–1985
MPL   Jean Jacques Migne, *Patrologiae cursus completus*, ser.I: *Patrologia latina*. Paris, 1844–64
Abbo of Fleury. *Apologeticus. MPL* 139, cols. 461–72.
Adalbero of Laon. *Adalberon de Laon, Poème au roi Robert*. Ed. and trans. Claude Carozzi. Paris, 1979.
Adalbert of Prague. [Johannes Canaparius,] *Adalberti Pragensis episcopi . . . vita prior*. Ed. Jadwiga Karwasińska. Monumenta Poloniae Historica ser. altera, vol. 4, fasc. 1. Warsaw, 1962.
Ademar of Chabannes. *Adémar de Chabannes, Chronique (Chronica)*. Ed. Jules Chavanon. Collection de textes pour servir à l'étude et à l'enseignement de l'histoire. Paris, 1897.
Aimoin of Fleury. *Vita sancti Abbonis. MPL* 139, cols. 387–414.
Alpert of St. Symphorian at Metz. *Libellus de episcopis Mettensibus. MGH SS* 4, pp. 697–700.
———. *De diversitate temporum. MGH SS* 4, pp. 700–723. (Republished with a Dutch translation by Hans van Rij and Anna Sapir Abulafia, Amsterdam, 1980.)
Andrew of Fleury. *André de Fleury, Vie de Gauzlin abbé de Fleury*. Ed. Robert-Henri Bautier and Gillette Labory. Sources d'histoire médiévale, 2. Paris, 1969.
Anselm of Besate. *Rhetorimachia. Gunzo. Epistola ad Augienses und Anselm von*

Besate. *Rhetorimachia.* Ed. Karl Manitius. *MGH Quellen zur Geistesgeschichte des Mittelalters.* 2. Weimar, 1958.

Anselm of Liège. *Gesta episcoporum Leodicensium. MGH SS* 7, pp. 191–234.

Benedict of Monte Soratte. *Il "Chronicon" di Benedetto monaco di S. Andrea del Soratte.* Ed. Giuseppe Zucchetti. Fonti per la storia d'Italia, 55. Rome, 1920.

Benedict of Nursia. *Benedicti Regula.* Ed. Rudolf Hanslik. Corpus scriptorum ecclesiasticorum latinorum, 75. 2d ed. Vienna, 1977. (Other editions include: A. Lentini, ed., Monte Cassino, 1980; and Eugène Manning, ed., Westmalle, 1980.)

Bern of Reichenau. *Die Briefe des Abtes Bern von Reichenau.* Ed. Franz-Josef Schmale. Veröffentlichungen der Kommission . . . Baden-Württemberg. Series A, vol. 6. Stuttgart, 1961.

Brun of Querfurt. *Vita altera Adalberti Pragensis Episcopi.* Ed. Hedvigis Karwasińska. Monumenta Historica Poloniae ser. altera, vol. 4, fasc. 2. Warsaw, 1969.

———. *Vita vel passio sanctorum Benedicti et Iohannis sociorumque suorum (= Vita quinque fratrum).* Ed. H. Karwasińska. Monumenta Historica Poloniae, series altera, vol. 4, fasc. 3. Warsaw, 1973.

Burchard of Worms. *Decretum. MPL* 140, cols. 537–1058.

———. *Lex familiae Wormacensis ecclesiae ("Hofrecht"). MGH* Constitutiones 1, pp. 639–44, no. 438.

Cambrai. *Gesta pontificum Cameracensium. MGH SS* 7, pp. 402–89.

Carmina Cantabrigiensia. Ed. Karl Strecker. *MGH SSRG* 40, 1926.

Constantine of St. Symphorian at Metz. *Vita Adalberonis II Mettensis episcopi. MGH SS* 4, pp. 659–72.

Conventum inter Guillelmum Aquitanorum comes [!] et Hugonem Chiliarchum. Ed. Jane Martindale. *The English Historical Review* 84 (1969), pp. 538–48. (The "conventum" is actually a report of complaints against William for not honoring his obligations.)

Corpus consuetudinum monasticarum (Monastic customs). Ed. Kassius Hallinger. Vol. 7, fasc. 3, *Consuetudines saeculi X–XI–XII.* Ed. Kassius Hallinger. Seigburg, 1984. (Begins with Fleury, 10th century.) Vol. 10, *Liber tramitis Odilonis abattis.* Ed. Petrus Dinter. Siegburg, 1980. (So-called *consuetudines Farfenses,* compiled at Farfa, containing many of the Cluniac customs of Odilo's time.)

Decretales Pseudo-Isidorianae et Capitula Angilramni. Ed. Paul Hinschius. Leipzig, 1863; Aalen, 1963.

Eberwin of Treves. *Vita sancti Simeonis (Trevirensis).* Edition: *Acta Sanctorum (Bollandiana), Iunius* I. Antwerp, 1695. Reprint: Brussels, 1969, pp. 86–92.

Ekkehard IV of Saint Gall. *St. Galler Klostergeschichten (Casus s. Galli).* Ed. Hans F. Haefele (with German translation). Ausgewählte Quellen zur deutschen Geschichte des Mittelalters, vol. 10. Darmstadt, 1980.

Flodoard of Reims. *Historia Remensis ecclesiae. MGH SS* 13, pp. 409–599.

———. *Annales. Les annales de Flodoard.* Ed. Philippe Lauer. Collection de textes pour servir à l'étude et à l'enseignement de l'histoire. Paris, 1905.

Flothilda. *Visions de Flothilde.* Appendix 2 of: *Les annales de Flodoard* (see previous entry), 170–76.

Fulbert of Chartres. *The Letters and Poems of Fulbert of Chartres.* Ed. and trans. Frederic Behrends. Oxford, 1976.

Gerbert of Aurillac. *The Letters of Gerbert with His Privileges As Sylvester II*. Ed. Harriet Pratt Lattin. New York, 1961.

———. *Die Briefsammlung Gerberts von Reims*. Ed. Fritz Weigle. MGH, *Die Briefe der deutschen Kaiserzeit*, 2. Munich, 1966.

Gerhard of Augsburg. *Vita Oudalrici Augustensis episcopi. MGH SS* 4, pp. 381–419.

Helgald of Fleury. *Helgaud de Fleury, Vie de Robert le Pieux (Epitoma regis Rotberti Pii)*. Ed. Robert-Henri Bautier and Gillette Labory. Sources d'histoire médiévale, 1. Paris, 1965.

Hrotsvith of Gandersheim. *Hrotsvithae opera*. Ed. Helene Homeyer. Munich, 1970.

Hugh of Farfa. *Destructio monasterii Farfensis. MGH SS* 11, pp. 532–44.

John (the Roman). *Iohannes (Romanus), Vita Odonis abbatis Cluniacensis. MPL* 133, cols. 43–86.

John of Saint Arnulf at Metz. *Vita Iohannis Gorziensis abbatis. MGH SS* 4, pp. 337–77.

———. *Vita et miracula Glodesindis. MPL* 137, cols. 211–18.

Land registers: Brescia. *Inventari altomedievali de terre, coloni e rendite*. Ed. Andrea Castagnetti et al. Fonti per la storia d'Italia, 104. Rome, 1979. (See especially no. 5, pp. 43–94: *Santa Giulia di Brescia*, ed. Gianfranco Pasquali.)

Land registers: Farfa (Forcone). *Il regesto di Farfa*. Ed. Ignazio Giorgi and Ugo Balzani. Vol. 5. Rome, 1892, pp. 254–79.

Land registers: Prüm. *Das Prümer Urbar*. Ed. Ingo Schab. Rheinische Urbare, 5. Publikationen . . . Rheinische Geschichtskunde, 20. Düsseldorf, 1983.

Liutprand of Cremona. *Die Werke Liudprands von Cremona*. Ed. Joseph Becker. *MGH SSRG* 41. 3d ed. Hannover, 1977.

Matilda, Queen. *Vita Mahtildis antiquior. MGH SS* 10, pp. 575–82.

Odilo of Cluny. *Epitaphium domine Adelheide auguste*. Ed. Herbert Paulhart. In *Mitteilungen des Instituts für österr: Geschichtsforschung*. Ergänzungsband 20, fasc. 2. Graz and Cologne, 1962.

Odo of Cluny. *Vita Geraldi Auriliacensis comitis. MPL* 133, cols. 639–704.

Odorannus of Saint-Pierre-le-Vif at Sens. *Opera omnia*. Ed. and trans. Robert-Henri Bautier and Monique Gilles. Sources d'histoire médiévale, 4. Paris, 1972.

Petrus Damiani. *Vita beati Romualdi*. Ed. Giovanni Tabacco. Fonti per la storia d'Italia, 94. Rome, 1957.

Pontificale. *Le Pontifical romano-germanique du dixième siècle*. Ed. Cyrille Vogel and Reinhard Elze. Studi e testi, 226, 227, 269. 3 vols. Vatican, 1963–72.

Pseudo-Dionysius. See Decretales.

Raker of Verona. Letters. *Die Briefe des Bischofs Rather von Verona*. Ed. Fritz Weigle. MGH, *Die Briefe der deutschen Kaiserzeit*, 1. Munich, 1949, 1979.

———. *Praeloquia*. Ed. Petrus L. D. Reid et al. Corpus Christianorum, continuatio mediaevalis, t. 46A. Turnhout, 1984.

Regino of Prüm. *Libri duo de synodalibus causis et disciplinis ecclesiasticis*. Ed. F. G. A. Wasserschleben. Leipzig, 1840. Reprint Graz, 1964.

———. *Regionis abbatis Prumensis Chronicon cum continuatione Treverensi*. Ed. Fridericus Kurze. *MGH SSRG* 50. Hannover, 1890.

Richer. *Historiae. Histoire de France (888–995)*. Ed. and trans. Robert Latouche. Vol. 1, Paris, 1930. Vol. 2, 2d ed., Paris, 1964.

Rodulfus Glaber. *Historiaum libri quinque.* Ed. and tr. John France. Oxford Medieval Texts. Oxford, 1989.

———. *Vita domni Willelmi abbatis.* Ed. Neithard Bulst. *Deutsches Archiv* 30 (1974), pp. 462–87.

"Ruodlieb" (poem). *The Ruodlieb.* Ed. Gordon B. Ford, Jr. Leiden, 1960.

———. *The Ruodlieb.* Ed. and trans. C. W. Grocock. Oak Park, Ill., and Warminster, England, 1985. (For another edition, with German translation, see below, *Waltharius,* etc., ed. Langosch, pp. 85–215.)

Ruotger. *Ruotgers Lebensbeschreibung des Erzbischofs Bruno von Köln.* Ed. Irene Ott. *MGH SSRG,* n.s. 10. Weimar, 1951.

Die Tegernseer Briefsammlung (Froumund). Ed. Karl Strecker. *MGH Epistolae selectae,* 3. Berlin, 1925.

Thangmar of Hildesheim. *Vita sancti Bernwardi episcopi Hildesheimensis. MGH SS* 4, pp. 757–82.

Thietmar of Merseburg. *Thietmarus Merseburgensis, Chronicon.* Ed. Robert Holtzmann. *MGH SSRG,* n.s. 9. Berlin, 1935.

"Unibos" (poem). See below, *Waltharius, Ruodlieb, Märchenepen,* pp. 251–315.

"Walthari" (poem) (*Waltharilied*). Ed. Karl Strecker. *MGH Poetae Latini medii aevi,* t. 6, fasc. 1. Weimar, 1951. Reprint Munich, 1978. (Erroneously dated to the end of the 9th century. On the authorship, see *Mittelateinisches Jahrbuch* 18, 1983).

———. *Waltharius, Ruodlieb, Märchenepen.* Ed. Karl Langosch. 3d. ed. Darmstadt, 1976, pp. 5–83. (Latin-German.)

Widukind of Corvey. *Die Sachsengeschichte des Widukind von Korvei.* Ed. Paul Hirsch and Hans-Eberhard Lohmann. *MGH SSRG* 60. Hannover, 1935, 1977.

Wipo. *Opera: Gesta Chuonradi II imperatoris, Tetralogus, Proverbia.* Ed. Harry Bresslau. *MGH SSRG* 61. Hannover, 1915, 1977.

Wolfhere of Hildesheim. *Vita Godehardi episcopi prior. MGH SS* 11, pp. 167–96.

SECONDARY SOURCES
General

Bloch, Marc. *Feudal Society.* Trans. L. A. Manyon. Chicago, 1961.

Boutruche, Robert. *Seigneurie et féodalité.* Vol. 1. *Le premier âge des liens d'homme à homme.* Paris, 1959.

Duby, Georges. *The Chivalrous Society.* Trans. Cynthia Postan. London, 1977.

———. *Hommes et structures du moyen âge.* Paris, 1979.

———. *Rural Economy and Country Life in the Medieval West.* Trans. Cynthia Postan. Columbia, S.C., 1968.

Fossier, Robert. *Enfance de l'Europe, Xe–XIIe siècles.* 2 vols. Paris, 1982. (With bibliography.)

I laici nella "societas christiana" dei secoli XI e XII. Miscellanea del Centro di Studi Medioevali 5. Milan, 1968. (Articles.)

Lopez, Robert Sabatino. *The Tenth Century: How Dark the Dark Ages?* New York, 1959. (Extracts of translated primary sources, and introduction.)

Poly, Jean-Pierre, and Bournazel, Eric. *La mutation féodale (Xe–XIIe siècles).* Nouvelle Clio, 16. Paris, 1980.

I problemi comuni dell'Europa post-carolingia. Settimane di Studio del Centro italiano di studi sull'Alto Medioevo, no. 2, 1954. Spoleto, 1955.

Riché, Pierre. *Daily Life in the World of Charlemagne.* Trans. Jo Ann McNamara. Philadelphia, 1978.

Sellin, Volker. "Mentalität und Mentalitätsgeschichte." *Historische Zeitschrift* 241 (1985), pp. 555–98. (Quotes further articles on the topic.)

Structures féodales et féodalisme dans l'Occident méditerranéen (Xe–XIIIe siècles). Collection de l'Ecole française de Rome, 44. Rome, 1980. (A rich collection of articles reporting on a colloquium in Rome, 1978.)

White, Lynn, Jr. *Medieval Technology and Social Change.* Oxford, 1962.

Regional

Bonnassie, Pierre. *La Catalogne du milieu du IXe à la fin du XIe siècle.* Publications de l'Université Toulouse—Le Mirail, série A, t. 23, 29. 2 vols. Toulouse, 1975, 1976.

Devailly, Guy. *Le Berry du Xe siècle au milieu du XIIIe.* Ecole pratique des Hautes Etudes—Sorbonne, VIe section. Civilisation et société, 19. Paris and The Hague, 1973.

Dion, Roger. *Histoire de la vigne et du vin en France des origines au XIXe siècle.* Paris, 1959.

Duby, Georges. *La société aux XIe et XIIe siècles dans la région mâconnaise.* 2d ed. Paris, 1971.

Fossier, Robert. *La terre et les hommes en Picardie jusqu'à la fin du XIIIe siècle.* 2 vols. Paris, 1968.

Fumagalli, Vito. *Terra e società nell'Italia Padana: I secoli IX e X.* Torino, 1976.

Jarnut, Jörg. *Bergamo 568–1098.* Vierteljahrschrift für Sozial- und Wirtschaftsgeschichte, Beiheft 67. Wiesbaden, 1979.

Leyser, Karl. *Rule and Conflict in an Early Medieval Society: Ottonian Saxony.* London, 1979.

Magnou-Nortier, Elisabeth. *La société laïque et l'Eglise dans la province ecclésiastique de Narbonne (zone cispyrénéene) de la fin du VIIIe à la fin du XIe siècle.* Publications de l'Université Toulouse–Le Mirail, series A, 20. Toulouse, 1974.

Poly, Jean-Pierre. *La Provence et la société féodale, 879–1166.* Paris, 1976.

Schreiber, Georg. *Deutsche Weingeschichte: Der Wein in Volksleben, Kult und Wirtschaft.* Cologne, 1980.

Toubert, Pierre. *Les structures du Latium médiéval: Le Latium méridional et la Sabine du IXe siècle à la fin du XIIe siècle.* Bibliothèque des Ecoles Françaises d'Athènes et de Rome, 221. 2 vols. Rome, 1973.

SOURCES BY CHAPTER
Chapter 1: Order as Rank Order
General

Boshof, Egon, "Köln, Mainz, Trier." *Jahrbuch des Kölnischen Geschichtsvereines* 49 (1978), pp. 19–48.

Brown, Elizabeth A. R. "Georges Duby and the Three Orders." *Viator* 17 (1986), pp. 51–64. (Quotes further publications on the topic.)

Callahan, Daniel F. "The Sermons of Adémar of Chabannes and the Cult of St. Martial of Limoges." *Revue Bénédictine* 86 (1976), pp. 251–95.

Duby, Georges. *The Three Orders: Feudal Society Imagined.* Trans. Arthur Goldhammer. Chicago, 1980, 1982, 1984.

Dvornik, Francis. *The Idea of Apostolicity in Byzantium, and the Legend of the Apostle Andrew.* Cambridge, Mass., 1958.

Notes

(Peter Damian) Petrus Damiani, *Opusculum* XXII, *MPL* 145, col. 466, c. 2.

(Fulbert of Chartres on Châlons) Fulbert (see Primary Sources), p. 62 no. 34.

(Pope John XIII for Magdeburg) Harald Zimmermann, *Papsturkunden 896–1046,* vol. 1 (Vienna, 1984), p. 348 no. 177.

(Pope Benedict VII for Magdeburg) Zimmerman, *Papsturkunden,* vol. 1, p. 530 (on the question of an interpolation); p. 531 no. 270.

(Martial) Gregory of Tours, Historia Francorum 1, c. 30, *MGH SS rerum Merovingicarum* 1, p. 48; Ademar of Chabannes, *Epistola de apostolatu s. Martialis, MPL* 141, col. 89–112.

(Gerbert of Aurillac) Gerbert (see Primary Sources), ed. Weigle, p. 99 no. 69 (986).

(John XIII for Fulda) Zimmermann, *Papsturkunden,* vol. 1, p. 395 no. 199.

(Assembly of relics at Cambrai) *Gesta episcoporum Cameracensium,* 3, c. 49, *MGH SS* 7, p. 484.

(Synod at Frankfurt) Wolfhere (see Primary Sources), c. 31, p. 190.

(Synod of Pavia) *MGH Constitutiones* 1, p. 94 no. 48.

(Conversi, etc.) Wolfgang Teske, "Laien, Laienmönche und Laienbrüder in der Abtei Cluny, I," *Frühmittelalterliche Studien* 10 (1976), pp. 248–322. (See also *Corpus consuetudinum* [Primary Sources] and the following chapter.)

(John I, Abbot of Gorze) John of Saint Arnulf at Metz (see Primary Sources), p. 358, c. 76.

(Theory of nonsuperiority) Innocent III, December 1202, to Count William of Montpellier, *MPL* 214, col. 1132 B; *Corpus Iuris Canonici,* ed. Aemilius Friedberg, 2 (Leipzig, 1879, Graz, 1959), p. 715 (X 4.17.13).

(Charles the Simple and Hagano) Richer (see Primary Sources) 1, c. 16, ed. Latouche, p. 1, 40.

Chapter 2: Social Gestures
General

Amira, Karl von. *Der Stab in der germanischen Rechtssymbolik.* Abhandlungen der königlich-Bayerischen Akademie der Wissenschaften, philos.-philol. u. hist. Kl., 25, fasc. 1. Munich, 1911.

Le Goff, Jacques. "The Symbolic Ritual of Vassality." In idem, *Time Work and Culture in the Middle Ages.* Trans. Arthur Goldhammer. Chicago, 1980. (First appeared in *Simboli e simbologia* [see below], pp. 679–88.)

Rouche, Michel. "La matricule des pauvres." In *Etudes sur l'histoire de la pauvreté* 1. Publications de la Sorbonne, Etudes, 8. Paris, 1974, pp. 83–110.

Schmidt-Wiegand, Ruth. "Gebärdensprache im mittelalterlichen Recht." *Frühmittelalterliche Studien* 16 (1982), pp. 363–79.

Simboli e simbologia nell'Alto Medioevo. Settimane di Studio, Spoleto, 23, 1975. 2 vols. Spoleto, 1976.

Vercauteren, Fernand. "Avec le sourire." *Mélanges Rita Lejeune* 1. Brussels, 1969, pp. 45–56.

Vogel, Cyrille. "Les rites de la pénitence publique au Xe et XIe siècle." In *Mélanges René Crozet*, 1. Poitiers, 1966, pp. 137–44.

Notes

(Bruno of Cologne) Ruotger (see Primary Sources), p. 12, c. 12.

(Arno Borst) Borst, *Lebensformen im Mittelalter* (Frankfurt, 1973), p. 485.

(Augustine on signs) *De doctrina christiana,* 2, c. 1, *Corpus scriptorum ecclesiasticorum latinorum,* vol. 80. Ed. W. Green (Vienna, 1963), p. 33.

(Eagles of Aix-la-Chapelle) Thietmar (see Primary Sources), 3, c. 8. ed. Holtzmann p. 106; Richer 3, c. 71, ed. Latouche 2, p. 88.

(Otto II and Hugh Capet) Richer 3, c. 85, ed. Latouche 2, p. 108.

(Otto III at table) Thietmar 4, c. 47, ed. Holtzmann, p. 184.

(Peace movement, 1033) Rodulfus Glaber (see Primary Sources) 4, c. 5, ed. France; p. 194–99.

(Henry II and Heribert of Cologne) Lantbert of Deutz, *Vita Heriberti Coloniensis archiepiscopi, MGH SS* 4, p. 749, c. 10.

(Otto I and Notker of Saint Gall) Ekkehard (see Primary Sources), c. 133, ed. Haefele, p. 258.

(Ekkehard in Ingelheim, 1030) Ekkehard (see Primary Sources), c. 66, ed. Haefele, p. 142.

(Robert the Pious at table) Helgald (see Primary Sources), p. 64, c. 5.

(Aid to the needy) Georges Duby, *Guerriers et paysans* (Paris, 1973), p. 261.

(Robert the Pious and the paupers) Helgald p. 104, c. 21.

(Death of archbishop Walthard of Magdeburg) Thietmar (see Primary Sources) 6, c. 73, ed. Holtzmann, p. 362.

(Death of a count) Richer (see Primary Sources) 4, c. 94, ed. Latouche 2, pp. 300 f.

(Mutiny of Ravenna 1026) Wipo (see Primary Sources), Gesta c. 13, ed. Bresslau, p. 35.

(Crosier as evidence of nomination) Letald of Saint Mesmin at Micy, *Miracula sancti Maximini,* c. 19, *MPL* 137, col. 805.

(Jurisdiction over Gandersheim) Thangmar (see Primary Sources), p. 777, c. 43.

(Lance as a symbol of investiture) Thietmar (see Primary Sources) 5, c. 21, ed. Holtzmann, pp. 214, 216.

Chapter 3: Representation
General

Berlière, Ursmer. "Les processions des croix banales." *Académie Royale de Belgique: Bulletin de la classe des lettres,* série 5, t. 8 (Brussels, 1922), pp. 419–46.

Brühl, Carlrichard. *Fodrum, Gistum, Servitium regis.* Kölner Historische Abhandlungen, 14. 2 vols. Cologne, 1968. (Food supply due to the King's table.)

Heitz, Carol. "Symbolisme et architecture: Les nombres et l'architecture du Haut

Moyen Age." In *Simboli e simbologia* (see chap. 2), pp. 387–420. (See also Horn and Born (below, chap. 12), vol. 1, pp. 118–19, for further literature.)

Willmes, Peter. *Der Herrscher-"Adventus" im Kloster des Frühmittelalters.* Münstersche Mittelalterschriften, 22. Munich, 1976.

Notes

(Salomo of Constance and the chamberlains) Ekkehard (see Primary Sources), c. 12, ed. Haefele, p. 36.

(Count Erluin) Dudo of Saint Quentin, *Gesta Normanniae ducum* 3, MPL 141, col. 677.

(Duke William in Limoges) Ademar (see Primary Sources) 3, c. 41, ed. Chavanon, p. 163.

(Letter of Abbo of Fleury) Aimoin (see Primary Sources), p. 399, c. 10.

(Louis III, 905) Liutprand (see Primary Sources), *Antapodosis,* p. 54, c. 39.

(Drinking bouts) Constantine (see Primary Sources), p. 669, c. 29; Atto of Vercelli, *Polypticum,* trans. G. Goetz, in *Abhandlungen der Sächsischen Akademie der Wissenschaften, philos.-hist. Kl.,* vol. 37, fasc. 2 (Leipzig, 1922), p. 60, c. 8; Alpert (see Primary Sources), *De diversitate temporum,* 2, c. 20, MGH SS 4, p. 719.

(Precious garments) Abbo, *Bella Parisiacae urbis* 2, 606 ff, ed. H. Waquet (Paris, 1964), p. 112; Helgald (see Primary Sources), p. 64, c. 5.

(Horses of Italian bishops) Rather (see Primary Sources), *Praeloquia* 5, c. 9 and 12, pp. 149–50.

(A Cluniac as a *miles*) Adalbero of Laon (see Primary Sources) 8, vv. 96–104.

(Rather on episcopal garments) Rather (see Primary Sources), *Praeloquia* 5, c. 6, pp. 146, 149, 150, 157.

(Gerbert) Gerbert (see Primary Sources), *Briefsammlung,* ed. Weigle, p. 40 no. 17, p. 63 no. 35.

(Helgald of Fleury) Helgaud (see Primary Sources), c. 7, ed. Bautier-Labory, pp. 66–67, cf. p. 18 and n. 4.

(Ademar of Chabannes on Henry II) Ademar (see Primary Sources) 3, c. 37, ed. Chavanon, p. 160.

Chapter 4: Family and Clan
General

Bouchard, Constance B. "Consanguinity and Noble Marriages in the Tenth and Eleventh Centuries." *Speculum* 56 (1981), pp. 268–87.

Duby, Georges. *Medieval Marriage: Two Models from Twelfth-Century France.* The Johns Hopkins Symposia, 11. Baltimore and London, 1978.

Famille et parenté dans l'Occident médiéval. Colloque, Paris, 1974. Communications and discussions. Ed. Georges Duby and Jacques Le Goff. Rome, 1977. (Jean-Claude Maire-Vigueur gives a good summary in "A propos d'un colloque sur famille et parenté," *Studi Medievali,* ser. 3, vol. 16, no. 1, 1975, pp. 407–15.)

Il matrimonio nella società altomedievale. Settimane di Studio, Spoleto, 24, 1976. 2 vols. Spoleto, 1977.

Schmid, Karl. *Gebetsgedenken und adliges Selbstverständnis im Mittelalter.* Sigmaringen, 1983. (Schmid's selected articles. See especially "Zur Problematik von Familie, Sippe und Geschlecht, Haus und Dynastie beim mittelalterlichen Adel," pp. 183–239.)

Wemple, Suzanne Fonay. *Women in Frankish Society: Marriage and the Cloister, 500 to 900.* Philadelphia, 1981.

Notes

(Picardy) Fossier, Picardie (see Secondary Sources, Regional), 1, p. 256.

(Queen Emma's complaint) Gerbert (see Primary Sources), *Briefsammlung,* ed. Weigle, p. 146 no. 119 (988), p. 127 no. 97 (986–87).

(Alpert of Saint Symphorian) Alpert (see Primary Sources), 2, c. 9, p. 714.

(Henry I and Hatheburg) Thietmar (see Primary Sources) 1, c. 5 and 9, ed. Holtzmann, pp. 8, 14.

(Exogamy) Quoted from Claude Lévi-Strauss, *Les structures élémentaires de la parenté* (Paris, 1949), p. 593. (*The Elementary Structures of Kinship,* trans. James Harle Bell, John Richard von Sturmen, and Rodney Needham, [Boston, 1969].)

Chapter 5: Patriarchal Lordship
General

d'Alverny, Marie-Thérèse. "Comment les théologiens et les philosophes voient la femme." In *La femme dans les civilisations des Xe–XIIIe siècles—Cahiers de civilisation médiévale* 20 (1977), pp. 105–29.

Duby, Georges. "Youth in Aristocratic Society: Northwestern France in the Twelfth Century," in idem, *Chivalrous Society* (see Secondary Sources, General), pp. 112–22.

Ennen, Edith. *Frauen im Mittelalter.* Munich, 1984.

La Femme (II). Recueils de la Société Jean Bodin, 12. Brussels, 1962. (See especially François-Louis Ganshof, "Le statut de la femme dans la monarchie franque," pp. 5–58.)

Luzzatto, Gino. *Dai servi della gleba agli albori del capitalismo.* Bari, 1966.

Thieme, Hans. "Die Rechtsstellung der Frau in Deutschland." In *La Femme* (see above), pp. 351–76.

Notes

(Definition of "family") Ulpian, Digestum 50, 16, 195, 2; *Corpus iuris civilis* 1, ed. Th. Mommsen and P. Krüger (Berlin, 1902), p. 864 s.

(Karl Schmid) Schmid, *Gebetsgedenken* (see chap. 4), p. 231.

(Rodulfus Glaber on a family feud) Rodulfus Glaber (see Primary Sources) 2, c. 10 (21), ed. France, pp. 88–89.

(Thietmar on adultery) Thietmar (see Primary Sources) 8, c. 3, ed. Holtzmann, pp. 494–96.

(Ruodlieb) "Ruodlieb" (see Primary Sources) 14 (15) vv. 70–87, ed. Ford, p. 92.

(William of Aquitaine and Hugh of Lusignan) *Conventum . . .* (see Primary Sources), p. 542.

(Waltharius) Walthari (see Primary Sources), ed. *MGH,* Poetae 6/1, pp. 29–30.

(Monks of Farfa) Hugh of Farfa (see Primary Sources), c. 6, 13, pp. 535, 538.

(Cathedral of Arezzo) Harry Bresslau, "Chronik des Capitels zu Arezzo," *Neues Archiv* 5 (1880), pp. 442–51.

Chapter 6: The Familial Model

General

Berlière, Ursmer. *La Familia dans les monastères bénédictins du Moyen Age*. Académie Royale de Belgique, Classe des Lettres et Sciences morales et politiques, Mémoires, series 2, vol. 29, fasc. 2. Brussels, 1931.

Bosl, Karl. "Die 'familia' als Grundstruktur der mittelalterlichen Gesellschaft." *Zeitschrift für Bayerische Landesgeschichte* 38 (1975), pp. 403–24.

Herlihy, David. *Medieval Households*. Studies in Cultural History. Cambridge, Mass., and London, 1985.

Kuchenbuch, Ludolf. *Bäuerliche Gesellschaft und Klosterherrschaft im 9. Jahrhundert: Studien zur Sozialstruktur der Familia der Abtei Prüm. Vierteljahrsschrift für Sozial- und Wirtschaftsgeschichte*, suppl. 66. Wiesbaden, 1978.

———. "Die Klostergrundherrschaft im Frühmittelalter: Eine Zwischenbilanz." In *Herrschaft und Kirche*. Ed. Friedrich Prinz. Monographien zur Geschichte des Mittelalters, 33. Stuttgart, 1988, pp. 297–343. (Includes a bibliography of modern works.)

Lynch, Joseph H. *Godparents and Kinship in Early Medieval Europe*. Princeton, 1986.

Meersseman, Gilles Gerard. *Ordo fraternitatis: Confraternite e pietà dei laici nel medioevo*. Italia Sacra, 24–26. 3 vols. Rome, 1977. Vol. 1, pp. 35–67, 95–112.

Notes

(Forcone) Land registers: Farfa (see Primary Sources).

(Mâconnais) Georges Duby, *La société aux XIe et XIIe siècles dans la région mâconnaise* (Paris, 1953, 1971), pp. 8–9.

(Thietmar and Magdeburg) Thietmar (see Primary Sources) 4, c. 16; 7, c. 33; 6, c. 18, ed. Holtzmann, pp. 150, 438, 294–98.

(Godparenthood of monks) Richer (see Primary Sources) 3, c. 35, ed. Latouche 2, pp. 42–44.

(Kindred of translated saints) Klemens Honselmann, "Reliquientranslationen nach Sachsen," in: *Das erste Jahrtausend*, Text (Düsseldorf, 1962), p. 192.

(Family of kings) Franz Dölger, "Die 'Familie der Könige im Mittelalter," in: *Byzanz und die europäische Staatenwelt* (Ettal, 1953), pp. 34–69; Arno Borst, *Lebensformen im Mittelalter* (Frankfurt, 1973), p. 488.

Chapter 7: The Noble

Research on the meaning of the word *nobilis* is scarce. Much has been done on nobility as a social group. For this we give some examples.

General

The Medieval Nobility. Ed. by Timothy Reuter. Europe in the Middle Ages, Selected Studies, 14. Amsterdam, New York, and Oxford, 1978. (Instructive essays by continental authors, in English.)

Bouchard, Constance B. "The Origins of the French Nobility: A Reassessment." *The American Historical Review* 86 (1981), pp. 501–32.

Brown, Elizabeth. "The Tyranny of a Construct: Feudalism and Historians of Medieval Europe." *The American Historical Review* 79 (1974), pp. 1063–88.

Ganshof, François-Louis. "Les relations féodo-vassaliques aux temps post-carolingiens." In *I problemi comuni* (see Secondary Sources, General), pp. 67–114.

Leyser, Karl J. "The German Aristocracy from the Ninth to the Early Twelfth Century." *Past and Present* 41 (December 1968), pp. 25–53. Reprinted in idem, *Medieval Germany and Its Neighbours (900–1250)*. London, 1982, pp. 161–89.

———. *Rule and Conflict* (see Secondary Sources, Regional).

Oexle, Otto Gerhard. "Memoria und Memorialüberlieferung im früheren Mittelalter." *Frümittelalterliche Studien* 10 (1976), pp. 70–95.

Schmid, Karl. *Gebetsgedenken* (see chap. 4).

Werner, Karl Ferdinand. "Adel." In *Lexikon des Mittelalters* 1. Munich and Zurich, 1977, cols. 119–28. Reprinted in Werner, *Vom Frankenreich zur Entfaltung Deutschlands und Frankreichs*. Sigmaringen, 1984, pp.12–21.

Notes

(*Nobilis, nobilior, nobilissimus*) Josef Fleckenstein, "Die Enstehung des niederen Adels und das Rittertum," in *Herrschaft und Stand,* Veröffentlichungen des M. Planck-Instituts für Geschichte, 51 (1977), p. 18 (on the Carolingian age).

(Ekkar, son of Liudolf) Widukind 2, c. 4, ed. P. Hirsch and H.-E. Lohmann, p. 71.

(Practical knowledge) John of Saint Arnulf at Metz (see Primary Sources), p. 340, c. 11.

(Cambrai 1012) *Gesta episcoporum Cameracensium* 1, c. 120, *MGH SS* 7, p. 454.

(Bruno's ancestors) Ruotger (see Primary Sources) c. 14.

(African hermit) Rodulfus Glaber, *Historiae* 5, c. 1 (13), pp. 234–37. Another version gives Iotsaldus, *Vita Odilonis abbatis* (Cluny), 2, c. 13, *MPL* 142, cols. 926–27.

(Thietmar on intercessory prayer) Thietmar (see Primary Sources), 4, c. 75, p. 218.

(Karl Schmid on necrologies) Schmid, *Gebetsgedenken* (see chapter 4), p. 383.

Chapter 8: The King
General

Das Königtum: Seine geistigen und rechtlichen Grundlagen. Vorträge und Forschungen, 3. Lindau and Constance, 1956. (Essays.)

Beumann, Helmuth: "Zur Entwicklung transpersonaler Staatsauffassungen." In *Das Königtum* (see above), pp. 185–224.

Bloch, Marc. *The Royal Touch: Sacred Monarchy and Scrofula in England and France.* Trans. J. E. Anderson. London, 1973.

Hauck, Karl. "Tiergärten im Pfalzbereich." In *Deutsche Königspfalzen.* Vol 1. Veröffentlichungen des M. Planck-Instituts für Geschichte, 11/1. Göttingen, 1963, pp. 30–74.

Mitteis, Heinrich. "Formen der Adelsherrschaft im Mittelalter." In idem, *Die Rechtsidee in der Geschichte.* Weimar, 1957, pp. 636–68. (Monarchy and aristocratic oligarchy.)

Vogelsang, Thilo. *Die Frau als Herrscherin im hohen Mittelalter: Studien zur "consors regni"-Formel.* Göttinger Bausteine, 7. Göttingen, 1954.

Notes

(Heinrich Mitteis) Mitteis (see above), pp. 643–44.

(Liutprand of Cremona) Liutprand (see Primary Sources), p. 116. *Antapodosis* 4, 23; *Opera,* ed. Becker, p. 116.

(Synod of Hohenaltheim) *MGH Constitutiones* 1, pp. 620–27.

(Neo-Carolingian kingship) Jean François Lemarignier, *Le gouvernement royal aux premiers temps capétiens* (Paris, 1965), p. 168.

(Surname "simplex") Bernd Schneidmüller, in *Schweizerische Zeitschrift für Geschichte* 28 (1978), pp. 62–66.

(Synod of Trosly) Joannes Dominicus Mansi, *Sacrorum conciliorum nova et amplissima collectio,* 18A. (Paris, 1902), cols. 263–308.

("Cyprian") *Cypriani opera omnia,* ed. Giulelmus Hartel, in *Corpus scroptorum ecclesiasticorum Latinorum* III, 3 (Vienna, 1871), pp. 166–67.

Chapter 9: The Bishop
General

Giese, Wolfgang. "Zur Bautätigkeit von Bischöfen und Äbten des 10. bis. 12. Jahrhunderts." *Deutsche Archiv* 38 (1982), p. 388–438.

Kaiser, Reinhold. *Bischofsherrschaft zwischen Königtum und Fürstenmacht.* Pariser Historische Studien, 17. Bonn, 1981.

La Maison d'Ardennes, Xe–XIe siècles. Publications . . . Institut Grand-Ducal de Luxembourg, 95. Luxemburg, 1981.

Parisse, Michel. *La noblesse lorraine.* Vol. 1. Paris, 1976.

Prinz, Friedrich. *Klerus und Krieg im früheren Mittelalter.* Monographien zur Geschichte des Mittelalters, 2. Stuttgart, 1971.

Renn, Heinz. *Das erste Luxemburger Grafenhaus (963–1136). Rheinisches Archiv,* 39. Bonn, 1941.

Scheibelreiter, Georg. "The Death of the Bishop in the Early Middle Ages." In *The End of Strife* (Colloquium, Durham, U.K., 1981). Ed. David Loades. Edinburgh, 1984, pp. 32–43.

Schmid, Paul. *Der Begriff der kanonischen Wahl in den Anfängen des Investiturstreits.* Stuttgart, 1926.

Schulte, Aloys. *Der Adel und die deutsche Kirche in Mittelalter.* Kirchenrechtliche Abhandlungen, 63/64. Stuttgart, 1910. 3d ed. Darmstadt, 1958.

Notes

(Aloys Schulte) See sec. A above.

(Non-noble bishops) Jane Martindale, "The French Aristocracy in the Early Middle Ages," *Past and Present* 75 (May 1977), pp. 35–36.

(Meinwerk in Paderborn) Thietmar (see Primary Sources), 6, c. 40, ed. Holtzmann, pp. 322–23.

(Malcalanus's treatise) "Dialogus de statu sanctae ecclesiae," ed. Heinz Löwe, *Deutsches Archiv* 17 (1961), pp. 68–90.

(Church and lay power) Auguste Dumas, in Emile Amann, *A. Dumas: L'Eglise au pouvoir des laïques*, Histoire de l'Eglise 7 (Paris, 1948), p. 215.
(Otto's letter to Heribert) Lantbert of Deutz, *Vita Heriberti archiepiscopi Coloniensis*, c. 5, *MGH SS* 4, p. 743.
(Bishopric of Verdun) *Gesta episcoporum Virdunensium, Continuato*, c. 4–5, *MGH SS* 4, p. 47.
(Friedrich Prinz) *Klerus and Krieg* (see above), p. 148.

Chapter 10: Worldly Clerics
General

Felten, Franz Josef. *Äbte und Laienäbte im Frankenreich*. Monographien zur Geschichte des Mittelalters, 20. Stuttgart, 1980. (Ends with the death of Louis the Pious; a new evaluation of the irregularity of abbots.)
Herkommer, Lotte. *Untersuchungen zur Abtsnachfolge unter den Ottonen*. Veröffentlichungen der Kommission für geschichtliche Landeskunde Baden-Württemberg, vol. 75. Stuttgart, 1973.
Parisse, Michel. "Les chanoinesses dans l'Empire germanique (IXe–XIe siècles)." *Francia* 6 (1978), pp. 107–26.
Siegwart, Josef. *Die Chorherren- und Chorfrauengemeinschaften in der deutschsprachigen Schweiz . . . , mit einem Überblick über die deutsche Kanonikerreform des 10. und 11. Jahrhunderts*. Fribourg, 1962.
Wollasch, Joachim. "Parenté noble et monachisme reformateur." *Revue Historique*, year 104, vol. 264 (1980), pp. 3–24.

Notes

(Chess poem) *MGH Poetae Latini* vol. 5, fasc. 3 (Munich, 1979), pp. 652–55.
(Aschaffenburg quarrel) *Urkundenbuch des Stifts St. Peter und Alexander zu Aschaffenburg*, vol. 1: 861–1325, ed. Matthias Thiel (Aschaffenburg, 1986), pp. 27–39 nr. 8.
(Rules of Aix-la-Chapelle) *MGH Concilia* 2 (Karol.1), Canons: pp. 397–421; Canonesses: pp. 421–55.
(Lifestyle of canonesses) Parisse (see above), p. 117.
(Gandersheim quarrel) Thangmar (see Primary Sources), *MGH SS* 4, pp. 764–69, c. 13–23; Wolfhere, (see Primary Sources), *MGH SS* 11, pp. 188–89, 192–94, c. 29, 34, 36.
(Charter of Wido of Anjoy) Olivier Guillot, *Le comte d'Anjou et son entourage au XIe siècle*, vol. 1 (Paris, 1972), p. 140 and n. 46.
(Castle in Berry) Andrew (see Primary Sources), c. 45, p. 84.
(Gauzlin of Fleury) Andrew (see Primary Sources), c. 3A, p. 38; c. 18A, pp. 50–52.

Chapter 11: Hermits and Reformers
General

Il monachesimo nell'alto Medioevo e la formazione della civiltà occidentale. Settimane di Studio, Spoleto, 4, 1956. Spoleto, 1957.
Benedictine Culture 750–1050. Ed. W. Lourdaux and D. Verhelst. Mediaevalia Lovaniensia, ser. 1, Studia, 11. Leuven, 1983.

Bulst, Neithard. *Untersuchungen zu den Klosterreformen Wilhelms von Dijon.* Pariser Historische Studien, 11. Bonn, 1973.

Cluniac Monasticism in the Central Middle Ages. Ed. Noreen Hunt. London, 1971. (Essays by continental authors, in English.)

Cluny. *Beiträge. . . .* Ed. Helmut Richter. Wege der Forschung, 241. Darmstadt, 1975.

Constable, Giles. "*Famuli* and *Conversi* at Cluny." *Revue Bénédictine* 83 (1973), pp. 326–50. Reprint in idem, *Cluniac Studies.* Collected Studies Series, 109. London, 1980.

Grundmann, Herbert. "Adelsbekehrungen im Hochmittelalter: *Conversi* und *nutriti* im Kloster." In idem, *Ausgewählte Aufsätze,* Schriften der MGH, no. 28, vol. 1 (Stuttgart, 1976), pp. 125–49.

————. "Deutsche Eremiten, Einsiedler und Klausner im Hochmittelalter (10.–12. Jahrhundert)." In idem, *Ausgewählte Aufsätze,* 1, pp. 93–124.

Hallinger, Kassius. *Gorze-Kluny: Studien zu den monastischen Lebensformen und Gegensätzen im Hochmittelalter.* Studia Anselmiana, 22–25. 2 vols. Rome, 1950, 1951.

Poulin, Joseph-Claude. *L'Idéal de Sainteté dans l'Aquitaine carolingienne d'après les sources hagiographiques (750–950).* Quebec, 1975.

Rosenwein, Barbara H. *Rhinoceros Bound: Cluny in the Tenth Century.* Philadelphia, 1982.

Tabacco, Giovanni. "Eremo e cenobio." In *Spiritualità cluniacense.* Convegni del centro di studi . . . Todi, vol. 2, 1958. Todi, 1960, pp. 326–335.

Teske, Wolfgang. "Laien, Laienmönche" (see chap. 1, note to "Conversi").

Wollasch, Joachim. "Parenté noble et monachisme réformateur." *Revue Historique.* Année 104, t. 264 (1980), pp. 3–24.

Notes

(Golden Age) Petrus Damiani, *Vita beati Romualdi* (see Primary Sources), pp. 105–6.

(Signs in Saint Gall) Walter Jarecki, *Signa loquendi,* Saecula spiritualia 4 (1981), p. 124 nr. 17, p. 136 nr. 82.

(Dream of Otto III) Rodulfus Glaber (see Primary Sources) 1, c. (14), ed. Prou, pp. 28–30.

(Antisecular protest) Kassius Hallinger, *Zur geistigen Welt der Anfänge Klunys,* in Cluny, *Beiträge* . . . (see above), p. 114.

(*Consuetudines* of Cluny) *Liber tramitis* (see Primary Sources, *Corpus consuetudinum*), p. 5 (preface).

Chapter 12: Monastic Life
General

Berlière, Ursmer. "Le nombre des moines dans les anciens monastères." *Revue Bénédictine* 41 (1929), pp. 231–61; 42 (1930), pp. 11–42.

Hallinger, Kassius. "The Spiritual Life of Cluny in the Early Days." In *Cluniac Monasticism* (see chap. 11), pp. 29–55.

Horn, Walter, and Ernest Born. *The Plan of St. Gall.* 3 vols. Berkeley, Los Angeles, and London, 1979. (A fundamental work on the Plan, with many observations on monastic life and buildings. On the date of the plan, see also Warren Sanderson, in *Speculum* 60 [1985], pp. 615–32.)

Ovitt, George, Jr. "Manual Labor and Early Medieval Monasticism." *Viator* 17 (1986), pp. 1–18.

Spiritualità cluniacense. Convegni . . . sulla spiritualità medievale, 22, Todi, 1958. Todi, 1960.

Zimmerman, Gerd. *Ordensleben und Lebensstandard: Die cura corporis in den Ordensvorschriften des abendländischen Hochmittelalters*. Beiträge zur Geschichte des Alten Mönchtums, 32. Münster, 1973. (Standard work on precepts concerning material existence in the Cluniac monasteries.)

Notes

(Purpose of *oblatio puerorum*) Consuetudines Udalrici, *MPL* 149, pp. 635–36. See Teske, "Laien, Laienmönche" (chap 1, note for "Conversi"), p. 282.

(Buildings at Cluny [II]) A description is given in the *Liber tramitis* (see Primary Sources, *Corpus consuetudinum*), 2, c.1 (142), pp. 203–5. Also in Horn and Born, vol. 2, pp. 233–34, with English translation. Reports on the excavations of the Medieval Academy of America summarized by Kenneth John Conant, in *Speculum* 29 (1954), pp. 1–43, with 16 plates.

(Wigo of Tegernsee at Feuchtwangen) *Die Tegernseer Briefsammlung* (see Primary Sources), p. 4 no. 2.

(Beans or vegetables?) Zimmerman (see above), 1, p. 281.

Chapter 13: Education and School in the Monastery
General

Bischoff, Bernhard. "Das griechische Element in der abendländischen Bildung des Mittelalters." In idem, *Mittelalterliche Studien*, 2. Stuttgart, 1967, pp. 246–75.

Glauche, Günter. *Schullektüre im Mittelalter*. Münchener Beiträge zur Mediävistik- und Renaissanceforschung, 5. Munich, 1970.

Riché, Pierre. *Les écoles et l'enseignement dans l'Occident chrétien de la fin du Ve siècle au milieu du XIe siècle*. Paris, 1979.

La scuola nell'Occidente latino dell'Alto Medioevo. Settimane di Studio, Spoleto, 19, 1971. Spoleto, 1972.

The Seven Liberal Arts in the Middle Ages. Ed. David L. Wagner. Bloomington, 1983. (Instructive essays on the individual arts.)

Stotz, Peter. "Dichten als Schulfach—Aspekte mittelalterlicher Schuldichtung." *Mittellateinisches Jahrbuch* 16 (1981), pp. 1–16.

Notes

(Aimoin of Fleury on copying the ancients) Aimoin, *Historia Francorum*, *MPL* 139, col. 628.

Chapter 14: Popular Beliefs
General

La culture populaire au moyen âge. 4th colloquium, Montreal, 1977. Montreal, 1979.

Liber miraculorum sancte Fidis. Ed. A[uguste] Bouillet. Collection de textes pour servir à l'étude et à l'enseignement de l'histoire. Paris, 1897.

See also Primary Sources: Burchard, *Decretum;* Regino, *De synodalibus causis;* and Flothilda.

Blöcker, Monica. "Wetterzauber: Zu einem Glaubenskomplex des frühen Mittelalters." *Francia* 9 (1981), pp. 117–31.

Demm, Eberhard. "Zur Rolle des Wunders in der Heiligkeitskonzeption des Mittelalters." *Archiv für Kulturgeschichte* 57 (1975), pp. 300–344.

Fichtenau, Heinrich. "Zum Reliquienwesen des früheren Mittelalters." In idem, *Beiträge zur Mediävistik,* 1. Stuttgart, 1975, pp. 108–44.

Gaudemet, Jean. "Les ordalies au Moyen Age: doctrine, législation et pratique canoniques." In idem, *La société ecclésiastique dans l'Occident médiéval.* Reprint (XV), London, 1980, pp. 99–135.

Geary, Patrick J. *Furta sacra: Thefts of Relics in the Central Middle Ages.* Princeton, 1978.

———. "Humiliation of saints." In Stephen Wilson, ed. *Saints and Their Cults: Studies in Religious Sociology, Folklore and History.* Cambridge, 1983, pp. 123–140.

———. "La coercition des saints dans la pratique religieuse médiévale." In *La culture populaire* (see above), pp. 145–61.

Harmening, Dieter. *Superstitio.* Berlin, 1979.

Manitius, Karl. "Rhetorik und Magie bei Anselm von Besate." *Deutsches Archiv* 12 (1956), pp. 52–72.

Nottarp, Hermann. *Gottesurteile.* Bamberg, 1949.

Poulin, Joseph-Claude. "Entre magie et religion." In *La culture populaire* (above), pp. 121–43.

Sigal, Pierre-André. *L'homme et le miracle dans la France médiévale (XIe-XIIe siècle).* Paris, 1985.

Ward, Benedicta. *Miracles and the Medieval Mind: Theory, Record and Event.* Aldershot, 1982, 1987.

Notes

(Christ in majesty) Etienne Delaruelle, "La culture religieuse des laïcs en France aux XIe et XIIe siècles," in *I laici* (see Secondary Sources, General), pp. 522–53.

(*Eulogiae* given before a battle) Aimoin of Fleury, *De miraculis s. Benedicti* 1, c. 16 (30), *MPL* 139, col. 820.

(Saints as legal subjects) Hans Hattenhauer, *Das Recht der Heiligen,* Schriften zur Rechtsgeschichte 12 (1976), p. 69.

Chapter 15: Peasant Existence
General

Agricoltura e mondo rurale in Occidente nell'alto medioevo. Settimane di Studio, Spoleto, 13, 1965. 2 vols. Spoleto, 1966.

Cristianizzazione e organizzazione ecclesiastica delle campagne nell'alto medioevo. Settimane di Studio, Spoleto, 28, 1980. 2 vols. Spoleto, 1982.

Déléage, André. *La vie rurale en Bourgogne jusqu'au début du onzième siècle.* 3 vols. Mâcon, 1941.

Dollinger, Philippe. *L'évolution des classes rurales en Bavière jusqu'au milieu du XIIe siècle.* Paris, 1949.

Duby, Georges. "Le problème des techniques agricoles." In *Agricoltura e mondo rurale,* Settimane di Studio, Spoleto, 13, 1965. Spoleto, 1966, pp. 108–21.

Fichtenau, Heinrich. "Wald und Waldnützung" (im 10. Jahrhundert). In idem, *Beiträge zur Mediävistik,* 3, 1986, pp. 108–21.

Finó, Jean-Paul. *Forteresses de la France médiévale: Construction, attaque, défense.* 3d ed. Paris, 1977.

Fossier, Robert. *Peasant Life in the Medieval West.* Trans. Juliet Vale. Oxford and New York, 1988. (Pp. 196–207: select bibliography.)

Gille, Bertrand. "Recherches sur les instruments du labour au moyen âge." *Bibliothèque de l'Ecole des Chartes* 120 (1962), pp. 5–38.

Higounet, Charles. "Les forêts de l'Europe occidentale du Ve au XIe siècle." In *Agricoltura e mondo rurale,* Settimane di Studio, Spoleto, 13, 1965. Spoleto, 1966, pp. 343–98.

Medioevo rurale. Ed. Vito Fumagalli and Gabriella Rossetti. Bologna, 1980.

Montanari, Massimo. *L'alimentazione contadina nell'alto Medioevo.* Nuovo Medioevo, 11. Naples, 1979.

Rösener, Werner. *Bauern im Mittelalter.* Munich, 1985. (Instructive, with a good bibliography.)

Settia, Aldo A. *Castelli e villaggi nell'Italia padana: Popolamento, potere e sicurezza fra IX e XIII secolo.* Naples, 1984.

Sprandel, Rolf. *Das Eisengewerbe im Mittelalter.* Stuttgart, 1968.

Unibos. See Primary Sources, "Walthari," *Waltharius,* ed. Langosch, pp. 251–305.

Notes

("Agricultural revolution") Lynn White, Jr., *Medieval Technology* (see Secondary Sources, General), chap. 2; idem in *Europäische Wirtschaftsgeschichte: Mittelalter,* ed. C. Cipolla and K. Borchardt (Stuttgart and New York, 1978), p. 93; and idem in *Mediaevalia et Humanistica* 9 (1955), p. 28 (on the far-reaching consequences of legume cultivation).

(Prüm in the 13th century) Dieter Hägermann, "Eine Grundherrschaft des 13. Jahrhunderts im Spiegel des Frühmittelalters," *Rheinische Vierteljahrsblätter* 45 (1981), pp. 16, 21.

(Reasons for castle-building in France and Italy) Godefroid Kurth, *Notger de Liège,* vol. 1 (1905), p. 25.

(*Incastellamento*) Toubert, *Latium* (see Secondary Sources, Regional); and the reviews by Pierre Bonnassie, "Le Latium au coeur du Moyen Age," *Revue Historique* 259 (1978), pp. 491–500; and Hartmut Hoffmann, "Der Kirchenstaat im hohen Mittelalter," *Quellen und Forschungen aus italienischen Archiven und Bibliotheken* 57 (1977), pp. 1–45.

Chapter 16: Stratification and Mobility

Bosl, Karl. *Gesellschaftsgeschichte Italiens im Mittelalter.* Monographien zur Geschichte des Mittelalters, 26. Stuttgart, 1982.

———. "Potens und pauper." In idem, *Frühformen der Gesellschaft im mittelalterlichen Europa.* Munich, 1964, pp. 106–34.

Etudes sur l'histoire de la pauvreté (Moyen Age—XVIe siècle). Ed. Michel Mollat. Publications de la Sorbonne, Etudes, VIII/1–2. Vol. 1, Paris, 1974.

Freed, John B. "The Formation of the Salzburg Ministerialage in the Tenth and Eleventh Centuries: An Example of Upward Social Mobility in the Early Middle Ages." *Viator* 9 (1978), pp. 67–102.

Mollat, Michel. *The Poor in the Middle Ages: An Essay in Social History.* Trans. Arthur Goldhammer. New Haven, 1986.

Verlinden, Charles. *L'esclavage dans l'Europe médiévale.* 2 vols. Bruges, 1955, Ghent, 1977.

Chapter 17: Disorder and Public Coercion
General

Adso Dervensis. *De ortu et tempore Antichristi.* . . . Ed. D. Verhelst. *Corpus Christianorum, continuatio mediaevalis,* t. 45. Turnhout, 1976.

Attonis qui fertur Polipticum quod appellatur Perpendiculum, ed. Georg Goetz. Abhandlungen der Sächsischen Akademie der Wissenschaften, phil.-hist. Kl., 37, no. 2. Leipzig, 1922. (See also Percy Ernst Schramm, *Beiträge zur allgemeinen Geschichte,* 3, Stuttgart 1969, pp. 17–29.)

Konrad, Robert. *De ortu et tempore Antichristi: Antichristvorstellungen und Geschichtsbild des Abtes Adso von Montier-en-Der.* Münchener historische Studien, Abteilung mittelalterliche Geschichte, 1. Kallmünz, 1964.

Lambert, Malcolm. *Medieval Heresy: Popular Movements from Bogomils to Hus.* London, 1977. (See the synopsis on pp. 357–63.)

Otloh of Saint Emmeram at Ratisbon. *Liber de temptationibus suis.* MPL 146, cols. 32–33.

Notes

(Defeat by the Frisians) Alpert (see Primary Sources), *De diversitate temporum,* 2, c. 21, *MGH SS* 4, pp. 719–20.

(Panic of soldiers) Anselm of Liège, c. 24, *MGH SS* 7, p. 202; Fulbert (see Primary Sources), nos. 10, 99, 100, pp. 20, 178–82.

(Eblus of Limoges, Elias I of Périgord, Count William of Poitiers) Ademar (see Primary Sources) 3, c. 25, 28, ed. Chavanon, pp. 147, 150.

(Bishop Fulbert of Chartres) Fulbert (see Primary Sources), no. 10, p. 22.

(Ineffectiveness of excommunications) "Dialogus de statu sanctae Ecclesiae," ed. Heinz Löwe, *Deutsches Archiv* 17 (1961), p. 83.

(Castellan Walter): *Les annales de Saint-Pierre de Gand et de Saint-Amand.* Ed. Philippe Grierson. Brussels, 1937, p. 155.

(Curse formula) Synod of Reims (900), Johannes Dominicus Mansi, *Sacrorum conciliorum nova et amplissima collectio* 18A, cols. 183–84.

(Krumbacher) Karl Krumbacher, *Geschichte der byzantinischen Literatur* (1891), p. 44.

Chapter 18: Lies and Deceit

(Hatto and Adalbert) Otto of Freising, Chronica, 6, c. 15, ed. Adolf Hofmeister, *MGH SSRG* 45, 2d ed. 1912, pp. 274–75.

(Gerbert's letters) Gerbert, *Briefsammlung* (see Primary Sources), nos. 32, 33, 158, 159, 163, 178 (Bobbio); for his self-criticism, see nos. 167, 172; letters for Adalbero of Reims, see nos. 54, 57.

(Brun of Cologne, Hugh of Francia) Thietmar (see Primary Sources), 2, c. 23, pp. 66–67.

(Archbishop William of Mainz on his family): William's letter to Pope Agapet II (955), *Monumenta Moguntina,* ed. Philipp Jaffé, Bibliotheca rerum Germanicarum 3 (Berlin, 1866), p. 348 no. 18.

Chapter 19: Unlawful Power
General

Boussard, Jacques. "Services féodaux, milices et mercennaires dans les armées, en France, aux Xe et XIe siècles." In *Ordinamenti militari in Occidente nell'alto Medioevo.* Settimane di Studio, Spoleto, 15, 1967. Spoleto, 1968, vol. 1, pp. 131–68.

Vita Burchardi Wormatiensis episcopi. MGH SS 4, pp. 830–46. See especially c. 6, pp. 835–36 (on "robbers" in Worms).

Notes

(Burning of Strassburg cathedral) Thietmar (see Primary Sources) 6, c. 51, pp. 338–39.

(Ostentative destructions) Toubert, *Latium* (see Secondary Sources, Regional) 1, pp. 357–38.

(Wichmann and Balderich): Alpert (see Primary Sources) *De diversitate temporum,* 2, c. 1, *MGH SS* 4, p. 710.

(Decrees of Steele, 938) Widukind (see Primary Sources) 2, c. 10, p. 74.

(Report of a vision, around 900) William of Malmesbury, *Gesta regum Anglorum* 2, c. 111, *MGH SS* 10, p. 458.

("Evil Christians"). Hagen Keller, *Adelsherrschaft und städtische Gesellschaft in Oberitalien,* Bibliothek des Deutschen Historischen Instituts in Rom, 52 (1979), p. 152.

("Robbers" in Frisia) Alpert (see Primary Sources) *De diversitate* 2, 20, *MGH SS* 4, p. 718.

(Cannibalism) Rodulfus Glaber, *Historiae,* 4, c. 4 (10), ed. France, pp. 188–89.

(Peace of God) Rodulfus Glaber (see Primary Sources) *Historiae* 4, c. 5, pp. 194–99. See also Hartmut Hoffmann, *Gottesfriede und Treuga Dei,* Schriften der *MGH,* 20, Stuttgart, 1964.

Epilogue: A Look into the Future of the Past

(Critics on laical domination of churches) Kassius Hallinger, "Zur geistigen Welt der Anfänge Klunys," in Cluny, *Beitrage . . . ,* Wege der Forschung 241 (Darmstadt, 1975), p. 117.

(Reform of knighthood) Carl Erdmann, *Die Entstehung des Kreuzzugsgedankens* (1935), quoted by Joachim Bumke, "Der adlige Ritter," in *Das Rittertum im Mittelalter,* Wege der Forschung 349 (Darmstadt, 1976), p. 285.

INDEX

Abbo of Fleury, 6, 16, 56, 198, 218, 235, 238–40, 286, 289, 294–95, 298, 322, 388, 395, 409, 413, 427

Abbot primate, 16–18

Abbots, 18, 20–21; appointments of, 233–35; diet of, 280–81; lay, 232–34; relations with bishop, 239–41; role of in monastery, 121–22, 232–33, 274–75, 279

Adalbero I of Metz, 119, 185, 200–209, 222, 256

Adalbero II of Metz, 119, 184, 187–88, 191, 197, 205, 215

Adalbero of Laon, 4–6, 27, 68, 70, 89, 114, 166, 187, 196, 238, 258, 361, 384, 403

Adalbero of Reims, 222, 399, 411–12

Adalbert of Prague, 66–67, 198, 264

Adalbert (son of Berengar), 48, 92, 406–8

Adelheid, Empress, 62, 89, 167, 177, 179–80, 326, 368

Ademar of Chabannes, 14–15, 75–76, 89, 141, 198, 264, 404, 414, 431

Adso of Montierender, 287–88, 314–15

Agapet II, Pope, 204

Agriculture: cultivation of bread, 342–43, 345, cultivation of legumes, 342–44, cultivation of wine, 343, 345; implements of, 336–38; in Italty, 358; practice of half-cultivation, 364; three-field system, 344

Aimoin of Fleury, 48, 198, 286

Aix-la-Chapelle, 32, 160–63, 222, 225; Rule of, 223, 225–27, 230; synod of, 222

Allegory, 306

Alphabet, symbolism of the, 71

Anathema, 392–93, 396–97, 414

Andrew, Saint, 12–14

Angers, 232, 235, 327. See also Saint-Aubin

Angilbert, 76, 252, 269

Animals, domestic, 334–36; husbandry of, 338, 341, 345

Anjou, 190, 235, 435

Annales school, xvii

Annappes, 334, 337, 345–46

Ansegis of Sens, 12

Anselm of Besate, 88–89, 294, 297–98, 322

Anticlericalism, 397–98

Aquileia, 12, 20, 54

Aquitaine, 13–14, 65, 184, 269, 410, 425; feudalism in, 156; widows in, 110

Architecture, 71–72; and Lombard construction form, 272. *See also* Churches; City walls; Cluny; Monasteries; Saint Gall

Ardennes, the, 119, 187, 191, 412

Areligiosity, 399–400

Arles, 12, 397

Arnolf of Saint Emmeram, 72, 313–15

Arnulf of Orleans, 239

Arnulf of Reims, 154, 159–60, 192, 204, 396, 414, 426

Arnulf of Tours, 116

Arras, 215, 240

Arval Brethren, 321

Aschaffenburg, 224–26, 229

Astronomy, 299

Atto Adalbert of Canossa, 29, 88, 155

Atto of Vercelli, 7, 60, 77, 87, 116, 118, 121, 214, 220, 307, 311, 314, 384–85, 389, 410, 422

Augsburg, 19, 48, 54, 160, 172, 187, 287

Augustine, Saint, 32, 388

Aurillac, 148, 184

Auxerre, 263, 423

Balderich of Liège, 198, 206, 307, 423–25, 427

Baldwin of Flanders, 232, 427

Bamberg, 19, 37, 47, 203, 222, 328, 375

Banquets, 27–28, 58–61, 87, 128, 199. *See also* Meals

Barcelona, 116, 191, 207
Beatrix of Upper Lorraine, 180, 197
Benedict V, Pope, 46
Benedict VIII, Pope, 11
Benedict VIII, Pope, 116, 373–74, 376
Benedict of Aniane, 227, 230, 251–52, 256,
  261, 269, 272
Benedict of Nursia, Saint, 15, 20, 227, 230,
  238–40, 246, 248–49, 251–52, 254,
  258–59, 261–62, 270, 274, 277, 279,
  282, 284, 288–89, 293–95, 323, 405;
  Rule of, 21–22, 36–37, 39–40, 68, 70,
  74, 77, 121–22, 128, 230, 233, 237, 240,
  247, 251, 255–59, 263, 266–67, 270,
  274, 277–79, 285, 289, 300, 389
Berengar II, King, 48, 53, 92, 179, 196, 374,
  422
Berengar of Cambrai, 207, 430
Bergamo, 338, 343, 353, 360, 366
Berlière, Dom, 125
Bernward of Hildesheim, 47, 72, 204, 228,
  376
Bertha (wife of Robert II), 95, 167, 178
Besalù, 191
Bèze, (monastery), 55, 263, 270
Bishops, 5, 9, 18; appointment of, 191–92;
  family politics of, 186–91, 198–99; and
  kinship, 183–85; as building commission-
  ers, 202–3; "courts" of, 199, 209; death
  of, 47, 213–16; election of, 193–95; gift
  giving among, 199–200; military activities
  of, 207–10; role in monastery, 121; pas-
  toral duties of, 210–13; social origins of,
  182–83; suffragans, 18; virtues of, 197–
  98
Blessings, 313
Bloch, Marc, xvii, 81–82, 136, 138, 162,
  435–37
Blood feuds, 87, 423, 426
Bobbio. See Gerbert of Aurillac
Bogomils, 402
Boniface, Saint, 16, 131
Boniface of Canossa, 108, 163
Bonn, 329–30; Treaty of, 26
Bonnassie, Pierre, xvi
Book of Ceremonies, 8
Books, 9, 287–90
Borst, Arno, 31, 131
Boso of Tuscany, 66, 331
Bourges, 239; synod of, 94–95
Bremen, 150, 222
Brescia, 338, 345
Brun of Querfort, 147, 174, 192

Bruno of Augsburg, 19, 30
Bruno of Cologne, 61, 145–46, 197, 200,
  204, 208, 213, 215, 248, 286–87, 291,
  293, 416
Burchard of Worms, 11, 13, 70, 90, 104–5,
  142, 186, 197, 201, 288, 315, 388, 390,
  414, 429
Burghers, 202

Calabria, 386
Cambrai, 17–18, 33, 108–10, 143, 214–15,
  236, 240, 270, 327, 425
Campo, 116
Canonesses, 227
Canons, 223–27
Canossa, 88, 365
Capua, 317
Carcassonne, 199
Carolingians (family), 26, 131, 171, 205
Carthusians, 71
Castille, 93
Castles, 93: construction of, 206–7, 355–56,
  424; in Catalonia, 142; in France, 354–
  56; in Germany, 356–58; Mottes, 355–56,
  358; politics of, 425. See also Incastella-
  mento
Catalonia, 156, 343, 372; castles in, 142;
  classes of nobility in, 138; family in, 83,
  94; irrigation in, 342; legal status of
  women in, 108–9
Cathedral chapter, 222
Centula, 75, 252, 269, 334
Cerdaña, 189, 191
Châlons-sur-Marne, 8
Chamberlains, 177
Champeaux, 262, 295
Charlemagne, 45, 66, 91, 153, 158, 163,
  165, 278, 280, 345
Charles III, 26, 311
Charles III (the Simple), 26, 28, 45, 169,
  171–72, 174, 203, 328, 428
Charles of Lorraine, 24, 94, 215, 410–11,
  415, 421
Charles the Bald, 152, 392
Charles the Great, 127
Charroux, synod of, 362
Chartres, 53, 74, 235, 263, 271, 412
Chivalry, 61
Chronicle of Frafa, 116
Churches: construction of, 202, 209; dedica-
  tions of, 211–12; donations to, 219, en-
  dowment of, 148–49
Cistercians, 71, 77

City walls, construction of, 202
Classe, 248
Clemens, Saint, 404
Clergy, secular, 218–22; attitude toward poor, 368; criteria of rank among, 7; and military, 219; in warfare, 237–39
Clermont, 15
Clothing, 4, 32, 45, 64–69
Clovis, 169
Cluniacs, 114, 238, 387. See also Cluny
Cluny, 15, 17, 21, 60, 73, 75, 149–51, 232, 252, 255–56, 258, 263–64, 268, 270, 276, 281–82, 285, 292, 349, 373, 385, 425; Cluny II, 72, 272, Cluny III, 72; Building plans of, 273–75; monasticism of, 6, 31, 37, 39, 68–70, 218, 231, 234, 238, 251, 253. See also Cluniacs
Clusa, 294
Cologne, 11, 18–19, 30, 42, 144, 329
Como, 422
Companio, meaning of, 58
Concordat of Worms, 181
Confraternities, 127–29
Conques, 305, 331
Conrad I, 62, 157, 164
Conrad II, 18–19, 40, 46, 158, 173, 176, 179, 201, 231, 400, 420, 425
Conradines, 144
Conrad of Burgundy, 257, 407
Conrad of Corinthia, 95, 401
Constance, Queen, 65, 177, 179–80, 402
Constantia, 405
Constantine, 215–16
Constantine Prophyrogennetos, 8
Constantinople, 8, 13, 63
Consuetudines, 33, 252, 254, 256–60, 265, 277, 279–80, 282–83; meaning of, 30–31
Corbie, 269, 278, 370
Cordoba, 419
Coregency, 171–73, 175–76
Corvey, 357
Coseigneurie, 85
Cotrone, 48, 92
Council of Aix-la-Chapelle, 126
Councile of Trent, 104
Cremona, 214, 288
Creussen, 357–58
Criminals, 44; in monastery, 267–68; robbers, 428. See also Homicide
Crosier, symbolism of, 46–47
Cunibert, Saint, 42
Cunning, 384; praise of, 406–9

Cyprian, 175
Czechs, 248

Danes, 397, 399
Deacons, 21
Death: burial ceremonies, 43; commemoration of, 150–52; mourning, 42–43; of bishops, 47, 213–16; spirits of, 316–17
Demons, 320–21
Devil, the, 311–14, 318, 383–84
Dietrich of Metz, 92, 410, 412
Dietrich of Trier, 11, 187
Dijon, 40, 73, 263, 425
Dionysius, Saint, 15, 326, 404
Disgrace, display of, 35–36
Divorce, 95–103
Dölger, Franz, 131
Domus, meaning of, 101–2
Donatus, 289
Dortmund, synod of, 41, 95, 128, 150
Dowry, 114, 116; dos, 103–4, 124
Drinking bouts, 27, 60–63, 87, 149, 279, 282–83; caritas, 39, 282; Minnetrinken, 60
Duby, Georges, 4, 40–41, 64, 67, 126, 137, 345
Dudo of Saint-Quentin, 37, 145, 147, 409
Duels, 311, 414
Dumas, Auguste, 189
Durandus of Liège, 375

Eberhard of Franconia, 139
Eblus of Limoges, 390
Ebo of Reims, 182
"Ecbasis captivi," 230
Edgitha, 92
Education, 210; classical, 290–92; liberal arts, 295–300; of the laity, 305; program of, 285; purpose of, 285–86
Eichstätt, 202, 226, 291, 375
Einsiedeln, 238, 408
Ekkehard of Meissen, 25
Ekkehard of Schleswig, 369
Ekkehard IV of Saint Gall, 40, 53, 231, 261, 291, 293, 383, 406–7
Elias of Perigord, 391
Elites, and bishops, 220–21
Emma, Queen, 89–90
Emmeram, Saint, 60
Emperors, 165–66; dynastic politics, 89
Engelbert of Saint Gall, 237
Eparchius, Saint, 415
Epiphanios of Cyprus, 8

Limoges, 14–15, 53, 89, 193, 234, 294, 372, 394; synod of, 24, 70, 268
Limousin, 15
Literacy, 289
Liturgy, 211
Liudolfing dynasty, 151, 159, 228. *See also* Ottonians
Liudolf of Swabia, 112, 140, 225, 287
Liuthar, 161
Liutizi, 248, 335
Liutprand of Cremona, 8, 45, 58–59, 66, 68, 159, 161, 163, 168, 170, 178–79, 207, 293, 311, 316, 390, 409–10, 412, 421–22
Llès, 343
Lobbes, 239, 264, 280
Lombardy, 86
Lomello, 153
Longsword, William, 26
Lorraine, 356
Lothair, King, 39, 91, 197, 215, 412
Lotharingians, 171
Lothar of Italy, 176, 178–80, 234, 419
Louis II the Stammerer, 169
Louis III, 57, 171
Louis IV d'Outremer, 94, 26, 162, 167, 170, 203, 313, 416, 419
Louis V, 174
Louis the German, 169
Louis the Pious, 127, 147, 173–74, 179, 182, 222, 348, 401
Louvain, 424
Loyalty, 409–12
Lübeck, Konrad: 17
Lucca, 220
Luke, Saint, 15
Lyons, 13

Mâcon, 92, 354–55, 425
Mâconnais, the, 86, 93, 126, 137, 154, 354–55, 364, 367, 373
Magdeburg, 10–11, 18–19, 25, 34, 47, 53, 59, 127, 166, 193–94, 328
Magic, 319–24; restorative, 4
magicians, 317
Magyars. *See* Hungarians
Maine, 354–55
Mainz, 11, 16, 19, 25, 37, 40, 228, 263, 401; pontifical of, 173
Maiolus of Cluny, 5, 272, 385
Malcalanus (pseud., Theophilus), 185

Mansus, 83
Mantua, 19
Marius, Saint, 309
Mark, Saint, 15
Marriage, 24, 89, 113–14; arranging of, 114; civil, 104; clerical, 115; politics of, 90–95; prohibitions on, 94–96; varieties of, 103–5
Mars, 314
Marseille, 276
Martial of Limoges, Saint, 14–15, 24, 57, 89, 264, 404
Martindale, Jane, 182
Mathematics, 298
Mathilda, Queen, 58, 62–63, 88, 91, 139, 176, 178, 229
Matricula, 41–42
Matthew, Saint, 12, 15
Maubeuge, 314
Maundy Thursday, 41
Mauritius, Saint, 316, 331–32
Meals, 7, 33, 41, 225, 227. *See also* Banquets
Meaux, 192
Medieval Academy of America, 272
Megingaud of Eichstätt, 24–25, 210
Meinwerk of Paderborn, 184, 249
Meissen, 47, 357
Mentalitiies, history of, xvii
Mermeunt, 323
Merseburg, siege of, 109
Merseburger Necrology, 151
Mettlach, 55
Metz, 35, 53, 91, 180, 187–88, 197
Michael, Saint, 61
Micy, 233, 280, 404
Mieszko I, 37, 163
Milan, 12, 189
Military affairs, and rank, 28
Military command, 48
Milo of Carcassonne, 236
Missionary activity, 12, 14, 210
Mitteis, Heinrich, 157
Modena, 129
Modus Liebinc, 405
Monasteries: and confraternity, 128; building plans, 272–73; danger of fire in, 271, 289; dormitories of, 269–70; entry into, 20, 266–67; governance of, 231–32; landholdings of, 344, 366; meals in, 274; meditation in, 275–76; obligations of

Paterfamilias, 97
Patriarch, role of, 83
Paul, Saint, 5, 12–13, 15, 314, 328
Pavia, 152, 163, 171, 204, 330, 385, 409;
   synod of, 20, 374, 376
Peace of God movement, 14, 34, 238, 317,
   383, 432–34
Peasantry, 4, 31; divisions in, 23; and free-
   dom, 364–65; and military service, 356–
   57; landholdings of, 346–50; prestige
   and, 362; religious instruction of, 305–7
Penance, 43–45, 278, 392, 413
Pepin, King, 32, 37
Périgueux, 14
Perugia, 240
Peter, Saint, 9–10, 12–15, 47, 70, 326, 330
Peter Damian, 7, 248
Peter of Vercelli, 316
Philip I, 12, 162
Philip II Augustus, 166
Picardy, 83, 154, 335, 348, 354
Pilgrimages, 55–56, 212, 329–30, 392. See
   also Processions
Pilgrim of Cologne, 18
Pistoia, 117
Pîtres, Edict of, 342
Plundering, 385
Poetry, 291–92, 296, 306, 403; pagan, 290
Poitiers, 15, 266, 327
Poitou, 266, 354
Polycarp, Saint, 13
Pomerania, 311
Ponthion, 32
Pontifex summus, 18
Pontificale Romano-Germanicum, 87, 114
Poor, the, 367–70; care of the, 40–41, 62,
   209–10
Population increases, 341–42, 352, 435
Po Valley, 338, 342, 365
Praise, giving of, 40–42
Prayer, 34, 42, 313
Prestige, 6–7, 123
Priests, 21; as monks, 266
Primate, title of, 10–11, 20
Prinz, Friedrich, 207
Processions: obligatory, 54; streets of, 54
Procopius, 399
Prostration, 37
Provence, 354, 428
Prüm, 74, 122, 139, 270, 338, 340, 344,
   348
Pseudo-Dionysius "the Areopagite," 5

Pseudo-Isidore, 9, 10, 129
Punishment, 390–91, 432

Queen: appearance of, 178–79; duties of,
   176–78, military skill of, 179; role of,
   175–76

Ramwold of Regensburg, 72
Rank order: of apostles, 12–15; among canons, 226–27; of churches, 8–10; of cities,
   8–10; criteria of, among clergy, 7; ecclesiastical disputes over, 10–12, 20–22;
   among ecclesiastics, 6, 67; within the estate, 363; and the family, 130–32; monas-
   tic, 17, 20, 122; in secular sphere, 22–29
Raoul, King, 52, 203
Rather of Verona, 5–6, 29, 37–38, 64, 67,
   69–70, 105–6, 115, 118, 144, 195–98,
   200, 204, 207, 209, 221–22, 226, 231,
   264, 267, 293–94, 305, 325, 368, 377–
   78, 382, 388, 398, 413
Ratisbon, siege of, 160
Ravenna, 12, 44, 48–49, 292
Reception, 51–54
Regensburg, 46, 60, 72, 314
Regenwala, 149
Reggio Emilia, 345
Regino of Prüm, 60, 102, 106, 167, 169,
   219, 267, 315, 375, 413
Registrum epistolarum, 36
Reichenau, 150, 270–71, 274, 305
Reichenhall, 82–83
Reims, 8–13, 16, 24, 26, 59, 70, 129, 154,
   164, 183–84, 187–89, 206, 219, 223,
   253, 298, 312, 331, 335, 394, 410–11,
   414, 419, 424
Reinilda, 110
Relics, 18, 321, 324–32, 413, 432–33; cult
   of, 316–17
Religio, 245–46
Remigius of Auxerre, 211, 312, 331
Remus, 9
Repression, 420–26
Retinues, 56–58
Rhetoric, 296–97
Ribagorça, 191
Richard of Normandy, 37, 92
Richer of Saint-Rémi, 24, 32–33, 39, 43, 45,
   162, 171, 174, 208, 296–97, 299, 310,
   408, 414, 421, 428
Richwin, 214

Sergius III, Pope, 321
Sermons, 210
Servants, 361–62, 369; dormitories of land-
less, 124–25; legal status of, 370–73;
marriage of, 124; social advancement of
373–78. *See also* Serfs
Seulf of Reims, 108
Signs, interpretation of, 320–21. *See also*
God
Silvester II, Pope, 11, 16–17, 47, 183. *See*
also Gerbert of Aurillac
Simeon of Trier, 317
Simon, Saint, 12
Sin, 43. *See also* Penance
Sittengeschichte, xx
Sixtus, Saint, 10, 13
Slaves, 371
Slavs, 173, 204, 215, 366, 372, 419–20
Slawniking (family), 192
Soissons, 8, 189, 297; battle of, 171–72
Song of Roland, 306
Sons, 111–15
Sophia, 25, 228–29
Spengler, Oswald, xvii
Speyer, 54, 296
Stade, 25
Staffs, symbolism of, 48–49
Statues, 331
Status, ecclesiastical marks of, 67–71
Stephen II, Pope, 32, 37
Stephen of Hungary, Saint, 15, 248
Stephen of Liège, 90
Strasbourg, 19, 309, 419
Sulpicius Severus, 208
Supernatural, 317
Swabia, 186, 419
Sword, symbolism of, 44–45, 65, 67
Symbolism, 32–33

Taktika, 7–8
Tammo of Niederaltaich, 312
Tarragona, 427
Tassilo of Bavaria, 38
Tegernsee, 74, 177, 236, 272, 280, 343, 368
Terracina, 56
Textiles, ecclesiastical, 73–74
Thangmar, 25, 47, 66, 112, 228
Thegan, 182, 186
Theodora, 178–79
Theophanu, Empress, 34, 89, 92, 175–76,
179–80, 319
Theophilus. *See* Malcalanus
Theophylactus (family), 351

Thiedlach of Worms, 202
Thietmar of Merseburg, 25, 32–33, 35, 42,
47–48, 59, 89, 91, 102, 110, 112, 127–
28, 150–51, 161, 166, 184, 189–90,
193–94, 202, 231, 253, 255, 316, 319–
20, 328, 355, 368, 397, 399, 407–8, 410,
416
Thietmar of Prague, 192
Thomas Aquinas, 87, 167, 382
Thomas, Saint, 12
Thor, 315
Thuringians, 420
Tivoli, 44
Tonsure, 70
Toubert, Pierre, 350–52
Tournus (monastery), 55
Tours, 15, 49
Toxandria, 190
Travelers, 273
Trebeta, 9
Trier, 9–11, 13, 17, 79, 54–55, 100, 222,
317
Trosly, synod of, 31, 174–75, 214, 239,
382–83, 412–13
Troyes, 192, 412, 425
Truth: literary, 404–5; popular notions of,
404. *See also* Lies
Tuscany, devastation of, 352
Tutilo of Saint Gall, 263

Udalrich of Augsburg, 58, 104, 149, 186–
87, 198, 208, 210–11, 214, 250, 253,
290, 306, 319
Ulpian, 97–98
Ulrich of Aix, 189
Unbelievers, 307–8
Unibos, 115, 334–38, 405
Urgel, 207
Ursmar, Saint, 314
Utrecht, 44, 307

Vassals: and social bonds, 87–88, 91, 123,
152–56; gestures of, 39
Vendôme, 392
Venice, 371
Vercelli, 389
Verden, 19
Verdun, 19, 187, 197, 411
Verona, 20, 52, 54, 67, 221–22, 395
Vexia, the, 330
Vézelay, 234, 257
Vich, 207
Vikings, 139, 171–72, 175